Nick Rider

short breaks in
NORTHERN FRANCE

'at low tide the sea recedes for miles,
and the placid channels, sandbanks and
expanses of marsh lavender present a
subtle, ever-changing mix of colours
fading into the horizon.'

CADOGANguides

Contents

About the author

Nick Rider's first experience of French food was a crêpe with jam from a stand in Brittany when he was six years old, made by a man with a beard in baggy brown shorts. Its impact has never been forgotten. More recently, he lived in Barcelona for ten years, and has travelled widely in Spain, France, Italy and Mexico, as well as writing, among other things, a Ph.D on Spanish history, a general index of movies, and articles on food, travel, history, music and art and design. He has also written the Cadogan Guide to the Yucatan and Southern Mexico.

Cadogan Guides
Network House, 1 Ariel Way, London W12 7SL
cadoganguides@morrispub.co.uk
www.cadoganguides.com

The Globe Pequot Press
246 Goose Lane, PO Box 480, Guilford, Connecticut 06437–0480

Copyright © Nick Rider 1996, 2001

Cover design by Kicca Tommasi
Book design by Andrew Barker
Cover photographs by John Ferro Sims and John Miller
Maps © Cadogan Guides, drawn by Map Creation Ltd and Tracey Ridgewell
Editorial Director: Vicki Ingle
Series Editor: Linda McQueen
Editor: Catherine Charles
Indexing and Proofreading: Judith Wardman
Production: Book Production Services

Printed in the UK by Cromwell Press
A catalogue record for this book is available from the British Library
ISBN 1–86011–814–3

The author and publishers have made every effort to ensure the accuracy of the information in this book at the time of going to press. However, they cannot accept any responsibility for any loss, injury or inconvenience resulting from the use of information contained in this guide.

Please help us to keep this guide up to date We have done our best to ensure that the information in this guide is correct at the time of going to press. But places and facilities are constantly changing, and standards and prices in hotels and restaurants fluctuate. We would be delighted to receive any comments concerning existing entries or omissions. Authors of the best letters will receive a copy of the Cadogan Guide of their choice.

Introduction

01

France is a country about which everyone has an opinion. Some still say it's an innately stylish place, the home of chic. No, say some, it's overrated. Some think the French are always hostile and unhelpful. No, say others, they're very charming. For British people, France is both well-known and unfamiliar. For, it's true, the French have their ways of doing things. Contrary to a prejudice that's frequently aired in the British press, they don't cultivate these distinctive habits just to annoy other people, and in my experience are generally perfectly charming about explaining and showing off their customs to foreign visitors, in a neighbourly way.

The distinctiveness of France, the multi-varied complexity of its culture and its determined ways of behaving, means that any visit there can give you an enjoyable blast of difference. Along the north coast of France or just a short distance inside the country there are small-town cafés, neat seaside towns that still have a definite season, bustling weekly street markets, stylish city shopping streets, and a natural, unpavemented countryside, all with the unequivocal stamp of Frenchness.

Visiting France has always been bound up with eating. Restaurant and hotel are both French words, and for foreigners and the French themselves the thousand varieties of French foods, how they are prepared and how they are eaten have long been essential parts of the nation's identity. For a long time French cuisine was considered the only proper cuisine, while all the rest was just food. More recently other places have come on a great deal, while it's sometimes said that French restaurants have become immobile and complacent. There are of course mediocre restaurants in France as there are everywhere else. On the whole, though, the standard of French country and small-town restaurants – especially compared with similar areas elsewhere in Europe – is still extremely high. French diners may often be a tad conservative when it comes to the dishes they will try, but they are also extremely demanding with regard to quality. And when this quality is maintained in a restaurant it's done by staying true to certain basic and very valid principles – following the seasons, using only fresh ingredients, whenever possible using only local produce; all things to be cherished, still more so in this age of food scares. Associated with this is a willingness to be near-endlessly painstaking, for perfectionism is one of the lesser-known but very marked French characteristics, and if France has been so important in the history of cuisine it is perhaps because it was the first country in Europe really to institutionalise taking trouble over its food. And one other aspect is a sense of luxury, for France enjoys its pleasures, and a pampering opulence is still a prime feature of fine French food today.

This guide is based on my shorter 1996 book *Lazy Days Out Across the Channel*, and like the earlier guide seeks to open up a range of attractive places within easy distance of the Channel ports, familiar and non-familiar – famous sites such as Monet's garden at Giverny, Mont St-Michel, the great cathedrals of Amiens, Bayeux or Rouen, beautifully tranquil countryside such as the Pays d'Auge or the Bay of the Somme, cities like Lille, and characterful small towns such as Eu. In restaurants, it does not aim to present a guide to all the thousands of eating-places across northern France, but a selection. Among the featured restaurants there are some of the region's premier chefs, such as Roland Gauthier at Montreuil, Jean-Pierre Dargent in Arras or

Patrice Kukurudz at Rouen, but also tiny inns lost in the countryside, small-town favourites, hip beach-resort brasseries. All of them, though, can provide a wonderful meal that's a rare pleasure, and well worth a detour.

Orientation

Eating Times, Restaurants and Brasseries

To say that the French are a nation of traditionalists is a statement that one could mull over at length, but it certainly does apply in one area: when to eat. A huge proportion of the population, and in rural areas just about everybody, sits down to lunch from 12.30 to 1pm, and for dinner from 8.30 to 9pm, and anywhere that calls itself a restaurant expects to serve food only around these times. To avoid disappointment, it's advisable to say 'when in Rome...' and adapt to this as much as possible. When, in the timings given in this book, it says that a restaurant is open noon–2pm and 7.30–9.30pm, this means that these are the times within which you can order a meal (although it's still not a good idea to try to get lunch after 1.30); it does not mean that you will have to leave at 2pm, for having sat down you can take as long as you like, and one positive feature of this attitude is that there is never any idea of squeezing you off a table in order to admit a 'second sitting'. In cities, eating times are more fluid, and in particular many restaurants may take orders until 10–11pm.

The traditional alternative to the French restaurant with its set timings has been the brasserie. Real city brasseries have a less formal style, have huge menus that include many snacks and one-course dishes as well as three-course meals – all-time brasserie classics include steaks, sandwiches, mussels and *frites* and French onion soup – and are genuinely open '*à toute heure*', at all hours, often till 2–3am. In country districts, however, especially in western Normandy, you may well find that even in a place that calls itself a brasserie they will look aghast at you if you try to order anything more than a coffee or a drink during the afternoon, so they can't be relied on. Increasingly fashionable are small *salon de thé*-type restaurants that particularly serve light one-course lunch menus of mixed salads, omelettes and so on, but so far these are very much a sophisticated urban phenomenon. One other consequence of the belief in regular eating habits is that Normans rarely snack between meals. The attitude changes in the north, towards Belgium, where *frites* or chip stands are fairly ubiquitous, and in Brittany with the bargain institution of the *crêperie*.

Menus and *Formules*

The set menu is the most common way of ordering a meal in French restaurants, with three or four courses (often including cheese) and coffee for a fixed price. Wines and other drinks are usually charged separately. Most restaurants offer a range of different menus of varying degrees of elaborateness, and this is nearly always the best-value way to eat. Ordering from the *carte*, which most restaurants also have, will always be more expensive. Brasseries generally list both set menus and a wide range of single dishes. Very cheap, bargain menus are often called *formules*.

Auberges du Terroir and *Fermes-auberges*

These two types of country restaurant both developed out of the enormous interest in France in fresh local produce and regional cooking. An *auberge du terroir* is officially recognised as serving only fresh produce from the surrounding area, although the way it uses them can be notably sophisticated. A *ferme-auberge* is a farm that also has a dining room where meals are served made only with the produce of the farm itself, and so tends to offer simple country cooking, although, again, the culinary inventiveness of French farming families can amaze you.

Hotels, *Logis* and *Chambre-d'Hôte*

France has a great many small-scale, local hotels throughout the country. *Logis de France* are not a chain but an association, of independent, usually family-run hotels with resident proprietors. *Logis* are graded, from one to three (and occasionally four) 'chimneys', and can be luxurious, in some cases, or quite basic; but *Logis* membership nearly always guarantees a certain reliable level of quality and individual service. *Chambre-d'hôte* is French for bed-and-breakfast (B&B), of which there is now a wide choice in France, including many spectacular examples that offer a far better deal than hotels. They do not usually provide evening meals, although they may be available by arrangement, particularly in country *chambre-d'hôte* with no restaurant nearby. One essential difference is that, in the prices given in this guide, hotel prices do not include breakfast, which is charged separately (*usually 30–40F/€4.57–6.1*); in *chambre-d'hôte* prices, on the other hand, breakfast is always included.

Information

France has a very well-developed network of tourist offices. Anyone who is interested in finding out about traditional food producers and farms that sell direct to the public will find that the local offices have plenty of relevant leaflets and lists of suitable places. The *Bienvenue à la Ferme* leaflets produced for most *départements* are especially useful.

Prices and the Euro

Prices are given in this guide as they are usually shown in France, that is, with the basic franc price and the new euro price calculated next to it, so that you get unwieldy figures like 200F/€30.49. One euro has a fixed value of 6.56F. The euro, however, will appear on the streets as an everyday currency on 1 January 2002, and is expected to replace the franc by March 2002 (*see* p.17). As the euro takes over and becomes the basis for pricing, these fractional euro prices will inevitably be rounded off (and probably upwards) by 1–2 euros, but until this happens it is impossible to predict just what the level of prices will be.

The Food and Drink of Northern France

Essential to the type of French cooking which is covered in this guide is the concept of *terroir*, which means earth, or rather the particular piece of earth of each place or region. Every *terroir* in France, every region, sometimes each small locality, has its own specialities, based on the products most suited to its soil, climate, even the lay of the land, and wherever possible you should make use of them: fish or shellfish on the coast, apples or leeks inland. There is also a concern to follow the seasons, out of a desire for genuine freshness and a simple, deep-rooted respect for the *terroir*.

Freshness and quality of ingredients is everything in good French cooking. This is the opposite of the kind of attitude that expects to have strawberries, tomatoes or sugarsnaps 365 days a year, flown in from any corner of the globe. There is still an enormous demand in France for local, premium-standard produce, even if it costs more, and a substantial part of French agriculture and fishing – in short, the much-decried ways of the traditional French farmer – is still geared to satisfying this need. There is an emphasis on obtaining fresh products as close to source as possible, directly from farms and independent producers, many of which are listed in this book. Such ingredients simply taste exactly as they should taste, and the difference this makes is exhilarating, so that even dishes that are otherwise very simply prepared can be spectacular.

Because of the notion of *terroir*, food in France – above all rural France – is still tremendously regionalised, sometimes to extremes: in Picardy virtually every restaurant has *ficelle picarde* somewhere on its menu, while if you cross the little River Bresle into Normandy cider and cream sauces suddenly appear on every side. Like all popular concepts *terroir* can be abused and trivialised, but at its best it creates a fascinating diversity. And in northern France it leads to local produce such as leeks, cabbage, carrots, meats and herbs being valued and used in a way that could inspire those restaurants in Britain that still dismiss them in favour of sun-dried tomatoes and shiitake mushrooms.

Among the most distinct and popular products of each *terroir* are its cheeses. Fine French cheeses are often the result of two distinct processes, the actual cheese-making on the farm or at the cooperative, and the maturing or *affinage* that takes place in a cheese cellar. *Affinage* is one of the greatest of French inventions, the delicate process by which cheeses are aged by being washed in different liquids – *eau-de-vie*, brine, beer – in special cellars to create subtle flavours. Some farm producers mature their own cheeses, but the best are produced in the cellars of craft cheese merchants, identified as a Maître Fromager Affineur. Any good *fromager* will have a choice of cheeses from around the country, but the most prominently displayed will generally be those from the local area. Cheeses are always *affiné* to reach their best at a certain time, and when buying cheese you will almost certainly be asked when you intend to eat it. Most Northern French and Norman cheeses are soft, and have a fairly short life (they are liable to become pretty odorous and acidic after about two weeks). Virtually all traditional northern and Norman cheeses are made with cows' milk, but some farms now produce good-quality *brebis* (ewe's-milk cheese) and especially *chèvre* (goats'-milk cheese), generally based on more traditional southern varieties.

Food Concerns

As has been well reported, there have been some cases of BSE in France, although the level of infection is still much lower than it has been in Britain. Obviously, given that so little is known for certain about this disease, it would be a brave individual who made any categorical statements on the safety of beef and veal. However, controls in France are now very rigorous, and the level of public concern within the country has subsided. Also, a common link between the restaurateurs included in this book is their commitment to quality ingredients sourced direct from local producers, often organic. Their establishments are of all places perhaps the most likely to use safe, uncontaminated ingredients.

Pas-de-Calais and Artois

The Pas-de-Calais (chapters 4–6 and 9–11) is the closest part of France to Britain both geographically and in its produce: northern vegetables such as cabbages, carrots, chicory, celeriac, shallots and especially leeks feature strongly. This has never been among France's most admired cuisines, but dishes are often satisfying and subtle. Among meats, lamb and duck are often more prominent than beef, there is plenty of pork-based *charcuterie*, game and rabbit are popular in season, and one of the specialities of the area is *volailles de Licques*, free-range poultry from around the little town of Licques, south of Calais, which is known for its low fat-content and full-bodied but delicate flavour. This usually means chicken (*poulet de Licques*) but there are also Licques turkeys (*dindes*). This is also a big fish-eating area, from wonderful sole, ling and sea bass to the many uses of mussels.

The region's most traditional drink is, as in Flanders, beer. One of the best of the local small-brewery labels to look out for is the deliciously full-bodied Ch'ti, brewed at Benifontaine near Lens.

Boulette d'Avesnes: A powerful hybrid cheese made with bits of Maroilles (*see below*) kneaded together with herbs and spices and then formed into a cone, coated in paprika and cured for another length of time, forming a very strong, spicy mix.

Caudière, chaudière, chaudrée: Fish stew, usually with sole and other types of fish, mussels, small eels, potatoes and white wine.

Flamiche, Tarte Flamiche, Flamique: Vegetable tart on a doughy base, rather like a quiche but often without the upturned rim, and frequently topped with leeks (flamiche de poireaux), cream and cheese. Flamiches are also found throughout Flanders and Picardy.

Maroilles: The classic cheese of northern France, with variants found from Picardy to Flanders. A strong cow's-milk cheese that's aged and washed for some time before eating, with a dark reddy-brown rind, a soft texture and (usually) a powerful smell. Some Maroilles is washed in beer during *affinage*, which gives it extra strength in taste and odour.

Rollot: Another northern washed cheese, strong and spicy like Maroilles, with a lighter, yellower rind. It is often round or heart-shaped.

Flanders

French Flanders (chapter 7 and, to some extent, chapter 8, Lille) is something of an anomaly in this book, as the least French part of the whole area from Belgium to Brittany, despite this area having been a part of France for over 300 years. Flemish country food makes use of beef, rabbit and chicken, carrots and leeks, with a certain un-French, hearty quality, and a lack of the usual Gallic complexity. Another 'oddity' of dining in Flanders features the *estaminet*, the time-honoured Flemish pub, which traditionally serves single-course, snack-type dishes – open sandwiches, platters of cold meats, plates of stew with chips – served with beer, produced in one of this small region's many excellent local breweries (or just across the border in Belgium), *see* p.61. Beer is much-used in local cooking, and is one of its most distinctive sources of flavour; another is the use of juniper, whether as juniper hips (*baies de genièvre*) or just as gin. True historic *estaminets* are no longer plentiful, but even conventional restaurants in this region are more likely to serve one-course dishes than is the case in most parts of France, and since the Flemish are big snackers (again in an un-French way) there are *frites*-stands everywhere. In Lille, cuisine is much more Frenchified, and more sophisticated.

Carbonnade (de boeuf): Beef braised in beer with onions.
Coq à la bière: Chicken cooked in beer with mushrooms.
Mimolette: A round cheese with an orange-coloured flesh, similar to Dutch Gouda or Edam, and a grey rind that is aged for over a year before eating. A powerful cheese (the strongest kind is called Vieux Lille or Vieux Puant ('Old Stinker') for reasons that can be imagined). General De Gaulle loved the stuff.
Potjevleesch, potje'vleesh: Mixed terrine of rabbit, veal, chicken, pork or combinations of the above, served in slices cold with *frites*.
Tartine: Open-faced sandwich on buttered bread, with different toppings.
Waterzooi: Creamy stew of chicken or river fish with vegetables.

Picardy

The traditional food of Picardy (chapters 12–13) is sturdy, country cuisine. Since a great deal of the area is wetland, duck is especially important, and features heavily on menus throughout the winter. Around the Bay of the Somme, fish and shellfish caught close offshore – shrimps, mussels, sole and *lieu* (pollack) – are spectacularly good. Most celebrated of all the bay's produce, though, is its lamb. The Bay of the Somme is one of the two main areas in northern France (the other being the Bay of Mont St-Michel) where sheep can be raised on salt marshes. Salt-marsh lamb or agneau de prés-salés has unusually lean meat and a sparer, saltier, more delicate flavour than most lamb, and is highly prized. Ham and other pork are also prominent, while around Amiens much is made of the vegetables grown in the *hortillons* or water-gardens beside the Somme. In almost perverse contrast to their Norman neighbours, Picards make strangely little use of butter.

Belval: Mild cows'-milk cheese, made in flat disks.

Ficelle Picarde: The ubiquitous Picard dish: a savoury crêpe filled with ham, mushrooms and onions (and sometimes also chicken) and baked in a cheese sauce.

Soupe Maraîchère/des Hortillons: Fresh garden vegetable soup (Amiens).

Normandy

Normandy is the area most featured in this book (chapters 14–32) and Norman cooking is one of the grand cuisines of France, with a distinct identity and its own favourite ingredients *du terroir*: apples, cider, cream and butter. This may sound pretty rich, but the dishes need not be overpowering: all they require is an able chef, as fine Norman cooking is a real test of skill.

The apparently simple basic repertoire of Norman cooking can be applied to all kinds of ingredients and leaves enormous scope for variation. Peasant in origin, it also provides a base for dishes of great sophistication. Standard Normande or Vallée d'Auge sauces can be used with chicken, veal, pork or other meats, while duck – as prominent here as it is in Picardy – might be served with a subtle reduction with just a hint of apple. Cattle in this major dairy area are more often served to eat as veal, from male calves, than as beef. Duck also features in one of the most rich and traditional of Norman dishes, characteristic of Rouen and the Seine Maritime, Caneton Rouennais, in which the bird is cooked unbled so that the meat is supremely tender and has an exceptionally dense flavour. In its most complete form, when the duck carcass is put through a special ornate press to extract the juices, this is one of the most elaborate dishes of French grand cuisine.

The most prominent Norman *charcuterie* are earthy varieties: *boudin noir* (black pudding) or *andouilles* and *andouillettes* (gut sausages), the very best of which come from the Vire area in southwest Normandy. Smoked meats are a speciality of the Cotentin, which produces delicious smoked ham. Normandy is also the source of some of the finest foie gras in France, and one of the widest varieties of duck and goose terrines and *rillettes*. The Bay of Mont St-Michel, meanwhile, is one of the areas where the much sought-after *pré-salé* or salt-marsh lamb is raised.

Normandy also has a long coastline, and everywhere that fish and shellfish are landed there are restaurants that try to make the best of them. Sole has traditionally been the most highly regarded fish in Norman cooking, especially along the coast of the Seine Maritime, but turbot, *turbotin* (small turbot), sea bass and sea bream (*daurade*) are all popular. Mussels – often cultivated semi-artificially on *bouchots* (posts driven into mud-flats just offshore) – are consumed in huge quantities. Shellfish are best around the Cotentin peninsula: the region's finest oysters come from St-Vaast-la-Hougue, followed by the Bay of Mont St-Michel and the Isigny-Grandcamp coast, while lobsters are generally better on the western Cotentin. In winter, *coquilles St-Jacques* (scallops) take pride of place in most coastal restaurants.

Given Normandy's huge importance in the cheese world it's only natural that restaurants here tend to keep up the proper tradition of the cheese course, which is under pressure in some more fashion-conscious parts of France. Desserts are another area in which Norman cooking comes into its own, with, once again, primary reliance on the classic ingredients: apples and cream, with liberal dashes of apple booze (calvados) to give added sparkle. *Tarte normande, tarte aux pommes, tarte tatin* or *tarte aux poires* (with pears) are standards throughout the region.

Barbue à l'oseille: Brill in a sorrel sauce.

Douillon aux Pommes (or **aux Poires**): Fruit dessert in which a whole baked apple or pear is surrounded by a ring-like pastry case.

Jambon au Cidre: Ham baked or simmered in cider.

Marmite Dieppoise: Fish and shellfish stew with white wine, leeks and cream. In Fécamp virtually the same dish is called a Marmite Fécampoise.

Moules à la crème (**normande**): Mussels cooked in white wine, onions and cream, sometimes with a touch of cider.

Omelette Normande: Probably with a filling of mushrooms and *crevettes* (shrimps) or a sweet filling of apples, cream and calvados.

Poulet, veau, etc. Vallée d'Auge: Meat served with a crème fraîche, calvados and onion sauce, with sautéed apples and mushrooms.

Salade Normande: Mixed salad (usually) with ham, potatoes and hard-boiled eggs.

Sauce Normande: Sauce with a base of cider and crème fraîche.

Sole Normande: Sole poached in cider and cream with shrimps; in more refined versions, oysters, *langoustines* and other shellfish may be added.

Teurgoule: Norman baked rice pudding with thick cinammon-flavoured crust.

Tripes à la mode de Caen: Classic Norman dish of beef tripe, onions, other vegetables and spices cooked in water, cider and calvados.

Normandy Cheeses

Camembert: The least historic of the Normandy cheeses (*see* p.242), but the best-known. Camembert can now be made virtually anywhere, but the authentic *appelation d'origine contrôlée* (AOC) local product is identified as Camembert de Normandie. In good Camembert the rind should have some browny-red colour in it, and it should have a noticeable but not over-strong smell.

Livarot: A cows'-milk cheese with its own AOC (made only in the Pays d'Auge) that is one of the oldest Normandy cheeses, and is quite pungent. With a thick yellowy-orange rind, it is always made in round disks wrapped in five strips of paper that are said to suggest military stripes, which is why it's sometimes called Le Colonel.

Neufchâtel: From the Pays de Bray (*see* p.167), this is the only one of the classic Normandy cheeses from north of the Seine. It's one of the least-known, but also one of the most satisfying, and different from cheeses from further south: it has a drier, powdery texture, a mild taste and a white, powdery rind. Neufchâtel was mentioned in documents from the early Middle Ages, but it only got its AOC in the 1970s. The cheese is made in a variety of shapes: cylinders (*bondes*), rectangles (*briquettes* and *carrés*) and, most distinctively, hearts (*coeurs*). This doesn't affect the flavour, which depends on its age and whether or not it's *affiné*.

Pavé d'Auge: Very similar to Pont-l'Evêque, but stronger and with a darker rind.

Petit Lisieux or **Vieux Lisieux**: Another Pays d'Auge cheese related to Pont-l'Evêque, but possibly older and certainly spicier and stronger smelling. A very robust, rich cheese.

Pont-l'Evêque: A tender cow's-milk cheese from the northern Pays d'Auge, where the AOC area is centred, although it is now made all over Normandy. It has been known since at least the 16th century. Softer in texture than Camembert and milder in flavour, but still with a noticeable tang, it is made in squares, with a whiteish-brown rind. It should not have a very strong smell.

Cider, *Pommeau* and Calvados

Normandy is the largest region of France that does not contain a single vineyard. It does, however, have quantities of cider farms, and cider is the region's traditional tipple. Cider farms come in all sizes: the largest are those in the northern Seine Maritime – like the giant Duché de Longueville estate, south of Dieppe, which represents Normandy cider in supermarkets around the world. In the Bessin, west of Bayeux, there are large, attractive and less 'industrial' farms, while in the Cotentin there are tiny small-holdings half-lost up winding lanes.

Many smaller producers only sell direct, not through shops, which gives an added interest to cider-hunting; tourist offices in cider-producing areas have leaflets indicating local farms open for direct sales. Many Normandy farmers produce a relatively coarse cider in barrels (*cidre tonneaux*), which is sold in bottles with screw caps, but their best cider is always the *cidre bouché* (corked cider), which has a light fizz or *pétillance* and is usually available either *doux* (sweet), *demi* or *brut* (dry). Traditionally, the most prestigious cider-producing area in Normandy has been the Pays d'Auge east of Caen, which – around Cambremer – is the only district with an AOC for ciders. Pays d'Auge ciders tend to be well-rounded, with a slightly more golden colour than many others, and often even the *brut* ciders still have a touch of sweetness. If you prefer a drier, cleaner flavour try the more astringent ciders from the stonier soils of the Cotentin to the west. Ciders are unpredictable, as apples are more susceptible than grapes to changes in the weather, so that ciders from the same patch of ground can vary a great deal from year to year. This only adds to the interest.

The apple harvest runs roughly from late September to November. Once the apples have been gathered and crushed, the dryness of cider can be deliberately varied by how long it is left to ferment in the barrel, although cider apples more than six months old must by law be made into calvados. Cider, once bottled, does not change significantly with age. Many farms now bottle up some very sweet *cidre nouveau* for sale at Christmas, but purists scoff at this as a crude imitation of the Beaujolais nouveau fad. *Demi* and *brut* ciders become available in March or April, so that the best time for tasting and buying is from mid-spring to early autumn. Large producers have ciders on sale all year round, but by October smaller farms may have sold out. Even very high-quality ciders, brought direct from the producers, are very cheap, at around 30F a bottle or less.

Very few Normandy farms produce only cider. Many also produce *pommeau*, a straight cider-and-calvados mix that makes an enjoyable, smooth liqueur. It can be quite sweet, and it's used a good deal in cooking because of the tangy flavour it gives to meat. Farms also often sell *poiré* (pear cider, or old English perry), fine cider vinegars and fresh apple juice. And lastly but most importantly there is calvados itself, *calva*: distilled apple juice or apple brandy, perhaps Normandy's greatest culinary invention and still the region's favourite after-dinner *digestif*. Good calvados is smoother than most whiskies and is the most fragrant of spirits.

As with ciders, calvados from the Pays d'Auge has traditionally been the most highly regarded, and there are two different AOC categories, one for calvados and another for Calvados du Pays d'Auge, which must be passed twice through the traditional pot still, a process called double distillation. Again, calvados is hugely variable, which leaves plenty of room for individual taste and discussion. Calvados also varies a great deal according to how long it is left to age in the barrel. 'Standard' calvados is aged for up to five years; beyond that it may be called Hors d'Age or identified more precisely as ten, 15, 20 or up to 50 years old. Well-aged fine calvados is a superbly complex drink, with a fascinating depth and variety of flavour.

A final great Normandy institution is the *trou normand*: a shot of calvados drunk between the first and second courses of a meal, in order to clear a 'hole' for the remaining courses. In Maupassant's time it was the custom at Norman country dinners for the men at least to take a straight slug of calvados between every course, and some traditional folk are still stout enough to keep this up today. The most common version of the *trou* found in restaurants today is a more refined equivalent: a little cup of apple sorbet, floating in calvados.

Brittany

Brittany only features briefly in this book, in chapter 33, St-Malo. This being an historic port city, its best food has always been heavily based on fresh fish and seafood, and the immediate differences between the local cuisine and that of other Atlantic coast regions are not that marked, although compared to Normandy you do notice a decrease in the use of apples. Oysters, from Cancale, and cod, whether fresh (*cabillaud*) or salt-cod (*morue*), have always been St-Malo specialities, at least until the recent cod crisis. One significant difference is in the number of crêperies.

Crêpes (de froment): Thin wheatflour pancakes, often with sugar in the mix, served with sweet fruit, chocolate and cream fillings, often with cream on top.

Galettes (de sarrasin): Thicker, savoury buckwheat pancakes, served with savoury fillings such as mushrooms, ham, eggs, cheese and so on.

Practicalities

03

Getting There

By Air from North America

Paris, as a major transatlantic destination, often benefits in the airline price wars. There are a good dozen charter and cut-rate scheduled flight options from the USA.

Agencies that have long had cheap flight options to Paris are: Uni-Travel, **t** (800) 325 2222; Council Travel, **t** (800) 223 7402; Access, **t** (800) 825 3633; Discount Travel International, **t** (800) 543 0110; or Last Minute Travel Club, **t** (800) 527 8646.

From Canada, there are decidedly fewer juicy options: Travel CUTS is a good place to start hunting for bargains, 187 College St, Toronto, Ont., M5T 1P7, **t** (416) 979 2406. Also try *www.lastminute.com*.

Paris has two airports: Charles de Gaulle, (north of Paris), also known as Roissy from the suburb in which it is located, **t** 01 49 75 15 15/ **t** 01 48 62 12 12, and Orly (south, and nearer the centre), **t** 01 49 75 15 15.

There are frequent flights to Paris on most of the major airlines. During off-peak periods (the winter months and fall) you should be able to get a scheduled economy flight from New York to Paris from as little as around $370–$460.

Check the Sunday-paper travel sections for the latest deals, and research your fare initially on some of the cheap-flight websites:
www.priceline.com
www.expedia.com
www.hotwire.com
www.bestfares.com
www.travelocity.com
www.eurovacations.com
www.cheaptrips.com

By Sea

The ferry is a good option if you're travelling by car or with young children (children of four–14 get reduced rates; under-fours go free), and if you want to do some shopping (it takes 35mins from Dover to Calais by Seacat). Fares can be expensive and do vary according to season and demand. The most expensive booking period runs from the first week of July to mid-August; other pricey times include Easter and the school holidays. Book as far ahead as possible and keep your eyes peeled for special offers. Some good-value five-day mini breaks for a car and up to nine people (Caen and Cherbourg from £65) and 10-day saver-breaks (Caen and Cherbourg from £88) are available.

Brittany Ferries, The Brittany Centre, Wharf Road, Portsmouth PO2 8RU, **t** (08705) 360 360, *www.brittany-ferries.com*. Sailings from Portsmouth to Caen (6hrs) and St-Malo, from Poole to Cherbourg (4¼hrs).

Condor Ferries, The Quay, Weymouth, Dorset DT4 8DX, **t** (01305) 761551, *www.condor ferries.co.uk*. Sailings from Weymouth and Poole to St-Malo.

Hoverspeed Ferries, International Hoverport, Dover CT17 9TG, **t** (08705) 240 241, **f** (01304) 240 088, *www.hoverspeed.co.uk*. Seacats Dover–Calais (35mins), Folkestone–Boulogne (55mins), Newhaven–Dieppe (2hrs).

P&O Portsmouth, Peninsular House, Wharf Rd, Portsmouth PO2 8TA, **t** (0870) 242 4999, **f** (02392) 864 211, *www.poportsmouth.com*. Day and night sailings from Portsmouth to Le Havre (5½hrs) and Cherbourg.

P&O Stena, Channel House, Channel View Rd, Dover CT17 9TJ, **t** (0870) 600 0600, **f** (01304) 863 464, *www.posl.com*. Ferry and superferry from Dover to Calais (45mins).

SeaFrance, Eastern Docks, Dover, Kent CT16 1JA, **t** (08705) 711 711, **f** (01304) 240033, *www.seafrance.com*. Sailings from Dover to Calais (1½hrs).

Useful Numbers

Parking information in Dover: **t** (0839) 401 570.
Shopping information in Calais: **t** (0839) 401 577.
Weather forecast for Dover: **t** (0839) 444 069.
Weather forecast for France: **t** (0891) 575 577.

By Train

Eurostar (**t** 0990 186 186) trains leave from London Waterloo or Ashford International, in Kent, direct to Paris (Gare du Nord; 3hrs; £79) and Lille (2hrs; £69). Fares are cheaper if booked at least seven days in advance and you include a Saturday night away. Check in 20mins before departure, or you will not be allowed on to the train.

Tour Operators and Special-interest Holidays

For a complete list of tour operators, see the Maison de France website at *www.franceguide. com* or the US website at *www.francetourism. com*, or get in touch with a French government tourist office (*see* p.18).

Andante, Grange Cottage, Winterbourne Dauntsey, Salisbury, Wiltshire SP4 6ER, **t** (01980) 610 555, **f** (01980) 610 002, *andante travel@virgin.net*. Archaeological, walking and historical study tours in Brittany.

Page & Moy, 135–40 London Rd, Leicester LE2 1EN, **t** (0116) 250 7000, **f** (0116) 250 7123. City breaks, gastronomy and cultural tours.

Custom Spa Vacations, 1318 Beacon St, Suite 20, Brookline, MA 02446, **t** 800 443 7727,

t (617) 566 5144, **f** (617) 731 0599, *www.spa tours.com*. Health spas in France including Deauville.

Galaxy Tours, P.O. Box 234, 997 Old Eagle School Rd, Suite 207, Wayne, PA 19087 0234, **t** 800 523 7287, **t** (610) 964 8010, **f** (610) 964 8220, *www.galaxytours.com*. First and Second World War veterans' tours.

Backroads, 801 Cedar St, Berkeley, CA 94701 1800, **t** 800 462 2848, **t** 800 GO ACTIVE, **f** (510) 527 1444, *www.backroads.com*. Bicycling, hiking and multisport holidays in France including Brittany and Normandy.

Brooks Country Cycling Tours, 140 W. 83rd St, New York, NY 10024, **t** (212) 874 5151, **f** (212) 874 5286, *brookscct@aol.com*. Guided cycling tours in Brittany and Normandy.

Details, advance reservations and car hire information are available at
Rail Europe, 179 Piccadilly, London W1V 0BA, **t** (08705) 848 848, *www.raileurope.co.uk*.
Rail Europe, 226 Westchester Av, White Plains, NY 10064, **t** (1 800) 438 7245, *www.raileurope.com*.

By Car

Putting your car on a Eurotunnel train is the most convenient way of crossing the Channel. It takes only 35mins to get through the tunnel from Folkestone to Calais, and there are up to four departures an hour, 365 days of the year. In low season, tickets for a car and passengers should cost around £170 return, rising to £200 return at peak times. If you travel at night (*10pm–6am*), it will be slightly cheaper. Special-offer day returns (look for them on the website) range from £15 to £50. The price for all tickets is per car less than 6.5m in length, plus the driver and all passengers.
Contact: Eurotunnel, **t** (0990) 353 535, *www.eurotunnel.com*.

If you prefer a dose of bracing sea air, you've plenty of choice, although changes and mergers may be on the horizon. Short ferry crossings currently include Dover–Calais with P&O Stena, **t** (0870) 600 0600, SeaFrance, **t** (08705) 711 711, or Hoverspeed, **t** (08705) 240 241, which offers the fastest crossing, at 35mins. *See* 'By Sea', above, for other routes.

Entry Formalities

Holders of full, valid EU, USA, Canadian, Australian and New Zealand passports do not need a visa to enter France for stays of up to three months. If you intend to stay longer, the law says you need a *carte de séjour*, a requirement EU citizens can easily get around as passports are rarely stamped. Non-EU citizens had best apply for an extended visa before leaving home. You can't get a *carte de séjour* without the visa. For further information contact your nearest French consulate.

Getting Around

By Train

The SNCF's France-wide information number is **t** 08 36 35 35 35 (3.35F/€0.51 per min), or check out *www.sncf.com* (you can book advance tickets from the USA or UK prior to departure on this website, and pay by credit card at an SNCF machine in France). The SNCF runs a decent and efficient network of trains through all the major cities. Prices have recently gone up but are still reasonable.

Tickets must be stamped in the little orange machines by the entrance to the lines that say *Compostez votre billet*. Any time you interrupt a journey until another day, you have to re-compost your ticket.

Nearly every station has large computerised lockers (*consignes automatiques*), but note that any recent terrorist activity in France tends to close them down across the board.

By Bus

There is no national bus network. Though local services can work out, do not count on seeing any part of rural France by public transport. The bus network is just about adequate between major cities and towns, but can be rotten in rural areas. More remote villages are linked to civilisation only once a week or not at all.

For details on local bus services, enquire at your local tourist office in France.

By Car

A car is the only way to see some of the remoter parts of France. Roads are generally excellently maintained, but anything of less status than a departmental route (D road) may be uncomfortably narrow.

Rules and Regulations

You will need your vehicle registration document, full driving licence and an up-to-date insurance certificate. If you're coming from the UK or Ireland, you'll need headlight converters to adjust the dip of the headlights to the right. Carrying a warning triangle is mandatory if you don't have hazard lights, and advisable even if you do. Drivers with a valid licence from an EU country, Canada, the USA or Australia do not need to have an international driving licence.

Speed limits are 130km/8omph (110km/h in wet weather) on the *autoroutes* (toll motorways); 110km/69mph on dual carriageways (divided highways and motorways without tolls); 90km/55mph on other roads; 50km/30mph in an 'urbanised area' – as soon as you pass a white sign with a town's name on it and until you pass another sign with the town's name barred. Fines for speeding, payable on the spot, begin at 1,300F/€198.17 and can reach an astronomical 10,000F/ €1524.39 if you fail the breathalyser (the limit is 0.05% alcohol).

If you wind up in an accident, you must fill out and sign a *constat amiable*. If your French isn't sufficient to deal with this, hold off until you find someone to translate for you so you don't accidentally incriminate yourself. If you have a breakdown and are a member of a motoring club affiliated with the Touring Club de France, ring the latter; if not, ring the police.

Watch out for the *Cédez le passage* (Give way) signs and be careful. Generally, as you'd expect, give priority to the main road, and to the left on roundabouts. If you are new to France, think of every intersection as a new and perilous experience. Watch out for Byzantine street-parking rules (do as the natives do, and be especially careful about village centres on market days). When you (inevitably) get lost in a town or city, the *Toutes directions* or *Autres directions* signs are like Get Out of Jail Free cards. Watch out for the tiny signs indicating which streets are meant for pedestrians only (with complicated schedules in even tinier print).

Petrol (*essence*) at the time of writing is 7.4F/€1.13 a litre for unleaded, 7.8F/€1.19 a litre leaded, 5.3F/€0.81 for diesel (gasoil), but varies considerably, with motorways always more expensive. Petrol stations keep shop hours (most close Sunday and/or Monday) and are rare in rural areas. If you come across a garage with petrol-pump attendants, they will expect a tip for oil, windscreen-cleaning or air.

Contact: Europ Assistance, Sussex House, Perrymount Rd, Haywards Heath, West Sussex RH16 1DN, **t** (01444) 442211. They offer help with insurance for travelling abroad.

Useful Websites

Route planner: *www.iti.fr*.
Autoroute information: *www.autoroutes.fr*.
Roads and traffic information: *www.equipment.gouv.fr*.

Health and Emergencies

Ambulance (SAMU) **t** 15
Police and ambulance **t** 17
Fire **t** 18

France has one of the best healthcare systems in the world. Local hospitals are the place to go in an emergency (*urgence*). Doctors take turns going on duty at night and on holidays: ring one to listen to the recorded message to find out what to do.

Pharmacists are trained to administer first aid, and dispense advice for minor problems. In rural areas there is always someone on duty if you ring the bell of a pharmacy; in cities, pharmacies are open on a rota and addresses are posted in their windows and in the local newspaper.

In France, however you're insured, you pay up front for everything, unless it's an emergency, when you will be billed later. Doctors will give you a brown and white *feuille de soins* with your prescription; take both to the pharmacy and keep the *feuille*, the various medicine stickers (*vignettes*) and prescriptions for insurance purposes at home.

Money and Banks

1 January 1999 saw the start of the transition to the euro (€). It became the official currency in France (and 10 other nations of the European Union) and the official exchange rate was set at €1=6.55957F. Shops and businesses are now obliged to indicate prices in both currencies. You can open euro accounts, and some places will accept payment in euros by cheque or credit card, although euro coins and notes will not be circulated until 2002. Until 2002, you'll still be using the franc (abbreviated with an F), which consists of 100 centimes. All prices in this guide are shown in francs and euros.

Major international credit cards are widely used in France, but smaller hotels and restaurants and B&Bs may not accept cards at all.

Under the Cirrus system, withdrawals in francs can be made from bank and post office automatic cash machines, using your UK PIN. The specific cards accepted are marked on each machine, and most give instructions in English. Credit card companies charge a fee for cash advances.

In the event of **lost or stolen credit cards**, call the following emergency numbers:

Mastercard t 0800 901 387
American Express Paris, **t** 01 47 77 72 00
Visa (Carte Bleue) Paris, **t** 01 42 77 11 90
Barclaycard t (00 44) 1604 230 230
  (UK number)

Banks are generally open 8.30am–12.30pm and 1.30–4pm; they close on Sunday, and most close either on Saturday or Monday as well. Exchange rates vary, and nearly all take a commission of varying proportions. *Bureaux de change* that do nothing but exchange money (and hotels and train stations) usually have the worst rates or take the heftiest commissions.

Opening Hours, Museums and National Holidays

While many **shops and supermarkets** are now open continuously Tues–Sat 9/10–7/7.30, businesses in smaller towns still close down for lunch (12/12.30–2/3 or, in summer, till 4). There are local exceptions, but nearly everything shuts down on Mondays, except for grocers and *supermarchés* that open in the afternoon. In many towns, Sunday morning is a big shopping period. Markets (daily in the cities, weekly in villages) are usually open mornings only, although clothes, flea and antique markets run into the afternoon.

Most **museums** close for lunch, and often all day on Mondays or Tuesdays, and sometimes for all of November or the entire winter. Hours change with the season: longer summer hours begin in May or June and last until the end of September – usually. Most museums close on national holidays. We've done our best to include opening hours in the text, but don't sue us if they're not exactly right. Most museums give discounts if you have a student ID card, or are an EU citizen under 18 or over 65 years old; most charge admissions ranging from 10 to 30F. We have indicated in the text when there is an admission charge (*adm*) and if it is particularly expensive (*adm exp*). National museums are free if you're under 18. **Churches** are usually open all day, but might only open for Mass. Sometimes notes on the door direct you to the *mairie* or priest's house (*presbytère*) where you can pick up the key. There are often admission fees for cloisters, crypts and special chapels.

On French national holidays, banks, shops, businesses and some museums close; but most restaurants stay open. The French have a healthy approach to holidays: if there is a holiday on a Tuesday or Thursday, they 'make the bridge' (*faire le pont*) to the weekend and make Monday or Friday a holiday too.

Post Offices, Telephones and the Internet

Known as the PTT or Bureaux de Poste, easily discernible by a blue bird on a yellow background, post offices are open in the cities Mon–Fri 8am–7pm, and Sat 8am–12 noon. In villages, offices may not open until 9am, then break for lunch, and close at 4.30 or 5pm. You can buy stamps in *tabacs* and post offices.

Nearly all public telephones have switched over from coins to *télécartes*, which you can purchase at any post office or newsstand for 40F/€6.1 for 50 *unités* or 96F/€14.63 for 120 *unités*.

The French have eliminated area codes, giving everyone a 10-digit telephone number with the following prefixes: Paris and Ile de France 01, Normandy and Brittany 02, Picardy and Flanders 03. If **ringing France from abroad**, the international dialling code is 33, and drop the first '0' of the number. For **international calls** from France, dial 00, wait for the change in the dial tone, then dial the country code (UK 44; US and Canada 1; Ireland 353; Australia 61; New Zealand 64), and then the local code (minus the 0 for UK numbers) and number. For directory enquiries, dial **t** 12, or try the free, slow, inefficient Minitel electronic directory in every post office.

Most cities and towns now have one or more Internet cafés.

Tipping

Almost all restaurants and cafés automatically add an extra 15 per cent to the bill, and there's no need to leave any more unless you care to or in recognition of special service. Taxi drivers will be happy with 10 per cent.

Tourist Information

Every city and town, and most villages, have a tourist information office, usually called a Syndicat d'Initiative or an Office de Tourisme. In smaller villages this service is provided by the town hall (*mairie*). They distribute free maps and town plans, and hotel, camping and self-catering accommodation lists for their area, and can inform you about sporting events, leisure activities, wine estates open for visits, and festivals.

French government tourist offices abroad:
Australia: 25 Bligh St, Level 22, NSW 2000 Sydney, **t** (02) 9231 5244, **f** (02) 9221 8682.
Canada: 1981 Av McGill College, No.490, Montreal, PQ H3A 2W9, **t** (514) 288 4264, **f** (514) 845 4868, *mfrance@attcanada.net*.
Ireland: 10 Suffolk St, Dublin 1, **t** (01) 679 0813, **f** (01) 679 0814, *frenchtouristoffice@tinet.ie*.
UK: 178 Piccadilly, London W1V 0AL, **t** 0891 244 123 (calls charged at 60p/min), *info@mdlf.co.uk*, *www.franceguide.com*.
Normandy Tourist Board, The Old Bakery, 44 Bath Hill, Keynsham, Bristol BS31 1HG, **t** (0117) 986 0386, *www.normandy-tourism.org*, *stevenrodgers@compuserve.com*.
Picardy Tourist Board, c/o THF, PO Box 21352, London WC2H 9SR, **t** (020) 7836 2232, *www.cr-picardie.fr*, *www.somme-tourisme.com*, *picardie@thehatfactory.com*.
USA: 444 Madison Av, New York, NY 10022, **t** (410) 286 8310, **f** (212) 838 7855, *info@france tourism.com*, *www.francetourism.com*.
676 N. Michigan Av, Chicago, IL 60611, **t** (312) 751 7800, **f** (312) 337 63 39, *fgto@mcs.net*.
9454 Wilshire Bd, Suite 715, Beverly Hills, CA 90212, **t** (310) 271 6665, **f** (310) 276 2835, *fgto@gte.net*.

Unavoidable:
Calais

04

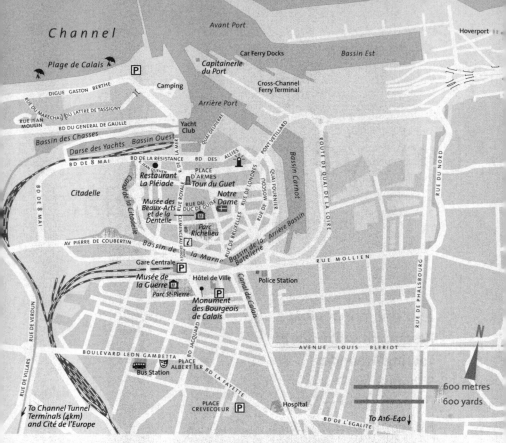

Channel

Avant Port

Hoverport

Plage de Calais

Car Ferry Docks

Bassin Est

Capitainerie
du Port

P

Camping

DIGUE GASTON BERTHE

Cross-Channel
Ferry Terminal

RUE DU MARECHAL DU LATTRE DE TASSIGNY

Arrière Port

RUE JEAN
MOULIN

BD DU GENERAL DE GAULLE

Yacht
Club

QUAI DELPIERRE

Bassin des Chasses

Darse des Yachts   Bassin Ouest

PONT VETILLARD

Bassin Carnot

ROUTE DE QUAI DE LA LOIRE

RUE DU NORD

Citadelle

BD DE 8 MAI

BD DE LA RESISTANCE

BD DES ALLIES

RUE DE LA MER

BD DE 8 MAI

Canal de la Citadelle

RUE JEAN QUEHEN

PLACE
D'ARMES

Restaurant
La Pléiade

Tour du Guet

RUE DE LONDRES

RUE DE BRUXELLES

QUAI FOURNIER

Musée des
Beaux-Arts
et de la
Dentelle

RUE DU
DUC DE GUISE

Notre
Dame

RUE DE MOSSON

M

RUE CLEMENCEAU BOSQUET

Parc
Richelieu

AV PIERRE DE COUBERTIN

Bassin de
la Marne

i

Bassin de la
Batellerie

Arrière Bassin

RUE MOLLIEN

Gare Centrale

P

RUE DE PHALSBOURG

Musée de
la Guerre

Hôtel de Ville

Police Station

Parc St-Pierre

P

RUE DE VERDUN

Monument
des Bourgeois
de Calais

Canal de Calais

BD JACQUARD

AVENUE   LOUIS   BLERIOT

N

BOULEVARD LEON GAMBETTA

PLACE
ALBERT 1ER

Bus Station

BD LA FAYETTE

RUE DE VILLARS

PLACE
CREVECOEUR

P

Hospital

600 metres

600 yards

To Channel Tunnel
Terminals (4km)
and Cité de l'Europe

BD DE L'EGALITE

To A16-E40 ↓

Ah, Calais. For Britain, the best-known, essential point of contact with France and
Continental Europe. A city rarely praised and rarely loved.

Calais is a gritty little working-class city, with a high level of unemployment and
famously argumentative dockers, part of a workaday France without any airs and
graces. Calais will never be put on any list of *villes de charme* or win any competition
for the *ville plus belle* or *plus fleurie*. Lately, instead, craggy Calais has been given a
fresh prominence in the eyes of the rest of France by its heroic football team, oddly
known as the CRUFC (from Calais Racing Union Football Club), the amateur side that
in a season of pure sporting romance in 1999–2000 got through to the final of the
French Cup by despatching a string of much more prestigious professional teams,
only to lose by one penalty to Nantes at the last hurdle, providing a whole new
source of local pride.

It's not that Calais isn't a historic town. Rather, Calais has suffered from an excess of
history, of the violent kind that has swept away whole centuries of its architecture,
often to be replaced by whatever could be put up most easily. And this history has
always, inescapably, been wound up with Britain.

Most recently, of course, Calais is best-known in Britain as Europe's largest discount
booze store, which only adds to its utilitarian feel. If all you want to do in Calais is
find the drinks warehouses, hypermarkets or shopping malls, fill up the car boot and

Getting There

The ferry terminals are all on the east side of Calais harbour; the Channel Tunnel terminal is west of the city at Coquelles. From the ferry terminals, follow the *Toutes Directions* sign to the first roundabout, and then take the exit for *centre ville*; for the large out-of-town stores, turn left at the first roundabout and follow the ring road instead. From the Shuttle terminal, you have the option of heading straight for Cité de l'Europe, joining the A16 *autoroute* and the ring road, or following signs for *centre ville* to get into town.

The main artery of Calais' old centre is the north-south street that's called at different points Rue de la Mer, Rue Royale and Boulevard Clémenceau. Parking is not usually too difficult in the city centre, and there is a large car park by the seaward end of Rue de la Mer on Boulevard de la Résistance. Rue Jean Quéhen, where La Pléiade restaurant is located, is the first turning on the right off Rue de la Mer, heading away from the sea.

Ferry companies provide complimentary or very cheap buses to the town centre for foot passengers. Calais also has good rail connections to Paris, the rest of France and other destinations from the Gare Centrale, near the Hôtel de Ville. Some London–Paris Eurostar trains also stop at Calais-Fréthun station outside the city; there are bus transfers between the Gare Centrale and Fréthun.

Tourist Information

Calais: 12 Bd Clémenceau, t 03 21 96 62 40, f 03 21 96 01 92, *www.ot-calais.fr*.

leave, then modern Calais' road system is organised to make this very easy to do. However, if you take the time to wander into town, central Calais also offers plenty of things to see and do in a day. As well as its megastores it has rows of bars and cafés and outside terraces, and beneath the surface there are all the everyday necessities of French life – *boulangeries, pâtisseries, traiteurs*, street markets. It has a lovely, unsung beach. And Calais has a quite exceptional range of fine places to eat, better than you might find in many higher chic-rated cities, which can justify a visit all by themselves. Of the impressive selection, one of the very best is M Eric Mémain's **La Pléiade**, a discreet little restaurant in the heart of the old town.

La Pléiade

32 Rue Jean Quéhen, t 03 21 34 03 70, f 03 21 34 03 13, E.Memain@lapleiade.com. Open Tues, Thurs, Fri and Sun 12–2.30 and 7.30–9.30, Wed 12–2.30, Sat 7.30–9.30; closed Mon. Menus 95F/€14.48, 125F/€19.05, 130F/€19.82 and 165F/€25.15; à la carte average 250F/€38.11.

The Rue Jean Quéhen is, like most of central Calais, a plain, workaday street of offices and apartment blocks, and the shop-like frontage of La Pléiade does not initially look much more distinctive. Inside, however, the traditional French restaurant comforts and customs are properly and smartly maintained: neat, classic décor, bowls of flowers on the tables, crisp linen and correct table settings. This traditionalism seems a little surprising, for Mme Delphine Mémain and her staff, who greet and serve with charm, style and attentiveness, are all young. The clientele – which usually seems to include a few Brits – is a wide mix, from families and business groups to young locals in jeans and black sweaters who drop in for a quick but superior lunch.

Neither trendy nor inflexibly old-fashioned, it's a restaurant with a certain timeless sense of intimacy. The first introduction to chef-proprietor Eric Mémain's cooking comes with the *mises-en-bouche*, the appetisers. On an autumn evening this might be a fabulously smooth and subtle *crème de coquilles St-Jacques*, a perfect mini-mix of flavours and textures.

A Calais native, Eric Mémain worked in Paris, Switzerland and various places around France before opening La Pléiade in the early 1990s. He is well schooled in the traditional dishes of northern France – fish stews, classic sauces – but is also always creating new dishes. A first course of freshwater crayfish ravioli with *girolles* mushrooms and a *jus de carapaces émulsionné* made with the seafood shells is hugely impressive. One of his frequent main courses features breast of the Pas-de-Calais' celebrated Licques chickens, artfully stuffed with *langoustines*. Another of his creations is sea bass steamed with dill and served with carefully simmered fennel and an oyster butter sauce.

This is exceptionally refined, subtle food, made with a skilful and light touch. It's also quite extraordinary value, and all the dishes on the set menus can also be ordered separately or as single courses, for not much extra expense.

To go with them there's a well-selected list of wines, all perfectly served. Desserts are as sybaritic and original as the earlier courses, as in a chicory ice-cream served with homemade biscuits and a decadently rich chocolate sauce. The coffee is accompanied by notably fruity *petit-fours* – as distinctive and finely crafted as the almost-forgotten *mises-en-bouche*.

Touring Around

Calais has two main parts. The medieval city of Calais was a fortified town built on a patch of hard ground surrounded by some of the many unstable water courses that criss-cross northern France and Flanders, which long ago were made into solid canals that ringed the old city like a moat and converted it into a quite distinct little island, as can easily be seen on any map. Directly to the south and some way inland there grew up an initially entirely separate community of St-Pierre, centred roughly where the junction of boulevards Jacquard and Lafayette is today, which expanded greatly with 19th-century industrialisation. Both halves were officially joined together in one city in 1885, and since then have been surrounded by a large 20th-century urban sprawl. The old city on the island is sometimes referred to as Calais-Nord, while the 'new' city in the former St-Pierre is Calais-Sud.

Not that either of them appears especially old to the visitor today. This is because Calais gives you a rapid and striking introduction to one of the less-publicised but pervasive features of northern France: 1940s reconstruction architecture. It is not widely appreciated in the English-speaking world just how much the north of France was devastated in the two World Wars. Whole cities from Normandy to Flanders were fought over and bombarded two or three times in just a few years, while others, considered transport hubs, were repeatedly bombed. The old quarters of the northern cities, based on brick and wood, burnt very easily when the firing started. Afterwards, some towns were the site of often astonishing restoration programmes – most remarkably Arras and St-Malo. Others were restored in large part, such as Rouen. After the Second World War, however, there were just too many places in urgent need of reconstruction and resources were too thin for this kind of work to go on everywhere, and entire districts or towns were rebuilt in a fairly uniform, practical style of straight lines, sloping tiled roofs and light grey stone or concrete walls. St-Lô and Tilly-sur-Seulles in Normandy are almost complete reconstruction towns. And one of the largest reconstruction cities is Calais.

Calais' particular catastrophe came in May 1940, when British and French troops were besieged within the city's centuries-old fortifications by relentless German air and artillery bombardment. The last-ditch defence of Calais significantly delayed the German advance, and played a major (some say essential) part in gaining time for the evacuation of the main Allied force to take place at Dunkerque to the east. It was also one of the better examples of Franco-British cooperation, with many heroic incidents such as that of the '1,000 volunteers of Calais', the French sailors who, offered the possibility of evacuation, volunteered to stay behind to fight as infantry. Calais was fought over again in September 1944, when Canadian troops ejected the Germans. By that time, virtually all of the historic architecture in the old city had been destroyed. Had this not happened visitors to the city today, instead of complaining about its greyness, would probably praise the charms of a town that curiously contained the largest (and only) concentration of English Tudor architecture in France.

Calais is a relative latecomer among the Channel ports, and is first mentioned in documents, as a subsidiary community of the much more important town of Boulogne, in 1180. In 1223 Philippe Hurepel or 'Frizzy-Hair', made Count of Boulogne by his father Philippe Auguste of France, first began to build up Calais as a fortified town with a castle on its western side. It soon became an important link in the wool trade between England and Flanders, and grew quite rapidly in the following century. More difficult contacts with the English came with the Hundred Years' War. In September 1346 Edward III, fresh from his victory at Crécy, besieged Calais. The city held out doggedly for all but a year until August 1347, when the starving Calaisiens asked for surrender terms. A vengeful Edward said that he would spare the people of Calais if six of its leading citizens, the famous Burghers of Calais, would come to present the keys of the city to him as beggars dressed only in their shirts. He sentenced the six to death, but was obliged to be merciful by the pleadings of his wife, Philippa of Hainault. Most of Calais' population, though, were expelled from the city, which would remain in English hands for the next 211 years.

It suffered a second, unsuccessful, siege in 1436, this time at the hands of the Duke of Burgundy who had fallen out with his former English allies. It was still a significant English possession in the early 16th century, and both Henry VIII and Mary Tudor sponsored substantial building work in the city. Then in 1558 the Duke of Guise, in a surprise attack, took Calais for France, supposedly leaving Mary Tudor to die with Calais written on her heart. This was not the end of Calais' travails, though, for it then became caught up in France's wars with the Spaniards in the Netherlands to the east.

A Spanish army took Calais in a bloody assault in 1596, and it was attacked again in 1638 and 1651, before the French frontier moved a safe distance away under Louis XIV. It then settled into its role as a port of passage for the English, and further major changes did not come until after the Napoleonic wars, when Calais – or rather, at that time, St-Pierre – became an important centre for the making of lace, helped by several families of English lacemakers from Nottingham who settled here. The arrival of a railway line from Paris in the 1840s, ahead of those to its competitors, cemented its position as the busiest of the French Channel ports. It also developed considerably as a commercial and fishing port, and was an early hub of the French labour movement, hence those obstreperous dockers.

Any visit to central Calais today concentrates on the **'old' city**, and particularly Rue de la Mer–Rue Royale–Boulevard Clémenceau, the main shopping, café and restaurant thoroughfare. The historic main square, **Place d'Armes**, still has its historic name but is the kind of place that – try as you might – does little to help you be nice about it. It's surrounded by grey shop-fronts and never quite seems sure whether it's a real square or just a car park. A plaque by a patch of grass indicates the site of an English Tudor belfry that was built for Mary I, and destroyed in 1940.

Looming up by the corner of Rue Royale there is a remarkable survivor of many battles, the battered but impressive watchtower, the **Tour de Guet** (38.5m), which has a vaguely Gothic base that formed part of the first defences of Calais built for Philippe Frizzy-Hair in 1224, and leads up bizarrely to a completely out-of-style bell tower, added in 1770. From the platform on the first storey Jean de Vienne, Governor of Calais, announced Edward III's surrender conditions to the people during the siege of 1347. A short walk from the far right corner of the Place d'Armes (looking from Rue Royale) is the 14th–15th-century church of **Notre-Dame**, which has the distinction of being the only English perpendicular Gothic church in France. It's another rare survivor from 1940, but was very badly damaged, and also is often closed (check with the tourist office on opening times). General de Gaulle was married here in 1921.

A few streets to the north on Boulevard des Alliés is Calais' lighthouse, the **Phare de Calais** (*normally open Oct–May Mon–Fri 2–5.30, Sat and Sun 10–12 and 2–5; June–Sept Mon–Fri 2–6.30, Sat and Sun 10–12 and 2–6.30; check with tourist office; adm*), which strangely towers up in the middle of the old town. The triangular Courgain district, between Boulevard des Alliés and the harbour, was one of the most traditional fishermen's quarters of Calais, and in post-1945 reconstruction an attempt was made to conserve something of its community feel in its very unusual apartment blocks, linked by small squares and passageways. It still contains good small fish restaurants.

However, the greatest monument of old Calais is reached by cutting back to the main street and following any of the streets on the western side of Royale/de la Mer to the end. This will take you to a broad esplanade and the moat-canal surrounding the massive low walls of the **Citadelle**, reached by a bridge. It was begun by the Duke of Guise in 1560, taking over and extending the site of the old castle, in order that the English would not be able to win the town back again. Subsequent rulers and generals extended it several times. The defenders of Calais made their last stand here in 1940, when its walls, like those of many other old French fortresses, showed themselves remarkably able to survive 20th-century technology, even though most of the buildings within them were destroyed. Today it's a very atmospheric park: an idea of its awesome size can be gained from the fact that inside it there is an entire sports stadium, built in 1965. Calais also has another unusual fortress-park inside the 17th-century walls of **Fort Nieulay**, near the western end of the main through-road through town, not far from the Tunnel terminal (*open April–Oct only*).

The old city also contains the **Musée des Beaux-Arts et de la Dentelle** (*open Mon, Wed–Fri 10–12 and 2–5.30, Sat 10–12 and 2–6.30, Sun 2–6.30; closed Tues; adm*), beside the Parc Richelieu at the southern end of Rue Royale, housed true to form in a dull 1960s building. The 'Museum of Fine Arts and Lace' is really three, not two, museums in one. Best-known is its sculpture collection, centred on the studies by Rodin for the *Burghers of Calais* monument nearby, which are interestingly exhibited alongside studies for similar monuments by more conventional sculptors of the time like Eude, Maillol and Carpeaux – making Rodin look all the more radical by comparison. The museum's Rodin collection also includes an impressive set of small busts, with a very fine self-portrait and one of his protégée/lover Camille Claudel. There is an unusual picture collection, from engagingly odd 17th- and 18th-century naive paintings from the Calais region to a few works by major artists such as Picasso and Dubuffet, although its more important contemporary works often seem to be somewhere else on loan. It also hosts regular shows of contemporary art. The largest section of the museum, however, is that given over to lace-making, and an enormous amount of information is given (in French) on the history and techniques of lace in general and Calais lace in particular. On show there are beautiful pieces of 19th-century lace, entire Belle Epoque outfits, theatrical costumes, wedding dresses, underwear and examples of the use of lace by couture designers from Worth through Dior and Givenchy to Christian Lacroix, all of which could make it quite a sexy museum if it was displayed with a little more style. On a more industrial level there's a giant 19th-century Jacquard lace-maker's loom. And, oddly placed in the middle of the lace section, perhaps because there was no obvious other place to put it, is a remarkable 1904 relief model of Calais, showing the city as it was before 1940, and with the old and new towns still entirely separate.

From the museum a short walk down Boulevard Clémenceau, past the tourist office, will take you to the large bridge that connects the old and new towns. Immediately visible on the other side and to the left is Calais' spectacular **Hôtel de Ville**, built in Flemish-revival style with a giant belfry and clocktower, visible for miles, that has long been a symbol of the city to ferry passengers arriving in the harbour. The town hall was begun in the 1890s to mark the joining of old Calais and St-Pierre, but was not finished until 1925; this was one building that was carefully restored after the Second World War. In the park-like square in front of it is Calais' most famous and precious monument, Rodin's extraordinary statue of the six *Bourgeois de Calais*, the Burghers of Calais, unveiled in 1894. When the city fathers commissioned it at the time of the 'unification' of Calais they were probably hoping for a conventional piece of patriotic sculpture, exalting the heroism of the six burghers who were ready to sacrifice themselves for their community. They got something quite different: it has no conventional heroism in it at all, but an immense, quiet intensity. It is also completely different from conventional group monuments in that each of the six figures is entirely individual, and they seem almost to be choreographed against each other, and yet still form a whole with a special sense of drama. Especially awe-inspiring is the figure of the leader, Eustache de St-Pierre, who seems to loom out from among the others, like an emphatic figure of wisdom.

Across the street to the west there is another, more bizarre monument, a huge, lushly romantic **Monument aux Morts**, epitomising the kind of melodramatic patriotic sculpture that Rodin avoided. It commemorates not the usual dead, since it was put up well before the First World War, but the fallen in all sorts of obscure colonial conflicts around France's empire during the 19th century, from Indochina to Madagascar, and passing by the Paris Commune of 1871. Behind the monument is the neatly maintained Parc St-Pierre, half-hidden inside of which is the entrance to the **Musée de la Guerre** (*open Feb, Mar, Oct and Nov Mon, Wed–Sun 11–5, last admission 4.15; April–Sept daily 10–6pm, last admission 5.15; adm*), Calais' 1939–45 war museum. It is so hidden because it occupies the concrete bunker that was once the command post for the German Navy in the Calais sector, which gives it extra atmosphere. Inside, there's a huge amount to see, with rooms of memorabilia on the two battles of Calais in 1940 and 1944, life under the Occupation, the German coastal defences, Calais when it was a major British base during the 1914–18 war and many other aspects of the city in the World Wars.

Below the park and the Hôtel de Ville, Boulevard Jacquard and further down Boulevard Lafayette form the high streets of non-ferry orientated Calais, with all the everyday stores such as Monoprix and shoe and clothes shops that you find in an everyday French city. The two boulevards meet at **Place Albert Ier**, surrounded by busy, lively bars, which is better known to locals as the Place du Théâtre because it is dominated by the very grand Beaux-Arts style theatre, opened in 1905. In front of the theatre there is also a very large and striking monument to Joseph-Marie Jacquard, whose invention of the Jacquard punch-card loom and its adaptation to lace-making made this district's fortune in the 19th century. The Jacquard loom was something of an Anglo-French collaboration, for he was greatly aided by two British engineers, Martyn and Ferguson, who are duly commemorated on the monument.

A few streets south of Boulevard Lafayette is the stadium where the mighty local amateur football team, the CRUFC, play their games. In general, though, there isn't much more to explore in the new town. It's a better bet on a decent day to head straight back to the old town and to the beach, one of Calais' lesser-known attractions. It's a fine, old-fashioned strip of sand, with several good restaurants and all the proper French crêpe- and *frite*-stands alongside it. At the western end it eventually runs into the less-developed beach and dunes at Sangatte, which is popular for sand-yachting. As the day draws in, if you're not due for a meal at one of the better restaurants in town, you can always head back to the Rue de la Mer, old Calais' bar and café row. It has English pubs, a place just called Le Pub, a giant brasserie called Le Bistrot, and the Kabylie Maghrebi restaurant, which has belly dancers every Wednesday. It's not the most chic place in France, but it's far from dull.

Shopping

The **Cité de l'Europe**, the continent's largest mall, right next to the Tunnel terminal, has a Toys'R'Us, Tesco, Oddbins, Le Chais, a vast Carrefour hypermarket, plus individual shops. Near **Fort Nieulay** is another concentration of stores: easy to spot from the main road are Sainsbury's and the Auchan hypermarket. In the industrial estates, especially the **Zone Marcel Doret**, on the ring road, are the real discount warehouses, like Eastenders. Note that the French-owned wine stores concentrate on French wines, while the British-owned outlets have the same multinational range you would find in Britain.

Calais still holds traditional street **markets**, in Place d'Armes (*Wed and Sat mornings*), and (with more stalls) in Place Crèvecoeur, off Bd Lafayette in the new town (*Thurs and Sat*).

Calais ✉ 62100

Le Bar à Vins, 52 Place d'Armes, **t** 03 21 96 96 31, **f** 03 21 34 68 22. A great little shop and convivial bar, where you can taste before you buy. Luc Gille stocks carefully selected wines from small producers around France, together with a still more select range of fine Normandy ciders and liqueurs. Among them are many organic wines. You can make great discoveries here. M Gille speaks good English and loves to talk wine.

Le Chais, 40 Rue de Phalsbourg, **t** 03 21 97 00 50, **f** 03 21 96 71 90. A long-established French wine merchant (also at Cité de l'Europe). To find it follow Rue Mollien eastwards and Rue de Phalsbourg is a wide turning on the right. The range of wines (no beers) is entirely French. Note that the stores close for lunch. *Open daily till 7; closed 12–2.*

Charcuterie Le Gars, 39 Rue Royale. Bright *charcuterie-traiteur* selling enticing made-up dishes, and a particularly good range of French sausages – *boudins noir* or *blanc*, *andouillettes*, *saucisson sec* – all homemade.

Eastenders, 14 Rue Gustave Courbet, Zone Marcel Doret, **t** 03 21 34 53 33. The king of cash-and-carry, in a giant warehouse just off the Calais ring road (plus two other outlets): popular, high-turnover wines dominate, but there are some rarer labels too. Hard to beat on price. *Open 24 hours a day, every day.*

Royal Dentelle, 37 Bd Jacquard, **t** 03 21 34 91 36. For a very traditional souvenir of Calais: handkerchiefs, lingerie, veils and other gift items, as well as different types of lace sold by the metre. There are smaller shops on Bd Clémenceau and Bd Lafayette.

Vignobles et Saveurs de France, Av Pierre de Coubertin, **t** 03 21 19 30 01. A small independent wine merchant specialising in quality French wines from small growers. Prices are very reasonable. Av Coubertin is near the Citadelle. *Closed Mon.*

The Wine & Beer Company, Rue de Judée, Zone Marcel Doret, **t** 03 21 82 93 64. A British-owned company with helpful staff and reliable quality: the stock comes from every continent, and the 'star buys' are worth checking out. This is their largest outlet in Calais (*open daily till 10pm*); there is another near Fort Nieulay (*open till 8pm*) and one on Rue de Phalsbourg (*open till 7pm*).

Where to Stay

Calais ✉ 62100

Hôtel Meurice, 5–7 Rue Edmond Roche, **t** 03 21 34 57 03, **f** 03 21 34 14 71, *www.hotel-meurice.fr* (*double rooms 430–560F/€65.55–85.37*). The classic Grand Hotel of Calais, where the famous and respectable have been staying since 1771 (although the present building is a reconstruction of the original, destroyed in 1940). It offers traditional, carpeted comfort, although the rooms have no great character. Popular, mainly with older guests. The old-fashioned wood-panelled dining room, **La Diligence**, offers traditionally elaborate French *haute cuisine* (*menus 140–350F/€21.34–53.35*).

Le George V, 36 Rue Royale, **t** 02 21 97 68 00, **f** 03 21 97 34 73, *www.georgev-calais.com* (*rooms 330–490F/€50.30–74.7*). Reliable comfort and convenience combined with a livelier, more relaxed atmosphere than the Meurice. The 42 rooms have been recently renovated, and are bright and spacious. It has two restaurants downstairs (*see below*).

Hôtel Pacific, 40 Rue du Duc de Guise, **t** 03 21 34 50 24, **f** 03 21 97 58 02, *www.cofrase.com/hotel/pacific* (*double rooms 260–311F/€39.63–47.41, breakfast extra*). A popular small hotel just off Rue Royale that's one of the city's best-value options (with, so far, no lift). The 17 rooms are plain but comfortable, and have good facilities. There are family rooms, the breakfast room is very warm and cosy, and M and Mme Duhamel are quietly hospitable. There's some indoor parking.

Hervelinghen ✉ 62179

La Leulène, 708 Rue Principale, **t** 03 21 82 47 30 (*rooms 320F/€48.78 for two, 450F/€68.6 for four*). An attractive converted farm around a traditional courtyard in this tiny village, c. 12km west of Calais between the A16 and the coast. The friendly Mme Petitprez has three prettily decorated B&B rooms. **Evening meals** (*80F/€12.2*) can be provided with prior notice. A very peaceful place to stay.

Marck ✉ 62730

Le Manoir de Meldick, 2528 Av du Général de Gaulle, Le Fort Vert, **t/f** 03 21 85 74 34 (*rooms 300F/€45.73 for two, 50F/€7.62 per additional person*). Popular B&B in an impressively big 1930s house not far from the dunes and the beach, a few minutes east of Calais. There are five rooms, including an enormous four-person family room. All the rooms are very spacious and attractively furnished. M and Mme Houzet are very hospitable, and there's a big garden around the house.

Eating Alternatives

Calais ✉ 62100

L'Aquar'aile, 255 Rue Jean Moulin, **t** 03 21 34 00 00, **f** 03 21 34 15 00 (*menus 130–230F/ €19.82–35.06*). Oddly located in a modern block behind the western end of the beach, this is Calais' *restaurant panoramique*, five floors up with fabulous views along the seafront and out to sea. Chef Fernand Leroy is one of the region's finest. There are spectacular *palettes de fruits de mer* (*98F/€14.94 or 198F/€30.18 per head*) and fine oysters. Leroy also makes much use of local dishes and produce: supreme of Licques chicken with a *crème de maroilles*, or roast trout with baby endives cooked in beer; game and forest mushrooms feature strongly from autumn to spring. *Closed Sun eve*.

Au Côte d'Argent, 1 Digue Gaston Berthe, **t** 03 21 34 68 07, **f** 03 21 96 42 10 (*menus 98–230F/€14.94–35.06*). Unmissable at the 'town' end of Calais beach, a real seaside restaurant with panoramic views and fine food. Chef Bertrand Lefebvre's menus feature almost as much meat as fish, especially local poultry – Licques chicken, duck, pigeon etc. The *menu douceur* might include *craquelot de fruits de mer* (smoked herring with mixed seafood), and *fricassée* of chicken in a curry sauce. It has many British regulars. *Closed Sun eve and Mon*.

Le George V, *see above* (*menus 170F/€25.91 and 285F/€43.45*). Large, traditional and high-quality restaurant, serving classic, sophisticated French cuisine. For a cheaper alternative there's **Le Petit Georges**, with a classic bistro-type menu: duck *à l'orange*, cod *bonne femme* or *moules marinières*. *Closed Sat lunch and Sun eve*.

Le Grand Bleu, 8 Rue Jean-Pierre Avron, Bassin de la Colonne, **t/f** 03 21 97 97 98 (*menus 130F/€19.82 and 160F/€24.39*). A gourmet restaurant next to the quayside fish market in the old fishing district of Courgain, on the east side of the port. Chef Michaël Olivier's bright, nautical restaurant serves almost entirely fish and seafood, featuring the wonderfully fresh local catch. The more complicated traditional fish dishes of the Pas-de-Calais are superbly done here. *Closed Sat lunch and (Oct–May only) Sun*.

L'Histoire Ancienne, 20 Rue Royale, **t** 03 21 34 11 20, **f** 03 21 96 19 58 (*weekday and off-peak menu du jour 63F/€9.6, other menus 99–158F/€15.09–24.09*). Cosy, old-fashioned restaurant with an able young chef, Patrick Comte, who has an interesting take on classic dishes: warm salad of St-Marcelin cheese with herbs, or skate wings in a cream sauce with grapefruit zest, pilau rice and chargrilled potatoes. Very good value for such distinctive cooking. *Closed Sun*.

Au Calice, 55 Bd Jacquard, **t** 03 21 34 51 78, **f** 03 21 97 69 81 (*menus 79–99F/€12.04– 15.09; plats du jour c. 50F/€7.62*). Big, snug and comfortable Flemish-style *estaminet* for quick snacks and lighter meals. There's a wide range of local and Belgian beers, and set menus, *plats du jour* or *flamiches*, omelettes and salads. *Open daily until 2am*.

Just Across the Water:
Boulogne

05

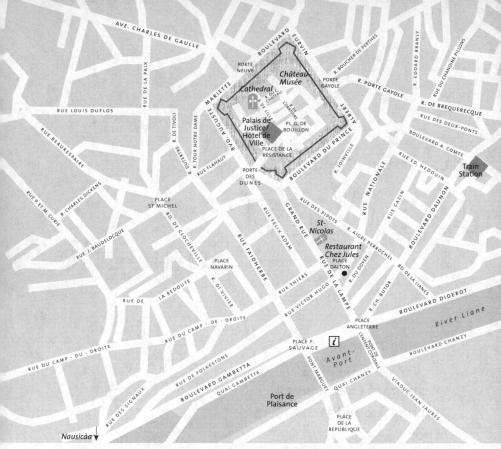

Nausicàa ↓

Most of the thousands of people who visit the Pas-de-Calais every year simply use it as a supermarket, or as a place to pass through quickly on the way to somewhere else. Of those who want to linger and explore, many are not sure where to choose – it's an area that has curiously few known landmarks. However, only just west of Calais and the Channel Tunnel there is a beautiful, sweeping coastline of dunes, cliffs, wind-blown coarse grass and long beaches, labelled the Côte d'Opale because of the sometimes iridescent, milky-green colour of its waters. Along it, there is a string of very individual, surprisingly out-of-the-way little beach towns. And just to the south is Boulogne, a town of real charm and personality.

Boulogne is the oldest of all the Channel ports: it was the main harbour for links with Roman Britain. Today it's the most important fishing port in France, and has an all-modern aquarium/nautical theme park. It's also an excellent place to experience *la vie française* and a great shopping destination, with a wonderful, bustling street market and several gourmet specialists – including one of France's very finest cheese emporia – as alternatives to the hustle of the hypermarkets.

And a trip to Boulogne and the Côte d'Opale is of course a treat for lovers of fine restaurants, of which there's no place better than **Chez Jules**, a classic brasserie-restaurant that has been welcoming locals and visitors alike from early morning until late at night since the 1890s.

Getting There

Two roads lead from Calais and the Channel Tunnel to Boulogne, the A16 *autoroute* (toll-free as far as Boulogne) and the more attractive and leisurely D940 along the coast. Just north of Boulogne the exit road from the *autoroute* (exit 3) joins the D940, so that both bring you into town along the boulevards Ste-Beuve and Gambetta, beside the river.

As you approach the port look out for an entrance on the right into a large car park along the quay, one of two good places to leave vehicles before exploring the town (the other is around the ramparts of the Haute-Ville, at the very top of Boulogne's hill, reached by following signs to St-Omer; either way, you have to do some walking uphill). From the quay walk up Rue de la Lampe to Place Dalton, the main square, where Chez Jules is impossible to miss on the righthand (downhill) side.

If you arrive by SeaCat, the terminal is, like the rest of the modern port, on the other side of the River Liane from the town. Follow signs for *centre ville*, which will take you round in a loop to cross the river and come up to the main quays from the south; on foot, walk across Pont Marguet, nearest the terminal.

Tourist Information

Boulogne-sur-Mer: Forum Jean Noël, Quai Gambetta, t 03 21 10 88 10, f 03 21 33 81 09, *boulogne@tourisme.norsys.fr*. The tourist office is by the quays, near the Pont Marguet (the last bridge, going seawards).
Ambleteuse: Place de la Mairie, t 03 21 83 50 05, f 03 21 87 65 01.
Wimereux: Quai Giard, t 03 21 83 27 17, f 03 21 32 76 91, *tourisme.wimereux@wanadoo.fr*.
Wissant: Site des Deux Caps, 1 Place de la Mairie, t 03 21 85 15 62, f 03 21 85 50 44.

Chez Jules

8–10 Place Dalton, t 03 21 31 54 12, f 03 21 33 85 47.
Open (service) Mon–Sat 9.30am–10pm, Sun 9.30am–2.30pm.
Closed 23 Dec–5 Jan. Menus 90F/€13.72, 120F/€18.29
(weekdays only), 145F/€22.11 and 225F/€34.30; à la carte average
(restaurant) 170F/€25.92.

Chez Jules is a local institution, with a big and positively brash 'Brasserie-Restaurant-Pizza' sign across the façade which announces the *trois formules* that Chez Jules proudly offers, so that there's something for everyone at all kinds of prices, from elaborate dishes to simple salads and pizzas, from full meals to snacks or a coffee and croissant. The pizzeria occupies part of the ground floor, with the brasserie alongside it, although both have the same plain tables and comfy leatherette seats, and the division doesn't seem too strict; in front there's an outside terrace, for a close-up view of Place Dalton's comings and goings. The smarter, pretty restaurant is on the floor above, with a view down over the square from some of its tables.

Throughout, there's the constant to-ing and fro-ing of a lively brasserie. As well as a fair number of British diners, a whole cross-section of Boulogne seems to come here, to be served by the bluff waiters who appear to know half their clientele personally. The busy restaurant is spacious, and you never feel cramped or hurried. A good deal of Chez Jules' movement centres around the wiry, effervescent owner, Claude Leleu, who seems to do so much meeting and greeting that he might be mistaken for the mayor. While he presides behind the bar, his son Philippe is in charge of the kitchen.

Millefeuille de la Mer

Serves 6–8

650g/1½lb shell-on prawns, preferably with heads
500g/1lb 2oz leeks (white parts), well washed
100g/3½oz butter
100g/3½oz crème fraîche
1kg/2¼lb spinach, stemmed, washed and spun dry
30g/1oz ground almonds
2 carrots, cut in thin matchsticks
2 courgettes, cut in thin matchsticks
1 celery stick, cut in thin matchsticks
225g/8oz crab meat
8 large scallops without roe
6–8 sheets *feuilles de brick*, or filo pastry (*feuilles de brick* is slightly thicker)
chopped chervil
salt and pepper

For the sauce:
15ml/1tablespoon oil
3 shallots, finely chopped
100ml/3½fl oz dry white wine
150g/5½oz crème fraîche or double cream
50g/1¾oz cold unsalted butter, diced

Peel the prawns, keeping the shells for the sauce. Reserve, covered, in the fridge. For the sauce, heat the oil in a saucepan over a medium heat and add the prawn shells. Cook, stirring, until lightly coloured and beginning to stick. Add the shallots

The menus are long, with loads of choices from the simple to the sophisticated: 'welsh rarebit', chicken and chips, pizzas, and even paella. The Leleus take good advantage of the unbeatable supply of fresh fish. In the restaurant, turbot, sole, skate or whatever is best that day can be had simply poached or steamed with a classic sauce, but some of the most popular dishes are the elaborate specialities such as *la pêche miraculeuse*, a marvellous brochette of succulent chunks of monkfish, scallops, salmon and prawns, or the rich *pot au feu de la mer* of cod, monkfish, prawns, mussels, scallops, various vegetables and more. Plus, there are the daily specials: a deliciously satisfying *blanquette de poisson* with salmon and monkfish, or the intricate starter *millefeuille de la mer*, which has to be ordered in advance. And there's excellent shellfish, whether, oysters, *moules-frites*, or extravagant *plateaux de fruits de mer*.

Meat dishes include steaks, rack of lamb with thyme, or duck in cider, and recently in winter Philippe Leleu has introduced a good deal of game and venison. The same energetic concern for quality is notable in everything, in starters such as a warm goats'-cheese salad or the ample and ambitious wine list. And there's also excellent coffee, to help you settle in after a feast chez Jules and watch Boulogne go by.

and cook for a minute or two. Add the wine, let it bubble and pour over 1 litre/
1¾pints water. Bring to a boil, reduce the heat and simmer for 25 minutes. Strain the
stock into a clean saucepan, discarding the solids. Boil to reduce by half and stir in
the cream. Continue boiling gently to reduce by one-quarter. Set the sauce aside.

Thinly slice the leeks. Melt half of the butter in a saucepan set over a medium heat.
Add the leeks and cook for about 5 minutes, stirring frequently. Add the crème
fraîche and continue cooking until the cream is thick and reduced and the leeks soft.
Season with salt and pepper and set aside.

Cook the spinach in a large saucepan until wilted, turning to move the uncooked
parts to the bottom of the pan, or steam or microwave it. Drain well, pressing to
extract as much water as possible, and chop finely. Melt the remaining butter, add
the spinach and ground almonds, season with salt and pepper and set aside.

Steam the carrot, courgette and celery matchsticks until just tender.

Preheat the oven to 200°C/400°F/Gas mark 6. Butter the bottom of a 23–25cm/
9–10in springform mould. Mix the crab meat with 2–3 tablespoons of the sauce. Slice
the scallops crossways into 3 discs.

Cut the *feuilles de brick* in 6 rounds the size of your mould. Set the mould on a
baking tray. Start with a round of pastry. Top with the crab meat mixture, spreading
it out, another pastry round, spread the spinach, top with pastry, layer the prawns,
another pastry round, the vegetable matchsticks, pastry, and the scallop discs, the
last pastry round and top with the leeks. Bake for 25 minutes, until nicely browned.

Meanwhile, finish the sauce. Whisk in the butter, by bits, to make a silky sauce with
a syrupy consistency. Taste and season, if needed (if too salty, whisk in a little more
cream or butter). Pour in a warm serving jug.

To serve, transfer the mould to a warm serving plate and remove the edge. Sprinkle
with the chopped chervil. Cut in wedges and surround each portion with sauce.

Touring Around

From Calais or the Tunnel Terminal on the A16, take the road west at exit 7 until you
come to a fork, from which one road leads to Cap Gris-Nez and the other, the D238,
runs north up to the little town of **Wissant**, seemingly half-swallowed up amid the
sand dunes. The name comes from the old Flemish for 'White Sand': in front and on
either side is a vast expanse of white beach and dunes, popular with sand-yachters
and windsurfers. Wissant has a claim to being almost as old a Channel port as
Boulogne, for it is believed that Julius Caesar used it for his second invasion of Britain
in 54 BC; it was an important port in the early Middle Ages, and Thomas à Becket
passed through here in 1170 on his last journey back to Canterbury. By the 16th
century, however, the harbour had entirely silted up. Since then the fishermen have
had to drag their distinctive little boats – *flobarts* – backwards and forwards across
the beach. Fewer locals work in fishing today, but they still haul their *flobarts* to and
from the sea with tractors, and keep them in their back gardens the rest of the time.
The town has a clutch of hotels and crêperies, *moules-frites* stands and little bars.

The view along the beach at Wissant is framed at either end by **Cap Blanc-Nez** to the east and the much taller **Cap Gris-Nez** to the west, their white chalk cliffs a perfect mirror to the Kent cliffs that can usually be seen across the Channel. From Wissant there's a great walk to Cap Gris-Nez along the beach (for most of the way) or the GR coastal footpath, over dunes, grassy cliffs and bits of German blockhouses. A lazier alternative is to drive around to the cape on the D940 from Wissant. At Cap Gris-Nez there's a lighthouse, the modern Channel shipping control station with its thicket of aerials, great views and another fine sandy beach. At Audinghen, where the cape road meets the D940 Boulogne road, there's a small **Musée du Mur de l'Atlantique** (*open April–Sept daily 9–7; Oct–Mar daily 9–12 and 2–6; adm*), the main exhibits of which are two of the huge guns installed there to bombard Dover.

The D940 rejoins the coast just above **Ambleteuse**, a beach village among the dunes, with a strip of shingle, sand and rock pools (good for windsurfing, crabbing and windswept walks in winter), beside the estuary of the River Slack which has created a small-scale salt-marsh, with lots of birds (the estuary is a protected nature reserve). The scene is dramatically topped off by **Fort Vauban** (*open for guided tours Easter–11 Nov Sun 3–6.30; July and Aug Sat and Sun 3–6.30; adm*), the castle that dominates the seaward view. The Slack estuary had often been used as a landing point by English invaders, and in the 1680s Louis XIV's fortress-builder *extraordinaire*, Marshal Vauban, built this bastion here to prevent any further incursions. It's a wonderfully ghastly structure. Ambleteuse also has a small, private Second World War display, the **Musée 39–45** (*open April–Oct 10–1 and 2–6; Tues–Sun Nov–Mar 2–6; adm*).

Before it runs into Boulogne the coastal road meets **Wimereux**, a charming little Belle Epoque beach resort – it was once optimistically promoted as 'the Nice of the North' – with a slightly raffish air. Compact and friendly, with great views out to sea from its long prom, there are some great places to eat and stay, and shop.

Boulogne

If you arrive in Boulogne on a Wednesday or Saturday morning, make straight for the Grande Rue, the main street, and – just to one side of it and presided over by the grey, war-battered church of St-Nicolas – **Place Dalton**, site of one of the best traditional markets in this part of France. There are plenty of stalls selling fine cheeses, terrines, farmhouse sausages and a kaleidoscope of herbs, fresh flowers and pot plants; this being the north, it's especially good for local vegetables – carrots, chicory, shallots and endives – and sweets, biscuits and chocolates. Boulogne has its hypermarkets, mostly near the *autoroute* or the N42 St-Omer road, but the main town-centre shopping (especially good for chocolates) is just across the Grande Rue from the market, around **Rue Thiers** and **Rue Victor Hugo**. Anyone with the remotest liking for cheese will want to make the pilgrimage to the legendary *fromagerie* of Philippe Olivier (43 Rue Thiers, *see* below).

If Boulogne has more character than most other Channel ports, it is in good part because of its history. Whatever the claims of Wissant, it is known with certainty that Caesar sailed on his first invasion of Britain in 55 BC from the mouth of the River Liane, and that after their definitive conquest of Britain the following century the Romans built a fortress-town near its banks as their main base for communications with the new colony. After the fall of Rome Boulogne was semi-abandoned, but it revived in the early Middle Ages as the seat of a line of independent counts. Though not a Norman, Count Eustache II, 'As Grenons' ('Fine Moustaches'), of Boulogne went with William the Conqueror to Hastings; his son, Godefroy de Bouillon, was one of the leaders of the First Crusade. In 1214 Philippe Auguste of France established his authority over Boulogne, and from then on it was the main bastion of French power in the north, against challenges from the Counts of Flanders and, later, England and Spain. The king gave Boulogne to his second son Philippe Hurepel ('Frizzy Hair') who, in between plotting to take over the crown himself, substantially rebuilt the old town, and gave it the present castle and ramparts (1227–31). Marshal Vauban made some changes to the ramparts in the 1680s, but today large sections of the intact walls look much as they did in the 13th century, especially the Porte des Degrés on the west side.

To get to the **Haute-Ville**, the old walled town, walk straight up the steep Grande Rue. Before entering through Vauban's **Porte des Dunes**, spare a glance for the plaque on the tower to the right dedicated to François Pilâtre de Rozier, an early adventurer in cross-Channel flight. Pilâtre made the world's first manned balloon flight in November 1783 – two months after the Montgolfier brothers' first experiment with a duck, a sheep and a cockerel – and, 26 years old, was a superstar of his day. He attempted to cross the Channel in June 1785, leaving from this same tower to gain height, but his balloon caught fire and plummeted into the ground near Wimereux. Beneath the ramparts to the left of the Porte des Dunes is a broad esplanade with a large, odd monument of a man in a fez on top of a pyramid. This is **Auguste Mariette**, the father of French Egyptology, one of several engaging figures who gave Boulogne a notably individual cultural and intellectual life in the 19th century.

Through the gate you enter the heart of the old town, **Place de la Résistance** and, just beyond it, Place Godefroy de Bouillon, on the site of the crossroads that formed the centre of Roman Boulogne. To the left are the neoclassical Palais de Justice and Hôtel de Ville, attached to a massive stone belfry that's partly 12th-century and a rare survivor from before the arrival of Philip Frizzy-Hair. On the right in Place Godefroy de Bouillon is the **Hôtel Desandrouins**, an elegant 18th-century mansion that was used by Napoleon and Josephine as their residence during their extended stays in Boulogne while the Emperor sought the means to invade England.

The streets of the old town are narrow and cobbled, the tight ring of the ramparts creating an enclosed, hushed atmosphere. The **Rue de Lille**, the most important street running off Place Godefroy de Bouillon, was the *decumanus* of the Roman town. Today it contains antique and souvenir shops, restaurants and some irresistible chocolate shops and *pâtisseries*. No.58 is the oldest house in Boulogne, built as an inn for 16th-century travellers, and now occupied by a restaurant and wine bar (*see* below). Above the gate there is a scallop shell, indicating that it was used by pilgrims on their way to Santiago de Compostela. Just across the street is the **cathedral**, the giant dome of which can be seen from miles around but which, close-up, comes upon you almost by surprise. During the most radical phase of the French Revolution in 1793, the revolutionaries of Boulogne were not content with just desecrating their

12th-century abbey church, but actually destroyed it. In the 1820s the Catholic Church, reinstated and in truculent mood, decided to put the Godless to shame with this colossal edifice. Completed in 1866, the inside seems extraordinarily huge– the dome above all – but impressive rather than beautiful.

At the end of Rue de Lille is another gate, the Porte Neuve, and one of many points where there are steps up to the **ramparts**, a circuit of which is a special part of a meander around the Haute-Ville – the timeless streets of old Boulogne inside, and outside views over the rest of the town and out to sea. In the eastern corner is the well-preserved, monolithic castle of Philippe Hurepel, now the **Château-Musée** (*open Mon–Sat 10–12.30 and 2–5.30, Sun 10–12.30 and 2.30–5.30; closed Tues; adm*). The collection is a real hotchpotch, put together out of donations from a string of local private collectors and savants. There are, for example, mummies and other Egyptian relics from the great Mariette, some very fine 18th-century porcelain, and, oddest of all, a remarkable collection of Inuit and Native American masks acquired by a local anthropologist, Alphonse Pinart, on an expedition to Alaska in 1871. The most inter-esting part of the castle itself, seen as you near the end of the visit, is the Salle de la Barbière, a fine vaulted Gothic hall.

From the Haute-Ville, walk back down the hill into the shopping streets of the new town, down the Grande Rue or the parallel Rue Félix Adam. At the river, turn right for a walk along the busy quays of the port. Unmissable at the end of the riverfront is the modernistic geometry of Boulogne's most innovative attraction, the curiously named **Nausicaá** 'sea experience museum' (*open Sept–June daily 9.30–6.30; July and Aug daily 9.30–8; closed Dec 25 and three weeks Jan; adm, group discounts, t 03 21 30 99 99*). This all-modern aquarium has been a big hit since it opened in 1991, especially with British visitors. It succeeds in providing a wealth of ecological information about the sea in enjoyable form, through dynamic multi-media displays (with good provision for different languages). As well as fish and sea creatures from across the world, there are theme-park-ride exhibits: the deck of a trawler in a storm, or a sealed 'tropical envi-ronment' in which to warm up in mid-winter. There's also a tank where kids can touch rays, skate and the like, if not the sharks that are always among the main attractions. A full visit to Nausicaá takes at least two hours, and there are cafés and a restaurant (run by the prestigious Matelote across the street). Just next to the museum is Boulogne's fairly clean but often unnoticed beach.

On the north side of Boulogne, just off the Calais road, next to the main British war cemetery in the area, is another of the town's most visible landmarks, the **Colonne de la Grande-Armée** (*open Oct–April Thurs–Mon 9–12 and 2–5; May–Sept daily 9–12 and 2–9; adm*), one of the greatest monuments ever raised to a non-event. From 1803 to 1804 Napoleon kept an army of 200,000 men encamped at Boulogne for months on end while he tried to work out a way of invading England, until he finally gave up the idea and marched them off to greater glory in Germany. The men, however, had had such a good time that they voted to erect a memorial to their stay, and all the officers chipped in to pay for this column, with a statue of the Emperor on top; it was finally completed under Louis-Philippe in 1841. Today, it's possible to climb up the 263 steps inside for a panoramic view over Boulogne and the Côte d'Opale.

Shopping

The market aside, Rue Thiers, the Grande Rue and the Haute Ville contain Boulogne's most interesting concentrations of shops. Rue Victor Hugo, parallel to Rue Thiers, contains rather duller fashion stores and banks. Boulogne's largest hypermarket, Auchan, is on the way out of town on the N42 towards St-Omer.

Boulogne-sur-Mer ✉ 62200

Boucherie du Centre, 48 Rue Thiers, t 03 21 32 02 93. A fine traditional butcher with a superior quality range of local produce – especially Licques chickens (31F/€4.73 each) and Pérard fish soup from Le Touquet, celebrated as the best in France (*see* p.94).

La Cave du Fromager, 23 and 30 Rue de Lille, t 03 21 80 49 69. Marie-Renée Fremont's small shop stands out by also having a cheese-based restaurant just across the street. She has a fine selection of Maroilles and other local cheeses, plus others from all over France, and some fine wines. Another speciality is own-made cheese pastries, such as a delicious *goyère aux maroilles*, *feuilleté de chèvre/brie* and Roquefort tarts (*33F/€5.03 for a family-sized model*).

Charcuterie-Traiteur Bourgeois, 1 Grande Rue, t 03 21 31 53 57. A delightful traditional *traiteur* selling a wonderful range of made-up dishes, and also packed with other enticing gourmet items – traditional sausages like *boudins noir et blanc*, fine wines, and quails' eggs (*18 for 30F/€4.57*). The courteous staff speak English.

Les Chocolats de Beussent, 56 Rue Thiers, t 03 21 92 44 00. If you can't get to the little shop in Beussent (*see* p.94), this attractive *chocolaterie* also sells their luxurious hand-made chocolates.

Philippe Olivier, 43–45 Rue Thiers, t 03 21 31 94 74, f 03 21 30 76 57. The most famous – and most enterprising – *fromagerie* in northern France has around 300 varieties of cheese in stock at any one time, but both the shop and the *caves* beneath are surprisingly small, for M. Olivier believes that any change in scale could lead to a compromise on quality. All the cheeses – and the equally fine butter – are made with entirely non-industrial methods, and the range changes continually, for he is always researching into new varieties and producers in France, Italy and even Britain. Olivier is especially strong in local, northern French cheeses such as Maroilles and Rollot. The highly knowledgeable staff are never too busy to answer any queries. To complete their cheese education, clients can also receive a regular newsletter.

Saveurs et Traditions, 26 Grande Rue, t 03 21 31 19 64. An unobtrusive little shop, just up the hill from Place Dalton, which is dedicated to showcasing the products of small producers around the Pas-de-Calais, many of whom use little-known traditional recipes: M Hubert Delomel's Perlé raspberry or blackcurrant champagne from Loison-sur-Créquoise (*see* p.104), Artois ciders, natural sodas and lemonades, many kinds of honey and mead, waffles, farm-made terrines, jams and natural cosmetics.

Wimereux ✉ 62930

Mille Vignes, 90 Rue Carnot, t 03 21 32 60 13, f 03 21 32 56 37, *www.millevignes.com*. An exceptional small wine merchant, run by amiable Englishman Nick Sweet. The great majority of the wines come from small producers, and Rhône and other southern French wines are a particular speciality; there's also a substantial choice of burgundies and champagnes. Prices run from around 25F/€3.81 to 1,500F/€228.67 or more. You won't find the obvious names here but this is an excellent place to discover some interesting new wines. Prices may not be quite as low as in the wine warehouses, but the quality is worth it. Mille Vignes has only wines and champagnes, and no beers or spirits.

Le Terroir, 16 Rue Carnot, t 03 21 32 41 33. From the outside this looks pretty much like a normal corner grocery store, but once inside you discover a variety that defies description, much of it dictated by the passionate interests of owner Auguste Corteyn. His collection of fine wines and rare alcohol almost qualifies it as a museum: fine wines from every year since 1940, single bottles from as far back as 1873, a collection of *première* armagnacs going back to 1923, rare rums and gins from around the world, and, of course, a well-selected stock of more current fine wines and liqueurs. The foods, perhaps more the domain of Mme Corteyn, include terrines, fish soups, all sorts of biscuits, fresh fruit and veg, superior farmhouse cheeses and much more.

Where to Stay

Boulogne-sur-Mer ✉ 62200
Hôtel de la Matelote, 70 Bd Ste-Beuve, t 03 21 30 33 33, f 03 21 30 87 40, *www.la-matelote.com* (*rooms from 520F/€79.27; 'Supérieure' rooms from 620F/€94.52*). The most luxurious option in Boulogne town: opened in 1999 by chef Tony Lestienne next door to his acclaimed restaurant, La Matelote offers a very high level of accommodation in its 29 rooms, with superior facilities for business travellers and extra comfort for those more at their ease (off-street parking, multi-channel TV, and so on). A drawback could be its rather out-of-the-way location, opposite the Nausicaá centre and a little away from the centre of town. There's no direct communication between hotel and restaurant, but demi-pension packages are available.

Le Chatelet, 32 Rue de l'Oratoire, t 03 21 30 09 04 (*double or twin rooms 350F/€53.36, extra beds 50F/€7.62 each*). The distinctive, recently opened *chambre-d'hôte* run by Paul Desgris and his Welsh wife Lynda, in the narrow streets of Boulogne's Haute Ville, occupies part of a 17th-century former convent, with an imposing gateway that leads into a sunny garden courtyard for summer breakfasts. Inside there are four rooms, each differently and imaginatively decorated with antiques – plus British and French TV and a video library.

Mme Delabie, 26 Rue Flahaut, t 03 21 31 88 74 (*300–350F/€45.73–53.36 for two*). A very charming B&B in an 1841 house just outside the ramparts of Boulogne's old town, at the top of the hill. The beautiful woodwork and staircase and massive door on to the street are all original, while the rest of the rambling house has been fully renovated. Cosiness is its keynote: Mme Delabie and her husband are both elderly, and very welcoming, and particularly like to have

families as guests. There are five spacious rooms including a large family room. They have many regular customers, so book early, above all for weekends. *Closed Jan.*

Wierre-Effroy ✉ 62720
La Ferme du Vert, t 03 21 87 67 00, f 03 21 83 22 62, *ferme.du.vert@wanadoo.fr* (*rooms 340–560F/€51.83–85.37; suite 660–870F/€100.62–132.63*). Another big, old stone courtyard farm, where M et Mme Bernard began taking in guests on a small scale some years ago, and which has metamorphosed into a full-time, but unusual, Logis hotel. The 15 rooms are fully modernised, but retain timber beams and other farmhouse features, and are extremely spacious – there is also a two-room suite filling a whole floor of one building with room for up to five. In another building is the pretty **restaurant** (*menus 130–230F/€19.82–35.06*), and there's a large garden. British guests make up around 60 per cent of the clientele. *Closed 15 Dec–15 Jan.*

Ferme-Auberge de la Raterie, t 03 21 92 80 90, f 03 21 87 29 30, *www.ferm-auberge-lara-terie.com* (*rooms 250–450F/€38.11–68.60*). La Raterie, in the village of Wierre-Effroy around 10km northeast of Boulogne, may not immediately match your idea of a *ferme-auberge*: first opened on a small scale in the 1980s, it now has 20 rooms (so that it qualifies as a hotel), and has restaurant space for 160 diners. The farm is a huge, rambling complex around a courtyard, with a big garden for outdoor breakfasts or lounging around in summer: rooms vary according to where they are and when they were converted. The most attractive are those in the main farmhouse, in comfortable, old-fashioned style; the newer rooms in the former outbuildings don't have as much character, but offer good facilities for families, while some large rooms have luxurious massage showers. There is also an impressive farmhouse restaurant (*see below*).

Wimereux ✉ 62930
Hôtel L'Atlantic, Digue de Mer, t 03 21 32 41 01, f 03 21 87 46 17, *www.hotel.atlantic.fr* (*rooms with sea view 490–750F/€74.70–114.34; landside rooms 395F/€60.22*). With its smartly

restored sky blue-and-white façade presiding over Wimereux's seafront, and fresh, spacious lounges, L'Atlantic has a real feel of the seaside about it, and is run with style by chef-proprietor Alain Delpierre. It's best known for his esteemed restaurant (*see below*), but above it there are modern, comfortable rooms with sea views and, in the best of them, balconies.

La Goelette, 13 Digue de Mer, **t** 03 21 32 66 44, **f** 03 21 33 77 54, *lagoelette.ifrance.com* (*rooms with sea view 400F/€60.98, July and Aug 500F/€76.22; courtyard rooms 300F/€45.73, July and Aug 400F/€60.98*). A delightful *chambre-d'hôtes* on Wimereux's seafront, run by the charming Mary Avot, a very good English-speaker who has redecorated this old seaside villa with style and flair, using wooden floors, antiques and bright linens. The two rooms facing the sea (one double, one twin) are spectacular, with wonderful views of the beach as you wake up. The two rooms facing on to an interior patio are smaller and not quite so special, but still pretty and comfortable; taking both of them is a good option for families. Abundant and excellent breakfasts are served in a pretty room that faces the sea, and at night you'll find a chocolate bar on your pillow.

Hôtel du Centre, 78 Rue Carnot, **t** 03 21 32 41 08, **f** 03 21 33 82 48, *hotel.du.centre@wanadoo.fr* (*rooms from 260F/€39.64*). A long-term favourite with Brits, the Centre couldn't look more like a classic French small-town hotel if it was a film set. Combined with this traditional feel are a full range of comforts, and all the 23 rooms have been completely renovated for 2001. The restaurant (*see below*) is permanently popular, and there's a pretty garden terrace, but what regulars appreciate most is the warm, welcoming atmosphere of this family-run hotel.

Hesdin-l'Abbé ✉ 62360

Hôtel Cléry Château d'Hesdin-l'Abbé, Rue du Château, **t** 03 21 83 19 83, **f** 03 21 87 52 59 (*standard and Confort rooms 328–650F/ €50–99.09, Grand Confort rooms and Junior Suites low season from 620F/€94.52; midsummer from 845F/€128.82*). An 18th-century Louis XV château, in a village a few

kilometres southeast of Boulogne, which was transformed in the 1990s into a smart country-house hotel. It stands in an extensive park: rooms are divided between the main château and the former stables. The very large 'Grand Confort' and Junior Suite rooms have a real touch of luxury; standard and 'Confort' rooms are more conventional, but still very comfortable. The lounges and public rooms exude cosy opulence, and there's a fine if expensive **restaurant**, with notably elaborate (even for France) gourmet menus.

Eating Alternative

Boulogne-sur-Mer ✉ 62200

Boulogne's restaurants make more provision than is usual in France for vegetarians – perhaps because of the number of British visitors passing through.

La Matelote, 80 Bd Ste-Beuve, **t** 03 21 30 17 97 (*menus 150–365F/€22.87–55.64*). Regarded as Boulogne's premier restaurant, the Matelote is a little outside the town centre on the quayside boulevard, opposite Nausicaá. Chef Tony Lestienne's great fortes are fish, and every day there's a choice of several fabulously fresh varieties such as turbot, cod, sole, lobster and *langoustines*, as well as new creations such as monkfish *à la poêle posés sur une piperade aux olives et copeaux de parmesan, huile d'olive à basilic* and many other exquisite delicacies. There is now a hotel alongside (*see above*), and Lestienne also oversees the simpler, but still sophisticated, **Restaurant de Nausicaá** (**t** 03 21 33 24 24) (*menus 105–165F/€16.01–25.15*).

Estaminet du Château, 2 Rue du Château, **t** 03 21 91 49 66 (*menus 70–175F/ €10.67–26.68*). An attractive, *sympa* and well-priced small bistro in the Haute-Ville, tucked into a narrow street between the cathedral and the château-museum. The menus and *à la carte* offer loads of choice, with a good range for vegetarians. The excellent wine selection includes those produced by master Frenchman G. Depardieu. *Open daily 11.15–3 and 7.30–10.*

Aux Pêcheurs d'Etaples, 31 Grande Rue, **t** 03 21 30 29 29 (*menus 85–130F/€12.96–19.82*). A classic Boulogne experience. This outlet of the Etaples fishermen's cooperative, right opposite Place Dalton, couldn't declare its business more emphatically: the entrance is dazzling in itself, since this is also a spectacular fishmongers', piled high with sole, turbot, red mullet, mussels and more, while all along one wall there is a tank of multi-coloured tropical fish (which don't generally feature on the menu). Beyond is the bright and suitably nautical dining room. The menu offers plenty of options, whether you feel like spending a little or a lot: from *moules-frites* (48F/€7.32) to gargantuan *plateaux de fruits de mer* (165F/€25.15 or 215F/€32.78 per head).

Au Bon Accueil, 55 Rue de Lille, t 03 21 80 37 41 (*menus 50–130F/€7.62–19.82*). In the heart of the Haute-Ville, opposite the Vole Hole, this long-running budget favourite looks almost impossibly unchanging and plain, a bit like everyone's image of a classic French bistro from the 1920s. However, the mainly female staff are young and bright. There are no surprises in the cooking: in the mainly meat selection (*78F/€11.89*), *côte de porc au maroilles*, or, in the all-fish list (*88F/€13.42*), variations on sole and skate. There's also *moules*, steak and omelettes with *frites* (*48F/€7.32*), and several vegetarian dishes.

The Vole Hole, 58 Rue de Lille, t 03 21 80 97 66. Occupying part of the oldest building in Boulogne, with its scallop shell above the gateway alongside to show that it was once on the road to Santiago, the Anglo-French Vole Hole bar is a perennially popular stop-off for visitors to Boulogne. To go with the intimate and ever-relaxed atmosphere there's a big choice of beers and fine wines, and a smaller choice of snacks.

Wierre-Effroy ✉ 62720

Ferme-Auberge de la Raterie, *see above* (*menus 109F/€16.62 and 155F/€23.63*). With a large dining room for groups, La Raterie has developed some way beyond a simple farmhouse *auberge*, but Mme Coquerelle makes it clear that all the food served still uses the farm's own produce, and that she herself, in a *tour-de-force* of sustained energy, is still in charge of all the cooking. Her menus feature classic country cooking, skilfully prepared –

pork, chickens, duck and vegetables, in hearty dishes such as an *assiette de terrines*, or roast farm chicken (a staple). Diners not in a big group are served in a pretty farmhouse dining room.

Marquise ✉ 62250

Le Grand Cerf, 34 Av Ferber, t 03 21 87 55 05, f 03 21 33 61 09 (*menus 135F/€20.58 (weekdays only), 175F/€26.68 and 255F/€38.87; bistro meals 90–140F/€13.72–21.34*). Stéphane Pruvot is one of the most able chefs in northern France, the creator of beautifully inventive dishes such as his sublime *aumônières* (filo parcels) of crab in shellfish essences. His restaurant occupies a grand old 18th-century coaching inn on the old road between Boulogne and Calais. At its best, a meal there is a truly memorable experience. In addition, the Grand Cerf also has a simpler bistro in the part of the building nearest the street, serving less expensive – and less interesting – food.

Wimereux ✉ 62930

Restaurant La Liègoise-Hôtel L'Atlantic, *see above* (*dining room menus 130F/€19.82 (weekday lunch only), 180F/€27.44, 240F/€36.59 and 400F/€60.98; brasserie lunch menu 105F/€16.01*). Alain Delpierre's restaurant in Wimereux's Atlantic hotel is one of the best-regarded in the region. Local fish and seafood, and the traditional cuisine of France's north coast, naturally rate highly among his sources of inspiration; among the specialities are *panaché* of turbot, and red mullet with a *poêlée* of foie gras. The elegant main dining room, with a fine outlook over the sea, is on the first floor; an interesting brasserie range is served in the ground floor terrace bar, also with sea view.

Hôtel du Centre, *see above* (*menus 105F/€16.01 and 175F/€26.68, plus generous à la carte*). Wimereux's Hôtel du Centre is like a piece of old France, and the dining room accordingly looks just like a 1930s bistro. Its food is similarly traditional, with good-value versions of such staples as *poulet rôti, moules, filet de cabillaud*, and so on. The atmosphere is relaxed and friendly, and loved by its British fans even more than by the locals.

The First Town in France:
St-Omer

06

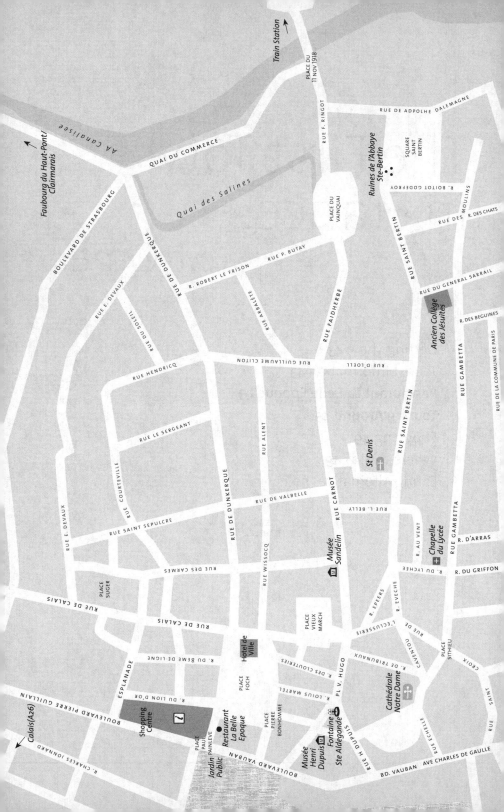

Getting There

St-Omer is about 30mins from Calais by *autoroute*. Whether you go direct to the town on the old N43 from Calais or come in from Boulogne and the A26 Calais–Paris *autoroute* via the N42, you will reach the same bypass around the town; follow signs for *centre ville* to come on to a long straight road along the north side of St-Omer, Avenue Joffre. After the Carrefour hypermarket, look for a broad turning to the right, also signposted *centre ville*, Boulevard Pierre Guillain. Follow this road into town and you will come up to the main square, Place Foch. On your right just as you enter the *place* there is another, smaller, square, Place Paul Painlevé, where the Belle Epoque is virtually in front of you, a little over to the right. Place Foch is also usually the best place to park, except on market days (Sat).

St-Omer also has train services, on the Calais–Lille line. The station is on the east side of the town, by the River Aa.

Tourist Information

St-Omer: 4 Rue du Lion d'Or, t 03 21 98 08 51, f 03 21 88 55 74. Since 2000 the tourist office is in St-Omer's latest addition, the glossy new shopping and cinema complex on the north side of Place Paul Painlevé, very near the Belle Epoque restaurant and Place Foch.
Eperlecques: 4 Rue de la Mairie, t 03 21 95 66 25, f 03 21 12 77 72.

Many people, having wandered across the Channel and arrived at St-Omer, describe it as the first real French small town they come upon. At its heart there is a broad, cobbled main square, with cafés around the sides and presided over by an imposing Hôtel de Ville, which hosts a vibrant weekly market; nearby are narrow streets with beautiful *pâtisseries*, *charcuteries* and other shops.

The idea that St-Omer should epitomise all that is French might seem strange, however, since it has only been part of France since 1678. For much of its history the town was attached to Flanders, and ruled successively by the counts of Flanders, the dukes of Burgundy and the kings of Spain, all of them in endless warfare with the kings of France. Like much of Flanders, St-Omer was partly built on water, and just to the east there is an atmospheric, silent landscape of marshes and polders, the Marais Audomarois, rich in wildlife, with a web of canals built up over centuries between reed beds and prolific vegetable gardens. The produce from these marsh-gardens – leeks, chicory, cauliflowers – has always been among the staples of food in St-Omer. Others are beef, rabbit, fish from the nearby ports, and beer, and locals very noticeably share the region's love of chocolate and other things sweet. For fine versions of local dishes in St-Omer you would have to look hard to do better than **La Belle Epoque**, an unassuming but very hospitable restaurant just off the main square.

La Belle Epoque

Place Paul Painlevé, t / f 03 21 38 22 93. Open May–Sept Mon, Wed–Sun 12–3 and 7–10.30; Oct–May Mon, Wed–Sat 12–3 and 7–10.30, Sun 12–3; closed Tues. Menus 98F/€14.94, 118F/€17.99 and 148F/€22.56; à la carte average 190F/€28.97.

Mme Dacheville does everything in the kitchen at the Belle Epoque, while her husband, with occasional help from two young waitresses, looks after front-of-house. On some days, she also takes the orders, lays the tables and serves as well, but will

Magret de Canard aux Pêches

Serves 2

2 peaches, halved and peeled
250ml/9fl oz fruity red wine
1 clove
pinch of ground cinnamon
1 large boneless French duck breast, about 350g/12oz
25g/1oz/2 tablespoons butter
15ml/1 tablespoon runny honey
1 tablespoon cognac
salt and pepper

Put the peaches in a plastic bag set in a dish, add the wine, clove and cinnamon, and marinate for 12 hours.

Score the fatty skin covering one side of the duck breast and season both sides. Set a sauté pan over medium heat, add the duck breast, skin-side down, and cook until it has rendered about ¾ of the fat, about 8 minutes. Pour off the rendered fat and cook the other side until golden, 2–3 minutes more, remove to a plate and keep warm.

Strain the marinade into the sauté pan and boil to reduce by one-quarter. Add the butter and honey, stir, and add the peaches. Simmer gently, uncovered, until the peaches are just tender, turning them once. Return the duck breast to the pan, skin side up, for 3–4 minutes to reheat (it should remain pink) and flame with the cognac.

To serve, slice the duck and divide between two warm plates. Garnish each with two peach halves and pour over the sauce.

In the restaurant, this is served with a purée of celeriac.

still agree very amiably to provide quite complex dishes at short notice late into the evening. She also manages to remain utterly charming and welcoming throughout, and, most important of all, the results of her cooking are excellent. There's no sign of anything being skimped under pressure, and even the *pâtisserie* is homemade. Moreover, she is used to the inability of British visitors to observe proper French hours (and the needs of those arriving late from or on their way to the Tunnel or a ferry), and is willing to serve food well outside the customary local closing times. Those given above are more guidelines than strict timings; if the Dachevilles are there in the middle of the afternoon, she may well be prepared to cook something up for you.

Thanks to its well-earned success, the restaurant was extended in 1998 and now fills two small 1900s townhouses. Inside, it's neatly comfortable, with plenty of flowers, white linen and smart red plush bench seats. Despite being a one-woman band, the menu offers an ample choice. Apart from dishes based on local fare, the other speciality is fish, with a list of specials that changes according to whatever's fresh that day, but might feature monkfish – especially an excellent *lotte à l'améri-caine*, cooked with tomatoes, garlic, shallots, brandy and white wine – or turbot or sometimes local trout from the River Hem. There are also several varieties of grilled steaks, lamb, turkey and so on.

The set menus are generous, and impressive value (the 98F menu includes an all-vegetarian combination). The 118F list might include for starters lobster soup, and an own-made *compôte de lapin aux fruits secs*, a smooth terrine with a fruity undertone, to be followed maybe by the classic Flemish *carbonnade de bœuf*, a fine, strong beef-and-beer stew. Full-bodied, traditional flavours are a characteristic of Mme Dacheville's cooking, but there's a good deal of imagination too. Fixtures on the 148F list are the deliciously light but flavoursome first course of a *gratin* of Chavignol and bacon salad, and the excellent rabbit with prunes and armagnac, one of her specialities. Added to them there are more recent creations such as *magret de canard flambé aux pêches* or, for fish-eaters, *sole aux crevettes sur fondue de poireaux*, in a cream and vermouth sauce.

The wine list is also sizeable for a small restaurant, with quality bottles from around 90F/€13.72, and the cheese selection includes some great, no-beating-about-the-bush local Rollot and Maroilles. More highlights arrive for dessert, such as homemade *nougat glacé* with fresh-fruit coulis or the delectably sticky chocolate mousse. And you'll not be obliged to hurry over your coffee, if you're not rushing to get away.

Touring Around

The main square, officially **Place Foch**, is still very much the hub of St-Omer, and almost inevitably features on any walk around the town. Like many town squares in Flanders and Artois it is strikingly large, built to accommodate the market. Today it also looks as if it was created around the **Hôtel de Ville** which occupies one side, although it is in fact much older. The town hall was only built in the 1830s, in the standard grand style for French public buildings. The biggest pavement cafés and bars are on the south, higher, side, with a balcony view over the rest of the square. It is busiest on Saturday mornings, when it's taken over by the **market** (there is also a smaller market on Wednesdays).

The stalls display local goods, notably fine chicory and other vegetables from the Marais, highly regarded because of the special qualities given by the rich soil of the drained marsh-gardens, which can produce several crops each year. In amongst the crowds there are also stalls with fresh herbs or homemade biscuits, or piled up with whole arrays of northern cheeses such as the strong, under-appreciated Maroilles, as well as others with all the non-food items that mark out a genuine town market, from baby clothes to books.

St-Omer was founded in 637 by Audomar (later St Omer), a monk sent to evangelize the pagan population of this region of bogs and swamps. He also founded an abbey, St-Bertin, which remained a powerful influence in the town until its dissolution during the Revolution. In the early Middle Ages St-Omer and Bruges were the two richest cities in Flanders, larger than Arras and many cities to the south; however, its position also put it square in the middle of the area chosen by France, England and later Spain as their prime battleground for nearly 400 years. When the town was finally secured for Louis XIV and France after a long siege in 1677, Marshal Vauban encased it in a massive set of new ramparts as part of his *pré carré* or 'square field', the line of forts built to protect the new frontier. They held the town like a clamp for two centuries. If you leave Place Foch by Place Painlevé, past the Belle Epoque restaurant, you will come to St-Omer's main park, the **Jardin Public**, which incorporates the only remaining section of Vauban's ramparts, a giant, monolithic screen of plain brick. The rest of the walls, remarkably, were entirely demolished during the 1880s and 1890s, and the only trace of them is the line of boulevards around the city centre.

The long streets that lead away east from Place Foch, especially Rue de Dunkerque, form St-Omer's main shopping centre, with the biggest concentration of high-street stores, *parfumeries*, and so on. The little streets that run off the square between the cafés on the south side, on the other hand, lead into **old St-Omer**, a small area with a distinctive charm that, it has to be said, is very French. Especially attractive are Rue des Clouteries, opposite the Hôtel de Ville, and the parallel Rue Louis Martel, two alley-like streets that now contain small, chic fashion shops – particularly on Rue des Clouteries – mixed in with bakers selling superb fresh bread and *charcuteries* full of bulging red sausages. Throughout the town centre the sweet tooth of northern France is catered for in a markedly high number of chocolate and cake shops.

Rue des Clouteries and Rue Louis Martel lead into the rectangular **Place Victor Hugo**. To the right there is a rather endearingly over-grand baroque fountain; leave the square to the left of the fountain, admiring its chubby cherubs on the way, and then turn left again, and you will come to St-Omer's greatest monument, the **cathedral**.

It was begun around 1200 on the site of three earlier churches, and was completed three hundred years later. It is the largest, grandest Gothic church in the Pas-de-Calais. Before going in, walk around the outside to get an idea of its monumentality: some of the lower, 13th-century sections are quite plain, almost similar to Romanesque, while the squared-off 15th-century tower is entirely a work of elaborate, Flamboyant late Gothic. Most impressively sculptural of all is the *portail royal* at the end of the south transept, on the opposite side from Place Victor Hugo, flanked by two massive, soaring towers. The cathedral has many treasures, of which perhaps finest of all is the truly magnificent organ that fills the whole of the west end of the nave, a superb piece of baroque woodcarving from 1717 that manages to combine perfectly with its medieval surroundings. It is regularly used for concerts. In the north transept, look up to see a wonderful and very rare astrological clock from 1558 – a fine illustration of Renaissance ideas of the world, and still in working order – beneath an intricate Flamboyant-Gothic rose window from the 1450s that, because the cathedral does not actually face due east as it should, beautifully catches the evening light.

Place Sithieu and the streets around it, down the steep slope from the eastern end of the cathedral, make up one of the oldest parts of St-Omer, a little knot of cobbled alleys full of fascinating, very old, sometimes precarious-looking structures. The long streets that lead eastwards from there are a mixture of plainish, largely 19th-century buildings, more elegant French 18th-century residences and some much grander brick edifices from the era when St-Omer was an important city of the Spanish Netherlands and a major centre of the Catholic church. Rue Gambetta is straddled by the various departments of the local *lycée*, the core of which consists of the former buildings of a Jesuit seminary. On Rue du Lycée, which turns north off Rue Gambetta, there looms up the giant mass of the **Chapelle du Lycée** (*open May–Sept some Sundays; inquire at the tourist office*), the extraordinary former chapel of the seminary. Built between 1615 and 1640 by the architect Du Blocq, himself a Jesuit, it's spectacular above all for its size, almost rivalling the cathedral, with a towering five-level brick and stone façade combining Flemish traditions with Italianate Jesuit baroque. Equally unusual are the two remarkably slim, flat-topped towers, difficult to appreciate from the street, that stand at the eastern end of the chapel. The interior is in Flemish *hallekerk* style with no transepts.

Rue du Lycée meets Rue St-Bertin, parallel to Rue Gambetta, where a right turn will take you to the **Ancien Collège des Jesuites**, also now part of the *lycée*. A plaque outside records that this was built as the English College, a reminder of a time when in England to be found to have come on a mission 'from St-Omer' was something like being discovered with credentials from the KGB at the height of the Cold War, and liable to much bloodier penalties. In 1592, as measures against Catholics in England became ever more restrictive, English Jesuits sought help to found a new college to educate the sons of Catholic families on safe soil. It was the most important of several English Colleges on Spanish territory, and lavishly endowed by Philip II of Spain himself and many of the Spanish aristocracy.

On the opposite side of Rue St-Bertin, just back towards the centre of town, a small side-courtyard contains the church of **St-Denis**, an attractive work of simple, 13th-century early Gothic, one of the oldest of St-Omer's remaining churches. It has a *Last Supper* from 1523 attributed to Della Robbia, although this has been contested. Following its final absorption into France St-Omer acquired its more Gallic appearance during the 18th century with a set of large Ancien Régime buildings, and in particular a number of *hôtels particuliers* or town residences that were built for the prosperous local bourgeois and aristocracy. There are several along Rue St-Bertin, and at no.20 is the soberly elegant **Hôtel de Bergues**, which was used to accommodate both George V and the Prince of Wales, the future Edward VIII, when they came to St-Omer on visits to the front during the First World War. The finest is the **Hôtel Sandelin**, on Rue Carnot, the parallel street to the north. Built for Marie-Josephe Sandelin, Comtesse de Fruges, in 1777, this very elegant Louis XVI-style mansion now houses the **Musée Sandelin** (*unfortunately it has fallen foul of a renovation programme that has become mired in political argument, and the most likely date offered for its reopening is mid-2003*), which, when you can see it, is one of the best of northern France's smaller museums. A prime attraction is the house itself, with original, delicately prettified décor from the era of Marie-Antoinette; the collection is also impressive, with fine 18th-century porcelain that ideally matches the setting, French, Dutch and Flemish paintings, and some remarkable medieval religious sculptures from abbeys near St-Omer. You can admire its august façade and grand entrance courtyard from the street. St-Omer has another museum, the **Musée Henri Dupuis** (*open Wed–Sun 10–12 and 2–6; adm*). Its curious collection mainly features birds, shells and other items amassed by the local naturalist after whom it is named, and is something of an acquired taste, but it does have some fine local ceramics and one very special feature in the shape of a beautiful, painstakingly restored Flemish kitchen from 1635.

At the very end of Rue St-Bertin, heading east, there is one more relic of medieval St-Omer, the ruins of the **Abbey of St-Bertin**, standing rather neglectedly within a small park. Built between 1326 and 1570 to replace St Audomar's original abbey, in an emphatic Gothic style similar to that of the great churches of Rouen, this was one of the largest building projects undertaken anywhere in France during the 14th century; most of it was energetically demolished during the 1790s, which is when the saints on the façade all had their heads knocked off, in a burst of revolutionary iconoclasm. Today only the main façade and part of the nave survive. Continue walking a little further from there, to the left of the abbey, to the **River Aa**, where a left turn will take you towards one more of St-Omer's unusual mix of neighbourhoods, the **Faubourg du Haut-Pont**. This characterful district of brick riverworkers' cottages, much of it from the 19th century, still has at least something of the feel of the French canal and riverside communities seen in Jean Vigo's *L'Atalante* or the films of Jean Renoir.

Outside St-Omer there are two more attractions that stand out, for curiosity value alone, among the great many Second World War sites in the Pas-de-Calais, and which exert an awful fascination for anyone interested in the development of destructive technology. About 10km to the north, near the village of Eperlecques, is the **Blockhaus d'Eperlecques** (*open Mar–Nov daily 10–6.30; adm*), one of the main bases for the launching of V2 missiles against London in 1944, which is now a museum. Five kilometres south of town between Helfaut and Wizernes is **La Coupole** (*open Oct–Mar daily 10–6; April–Sept daily 9–7; adm*), another V2 bunker which hosts a state-of-the-art display. Highly popular, this varied exhibit deals not just with the Nazi rocket programme but also with the subsequent career of Doctor Werner von Braun and the development of space travel, while another section graphically traces the story of the war and occupation in northern France, although the star of the show tends to be the journey down into the giant concrete pit of La Coupole itself.

Alternatively, between spring and autumn you can take a boat trip through the canals of the **Marais Audomarois**. Several companies run tours from villages around St-Omer, the most accessible of which is usually Isnor in Clairmarais (*t 03 21 39 15 15, www.isnor.fr; hour-long tours April–June, Sept and Oct Sat, Sun and hols hourly 2–6; July and Aug daily 11am and hourly 2–6; adm*) on the east side of town, although in July and August some tours also pick up at the Haut-Pont in St Omer. They use open boats (the closed launches of other companies may be weather-proof, but they have much less charm). To get to the main landing point, follow the road to the right of the railway station across the Aa from central St-Omer. Commentaries on the flora, fauna and the many legends associated with this strange, flat space are given in English if there are enough people who require it. Canals to drain the marshes, known by their Flemish name *watergangs*, began to be built in Audomar's time, and have been added to ever since. It's a different, tranquil world of rushes, lilies and marsh flowers, inhabited by grebes, ducks and herons. During the day, there are also the *maraîchers*, the cultivators of the marsh allotments. Few now live full-time in the little houses along the banks, but they still take their produce to market in silent punt-like boats.

Shopping

St-Omer has a choice of hypermarkets: Carrefour is north of town, by the main road from Calais and the *autoroute*; Auchan is to the south, by the main roundabout in the direction of La Coupole and the *autoroute* south (*both open Mon–Sat till 10pm*).

St-Omer ✉ 62500
La Cave Gourmande, 11 Rue Louis Martel, t 03 21 93 22 00. A comprehensive selection of French delicacies.
Les Chocolats de Beussent, 30 Rue des Clouteries, t 03 21 12 66 82. Another outlet for the wonderful handmade chocolates from Beussent (*see* p.94).
Le Clair'Marais, 100 Route de Clairmarais, t 03 21 88 07 26. A small greengrocer and food store beside the road between St-Omer and the main landing stage for boat trips into the Marais, where you can regularly get fine marsh grown vegetables.
Le Marché du Quai – La Ferme, 4 Quai du Commerce, t 03 21 39 62 36. Should you pass this barn of a store by accident, on the riverside quay leading to the Faubourg du Haut-Pont, you might just dismiss it as a simple local supermarket. Go inside, however, and you find a panoramic selection of cheeses, many of which have been matured in the company's own cellars. Particularly impressive is the range of fine cheeses from small producers in the Pas-de-Calais. There are also local vegetables, meats – sausages, hams, Licques chickens – and good wines, ciders and liqueurs.

Houlle ✉ 62910
Destillerie Persyn, 19 Route de Watten, t 03 21 93 01 71, f 03 21 39 25 36. A scent of gin wafts over the centre of the village of Houlle. This is because it is home to this tiny distillery, the only one in the Pas-de-Calais, where fine gins have been made since 1812. Visitors can take a tour of the distillery (*reservation necessary; adm*), including a tasting – which can be a bit of a test, as there are over seven varieties and they won't let you get away with trying just one or two. You don't have to take the tour, to buy at the distillery shop; bottles of gin cost from 91F/€13.87.

Where to Stay

Muncq-Nieurlet ✉ 62980
Mme Françoise Breton, Ferme de la Motte Obin, Rue du Bourg, t 03 21 82 79 83 (*double rooms 210F/€32.01*). Mme Breton's farmhouse is reached from the road between the villages of Muncq-Nieurlet and Ruminghem, about 15km north of St-Omer and 30km from Calais. Turn through the centuries-old gate into the farm and you enter a sweeping timber and brick courtyard, with the house in one corner and giant old stables around the other sides. Mme Breton, an elderly widow, now lives in this venerable pile by herself, but this doesn't seem to faze her; she loves to have guests, to whom she will talk at length (in French). The two rooms are big, characterful and comfortable, and each have space for children's beds. She also serves ample country meals (*90–100F/€13.72–15.24*), which are praised to the skies by former guests. *Closed 1 Nov–1 April.*

Zouafques ✉ 62890
La Ferme de Wolphus, Route Nationale 43, t/f 03 21 35 61 61, *ferme.de.wolphus@wanadoo.fr* (*double rooms 225–250F/€34.30–38.11, rooms for four 400F/€60.98*). A popular B&B off the N43 south of Ardres. A little functional but made comfortable and welcoming by the friendly owners. The three guest rooms, in a former outhouse, are simply decorated in modern style; one has space for up to four and all have access to a kitchenette. There are also two self-contained *gîtes*. Owner Jean-Jacques Behagel also sells wine and honey.

St-Omer ✉ 62500
Hôtel Le Bretagne, 2 Place du Vainquai, t 03 21 38 25 78, f 03 21 93 51 22 (*double rooms 320–480F/€48.78–73.18*). A modern 75-room hotel on the eastern side of St-Omer, near the ruins of St-Bertin abbey, around a 10–15min walk from the centre. The large ground floor **restaurant** offers both a brasserie list and a fairly sophisticated *à la carte* (*menus 90–180F/€13.72–27.44*).
Hôtel St-Louis, 25 Rue d'Arras, t 03 21 38 35 21, f 03 21 38 57 26, *www.hotel-saintlouis.com* (*double rooms 290–330F/€44.21–50.31*) . A

pleasant, unfussy and comfortable small-town Logis hotel in a much-renovated old coaching inn a short walk from the cathedral and Place Foch. Service is warm, and the St-Louis has a livelier restaurant, **Le Flaubert** (*see* below), than many Logis hotels.

Tilques ✉ 62500

Hôtel Château de Tilques, t 03 21 88 99 99, **f** 03 21 38 34 23, *www.chateautilques.com* (*double rooms from 750F/€114.34, luxury rooms 1,050F/€160.07*). The luxury option in the St-Omer area, a plush 53-room country house hotel in its own grounds. The current château was built in the late 19th century in mock-Flemish baronial style, but the manor on which it stands, just north of St-Omer, is centuries older. The 30 rooms in the château are traditional in style, while the 'garden rooms' in an adjoining building are a little more modern and bigger; all offer every kind of comfort. In the former stables there's a much admired restaurant (*see* below).

Eating Alternatives

Houlle ✉ 62910

L'Auberge de l'Etang Poupart, 12 Impasse des Etangs, **t** 03 21 93 05 26 (*menus from 110F/ €16.77*). A winding (but signposted) lane leads out of the marshlands village of Houlle, about 6km north of St-Omer, to end at this restaurant in a very pretty, flower-bedecked old *marais* farmhouse, with – as the name suggests – a large placid *étang* (pond) at the back, alongside which there are tables in summer. Inside, the dining room is cosy and rustic, and there is nothing crude about chef-owner Jérôme Delplace's cooking either. He sticks to traditional dishes – *carbonnade, andouilles,* fish soups – with, since this is a *restaurant du terroir*, a firm emphasis on fresh local produce.

Clairmarais ✉ 62500

Auberge des Nénuphars, 60 Route de St-Omer, **t/f** 03 21 38 24 84 (*menus 60–130F/ €9.15–19.82*). Another *marais auberge,* easy to find on the D209 as it continues out from St-Omer past the boat-landings in Clairmarais. The laidback little inn occupies a low house with a dining room in a big glass conservatory and more tables outside in the garden; it stands alongside a big, placid *étang*, with ducks, geese and a landing stage – from where boat trips are sometimes available – while all around it there are plots full of exuberant crops of vegetables.

St-Omer ✉ 62500

Le Cygne, 8 Rue Caventou, **t** 03 21 98 20 52, **f** 03 21 95 57 12 (*5 different menus 75–265F/ €11.43–40.40*). A pretty town restaurant with rather fluffy bourgeois décor – lace curtains, white table settings – but relaxed and comfortable nonetheless. It stands on one of the narrow old streets just east of the cathedral, looking down the long slope of Rue St-Bertin. The cuisine covers an interesting variety, from local dishes such as cod baked in white beer or an excellent *salade maraîchère* with local vegetables and foie gras, to others with daringly exotic touches.

Restaurant Le Flaubert, *see* above, Hôtel St-Louis (*restaurant menus 79–160F/ €12.04–24.39; brasserie dishes 20–25F/ €3.05–3.81*). One half of this popular restaurant is a conventional dining room, with a good-value range of fairly substantial classic dishes. A hearty Alsatian meat *choucroute* is the house speciality, but there's also an ample range of salads. The other half is a relaxed bar-brasserie-'sandwicherie', a favourite with students from the *lycée*.

Au Petit St-Pierre, 27 Quai du Haut-Pont, **t** 03 21 38 01 44 (*menu 97F/€14.79*). On the quay in the Faubourg du Haut-Pont, the bluff and basic St-Pierre is the first place to go in St Omer to find the most traditional northern, Artois and Flemish specialities. The set menu is superb value. *Lunch only*.

Tilques ✉ 62500

Hôtel Château de Tilques, *see* above (*lunch menus 130F/€19.82, Sun 165F/€25.15; dinner menus 220F/€33.54, Sun 250F/€38.11*). The restaurant in the converted former stables of the château, presided over by chef Patrick Hittos (and where Jamie Oliver once spent some time), offers a notably opulent repertoire that combines French *haute cuisine* with some more exotic touches: rabbit pâté with mango and tarragon vinegar. Prices are surprisingly accessible. There's also a refined wine list, and a wine shop.

In the Flemish Mountains:

Cassel and the Monts de Flandre

07

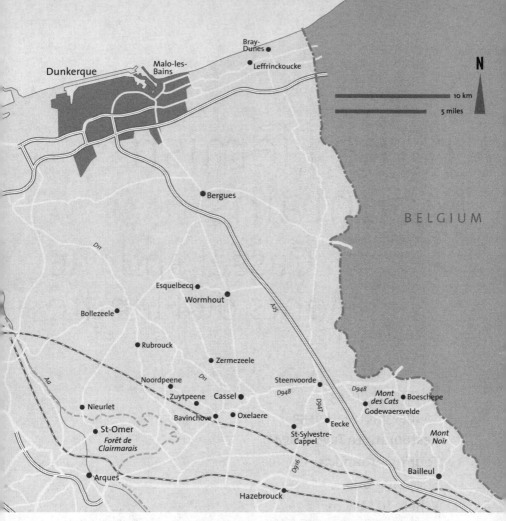

All over the European continent there are little patches where the official frontiers and the extent of the communities on the ground don't quite coincide, where those who drew up the border lines never took much care to ensure that speakers of one language were all on one side while those of a neighbouring culture were all on the other.

Such a place is French Flanders, the compact strip of land between Lille, St-Omer, the sea and the Belgian border. A glance at the map and the place names – Zermezeele, Boeschepe, Godewaersvelde, all about as Gallic as Rembrandt's nose – is enough to show that this is not one of the historic heartlands of French culture. And yet this has been a part of France since the 1670s, when it was seized by Louis XIV. Today, it's a curious but distinct mix: French in language, but still Flemish in many of its customs.

In France it is virtually obligatory in any reference to Flanders to quote from the Jacques Brel song 'Le Plat Pays' ('The Flat Country'), which raised flatness to the level

Getting There

The quickest way to drive from Calais and the Tunnel to the Monts de Flandre is to take the A16 *autoroute* eastwards to Dunkerque, and then follow the signs for Lille on to the A25 *autoroute* south (both motorways are toll-free in this area). Leave the A25 at junction 13 (Steenvoorde) to get on to roads to the right for Cassel (7km) or Hazebrouck (12km). It's quite easy to get to Cassel in about 45mins, while Hazebrouck takes a little longer. A more leisurely and rural route, only a bit slower, is to leave the A16 west of Dunkerque at junction 24, head south on the D600 signposted to St-Omer for about 4km and then look for the little D11 to the left, for Cassel, via various villages and flat Flanders fields.

This area has reasonable local rail connections. Local trains on the Calais–Lille and Dunkerque–Lille lines stop at Hazebrouck, and Dunkerque–Hazebrouck–Lille trains stop at Bailleul and Bavinchove, the station for Cassel, which is 3½km away on the top of its hill.

Tourist Information

Bailleul: Office de Tourisme des Monts de Flandre, 3 Grand'Place, t 03 28 43 81 00, f 03 28 43 81 01, *bailleul@tourisme.norsys.fr*. The largest and most comprehensive tourist office for the whole area, opposite the Hôtel de Ville on the main square.
Cassel: 28 Grand'Place, t 03 28 40 52 55, f 03 28 40 59 17.
Esquelbecq: Place Bergerot, t 03 28 62 88 57, f 03 28 49 74 84.
Hazebrouck: Grand'Place, t 03 28 49 59 89, f 03 28 49 53 04.
Steenvoorde: Maison de Flandre, Place Dr J.F. Ryckewaert, t 03 28 49 97 98, f 03 28 49 74 84.
Wormhout: Place du Général de Gaulle, t/f 03 28 62 81 23.

of a poetic image; and flatness is certainly its most overriding characteristic. However, Flanders does have some substantial hills, and the Monts de Flandre are the reason why France wanted the area in the first place. Under 200m high, they are actually very steep; rising up out of the flat, wet Flemish plain. The abrupt contrast between the hills and the plains creates a strangely awesome landscape, a favourite with walkers. The Monts also have wonderful views, and especially clear light and air that's kept alive by the uninterrupted winds. Their peculiar prominence has also given them a special role in the area's folklore, religion and war. And on top of the tallest of them all is the little walled hill town of Cassel, one of the most atypically characterful historic towns in northeast France.

The idiosyncratic identity of French Flanders is also illustrated by the huge windmills on many of the hills, which stand out like giant sailed monuments against the sky. There is a distinctive architecture, of step gables, belfries, rectangular churches, small brick houses, painted shutters and lace curtains. There are traditional Flemish games, the *carillons* of little bells that peal from the belfries, and a dense folklore of Carnival and giants that is celebrated each year. And as soon as you cross the River Aa by St-Omer the food changes, taking on more of a straightforward heartiness – although still a little more refined than in Belgium. The favourite drink of this *terroir* is beer, produced by small traditional breweries, and sampled at its best in *estaminets*, snug, wooden-tabled old pubs that are perhaps French Flanders' most cherished institution. One of the most atmospheric places in which to find the full range of the region's cuisine and its finest beers is **La Taverne**, in the old Flemish crossroads town of Hazebrouck.

La Taverne

61 Grand'Place, Hazebrouck, t 03 28 41 63 09. Open Tues–Sat
11am–10pm, Sun 11am–2.30pm. Closed Sun eve and Mon.
Menus 98F/€14.94, 105F/€16.01 and 145F/€22.11;
à la carte average 180F/€27.44.

Hazebrouck's Grand'Place is an imposingly large open space to which people from round about have been coming to do business and keep up with what's going on for centuries. The style of the square is mirrored by the most impressive of the several restaurants around it, La Taverne, quickly recognisable by its soaring Flemish stepped-gable brick façade and elegantly arching entrance.

Its narrow frontage leads into a giant barn of old dark wood, with a semi-baronial ceiling inset with diamonds of stained glass. On one side there's a solid, carved-wood bar, with barrels hanging from the roof above it, while around the walls there are curiosities such as lace trimmings, figures of pixies and other folkloric characters, and Flemish bar-room games. Hazebrouck is a businesslike sort of place, and La Taverne can get impressively bustling and noisy when the midday crowds pile in. It's also spacious enough to be an easy place to settle into amid the warm fug for a convivial winter afternoon spent sampling the beers, or trying out some of those incomprehensible games.

Table settings, meanwhile, are traditionally neat, with red undercloths and white linen, and a pretty menu with a picture of a Flanders hill. Service by owner Bernard Dentener and his staff is charming, fast when it needs to be, and quietly solicitous, creating an easygoing brasserie atmosphere. Look around the restaurant and you may just as well see big groups sitting down to a hefty lunch, twos and threes of plump, suited men setting about their own piles of *frites* and *potjevleesch*, and young women on their own who come in for a quick bite.

La Taverne is a good place to appreciate the essential features of Flemish cooking, its comfort-food quality among them. The sometimes compulsive intricacy of much *cuisine française* is largely absent, and in its place there are many dishes that are simply satisfying, warming nosh, served with the obligatory heaps of *frites*. Quality stems from the good fresh ingredients and proper care in preparation. Many of the most traditional local dishes were first served (other than as home cooking) in *estaminets* or pubs: *tartines* (open sandwiches with meat, cheese or other toppings), quiches, savoury tarts and *flamiches*, large platters of *frites* and *potjevleesch* (mixed terrines of rabbit, chicken and veal), and *waterzooi* chicken soup. Mustard pots stand on every table, to go with the *potjevleesch*. Among La Taverne's specialities are an excellent range of quiches and *flamiches* with a wide choice of fillings, some of which always feature on the set menus: *quiche de l'Abbaye à la Leffe* (made with Mont des Cats cheese and Leffe beer) has an interestingly beery tang.

In addition, since the 1980s La Taverne has also offered a full restaurant-brasserie menu, which in the last few years has become increasingly sophisticated. Apart from a fine version of the classic Flemish *carbonnade* and other beer-based choices, many of the most interesting dishes feature one of the lesser-known but most original elements in the region's cooking, juniper berries (*genièvre*), and sometimes even straight gin. *Andouillettes de Cambrai au Wambrechies* (Cambrai sausages cooked in Belgian Wambrechies gin and juniper) is a fine Brueghel-esque combination. To finish there are sorbets, and a lot of over-the-top, old-fashioned, creamy desserts, which go rather well with the décor.

The subtleties missing from Flemish food tend to be deferred to the beers, which are wonderful. La Taverne has around 20 in bottles and several on draught, all from small breweries either in northern France or nearby across the border in Belgium. Discoveries, such as the full-bodied but soft Trois Monts from St-Sylvestre Cappel, Zannekin, La Choulette or Grain d'Orge, make this a beer-taster's heaven; note too, that La Taverne – rather unusually for a restaurant in Flanders – also has a decent wine list.

Touring Around

The natural centre of the Monts de Flandre and obvious focus for visitors is **Cassel**, perched atop Mont-Cassel (176m), the highest point in Flanders. This may not seem much of a height by international standards, but as you climb the winding lanes that lead up from the plain it looks huge: the town is clustered together in almost unreal fashion at the top, behind its old fortified gates, to complete the theatrical impression. At its core there is an expansive and attractive Grand'Place, and, at the very peak, a remarkable windmill, a statue of Marshal Foch and the Kasteelhof, French Flanders' most famous *estaminet*. That the top of the town is marked by a windmill is another of its eccentricities. Around and below, the houses of Cassel are packed precipitously along the hillsides, their steep-sloped grey- and red-tiled roofs sometimes seeming impossibly close together, mixed in with vegetable allotments and footpaths, while all around the green and brown Flanders plains stretch away for ever.

The height of Mont-Cassel in a flat country has always made it especially important in wars, which Flanders has probably seen more of than any other part of Europe. It was a stronghold of a Gaulish tribe called the Morins, and the Romans seized the hill and built a fortress here in the time of Julius Caesar. Cassel was fought over many times in the Middle Ages. Then, in the 1670s as Louis XIV was driving French frontiers relentlessly eastwards, his Generals informed him that the Monts de Flandre, which until then had with the rest of Flanders formed part of the Spanish Netherlands, were a strategic property that France should definitely possess. In 1677 a mixed Spanish and Dutch army was defeated by the French at Zuytpeene, just south of Cassel, and the following year western Flanders was attached to France for ever. For a long time this meant little to most of the population, who remained predominantly Flemish-speaking at least until the Third Republic imposed universal education in French in the 1880s, and in many communities until decades after that.

This did not end Cassel's military role. In 1914 it became the headquarters of the French General (later Marshal) Foch in the Battle of the Yser, in which his armies halted the Germans' attempts to cut around the flank of the allied lines. The last time Cassel saw heavy fighting was in May 1940, when both its hill and the Mont des Cats further east were important strongpoints in British attempts to slow down the German advance on Dunkerque, and were only given up after a ferocious three-day battle. There is a British war cemetery attached to the town cemetery, beside the road in from Bailleul and Steenvoorde on the east side of town.

The obvious place to begin exploring Cassel is the **Grand'Place**, which itself slopes up and down over different levels and terraces. It contains the town's most distinguished buildings, a mix of very French Ancien Régime styles with others that are far more Netherlandish, as well as others in functional brick that date from the 1950s. Cassel is another of the towns that needed a great deal of reconstruction work after 1945 and, although not everything could be restored, the result is still impressive. Grandest of all the mansions is the **Hôtel de la Noble Cour** on the west side (also known as the **Landshuys**), built during the years of Spanish rule at the end of the 16th century. Beneath a typically Flemish gable roof, it has an elegant, much more French-Renaissance-influenced main façade; its most curious features, though, are the grotesque heads carved at the foot of each of its main windows, mythical beasts and figures that often look distinctly devilish. The Noble Cour was built as the courthouse of the Lordship of Cassel, which had authority over the whole territory between St-Omer and Ypres, but now houses the **Musée de Flandre** (*open during exhibitions Wed–Sun 2–6; usually free*). This folk and social history museum has been under restoration for some time, but during temporary exhibitions you get a chance to see the interior of the building. Other façades on the Grand'Place provide something of a run-through of Cassel's history: the **Taverne Flamande** restaurant, built in a 'neo-Flemish' style in the 1930s, stands next to a finely proportioned Louis-XVI-model *hôtel*. One building that was irredeemably lost in 1940 was the famous 1634 town hall, which was replaced by the current, rather plain brick Hôtel de Ville that houses the tourist office. All around the square there are attractive cafés and restaurants – the **Café de l'Hôtel de Ville** and the **Crêperie du Mont** are two of the most enjoyable – with plenty of outside terrace-space when the weather's suitable.

One street back from the Grand'Place, but dominating the view towards the southern end of the square, is Cassel's main church, the **Collégiale de Notre-Dame**. Parts of this giant brick temple date from the 11th century, but the greater part of it is a sombre 16th-century Gothic *hallekerk* or hall-church, a huge rectangular space with three naves of equal length instead of the usual cross-pattern, a church style peculiar to Flanders that – prior to the French takeover – also spread westwards into Artois. Notre-Dame is in serious need of restoration, but inside there is still some very fine stained glass. Right behind it there is also the impressive Flemish Baroque façade of the one-time **Jesuit Church**, which now provides a very grand location for a garage. There are several more churches and small chapels around Cassel, which for centuries was an important pilgrimage centre; the tourist office has a full list.

From the main porch of Notre-Dame, a walk along the street sloping up to the right out of the Grand'Place, Rue de Bergues, will take you on a circuit around the line of Cassel's 16th–17th-century **ramparts**, which once enclosed the tiny fortified town. The corner of the Route de Dunkerque, right next to the church, marks the site of the **Porte de Dunkerque**, now mostly demolished; further up Rue de Bergues, at the corner of Rue Profonde ('Deep Street'), there remains from the old **Porte de Bergues** a strange little watchtower, with wonderful views over a near-360° circle. And, as in much of Cassel atop its hill, it's often invigoratingly windy. Continuing along Rue de Bergues will take you into a large, sloping square that's now primarily a car park. This is Place du Général Vandamme, named after a Napoleonic commander born in the town. From there, the little alley of Rue St Nicolas strikes up steeply toward the Kasteelhof *estaminet* and the very top of the hill.

The top of the hill naturally gives the very best **views** of all, especially from the eastern side by the Foch statue, where the Marshal, atop his horse, scans the horizon endlessly for signs of any new invading armies. The statue is ringed by an indicator board, showing distances to innumerable places near and far. According to a local saying, from the summit of Mont-Cassel it's possible to see five kingdoms: France, Belgium, Holland, Britain and the Kingdom of Heaven. There's also a very fine view from the windows of the Kasteelhof, for many as much a point of pilgrimage as anything else in Cassel. Dominating the view in a westerly direction is the magnificent 16th-century windmill, the **Moulin de Cassel** (*open Sat and Sun 10–6*), beautifully restored and now very much in use; you can even buy freshly ground flour. To the left of the mill is the site of the former château of Cassel, destroyed in the 18th century, and now a small park, the **Jardin Public**, containing the Monument des Trois Batailles, commemorating three conflicts in the hill's history (in 1071, 1328 and 1677). On one side of the esplanade there is also a large but now rather decayed 1920s building known as the 'casino'. Built in an attempt to give Cassel a Grand Hotel, but long closed, its main purpose today is to hold up the transmitters of a local bilingual radio station. Just below it, on the town side of the Jardin Public, a path leads steeply down through the 1621 **Porte du Château**, flanked by two very solid turrets and the only substantial part of the old castle still standing. This path runs into the equally steep and narrow Rue de Château, which leads back to the Grand'Place.

Cassel is a town of alleys and brick courtyards, hidden spaces and gardens. To follow a popular route through town head out of the inner ring of streets from Place Vandamme northwest down Rue Bollaert le Gavrian, the St-Omer road. A short distance from the *place* there is an opening on the left into a very narrow alley which, surprisingly, is the beginning of the **Chemin des Remparts**, a paved path that runs just below the line of the old fortifications along the western side of town, in between houses and vegetable patches, with more superb views along the way. In Cassel the town fades away quickly into open country as soon as you leave the main streets behind. Along the way the Chemin meets the **Chemin d'Aire**, with the Porte d'Aire, the most complete survivor of the 17th-century gates. Beyond it, the path continues through more allotments and over a little bridge to emerge beyond the southeast corner of the Grand'Place, via another very tiny alley. The whole area in and around Cassel is criss-crossed with paths, and the tourist office has good leaflets indicating most of them.

Two roads lead eastwards from Cassel. The D948 runs straight to Steenvoorde, where the eye is grabbed by two of the largest Flanders windmills, which dominate the town. An alternative is to take the Bailleul road southeast through St-Sylvestre-Cappel – site of one of the area's best breweries – and turn off left on to the country road that leads, via the attractive village of Eecke, to **Godewaersvelde**. As well as having one of the region's most incorrigibly un-French names, this little village 5km from the Belgian border is one of the most characteristically Flemish in the whole area, with a long winding street through the middle, a big hall-church and little brick and tile houses with lace curtains. It's a centre for French Flanders' mild-mannered nationalist movement which, fittingly, is based in a bar, the wonderful **Het Blauwershof**. With its green-white-and-red shutters, wooden panelling, copper stoves, beer-pumps and wonderful beer this venerable place perhaps outdoes the better-known Kasteelhof in Cassel as an image of the traditional *estaminet*, and itself provides a reason for visiting the village. The black-on-yellow Lion of Flanders, and signs announcing Flemish language classes and other events, are displayed, but there's no great atmosphere of militancy, and the main language spoken still seems to be French.

Just southeast of Godewaersvelde is **Mont des Cats**, most dramatically steep of the Monts de Flandre, which is reached via a narrow lane that winds up through the curious tiny village that clings to the green flank of the hill (or a similar road from the Bailleul side). The mountain's name is derived from that of a Germanic people known as the 'Cattes', who made it their stronghold in the 5th century AD. Both roads turn through tight loops as they climb to the top of the mountain (158m), from where there are wonderful views into Belgium, and a massive, brick-faced monastery, the **Abbaye de Notre Dame du Mont** (*a small visitor centre has an exhibition on the life of the community, t 03 28 42 52 50; the public can attend Mass in the chapel on Sun*). This is not a medieval foundation, but was established in 1826 as part of the restoration of Catholicism following the Revolution. Restored in turn after 1918 and 1945, the abbey has a neo-Gothic, dark aspect, a cross between a cathedral, a castle and a Victorian textile mill. Inside – a religious centre since time immemorial – there is still a functioning closed community of Trappist monks. The monks make their own cheese, which is on sale at the shop next to the Hostellerie du Mont des Cats (*see* below).

Further on are some more of Flanders' mountains. On the very line of the Belgian frontier is **Mont Noir**, famous to French readers as the childhood home of the novelist Marguerite Yourcenar. The château where she lived is no longer there – it was obliterated in the First World War – but the summit has been made into an attractive park in her memory. There is also a large **British war cemetery**, mostly containing the graves of men who died in the battle to hold Mont Noir in April 1918 – one of many cemeteries and memorials in this area, which formed part of the 1914–18 front line for long periods. On the way up to the top of the hill from Boeschepe is an especially magnificent windmill, the **Ondankmeulen**, built in 1802 and still in regular use. Like others nearby, it is particularly impressive when the weather closes in and the wind strikes up, which happens fairly frequently around here.

The villages north and west of Cassel also have their points to explore, amid a landscape that runs down from the hills to roll gently for a while before becoming completely flat. Little **Zermezeele**, about 4km north of Cassel, has the personal chapel of a 15th-century *seigneur* incorporated into its church; further north again is the fascinating village of **Esquelbecq**, built around an impressively large square with a very Flemish-looking château from 1606 on one side and a giant 16th-century *hallekerk* church with walls of elaborately patterned decorative brickwork – and a fine *carillon* – on the other. The château is not open to the public, but its exterior can well be appreciated from the square, all up-and-down pepper-pot turrets that make it an ideal candidate for a ghastly grange. A barn near Esquelbecq was the site of the

Flemish Festivals

Nearly every town and village in French Flanders has its set of **giants**, huge wood and papier-mâché figures commonly associated (half-seriously) with some legend of the origin of the community. Lovingly maintained, they are generally paraded around town during Carnival, in the spring, and on certain other set days each year, depending on each town's particular calendar of events. The parades are made up of loopy-sounding marching bands in jokey outfits which make their way around amid general partying and much sampling of the local brew.

These festivals are also the occasions for bringing to the fore the strange range of **Flemish games**, such as Flemish archery (firing an arrow straight up into the air to hit a target dangling from a crane), Flemish bowls (played with round slabs, which look a bit like uncut cheeses, instead of balls) and many more. There are also games that can be played at any time of year in *estaminets*, such as putbak, a quoits-like game that involves throwing balls into the mouth of a metal frog.

The following are just a few of the larger giants' parades:

Bailleul's Carnival is one of the biggest and most boisterous, and all the attention is focused on Gargantua, the only sitting giant in Flanders, who is paraded on the Sunday before Mardi-Gras.

Cassel's giants are a couple, Reuze-Papa and Reuze-Maman. Reuze-Papa, who looks like a Roman soldier, makes his first appearance of the year on the Carnival Sunday before Shrove Tuesday, and both come out together on Easter Monday.

Hazebrouck's giant, Roland, comes out – very unusually – in the middle of Lent, and then has another, more important, parade with his family, the Tijse-Tajse, on the first weekend in July.

Steenvoorde has several giants who appear at several times each year, including Yan den Houtkapper (Jan the Woodcutter), a woodcutter who supposedly made a pair of clogs for Charlemagne, and was rewarded with a magic breastplate. Two other major occasions are the International Giants Summer Carnival in late April, and the Hop Festival on the first Sunday in October.

In **Wormhout**, the 'Roi des Mitrons' parades with his band, the 'Bande des Mitrons', on Carnival Sunday.

'Wormhout Massacre' in May 1940, when some 80 British prisoners were massacred by German SS troops.

To the west, **Bollezeele** has an especially grand late-Gothic church, completed in 1606 but extended in the 1870s. This was necessary to accommodate pilgrims to Notre Dame de Bollezeele, a figure of the Virgin that has been a major focus of Catholic devotion throughout Flanders since the Middle Ages. About 3km to the south is **Rubrouck**, an ancient village full of medieval details that also houses one of the region's most bizarre sights. The village was the home of Friar Guillaume de Rubrouck, who in the 13th century travelled all the way to Mongolia, to the court of Genghis Khan. To commemorate its most distinguished son little Rubrouck now has the **Maison Guillaume de Rubrouck** (*t 03 28 43 03 83; open Feb–Nov Sat and Sun 2–5; adm*), which consists of none other than two genuine round Mongol yurt tents, plonked in a Flanders field. Inside, there is an exhibition on Mongolian life and culture. Just to the south again are **Noordpeene** and **Zuytpeene**, site of the battle that secured Cassel and its surrounding villages for France in 1677.

Of the larger towns in the south of French Flanders, **Bailleul** is an ancient community that was one of the wealthiest trading towns in Flanders in the Middle Ages, when it had particularly close links with England. It was devastated in the First World War, but a prodigious effort was made at restoration. Like all old Flemish merchant towns it has a very big Grand'Place, or market square, which post-1918 regained a remarkable number of its Flemish stepped-brick façades, which make it something like a smaller, more industrial Arras. Above all, Bailleul's magnificent Gothic **Hôtel de Ville** was restored almost completely, together with its 13th-century main hall and giant tower-belfry, **Le Beffroi**, which can be climbed to enjoy the view (*open June–Sept Sat 3pm, Sun 11am; July and Aug daily 4.30pm; enquire at tourist office*). Just off the square there is also a more than usually interesting local museum, the **Musée Benoît Depuydt** (*open Mon, Wed–Sun 2–5.30; adm*). As well as an impressive collection of 17th- and 18th-century Flemish furniture, costumes, local lace and household items, it also contains Italian ceramics and a surprising picture collection, with fine works by many Flemish artists such as Gérard David and Pieter Brueghel II, including a remarkable Brueghelesque image of Bailleul in 1621 by Jacob Savery. Bailleul is also one of the towns of French Flanders most dedicated to keeping up its traditions: its food, its Carnival, and its markets.

Hazebrouck itself, 13km west of Bailleul, was a well-known communications centre in the First World War, but was more heavily knocked around in the Second. It too has been much restored and rebuilt, but amid the modern town there are still many relics of old Flanders, such as the 15th-century church of **St-Eloi**, with a turreted tower added in 1532, and the former **Augustinian Convent**, from 1518. Hazebrouck's main attractions, though, are its restaurants and busy street activity, centred around one of the largest Flemish Grand'Places, dominated by a 19th-century neoclassical **town hall** that could easily be mistaken for a national parliament. The square is at its liveliest during the great weekly markets, which in both Hazebrouck and Bailleul, due to a curious Flemish tradition, are on Tuesdays.

Shopping

St-Sylvestre-Cappel ✉ 59114
Brasserie St-Sylvestre, 1 Rue de la Chapelle, **t** 03 28 40 15 49, **f** 03 28 40 13 44. A well-established traditional brewer which produces the satisfying Trois Monts, as well as other refined brews. *Open Tues–Fri 8–12.30 and 2–5.30, Sat 8–12; brewery tours on an occasional basis.*

Esquelbecq ✉ 56470
Brasserie Thiriez, 22 Rue de Wormhout, **t/f** 03 28 62 88 44. Often known as the 'Brasserie d'Esquelbecq', this micro-brewery uses traditional Flemish brewing techniques. It produces four main beers and several special-occasion brews such as the hefty Bière de Noel. There's an attractive *estaminet*/shop, where you can sample the product together with local snacks. *Open Mon–Sat 10–1 and 2–7, and some Sundays in summer; guided tours by reservation; adm.*

Bailleul ✉ 59270
Aux Délices Bailleulois, 10 Grand'Place, **t** 03 28 49 29 47. An attractive shop on the main square with a complete range of local food products – and of course beers.
Ferme de Beck Eeckelstraete, **t** 03 28 49 03 90, **f** 03 28 42 28 32. On the ouskirts of Bailleul, Christiane and Denis Beck brew their own fine traditional beer, Hommelpap. This is also a dairy farm, so butter and other farm produce is also on sale. *Open for sampling, along with a traditional supper, Mar–Nov Sat from 7pm, Sun from 5pm.*

Oxelaere ✉ 59670
Ferme des Templiers, La Place, **t** 03 28 40 50 37. Marie-Christine and Philippe Dubois produce a fine traditional cheese, Boulet de Cassel: creamy, rich and with a thick rind similar to Dutch cheeses like Gouda. The farm shop also sells their butter, preserves, and homemade waffles and biscuits, such as the Flemish pre-Christmas speciality *strynt'jes* (rather like a small, crisp waffle), together with local beers, *potjevleesch* and other *charcuterie*. The farm is signposted, near the centre of Oxelaere just south of Cassel. *Guided tours by reservation.*

Godewaersvelde ✉ 59270
Fromagerie du Mont des Cats, Le Mont des Cats, **t** (via L'Hostellerie) 03 28 42 51 44. All the fine cheese on sale is made by the monks. The shop also sells a small selection of farm-made biscuits, beers and other local produce. *Closed Sun am, Mon and Tues.*

Where to Stay

Hazebrouck ✉ 59190
Auberge de la Forêt, La Motte au Bois, **t** 03 28 48 08 78, **f** 03 28 40 77 76 (*rooms 220–340F/ €33.54–51.83*). A 12-room Logis in a Flemish-style brick chalet in the centre of this village, about 4km south of Hazebrouck. The rooms have recently been renovated, and the **restaurant** (*menus 140–290F/€21.34–44.21*) serves above-average local and French fare.

Boeschepe ✉ 59299
Auberge du Vert Mont, Route du Mont Noir, **t** 03 28 49 41 26, **f** 03 28 49 48 58 (*rooms 280–340F/€42.69–51.83*). An unusual Logis hotel in its own grounds on the slopes of the Mont Noir, with tennis courts, spectacular views, and health farm facilities such as a sauna, a hammam and massage treatments. The **restaurant** (*menus from 90F/€13.72*) serves conventional local fare.

Bollezeele ✉ 59470
Hostellerie St Louis, 47 Rue de l'Église, **t** 03 28 68 81 83, **f** 03 28 68 01 17 (*rooms 320–450F/ €48.78–68.60 for two*). A superior Logis hotel in a rambling 18th-century residence on the main street, surrounded by a large, attractive garden. The well-appointed rooms are mostly in the 19th-century wings. The **restaurant** (*menus 140–320F/€21.34–48.78*) serves traditional French and local dishes.
Le Pantgat Hof, 27 Rue de Metz, **t** 03 28 68 00 87 (*rooms 240F/€36.59 for two, 320F/ €48.78 for three; two-room suite from 420F/ €64.03 for four or five; one of the doubles has full disabled access*). An impressive *chambre-d'hôte* with five rooms in a large farm 2km outside Bollezeele. **Evening meals** available by arrangement (*95F/€14.48*). The owners, M and Mme Chiloup-Gey, run an art workshop and offer guided walks and pony rides.

Cassel ✉ 59670

M and Mme Woestelandt, 1516 Route d'Hazebrouck, **t** 03 28 42 41 15, **f** 03 28 42 41 15 (*rooms 220F/€33.54 for two*). A comfortable B&B on the road south of Cassel past Oxelaere, in a tranquil old Flemish farm with a lovely garden and a pond. The attractive rooms, in an old brick barn, have good facilities. There are also two self-contained *gîtes*, one with space for four, the other for eight.

Hôtel Le Foch, 41 Grand'Place, **t** 03 28 42 47 73 (*rooms 180F/€27.44, breakfast 40F/€6.10*). More a local restaurant than an hotel, with two simple rooms and two studio-like, double rooms with kitchenettes.

Eating Alternatives

A feature of Flanders is the *estaminet*, which traditionally serves hearty, snack-type dishes.

Godewaersvelde ✉ 59270

L'Hostellerie du Mont des Cats, Le Mont des Cats, **t** 03 28 42 51 44, **f** 03 28 42 52 05 (*menu 140F/€21.34*). This big eating-house for pilgrims and tourists serves unadventurous country cooking: the Assiette de l'Abbaye – a snack with bacon and Mont des Cats cheese – *magret de canard*, or Flemish sausages. There is a sweeping view from the dining room or the larger outside *terrasse*.

L'Auberge du Catsberg, 1487 Route de l'Abbaye, **t** 03 28 42 59 59, **f** 03 28 43 30 44 (*menu 89F/€13.57; plat du jour 45F/€6.86*). A little below the abbey on the north side of the Mont des Cats, but still with a fine view, this is a convivial little country bar-restaurant offering local classics such as *carbonnade*, *potjevleesch* and *coq à la bière*. *Closed Mon*.

Au Roi du Potje Vleesch, 31 Rue du Mont des Cats, **t** 03 28 42 52 56 (*dishes c. 40–60F/ €6.10–9.15*). Almost as pretty as the Blauwershof, with a slightly wider choice of Flemish specialities: especially good meats and local *charcuterie*. It also has a shop selling meats, beers, cheese and other Flanders products. *Closed Mon*.

Het Blauwershof, 9 Rue d'Eecke, **t** 03 28 49 45 11 (*dishes c. 20–65F/€3.05–9.91*). A wonderfully relaxing bar where you can easily settle in for a whole afternoon. There are three

beers on tap, close to 30 French and Belgian beers in bottles and a big choice of gins and spirits. The food is hearty: *coq à la bière*, *flamiches* and *tartines*, all served with huge bowls of *frites*. There's the full range of traditional Flemish bar games, and you can pick up leaflets about the area. *Closed Mon*.

Eecke ✉ 59114

Brasserie St-Georges, 5 Rue de Caestre, **t** 03 28 40 13 71, **f** 03 28 40 27 06 (*dishes c. 65F/€9.91*). The brasserie retains the essential features of an *estaminet*, but is much bigger than the norm. There are over 60 bottled beers, with five on draught. The broad food range includes less common Flemish dishes such as ham in beer and *standevleesch* (cooked *charcuterie*, pork, melted Maroilles cheese and cumin, served with salad). *Open Fri eve, Sat, Sun, public hols and eves of public hols*.

Bavinchove ✉ 59670

In den Goedendag, 1 Kerke Plaetse, **t/f** 03 28 48 49 18 (*dishes c. 50F/€7.62*). In a little village south of Cassel, this is a classic country *estaminet*, with good *tartines*, *potjevleesch*, other hearty dishes and fine beers.

Cassel ✉ 59670

La Taverne Flamande, 34 Grand'Place, **t** 03 28 42 42 59, **f** 03 28 40 51 84 (*menus 68–99F/ €10.37–15.09*). In one of the most distinguished buildings on the main square, with a Flemish gable roof and flower-filled windows. The dining room has a fine view. Service is low-key but charming, and the set menus are great value: regulars include a deliciously warming cheese *flamiche*, and pork cooked with juniper, with great baked apple tarts to finish. As well as the inevitable local beers, there's a decent wine list.

'T Kasteelhof, 8 Rue St Nicolas (*face au moulin*), **t** 03 28 40 59 29 (*dishes c. 35–54F/ €5.34–8.23*). With a great location, next to the mill on Mont-Cassel, and a wonderful view. Dishes includes plenty of Flemish favourites such as *tartes flamandes* with *frites*, *andouillette à la flamande*, *flamiches*, omelettes, crêpes and *tartines*; or *lapin à la moutarde* (order two days ahead) and chicken *waterzooi*. *Open June–Aug and local school hols daily; Sept–May Thurs–Sun*.

Metropolitan France:

Lille

08

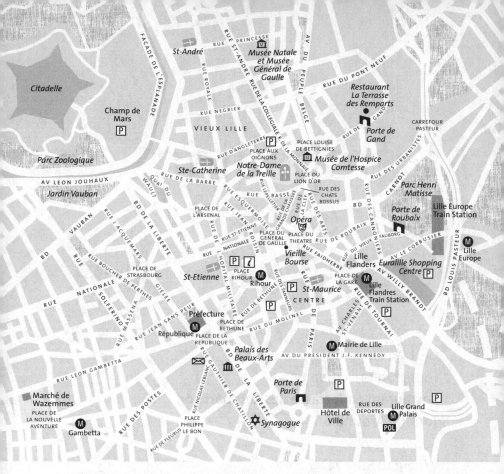

Citadelle

Champ de Mars ![P]

Parc Zoologique

AV LEON JOUHAUX

Jardin Vauban

St-André ✚

RUE PRINCESSE
RUE ST-ANDRÉ
FAÇADE DE L'ESPLANADE
RUE ROYALE

Musée Natale et Musée Général de Gaulle ![M]

AV DU PEUPLE BELGE

Restaurant La Terrasse des Remparts ![i]

RUE DU PONT NEUF

RUE DE GAND

Porte de Gand

CARREFOUR PASTEUR

RUE NEGRIER

VIEUX LILLE

RUE DE LA COLLÉGIALE & DE LA MONNAIE

PLACE AUX OIGNONS

PLACE LOUISE DE BETTIGNIES

Musée de l'Hospice Comtesse

RUE DES URBANISTES

Ste-Catherine

RUE DE LA BARRE

QUAI DU WAULT

Notre-Dame de la Treille ✚

RUE D'ANGLETERRE

PLACE DU LION D'OR

RUE DES CHATS BOSSUS

Parc Henri Matisse

RUE DES CANONNIERS

CARNOT

BD DE LA LIBERTÉ

PLACE DE L'ARSENAL

RUE ESQUERMOISE

RUE LEPELLETIER

RUE BASSE

RUE DE LA GRANDE CHAUSSÉE

RUE DE LA CLEF

RUE DES ARTS

Opéra

PLACE DU GÉNÉRAL DE GAULLE

PLACE DU THEATRE

Porte de Roubaix

BD DES

FAUBOURG

Lille Europe Train Station

AV LE CORBUSIER

VAUBAN

RUE J. JACQUEMARS

RUE JEAN ROISIN

RUE NATIONALE

RUE ST-ETIENNE

Vieille Bourse

RUE FAIDHERBE

RUE DU VIEUX

Lille Flanders

Euralille Shopping Centre ![P]

![M] Lille Europe

BD LOUIS PASTEUR

RUE BOUCHER DE PERTHES

GIELÉE

PLACE DE STRASBOURG

St-Etienne

RUE DE L'HOPITAL MILITAIRE

![P] ![i]

PLACE RIHOUR

Rihour ![M]

RUE DES TANNEURS

St-Maurice ✚

PLACE DE LA GARE

![M] Lille Flandres Train Station

AV WILLY BRANDT

NATIONALE

SOLFERINO

RUE MASSENA

RUE JEAN SANS PEUR

Préfecture

![M] République

PLACE DE BÉTHUNE

RUE DE BÉTHUNE

CENTRE

RUE DU MOLINEL

RUE DE PARIS

AV CHARLES ST-VENANT

RUE DE TOURNAI

RUE LEON GAMBETTA

PLACE DE LA RÉPUBLIQUE

✉ 🏛

Palais des Beaux-Arts

AV DU PRESIDENT J.F. KENNEDY

![M] Mairie de Lille

Marché de Wazemmes

PLACE DE LA NOUVELLE AVENTURE

![M] Gambetta

RUE DES POSTES

RUE NICOLAS LEBLANC

RUE GAUTHIER DE CHATILLON

BD DE LA LIBERTÉ

PLACE PHILIPPE LE BON

RUE DE FLEURUS

✡ Synagogue

Porte de Paris 🏛

![P]

Hôtel de Ville

RUE DES DEPORTES

![M] Lille Grand Palais

![P]

POL

The fourth-largest city in France, Lille was once its great industrial textile centre, while around it was the country's largest coalfield. In the last few decades, however, the city has been comprehensively cleaned up, to reveal an elegant, still businesslike city beneath the old factory soot. Lille is also a frontier city, the one-time capital of Flanders, and at its heart there is an old 16th–17th-century Flemish town of great charm. The Eurostar has transformed access to Lille from Britain, and a visit there provides an enjoyable immersion in French urban life. It's a very lively city, with a huge student population. At its core are the city's three central squares, where, true to its old merchant heart, Lille holds the largest antiques and flea market in Europe each year in early September, the Braderie. It has some luxurious food shops, and is a shopping mecca in other ways too. Because of Lille's long position as a textile centre, it has a concentration of high-chic fashion stores.

In food, Lille offers all the diversity of a modern city, where restaurant-going seems to be the number-one social activity. Local Flemish tradition – especially the superb beers – lives alongside a range of more eclectic French and international influences. One of the city's most imaginative and engaging modern restaurants, in one of its most attractive settings, is **La Terrasse des Remparts**, installed right on top of one of the old gates built by the Spaniards in the 1620s to defend the city.

Getting There

On Eurostar from London or Brussels or the TGV from Paris (Gare du Nord) and other parts of France, you arrive at the new Lille-Europe station, on the eastern side of the city centre. It's an easy walk from there to the heart of town: walk downhill along Rue Le Corbusier, which leads in about 130 metres to the old station, Gare Lille-Flandres on Place de la Gare, which still handles local trains. From there, along Rue Faidherbe, it's a few minutes' walk to Lille's three central squares. A right turn up Rue de la Bourse will take you eventually to Rue de Gand and the Terrasse des Remparts.

Alternatively cut across the Parc Henri Matisse, and through the Porte de Roubaix. A turn up any of the (not so scenic) streets on the right will take you towards Vieux Lille, and the Rue de Gand.

From Calais leave the A25 *autoroute* at the Lille-Centre exit which will take you via some twists on to Rue Nationale. From Paris and the south on the A1, follow the signs on to Lille

Périphérique-Sud and then Lille-Centre. There are several underground car parks in the city centre (c. *60F/€9.15 per day*).

Lille has a small airport at Lesquin, 10km south of the city, from where is a shuttle bus to the city centre and Lille-Europe station (airport information t 03 20 49 68 68).

Central Lille is easy to get around on foot, but taxis are plentiful and there is a good public transport system. There are two Métro lines, which cross each other at Gare Lille-Flandres, and many bus routes. Tickets are sold from automatic machines at Métro stations and some bus stops, and the tourist office. The best ticket to get is the *Pass' Journée* (or *Ticket une journée*), which gives unlimited travel on the Métro and buses.

Tourist Information

Lille: Palais Rihour, Place Rihour, t 03 20 21 94 21, f 03 20 21 94 20, *www.lilletourism.com*. The tourist office offers an excellent range of guided tours, many in English.

La Terrasse des Remparts

Logis de la Porte de Gand, Rue de Gand, t 03 20 06 74 74, f 03 20 06 74 70, www.lecocq.fr/remparts. Open Mon–Sat 12–2 and 8–11, Sun 12–2 and 8–10. Menus 98F/€14.94 (Mon–Sat midday only) and 153F/€23.32.

The Terrasse des Remparts has a location that any restaurant-owner would die for, in the old Salle de Garde (guardhouse) on top of the elegant Porte de Gand, which completely dominates the long Rue de Gand. Come around Christmas time, when cascades of lights tumble down the front of the gate, and the effect is dazzling.

Inside the restaurant, reached via an impressive stairway, the old military brickwork has been imaginatively combined with a conservatory-style roof, blonde-wood tables and sleek blue-plush chairs to create an exceptionally pretty and stylish modern space. Towards the rear of the gate there is also a small walled garden with a view along part of the ramparts. Fellow diners are likely to be a broad mix: casually and/or trendily dressed 20-somethings, business people, middle-aged couples. Service is buzzily efficient, but if you wish to take your time no one will hurry you along.

The chef, Phay Vanh Bouakhasith, is of Laotian descent, and while his training and the overall direction of the restaurant are clearly predominantly French he regularly mixes in a few more global ingredients – Asian spices, citrus juices – as is now quite fashionable. Several dishes on the menu are identified as *cuisine légère*, or light dishes, which are equally in demand from urban customers.

The Terrasse's menus present an imaginative, fresh and skilful combination which allies northern French traditions with a range of other influences. There are always traditional local dishes, such as a gratin of Maroilles cheese with chopped pears, a terrine of leeks and eels with a Houlle gin vinaigrette, or sea bass cooked with Ch'ti beer and served with a fennel compote, and others from a pan-French range, such as *brochettes* of *coquille St-Jacques* with basil. One dish in particular to look out for is *cuisse de poulet de Licques grillé au citron vert*, which for added exoticism comes with a tequila jus.

You can choose from the whole menu for a set price, with supplements for more elaborate dishes. The straightforward wine list is just one page and easy to handle. There is not usually a cheese course unless you ask for it, and desserts come rather curiously from a lavish self-service pâtisserie buffet.

Touring Around

The heart of Lille is its three main squares, and above all the **Grand'Place**, whose official title is Place Général de Gaulle, in memory of the city's most famous son. On the north side, towards Vieux Lille, it's lined by an up-and-down row of old houses, all with different roof lines, while to the south the eye is grabbed by the giant façade of the Voix du Nord newspaper building, built in the 1920s in a curious Flemish revival-art deco style with a huge stepped gable in grey concrete. Next to it, Lille's main theatre, the Théâtre du Nord, is housed in the surprisingly elegant building that was designed as the Grand'Garde, the central guardhouse for the city's army garrison. In the middle of the square there is a patriotic monument, the column of the Déesse, commemorating the resistance of Lille during its siege by the Austrians in 1792.

The most striking building on the square, and Lille's greatest treasure, is the **Vieille Bourse** or 'Old Exchange' (1652–3) along the eastern side. Rising up through three floors to a grey slate roof, it's a classic of Flemish burgher baroque, a fascinating combination of solidity and tangled, intricate carvings in the shape of caryatids and other mythical creatures. It has been beautifully restored so that the red, ochre and black of its façades gleam out. The Bourse was built at the highest point of Lille's wealth and importance as a major city of the then-Spanish Netherlands. Crests sit above each of its four entrances: on the north side is a blue-and-yellow shield of the city's merchants; facing the Grand'Place is the white fleur-de-lys on red of the City of Lille itself; on the south side there is the black lion on gold of the Counts of Flanders; and above the Place du Théâtre entrance is the multi-quartered coat of arms of the Habsburg monarchs of Spain. The Bourse's ground floor consisted of 24 small shops that were occupied by the city's principal merchants, around a galleried central court-yard which now contains stalls selling flowers and second-hand books (*daily exc Mon*).

The Grand'Place is full of movement at all times of day, but it comes particularly alive at certain times of the year. At the end of April it hosts a dazzling flower market, June sees the Fêtes de Lille, and in the first weekend of September each year the Grand'Place and Place Rihour are the centre of the **Braderie**, Lille's extraordinary flea market. The origins of this event are a medieval law that allowed servants to sell their masters' old clothes and other oddments on the street once a year: since then everyone in the city has had the right to set up a stall on these two days every September. There are hundreds of them, and people selling Pokemon cards or piles of old junk rub shoulders with serious antique dealers who descend on Lille from across Europe, together with an estimated one million visitors. All sorts of other events are organised to go with it, and this is also a traditional time to eat *moules* and *frites*. The square is also especially lovely around Christmas time, when a **Christmas fair** takes over Place Rihour, and the Grand'Place, lined with lights, has as its centrepiece the Grande Roue, a giant ferris wheel.

From the corner of the square by the Grand'Garde little café-lined Rue Rihour leads through to Place Rihour. Stripped of markets and Christmas fairs the square is actually pretty much of a mess. The tourist office on the north side occupies the irregular remaining parts of the Palais Rihour, the sole architectural reminder of Lille's medieval period. It's a much-battered building: in the 17th century it was made into Lille's town hall, but was damaged by a fire in 1700; major alterations were carried out in the 19th century, but it was then caught by another fire in 1916 while Lille was under German occupation. It's hard to get a good idea of its overall structure from what's left, but some of its Flamboyant Gothic features can be seen: the tourist office is in a former chapel. Overshadowing the Palais is the huge, sombre mass of Lille's war memorial, erected in the 1920s.

The third of the main squares, **Place du Théâtre**, is a more orderly space. Facing the Bourse are two giant buildings from among Lille's singularly quirky collection of early 20th-century architecture, both by the same architect, Louis-Marie Cordonnier. The huge **Opéra** was designed to replace a much smaller 18th-century theatre that had given the square its name, and which had burnt down in 1903. He and his patrons chose to use an extravagant neo-Louis XVI baroque style, but its completion was interrupted by the First World War, so that by the time it opened in 1923 it appeared still more out of its time. Earlier in the 1900s Cordonnier had also built the Chambre de Commerce further along the square, only this time in Flemish-revival style with massive towering belfry.

The Grand'Place is one of the oldest parts of Lille, and was used as a market from the earliest days of the city, but it was outside the early walled town, which was centred to the north, around a castle where Notre-Dame de la Treille is today, on a semi-island surrounded by different streams of the River Deule (Lille and its Flemish name, 'T Rijsel, both derive from words for island). Since then the Deule has been confined in canals that run around the north of the city.

Vieux Lille, the area around the oldest core of the city northeast of the three squares, has been the greatest beneficiary of Lille's clean-up. It's a great area for wandering in no particular direction, with charming narrow streets and old Flemish houses, most of them now beautifully restored, often with elaborate carved details picked out in reds, yellows, blues, greens and more. This is also Lille's most chic shopping area. There are many routes into the old town, but the most historic is to turn right at the north end of the Grand'Place along Rue de la Bourse to enter Rue de la

Grande Chaussée, which began life as the main path between the walled town and the Grand'Place market. It ends when it meets Rue des Chats Bossus, where in front of you is L'Huitrière, France's most magnificently ornate fishmongers' (and restaurant, *see* pp.72 and 73–4). Another great street to wander up is Rue Esquermoise, north from the Grand'Place, which contains the Pâtisserie Meert, as fabulous a temple to cakes and chocolate as the Huitrière is to fish. Rue Basse and Rue Lepelletier are two of the most attractive streets in the old town, with fashion by young designers, antiques shops, gift shops and some great bars and restaurants.

From Rue Basse, a turn north up Rue Cirque will take you to the semi-circular space that surrounds Lille's curiously unknown cathedral, **Notre-Dame de la Treille**, the first sight of which may come as a shock, for it's quite easy to think that part of the west front, facing you, is covered in plastic sheeting. A strange tale is attached to this building. Lille had never had a cathedral, and in the 19th century a competition was launched to find a suitable design. The winner was a scheme submitted by two English architects, and when it became public that foreign architects had won the prize, the whole process descended into chaos. Work on the cathedral went on for decades, before stumbling to a complete halt in 1947. For years, the west front was simply bricked up. La Treille was finally given its west façade in 1999, to a design by architect PL Carlier so radical and so at variance with Victorian Gothic that the cathedral can still appear vaguely 'unfinished'. The 'plastic' façade is actually translucent glass, around a rose window by the artist Kijno and, however odd it looks from the outside, the effect from inside the cathedral is stunning.

Rue des Chats Bossus ends at the very pretty Place du Lion d'Or, where to the right is **Rue de la Monnaie**, one of Vieux Lille's most elegant streets of. It has some of the most charming Flemish ornamented gables, and several small designer shops, but Rue de la Monnaie – so named because it once housed Louis XIV's mint – stands out most as Lille's street of fabrics and interior design. Just above Place du Lion d'Or, the **Musée de l'Hospice Comtesse** (*open Mon 2–6, Wed, Thurs, Sat and Sun 10–6, Fri 10–7; closed Tues; adm*) occupies a hospital founded in 1237 as a refuge for the poor and sick, although most of the present building dates from the 15th and 17th centuries. One of its great attractions is its beautifully calm old Flemish interior: the refectory, parlour and dormitories now house the museum exhibits, while the enormous Gothic main hall, where the sick were actually treated, is used for a variety of public events. The museum's collection is an illuminating display of the arts and crafts of Lille and the Low Countries from the 15th to the 17th centuries – paintings, faïence pottery, wood carvings, tapestries, and a rare collection of early musical instruments among them.

The Place du Lion d'Or runs indistinguishably into Place Louise de Bettignies. In the early 17th century the flat strip of land alongside it that is now called Place du Peuple Belge was still an open canal, where goods were loaded and unloaded, making it one of the most important parts of the merchant city. The most striking of the square's 17th-century buildings is the Maison de Gilles de la Boë, built for a wealthy merchant in 1636, and now suitably occupied by a fashion shop. Designed by Julien Destrez, it looks almost like a miniature dry run for the same architect's Vieille Bourse of 15 years later. Away on the eastern side of Place du Peuple Belge is the Rue de Gand, with the

Porte de Gand impossible to miss at its far end. This is the finest of the city's Spanish gates, solid and beautifully proportioned. Rue de Gand is one of the liveliest streets of Vieux Lille, the district's restaurant row.

Beyond Place du Peuple Belge Rue du Pont Neuf (or up Rue Royale from Rue Esquermoise), you enter an area which takes on a different feel because its streets are long and straight. It corresponds to Louis XIV's 'extension' of Vieux Lille, laid out after the takeover of 1667. The lower end of Rue Royale now forms one of Lille's more stylish and popular night-time bar areas, with several buzzing venues. Nearby on Rue d'Angleterre (so named because Thomas à Becket is said to have stayed there once) is L'Angle Saxo, Lille's foremost live jazz club. In complete contrast, tucked away just west of Rue Royale is Lille's oldest church, Ste-Catherine, a rectangular Flemish *hallekerk* begun in 1288, with an impressively monolithic tower added in the 16th century. A walk several blocks up Rue Royale and right along Rue Princesse meanwhile will take you to the **Maison Natale du Général De Gaulle**, a shrine to the great man who was born here in 1890 (*open Wed–Sun 10–12 and 2–5; closed Mon, Tues and hols; adm*).

The areas of Lille south of the three main squares are mostly made up of post-1667 French extensions to the city, although the Rue de Béthune, now one of Lille's busiest, un-chic shopping streets, was laid out under Spanish rule. From Place du Theâtre Rue Faidherbe runs down to the dainty old railway station, Lille-Flandres, which is surrounded by cheap hotels and brasseries. The building was actually the first Gare du Nord of Paris, and when it proved too small in 1862 it was dismantled and handed over for rebuilding in Lille. To the east is what could be called 'Mitterrand's Lille'. Looming up over the old station is the awesome mass of the 1994 Euralille shopping mall, while beyond are the modernistic roofs of the new Lille-Europe station.

Running due south from the other corner of Place du Theâtre, **Rue de Paris** existed before 1667 but was largely rebuilt in the following years to form the central spine of the additions made by the French in the south of Lille. It still contains, though, some older, heavy-timbered houses, and towards the north end is the 15th-century church of St-Maurice, the finest surviving Gothic building in the city. Rue de Paris continues down to the **Porte de Paris**, a suitably Parisian baroque triumphal arch erected in the 1680s to celebrate the French conquest of Lille. The Sun King's monument is now overshadowed by the immensity of the quite extraordinary **Hôtel de Ville**. Despite initial appearances it was only commissioned after the First World War and built from 1924 to 1928, to replace the by-then unusable Palais Rihour. Its style could maybe be described as Flemish revival-art deco-modernist-Gothic, and topping it off there's the tallest of all Flanders' many belfries, 107 metres high, which has become one of the city's inescapable landmarks.

To the west of this area and the old town is 19th-century Lille, made up of typically broad, straight boulevards, the most important of them Boulevard de la Liberté. Its centrepiece is the large Place de la République, flanked on two sides by two very large, equally typically French public buildings in the ornately bloated Beaux-Arts style favoured by official France from the Second Empire to the 1900s, the Préfecture to the north and the **Palais des Beaux-Arts** to the south (*open Mon 2–6, Wed, Thurs, Sat and Sun 10–6, Fri 10–7; closed Tues; adm*). Often described as the second-most important museum in France after the Louvre, Lille's Beaux-Arts has recently been given a very comprehensive and expensive renovation, completed in 1997, to the extent that its stylish new spaces and lighting effects can outshine some of the collections. It has several real masterpieces, but as with many French regional museums it's also very patchy. As is often the case, too, many of its most impressive works have some local connection. Flanders' 17th-century Golden Age is heavily represented, with major works especially by Rubens – above all his 1616 *Descent from the Cross*, originally painted for the Church of the Capuchins here in Lille – and Van Dyck. Standing out among an otherwise rather routine display of French 18th-century painting is one of the museum's great treasures, David's 1781 *Belisarius requesting charity*,which is credited with initiating the vogue for neoclassical history painting in France.

The collection of French Romantic and 19th-century painting is a very individual mixture. Highlights among the works by local artists are those of Lille-born Louis-Léopold Boilly (1761–1845). More celebrated are Courbet's superb 1849 *Après Dîaner à Ornans*, one of the groundbreaking works of realism, and Delacroix's lush *Medea*. The Impressionists are decently represented by Manet, several Monets, Sisley landscapes and a little-known Toulouse-Lautrec, *Dans l'Atelier, la pose de la modèle*. The works of the Symbolists are highly engaging, including a very passionate 1868 *Le Baiser* ('The Kiss') by Lille-born Carolus-Duran, and sexually charged Romantic-Symbolist paintings by Alfred Agache, also from Lille.

The non-French pictures are another varied bag, including an El Greco, a Veronese, a Raphael cartoon, and a wonderful *Portrait of a Venetian Senator* by Tintoretto. Among them, however, are by far the finest pictures in the whole museum, its two Goyas, *Time (The Old Women)* and *The Letter (The Young Women)*, both ferocious images, full of the disturbing qualities characteristic of the artist's later work. Beyond them a few contemporary works by Sonia Delaunay, Léger, Braque, Picasso and other major 20th-century names come as a surprise in a museum dominated by historic art.

The museum's huge ceramics collection includes the renowned ceramics styles of the Netherlands (north and south) and northern France from the 17th and 18th centuries – Delftware, the Lille and Arras blue and white faience. The museum also contains one of France's largest stores of 19th-century monumental sculpture, but this rarely appeals to modern tastes except as kitsch.

In the basement there are artefacts from ancient Greece and Egypt, some local Roman finds, and a magnificent collection of medieval and early Renaissance art and craftwork. There is also an extraordinary collection of 17th–18th-century relief models of the fortified cities of northern France and the Netherlands. These plans – with streets, churches, individual houses, streams, etc. faithfully reproduced – represent a remarkable historical picture of these towns before the arrival of modern industry, and in some cases, as with Ypres or Calais, provide the only comprehensive image of what the old towns looked like before the devastation of the 20th-century wars.

If as you leave the museum you turn left down Rue Gauthier de Châtillon, cross the street and go up Rue Nicolas Leblanc you will come to the circular Place Philippe Le Bon, across which and a little way along Rue Fleurus is another of Lille's architectural oddities, the **Maison Colliot**, the city's only complete art nouveau building. It was designed in 1898 by Hector Guimard, author of the famous Paris Métro entrances, and is one of the most unusual of all his unusual buildings, curving and asymmetrical at every point, with a strange recessed façade filled by upper-storey balconies at an abrupt angle to the main construction, and great details in tile, glass and metal. Sadly the building is looking rather neglected, and in need of repair.

Place Philippe Le Bon is traversed by Rue Solférino, a walk up which and then left along Rue Léon Gambetta, will take you to the Wazemmes district and the Place de la Nouvelle Aventure, home of Lille's celebrated flea market, held on Tuesday, Thursday and Sunday mornings and best-known as the **Marché de Wazemmes** (from the city centre, take the Métro, to Gambetta station). Alternatively, if you continue up Rue Solférino towards the junction with Rue Nationale you will enter the Quartier Solférino, which is above all the 'student quarter' of Lille, and the favourite area for cheap socialising. Streets like Rue Massena contain a string of pubs and club-type bars, while along Solférino itself there are any number of Algerian couscous houses, bargain bistros, Chinese restaurants and other ethnic and budget eating-places.

A walk to the top of Rue Solférino or Rue Liberté will take you to the largest open space within the city, the parks and gardens around the vast Citadelle. A giant five-pointed brick star on the ground, 2,200m round, it was begun immediately after the French took the city in 1667. It was the largest of all the many fortresses built by the great Marshal Vauban, who declared it his 'Queen of Citadels'. The Citadelle itself is still a French army establishment and can only be visited with guided tours booked through the tourist office (*April–June, and Sept-Oct Sun pm only*). Around it, though, there is a peaceful park and Lille's zoo.

Outside central Lille the other towns of the Lille-Métropole conurbation do not have too much to see, although Roubaix is shortly due to have a much-advertised new textile museum, the Musée d'Art et d'Industrie. For most visitors the main attraction in the Métropole is the **Musée d'Art Moderne de Lille Métropole** (*open Mon, Wed–Sun 10–6; closed Tues; adm*) in Villeneuve d'Ascq just east of Lille, the region's official contemporary art showcase. From Place Rihour take the yellow Métro line, direction 4 Cantons, to Pont du Bois, and from outside the station take the 41 bus four stops to Parc Urbain-Musée. The stops are clearly signposted, although the museum itself is not indicated at its bus stop; take the sloping footpath behind the stop to reach it.

Opened in 1983 in this otherwise unlovely suburb, in an effort to take culture to the masses, the museum stands in an attractive park which also functions as a sculpture garden, with impressive large pieces by Calder, Lipschitz and others. The low-standing brick museum is a tad dated from the outside, but makes a fine, intricate exhibition space within. Like the Beaux-Arts, the museum has its high points. It's extremely strong in Cubism, with fine works by Braque, Picasso and especially Léger; Modigliani is another artist well represented, and there are works by Miró, Joaquim Torres-García, Rouault and Van Dongen. The more contemporary work includes some lively installation work. The star exhibit is a wonderful installation called Exploded Cabins V2 42 by Daniel Buren, a room containing three wooden box structures, one inside the other, which you can walk inside, with walls of multi-coloured plexiglass that produce fascinating, shifting colour effects.

Shopping

Vieux Lille is both the most attractive area for window shopping, and has a wonderful concentration of individual shops. Rue de la Grande Chaussée, Rue des Chats Bossus and Rue Lepelletier are the most important fashion streets, while the best places to look for contemporary design items are Rue de la Monnaie and the little streets near Notre-Dame de la Treille.

For cheaper, more everyday shopping the best areas are the streets south of the Grand'Place, and Rue Gambetta near Rue Solférino. And for complete convenience there's Euralille, but note that even this mega-mall doesn't open on Sundays.

Lille ✉ 59800

Les Bons Pâturages, 54 Rue Basse, t 03 20 55 60 28. In the heart of Vieux Lille, a master cheese merchant with an excellent range of local cheeses – Maroilles, Mimolette, Vieux-Lille – all skilfully *affinés* on the premises, as well as an inventive range of tarts, quiches and cheese terrines.

Boulangerie Leroy, 118 Rue Esquermoise, t 03 20 55 35 55. A wonderful array of fine fresh breads and *pâtisseries*, from old favourites like baguettes, *pains de campagne* and croissants to half-forgotten traditional breads like *carré de Lille*. Plus, there's an excellent range of local beers and gins.

Le Cèdre Rouge, Parvis de la Treille, t 03 20 51 96 96. On the square next to the cathedral, this attractive shop has a wide range of modern design and household items from elegant, beautifully made wooden furniture and striking lamps to fine glass, ceramics and smaller accessories.

A l'Huitrière, 3 Rue des Chats Bossus, t 03 20 55 43 41, f 03 20 55 23 10. Considered both the premier restaurant in Lille and the most spectacular fish shop in France, this is an essential sight of the city even if you aren't buying. The 1928 art deco tiling is extraordinary: on the façade are scenes of undersea life, grapes as symbols of abundance, and huge lobsters surrounded by curly mosaics of steam, while the interior, behind stained-glass windows, features Breton fishing scenes. Below them are some of the world's finest oysters, lobsters, prawns, sea bass and more. There are also non-seafood delicacies such as Licques chickens and other poultry, pâtés and terrines, the house foie gras, exquisite desserts and Périgord truffles.

Jean Maniglier, 89–95 Rue de la Monnaie, t 03 20 13 05 05. A home accessory shop which stands out for the sheer class and variety of its stock. A grand emporium of luxury: Toulemonde Brochart contemporary carpets, tableware, lighting and superb fabrics. There is also a collection of oriental carpets, and some smaller gift items.

Pâtisserie Meert, 27 Rue Esquermoise, t 03 20 57 07 44, f 03 20 54 93 19. An astonishing temple to chocolate-and-cream indulgence, a piece of old-world luxury right down to the uniformed young lad to open the door for you and décor that wouldn't shame an opera house: elaborate ceiling mouldings, intricate metal balconies, wonderful mirrors and carved and gilded cabinets. The all house-made chocolates, cakes, pastries and ice-creams on display are no less magical than the décor, and purchases are beautifully wrapped and presented. There's also a *salon de thé*. Catch Meert's window displays before Christmas, when they are still more tastefully magnificent than ever.

Paul, 8–12 Rue de Paris, t 03 20 74 50 67. Impossible to miss on the corner of Rue de Paris, opposite the Vieille Bourse, Paul is another prestige establishment that covers the whole *boulangerie-pâtisserie-chocolaterie* field: superb breads, delicious *gâteaux*, pastries and endless combinations of chocolate. The pastry, especially, is marvellous.

Le Savour Club, 46 Rue Négrier, t 03 20 74 33 44, f 03 20 55 62 02, *www.le-savour-club.fr*. Lille's foremost wine repository, a branch of the Paris-based organisation that French oenophiles swear by. You won't find the bargain offers of Calais wine dealers here, but you can discover very fine wines at still reasonable prices. All the labels on their lists are selected by experts, and the resident staff are knowledgeable and helpful; there's a superior selection of whiskies and liqueurs, and a respectable interest is even shown in non-French wines. Members of the 'club' receive a newsletter, discounts, regular special selections and other perks.

Where to Stay

Lille ✉ 59800

Hôtel Carlton, 3 Rue de Paris, **t** 03 20 13 33 13, **f** 03 20 51 48 17, *www.carltonlille.fr* (*double rooms 1,080F/€164.63, breakfast 85F/€12.96*). The luxury choice in Lille, an old-style grand hotel that has been dominating one side of Place du Théâtre since the end of the 19th century. Its 60 rather flowery rooms come with a comprehensive range of modern comforts and perfect soundproofing, and service is very smooth. The hotel also has a fine restaurant, and a cocktail bar.

Hôtel de la Treille, 7–9 Place Louise de Bettignies, **t** 03 20 55 45 46, **f** 03 20 51 51 69 (*double rooms 460–500F/€70.12–76.22 during the week, 420–500F/€64.02–76.22 at weekends*). A 40-room hotel in a great location, in a 17th-century house on one of Vieux Lille's main squares, ideally placed for shopping and the restaurants of Rue de Gand: some rooms look out on to Place Louise de Bettignies, while others have views of Notre-Dame de la Treille. The modernised rooms do not have the same character, but are bright and functionally comfortable.

Hôtel de la Paix, 46 bis Rue de Paris, 59800 Lille, **t** 03 20 54 63 93, **f** 03 20 63 98 97 (*double rooms 400–450F/€60.98–68.6*). A short walk from Place du Théâtre, with a discreet exterior. Fully renovated in the last few years, with an eye to style and character as well as comfort. Each of the 36 rooms has been individually decorated with prints by a different artist, personally selected by the owner. Staff are professional and helpful.

Hôtel Brueghel, 5 Parvis St-Maurice, **t** 03 20 06 06 69, **f** 03 20 63 25 27 (*double rooms 370–445F/€56.4–67.83*). A characterful mid-range hotel which fills a seven-storey 1900s brick apartment block alongside the church of St-Maurice, with wonderful views of the church's Gothic façade from several rooms; in the lobby, pot plants, an engaging collection of bric-à-brac and an antique lift set the cosily original tone. Some of the 70 rooms are all-white with modern sea grass flooring, others in colours and carpets. The bathrooms could be better laid out, and it seems oddly difficult to get enough towels, but staff are charming and helpful.

M and Mme Goblot, 51 Rue Négrier, **t** 03 20 51 39 09 (*rooms 255F/€38.87 for two*). A charming two-room B&B in an 18th-century house in one of the 'French' streets just north of Vieux Lille. The rooms are packed with an unclassifiable mix of antiques, books and other accumulated objects, and the old house is quite creaky, but the elderly Rémi and Any Goblot are kindness itself – to the point of having a video library for rainy days, with films carefully catalogued into different languages.

Janine Hulin, 28 Rue des Hannetons, **t/f** 03 20 53 46 12 (*rooms c. 260F/€39.63 for two*). Mme Hulin could be a candidate for the perfect B&B host: warm, chatty, interested and endlessly helpful (she speaks some English). Her house, full of flowers and plants, is in a quiet area outside the city centre, reachable in about 10–15 minutes by Métro and bus (depending on the traffic), but she goes to great lengths to explain the route, and will drive to the Métro station to pick up lost guests. There are two comfortable rooms, and breakfast is served in her bright kitchen, looking out on to a pretty garden, which you can also make use of in summer.

Central Hôtel, 91 Rue Boucher de Perthes, **t** 03 20 54 64 63, **f** 03 20 30 03 91 (*rooms 185–260F/€28.2–39.63 for two*). A characterful old building in the middle of the bar- and restaurant-filled student quarter around Rue Solférino. There's nothing special about the décor, but the rooms have been recently renovated and most now have their own showers. Breakfast is served in a cosy little room on the ground floor, where **meals** are served in the evenings (*90F/€13.72*).

Eating Alternatives

Lille ✉ 59800

A l'Huitrière, *see above* (*gourmet menu 580F/€88.41*). One of France's grand culinary monuments, a place of pilgrimage for wealthy seafood lovers for nearly a century. It's a little odd to see well-dressed diners walking through a fish sho to eatp, but this is what you do here, as the plush dining room is at the back of the magnificent *poissonerie*. L'Huitrière is not a place to come to looking for experimental cooking, but to find supreme-quality fish and seafood in perfect versions of the most traditional, frankly conservative styles – oysters, *coquilles St-Jacques à la fleur de thym, lotte aux morilles*, fabulous seafood salads. There are also meat dishes and the maison's famed foie gras, but not to have seafood here seems somehow to miss the point. Service, wines and so on are of a quality to match the price. *Closed Sun evenings.*

La Cave aux Fioles, 39 Rue de Gand, t 03 20 55 18 43, f 03 20 74 99 54 (*menus 60F/€9.15, 120F/€18.3 and 190F/€28.96*). A great Vieux Lille restaurant that ably combines the historic charm of its 18th-century building with a Gallic sense of bohemian cool, helped along by a (sometimes live) jazz soundtrack. The fare combines dishes with a local touch – Licques turkey with fennel, cod fillet cooked in Kriek beer – with others that experiment with sweet and sour flavours. The owners are laidback but professional and welcoming, and will advise on the current star dishes and (also excellent) wine selection. *Closed Sat midday, and Sun.*

Le Pourquoi Pas, 62 Rue de Gand, t 03 20 06 25 86 (*lunch menu 70F/€10.67; menus 110–180F/€16.77–27.44*). A popular, intimate restaurant with very much the look of a romantic rendezvous (subtle red walls, candlelight, mellow music). Service is unfussily charming. Modish sweet-and-sour combinations are a house touch, as in a *nage* of shellfish with limes, and there are vegetarian choices (*brique de chèvre chaud* with juniper) and salads as well as more conventional French fare such as *gigot* of lamb with garlic. *Closed Sat and Sun midday.*

L'Ecume des Mers, 10 Rue des Pas, t 03 20 54 95 40, f 03 20 54 96 66 (*lunch menu 98F/ €14.94, menu 130F/€19.82*). In one of the streets north of the main squares near Rue Esquermoise, this is an offshoot of the legendary Huitrière (*see* above), which allows you to sample similar fine seafood but more simply presented, in a more relaxed atmosphere and at a more mid-range price. The interior is bright and pretty, suitably nautical-looking in blue and white. The cooking is conservative, but extremely well done: typical dishes include fine

oysters, fillets of John Dory in a ginger vinaigrette, a delicate salt cod with aioli and a superb *plateau des crustacés* (*300F/€45.73*). *Closed Sun evenings.*

Brasserie de la Paix, 25 Place Rihour, t 03 20 54 70 41, f 03 20 40 02 27 (*menu 94F/€14.33*). The most distinguished of the brasseries around Place Rihour, with a magnificent 1930s interior of mahogany, mirrors and tiles. The food is equally classic: *moules marinière*, soups, fish and meat grills, with especially good seafood. (Other brasseries on the square have lower prices, and longer opening hours.) *Closed Sun.*

Les Compagnons de la Grappe, 26 Rue Lepelletier, t 03 20 21 02 79 (*lunch menus 55F/€8.38 and 70F/€10.67; à la carte under 100F/€15.24*). A very pretty, convivial bar-restaurant reached down a passageway off Rue Lepelletier, open late, and with a small courtyard with terrace tables. The food consists mainly of healthy local favourites, presented in a light modern way: *tarte au Maroilles*, salmon salads and classic *carbonnade*. Another asset is the carefully selected wine list, featuring many fine wines from small, little-known producers from all over France. *Open Mon–Sat till 2am ; closed Sun.*

Estaminet 'T Rijsel, 25 Rue de Gand, t 03 20 15 88 75, f 03 28 36 82 76 (*lunch menu 66F/ €10.06*). An embassy for the traditional Flemish village *estaminet* ('T Rijsel is Flemish for Lille), with plain wooden tables and bar, farmhouse furniture, and old bric-à-brac and heraldic crests on the walls. It has an excellent selection of local and Belgian beers, and the food consists of light versions of local classics, as in the tasty *poulet au maroilles*, and a range of traditional snacks. It's cramped and very popular, so get there early to grab a table. It's more a restaurant than a bar, so it doesn't open in the afternoons. *Closed Sun, Mon, and Aug.*

La Ducasse, 95 Rue Solférino, t 03 20 57 34 10 (*dishes from 35F/€5.34*). A cosy Flemish *estaminet*-style bar-restaurant, with the requisite plain wood tables and antique fittings. On the menu are enjoyable versions of local classics such as *flamiches* as well as salads and more elaborate possibilities such as *cassolette de mer* (seafood stew), and a few good vegetarian main courses.

The Pleasures of the Grand'Place:

Arras

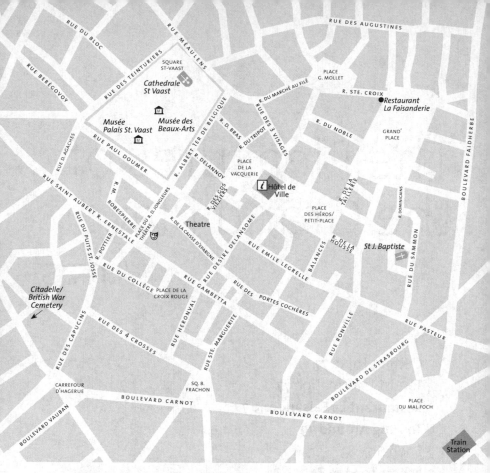

France's northern region has a jewel of a city, Arras. Its three great squares are an interlocking, harmonious ensemble of medieval and 16th-century buildings. Built to hold markets, they are a remarkable reminder of the years when the merchant cities of northern France and Flanders were the great trading centres of northern Europe. The capital of Artois, and always French-speaking, Arras nevertheless long looked to Flanders for its political allegiance, and many parts of the old city have a distinctly Flemish appearance, while others nearby have a more classical French elegance.

Restored with astonishing success after the First World War, the centre of Arras is full of unusual features. Beneath the squares there is a labyrinth of cellars and tunnels, used over the years as chalk mines, wine stores, refuse dumps or refuges. Above, Arras still hosts a giant, sprawling market of a kind that you might no longer expect to find in a modern city, and has many individual and opulent shops. And in the squares themselves, soberly beautiful on a winter's day or more animated when the market is in session, there is a relaxed, appealing atmosphere in the cafés and restaurants beneath the arcades. Arras also has another very special hedonistic attraction in **La Faisanderie**, situated in a house right on the Grand'Place. Jean-Pierre Dargent is one of the premier chefs of northern France. Greatly admired by other chefs, he has been working here for more than a decade, and remains constantly creative.

Getting There

Arras is about one hour's drive from Calais by *autoroute*, or 1½hrs by slower roads. Whichever direction you approach from, you will inevitably arrive on the ring of boulevards around the city centre. From the A26 *autoroute*, shortly after joining the boulevards (here Av P. Michonneau), you will come to a broad junction with a sign to the right indicating Grand'Place (from Calais and Boulogne on the N39, turn left at the boulevards and follow them round clockwise until you reach the same junction). This turning will take you very abruptly into the great expanse of the square, where La Faisanderie is almost directly in front of you in the opposite corner. You can either park in the square itself or in the car park beneath it.

Arras has good train connections to Calais, Amiens and several other cities and is on the Paris-Lille TGV line. The station is just outside the ring of boulevards on Place Foch, within easy walking distance of the central squares.

Tourist Information

Arras: Hôtel de Ville, Place des Héros, t 03 21 51 26 95, f 03 21 71 07 34, *www.ot-arras.fr* (open May–Sept Mon–Sat 9–6.30, Sun 10–1 and 2.30–6.30; Oct–April Mon–Sat 9–12 and 2–6, Sun 10–12.30 and 3–6.30; closed 25 Dec and 1 Jan). The tourist office is also the starting point for a range of tours around the city.

La Faisanderie

45 Grand'Place, t 03 21 48 20 76, f 03 21 50 89 18. Open Tues–Sat 12–2 and 7–9.30, Sun 12–2. Closed two weeks Feb and three weeks Aug. Book always. Menus 215F/€32.78 and 325F/€49.55; children's menu; à la carte average 450F/€68.60.

The entrance to La Faisanderie is via a hallway with classic, pastel-shaded French bourgeois décor. To eat, you must descend a wide spiral staircase into an elegantly restored, airy, barrel-roofed cellar, one of the many *caves* beneath the Grand'Place, with bare brick walls that give it a light, modern feel, and colour provided by paintings (for sale), and an abundance of flowers. The cellar used to be a stable, but you would never know it. The staff are smoothly professional and warmly welcoming.

Like his friend Roland Gauthier in Montreuil, Jean-Pierre Dargent is originally from another part of France entirely – the Hautes-Pyrénées – but nonetheless uses predominantly northern ingredients, and produces spectacular versions of traditional northern French dishes. The menu changes frequently with the seasons. In the vast wine list, as well as French bottles there are a few international wines, plus traditional beers from small local breweries.

The culinary innovations can be seen right away in the appetisers. Jean-Pierre likes to experiment, and they change every day: perhaps a cauliflower mousse with smoked haddock. While you're savouring this minor marvel the bread trolley arrives, offering a choice of seven superb freshly baked breads all made on the premises (it will come round again, so you can try a selection).

For first courses, there might be a lobster risotto with stuffed tomatoes, or hare terrine with forest mushrooms. Late autumn and early winter are especially good times to eat here, because Jean-Pierre Dargent does extraordinary things with mushrooms of all kinds. His *crème mousseuse de girolles et profiterolles de foie gras* is a true

Tartelette de Crevettes à l'Œuf Poché, Crème de Maroilles
(Prawn Tartlets with Poached Eggs and Maroilles Cheese Sauce)

Serves 4

225g/8oz shortcrust or puff pastry

1 large leek, trimmed and washed

100g/3½oz small cooked, peeled shrimps or prawns

4 eggs

100ml/3½fl oz beer

50g/1¾oz butter, plus more for cooking

150g/5½oz Maroilles cheese without rind, diced

5ml/1 tsp Dijon mustard

cayenne pepper

Preheat the oven to 190°C/375°F/Gas 5. Roll out the pastry on a lightly floured surface to a thickness of about 3mm/1/8in and use to line 4 tartlet tins, 10cm/4in diameter. Prick the bases, line the pastry cases with foil and fill with baking beans or weights. Place on a baking sheet and bake 15mins until the edges are golden. Remove the foil and beans and continue baking for 5–7mins, until the pastry is deep golden brown. Cool on a wire rack.

Meanwhile, slice the leek thinly and steam until tender. Refresh in cold water and drain. Put the beer in a saucepan with the 50g/1¾oz butter, the cheese and the mustard and set over a gentle heat. Cook, stirring constantly, until melted and well amalgamated. Season with cayenne pepper.

Bring a saucepan of salted water to a simmer and add a small splash of vinegar. Stir the water into a whirlpool and add the eggs, one at a time. Poach the eggs for a few minutes until the white is set and the yolk still runny. Remove with a slotted spoon. Refresh in cold water, drain and trim off the trailing edges of white.

To serve, preheat a hot grill. Melt a small knob of butter in a frying pan or saucepan, add the leek and prawns, heat through and divide the mixture between the tartlet cases. Place an egg on each and cover with the cheese sauce. Place under the grill to brown the tops and serve the tartlets at once on warm plates.

demonstration of what gourmet cooking is all about, a fabulous combination of tastes and textures. At its heart, preparing the way for the other elements, is perhaps the best mushroom soup ever made. Among main courses, there might be fillet of *sandre* (pike-perch) in a red wine butter with beef *persillade* and herby potato gnocchi. Meat dishes are just as delicious: roast partridge comes with a hearty mix of pears, figs, almonds and *girolle* mushrooms, which complement each other perfectly.

This is clever food, and it's hugely enjoyable. The cheese selection is also fabulous, but if you were tempted to come in just for one course, it might be dessert. A dark chocolate mousse with coffee parfait is decadent, with a slight tang of bitter oranges in the mousse; it is matched by the lemon ice cream *à la crème de thé*, which is pure nectar, and quite addictive. And then, finally, among the *petit-fours* that come with your coffee there arrives a little blackcurrant tart as a final touch to a superb meal.

Touring Around

When you first enter the **Grand'Place**, you will be immediately knocked back by its size. It is lined by Flemish-style houses that are all four storeys high, with curving gables. Their first floors jut out over the pavement, supported by slender stone columns, creating arcades that once sheltered market traders and their wares from the rain. From the corner of the square furthest from the main traffic entrance a little street, Rue de la Taillerie, connects through into the more intimate **Place des Héros**, better known as the **Petit-Place**, which is dominated by the soaring Gothic Hôtel de Ville. Behind the town hall is the third square, the plainer **Place de la Vacquerie**.

A market was first recorded on the site of the Grand'Place in the year 828. The size of the square is an indication of just how important Arras was during its Golden Age, in the 14th and 15th centuries. Merchants from all over the continent came to buy and sell here, and Arras tapestries – such as the 'arras' behind which Polonius is hiding when he is stabbed in *Hamlet* – were prized luxuries as far away as Byzantium.

The *places* today look very much as they have done for the last few hundred years, but a great deal is actually reconstruction – perhaps the greatest of all the restoration projects carried out in France following the world wars. During the First World War Arras had the misfortune of becoming part of the front line, and was incessantly pounded by German artillery – photographs in the town hall vividly reveal the extent of the devastation. As the dust settled the decision was taken to rebuild it exactly as it had been, to the extent of recovering individual bricks from the rubble and returning them to their exact former location. The result is extraordinarily effective.

The houses in the *places* are aligned with such simple harmony that at first sight they can appear quite uniform, but this impression rapidly disappears. Some have brick façades, others stone, and the spirals and other decoration on their gables are endlessly varied. Look above the arcades and you see all sorts of fascinating details: a mermaid on no.11 in the Petit-Place, the Three Kings in Rue de la Taillerie between the two squares, a cauldron, probably once a shop sign, at no.32 Grand'Place. The north side of the Grand'Place is especially beautiful, with gables and façades that are all differently, and delicately, coloured. It contains the oldest house in Arras, at no.49, now the Trois Luppars hotel, a wonderful semi-Gothic townhouse from 1467 with a watchtower in the middle of its distinctive stepped-gable roof.

The best times to see the *places* are on Wednesday and especially Saturday mornings, when they regain their original function and some of their 14th-century bustle with one of the largest **markets** in France. It no longer fills the whole of all three squares, but is still huge, and enormously varied. Foods, farm-fresh vegetables, flowers, stacks of cheeses and even a few live chickens can be found in Place de la Vacquerie, where the countryside meets the city; in the Petit-Place there are rows and rows of cheap jackets and other clothing, more great cheese and flower stalls, and any number of stands to answer an apparently limitless local demand for spit-roast chicken, which throw out wafts of warmth in winter. In the Grand'Place, meanwhile, you might come across clothes, tableware, antiques or old buttons, more foodstuffs and many other stalls that defy categorisation. Pre-Christmas, all three squares take on an extra gleam, with traders offering trees and bright mountains of decorations beneath the festive lights.

There are also interesting **shops** around the squares: the wonderful *fromagerie* of Jean-Claude Leclercq is on the corner of the Petit-Place and Rue de la Taillerie; the Cotellerie Caudron on Place de la Vacquerie is an impressive old family business that is the sole current manufacturer of true Arras blue porcelain (for both *see* p.83). A little clutch of interesting souvenir and oddments shops can also be found by walking on past the Cotellerie, down Rue des Grands Viéziers and across Rue Paul Doumer.

The grandest piece of post-war reconstruction in Arras is the **Hôtel de Ville**, one of the finest pieces of civil Gothic architecture in Europe: grandest of all is the central section, built very quickly between 1502 and 1506 in a Flamboyant style with elaborate traceries and pinnacles and a peppering of tiny dormer windows in the roof. The giant belfry behind it, celebrated in a poem by Verlaine, was built separately and took much longer (1462–1554). Both had to be painstakingly restored during the 1920s.

As you enter through the main porch, look left to meet Arras' good-natured giants, Colas and Jacqueline and their daughter, who are paraded around the city during the main *fêtes* in June and at the end of August. Buy tickets for the Hôtel de Ville from the tourist office beneath the porch. From the basement a lift (usually) takes you straight up – with some steps at the end – to the top of the **Belfry** (*closed for restoration; due to reopen summer 2001; opening times as for tourist office; adm included with Boves ticket*), for a panoramic view. When you come down, you're allowed to wander around the town hall if there are no meetings in progress. Inside, no real attempt was made to duplicate the pre-1914 décor, but the 1920s-style substitutes give the place an engaging charm. The **Salle des Mariages** has pretty murals with Isadora Duncanesque Grecian maidens on the subject of 'Spring', which make it popular for nuptials; the beautiful main hall has still larger murals of 15th-century life in Arras by the artist Hoffbauer, in a style somewhere between Brueghel and Arthur Rackham.

From the basement of the Hôtel de Ville you can also begin a tour of the **Boves** (*opening times as for tourist office; tours last c. 30–45mins; English-speaking guides available; on Fri and Sat (exc Aug) there's a night-time tour at 6.45, with actors re-enacting chapters in the catacombs' long and tortuous history; reservations advisable, from tourist office; adm*), the bizarre catacomb of tunnels that extends through the chalk beneath Arras. Some tunnels existed here in Roman times, and many more were opened up during the Middle Ages. They extend downwards through three levels, and without a guide you would easily get lost. Until 1982 everyone in Arras had a right of access to them. Since then the bottom levels have been closed for safety, except to tour groups, but many parts of the first level are still in private use, and entrances to these cellars can be seen all around the Grand'Place. The Boves have been used for all kinds of different purposes. The temperature and humidity make them perfect for storing wine, and many Arras porcelain merchants routinely threw all their damaged stock down them. During the Revolutionary Terror of the 1790s, Catholics held secret services here. The caverns were greatly extended frrom 1916 to 1917 by British troops, who used them as a safe means of getting to the trenches just east of Arras; long-forgotten sections of the wartime tunnels are still being discovered.

From the Hôtel de Ville, walk across Place de la Vacquerie, past the Cotellerie Caudron, and turn right at Rue Paul Doumer to the **Musée des Beaux-Arts** (*open April–Sept Mon, Wed, Fri and Sat 10–12 and 2–6, Thurs 10–6, Sun 10–12 and 3–6; Oct–Mar Mon, Wed and Fri 10–12 and 2–5, Thurs 10–5, Sat and Sun 10–12 and 2–6; closed Tues; adm*), which occupies the former Benedictine Abbey of St-Vaast, which somewhat surprisingly is a giant neoclassical edifice, vast by name and vast by nature, completed in 1783. The abbey was founded in the 7th century, and St-Vaast was one of the most important institutions in Arras throughout its history. In the 1740s, however, it was decided to knock down its early-medieval buildings and replace them with this all-new abbey (it is believed that one of the prime movers was the Cardinal de Rohan, Abbot of St-Vaast and one of the most worldly clerics of the Ancien Régime, and it looks more like a palace than a monastery). The museum collection is mixed, with a sizeable amount of unexceptional painting. There is a beautiful collection of fine 18th-century Arras and Tournai porcelain, a major Brueghel (the *Bethlehem Census*) and several landscapes by Corot, who often painted in the town. The museum's greatest artefacts, though, are its medieval sculptures. The 1446 tomb sculpture of Guillaume Lefranchois, a Canon of Béthune, is extraordinary and still shocking: a decomposing skeleton, a classic product of the anguished late-medieval mind. Completely different is the 14th-century *Head of a Woman*, believed also to be from a tomb, a face so serenely beautiful it seems timeless. The museum has, though, only one Arras tapestry – there are very few still in existence – *St-Vaast and the Bear*, with a delightfully worked, almost abstract background.

Alongside the museum is the **cathedral**, in a similar neoclassical style. If the Cardinal de Rohan did not like Arras' antique abbey, he was no more taken with the Gothic abbey church, and in the 1770s work on a new one was begun by Constant d'Ivry, one of the most important architects of the day. Unfinished at the time of the Revolution, it was completed in 1833, and then had to be rebuilt after 1918. It's a huge building, plain and white, and frankly unwelcoming.

The architectural mix of Arras closely reflects the course of its history. Originally a Roman town, from the 13th century it was ruled in turn by the counts of Artois, the dukes of Burgundy and the kings of Spain. Its incorporation into France in 1659 was initially highly unpopular. In the following decade Marshal Vauban arrived to give Arras a set of his ramparts, both as a defence against invaders and to keep a check on the local population. Then, in the 18th century, finally integrated as a French provincial capital, Arras acquired the 'Parisian-style' *hôtels particuliers* and neoclassical piles of every other French city under the Ancien Régime. Arras was noticeably effervescent in the years before the Revolution. As well as the Cardinal de Rohan, it had a large number of the lawyers, officials and aspiring intellectuals who were the core of provincial cultural life, and the chief enthusiasts for 'enlightened' ideas.

To enter another piece of 18th-century Arras, cross Rue Paul Doumer from the Musée des Beaux-Arts and veer to the left to come to the **Place du Théâtre**, with several fine buildings such as the Hôtel de Guines, on Rue des Jongleurs, and the gracious theatre. Just off the square is the former home of one of the rising personalities of Arras at that time, in the street now named after him, Rue

Maximilien-Robespierre. **Robespierre** lived in this house in the 1780s while he was establishing his reputation as a ferocious advocate, before going off to use his talents on a wider stage. Arras has never known quite what to do with its most famous son, or his house: being the home town of a man widely credited with the invention of modern totalitarianism is not easy to handle. For years the house was tightly shut-tered up, and the only voices calling for it to be made a memorial were those of the most incorrigible Stalinists in the French Communist Party. In 1999, however, and quite bizarrely, the city ceded the house to the Compagnons du Tour de France, a club of cycling fanatics, who use half of it to house an exhibition on their own special passion and have opened up the rest as the **Maison Robespierre** (*open April–Sept Tues–Sun 2–6.30; Oct–Mar Tues and Thurs 2–5.30, Sat and Sun 3–6.30*), with a few arte-facts – some clothes and documents – and information on the Revolutionary era.

Another 18th-century addition to Arras is the **Basse-Ville** – past the Place du Théâtre and a little to the right. The product of an early foray into town planning, begun in the 1750s, it has streets intersecting in a grid, centred on **Place Victor Hugo**, a wide, octag-onal square with an obelisk in the middle, an idea quintessentially of the Enlightenment era. From there, continuing roughly in the same direction, you will eventually come to the boulevards around the line of Marshal Vauban's ramparts, demolished in the last century. In the southwest corner, however, is his **Citadelle**, still in use by the French military.

Towards the northwest, the boulevard leads up to the only surviving part of Arras' walls, the Bastion des Chouettes, now landscaped into a tranquil park. Mid-way between the Bastion and the Citadelle on the outer side of the boulevard is the **First World War British Cemetery**, one of the largest and most overwhelming of so many in the area. It contains over 2,600 graves, and around the walls there are the names of nearly 40,000 men with no known grave, in lists that go on and on until it's impos-sible to take any more.

Arras and the territory to the east and north formed one of the most bitterly contested battlegrounds of the First World War, and there seem to be green-sign-posted Commonwealth cemeteries in virtually every village, as well as the giant French cemetery at Notre-Dame de Lorette (20,000 graves). Even those without any special interest in the Great War might appreciate a trip out to Vimy Ridge, north of Arras off the N17 Lens road. Taken by the Canadian army in 1917, it is now the **Canadian National Memorial** (*open daily sunrise–sunset; tours April–Nov daily 10–6*). All the war cemeteries were ceded by France in perpetuity, but no other country has made quite so much of this as Canada. Vimy Ridge is a Canadian National Park, a little piece of Canada: everything is rigorously bilingual, and the well-organised free guided tours are given by French- and English-speaking Canadian students. The park is immacu-lately maintained: near the top of the steep ridge many of the trenches, terrifyingly close together, and grassed-over craters have been preserved, and from the peak, by the sombre 1936 memorial, you can well appreciate why it was considered strategic, for it has a view eastwards for miles over France's traditional industrial heartland, looking surprisingly green from this distance.

Shopping

The city's main centre for more conventional and fashion shopping is **Rue Gambetta** and pedestrianised **Rue Ronville** which runs off it.

Arras ✉ 62000

Charcuterie Bernard Briet, 10 Rue de la Housse, t/f 03 21 51 12 83. A quite magnificent old shop (founded 1879) just off the Petit-Place, selling a whole range of local delicacies: fine wines, excellent beers, preserves, biscuits, and a wonderful selection of cold meats. The speciality is *andouillettes d'Arras*, and the array of *traiteur* dishes is a dazzling sight.

Cotellerie-Porcelaine Caudron, 15 Place de la Vacquerie, t 03 21 71 14 23. The Caudron family first opened their porcelain shop in 1845, and the correct formula for Bleu d'Arras was re-established here in the 1960s. All the pieces are made in their small workshops outside town: cheaper designs use ready-made plates, but the tableware series are entirely handmade and hand-painted. The charming old shop is worth a visit in itself. It also stocks silverware and fine glass.

Fromagerie Jean-Claude Leclercq, 39 Place des Héros, t 03 21 71 47 85, f 03 21 23 66 41. Arras' *premier* master cheese-merchant, in a beautiful shop on the corner of the Petit-Place. All the cheeses are matured and carefully tended in the *caves* beneath the shop; those on display include a comprehensive selection of northern cheeses and many from other parts of France.

Pâtisserie Yannick Delestrez, 50 Place des Héros, t 03 21 71 53 20. The Delestrez pastry and chocolate palace specializes in the city's own most traditional sweetmeats: *coeur d'Arras* – spicy, heart-shaped almond biscuits – and chocolate *rats d'Arras* (the rat has been a symbol of Arras since the 14th century). The beautiful old shop also contains an eye-catching display of other chocolates and cakes, as well as fine *traiteur* dishes.

Restocave, 4 Rue du Marché au Filé, t via Ostel des Trois Luppars 02 21 07 41 41. Robert de Troy, ex-restaurateur, owner of the Trois Luppars hotel and award-winning *sommelier*, has accumulated an extraordinary wine collection in these 15th-century cellars, reached by a narrow entry off a small street by the Hôtel de Ville (a van parked in front often helps you find it). The cellars seem to stretch into subterranean infinity: there are 1,200 different wines, with every kind of French wine – at least one from every year since 1833 – and others from all over the world. Prices run from 12F/€1.83 to many thousands. *Open Sat only 10–1 and 3–8.*

Where to Stay

Arras ✉ 62000

Hôtel de l'Univers, 3–5 Place de la Croix Rouge, t 03 21 71 34 01, f 03 21 71 41 42, *hotelunivers.arras@wanadoo.fr (double rooms 650F/€99.09)*. Occupying a grand town mansion in the centre, on the site of a 17th-century convent, this is one of the city's classic hotels. Now affiliated to the Best Western chain, it has been renovated and redecorated with an imaginative combination of classic and modern designs. Service is excellent, and the smoothly elegant restaurant (*see* below) has its own fan club. One of the region's star hotels.

Hôtel Astoria-Carnot, 10–12 Place du Maréchal Foch, t 03 21 71 08 14, f 03 21 71 60 95 (*double rooms c. 300F/€45.73*). Big and bright, and one of a small clutch of hotels on the square facing the railway station. Well run with 29 good value and recently modernised rooms. There's a big, bustling **brasserie** (*lunch menu 70F/€10.67*) that's open late and is great for snacks and light meals.

Ostel des Trois Luppars, 49 Grand'Place, t 03 21 07 41 41, f 03 21 24 24 80 (*double rooms 300F/€45.73, breakfast 40F/€6.10 extra*). The most characterful hotel in Arras, in the oldest building on the Grand'Place, a magnificent Flemish-Gothic townhouse from 1467 (now with lift). 'Luppars' is old Flemish for wolves, three of which are carved into the façade. All the 42 rooms, some of them in the eaves, have been comfortably re-equipped with modern facilities, and there's a sauna. The De Troy family, who run it, are very friendly.

OK Pub, 8 Place de la Vacquerie, t 03 21 21 30 60, f 03 21 21 30 61 (*rooms 150–340F/ €22.87–51.83; apartments 240F/€36.59 a night; weekly rates available*). A 16-room, rambling hotel above the convivial OK Pub (*see* below) – a good budget choice. Seven rooms are self-contained little apartments with kitchenettes. There's no lift in the main building, but there is wheelchair access via a roundabout route using the adjoining building. There are two outside terraces.

St-Nicolas-les-Arras ✉ 62223

Mme Antoinette Lesueur, Route de Roclincourt, **t** 03 21 55 27 85 (*double rooms 200F/€30.49*). Mme Lesueur offers three rooms as *chambre-d'hôte* on her big old farm, standing up out of the Artois plain between the villages of St-Nicolas-les-Arras and Roclincourt. It's only around 3km north of central Arras, but feels very rural. The rooms are straightforwardly comfortable: all have showers, but toilets are shared.

Fampoux ✉ 62118

M and Mme Peugniez, 17 Rue Verlaine, **t/f** 03 21 55 00 90 (*double rooms 200F/€30.49, one room for four 240F/€36.59*). A big, brick 19th-century farmhouse in the middle of Fampoux, 8km east of Arras south of the Douai road, with five simple but spacious and cosy rooms available as *chambres-d'hôte*. Fampoux is a classic, quiet Artois village, with a big old brewery across the street from the farm; it also stands virtually on the First World War front line.

Eating Alternatives

Arras ✉ 62000

Hôtel de l'Univers, *see* above (*menus 185–260F/€28.20–39.64*). The hotel's highly regarded restaurant is a rather plush, comfortable space where rather intricate, sophisticated dishes are served. The hushed atmosphere could be recommended for a particularly snug dinner for two.

Aux Grandes Arcades, 8–12 Grand'Place, **t** 03 21 23 30 89, **f** 03 21 71 50 94 (*menus from 100F/€15.24*). Impossible to miss on the Grand'Place, the giant Grandes Arcades offers two complete dining rooms, one with a traditional *à la carte* menu and a few set menus of northern dishes and French classics, the other with a long brasserie menu.

The food can be unexceptional, but the buzzing atmosphere, view of the *place* and outside terrace easily make up for it.

La Coupole d'Arras, 26 Bd de Strasbourg, **t** 03 21 71 88 44 (*dishes c. 135F/€20.58; menu 125F/€19.06*). Like its Parisian namesake, a traditional brasserie in the grand manner, with ranks of tables, fast-moving waiters and a giant menu offering a pretty unchanging choice of classics such as fish *choucroute*, veal kidneys in mustard sauce, steaks, mussels and a whole range of smaller dishes such as salads, onion soup and snacks.

La Rapière, 44 Grand'Place, **t** 03 21 55 09 92, **f** 03 21 22 24 29 (*menus 88–210F/€13.42–32.01*). In one of the old shop-fronts in the arcades, this excellent-value restaurant has bright, contemporary décor and highly regarded food, which is an enjoyable mixture of northern French tradition and sophisticated modern touches. The staff are charming, and it's popular with locals.

OK Pub, *see* above (*menus 65–150F/€9.91–22.87*). It proudly claims to have been 'the first pub in the Pas-de-Calais' (since 1967), but it's not really recognisable as an English pub, with its long bar, alcoves, and a choice of cocktails, whiskies and some 300-plus beers. Brash, lively and friendly, it also serves a big range of snacks such as sandwiches, *croques*, salads and pizza, and has an outside terrace. There's also a much neater dining area to the left of the bar, with a sizeable, good-value, brasserie menu.

Le Louisiane, 12 Rue de la Taillerie, **t** 03 21 23 18 00, *louisarr@caramail.com*. A comfortable and convivial cocktail-and-music bar on the street between the Grande and Petit *places*, with pool tables and a pleasant ambience. There's a big choice of cocktails, whiskies, beers and other drinkables, plus snacks. Live music (usually jazz) most evenings.

Taverne du Ch'ti, 17 Place du Héros, **t** 03 21 23 20 38, **f** 03 21 23 20 38. The Ch'ti stands out as an unfancified, smoke-filled French student café, utterly laidback and the kind of place where you can sit for hours. The barman nurtures a strange devotion to country & western music. The excellent, wheatey Ch'ti beer, brewed at Benifontaine near Lens, is on tap, and to eat there's a simple range of snacks such as *croques* and sandwiches.

Small Town Gem:
Montreuil

10

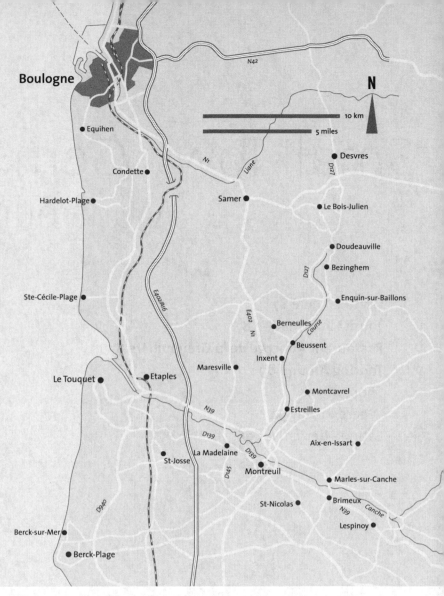

Boulogne

N42

N

Equihen

Desvres

Condette

N1

Liane

D127

Hardelot-Plage

Samer

Le Bois-Julien

Doudeauville

Bezinghem

D127

Ste-Cécile-Plage

E402/A16

Enquin-sur-Baillons

E402
N1

Berneulles

Course

Beussent

Inxent

Maresville

Montcavrel

Le Touquet

Etaples

Estreilles

N39

Aix-en-Issart

D139

La Madelaine

D39

St-Josse

D145

Marles-sur-Canche

Montreuil

Brimeux

Canche

D940

St-Nicolas

N39

Lespinoy

Berck-sur-Mer

Berck-Plage

10 km

5 miles

The countryside just south of Boulogne has provided the first taste of France for many British travellers for a very long time. Its place names can be familiar, and it might not seem an obvious place to look for the peace and timeless atmosphere associated with a classic image of the French countryside. Away from the main routes, though, there are any number of quiet villages with farmers going about their business, and lush, green valleys producing fine local meats and cheeses. And, on a rock above the wooded valley of the Canche, there is Montreuil, called sur-Mer despite the absence of any sea, a historic walled town still contained within its ramparts as it was in the 16th century, and showing no inclination to outgrow them.

Getting There

The A16 *autoroute* (toll road from Boulogne) passes between Montreuil and the sea. The road in from the motorway (exit 26) and all the other roads south, from Calais, Boulogne, Le Touquet or St-Omer, join up just north of Montreuil in the N1, which makes a wide eastward loop around the town. Instead of staying on this road take the turn into Montreuil and carry on through the ramparts and the old town on to the Abbeville road. On the south side of Montreuil look for a sharp right turn signposted to La Madelaine-sous-Montreuil. In the village there is another right turn, with a sign for the Auberge de la Grenouillère, which is at the very end of this lane.

Tourist Information

Montreuil: 21 Rue Carnot, t 03 21 06 04 27, f 03 21 06 57 85. The main information office for the area is beside the grassy esplanade near the Citadelle of Montreuil, and the Château de Montreuil hotel.
Berck-sur-Mer: 5 Av Francis Tetegrain, t 03 21 09 50 00, f 03 21 09 15 60.
Etaples: Bd Bigot Descelers, t 03 21 09 56 94, f 03 21 09 76 96.
Hucqueliers: 14 Grand Place, t/f 03 21 81 98 14.
Le Touquet: Palais de l'Europe, Place de l'Hermitage, t 03 21 06 72 00, f 03 21 06 72 01.
Vallée de la Course: 316 Rue du Village, Bernieulles, t 03 21 90 72 53. Bernieulles is 2km west of Beussent.

It receives its fair share of visitors, and yet nothing seems to disturb its placid pace and very refreshing small-town atmosphere.

Montreuil also makes an ideal destination for those in search of a pampering, utterly relaxing break within a very easy distance of a Channel crossing, since, thanks to its charms and well-established status as a travellers' rest, the town – and the delightful countryside of the Course and Canche valleys around it – possess an exceptional range of places to eat and stay. In particular, just outside Montreuil, there is a superb restaurant-hotel in a quite ravishing location.

The **Auberge de la Grenouillère** ('The Froggery') is in La Madelaine-sous-Montreuil, a village at the bottom of Montreuil's crag with a special view up to the town's remarkable ramparts. It occupies a beautifully restored old farmhouse – with entirely unique décor – by the River Canche, amid woods and lush meadows. Inside, award-winning chef Roland Gauthier creates endlessly inventive, richly enjoyable dishes based on a supremely skilful working of seasonal, local ingredients. For a combination of pure pleasure, comfort and rural calm, it's hard to beat.

Auberge de la Grenouillère

La Madelaine-sous-Montreuil, t 03 21 06 07 22, f 03 21 86 36 36,
www.lagrenouillere.fr, auberge.de.la.grenouillere@wanadoo.fr.
Open Sept–June Mon, Thurs–Sun 12–3.30 and 7.15–9.30;
July and Aug daily. Closed Jan. Book always. Menus 160F/€24.39
(not available Sat eve, Sun, public hols), 290F/€44.21 and 400F/€60.98;
à la carte average 400F/€60.98.

The winding lane that takes you down to the Auberge de la Grenouillère runs past the houses of the village of La Madelaine-sous-Montreuil, eventually petering out beside the bright waters of the Canche. There are trees all around, and fine horses in a

Sorbet à la Betterave Rouge (Beetroot Sorbet)

Serves 8–10

A juice extractor makes easy work of this sorbet or, if that is not an option, purée the beetroots in a blender or food processor. Serve the sorbet for dessert – this restaurant is known for novelty puddings – or alternatively as a refreshing starter or palate cleanser.

1litre/1¾ pints fresh beetroot juice (from about 22 medium-sized peeled beetroots)
200ml/7fl oz crème de cassis (blackcurrant liqueur)
450g/1lb caster sugar
juice of ½ lemon

Sieve the beetroot juice through a chinois or fine-mesh sieve and chill. Combine with the crème de cassis, sugar and lemon juice. Freeze the mixture in an ice-cream machine according to manufacturer's instructions. Serve immediately or freeze in an airtight container. If made ahead of time, remove from the freezer 20–30 mins before serving.

little field beside the river. The restaurant is just to your left, in a traditional Picard-style one-storey farmhouse, with red roofs and white walls, around a courtyard with tables, sunshades and flowers, a little pocket of plenty even in December. It is quite exceptionally pretty, and just as lovely and very comfortable inside, with dark wooden beams, tiles, more flowers and white linen. In winter, there's also a log fire. The unique feature of the décor is that the walls of the 'Froggery' are covered in whimsical pictures of very human-looking frogs, illustrating one of La Fontaine's fables about a frog who wanted to be as big as an ox and ate so much he exploded, painted during the 1930s by Frank Reynolds, once art director of *Punch*, and a friend of the then owner.

Roland Gauthier, who once worked at the Connaught Hotel in London, recently celebrated his 20th year at the Grenouillère. His cooking has won great praise, but there's no culinary grandstanding here: he still takes the orders himself, and does so with a quiet charm. Nor, despite its possession of a Michelin star, is there anything stiff or formal about the restaurant: the clientele are a broad mix, and it's not a place where anyone need feel inhibited. The menus, which change monthly, are strictly seasonal, and employ almost entirely local, *du terroir*, ingredients. This means that in autumn they may heavily feature game and duck, and sea bass and other fish from local ports; at other times, they might include more salt-marsh lamb or mackerel or river fish. Also, although he himself is originally from the Jura, he often presents versions of local northern dishes, such as the *caudière*, the classic fishermen's stew of the Pas-de-Calais.

The subtlety of the cooking is already announced by the appetisers, which on an autumn day included a bacon and seafood mousse that's a bravura combination of sweet and savoury flavours. The main weekday menu is *du terroir*, while there is also a four-course menu *terre et mer*: both offer plenty of enticing choices. Among the starters might be a wonderfully smooth, fragrant pumpkin and almond soup, or supremely delicate *cromesquis* (small profiterole-like balls) of warm foie gras. If it features among the fish courses, in season, don't miss the St-Jacques with cep mushrooms and endives *confits*, a fabulous multi-layered complex of flavours that goes far beyond any of its individual ingredients.

Seasonings and methods are complex, but one of the most outstanding qualities of Roland Gauthier's cooking is an exceptional combination of strong, earthy, very enjoyable flavours and others of great delicacy. In Baie de la Somme *pré-salé* lamb with haricot beans and *confit* of garlic, for example, the meat is saltily powerful yet at the same time has a much more refined, elusive flavour than more conventional lamb, with tones that waft around the tongue. Also, the reliance on the local *terroir* – so no Mediterranean tomatoes, courgettes or other products out of season – means that you are presented with continuously surprising, delicious combinations of often-undervalued northern European products.

The cheeseboard (*40F/€6.10 extra on some menus*) is another original, an impressive all-regional selection that includes Vieux Boulonnais, Pavé du Nord and many other often-neglected northern cheeses instead of just the usual standards; and there is an exhaustive, if expensive, wine cellar. Especially spectacular, though, are the desserts, another Gauthier forte – he devotes special care to them, since, he says, as the *coup de grâce* of a meal, they are often what lingers most in the mind. *Crème brûlée* comes with grilled oats, giving a completely new tone to an old standard; damson tarts are a little explosion of fresh fruit in the mouth; and maize ice-cream with a nougatine of polenta and bitter caramel mousse is a delectable, completely surprising and hugely inventive creation.

If the weather's suitable, go into the courtyard for coffee and *petit-fours*, and watch the breeze in the trees. Afterwards, take a wander down the path alongside the soothing river. And, for a longer rural idyll, take advantage of the Grenouillère's guest rooms, which need to be booked well in advance.

Touring Around

It's possible to get from Calais or Boulogne to Montreuil in about half an hour on the A16, or even on the N1 unless you get stuck behind a line of trucks, but an incomparably more attractive route is the little D127 road which runs roughly parallel to the main roads down the valley of the **River Course**, just inland. To get on to it, turn off the N1 in Samer on to the road to Desvres, and then, in a switchback section with great views north over the valley of the Liane, look for a tiny lane off to the right, with signs to Doudeauville and Bois-Julien, that disappears into the trees straight up a steep hill. At the top, follow another sign right to Doudeauville and you will be delivered into a green, narrow valley that is immediately so different from the semi-industrial small towns straggling south from Boulogne that it can feel like a lost world. The river is a quick-flowing, burbling stream. Hunkered down alongside it there are villages of white, red-roofed one-storey cottages, surrounded by the trademark flowers of the Artois valleys.

The Course has been discovered by a fair number of British travellers (there are very *gentils* little signs, here and there, reminding you to drive on the right), but it manages to remain a very genuinely rural, sleepy stretch of French countryside, with tree-clad villages with old-fashioned bars and other more hidden attractions spread along the valley. Several have unfussy restaurants and small *auberge* hotels, which make great places to stop and drink in the atmosphere.

Near Enquin-Baillons a road cuts eastwards up to the Haut-Pays, the flatter 'High Country' above the valley, centred around **Hucqueliers**, an attractive large village with some distinguished 16th–18th-century buildings. Further south back in the main valley there is **Beussent**, home of – to the left just before you enter the village from the north, and easy to miss – **Les Chocolats de Beussent**, a high-quality craft chocolate-maker that has become the Course valley's major 'industry'. From Beussent another narrow lane turns off to the east and runs across the river and then away from the Course to enter a branch valley that seems almost wild and uninhabited, with only a few isolated farms such as Le Fond des Communes, producer of fine fresh chèvre and butter.

Further south, just past Estréelles, the Course valley road brings you back to the main N1. **Montreuil-sur-Mer** is just a little further south, the old *ville-haute* atop its impressively steep hill reached via a hairpin road that brings you up to the main gate, the Porte de Boulogne, in the town ramparts. Beyond the gate the road winds round again to the right, as it has since the 19th century to avoid one of Montreuil's most famous streets, the Cavée St-Firmin, a precipitous cobbled incline, lined with quaint white houses with roofs each at a different level, which caused havoc among the carriages of 18th-century British travellers when they had to negotiate it en route to Paris.

It is believed that the site of Montreuil was already occupied in Roman times, although the town was actually founded in the 7th century by monks. It grew to be of most interest, however, to the region's warriors, and the first fortifications appeared 200 years later. It's not hard to see why, for the crag on which the *ville-haute* stands has a commanding view in every direction, and especially along the valley of the Canche.

It was also an important port, which is why, against all visible evidence, it still retains the title 'sur-Mer'. The harbour was one of the wealthiest in northern Europe during the 13th century, trading in grains, wines and wool, but the Canche had already begun to silt up, and by 1400 was virtually impassable. Today if you look from Montreuil out towards the sea, now 15km away, across the fields and thick woods where the port's traffic once came and went, you can only marvel at the capacity of this stretch of coast to shift and change.

Montreuil's position as a harbour and fortress long gave it a torrid and violent history. For two centuries it had the eccentric status of being the only port in France, for in the years when the theoretical 'kings of France' were consistently abused or ignored by over-mighty vassals such as the dukes of Normandy this was the only outlet to the sea under their direct jurisdiction. This situation ended after 1200 when Philippe Auguste seized control of Normandy and Boulogne, but Montreuil nonetheless remained a much-desired stronghold in all the wars that criss-crossed the region. Its greatest catastrophe came during the wars between François I of France and the Holy Roman Emperor Charles V. In 1537 an Imperial army besieged Montreuil and destroyed virtually the entire town. After it was recovered, François I ordered it rebuilt in a radically different manner, abandoning the old lower town alongside the now-useless river and retreating to the *ville-haute* on top of the hill, to be surrounded by the ramparts that are now Montreuil's most exceptional feature. The townspeople were required to take part in the building work, which continued off and on for over a hundred years.

In the 17th century, though, as the French frontier moved away to the east and the sea receded further to the west, Montreuil was allowed to slip into being a quiet backwater, which is why most of the town, remarkably, is still contained within the 16th-century walls. It was still a stop for the Paris–Calais mail coaches, and as such was visited by Victor Hugo, who set part of *Les Misérables* here, as the town where Jean Valjean briefly achieves peace and prosperity under the name of M. Madeleine, and even becomes mayor (recently some in the town have begun to milk its Mis-potential, and a *Les Misérables son et lumière* is now presented each summer, on the last weekend in July and the first in August).

If you arrive in Montreuil on a Saturday morning, carry on straight along the main street past the centre to the south side of the *ville-haute* and Place Charles-de-Gaulle, commonly called the **Grande-Place**, a wide, rambling square that's the site of the weekly **market**. This is a real small-town country market, with stalls in no apparent order offering excellent local vegetables, fresh herbs, CDs, very good, strong cheese and terrines, farm eggs, computer games and shoelaces. Around the square there are plenty of bars and cafés, bustling with shouted conversations on market days, tranquil again after the stalls have packed up.

Overlooking the scene from one side of the square, perhaps with a little admiration, is Field Marshal Sir Douglas Haig, atop a horse, a statue placed here in commemoration of the fact that during the First World War (from 1916 to 1918) little Montreuil was the headquarters of the British Army in France. One of the main buildings they used was the one behind him, since converted into a rather odd-looking theatre. Haig himself stayed at the Château de Beaurepaire (*not open to visitors*), in St-Nicolas, just south of the town. He was a familiar figure in the countryside around Montreuil, for he used to exercise by going riding every morning, always accompanied by several officers and a troop of lancers, and preceded by another horseman carrying a Union flag.

The market finishes in good time to go down through the gate in the ramparts on one side of the Grande-Place to the Grenouillère for lunch. Afterwards, or before lunch if it isn't market day, head back into the rest of Montreuil, north of the square. The intertwining streets and squares of the old town are narrow, small-scale and have enormous charm. As a town upon a hill it has a noticeably airy feel, an impression helped by its mostly whitewashed or light-grey stucco buildings. The little white cottages in the oldest streets sometimes look as if they should be in a fishing town, perhaps some kind of hangover from when it was 'sur-Mer'. The main streets are busy at the end of the school day, when crowds of children mill around waiting for buses to take them back to the surrounding villages. At other times the streets are often quiet as a mouse.

The main through street, the old Paris road that is now called Rue Pierre Ledent, runs through the western side of the *ville-haute*. Just off it is **Place Darnetal**, a very pretty square with lime trees and an engagingly twee fountain in the middle. The 16th-century half-timbered houses and Les Hauts de Montreuil hotel across on the other side of Rue Pierre Ledent are the oldest buildings in the town, parts of which may even be survivors from before 1537. From Place Darnetal a little street connects with the main square, **Place Gambetta**.

Montreuil has a curious range of churches. **St-Saulve** on Place Gambetta is the largest, a fine early-Gothic pile, which only half survived the great sack of 1537. The 15th-century main façade and nave are both beautiful, but the choir and the transepts were all destroyed, leaving it only half its previous size, and the sections rebuilt or added at different times since then look like nothing more than attempts to put on a brave face. Inside, though, its battered state can make it strangely atmospheric. Across the square is the **Chapelle de l'Hôtel-Dieu**, a building rarely open to the public, although this does not matter much since its main features are all on the outside. The hospital it serves is 15th-century, but the chapel was built in the 1870s by Clovis Normand, a local architect and Gothic revivalist of the school of Viollet-le-Duc, and is a pure medievalist fantasy, with a mass of luxuriantly sculpted Flamboyant Gothic details.

Go down the street to the right of the Hôtel-Dieu and you come to another quiet little square, with the **Chapelle de Ste-Austreberthe**, a simple, whitewashed late-medieval church. From there, Rue Porte Becquerelle and then Rue de Paon, to the right, will take you to the most picturesque part of Montreuil, with the little cobbled alleys of **Clape-en-Bas** and **Clape-en-Haut** huddled against the ramparts. The tiled roofs of the cottages that lean against each other along the steep streets seem almost to touch the ground, and each door is painted a different colour. Ungraciously, the names of the streets mean roughly Lower Drain and Upper Drain, referring to the gutters – the remains of open sewers – that still run down the middle of them. Several of the houses are used as craft workshops or bars during the summer, which keeps the area lively, but on other days they might be as slow-moving as the rest of the town.

On the corner of Rue de Paon at the foot of Clape-en-Bas is the **Musée Roger Rodière** (*open July–Aug daily 3–6; adm*), Montreuil's local museum, housed in an 18th-century former chapel, with a curious little collection that includes medieval religious sculptures, old coins, paintings by (very) local artists and relics of the First World War British 'occupation'.

Late afternoon, when the shadows are beginning to become more noticeable, is a good time to approach Montreuil's most special attraction, the walk around the **ramparts**, which are accessible from many streets in the town. They form an unbroken loop, and as you go around it the circuit seems to accentuate the smallness of Montreuil, confining it still more upon its hill. They extend for three kilometres, and the full walk takes about an hour, but along the way there are plenty of places to stop. And, despite the walls' original purpose, they are wonderfully peaceful, overgrown with grass and ivy along the top, with at some points a sheer drop beneath you. All around the views are superb: inwards, over the streets of Montreuil; northwards, over lower Montreuil and the Canche; westwards, towards the sea, the lower Canche and superb, gold-lit sunsets. By the **Porte de Boulogne**, rebuilt in the 1820s, you look down over lush flowerbeds by the roadside, which soften the town walls' naturally forbidding glare.

In the northwest corner of the ramparts, beyond an especially attractive, grassy area that now also contains Montreuil's tourist office, a little bridge leads to the **Citadelle** (*open Nov–Mar Mon, Wed–Sun 10–12 and 2–5; April–Oct daily 10–12 and 2–6; adm; tour commentaries, on cassette, available in English*). It was built, still more than the rest of Montreuil, to dominate the approaches along the Canche, and so has a still better view. Since it was attacked, damaged, rebuilt and added to over the centuries, different parts of it vary in age enormously, from the first Montreuil of the 9th century, through two massive towers built for Philippe Auguste, and a 17th-century entrance by the ever-present Marshal Vauban. The **Tour de la Reine Berthe** is where one of France's least distinguished kings, Philippe I, is supposed to have confined his Dutch Queen Berthe in 1091 after he had repudiated her to marry another, Bertrade de Montfort.

After exploring old Montreuil it's also worth wandering into the soft, green country-side of the lower Canche below La Madelaine, along the line of the one-time harbour. It's a curious landscape, visibly a low-lying dip and yet just as obviously an area that has been 'inland' for centuries, and with some deliciously pretty and calm villages among the woods and fields. And a visit to Montreuil can include a trip to the beach. **Etaples**, on the north side of the mouth of the Canche, has a beach but is very much a working fishing port, quite rough and ready, and with great fish restaurants.

To the south, and by complete contrast, is the eccentrically glitzy resort of **Le Touquet**, an artificial town created in the 1890s as a rival to Deauville and other fashionable spots further south, and long successful with wealthy Brits. Its art deco architecture, casino and giant grand hotels give it a vaguely Noël Coward air, but it also still has obvious cachet, with some giant houses to be glimpsed among the pines that surround the town, and many fine shops.

Some 10km further south again is **Berck-sur-Mer**, a more low-key old-fashioned French holiday town, with the necessary long prom, *frites* stands and giant sandy beach (the sea departs for the horizon at low tide), very popular with windsurfers and sandyachters, and a good place to watch the sun go down over the Channel.

Shopping

Montreuil-sur-Mer ✉ 62170

Vinophilie, 2 Rue du Grand Sermon, t 03 21 06
01 54, f 03 21 06 70 10, *www.vinophilie.com*.
In an ancient alley near the Citadelle at the
top of Montreuil, this modern wine
merchant has a broad selection of high-
quality French wines, displayed in renovated
old *caves*. There's a particularly impressive
choice of *grands crus*, and fine champagnes,
plus some spirits, liqueurs, and other gifts.

Beussent ✉ 62170

Les Chocolats de Beussent, 66 Route de
Desvres, t 03 21 86 17 62, f 03 21 81 85 49.
A remarkably successful cottage industry,
the Beussent *chocolaterie* produces a
complete range of filled chocolates, pralines,
chocolate bars, cooking chocolate and other
goodies, all handmade in its workshop.
So successful has it become that it now has
outlets in Boulogne, St-Omer and other
towns, but this is the most charming place
to try the range. *Open (shop) Mon–Sat 9–12
and 2–7; (tours) Sept–mid-July Mon–Sat
3.30–7; mid-July–Aug Mon–Sat 9–12 and 2–7.*

Le Touquet ✉ 62520

Maison Pérard, 67 Rue de Metz, t 03 21 05 13 33.
Widely accorded the accolade of producing
the finest *soupe de poisson* in France, for you
to take away. Sceptics can sample the soup
before buying. There is also wonderful *soupe
de crabe*, sauces, bunches of dried *salicornes*
(seaweed) and other fish-related produce
and preserves, all of the very highest quality.

Berck-sur-Mer ✉ 62600

Le Succès Berckois, 56 Rue Carnot, t 03 21 09 61
30, f 03 21 94 17 94, *www.succesberckois.com*.
Another remarkable family firm. *Succès* and
berlingots are boiled sweets, and the Matifas
family have made them to their own recipes
since the 1920s, in a huge variety of fruit,
herby and flower-based flavours – the range
changes all the time, as they are continually
introducing and experimenting with new
mixtures. They have won the award for the
best sweet in France. Not to be left behind,
they are now on the Internet.

Montcavrel ✉ 62170

Le Fond des Communes, Route de Beussent,
t 03 21 06 21 73. Eliane and Louise Leviel
produce excellent *chèvre*, butter and cows'-
milk cheese on this remote farm in one of
the side valleys of the Course. Among their
specialities are *aperichèvres*, assorted appetisers on a *chèvre* base. They also sell at the
market in Le Touquet (*Mon, Thurs, Sat*). To
find it, take the lane across the river in
Beussent (past the Restaurant Lignier), and
then follow an even smaller hill road to the
right, towards Montcavrel. *Tours of the farm
Feb–Nov daily exc Sun.*

Where to Stay

Montreuil-sur-Mer ✉ 62170

Château de Montreuil, Chaussée des Capucins,
t 03 21 81 53 04, f 03 21 81 36 43, *www.relais-
chateaux.fr/montreuil (double rooms
860–1,400F/€131.11–213.43). The* luxury
option in Montreuil, although it's actually a
rather large, late-19th-century seaside-type
villa, surrounded by a flower-filled garden.
Chef-proprietor Christian Germain trained
with the Roux brothers in England, his wife
Lindsay is English and at any time half or
more of the clientele are likely to be so too.
The attraction is its complete comfort: the
14 rooms, all different and with many special
decorative touches, are not cheap, but in
return you get true luxury. And to go with
the rooms, of course, there is Christian
Germain's renowned cooking (*see below*).

Auberge de la Grenouillère, La Madelaine-
sous-Montreuil, t 03 21 06 07 22, f 03 21 86
36 36, *www.lagrenouillere.fr (double rooms
400F/€60.98 a night, twin room 500F/€76.22,
suite 600F/€91.47; gourmet winter package
of meal and room 400F/ €60.98). The*
Grenouillère's four utterly charming guest
rooms are built into the eaves of the old
farmhouse, and combine antique furniture
with excellent bathrooms and fittings to
create the feel of a romantic hideaway.

Les Hauts de Montreuil, 21–23 Rue Pierre
Ledent, t 03 21 81 95 92, f 03 21 86 28 83
(*doubles 495–550F/€75.46–83.85). The* oldest
house in Montreuil, said to date from 1537, is
impossible to miss on the main street. Its

owner, Jacques Gantiez, works hard to make the most of his ancient property, with a borderline-brashness that might horrify historic purists, and offers a whole range of eating possibilities (*see below*). The renovated interior is cosy, and the atmosphere is convivial despite (or because of) the touristy touches. The 27 hotel rooms have plenty of charm, and very good facilities.

Hucqueliers ✉ 62650

Le Clos, 19 Rue de l'Eglise, **t** 03 21 86 37 10, **f** 03 21 86 37 18 (*twin rooms plus lounge and kitchenette 320F/ €48.78 B&B; the 'Grand Clos' plus lounge with sofabed and bunkbeds 390F/€59.46 for two, B&B*). A superior *chambre-d'hôtes* in the centre of Hucqueliers, in the Haut-Pays above the Course valley. The 19th-century house was once the home of the local notary and has a front courtyard, stable blocks and walled garden. Four of the six rooms are more or less self-contained apartments, giving the option of B&B or self-catering. In another wing there are two romantic double rooms. Facilities include a lounge, multi-channel TV, music, books and games. Owners Alain and Isabelle Bertin (who speak very good English) take great care of their guests, offering to babysit and book golf courses, taxis or anything else you might need.

Maresville ✉ 62630

Ferme-Auberge des Chartroux, **t** 03 21 86 70 68, **f** 03 21 86 70 38 (*rooms 280–430F/ €42.69–65.55, breakfast 35F/€5.34 extra*). Mme Delianne's *ferme-auberge*, deep in the countryside about 7km northwest of Montreuil, is a member of Logis de France, but feels more like a warm B&B than a hotel, and is very peaceful. The cosy rooms are spread about the former farm buildings and yard. Meals can be ordered in the restaurant (*see below*). *Closed two weeks in Nov and two weeks in Jan.*

St-Josse ✉ 62170

La Ferme du Tertre, 77 Chaussée de l'Avant Pays, **t/f** 03 21 09 09 13 (*double rooms 290F/ €44.21; 360F/€54.88 for three; 430F/€65.55 for four, with a kitchenette*). A stylish, charming

chambre-d'hôte run by Sabine and Alain Pretre in a former farm on the lane between La Madelaine and St-Josse, with distinctive bright blue and white painted gates. The smart modern rooms, with excellent facilities, are in one of the ex-farm buildings, each with its own french-window entrance from the garden. A fully independent *gîte* (for up to eight) is also available. Breakfast can be served in the garden. There are two ponds with ducks, swans and geese, both good for fishing.

Les Peupliers, 8 Allée des Peupliers, **t** 03 21 94 39 47 (*rooms 260F/€39.64, plus 70F/€10.67 per child*). B&B rooms in a modern house in the marshlands north of St-Josse, run by Mme Lepretre. The six rooms, most with twin beds, are simple but comfortable, with plenty of space, and have access to a kitchen. The house has ample grounds, and there's a pond with swans.

Inxent ✉ 62170

Auberge d'Inxent, **t** 03 21 90 71 19, **f** 03 21 86 31 67 (*rooms 295–370F/€44.97–56.4, breakfast 40F/€6.1*). A pretty old Course valley village inn, with clumps of geraniums at every window. It was picked out as a model of a French country *auberge* years ago by no less than Elizabeth David, and despite several changes of ownership its **restaurant** (*menus 85–125F/€12.96–19.06*) still places a fine emphasis on fresh local produce. The six charming guest rooms have pretty, traditional décor and good facilities, with views of the garden, village and river.

Bezinghem ✉ 62650

Ferme-Auberge des Granges, **t/f** 03 21 90 93 19 (*double rooms 250F/€38.11*). A rambling whitewashed farm – still very much in operation – in the rural heart of the Course valley, with six B&B rooms, five doubles and one for three. They're simple, but attractively and comfortably decorated, and well-priced. There are mountain bikes for hire for exploring the surrounding area. This is also a *ferme-auberge*, with a **dining room** offering fresh country cooking, especially traditional *tartes* cooked in a wood oven (*menu 95F/€14.48*). Meals must be booked in advance.

Eating Alternatives

Montreuil-sur-Mer ✉ 62170

Château de Montreuil, *see above (menus 200–400F/€30.49–60.98)*. Unreservedly top-drawer country-house hotel, with a very high reputation under Chef Christian Germain, who worked with the Roux brothers in Britain for some years before coming to Montreuil. His cooking combines French traditions with imaginative touches: local meats, fish and seafood are often presented with adventurous spicings, and there is a formidable Philippe Olivier cheese-board and a fine wine cellar.

Les Hauts de Montreuil, *see above (menus 160–460F/€24.39–70.13)*. This imposing 16th-century inn offers a whole variety of possibilities: the main restaurant, a bar-brasserie, and a wine and cocktail bar with a Caribbean flavour. There's also a shop selling wines and local food specialities, and this is the home of Montreuil's own beers. For all the hard sell, and high prices, the restaurant has a good reputation, especially for local specialities: Licques chicken, duck and lamb, and fish and seafood from Etaples.

Le Darnétal, Place Darnétal, **t** 03 21 06 04 87, **f** 03 21 86 64 67 *(menus 100–196F/ €15.24–25.76)*. A popular restaurant in the centre of old Montreuil, with a snug dining room full of flowers and an eccentric clutter of antiques. M and Mme Vernay extend a warm welcome. Highlights of their menus are some refined fish and seafood dishes – *paupiette d'aile de raie aux poireaux et moules* – or poultry – fillet of duck in red wine with *baies de cassis*; there are also classics such as *coq au vin*. There are four simple guest rooms upstairs *(from 220F/€33.54)*.

Auberge du Vieux Logis, La Madelaine-sous-Montreuil, **t** 03 21 06 10 92 *(menus 105–175F/ €16.01–26.68)*. In the middle of La Madelaine, near the turning for La Grenouillère, this is a cosy, friendly village bistro, with an outside terrace when the weather allows. The food is of a high standard, and the set menus might include *truite rôtie aux amandes* or a hearty *caudière étaploise* (fish stew). There are also good lighter dishes – salads and enjoyable mixed *assiettes* – for around 50F/€7.62.

Beussent ✉ 62170

Restaurant Lignier, Place de la Mairie, **t** 03 21 90 71 65 *(menus 98–210F/€14.94–32.01)*. A long-established country restaurant by the banks of the Course, popular with locals. Beyond the old-fashioned bar the two dining rooms serve homemade terrines, local trout, game, and classic meat favourites grilled over a wood fire, along with superior cheese and wine selections. *Closed Sun eve and Wed.*

Berck-sur-Mer ✉ 62600

L'Auberge du Bois, 145 Av du Docteur Quettier, **t** 03 21 09 03 43 *(menus 90–155F/ €13.72–23.63)*. A long-standing favourite: a simple place for bargain seafood specialities – *choucroute de la mer* (125F/€19.06) and a still heftier *plâteau de fruits de mer* (150F/€22.81). There are also other fine fish choices and some meat dishes. It's some way from Berck beach, on one of the main avenues running inland.

Maresville ✉ 62630

Ferme-Auberge des Chartroux, *see above (menus 98F/€14.94 and 138F/€21.04)*. A superior *ferme-auberge* in an impressively rambling farm. The produce used – especially the fine lamb, for which it is renowned – still comes from the farm, but the magnificent dining rooms are neatly pretty as well as rustic, and Mme Delianne and her family run the place with sophisticated charm. Other specialities include farm chicken in cider, and juicy onion tarts. Reservations essential. *Closed two weeks in Nov and two weeks in Jan.*

St-Josse ✉ 62170

Le Relais de St-Josse, Grand'Place, **t** 03 21 94 61 75 *(menus 108–215F/€16.46–32.78; weekday lunch 75F/€11.43)*. In a low, old inn building that's clad in geraniums for much of the year, the dining room is neat and simple, but Etienne and Fabienne Delmer's menus have a touch of grandeur. Local meats are a strong point, and the homemade pâtés and terrines are superb. For something simpler there are excellent fish dishes, grills, omelettes and light *assiettes*.

On the Back Roads of Artois:

Hesdin and the Sept Vallées

11

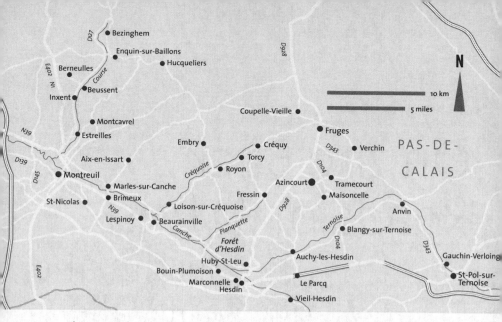

The countryside inland in the Pas-de-Calais, east of the main roads south, at first glance looks like an open expanse of rolling downs with few trees and giant fields patrolled by lonely tractors, and always wind-blasted when the winter weather sets in. Explore a little, though, and you find that the downland is divided by a string of sheltered, mellow valleys, some open, some steep-sided, lined by groves of trees and with fast-flowing rivers, babbling becks and waterfalls and large, placid ponds. The landscape suddenly seems abundant and richly varied.

Away from the main roads, this area – known as the Sept Vallées or Sept Vallées of Artois – you will come upon villages of neat, whitewashed cottages with red-tiled roofs and surrounded by colourful flowers, and so peaceful they seem lost to the world. Each has its individual quirks and features – a tumbledown château glimpsed through trees, a bizarrely shaped church porch, even a piano bar in the middle of nowhere. And, like any other part of rural France, the region has its traditions and special foods – especially cheeses, *charcuterie* and unusual liqueurs.

For centuries this area was also part of Europe's greatest battleground, fought over time and again by France, England, Spain and other powers. Its towns and villages have been conquered and re-taken many times, and this past is reflected in historic buildings found by market squares, or in battlefields such as Azincourt (Agincourt), still visible amid the rural quiet.

Roads wind up and around hills through the Artois valleys, interconnected by tiny, often sunken lanes, making them ideal for anyone who likes just wandering and taking each place as they find them. For thorough orientation, local tourist offices have plenty of literature, including lists of traditional food and craft outlets. And, as a focus when exploring, a natural point to aim for is Hesdin, the valleys' main town, which was built as a Spanish stronghold, and became a garrison town of the Ancien Régime. It has several very enjoyable places to eat, and, in **L'Ecurie**, an excellent showcase for the region's produce and cuisine.

Getting There

To reach the Sept Vallées from Calais or Boulogne, take the A16 or N1 south to Montreuil, and turn left on to the N39, sign-posted for Hesdin. As you enter Hesdin on this road, called Avenue François Mitterrand in town, you will come to a triangular park with a war memorial and a car park; park here, and walk the short distance up Rue André Fréville to Place d'Armes, the main square and undisputed centre of town. L'Ecurie is a further short walk away down Rue Jacquemont, one of the turnings off the square to the right.

Tourist Information

Hesdin: Office du Tourisme des Sept Vallées, Hôtel de Ville, Place d'Armes, **t** 03 21 86 19 19,

f 03 21 86 04 05. The central information office for the Sept Vallées, prominently located in Hesdin's Hôtel de Ville. Some information can also be found at *www.pas-de-calais.com*.

Azincourt: 22 Rue Charles VI, **t** 03 21 04 41 12, **f** 03 21 47 13 12.

Beaurainville-Vallée de la Créquoise: La Mairie, Beaurainville, **t** 03 21 90 30 63, **f** 03 21 90 02 88.

Blangy-sur-Ternoise: La Mairie, **t** 03 21 41 92 38, **f** 03 21 47 25 57.

Brimeux: La Mairie, **t** 03 21 06 07 95, **f** 03 21 86 38 78.

Fressin: 8 Rue Principale, **t/f** 03 21 86 56 11.

Fruges: Hôtel de Ville, **t** 03 21 04 02 65, **f** 03 21 47 30 07.

St-Pol-sur-Ternoise: Place de l'Hôtel de Ville, **t** 03 21 47 08 08, **f** 03 21 47 50 33.

L'Ecurie

*17 Rue Jacquemont, Hesdin, **t/f** 03 21 86 86 86.*
Open mid-Sept–mid-June Tues–Sun 12–2 and 7.15–10;
mid-June–mid-Sept daily 12–2 and 7.15–10. Book weekends.
Menus 88F/€13.42 (Tues–Fri and Sat lunch only), 108F/€16.46
and 138F/€21.04; à la carte average 150F/€22.87.

L'Ecurie occupies a 16th-century former stables (*écurie*) near Hesdin's Place d'Armes, which by the 1930s, as an old photograph on the wall shows, had moved on to house a garage at one end and a café at the other. The old building has been neatly restored, making good use of the plain brick and stone of its entrance to give an uncluttered sense of style. Inside, there's a small bar, and a combination of classic features – 19th-century prints, flowers, neat table settings – and more modern touches – lemon walls, wicker chairs, staff in casual clothes. The atmosphere is bright and airy. This mix of tradition and innovation is characteristic of the restaurant throughout.

The men behind L'Ecurie, chef Jean-Luc Lecoutre and maître-d Michel Cadet, are both from the Sept Vallées but worked in several first-rank restaurants around the north – including the august Huitrière in Lille – before opening up here in 1997, believing that there was a space in Hesdin and the Valleys for a more imaginative, quality restaurant that made the most of local produce and culinary traditions. As Cadet puts it, they know that in a country setting they cannot be too experimental, for fear of alienating their clientele, but they still always try to be creative in their approach to food. And this winning combination of satisfying but refined food presented in a relaxed style (and at very reasonable prices) has clearly hit the mark. It's a place that the whole town seems to enjoy – men in suits, families, men on their own, pairs of elderly ladies or young women, and passing tourists.

As you wait to order, the arrival of some delicious freshly baked bread rolls gives an indication of the Ecurie's attention to detail and quality. Jean-Luc Lecoutre presents creative dishes, but his cooking is very much based in northern French cuisine, with a liking for strong, vigorous flavours, a rich sense of meatiness and earthiness, and a great use of northern ingredients such as green vegetables, duck, local fish, beer and juniper berries. From the *menu terroir et région*, a *ballotin croustillant* (crispy filo parcel) of *coquilles St-Jacques* and smoked ling with juniper is an inventive and enjoyable mix of a rich, almost meaty sauce, crisp but ultra-light pastry and fine seafood. To follow, fillet of duck *aux agrumes et écorces confites* (with citrus and preserved zest) is a new take on traditional duck *à l'orange* – with a much more subtle, bitter flavour thanks to the use of zest, and complemented by an accompaniment of northern veg – baked onion, potato *gratin* and carrot mousse.

The cheese course is also imaginative – warm Belval on very spicy *pain d'épices* on an autumn day – and the wine list is, like the menus, shorter than some but skilfully selected. To finish up, there are some notably elaborate, creamy desserts and fresh-fruit sorbets. On a weekday at around 2pm many of your fellow diners will get up and go back to their business, but for those with no demands on their time there's no pressure to move on.

Touring Around

The valley of the Canche, running inland from Le Touquet past Montreuil, is the largest of the Artois valleys and the area's main artery. From Montreuil the N39 towards Hesdin runs parallel to the river, rolling up and down hills along the wooded banks through a line of relatively busy villages, several of which have their particular attractions. The Canche here is quite wide and slow-moving, and at **Brimeux** forms several large, mysterious-looking ponds surrounded by willows and birches, and much-loved by local anglers (permits are required, obtainable from the town hall).

Everywhere there is colour, for the villagers of Artois are known for their love of flowers, and except in the very dead of winter virtually every house has bunches of geraniums, hydrangeas and wild flowers decorating their window sills. Further east along the Canche in **Bouin-Plumoison** – or 'goose-pluckers', a reference to the villagers' early occupation – there is the **Musée de l'Abeille d'Opale**, a private operation dedicated to maintaining interest in one of the Pas-de-Calais' oldest traditions, beekeeping, and (as Thierry Apiculture) production of fine honey and things derived from it, especially *hydromel* or fermented honey, otherwise known as mead. Billed here as 'the drink of the Gauls', it has been made in this area for centuries, and recently achieved something of a revival. In the same village there is also the **Maison de l'Artesanat et du Terroir**, a display space for the area's crafts and distinctive foods.

Beyond Bouin the road approaches Hesdin. Although it now has the appearance of an historic old community the capital of the Sept Vallées was once a 'new town', transplanted from its original location a few kilometres to the east in 1554 on the orders of the Emperor Charles V. The great Franco-Spanish wars that long dominated the life of Flanders and Artois began when Charles fortuitously inherited both Spain and Burgundy, so that his territories effectively surrounded France. For the next century and a half, every French king took it as his aim to break this ring around them, a goal finally achieved between 1640 and 1680 by Louis XIV, with help from Richelieu and Mazarin. A hundred years earlier, though, the great Charles carried all before him, and in 1553, after their French garrisons had obstructed his troops once too often, he ordered that both Thérouanne to the north and the first Hesdin, an historic and wealthy town, be razed down to the last brick, and a new Hesdin created to the west. For the next decades, until a French army took it by siege in 1639, it would be the main bastion of Spanish power in Artois, face-to-face with the French stronghold at Montreuil, with regular skirmishes along the valley between them.

Hesdin today is a very attractive little town, at the meeting-point of the Canche and Ternoise valleys, with monuments that reflect its special history. The main square, **Place d'Armes**, which seems almost too big for the town, is dominated by a grand, Flemish-looking brick **Hôtel de Ville**, begun in 1572 and fronted by a magnificently sculpted two-level Baroque stone porch (1629). At the very top there is a *fleur-de-lys*, added in the 18th century, but the coat-of-arms at the centre of the balcony is that of Spain, flanked by those of Hesdin and Artois, and the figures on the sides of the upper level represent Philippe IV of Spain and his French queen Isabelle, surrounded by the cardinal virtues. Nearby is the massive church of **Notre-Dame**, built between 1565 and 1585 in the Flemish Hallekerk style as a rectangular hall instead of in the shape of a cross. Its brick façade is mainly very late-Gothic, but it has an impressive Renaissance-style stone porch, surmounted, again, by the Spanish Habsburg arms. Inside, there is some very fine Baroque woodwork.

Next to the church is the **river**, which runs through the middle of the town under little hump-backed bridges, sometimes disappearing under buildings and then re-emerging beside houses and the winding, cobbled streets. At No.11 Rue Daniel Lereuil is the birthplace of the **Abbé Prévost**, born 1697, famously un-devout and misbe-having priest and author of *Manon Lescaut*, while north of Place d'Armes in Rue Prévost is the **Hospice St-Jean**, formerly the Jesuit college where the future Abbé studied, begun in 1562 but with a distinguished neoclassical façade added in 1746.

Hesdin is busiest on Thursdays, when farmers from all around the valleys descend on the square for the area's most important and vigorous **market**. The town is also known for two kinds of food, a morish crunchy chocolate called a *pavé hesdinoise*, in the shape of an Artois roof tile, and *charcuterie*, often made with beer and honey, which can be found in the market and many shops near the square. And, after wandering through the streets of Hesdin, you can also walk all the way around it along a lovely beech-lined footpath, the **Tour-de-Chaussée**, created in the 17th century by travelling merchants to avoid passing through the town and paying the dues it was entitled to charge.

From Hesdin it's possible to head out into the Sept Vallées in any direction. One circular route continues along the N39 east, toward St-Pol-sur-Ternoise. On the way, pay at least some respect to tiny **Vieil-Hesdin**, site of what was, until it incurred Charles V's wrath, one of the region's richest towns. It also contained a famously palatial castle, the ruins of which are still visible, and the '**Park of Marvels**', a giant pleasure garden created at the beginning of the 14th century by Richard, Count of Artois. Stretching all the way to the Ternoise, and landscaped to create all kinds of visual tricks, it contained exotic beasts, elaborate fountains, bizarre statues and even jokes such as bridges that gave way when you trod on them, for which it was renowned throughout Europe. The dukes of Burgundy frequently used it for extravagant entertaining, but later it, too, was obliterated on the Emperor's orders, and only the name of the village of Le Parcq remains. Not far away is another idiosyncratic village, **Auchy-les-Hesdin**, with a 19th-century cotton mill – long closed down – built within the remains of a medieval abbey, and a superb Gothic church.

St-Pol-sur-Ternoise is quite a large, plain town, which had the misfortune to be badly battered twice the last time Artois was a battlefield, in both 1940 and 1944. A turn to the northwest, though, on to the D343 signposted to Anvin, will take you back into the **Ternoise**, a broad, misty valley with rambling, widely dispersed villages, such as Gauchin-Verloingt, apparently lost in green tranquillity. Anvin and, further west, **Blangy-sur-Ternoise** both have fine, but very different, 16th-century churches, the former late-Gothic, the second more eclectic. Blangy is also the place where Henry V of England and his army crossed the River Ternoise in October 1415, on their way to Azincourt (better known in English spelt with a G), where they would defeat a French force five times larger in one rain-soaked day. It's now reached by turning north on to the little D104 in Blangy.

In **Azincourt** there has for some years been a small museum, in the same building as the tourist office, which, like the stand-up figures of medieval knights by the roadsides around the village, was an entirely local initiative (governments rarely commemorate defeats). However, local officialdom has now swallowed its pride and recognised the potential of the site, and July 2001 will see the opening of a purpose-built **museum and visitor centre** (*open April–Oct daily 9–6; Nov–Mar daily 10–5; adm; family and group discounts*). This inspires differing feelings, since the old museum, with its imaginative (sometimes shameless) use of any material the local organisers had to hand, has a charm of its own, but the new centre promises to be a state-of-the-art, detailed display with new videos, interactive exhibits and so on. Whichever museum is open when you arrive in Azincourt, it's a good idea to visit it to get an idea of the main events of 1415 before walking or driving to the battleground. The Azincourt battlefield itself is remarkable: perhaps due to its compact size, it's possible to recognise the outlines of what happened there nearly 600 years ago more easily than at the sites of many far more recent events. The forests either side of the field, which hemmed in the French horsemen and made it impossible for them to use most of their strength, have gone, but the track along which carts ran – keeping the English archers supplied with arrows as they poured them into the French knights sliding and falling in the mud – is still there, now the road past the neighbouring village of Maisoncelle. Nowadays Azincourt also hosts a biennial international archery competition, next due in May 2002.

From Azincourt take the main D928 south towards Hesdin, then turn off right on to yet another tiny lane to enter another valley, the Planquette, and reach **Fressin**, known to students of French literature as the long-time home of Georges Bernanos and the background to many of his novels. Also, in among the trees just to the west, beyond the end of the village's long main street, there are the romantic ruins of a **castle** (*open April–Sept; adm*) that was once the seat of the Créquy, one of the grandest Artois families from the Middle Ages right up until the Ancien Régime, and servants at different times of both the kings of France and the dukes of Burgundy. Fressin has one of the finest of the valley churches, **St-Martin**, most unusual because its interior is entirely washed down in white. Especially beautiful is the funeral chapel of the Créquys, first built by a widow, Jeanne de Roye, for her husband and two others of the clan who died at Azincourt, and with some superb lattice-work Gothic carving. The rest of the church is actually later, with almost English-style columns added by a 16th-century Créquy who was ambassador to England.

As you leave the church, not far away downhill on Fressin's main street are **Les Caves du Vieux Chai**, the Glaçon family's also-historic wine *cave*, with a particularly good range of Bordeaux. Near the entrance there's a photo of M. Paul Glaçon shaking hands with Gérard Depardieu, a man who's known to know a few things about wine.

North of Fressin the road winds on up to Créquy village, at the head of the Créquoise, perhaps the most idyllic of all the Sept Vallées. The valley sides wind and dip and are very green, while the river sparkles and rushes along the roadside and past the village churches and flowerbeds. Just outside Créquy to the north is the **Sire de Créquy** farm, which produces a unique cheese with the same name, after a 13th-century Créquy, Raoul, who went off to the Crusades, was captured and believed lost forever, and then returned to claim his 'widow' on the day she was due to remarry (this story is also re-enacted in a cute *son et lumière* pageant in Fressin in early July). Visitors can have meals at the farm's *auberge* as well as tasting and buying.

A little way downriver in **Torcy** there is a piano bar and cabaret, **Le Baladin**, a very original combination of nightspot and village *crêperie*, which livens up every weekend; from there it's a further couple of kilometres to **Royon**, an exceptionally pretty village with the river running through the middle and a very fine Flamboyant-Gothic church from the 1540s. If you take a turn right there through Embry (on the Hucqueliers road), look out for its very odd but engaging whitewashed chapel, with a 19th-century wrought-iron porch that looks almost like a gazebo. Back in the main Créquoise valley, the road eventually winds down to **Loison-sur-Créquoise**, with a 12th-century Knights Templars' manor, **La Commanderie**, that is now an exceptional B&B. Loison is also the sole home of another special product, *perlé de groseille* or *de framboise*, a kind of redcurrant or raspberry champagne, and an enjoyably smooth, refreshing creation that's available at the **Maison du Perlé**, easy to find by the roadside. Owner Hubert Delomel also offers tours and bikes to hire to ride through the surrounding woods. Below Loison the Créquoise runs into the Canche and the road meets the D113, which to the right will take you back to Montreuil along a leafier, emptier route than the N39, with the option of a detour up one more steep, intimate, wooded valley, the Bras de Brosne, via the beautifully out-of-the-way hamlet of **Marles-sur-Canche**.

Shopping

Many products of the Sept Vallées can also be bought at Saveurs et Traditions in Boulogne (*see* p.37).

Créquy ✉ 62310

Les Brebis d'Esgranges, Ferme du Bois d'Esgranges, t/f 03 21 81 13 14. A small farm near Créquy which produces its own sheeps'-milk cheeses (tomme, mild cheeses straight or with herbs, fromage frais or *demi-vieux*) and yogurts. *Open May–Oct, mostly afternoons, for tours and tastings.*

Fressin ✉ 62140

Les Caves du Vieux Chai, 20 Grand Rue, t 03 21 90 61 43, f 03 21 81 10 00. The Glaçon family have run this traditional wine merchant for four generations. Their great speciality is Bordeaux, where they have a vineyard, and there's an own-label champagne. *Guided tours of the fine old caves by reservation. Open Mon–Sat 9–12.30 and 2–6.30.*

Hesdin ✉ 62140

The Wine Society, 1 Rue de la Paroisse, t 03 21 86 52 07, f 03 21 86 52 13. Aimed squarely at the passing Brit trade – all signs are in English – but somewhat oddly placed on Hesdin's very French market square. An internationally orientated selection – with New World and other European as well as French wines – at French prices.

Distilleries Ryssen, 1 Rue de la Paroisse, t 03 21 81 61 70, f 03 21 81 13 21. Ryssen have produced their own distinctive *pastis* since 1829, as well as an interesting range of fruity liqueurs. Their Hesdin showroom also sells a range of wines.

Aix-en-Issart ✉ 62170

L'Egouttoir, 26 Rue Principale, t 03 21 86 07 41, f 03 21 86 32 93, *www.legouttoir.fr*. In their village workshop Gilbert and Xavier Brunel produce wooden furniture large and small in historic styles (especially Louis Philippe, Directory and Louis XV) and the similar traditional country styles that have never entirely fallen from fashion in these parts. Each piece, usually in oak, is beautifully finished, and items can be made to measure.

Verchin ✉ 62310

Ferme Bocquet, 25 Rue Maranville, t/f 03 21 04 43 66. On her farm a few kilometres north of Azincourt, Patricia Bocquet bakes wonderful breads, brioches, tarts and other delicacies using a a truly historic wood oven. You can sample the products on site, with local ciders and cheeses. *Open mid-Mar–mid-Nov daily 9–7; mid-Nov–mid-Mar closed Sun.*

Bouin-Plumoison ✉ 62140

Maison de l'Artesanat et du Terroir, 1395 Route Nationale, t/f 03 21 86 97 47, *www.maison-artisanatterroir.com*. Easy to find on the N39 in the middle of the village, this is an attractive showcase for local traditional craft products: dried flowers, wooden toys, painted textiles, ceramics, leather, and fine handmade country furniture, etc. There is also a variety of local foodstuffs: country breads, walnut cakes, liqueurs and *apéritifs*. *Open Jan Sat and Sun 2.30–7; Feb–Mar and Oct–Nov Sat, Sun and hols 2.30–7; April–June Mon, Wed–Sun 2.30–7; July and Aug daily 10.30–12 and 2.30–7; Sept and Dec daily 2.30–7.*

Musée de l'Abeille d'Opale/Thierry Apiculture, 923 Route Nationale, t 03 21 81 46 24, f 03 21 86 44 83. *Shop open Tues–Fri and Sun 2–7, Sat 10–7; museum open mid-June–mid-Sept Tues–Sat 2–7; mid-Sept–mid-June Sat, Sun and hols 2–7.* The Thierry family's curious and very informal 'museum' will tell you everything you ever wanted to know about beekeeping, including a tour of the hives. The shop also sells pollen, royal jelly, cosmetics, candles and mead (*hydromel*), and there's an annual 'Fête de la Miel', usually on the first weekend in September.

Loison-sur-Créquoise ✉ 62990

La Maison du Perlé de Groseille, 50 Rue Principale, t 03 21 81 30 85, f 03 21 86 05 80. Hubert Delomel has refined traditional recipes for simple fruit wines to create his unique *perlé de groseille* and *de framboise* – blackcurrant and raspberry champagne. The shop also sells ciders, preserves, terrines and his *eau-de-vie-de-cidre*, which can't be called calvados because this isn't Normandy, and because it's too strong. There is also a small crêperie, to accompany tastings.

Fruges ✉ 62310

Le Sire de Créquy, Route de Créquy, **t** 03 21 90 60 24, **f** 03 21 86 27 72. The farm, which has an *auberge*-style restaurant (*see* below), produces its very own fine cheese, a variation on the region's traditional Rollot, a pungent, spicy, strong cheese with an orange rind and a shortish life. Tours of the *fromagerie* and its *caves* include a video on the history of the cheese.

Where to Stay

Auchy-les-Hesdin ✉ 62770

Auberge le Monastère, **t** 03 21 04 83 54, **f** 03 21 41 39 17 (*double rooms 255F/€38.87, 325F/ €49.55 for three; breakfast 40F/€6.10*). A very convivial and welcoming hotel-restaurant near the medieval church and old cotton mills. It's best known for its food (*see* below), but it's also a Logis hotel, with 10 simple, comfortable rooms and a pretty garden.

Loison-sur-Créquoise ✉ 62990

La Commanderie, Allée des Templiers, **t** 03 21 86 49 87 (*double/twin rooms 350–400F/ €53.36–60.98; suite 500F/€76.22*). A gem of a *chambre-d'hôte*. The main house of this giant farm was originally a 12th-century lodge for the Knights Templar, and the hall-living room-games room, open for guests' use, is wonderfully baronial; the location, by the Créquoise river, is just as delightful. The four rooms are quite luxurious, with loads of fresh flowers; the magnificent suite is almost a self-contained *gîte*, with its own breakfast room with view of the river, and access to a kitchenette. Owner Marie-Hélène Flament is friendly, and a bit of a character.

Azincourt ✉ 62310

La Gacogne, **t/f** 03 21 04 45 61 (*double rooms 300F/€45.73, double with extra single bed 350F/€53.36*). This likeable *chambre-d'hôte* is on the very edge of the Azincourt battle-field, and owners M and Mme Fenet are great enthusiasts for local history. Their own house, with an unusual tower in which breakfast is served, dates from the 18th century. The four charming guest rooms are

in a pretty converted farm building along-side, with its own lounge with fireplace.

Hesdin ✉ 62140

Hôtel les Flandres, 20–22 Rue d'Arras, **t** 03 21 86 80 21, **f** 03 21 86 28 01 (*double rooms 310F/ €47.26, breakfast 45F/€6.86*). This Logis hotel is very used to British guests, and service is friendly, relaxed, and bordering on eccentric. The reception area also serves as an unfussy bar, and the **restaurant** (*menus 96–170F/ €14.64–25.92*) offers ample menus concen-trating on traditional local dishes (*from 80F/€12.20, weekday lunch only*). The 14 rooms are cosily comfortable.

Gauchin-Verloingt ✉ 62130

Le Loubarré, 550 Rue des Montifaux, **t** 03 21 03 05 05, **f** 03 21 41 26 76, *MCVion.Loubarre@ wanadoo.fr* (*rooms 240F/€36.59 for two, 320F/€48.78 for three; children under five free*). M and Mme Vion's grand old manor house, with pointed turrets and a neo-classical portico, is made up of different sections dating from the 17th to the 19th centuries, and is stuffed with antiques and other curiosities; outside, there is a big, wooded garden with a few goats. The four big B&B rooms are in a former outhouse, and have simple, old-fashioned country furniture and good showers. To find it, take the D343 north from St-Pol and follow the *chambre-d'hôte* signs through the village, via several twists, turns and dips.

Marles-sur-Canche ✉ 62170

Manoir Francis, 1 Rue de l'Eglise, **t** 03 21 81 38 80, **f** 03 21 81 38 56 (*double rooms, 300F/ €45.73, family room 440F/ €67.08 for four*). A ravishing B&B in a tiny, utterly tranquil village that's well-placed for both Montreuil and the Sept Vallées. The giant castle-like manor-farm, built in 1662, has a broad, circular yard, whitewashed walls and stone flags. The charming owner, Dominique Leroy, ensures it feels very warm and homely (as well as collecting antiques, another of her interests is rescuing animals, so there is a varied collection of cats, dogs, ducks and other fauna). The breakfast room, kitchen and winding staircases are all delightful, as are the three rooms.

Eating Alternatives

Auchy-les-Hesdin ✉ 62770

Auberge le Monastère, *see above (menus 125–275F/€19.06–41.92).* That the bar is also the village *café-tabac* gives some idea of the amiable feel of the Monastère, and it is also a 'piano bar', since owner Jean-Robert Marecaux is a jazz fan, and plays the clarinet. Meals, served in a pretty old dining room with a giant open fireplace, include sophisticated original creations – with plenty of fine fish and seafood – and meaty *terroir* dishes, with generous menus. Its fans come for the atmosphere, but the food is good, too. The Monastère also has guest rooms *(see above). Closed Mon.*

Fruges ✉ 62310

Auberge du Sire de Créquy, Route de Créquy, **t** 03 21 90 60 24, **f** 03 21 86 27 72 *(menus 60–150F/€9.15–22.87)* . A big old farm on a hill, a little north of Créquy on the road towards Fruges, which has a huge, simply decorated dining room and menus of stout, creamy, often cheesy country dishes – renowned *flamiches, carbonnades,* duck with walnut sauce – made with fresh produce, mostly from the farm itself. Reservations essential. The farm also produces its own Sire de Créquy cheese *(see p.103),* used in many dishes on the menu. *Closed Mon.*

Torcy ✉ 62310

Le Baladin, 62 Rue Principale, **t** 03 21 90 62 51 *(snacks from c. 50F/€7.62).* A complete surprise in a fabulous old barn-like building beside the road in Torcy that could truly be part of a rural idyll, overlooking the tumbling Créquoise. The Baladin is a bohemian *café-crêperie* and music bar which features a non-complacent range of music on many Saturdays all year (every Saturday in summer): jazz, blues, Celtic, rock and, recently, an African hip-hop group. At other times, there's a laidback atmosphere, good local beers and enjoyable crêpes, *galettes,* salads and other snacks, and maybe a larger *plat du jour. Open Sept–June Fri and Sat from 6pm, Sun and hols from noon; July and Aug Tues–Sat from 6pm, Sun and hols from noon.*

Hesdin ✉ 62140

La Garenne, Huby-St-Leu, **t** 03 21 86 95 09 *(menus 130–350F/€19.82–53.36).* Nothing quite prepares you for the discovery of La Garenne in the middle of the Artois countryside: a simple old, white-fronted country cottage with a leafy garden filled with a Disney-twee collection of gnomes and other details. Inside there's an extravagant combination of old-fashioned French *bourgeois* comfort and theatrical camp – pink linen, photos of theatre and movie stars, grand open fireplaces, loads of flowers, and much more. There are also comfortable lounges, with more log fires, where crêpes and drinks can be served outside restaurant hours. The food, like the décor, is more elaborate than the rural norm, and a little more expensive: fine fish and game dishes are specialities.

La Bretèche, 19 Rue du Général Daullé, **t** 03 21 86 80 87 *(menus 92F/€14.03, 134F/€20.43 (du terroir) and 178F/€27.14).* A comfortable traditional restaurant in the heart of Hesdin. Owners Fabien and Christine Oudart are young and only took over a few years ago. It's long been known as a showcase for the region's own cuisine, so go for the *menu du terroir,* including such specialities as warm duck pâté with juniper, or *crépinette de lapin cuisinée façon carbonnade* (with beer). *Closed Sept–June Wed.*

Café du Globe, Place d'Armes, **t** 03 21 86 82 65 *(three-course lunch menu 64F/€9.76, plats du jour c. 50F/€7.62).* An inescapable presence on Hesdin's market square: a big, all-day bar-brasserie which serves coffee, snacks, crêpes and larger dishes, and sees the whole of local life pass by.

Coupelle-Vieille ✉ 62310

Le Fournil, Route de St-Omer, **t** 03 21 04 47 13 *(menus 85F/€12.96, 125F/€19.06, 174F/€26.53).* On the D928 about 3km north of Fruges, this pleasant roadside inn, much recommended by locals, offers an interesting range of fare at accessible prices. Traditional favourites, especially in meats, are to the fore, but there's no lack of imagination or care in the presentation of such things as *suprème de pintade aux prunes,* and the quality wine list.

Land, Sea and Sky:
Baie de la Somme

12

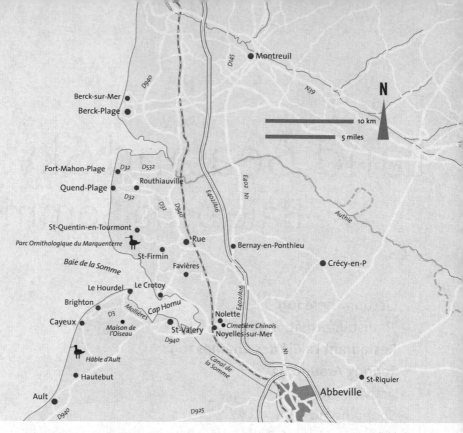

Seventy miles south of Calais there is a special, misty landscape of sand flats, water, dunes, salt marshes, giant skies and unbreakable stillness that is one of the least populated, least developed areas anywhere on the coast of France. The Bay of the Somme is a broad arc where at low tide the sea recedes for miles, and the placid channels, sandbanks and expanses of coarse grass, rushes and marsh lavender present a subtle, ever-changing, mix of colours fading into the horizon. Borders between earth, sea and sky are often hard to distinguish, and the light in the Bay has an opaque quality celebrated by writers from Jules Verne to Colette, and painters such as Degas and Seurat. The Bay is also exceptionally rich in birdlife.

The quiet little towns around the Bay can sometimes seem lost in the immensity of the landscape, as much left behind by history as they have been by the tide. They include, though, some of the oldest towns in France. St-Valery-sur-Somme, the largest, stands on a site occupied since the Stone Age, on one of the few rocky outcrops around the Bay. Locals believe William the Conqueror's enemy Harold of Wessex was imprisoned here, and the Conqueror himself passed through in 1066. Later St-Valery became a fishing port, a weekend retreat for the Amiens bourgeois and, briefly, a military camp. Nowadays, the main qualities of the ancient town are a sleepy tranquillity and an idiosyncratic charm.

The Baie de la Somme is also an area celebrated for its special produce – lamb raised on the salt marshes (*prés-salés*), duck when in season, leeks, celery and other greens,

Getting There

The coast road south from Calais and Boulogne via Le Touquet, the D940, runs directly to the Bay of the Somme, with turnings off to Le Crotoy and eventually St-Valery. If you are travelling on the A16 *autoroute* or the main N1 inland via Montreuil, turn off westwards near Bernay-en-Ponthieu (exit 24 on the A16), towards Rue, to join the D940. About 3km south of Rue there is a turning to the left signposted for Favières. If you are coming from the south there is a turning for Favières signposted right from the D940 just as it curves around the Bay near Noyelles. In Favières, La Clé des Champs is easy to find in the middle of the village.

The only Bay towns with conventional rail services are Noyelles and Rue, both stops on the Amiens–Abbeville–Boulogne local line.

Tourist Information

St-Valery-sur-Somme: 2 Place Guillaume-le-Conquérant, t 03 22 60 93 50, f 03 22 60 80 34. The most comprehensive in the area, the St-Valery tourist office is easy to find at the point where the road into town turns to run along the quay, by the mouth of the Somme Canal. Guided walks into the Baie de la Somme are run from an independent office, **Nature en Somme**, 9 Rue de la Ferté, t 03 22 60 75 75, just around the corner from the tourist office (*only fully staffed Sat 10.30–12.30 and 1.30–5.30*); for information you can also contact the tourist office, or better still the parent organisation, the **Centre Permanent d'Initiatives pour l'Environnement** (CPIE), 32 Route d'Amiens, ✉ 80480 Dury, t 03 22 34 24 27, *www.cpie80.com*. The CPIE also organises a variety of other guided trips, including walks in the Hable d'Ault bird reserve.

Ault: Rue du 11 Novembre, t 03 22 60 57 15, f 03 22 60 49 03.

Cayeux-sur-Mer: Bd du Général Sizaire, t 03 22 26 61 15, f 03 22 26 78 38.

Le Crotoy: 1 Rue Carnot, t 03 22 27 05 25, f 03 22 27 90 58. **Promenade en Baie**, 5 Chemin des Digues, t 03 22 27 47 36, also organises guided walks and other trips in the Bay.

Fort-Mahon: 1,000 Av de la Plage, t 03 22 23 36 00, f 03 22 23 93 40.

Quend-Plage: Place du 8 Mai, t 03 22 23 32 04, f 03 22 23 62 65.

Rue: Rue Porte de Bécray, t 03 22 25 69 94, f 03 22 25 76 26.

and fish and shellfish caught close offshore, shrimps, mussels, cockles, sole and *lieu* (pollack). It might be expected that in somewhere so apparently remote this food would be presented very simply, but, this being France, the Bay also has its well-tended restaurants. And, most surprising of all, deep in the marshes north of the Bay in the little village of Favières there is one, **La Clé des Champs**, where you can find a rare combination of the best of local produce, traditional Picard cooking and very sophisticated culinary skill, flair and imagination.

La Clé des Champs

Place des Frères Caudron, Favières, t 03 22 27 88 00, f 03 22 27 79 36. Open Tues–Sat 12–2 and 7–9, Sun 12–2; closed Mon, 1–15 Jan, first week Sept. Menus 90F/€13.72, 100F/€15.24 (both weekdays and Sat midday only), 150F/€22.88, 175F/€26.68, 205F/€31.25 and 250F/€38.11.

The narrow lanes that lead to Favières twist and bend and then bend again between low-lying fields, hedges and bunches of trees standing out against the flat horizon. Like most of the marshland communities it's a rambling place that doesn't

Assiette de Poissons de Petits Bateaux du Crotoy (Selection of Locally Caught Crotoy Fish)

Serves 4

1 medium carrot, cut in very thin matchsticks

1 celery stick, cut in thin matchsticks

1 leek (white part), cut in thin matchsticks

120ml/4fl oz Muscadet (dry white wine)

12 mussels, cleaned and debearded

400ml/14fl oz fish stock

1 shallot, finely chopped

4 plaice fillets, about 80g/3oz each (cut large fillets in half lengthways)

4 sole fillets, about 80g/3oz each (cut large fillets in half lengthways)

4 small turbot fillets, about 80g/3oz each (cut large fillets in half lengthways)

4 scallops

120g/4oz small raw prawns, shelled

200ml/7fl oz crème fraîche or double cream

100g/3½ oz cold butter, diced

salt and pepper

have the closely defined centre of other French villages, more a collection of farms and houses spread out along paths and roads. A few modern alterations aside, most are in the traditional style of the *maison picarde*, long, single-storey cottages with whitewashed walls and roofs of thatch or red tiles that hang down like sleep-heavy eyelids. And, in the area most like a centre, near the church, is La Clé des Champs, in one of the biggest Picard houses, clearly indicated by its own signposts. On Sundays the grass verges and the little triangular space in front that serves as a car park suddenly fill up, but on most days there will be scarcely any traffic around, except maybe the occasional chugging tractor.

The traditionally pretty décor of muted pinks and greens offsets the giant old farmhouse fireplace, and the carefully selected arrangements of seasonal wild flowers that beautifully catch the afternoon light. The staff are quietly courteous, and service follows all the proper rituals, with a deal of panache when main courses arrive. A massive and superior wine list (all French, naturally) and strikingly original *mises-en-bouche* of beetroot and mashed apple add immediate confirmation, if any were needed, that this is no backwoods operation.

Chef Bruno Flasque is as much a part of the *terroir* as the ingredients he uses, for he was actually born in this same house, when it was just the village *bar-tabac*, with a few *crêpes* cooked by his mother available at weekends. He has never worked outside the Baie de la Somme: after studying at the regional Hôtellerie school he cooked for a few years at Chez Mado in Le Crotoy, before taking over La Clé from his parents in 1985 with his wife Isabelle. He describes himself modestly as something of an autodidact, in which case, he must have made a very good teacher. Both he and his wife display plenty of the untiring care for detail that is one of the cornerstones of traditional

Steam the carrot, celery and leek separately until tender, about 8 minutes. Season and set aside.

Put 30ml/2tbsp of the wine in a small, stainless steel saucepan, add the mussels and set over a medium heat. Cook, tightly covered, for about 4 minutes, or until mussels open, shaking the pan occasionally. Strain the cooking liquid and reserve.

Put the fish stock, shallot and remaining wine in a stainless steel saucepan and bring to a simmer. Season the fish fillets and scallops.

Poach until they are opaque and cooked through, 7–8 minutes, adding the scallops and prawns after 3–4 minutes' cooking time. Carefully remove the fish and shellfish to a plate and cover to keep warm.

Boil the cooking liquid vigorously to reduce by half. Add the cream and the mussel cooking liquid and bring to a gentle boil. Whisk in the butter bit by bit, lifting the pan from the heat if the butter melts before it can be incorporated. Taste and season the sauce with salt and pepper as needed. Add the vegetables to the sauce and heat through.

To serve, pour a pool of sauce on to four warm plates, dividing the vegetables among them. Arrange the fish and scallops and garnish with the mussels in their shells and the prawns.

French catering, seen in four superb homemade breads, or the choice of five different coffees from around the world. Traditional Picard dishes are an essential part of his repertoire, along with classic French styles, but he's also highly imaginative. His cooking doesn't dither: strong, unabashed flavours turn up frequently, but his dishes are also subtle, delicate, refined and perfectly balanced. And, of course, he knows exactly where to find the very best products of the Bay, from salt-marsh lamb and sole and shrimps from Le Crotoy to celery, cress and summer asparagus.

There is no *à la carte*, only a series of set menus, but they offer a very broad choice, and – with the most sumptuous list still at 250F – are also quite phenomenal value. The 90F menu provides a delicious light, fresh meal, with a pretty definitive version of the local favourite *ficelle picarde* as a fixture, along with a fresh fish of the day. From the 150F list, a *tourte de canard sauvage aux champignons* is a wonderful duck pie, with perfect pastry, superbly bloody gravy and rafts of rich, warming autumnal flavours coming up from the bottom of the dish. Local fish *de petits bateaux*, caught inshore from small boats, are among the restaurant's prime staples, in a constantly changing range of combinations such as Le Crotoy sole with sancerre and mussels, or fillet of turbot with ginger and baked leeks. Complements and vegetables, such as the onion cake, celery and mushrooms that come with a main course of shoulder of beef, are fabulous, and can linger in the mind as much as the main dish.

A meal at La Clé des Champs makes an excellently sybaritic restorer after a walk around the Bay, with extra notes of luxury available, should you wish. Between the first and main courses there is the offer of an 'Interlude', a glass of sorbet with calvados, like a *trou Normand* – which, since this is Picardy, is cheating, but to be enjoyed nonetheless; while in between the excellent cheeses and the desserts comes a pre-dessert, a dainty dish of very fine homemade caramel ice-cream. The desserts themselves include a good choice of light, modern options, but M Flasque's superb versions of classic French puddings like *pain perdu* are hard to resist. Indulgently fruity and chocolatey, this is the ultimate Gallic comfort food. After which, and the choice of coffees, you can take a wander beneath Favières' waving poplars, to enjoy some more of the clean Bay air.

Touring Around

St-Valery-sur-Somme makes a natural focus for any visit to the Bay of the Somme. Spread along the side of the Bay, it consists of two halves, the old Ville-Haute on its hill, and the port and 'new town' (much of which is a few centuries old itself) beneath it to the east. The harbour is a very low-key affair: there are no docks or breakwaters, just a long **quay** winding round the shoreline from the end of the Somme Canal, alongside which a surprising number of fishing boats and small pleasure craft are moored in line. For several hours each day they rest on sand, and the only water to be seen is a shallow channel running out of the Canal. The quayside is a beguiling place to walk along, with a little gentle, unhurried activity usually in progress, and a few characterful bars with outside tables for taking in the scene. Within the last few years the building of the A16 *autoroute* has led to an increase in the Bay's popularity as a weekend destination for city-dwellers from the surrounding regions and even Paris, but this hasn't had too radical an effect on the town's atmosphere.

The quay runs into **Place des Pilotes**, which fills up with the main market on Sunday mornings, and a slightly smaller one on Wednesdays. West of the square, the road is closed to vehicles, and becomes the Quai Amiral Courbet, a tree-lined walkway where on Sunday evenings a large part of the town promenades up and down in positively Mediterranean fashion beside the water (or sand). Alongside there are several endearingly grand 1900s houses and villas, some notably ornate and some more discreet – the Guillaume de Normandy hotel by far the most extravagant – from a time when St-Valery enjoyed a brief vogue as a summer residence for affluent families from Amiens and other towns inland. Beneath the old town, the promenade simply runs out into the sand flats and the footpath to Cap Hornu.

St-Valery was a busy port in the early Middle Ages, when there was much less sand in the Bay. Thanks to its tides and the encroachment of the sandbanks it has been declining for much of the time since, but, against the odds, has never quite gone the way of Montreuil and other ex-harbours along this shifting coastline. The building of the Somme Canal at the beginning of the 19th century gave it a further reprieve, but traffic still did not become exactly intense, and the only interlude of concentrated activity came during the 1914–18 war when the British Army, stuck for alternatives, decided to use little St-Valery as a transit base for landing men and supplies from England.

At the eastern end of the quays, by the Somme Canal, stands the **Entrepôt des Sels**, a large 1736 salt warehouse built when salt was a royal monopoly. It sports a plaque indicating that William the Conqueror sailed from this spot on his way to Hastings in 1066. St-Valery was then in the midst of one of its greatest periods of activity. The rocky hill on which the old town stands was settled in the Neolithic era, and was used as a port by the Romans. In 611 an Irish monk called Walrick or Valerius (St Valery) came here, and founded an abbey that for some centuries was one of the most prestigious in the region. The town also became a stronghold. As the Bayeux Tapestry vividly recounts, a few years before 1066 Harold of Wessex, sent on a mission to Normandy by Edward the Confessor, was shipwrecked on the coast of France and held to ransom by Count Guy de Ponthieu, until the Count's powerful neighbour William of Normandy demanded his release. This was the first step in Harold's supposed debt of honour to William, which is made so much of in the tapestry. St-Valery was a prime possession of the Counts of Ponthieu, and it is believed that Harold was held here; just past the western end of the quays there are the remains of an ancient tower, the **Tour Harold**, where in local legend the Saxon earl was imprisoned. The Conqueror himself returned here by accident, and this is one of three places along the French coast that have monuments claiming to be his point of departure for England: Barfleur, where William himself embarked, Dives-sur-Mer, where he met up with his main force, and St-Valery, where the Norman fleet was obliged to put in by bad weather.

The little old town of St-Valery, the **Ville-Haute**, is one of the most charming and atmospheric of French walled towns. On market days the port area is sometimes vaguely busy; the old town scarcely ever. Its main entrance is the 16th-century **Porte de Nevers** at the end of Quai du Romerel, named after a family of local lords, some of whom still lived in the house above the gate until quite recently. It was badly damaged the last time St-Valery became a battle zone, in May 1940, but has been finely restored. The steep cobbled street beyond the gate leads to the **Eglise St-Martin**, an impressive church that conforms to none of the architectural rules: it has two complete naves of almost equal size, having had to be rebuilt several times after wars, fires and other catastrophes. The exterior, mostly from 1558, has some great gargoyles, and is made of stone and black flint in an eye-catching chessboard pattern typical of the Picardy coast. In the narrow streets near the church there are several houses in the same style. Next to the church is **Place St-Martin**, with a sheer drop on one side down to the quays, and a wonderful view over the Bay.

Because St-Valery peaked so early as a military stronghold no one ever saw a need to undertake any systematic renovation of its fortifications, and parts of its medieval walls are among the oldest still standing. The rough-brick **Porte Guillaume**, the western entrance to the Ville-Haute, now with flowers growing out of its towers, is definitely old enough to have been here when Duke William paid his visits. Joan of Arc was also brought through the gate as a prisoner in 1430, on her way to be handed over to the English in Rouen. Towards the Porte Guillaume the town is delightfully rural, and chickens and other animals scratch about in the gardens of many of the houses; roads that are ambitiously marked on the town map as 'rues' look more like grassy country lanes that no one has quite got round to finishing off. In Rue Brandt, on the south side of the Ville-Haute, there is a special garden, the **Herbarium** (*open May–12 Nov daily 10–12 and 3–6; adm*), within the one-time garden of an old convent-hospital, which seeks to preserve and revive the native plants and medicinal herbs that would have been seen in a medieval monastery garden.

A little way outside the Porte Guillaume are the walls of the old abbey, demolished after the Revolution, which now contain a luxurious private house. From there, a track leads through fields to the **Chapelle des Marins**, a 19th-century chapel in chessboard style built over the tomb of St Valery himself. Just beneath it there is a spring associated with the saint called the **Source de la Fidelité**, although the water is now murky enough to deter all but the most desperate pilgrims.

St-Valery also has an engaging folk museum, the **Musée Picarvie** (*5 Quai du Romerel; open mid-Feb–May and Sept–mid-Nov Mon, Wed–Sun 2–7; closed Tues; June–Aug daily 2–7; adm*), in the lower town. This is the work of an Abbeville builder, Paul Longuein, who over many years amassed a fascinating collection of over 6,000 items related to traditional crafts and every other aspect of life in the Picardy countryside, from tools, toys and cider presses to a whole schoolroom and shop interiors. One weekend in the middle of June each year, St-Valery holds its **Fêtes Guillaume-le-Conquérant**, when locals celebrate their most famous visitor by dressing up in medieval outfits, and enjoying parades, mock battles, music and fireworks.

The path along the Digue eventually comes to an end at **Le Hourdel**, a quite phenomenally calm and remote little fishing village with a lighthouse, a quay, a few boats and, for most of the day, no water. Past Le Hourdel the nature of the coast changes rapidly, from the marshy, placid bay to an endless bar of shingle and mounting waves along the edge of the open sea. If you have a car or bike, take the narrow coast route down to Cayeux, the Route Blanche, a mysterious-looking road between heather-clad dunes of brilliant white sand that often seem to threaten to envelop it completely. The shingle beach is usually deserted. Lost in the dunes is the curious little seaside village of **Brighton-les-Pins**, which once hoped to attract droves of English tourists with its name, and now looks a bit like a French town out of a Sam Shepherd story.

Beyond it is **Cayeux**, famous as a fishing port since the Middle Ages, which became a holiday resort in the 1900s. It has a long, rolling bank of a shingle and sand beach, with an old-fashioned seafront alongside that except in August seems far too big for the town. Just south of Cayeux is another area of marsh that forms the bird reserve of **Hable d'Ault**, tours of which are offered by the same CPIE organisation that runs the Nature en Somme office.

On the D3, slightly inland between St-Valery and Cayeux, the **Maison de l'Oiseau** (*open mid-Feb–June and Sept–mid-Nov daily 10–6; July–Aug daily 10–7; adm*) is an ornithological study centre in an old Picard farmhouse, with displays on the marsh birdlife that are heavily advertised but rather expensive.

Alternatively, take the road east from St-Valery, past Noyelles and more views over the *mollières* (salt marshes) to reach the north side of the Bay. Along the way, near Noyelles, a sign saying **Cimetière Chinois** points towards one of the area's strangest sites. When St-Valery was a British base during the First World War it was staffed, bizarrely, by Chinese labourers. In 1915 Britain began to recruit workers in China to make up for a labour shortage behind the lines, and at one time the 'Chinese Labour Corps' had over 90,000 men fetching and carrying for the army in France. Quite a few died here, due to disease more than enemy action, and are buried in the Chinese Cemetery at Nolette. It's one of the strangest of the many plots run by the Commonwealth War Graves Commission in France, and one of the saddest, for few relatives can ever have come to visit these graves.

Le Crotoy is known in French history as the place where Joan of Arc was first imprisoned after her capture by the Burgundians in 1430, but it also enjoyed a certain fashionable vogue at the end of the 19th century as a summer resort. Colette extolled the virtues of its light and giant skies, Seurat came to paint, Toulouse-Lautrec visited, and the Caudron brothers carried out some of the first experiments in French aviation on the sands. One of its first and most regular visitors was Jules Verne, who came here from Amiens virtually every summer; while here he spent a lot of time with the inventor and experimenter in submarining, Jacques-François Conseil, who provided much of the inspiration for *Twenty Thousand Leagues Under the Sea*. Thanks to its past Le Crotoy has elegant Belle Epoque houses and a casino, as well as a charming little fishing harbour and a giant beach.

North of Le Crotoy the flat marsh fields – all land given up by the sea over several centuries – are occupied only by very quiet villages like Favières or St-Firmin, and isolated farms next to clumps of trees. Inland the main centre in the northern Bay is **Rue**, a very likeable place that has all the amiable, everyday placidity of a classic French country town. It is another town that became an important baronial seat in the early Middle Ages, when it had access to the sea, and due to this former status it has some very fine architecture, especially the massive 15th-century Belfry, the Chapelle de l'Hospice and the superb 15th–16th-century Gothic Chapelle du St-Esprit.

From the D940 north of Rue another road, the D32, cuts west across to the sea and **Fort-Mahon Plage**, one of those curious little isolated seaside resorts that crop up around the French coasts, with a traditional promenade, rows of second homes and a golf course apparently half-hidden among the sand dunes. The similar but still smaller community of **Quend-Plage** stands just to the south. Quite lively each summer, out of season both have a quirky, almost wistful remoteness.

Between Le Crotoy and Fort-Mahon is one of the Bay's foremost attractions, recommended to anyone who wishes to see some of the local birdlife. The wildlife reserve of **Marquenterre** (*t 03 22 25 03 06; open mid-Mar–mid-Nov daily; mid-Nov–mid-Mar Sun and hols; April–Sept 9.30–7, last admission 5; Oct–Mar 10–6, last admission 4; adm exp*) occupies one of the most beautiful areas around the Bay, a 2,300-hectare stretch of marsh, lake and dunes. It's extremely well-organised for visitors, with a clear *parcours d'initiation* path with good viewpoints from which you can see plenty of duck, geese, herons, waders and, with luck, polecats and wild boar. A walk around it takes about an hour, or more. Those who wish to see more can follow longer paths into the reserve, to look for rarer species such as storks and spoonbill.

Activities

For exploring the Bay of the Somme outside St-Valery, there are alternatives to walking or driving. Railway enthusiasts and many others drool over the **Chemin de Fer de la Baie de la Somme**, a genuine 1900s narrow-gauge steam railway that runs from Le Crotoy through Noyelles and St-Valery to Cayeux (*three trains each afternoon April–Sept Sun and usually Wed and Sat; July and Aug daily exc Mon*). In St-Valery, the little station is right at the Canal end of the quays (information **t** 03 22 26 96 96). **Cycles** can be hired from Au Vélocipède, 1 Rue du Puits Salé, **t** 03 22 26 96 80, near the church in the Ville-Haute, and there is a centre on the quays offering **kayaks** for rent and guided trips; the tourist office has details. The north side of the Bay, where the sand is firmer, is popular for **sandyachting**.

There are a great many **walks around the Bay**, and tourist offices have handy booklets that show a range of accessible paths. An easy and popular (if muddy) walk at low tide is simply to follow the well-marked path from the end of the quays, past the little resort development at Cap Hornu and along the *digue* or dike beside the *mollières* (salt marshes) towards the mouth of the Bay. The full distance is nearly 10km. The patterns of the channels and swathes of grasses and marsh flowers are infinitely variable; at times, there's a strong sea wind; otherwise the stillness is impenetrable. Birdlife includes virtually every kind of European wetland and wading bird, but especially oystercatchers, avocets, wild geese and ducks.

There are also paths that cross the sandbanks and marshes, but **walks into the Bay** itself should *never be attempted without a guide*; there are dangerous patches of quicksand, and, while the sea may often be lost to view, it can also return with remarkable speed. Guided walks into the Bay are run from the little **Nature en Somme** office in St-Valery (*see* p.109). They normally last about three hours and cover about 7km. Even if you only walk along the Bay shore, it's still advisable to have with you a current tide table, available from the tourist office.

At Le Crotoy, Fort-Mahon and in St-Quentin-en-Tourmont, near Marquenterre, there are also centres that offer **pony-trekking** through the empty dunes; local tourist offices have all the details.

Shopping

The Baie de la Somme is not one of the great shopping centres of France, so for anyone looking for local foods and produce all attention is concentrated on the weekly town markets. The Place des Pilotes market in **St-Valery** (Sun morning, with a smaller gathering Wed) is one of the liveliest, with spectacular displays of mussels and Somme Bay shrimps, known as *sauterelles*, as well as more portable things such as pâtés and terrines. **Le Crotoy** has a fine market (June–Sept Fri mornings and Tues), that's especially good for fresh fish. The Saturday market in **Rue**'s Place Verdun is a real country market, with wonderful fresh vegetables, superb breads, cakes, cheeses and all kinds of derivatives of duck.

Where to Stay

Favières ✉ 80120
Mme Claudine Roussel, 773 Rue de Romaine, **t/f** 03 22 27 21 07 (*double rooms 280F/ €42.69*). Mme Roussel has four B&B rooms in her pretty, modernised Picard farmhouse right in the middle of Favières (and within walking distance of the Clé des Champs). The rooms are all bright and comfortable, and it's excellent for anyone interested in walking in the marshes, or just looking for complete rural tranquillity.

St-Valery-sur-Somme ✉ 80230
M and Mme Deloison, 1 Quai du Romerel, **t/f** 03 22 26 92 17 (*rooms 280F/€42.69 for two, 320F/€48.78 for three; apartment 900F/€137.20 for one night, 1,600F/€243.92 for two, 700F/€106.71 per night for four nights or more*). Escapees from the city, the Deloisons make driftwood sculptures and have an antiques and second-hand shop next to the quay and market square in St-Valery (easily locatable by the plain sign *Brocante*), and they and their kids live above

the shop. Their B&B rooms are next door in a creaky 19th-century house. The rooms are a tad untidy, and there are bikes, old toys and bird sculptures in the hallway, but they have loads of engaging features, and the top-floor double has wonderful views across the Bay and up river. Thre is also a rather different and quite superb self-contained apartment available for weekend and short-term stays. With a striking contemporary design and more great Bay views – it has been featured in French style magazines – it has two very comfortable double rooms and space for up to six.

La Gribane, 297 Quai Jeanne d'Arc, **t** 03 22 60 97 55 (*doubles 390F/€59.46; suite, with the option of a kitchenette, 450F/€68.60 for two, 750F/€114.34 for four*). A really lovely B&B in one of the elaborate 1900s villas along the bayfront in St-Valery, which Michèle and Jean-Pierre Douchet have beautifully restored with a mix of tasteful modern style and a few maritime accessories (sea shells, sea pictures) to suit the setting. The guest rooms fill with light, and looking out at the endless view over the still Bay is wonderful for clearing the head. There's also a pretty garden, evening meals are available on request, and delicious fresh breakfasts are served in another big, bright room with a view of the Bay.

Le Relais Guillaume de Normandie, 46 Quai du Romerel, **t** 03 22 60 82 36, **f** 03 22 60 81 82 (*rooms 300–360F/€45.73–54.88*). St-Valery's most distinctive hotel, a large, elaborate house and garden in a style that's a mix of neo-Gothic, art-nouveau and Norman/Picard traditional, several storeys high and topped off with roofs that in parts are almost pagoda-like. It has a fairy-tale appearance, especially the tower up one side with its spiral staircase; local legend maintains the house was built in the 1890s for an English Lord who set up his French mistress here and maintained trysts with her every weekend, although it seems more likely it was put up for an Amiens textile magnate. The 14 rooms are not quite as spectacular as the public areas and are a little small, so that they could be described as 'snugly comfortable', but still have their characterfully creaking woodwork and ornate touches like

red-flock wallpaper. Some rooms also have great views of the Bay. For the restaurant, see below.

M and Mme Servant, 117 Rue au Feurre, **t** 03 22 60 97 56 (*rooms 290–300F/€44.21–45.73*). A pretty *chambre-d'hôte* with three rooms and one family-sized two-room suite, in a gracious, big old house in the middle of the old Ville-Haute. The owners are charming, and there's a flowery garden in front of the house, which you are free to use.

Rue ✉ 80120

Le Lion d'Or, 5 Rue de la Barrière, **t** 03 22 25 74 18, **f** 03 22 25 66 63 (*double rooms 300–500F/€45.73–76.22*). A pleasant, traditional family-run little Logis de France hotel, in a partly half-timbered old inn on the main street of Rue, well-placed for the Baie de la Somme or the Montreuil area. Some of the 16 recently renovated rooms are smallish, but they're all well-equipped and distinctly cosy, and the owners, M and Mme Vandeville, make everyone very welcome. The equally comfortable **restaurant** (*menus from 85F/€12.96*) keeps to an unchanging French-small-town style, with bargain menus featuring plenty of seafood, duck and (in season) game.

Ault ✉ 80460

La Catouillette, Hautebut, **t** 03 22 60 51 02, **f** 03 22 60 51 25 (*double room 300F/€45.73*). Mme Danielle Zuccheri lives alone with her dogs and cats in this modern house in the tiny village of Hautebut, on the very edge of the Hable d'Ault bird reserve. She has just one room which is big, very comfortable and well-equipped. There's a lovingly tended garden, with tables for breakfast outside in summer. Ideal for anyone interested in cycling, walking and especially bird-watching in the Somme marshes.

Eating Alternatives

Quend-Plage ✉ 80120

Auberge Le Fiacre, Hameau de Routhiauville, Rue des Pommiers, **t** 03 22 23 47 30, **f** 03 22 27 19 80 (*weekday lunch menu 115F/€17.53, other menus 165–230F/€25.15–35.06*). In an isolated location in the flat marsh country behind Fort-Mahon, this old farm has nevertheless been very smartly renovated, and the atmosphere has a distinct touch of plush and luxury. The restaurant has a high reputation for its refined, seasonally changing versions of local classics such as *ficelles picardes*, fine fish and seafood and Baie de la Somme lamb. Part of the Relais du Silence hotel group, the Fiacre also has 11 similarly smart **guest rooms** (*380–450F/€57.93–68.60*), all on the ground floor facing the large garden.

Fort-Mahon ✉ 80790

Auberge de la Louvière, 27 Rue de Robinson, **t** 03 22 27 71 53 (*menus 95–240F/ €14.48–36.59*). A very charming, simple, family-run restaurant surrounded by a garden in the little resort of Fort-Mahon, offering few *haute-cuisine* frills but a very likeable welcome. The ample menus offer a wide range, from local favourites such as *ficelles picardes*, grills and enjoyable fish and seafood up to quite opulent dishes. It's a little out of the way down a side street, but find the central avenue of Fort-Mahon and there are signs to direct you to it.

Le Crotoy ✉ 80550

Chez Mado, 6 Quai Léonard, **t** 03 22 27 81 22 (*weekdays and Sat lunch menu 90F/€13.72, other menus 130–290F/€19.82–44.21*). On the seafront in Le Crotoy and with a fabulous view of the bay from its first-floor *salle panoramique*, Chez Mado doesn't look like any average French seaside restaurant; built all of wood, it has big timber balconies along both floors, in a style that's a mixture of French nautical and Wild West. Inside, tables fill up on summer weekends with contented diners making their way through plates of quality fresh fish and seafood. Set menus offer lots of choices, with enjoyable favourites such as a *panaché de la mer*, sole, pollack, prawns and other assorted seafood simply cooked *au beurre blanc*; there's a menu dedicated to lobster (*450F/€68.60*).

St-Valery-sur-Somme ✉ 80230

Le Relais Guillaume de Normandie, *see above* (*menus 85–220F/€12.96–33.54*). The dining room at the Guillaume de Normandie,

appealingly old-fashioned-ornate with flock wallpaper and gilt fittings, matches the rest of the hotel, although the most beautiful part of it is the plainer conservatory section overlooking the Bay, with misty views to accompany your lunch. Menus feature a combination of local dishes and others from a more general French repertoire: an *assiette de fruits de mer* featuring prawns and Somme Bay shrimps, classic *ficelles picardes*, beautifully fresh fish dishes such as skate simmered in a delicately garlicky *crème d'ail doux* and particularly *pré-salé* lamb, the house's speciality, prepared in several different ways. There is a memorable cheese board. *Open July and Aug only*.

Relais Les Quatre Saisons, 2 Place Croix l'Abbé, **t** 03 22 60 51 01 (*menus 140F/€21.34, 190F/ €28.97 and 240F/€36.59*). This unostentatious little restaurant, on one side of a large, open square by the Cayeux road on the south side of St-Valery's Haute-Ville, is quite easy to miss, but has won praise for the quality of its cuisine, and especially its commitment to the finest quality, fresh ingredients. Local dishes and produce, naturally, are highlighted – rack of *pré-salé* lamb *aux herbes*, *blanquette* of squid – and the menu typically follows market availability. The well-aged, rustic setting is offset by neat yellow linen, and the restaurant has plenty of St-Valery's infinitely soothing calm.

Le Nicol's, 15 Rue de la Ferté, **t** 03 22 26 82 96 (*menus 78–160F/€11.89–24.39*). On the main street of St-Valery's 'new town', near the tourist office, Le Nicol's has all the look of a pretty French small-town restaurant – smart linen, flowers, neat table settings – but also presents some surprises. Excellent local fish and seafood are the mainstays of the kitchen, but the menus combine dishes based on local classics – *moules, filets de sole aux crevettes, pôelée de St-Jacques*, rich meat dishes like beef in a wine sauce – with radical touches like an inventive use of fruit, as in *ailes de raie à la framboise* (skate wings with a raspberry sauce). Chorizo and other Spanish ingredients also crop up in several dishes, and one of the house specialities is paella (*65F/€9.91*).

The Cathedral and the Canals:
Amiens

13

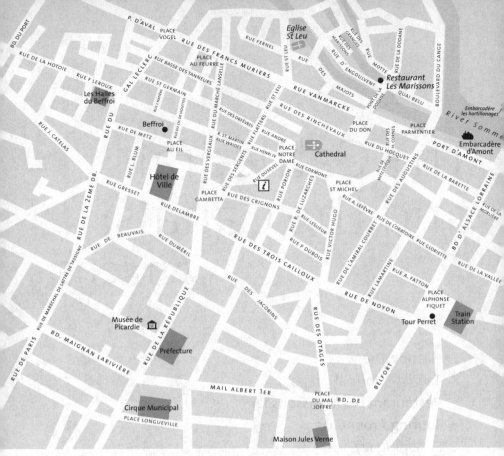

Amiens, capital of Picardy, is an historic city with a substantial modern sprawl and a charming and attractive heart. It was badly scarred in both world wars, but in the middle of town there are still small, atmospheric streets and squares along the banks of the River Somme, where the Roman city was founded. It also has fine shops, a large student population, and a sparky street, café and night life; one of the best of France's regional museums; and a great cathedral, France's largest, described by John Ruskin as the most perfect creation of medieval Christianity in northern Europe.

It is, though, Amiens' natural setting that most makes it such an engaging place to explore. In the 1470s, when it was one of the most important merchant cities in Europe, Louis XI of France called it 'my little Venice', and the reasons why are just as evident today. The Somme divides around a string of narrow islands, connected by footbridges and lined by old, steep-roofed houses with many-coloured façades that lean and bend. Just to the east the river runs through hundreds of man-made canals between drained marsh-gardens, the Hortillonages, which bring a stretch of silent, watery countryside right into the centre of the city. The produce from the dark, heavy soil of these allotments is a special feature of Amienois cooking. And in the heart of Amiens' canal district, in a former boatyard that once produced boats for working the Hortillonages, is **Les Marissons**, a strikingly attractive restaurant where chef Antoine Benoit creates refined dishes using the very best of local ingredients.

Getting There

Amiens has a fairly complicated road system, but if you come by car aim for *centre-ville* and the ring of boulevards, which as usual run around the core of town. Parking in the centre is restricted, with pay-and-display ticket machines on most streets, but outside the boulevards parking is free, so leave your car along or behind the boulevards on the south side, near the Cirque Municipal and the Mail Albert 1er. From there, it's an easy walk up Rue de la République to the centre of town. To go directly to Les Marissons, veer right at the end of Rue de la République up Rue des Sergents and Rue Dusevel to the cathedral, and then past the cathedral down to the canal

district, Quartier St-Leu. Les Marissons is next to the main bridge across the river to St-Leu, Pont de la Dodane. Amiens is 1½hrs' drive from Calais on the A16 *autoroute*, two hours by other roads, and 1¼hrs from Paris.

Amiens also has good train connections with Paris, Rouen, Calais, Lille and many other destinations. The station is beside the ring of boulevards, east of the city centre.

Tourist Information

Amiens: 6 bis Rue Dusevel, t 03 22 71 60 50, f 03 22 71 60 51, www.amiens.com (open April–Sept Mon–Sat 9.30–7, Sun 10–12 and 2–5; Oct–Mar Mon–Sat 9.30–6, Sun 10–12 and 2–5; closed 25 Dec and 1 Jan).

Les Marissons

Pont de la Dodane, Quartier St-Leu, t 03 22 92 96 66, f 03 22 91 50 50, www.les-marissons.fr. Open Mon–Fri 12–2 and 7.30–10, Sat 7.30–10; closed Sun and 24 Dec–3 Jan. Book always. Menus 120F/€18.29, 180F/€27.44, 220F/€33.54 and 295F/€44.97; à la carte average 400F/€60.98.

There has been a boatyard on the spot now occupied by Les Marissons – on a spit of land between two of the Somme canals by the bridge into the Quartier St-Leu – since the 1480s, and the main building was probably erected not long afterwards. It was first employed in making the long, narrow boats used for working the Hortillonages, and more recently served as an artist's studio. As a restaurant it's wonderfully pretty. Inside, the massive old timbers are offset by yellows and blues, in walls, floors and linen; everything is very elegantly and carefully presented, whether plates, settings, the armchairs where you can take an *apéritif* or the magnificent flower arrangements that all add to a discreetly indulgent ambience ideal for an intimate dinner. There are a few of the odd little accoutrements that often turn up even in the most tasteful settings in France – Cabotan puppets, an effigy of a duck hanging from the ceiling – but they're understated; the young but well-schooled waitresses are sweet and charming. When the weather's suitable there are also tables outside in the flower-lined garden-courtyard beside the canal, with a view across the river to the cathedral.

The boatyard was taken over by Antoine Benoit and his wife and converted into a restaurant in 1986. It has been acknowledged as Amiens' premier restaurant pretty much ever since. Wiry and softly spoken, M Benoit shows all the painstaking, quietly obsessive dedication to his craft of a true French chef, the kind of man who can discourse at some length on the varying textures of different kinds of fish. His greatest specialities are fish and duck, but his cooking is based above all on whatever's at its best in the market. Menus change daily, and this is a restaurant where it's always a good idea to ask which dishes are most recommended for that day – especially among the fish. (Mme Benoit speaks very competent English.)

Many of the dishes are also notably intricate, and often radical in their matches of ingredients. In *carpaccio de St-Jacques au piment d'Espelette et aux figues* raw, briny scallops are combined with fruit and chilli pepper, in a daring and memorable display of strong but surprisingly complementary flavours; *dos de turbotin à la fondue de poireaux* features beautiful fish with a truly fabulous leek sauce, smooth, supremely subtle and with a mysterious depth of seasoning. Les Marissons' house foie gras has a reputation all of its own, and in autumn dishes such as a fricassée of mixed wild mushrooms with *confit* of garlic are superb. Complex, delicate stuffings with roast meats are another Benoit forte, as in the satisfying saddle of rabbit stuffed with goats' cheese and rosemary.

The traditional French cheese course is something that's tending to be neglected in some more contemporary-style restaurants, but this is one place where it shouldn't be missed: the range and the quality are quite wonderful, from a perfect northern Maroilles to fine Fourme d'Ambert and other central and southern French cheeses. There's also an excellent wine list, with an unusually wide choice available in half-bottles or by the glass. Desserts are, like the other courses, highly inventive and enjoyable. And, when you haved finished your coffee, you need only wander a few metres from the comfort of Les Marissons to the riverside *terrasses* of Quai Bélu.

Touring Around

If you begin a visit to Amiens by leaving your car on the southern boulevards, near Mail Albert 1er, you will immediately notice the **Cirque Municipal**, an odd drum-like building with many ornate 19th-century details, which today is most often used for concerts. It is inseparably associated with one of Amiens' most celebrated residents, **Jules Verne**. He was actually born in Nantes, but in 1856 he came to Amiens for the wedding of a friend, and fell in love with the bride's sister, Honorine. They would be married for nearly 50 years. The couple lived here permanently from 1871, and Verne became an institution in the city. He was one of the first truly commercial authors – in 1862 he signed a contract with the publisher Hetzel to deliver three books a year – and by far the wealthiest writer of his day in France (if not Europe). The inventor of science fiction was also not the kind of author who hid himself away in his study; instead, he busied himself with every aspect of Amiens life, served on the city council, and in 1875 even produced a book called *An Ideal City: Amiens in the year 2000*, full of ideas (such as mechanised communal child-rearing) which so far have scarcely been taken up. Another of his great many interests was the circus, and in 1889 he badgered his fellow-councillors into giving Amiens one of the world's few permanent circus-halls.

In front of it there is a plaque that records that from the same spot, Place Longueville, the great man also made a flight in a balloon, in 1873. Just east of here at 44 Boulevard Jules Verne, parallel to the main boulevard, is the house where he died in 1905, although the **Maison Jules Verne** (*2 Rue Charles Dubois; guided tours Tues–Fri*

9–12 and 2–5.30, Sat and Sun 2–5.30; adm), where he actually lived most of the time, is just around the corner. Now a museum, several of the rooms are much as they were in the Vernes' time; there are models of flying machines, the *Nautilus* and other Vernian imaginings, and engaging displays on his life and times.

From the Circus cross the main boulevard and walk up Rue de la République (a route regularly taken by Verne on his constitutionals with his dog) to reach the **Musée de Picardie** (*open Tues–Sun 10–12.30 and 2–6; adm*). The grandest building in Amiens after the cathedral, it's a Second-Empire wedding cake of a museum, comparable to the Paris Opera, opened by Napoleon III in 1867 and with a large 'N' for Napoleon and 'E' for his Empress Eugénie built into the front. Inside it is still more imposing, with a giant main staircase and a vast Grand Salon with murals by the Symbolist artist Puvis de Chavannes. They present a fanciful vision of the prehistoric Picards, but their monumental size, style and curious stillness are very impressive, and they influenced Gauguin and many later artists. Finally, even if you don't feel like a coffee, take a look at the cafeteria, a neo-Gothic, neo-Byzantine extravaganza in red, blue and gold.

The museum collection is also highly impressive, especially since its greatest treasures are local. There are a great many fine **Roman artefacts**, many from excavations of the first Amiens, Samarobriva or 'Bridge-over-the-Somme', which in the 2nd century AD was the most important city in northern Gaul, twice the size of Paris. Other rooms contain wonderful **medieval sculptures** in wood and stone, mostly from Picardy and other parts of northern France; look out for the exquisitely modelled series of bas-reliefs on the *Life of Christ*, from around 1500. Most extraordinary, though, and unique, are the **Puys**, paintings offered to Amiens Cathedral during the 16th century by the Fraternity of Notre-Dame, an association of local merchants. It was the custom for each new master of the Fraternity to commission a painting, and together they present a panorama of Amiens and its burghers over more than a century. The artists were anonymous, but the paintings are superb – the *Vierge au Palmier* from 1520, for example, presents a vision of the city akin to Brueghel.

Beyond the Puys there are also several fine works by more familiar, 'named' artists – El Greco, Salvator Rosa, Frans Hals and other Dutch masters, Fragonard and Boucher. The more modern sections are not so eye-catching, but the museum has one great contemporary addition in *Wall Drawing 711*, a rotunda on the ground floor painted in 1992 by the American artist Sol LeWitt in a whole spectrum of colours in complex, interacting geometrical patterns.

Opposite the museum there is an elegant Louis XV *hôtel particulier* that now houses the **Prefecture of Picardy**, but as you continue towards the city centre the architecture becomes more plainly modern and uniform. Amiens was a wealthy textile town from the early Middle Ages, and attained its greatest prestige around the time when the Puys were painted. Much of old Amiens, however, was destroyed in just two days, 18 and 19 May 1940, when German bombers rained incendiaries on the city: the cathedral and many larger stone buildings emerged remarkably undamaged, but most of the old wooden houses in the centre went up like torches. Post-war, much of the city centre was rebuilt in a simple, unobtrusive modern style according to a plan by the architect Pierre Dufau.

Rue de la République ends when it meets the long, arterial street that, under different names, cuts across the city centre and forms its main commercial thorough-fare. (Look to the right and away in the distance, where the street is called Rue de Noyon, you can see the busy area around the train station, with, on the left, a distinctly odd-looking 1940s concrete skyscraper, the **Tour Perret**, built during the post-war reconstruction years.) The now-pedestrianised **Rue des Trois Cailloux** is the heart of Amiens' main shopping area. To the left, as Rue Delambre, the street leads to the very large **Hôtel de Ville**, rebuilt after the war. The square in front of the city hall was remodelled in the 1990s to an innovative, locally controversial design by the Catalan architect Joan Roig, with some intriguing inclined fountains; across Rue des Trois Cailloux from Rue de la République there is also a still more recent modernistic space, triangular **Place Gambetta**, completed only in 2000, which, however, has in the middle of it the **Horloge Dewailly**, an extravagantly elaborate 1890s Beaux-Arts style clock that has been lavishly restored in all its green, red and gold glory.

Walk around the Hôtel de Ville and you come to a survivor of the 1940 fires, the solid 15th-century belfry, **Le Beffroi**, once, as it looks, a prison. Close by there is a glass-walled modern market hall, **Les Halles du Beffroi**. This is not the most atmospheric of French markets, but it's a great place to find high-quality foods and local produce, especially the beautiful cheese stands of Gérard Quentin.

From there, walk back past the Beffroi and across a few more streets to approach the cathedral. For the moment continue past it across the *parvis* or square, go down the steps on the other side and turn right down little Rue des Rinchevaux to reach the riverside district and **Place du Don**, an attractive cobbled square with 16th-century houses on three sides, some original and some restored, and the river on the other. Virtually every house contains an antique shop, restaurant or bar with pavement tables, and this is a major centre of evening and night-life. Just off the square at 67 Rue du Don is the tiny shop of Jean-Pierre Facquier, only remaining maker of the traditional Amiens puppets, the Cabotans, at the centre of which is always Lafleur, a roguish, Mr Punch figure in a red suit, considered the archetypal Amiens and Picard character.

The many renovations in Amiens in the last few years have included what seems to be almost the handing-over of whole parts of the riverside to the university, and large sections of Rue Vanmarcke and its continuations, running west from Place du Don, now contain shiny new but fairly anonymous academic buildings. This college-spread has only increased the popularity of Place du Don and St-Leu across the river for studenty socialising, and there are plenty of buzzing bars, and a clutch of bigger discos mostly on Rue des Francs Mûriers. A more traditional note is struck in Place Parmentier, across the road from Place du Don, where on many Thursday and Saturday mornings vegetable and fruit growers from the Hortillonages tie up their boats packed with produce to sell direct (in June virtually all the growers take part in the Fête des Hortillons by the quay, one of France's most special markets). Look left from the quayside, towards Pont de la Dodane, and you see a man standing in mid-river, which never fails to entertain kids. This is actually a sculpture by the German artist Balkenhol, and if you look back at Place du Don you'll see two more of his strangely life-like figures on either side, a man and a woman.

And across the river is Amiens' engaging little Venice, the canalside quarter of **St-Leu**, spread across the islands in the Somme with little streets, alleys and bridges along and between the quiet waterways. This was formerly the weavers' and dyers' district, and the ne'er-do-well proletarian Lafleur is always seen as a native of St-Leu. It was less damaged than other areas in 1940, thanks to the river, but was run-down until restoration was begun in the 1980s, since when it has become newly fashionable. St-Leu's houses are endlessly varied: original half-timbered, stucco or plain brick, and with woodwork painted in greens, blues, ochres and reds. One at least, 56 Rue des Marissons, looks only two metres wide. And as you wander round – the only way to do it – you'll also find individual craft and antique shops, especially on Rue Motte and in the arcade behind Rue de la Dodane.

The great social focus of St-Leu is **Quai Bélu**, the picturesque stretch of quayside across from Place du Don, with restaurants, dance-bars, a music venue and more peaceful cafés that all have terrace tables beside the river whenever the weather's favourable. It's an extremely pretty spot, and a very relaxing place to find in the middle of a city. Near the eastern end of the *quai*, on the other side of the last bridge, there is a recent addition to the area, an unusually grand landing stage for local rowing clubs, the **Embarcadère d'Amont**, which is also the departure point for the Bateau Restaurant Le Picardie (**t** 03 22 92 16 40), which offers cruises on the Somme with dinner included. Although it was only built in 1998, the Embarcadère has elaborate Victorian-looking balustrades, arches and other decorative touches, in a neo-Vernian style that seems to have been taken up as the 'heritage style' of Amiens.

Immediately after lunch is the best time to visit the water gardens of the **Hortillonages**. To get to the landing-point, follow the signs along the river bank to the right from Place du Don, cross the Boulevard de Beauvillé bridge, and the entrance is on the right. Tours (*April–Oct daily from 2pm on demand; the last tour may leave anytime between 3–7; tours last c. 1hr; adm*) of some of the over 50km of channels are run by the association of allotment holders in their traditional long, black, motorised punts.

Vegetable plots on land drained from the Somme were known here in Roman times, and have been extended ever since. As in the Marais of St-Omer, this wet, green maze has given rise to its own legends, and has been used as a place of refuge, most recently by Resistance fighters in the Second World War. At the beginning of the 20th century nearly a thousand people lived on the Hortillonages, a separate community. Only a handful do so now, but many people work the plots or use them as a weekend retreat. As you travel almost at water level around the apparently endless, silent canals, you see some plots that are neat gardens, with clipped hedges and even garden gnomes, and others that are more reminiscent of a mangrove swamp. Some contain whole swathes of parsley or celery, others rows of bright flowers. There are birds everywhere, and on some plots also goats, kept to keep down the fast-growing marsh grass. It's a world of wonderful serenity, with its own fresh, still air.

This leaves till last the **cathedral**, up on its hill above Place du Don. For many it is the greatest of all Gothic cathedrals. Ruskin called the staggering **west façade**, with its hundreds of figures of saints, apostles and biblical scenes, 'the Bible in stone'. It entranced him particularly because he saw in it the perfect example of his idea of the medieval unity of art and craft, and indeed in the small roundels around the base of the three portals, portraying virtues and vices or the course of the seasons, you can see every element of 13th-century life represented. According to legend the central statue of Jesus, the *Beau Dieu*, was sculpted directly from a vision of Christ, and is extremely beautiful.

If you are disconcerted by the plain modern block at the foot of the cathedral, with its chocolate and souvenir shop, you are not alone. The ambitious plan of architect Bernard Huet for the renovation of the **cathedral square** has been hugely controversial, but was pushed through by the city nonetheless; the theory behind it was apparently that in the Middle Ages the space around the cathedral would have been smaller and more full of daily coming and going, and that by building on to the square some of this atmosphere would be regained; but the new buildings are loathed by most of Amiens. However, one other feature of the reconstruction work has been the comprehensive cleaning of the cathedral's west façade, and the result of this is staggering. It's now probably cleaner than at any time since it was first built, and the details of its many levels are hypnotic. The façade and all its figures were once painted in bright colours, and the original colours are now projected in a very state-of-the-art *son et lumière* back on to the façade, in an awe-inspiring, hugely effective spectacle (*mid-June–Sept and Christmas at sunset*).

When your neck can no longer stand craning up at the west façade, walk around the outside of the cathedral to take in its elaborate buttresses and gargoyles before going inside. It has to be said that from the outside, especially from a distance, it can look odd: it seems too tall for its length, and has a strange, slender spire, the **Flèche**, made of wood clad in lead, from 1529. Inside, though, Amiens Cathedral soars like no other. Vaults and columns give the impression of reaching up forever, and the high windows give the nave a special luminosity. It was begun in 1220 after Amiens had acquired the head of John the Baptist, brought here in dubious circumstances after the Fourth Crusade (it can still be seen in the cathedral treasury). Most of it was built within 50 years, which gives it an unusual unity of style. Also, unusually for a medieval building, it has a known first architect, Robert de Luzarches, who died in about 1225, and whose name is written in the centre of the great 'Labyrinth' in the intricate tiled floor.

Amiens Cathedral has many treasures, and it is only possible to mention a few of them here. If the façade is the Bible in stone, the **choir stalls** are the Bible in wood, carved by Amiens craftsmen between 1508 and 1522. The outside walls of the choir, in the Ambulatory, are just as impressive, and have also been finely restored. Two series of scenes in polychrome painted stone from the early 16th century depict the life of John the Baptist, on one side, and St Firmin, credited with having brought Christianity to Amiens, on the other. The detail and the colour of each scene are extraordinary, and, once again, they give a vivid picture of life at the time – look, for example, at the carving of the birth of St John, with the midwife bathing the baby. And, before you leave, look up to the three great **rose windows**. Much of their glass is no longer the original, but they are still breathtaking, more glass and light than stone. Afterwards, walk back down to Quai Bélu for a drink, and a great view of the cathedral from across the river.

Shopping

Amiens' culinary specialities are *macarons d'Amiens*, almond and fruit macaroons, known since at least 1855; and *pâté de canard d'Amiens*, first mentioned in 1643.

Rue des Trois Cailloux and Rue Delambre – really the same street – form the shopping heart of Amiens. The Les Halles market has many other fine stalls: La Corbeille Paysanne is a cooperative outlet for local farm produce.

Amiens ✉ 80000

Le Fromathèque Picard-Gérard Quentin, Marché des Halles du Beffroi, t 03 22 91 96 22. The two giant stands of master cheese-merchant Gérard Quentin stand out vividly among the many others in the Halles: superb arrays of cheeses – local Picard Belval or Riceys, and others from the rest of France.

H. Martigny et Fils, 12 Rue Albert Dauphin, t 03 22 91 57 51, f 03 22 80 85 51. Founded in 1850, and one of the most attractive fine wine and spirits merchants you could ever find, with bottle-racks arranged like books for browsing. There are wonderful French wines, especially from Bordeaux; and *c.* 150 whiskies, equally superb selections of champagne, calvados and brandies, plus over 180 beers. Many of the staff speak English, and are charming and knowledgeable. The shop is in a street alongside the Hôtel de Ville.

Schaetjens, 21 Rue des Trois Cailloux, t 03 22 91 32 73. Amiens' foremost *chocolatier-pâtissier-traiteur*, with dazzling window displays. All their *gâteaux*, pastries and chocolates are made by hand, and they claim proudly to be the most authentic makers of *macarons d'Amiens*. Also a renowned *traiteur*, producing the city's most celebrated duck pâté and a range of other savoury dishes. Upstairs there is an enticing *salon de thé*.

Jean Trogneaux, Parvis de la Cathédrale, t 03 22 72 07 72. The 'other' well-known macaroon-producer in town, run by the same family since 1872, has four shops in Amiens (the largest is at 1 Rue Delambre, near the Hôtel de Ville), and more in other cities. They also sell chocolates, chocolate *gâteaux* and especially *tuiles*, chocolate-coated almond biscuits.

Where to Stay

Amiens ✉ 80000

Relais Mercure Amiens Cathédrale, 17–19 Place au Feurre, t 03 22 22 00 20, f 03 22 91 86 57, *www.escalotel.com/relais.merc.amiens* (*double rooms 450–510F/€68.60–77.75*). When in 1998 the Mercure chain took over Amiens' former 18th-century coaching inn, Le Postillon, it adapted the rambling building – partly out of necessity, for it's a listed historic monument – with some taste and imagination. It combines something of the feel of a business hotel with modern comfort and the special features of an old *hôtel particulier* – a grand Louis XV façade, a courtyard with baroque fountain. There's a cocktail bar, 'Le Tour du Monde'.

Hôtel Alsace-Lorraine, 18 Rue de la Morlière, t/f 03 22 91 35 71 (*single rooms 180F/€27.44; double rooms 300–400F/€45.73–60.98; breakfast 35F/€5.34*). In a district of 19th century terraced houses just east of the boulevards – but still an easy walk from the cathedral and St-Leu – this hotel has a smart all-white interior and lots of fresh flowers. The 13 rooms have their foibles – some of the bathrooms are a little elderly – but the owners are charming, breakfasts are ample and the hotel is very popular. The larger, recently renovated rooms around the little courtyard are the best.

Hôtel Le Prieuré, 17 Rue Porion, t 03 22 92 27 67, f 03 22 92 46 16 (*double rooms 250–400F/ €38.11–60.98*). This distinctive hotel has rather been through the wars, but it is due to be fully open once again in May 2001. It has a superb location, right around a corner from the cathedral, and an enjoyable eccentricity. Some of the rooms are quite plain and simple, others are quite luxurious. A Logis de France hotel, the Prieuré also has a reliable, traditional **restaurant** (*closed during restoration; menus from 110F/€16.77*).

Hôtel de Normandie, 1 bis Rue Lamartine, t 03 22 91 74 99, f 03 22 92 06 56 (*double rooms 180–280F/€27.44–42.69; family rooms from 320F/€48.78*). A likeable and good value hotel in a rather grand Belle Epoque townhouse between the station and the centre. Its rooms are plain but comfortable, with good facilities. There's a very pretty breakfast room with restored art nouveau glass, and off-street parking for a small extra charge. The staff are unfussily friendly.

Hôtel au Spatial, 15 Rue Alexandre Fatton, t 03 22 91 53 23, f 03 22 92 27 87 (*double rooms from 260F/€39.64*). Under the same ownership as the Normandie, about 100m away, this is a plain, modern building, with simple, comfortable rooms with good facilities and free parking. The hotel's functional lines are softened by bright flower displays and the staff are charming and helpful.

Creuse ✉ 80480

Mme Monique Lemaître, 26 Rue Principale, t 03 22 38 91 50 (*double rooms 250F/€338.11; suite 350F/€53.36 for two, 500F/€76.22 for four*). A pleasant B&B in the peaceful village of Creuse, off the N29 about 12km west of Amiens. A big old Picard farmhouse, with red-tile roofs and single-storey wings around a lovely garden. The guest rooms are large and imaginatively decorated, with kilims and unusual antiques, and there's a delightful breakfast room. Mme Lemaître hosts special weekends for walkers and residential courses in painting, French and English. *Chambre-d'hôtes rooms available April–Oct; they can be rented on a longer-term basis in winter.*

Eating Alternatives

Amiens ✉ 80000

La Couronne, 64 Rue St-Leu, t 03 22 91 88 57 (*menus 92–180F/€14.03–27.44*). Philippe Gravier's snug restaurant has long been known in Amiens as one of the best places to find classic *cuisine française*: a little conservative, but of unfailingly high quality. Specialities include traditional leek quiches, homemade terrines, roast duck and lamb, fish with classic sauces and delicious, old-fashioned desserts, all made with wonderfully fresh ingredients and all excellent value. *Closed Sat and mid-July–mid-Aug.*

Du côté de Chez Swann, Esplanade de la Hotoie, t 03 22 91 37 05, f 03 22 72 46 60 (*menus 98–155F/ €14.94–23.63*). In a slightly out-of-the-way location beside the large, park of La Hotoie, west of the city centre, but

with a high reputation. Menus combine traditional local dishes – as in a satisfying *flamiche aux endives* – with inventive touches such as a *confit* of duck with a mustard-grain dressing. It's neatly comfortable and relaxed, with a small outside terrace looking across to the park. *Closed Sat midday, Sun, Mon eve.*

La Dent Creuse, 2 Rue Cormont, t 03 22 80 03 63, f 03 22 91 06 99 (*menus 98–135F/ €14.94–20.58, midday menu express 75F/ €11.43*). A pretty restaurant beside the cathedral, with charming, slightly old-fashioned service. Local classics are prepared with a refined touch, and some luxurious variations: roast sea bass with courgettes in a *crème de champagne* sauce. There's a wide choice of *grandes assiettes* combining salads with fish, duck, forest mushrooms, and so on (*from 72F/€10.98*). In summer there are tables outside. *Closed Sun eve.*

Le Pot d'Etain, 15 Quai Bélu, t/f 03 22 72 10 80. One of the best of the clutch of restaurants with waterside *terrasses* along Quai Bélu. Mainstays of the menu are a *rôtisserie* range, including good steaks and a hearty **grande rôtisserie** or mixed grill (*130F/€19.82*), and quality seafood, such as large *plateaux de fruits de mer* (*130F/€19.82*). Also *cassoulet*, a range of salads, and good wines.

Le T'chiot Zinc, 18 Rue de Noyon, t 03 22 91 43 79 (*menus 72–169F/€10.98–25.76*). A much-loved brasserie and *salon de thé* in an eccentric building near the station – it's much too tall for its (very narrow) width and the façade is an ornate extravaganza of neo-baroque columns. Exceptional value set menus offer local standards such as *ficelles picardes*, rabbit terrines, grilled fish or duck; there's also a fine *assiette des fruits de mer* (*99F/€15.09*). *Closed Sun and Mon midday.*

La Soupe à Cailloux, Place du Don, t/f 03 22 91 92 70 (*menus 72F/€10.98 and 110F/€16.77*). Amiens' most consistently popular relaxed, good-value bistro, in a great location by the river. Menus feature local standards: *tarte au maroilles* or a *cassoulet* of *moules*, and international creations like *lieu à la Thailandaise*. There are vegetarian choices on each menu. The house wine is pretty awful: this is somewhere where it's worth spending a little more. *Closed mid-Sept–May Mon.*

Normandy's Lost Frontier: Eu

14

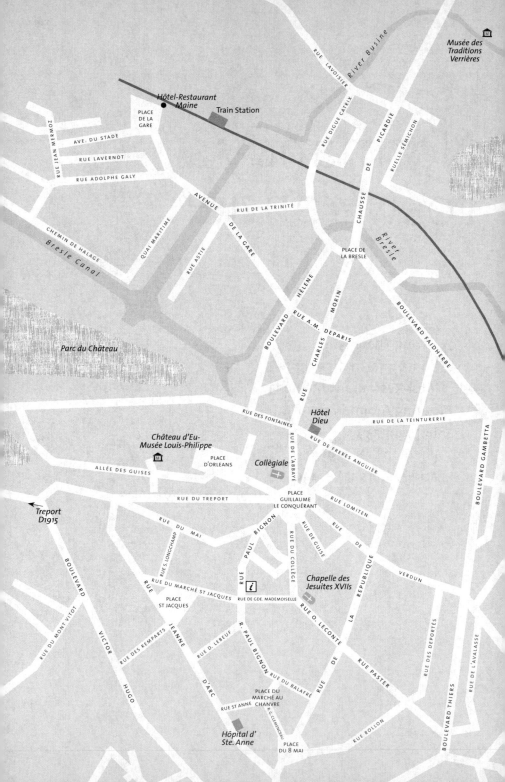

Musée des
Traditions
Verrières

RUE LAVOISIER

River Busine

Hôtel-Restaurant
Maine

Train Station

PLACE
DE LA
GARE

RUE JEAN MERMOZ

AVE. DU STADE

RUE LAVERNOT

RUE ADOLPHE GALY

CHEMIN DE HALAGE

Bresle Canal

QUAI MARITIME

AVENUE
DE LA GARE

RUE DE LA TRINITÉ

RUE ASTIE

RUE DIGUE CATRIX

CHAUSSE DE PICARDIE

RUELLE SEMICHON

River Bresle

PLACE DE
LA BRESLE

BOULEVARD FAIDHERBE

Parc du Château

BOULEVARD HÉLÈNE

RUE A.M. DEPARIS

RUE CHARLES MORIN

RUE DES FONTAINES

Hôtel
Dieu

RUE DE LA TEINTURERIE

Château d'Eu-
Musée Louis-Philippe

PLACE
D'ORLEANS

Collègiale

RUE DE L'ABBAYE

RUE DE FRERES ANGUIER

BOULEVARD GAMBETTA

ALLÉE DES GUISES

RUE DU TREPORT

PLACE
GUILLAUME
LE CONQUÉRANT

RUE LOMITEN

Treport
D1915

RUE DU MAI

RUE S. LONGCHAMP

RUE PAUL BIGNON

RUE DU COLLÈGE

RUE DE CUISE

RUE DE

VERDUN

BOULEVARD

RUE DU MARCHÉ ST JACQUES

RUE DE GDE. MADEMOISELLE

Chapelle des
Jesuites XVIIs

LA RÉPUBLIQUE

RUE

PLACE
ST JACQUES

RUE O. LECONTE

RUE DES DÉPORTÉS

VICTOR

RUE DU MONT VITOT

RUE DES REMPARTS

RUE D. LEBEUF

R. PAUL BIGNON

RUE DU BALAFRÉ

RUE DE

RUE PASTER

BOULEVARD THIERS

RUE DE L'AVALASSE

HUGO

JEANNE

D'ARC

RUE ST ANNE

PLACE DU
MARCHÉ AU
CHANVRE

R. CLERMINEAL

RUE ROLLON

Hôpital d'
Ste. Anne

PLACE
DU 8 MAI

Getting There

From St-Valery-sur-Somme (D940) or the main Calais–Boulogne road via Abbeville (D925), you will arrive at a large roundabout, Place Albert I. Carry straight on (the south exit, signposted *centre-ville*) to another round-about, Place de la Bresle, and take Bd Hélène, which leads off to the right. About 50m down on the right is Av de la Gare, which leads to the railway station and the Hôtel-Restaurant Maine, formerly the station hotel.

From Dieppe, on the D925, you will also come to a large roundabout, Place Charles-de-Gaulle, on the south side of town. Take the left exit, Bd Victor Hugo, following the signs for *centre-ville*. At the next roundabout the right exit will lead you into Place Guillaume-le-Conquérant, the centre of town, dominated by the church of the Collégiale in front of you. Go round the square and take the street down the hill to the right of the church, Rue de l'Abbaye, which leads straight into Rue Charles Morin. Second on the left on this street is Rue

Adjutant Deparis, which leads directly on to Av de la Gare.

Eu and Le Tréport still have (now rather infrequent) direct rail services from Paris, via Beauvais, making it possible to visit them from the capital even in one (pretty long) day trip. Parisian day-trippers, traditionally, go only to Le Tréport, and ignore Eu.

Tourist Information

Eu: 41 Rue Paul Bignon, t 02 35 86 04 68, f 02 35 50 16 03, *www.ville-eu.fr*. The tourist office has information on the whole of the Vallée de la Bresle, as well as special tours, walks and the possibilities of visiting sites and buildings with limited access.

Criel-sur-Mer: 85 Rue du 11 Novembre, t 02 35 86 56 91 (*open mid-April–mid-Sept only*).

Mers-les-Bains: 1 Rue Jules Barni, t 02 35 86 06 14.

Le Tréport: Quai Sadi Carnot, t 02 35 86 05 69, f 02 35 86 73 96, *www.ville-le-treport.fr*.

The valley of the river Bresle marks the northeast border of Normandy, a long, straight cleft lined with stretches of thick woodland. It has not been a real frontier between states since the 13th century, but nevertheless remains a significant dividing line: in food, in agriculture – between the grain fields of Picardy and the Norman pastures and orchards – and in the historical memory of the people. And, straddling the Bresle, there is the traditional main gateway to Normandy, the little town of Eu.

Today this town with its oddly monosyllabic name has a noticeably out-of-the-way feel, and is not very well known even in the rest of France. It's a relaxed, charming provincial town, its life centred on a main square that fills up with a market on some days and flocks of chattering *lycéens* on others. Eu has also cropped up in the history of both France and the British Isles a remarkable number of times and in a curious variety of circumstances, and hosted a whole gallery of heroes and villains. William the Conqueror was married here; later, it became a shrine to an Irish saint, and later still a summer residence of a French king, in which role it welcomed Queen Victoria.

This past has left Eu with a range of historic buildings, some hidden away, some of undeniable grandeur, exceptional for such a small, ordinary town. Perhaps in part because they still receive relatively few visitors, the Eudois are also particularly welcoming. Inland from the town there is the Forêt d'Eu, a long swathe of wild, almost virgin forest, ideal for walking, that contains within it a still only partially excavated Gallo-Roman city. Towards the sea is the Belle Epoque beach town of Le Tréport, with giant cliffs, a traditional promenade and a vigorously animated fishing harbour.

And Eu also has an exceptional restaurant, as unobtrusive and as idiosyncratic as the rest of town. The **Hôtel-Restaurant Maine**'s food and hospitality make it worth a stopover in Eu all by itself.

Hôtel-Restaurant Maine

20 Av de la Gare, t 02 35 86 16 64, f 02 35 50 86 25, hotelmaine@aol.com. Open Mon–Sat 12–2 and 7.30–9.30, Sun 12–2. Closed usually two to three weeks in Aug, check in advance. Book weekends. Menus 95F/€14.48 (Mon–Fri only), 140F/€21.35, 145F/€22.11 and 240F/€36.59.

A few trains still stop at Eu, even though most of the station has now been taken over by an insurance company. The Hôtel Maine, which until recently was still called the Hôtel de la Gare, is naturally enough alongside it, a plainish brick building with Mansart roof much like many other small station hotels put up around France at the end of the 19th century. Inside, the bar to the right of the entrance seems at first sight equally conventional, catering to a steady flow of locals. Look around, though, and you'll find a collection of modern designer lamps in the form of feet and other strange shapes, comic-strip pictures and some unusually comfortable furniture, indicating a quirky individuality you don't necessarily expect in a small-town restaurant. The distinctive tastes of Jean-Claude and Marie-Françoise Maine, owners since 1972, are just as present in the hotel upstairs, which since its recent makeover has an almost radically stylish, post-modern look.

The dining room is entirely different again: large and ornate to the point of being baroque, in apple green, with classic bourgeois mouldings in the first section and a magnificent, sinuous art nouveau fireplace and window frames in the larger end room. It's also very comfortable, and around the walls there's plenty of odd bric-à-brac and an eccentric collection of paintings, especially old portraits of stolid local burghers, to add to the interest while you're thinking about your meal.

This cheerfully eclectic décor is only part of the place's originality and charm. Jean-Claude, tall, wiry and with an ample grey walrus moustache, takes the orders, ambling from table to table and chatting with the clientele, many of them regulars. He does not cook himself (the current head chef is Vincent Lavaud), but is clearly a very able master of ceremonies, for over many years and with different personnel the restaurant has maintained a distinctive style and quality of cooking that would not be out of place in a major metropolitan eating house. It's rooted in French and local tradition, with a fine use of butter to introduce you to Normandy. There are two main menus at 140F/€21.35: 'du Pêcheur', all fish and seafood, and 'du Boucher', all meat, with four courses in each. The 'carte' also follows a set-price formula, with any three courses for 240F/€36.59 and any two for 145F/€22.11. Menus change completely with each season, providing a wonderfully varied and tempting choice (at an equally exceptional price). The Maines and their team stress the importance of taste, rather than complexity for its own sake, and finely marked flavours are as immediately apparent in all the hotel's

Salade Croquante à l'Huile de Noix et Caille Confite
(Salad of Preserved Quail with a Walnut Oil Dressing)

Serves 6

6 oven-ready quails

coarse sea salt

freshly ground pepper

10ml/2 teaspoons dried thyme

2 bay leaves, chopped or crumbled

3 garlic cloves, finely chopped

30ml/2 tablespoons cognac

goose fat, at room temperature

125g/4½oz mixed salad leaves, washed

12 quails' eggs, hard-boiled

fines herbes (chopped parsley, chive and tarragon)

For the vinaigrette

2 teaspoons white wine vinegar

30ml/2 tablespoons walnut oil

15ml/1 tablespoon vegetable oil

salt and pepper

Cure the quails a day ahead. Rub them generously with coarse salt and sprinkle with pepper, thyme, bay, garlic and cognac. Cover tightly and refrigerate overnight.

Preheat the oven to 150°C/300°F/Gas Mark 2. Rinse the quails and pat dry. Put them in a casserole into which they fit snugly and add enough goose fat to just cover them. Cover and cook for 1–1½ hours, until the meat is soft. Remove the birds from the fat and drain. When they are cool enough to handle, cut down the backbone, open them out and remove the main bones, leaving the legs intact.

For the vinaigrette, whisk a little salt and pepper into the vinegar, then whisk in the oils gradually.

Dress the salad leaves and divide among 6 plates. Place a quail on each and garnish with halved quails' eggs. Sprinkle with the herbs before serving.

dishes as the outstanding quality of every ingredient. A first course of a warm salad of *confit* of quails with quails' eggs and a hazelnut vinaigrette is perfectly matched, with a fragrant, nutty dressing. To follow, there's nearly always a fine lamb dish, with perfect-quality meat and rich but complex sauces and marinades, such as the curiously English *côtes d'agneau marinées*, lamb chops delicately marinated in mint. Alternatively, there are variants on classic dishes such as *jarret de porc en cocotte*, a casserole of pigs' knuckle and haricot beans, and superb steaks.

M Maine also takes good care of his wine list, and you can rely on his recommendations: to go with the meat, a supremely smooth Gigondas from the Rhône. The fish choices might includes delights such as a crab salad with artichoke hearts and a prawn dressing, or a *panaché* of salmon and whiting with a *badiane* (star anise) butter; some notably luxurious options highlight local fish and seafood.

The same attention to detail is seen in the cheese course – including a fabulously flavoured local Neufchâtel – and desserts, such as a delightfully refreshing (and boozy) apple *sorbet et calvados*. To finish, try one of Jean-Claude's great selection of calvados, such as the superbly fragrant Hors d'Age.

Touring Around

The first settlement of **Eu** appeared on a shelf of land above the Bresle, where the Château d'Eu and the church of the Collégiale stand today. It was occupied under the Romans, but the history of the town really begins in the 10th century, when the recently established dukes of Normandy built a castle here as the furthest defensive bastion of their new territories. It was also a port, with access to the sea along the Bresle. In 1050 William the Conqueror brought Matilda, daughter of the Count of Flanders, to the castle of Eu to marry him. Apparently she was none too keen on the match, and only submitted to it after William dragged her around her chambers by her hair. Romantic accounts traditionally claim that this was because he was so much in love he just couldn't take no for an answer, but it looks more like another example of the Conqueror's usual thuggery. An abbey was also founded near the castle, and the town of Eu grew up around the two. It has the oldest municipal charter of any town in Normandy, granted in 1151.

The town's central square, occupied by a wonderful market on Friday mornings, is **Place Guillaume-le-Conquérant**. It is dominated, however, by a great church dedicated to a more permanent resident of Eu, who was not Norman but Irish. This was **St Laurence O'Toole**, for centuries the only officially canonised Irish saint (since St Patrick, St Kevin and many others had never been formally recognised by the Vatican). He was Archbishop of Dublin at the time of the first Anglo-Norman invasion of Ireland in 1169, and in 1180 was sent to England by the Irish lords to intercede with Henri II. The King all but ignored him, and went off to Normandy; Laurence, old and sick, followed after him, but only got as far as the Abbey at Eu, where he died, and the rest, as they say, is history. He had supposedly stopped the day before on the crest just north of Eu, where the 19th-century Chapelle St-Laurent now stands out against the sky, and, looking down, said, 'there I will take my rest'; he was also said to have raised seven people from the dead, and his canonisation was begun very quickly, in part because of the papacy's own arguments with Henri II. Laurence's shrine at Eu immediately became an important pilgrimage centre, and remained so throughout the Middle Ages. More recently Eu has sought to revive its Irish links, and in a garden on the north side of the church there is now a Celtic cross in stone from St Laurence's birthplace in County Kildare, donated by a contemporary Dublin Archbishop.

Laurence's church, officially Notre-Dame-et-St-Laurent but better known locally as the **Collégiale**, was begun as a pilgrimage church in 1186, replacing the much smaller earlier abbey church, and first completed a hundred years later. Like many French churches battered by the Revolution it was restored during the 19th century by the great Gothic revivalist Eugène Viollet-le-Duc, who said that he had seen churches that were bigger or taller, but none that were more beautiful. Most of the nave is the original from the late 12th century; the choir and the apse, in contrast, are an extravagant work of Flamboyant Gothic, built after a major fire in 1426, and especially spectacular from the outside, with a tangle of buttresses to rival Notre-Dame in Paris. Even so, the different styles harmonise, and the building is superbly light.

The Collégiale has some fine baroque woodwork, especially the grand 1614 organ above the nave, and the statue of *Our Lady of Eu* in the Lady Chapel behind the choir. Its greatest treasure, though, is in a small chapel off to the right of the choir, an exquisite 16th-century *Entombment of Christ* in polychrome stone. The modelling and colour of the eight figures around the dead Christ are superb: look carefully at their marvellously expressive hands. Like much else in Eu, it is curiously little-known; it is believed to have been made in Burgundy, and no one knows how it got here. The 13th-century **tomb of St Laurence**, meanwhile, is in the vaulted crypt, which you enter from one side of the nave. The crypt is massive, built to accommodate a steady flow of pilgrims; desecrated during the Revolution, it was restored in the 1820s by Louis-Philippe, Duke of Orleans and later King of France, who lined it with the tombs of his ancestors, the counts of Eu and Artois.

In the later Middle Ages, Eu was another of the places where Joan of Arc was held on her way to her trial in Rouen, in 1430. Very little of the medieval town survives because, along with William the Conqueror's castle, it was burnt wholesale in 1475 on the orders of Louis XI of France, to prevent them falling into the hands of the English. Only the abbey and some churches remained intact. If, however, you walk from the south side of Place Guillaume up Eu's traditional main thoroughfare, **Rue Paul Bignon**, you enter an area of little winding streets built during a revival in the town's fortunes in the 16th and 17th centuries, with many fine Louis XIII-style merchants' houses in brick, with the occasional more elaborate ornamental detail. Rue Bignon, a charming, narrow street, also contains some great food shops, and the tourist office.

Overlooking a tiny square on Rue du Collège, which runs away from the main *place* just left of Rue Bignon, is the **Chapelle du Collège des Jesuites** (*open April–early Nov Mon–Sat 10–12 and 2.30–6.30*). This was built following Eu's next intervention in history, in the French Wars of Religion (1560–93). The title of Count of Eu had been passed around between several aristocratic dynasties, and in 1570 the then Countess, Catherine de Clèves, married Henri, Duc de Guise, known as le Balafré ('Scarface'), the foremost standard-bearer of intransigent Catholicism, and a perennial conspirator who played a significant part in the St Bartholomew's Day Massacre of Protestants in Paris in 1572. Guise decided to make Eu a powerhouse of the Counter-Reformation, and founded a Jesuit college here (alongside the chapel, and now the main *lycée*) in 1582. His wife Catherine was notorious for her '*galanteries*' with a string of lovers, from servants to gentlemen, some of whom were murdered on Guise's orders; nevertheless, she shared his religious ideas and, after he himself was assassinated by agents of Henri III in 1588, developed something of a cult to his memory. Reconciled to the former-Protestant Bourbon Henri IV, she lived to a great age, becoming known for her good works, and commissioned the chapel in Eu to be built between 1613 and 1624.

As in many other Jesuit churches built around that time, its design is based on the mother church of the order, the Gesù in Rome, made from brick and stone instead of marble, and with decoration that's similarly a mix of Italian Renaissance and more local influences. The fine carving on the façade was the work of some local sculptors, the brothers Anguier. Inside, the most prominent features by far are two giant, bombastic but very finely sculpted baroque **memorial tombs** in marble, made for Catherine de Clèves in 1627, one for herself and one for her husband. His is actually empty, since after his assassination Henri III had ordered that the Duke's remains be burnt and scattered in the Loire, to prevent them becoming a focus for his followers.

Thanks to the Guises and their successors, there were once so many churches and religious foundations in Eu that in 1650 the Mayor complained that they blocked off many of the town's streets. Most were demolished after the Revolution. Near the southern end of Rue Bignon, though, on the corner of Rue St-Anne and Rue Clemenceau, there is still the **Hôpital St-Anne**, now the tax office, built in 1664 as an almshouse for orphan girls. On Rue de l'Abbaye, downhill beside the Collégiale and on the right, is the beautiful **Hôtel-Dieu**, a convent and hospital from 1654, built around three sides of a garden courtyard in a happy combination of Norman half-timbering and more august, Louis XIII-style architecture.

The Guises were also responsible for the other building that, with the Collégiale, makes up the grand centrepiece of the town, facing the church across the broad and stately Place d'Orléans, the French-Renaissance style **Château d'Eu**, begun on the site of the earlier castle in 1578. What we see today represents only a part of the vast palace, with four sides around a great courtyard, that they had planned to create for themselves, for they were only able to complete part of one wing before le Balafré was murdered. In 1660 the château passed to Mademoiselle de Montpensier, known as la Grande Mademoiselle, cousin of Louis XIV, who was confined here by the Sun King to prevent her intriguing against him. It was she who first made it habitable, and added the elegant Le-Nôtre style French garden which forms the main part of the delightful park that sweeps away on its western side. The Château d'Eu is most associated, though, with Louis-Philippe of Orleans, who inherited it, together with the title of Count of Eu, in 1821.

Louis-Philippe loved Eu; not only did he amply restore his château and the crypt of the Collégiale, he also had the **Bresle Canal** built, restoring the town's access to the sea for the first time in centuries, in part in order that he could sail up it in his yacht. Moreover, it continued to be his favourite residence after the revolution of July 1830 catapulted him into power as France's 'Citizen King', considered an archetype of respectable virtues, and famous for never going out without his umbrella. Eu became for a while the virtual summer capital of France, and a new, rather barracks-like building, the Pavillon des Ministres, was put up next to the Collégiale to accommodate the members of the government who were obliged to decamp here for several weeks each year. In September 1843 Queen Victoria and Prince Albert arrived at the château for a week of picnics, parades, concerts and other entertainments. This was the first time a British monarch had set foot in France since Henry VIII's meeting with

François I at the Field of the Cloth of Gold in 1520, a fact that enables Eu to claim the title of 'Birthplace of the Entente Cordiale'. The visit had tremendous impact. Each day's events were followed with rapt attention by the local population, and in the following year every third girl born in Eu was named Victoria, Victoire or Victorine.

After Louis-Philippe was himself deposed by another revolution in 1848 Eu fell back into its more usual obscurity, but in the 1870s the Republic returned the château to the King's grandson, the Comte de Paris, pretender to the French throne, who again restored the house and gardens. Since 1964 it has belonged to the town, and part of it is now the Mairie, while the rest is the **Château d'Eu-Musée Louis-Philippe** (*open 15 Mar–31 Oct Mon, Wed–Sun 10–12 and 2–6; closed Tues; adm free while restoration work continues*). Maintaining such a large monument has been a heavy burden for a small town, and for some years parts of it have had a (quite engaging) tumbledown look, but a major restoration programme is now in progress. Unfortunately, while this goes on (probably until 2002–3), much of the château will be closed off, but visitors can see a free exhibition on the building and its history on the ground floor. Inside, some rooms still have the ornate 17th-century décor of the Grande Mademoiselle, while others were redecorated in the 1870s for the Comte de Paris by Viollet-le-Duc, with fascinating, multi-coloured designs on the borderline between Gothic revival and art nouveau. Most of the rooms, though, are as they were left by Louis-Philippe. He was an undemonstrative king, and his palace is accordingly cosy. He was also a man of his time, who installed in his château one of the earliest running-water systems, driven by mill-wheels on the canal, and one of the most eye-catching features of the building is its giant tangle of brass plumbing. There are, too, many souvenirs of the British visits, including paintings done at breakneck speed by Winterhalter and other artists in order that they could be shown to the royal couple before their departure. Behind the château, its lush green park (*open despite the restoration*) begins as a tranquil, formal garden, turning to beech woods the further you head into it.

The Bresle Valley is also known as the Vallée de la Verre, the valley of glass. **Glassmaking** has been carried on here since the Middle Ages, and the giant St-Gobain factory outside Mers-les-Bains now produces millions of Made-in-France glasses to send around the globe; at the same time, along the Bresle there are still small village glass workshops using semi-mechanised techniques. Eu now has a **Musée des Traditions Verrières** (*open May and Sept Sat, Sun and hols 2.30–6; June–Aug, Tues, Sat, Sun and hols 2.30–6; adm*), in a former barracks on Rue Sémichon, reached via a turning off the D1015 Gamaches road near Place Albert I. The informative, practical display on the whole history of glass is given a lively personal touch by the retired glassworkers who act as guides (they predictably don't know much English, but translated leaflets are provided, and English-speaking guides can sometimes be arranged via the tourist office). One of the specialities of the Bresle is fine bottle work (a proudly proclaimed statistic is that the valley produces 85 per cent of the world's perfume bottles), and one positively dazzling part of the museum is a room of delicately sculpted prototype flasks made for Givenchy, Chanel and all the *grand* names of *parfumerie*.

Glassmakers were first drawn to the Bresle Valley by its sandy soil and the abundant supply of wood, from what is still today one of the most heavily wooded parts of northern France. For a change from sightseeing, escape the town into the **Forêt d'Eu**, a wild, atmospheric expanse of deciduous forest of the kind that once covered much of northern Europe but which is now sadly rare, and home to a range of wildlife that includes deer and wild boar. It's wonderful for walking, and there are easy paths into the woods from the Beaumont road, off the D49 south, and from near St-Pierre-en-Val, off the D1314 to Neufchâtel (near which there are also *zones de silence*, closed off to all motor traffic). For a guide to these and longer routes ask for a walking map at the tourist office in Eu, which also organises walks led by foresters that end at a *carcahoux* or traditional woodcutters' hut deep in the woods, with a drink and maybe an opportunity to pick and cook the forest's prized wild mushrooms; riding is also popular, and the office has information on local riding centres. Further west, the roads that run alongside the forest drop down sometimes precipitously into the **Vallée de l'Yères**, a spectacularly pretty steep-sided, narrow valley possessed of an almost tangible, unmolested serenity, and which runs down to meet the sea at the little beach village of Criel-sur-Mer.

Just inside the Forêt d'Eu at Bois-l'Abbé, only 4km outside Eu itself, there is a major **Roman site** (*not yet fully open to the public, but tours with an archaeologist are run from the tourist office July–Sept Tues at 2pm, and occasionally at other times; adm*) that is almost a new discovery. The existence of Roman remains in the area has been vaguely known since the 18th century, but properly organised excavations have only got underway in the last decade; they have already unearthed a mass of ceramics, a temple, an amphitheatre with a capacity of 4–6,000 and, most unusually, a women's public bath, indicating a Gallo-Roman city of considerable size and sophistication. Finds from the digs are stored in the Hôtel-Dieu, which it is hoped to open as a permanent exhibition during 2002.

Alternatively, leave Eu in the opposite direction for the sea air of **Le Tréport**, where Prince Albert went swimming at seven in the morning. With an arching shingle beach beneath giant cliffs, it's a curious combination of a once quite genteel 19th-century resort and a busy, industrialised and gritty fishing port, with dainty architecture on one side and giant cranes on the other. Fabulously fresh fish and shellfish are landed and sold every day at stalls along the main Quai François I, and a near-unbroken line of seafood restaurants extends along the quay and round on to the beach front, nearly all offering the same, delicious range of lobsters, mussels, oysters, sole, and so on. Long a favourite escape for Parisians – the hoi-polloi, rather than the élite who make for Deauville – Le Tréport and its bustling restaurant strip still draw in the crowds on summer weekends, and by the beach there's also a casino, *frites* stands and all the other essentials of the French seaside. **Mers-les-Bains**, on the Picardy side of the Bresle, is quieter and has a rather better beach, but its greatest distinction is its extraordinary circa-1900 beachfront architecture, a line of *beaux-arts* to art deco follies, with elaborate turrets, gables and balconies and elaborate patterns in brick and wood, painted pink, cream, orange and duck-egg blue, that look like so many candy-coloured castles beneath the wheeling seagulls.

Shopping

The essential time to arrivein **Eu** is on Friday, when the town centre is virtually taken over by one of the best markets in northern Normandy. Stalls offer excellent farmhouse terrines, ciders, Neufchâtel and other fresh farm produce, plus everything else you might expect to find at a country market. At other times, Rue Paul Bignon is the place to head for, with at least three irresistible *boulangeries-pâtisseries* and equally fine *charcuteries*. There are also markets in **Le Tréport** (*Tues and Sat*) and fresh fish and shellfish are sold direct from the boats every day along Quai François I.

St-Martin-le-Gaillard ✉ 76260

Pascal Dumont, Hameau de Dragueville, **t** 02 35 50 93 44. On his farm outside the village of St Martin, M Dumont makes powerful *appelation contrôlée eau-de-vie de cidre*, a stronger variant on calvados, which is something of a speciality of the Vallée de l'Yères. *Closed Mon, and Sun in Aug.*

Where to Stay

Eu ✉ 76260

Le Domaine de Joinville, Route du Tréport, **t** 02 35 50 52 52, **f** 02 35 50 27 37, *www.chateauxhotels.com/joinville* (*double rooms 470–790F/€71.65–120.43; suites from 990F/€150.92*). One of the pavilions built for Louis-Philippe in the 1830s on the Château d'Eu estate, with its own grounds, now houses this luxury hotel. There are 20 rooms, six very ample suites, and a smart gourmet **restaurant** (*menus 135–450F/€20.58–68.60*). Decorated with traditional opulence, the Domaine naturally offers every comfort (and tennis courts, a fitness centre and so on).

Hôtel-Restaurant Maine, 20 Av de la Gare, **t** 02 35 86 16 94, **f** 02 35 86 16 64, *hotel-maine@aol.com* (*rooms 290–370F/ €44.21–56.41 for two*). A meal in Jean-Claude and Marie-Françoise Maine's art nouveau dining room doesn't prepare you at all for the rooms above, which could almost qualify the Maine as the Bresle Valley's one and only modernist hotel. Room doors are orange, with big silver numbers reaching from top to bottom: inside, some have modern iron-frame furniture and sometimes striking abstract paintings by the Maines' son, some are a slightly playful variant on a more traditional look. And all are very comfortable.

Manoir de Beaumont, **t** 02 35 50 91 91, *www.chez.com/demarquet* (*rooms 280F/ €42.69 for two, 320F/€48.78 for three, 70F/ €10.67 per additional person*). An extensively renovated hunting lodge and manor house in a superb location on a wooded hill just south of Eu, surrounded by its own gardens and grounds and with wonderful views. Rooms are deliciously comfortable, with antique furniture, lots of light and many extras, and the breakfast room and lounge are especially pretty. Catherine Demarquet and her husband will give you information on the activities and excursions available in the area, and there are bikes for guests' use.

Guerville ✉ 76340

Ferme de la Haye, **t** 03 22 26 14 26 (*rooms 230F/€35.06 for two, 360F/€54.88 for four*). A special *chambre-d'hôte* in an impressively big old farm, once a stud farm for racehorses, that is entirely within the Forêt d'Eu. M Jean Mairesse, who worked the farm before his retirement, is a craggy son of the Norman earth who in the evenings sits in traditional fashion on a stool beside the giant open fireplace to chew the fat (he knows some English); his wife Dominique is a sweet lady, and both, and their dog, are very welcoming. They have an eye for style, as seen in the attractive renovation of their one huge guest room. It's really a suite, with one giant double room, another with two singles, and an excellent bathroom, but is available for couples, even though they can't let the rooms separately as they lead off each other. It's a remarkable bargain. The location above all, surrounded by the forest, is wonderful, whether you want to go on long treks or just wander into the woods. Once you return to the farm in the evening you may not want to find your way out again, but this is not a problem as Mme Mairesse also provides excellent *table-d'hôte* meals of country cooking (*80F/€12.20*).

Mesnil-Val ✉ 76910

Hostellerie de la Vieille Ferme, 23 Rue de la Mer, Criel-sur-Mer, **t** 02 35 86 72 18, **f** 02 35 86 12 67 (*rooms 330–510F/€50.31–77.75*). This grand old half-timbered farmhouse from 1734 is now a classically picturesque country hotel. Most of its 33 rooms are in annexes behind the main house across a neat garden, and the most attractive on the ground floor have their own little garden terraces. Rooms are plainer in style than the rest of the hotel, but comfortable, and it's only a short walk from the beach at Criel-Plage. It also has a restaurant, *see* below. *Closed Sun eve, Mon (Oct–May only) and Jan.*

Le Tréport ✉ 76470

Le Prieuré Ste-Croix, t 02 35 86 14 77 (*rooms 260–360F/€39.64–48.78 for two*). A magnificent *chambre-d'hôte* in the former manor farm of the royal estate of the Château d'Eu, behind the château itself (the entrance is by the main roundabout on the D1915 Le Tréport road out of Eu), with an impressive courtyard and gardens of its own. Parts of it are medieval, while others are 16th- or 19th-century; all the beautiful old rooms have antique furnishings and modern bathrooms. The ground floor double 'room' is really a suite, with its own sitting room and access to a kitchenette.

Eating Alternatives

Eu ✉ 76260

La Bragance, Parc du Château, **t** 02 35 50 20 01 (*menu 100F/€15.24; dishes c. 50F/€7.62*). An attractive, unusual restaurant installed in the *glacière* or ice-house – a kind of giant brick igloo – and attached garden lodge built for Louis-Philippe by the entrance to the park beside the Château d'Eu. The young staff ensure a relaxed, *sympa* atmosphere. The food is light and modern, and based on fine fresh produce. A giant old wood-burning grill dominates one side of the dining room, and there is a great range of single-course dishes, such as mixed salads and *tartines*. In front there's a large, pretty terrace. *Closed Mon eve and Tues.*

Mesnil-Val ✉ 76910

Hostellerie de la Vieille Ferme, *see* above (*menus 120–239F/€18.29–36.44*). The lovely old dining room has the original black-and-white timbering and stone doorways, plus neat table settings and lots of fresh flowers. The kitchen concentrates on classic Norman fare, with a *menu du terroir* that includes *marmite pêcheur* and *poulet fermier vallée d'auge*, and a *menu de la côte d'albâtre* with more fresh local seafood. There's also a pretty garden. *Closed Sun eve, Mon (Oct–May only) and Jan.*

Le Tréport ✉ 76470

La Matelote, 34 Quai François I, **t** 02 35 86 01 13, **f** 02 35 86 17 02 (*menus 79F/€12.04 (Mon–Fri only) and 125–270F/€19.06–41.16*). One of the biggest and most comfortable of the seafood specialists along Tréport quay, with a first-floor *salle panoramique* with a view across the harbour to Mers-les-Bains. All the local seafood classics – fish and seafood stews, *moules* – are excellent, and for a feast you can tackle the superb *plateaux de fruits de mer* (*from 88F/€13.42*). *Closed Tues eve.*

Mon P'tit Bar, 3–5 Rue de la Rade, **t** 02 35 86 28 78 (*menus 68–150F/€10.37–22.87*). On the corner of one of the turnings off Quai François I – but still with a harbour view from many tables – this is a big, bright brasserie, with a busy, friendly feel and service genuinely *à toute heure*: enjoyable versions of local favourites – *moules*, lobster, grilled fish – and plenty of snacks and lighter dishes.

St-Martin-le-Gaillard ✉ 76260

Le Moulin de Becquerel, t 02 35 86 74 94, **f** 02 35 86 99 78 (*full meal c. 165F/€25.15*). Between St Martin-le-Gaillard and St-Sulpice, a steep driveway turns off west down to this restaurant in a fine old riverside mill, in its own grounds. The dining room is charming, and outside there are tables on a terrace. The menu features traditional Norman favourites, and is very good value. At weekends wedding parties and family outings may raise the volume a bit. *Closed June–Sept Sun eve and Mon; Oct–May Sun eve–Wed.*

Pirates, Painters and Gardens:

Dieppe and the Caux Maritime

Dieppe is a Channel port that's worth exploring. It's a small city, with a compact old centre of narrow streets and little alleys, and still a busy, living port. Its name comes from the Old Norse for 'deep', and the deep-water harbour, the mouth of the River Arques, comes right into the middle of town, lined with cafés, restaurants and shops, so that, uniquely among the Normandy ports, it has something of the bustle of a Mediterranean seaport town. Dieppe also has one of the very best town markets in Normandy, eye-catching food shops and a buzzing café- and night-life.

The town has always lived, in different ways, from the sea: Dieppe seamen sailed to Canada, while others brought back spices, ivory and other rarities from every point on the compass. Later, in the 1820s, Dieppe was the first town in France to follow Brighton and become a seaside resort. Its history has also been bound up with England. In the Middle Ages it was the chief port for English pilgrims on their way to Santiago or Rome, and post-Napoleon Dieppe had the first ever regular cross-Channel steam ferry service, in 1825. It was, too, an extraordinary focus of attraction for artists, British and French: Pissarro, Sickert and a long list of other painters all extolled the qualities of Dieppe's limpid, sea-coast light, and the town was a unique point of contact between the British and French art worlds.

The area stretching away to the west, with its distinctive small towns and villages, is known as the Caux Maritime. The shoreline consists of an almost continual line of cliffs, at the top of which you abruptly come to a massive, flat plateau, a land of giant, open horizons. Breaks in the cliff – of which Dieppe's own inlet is the largest – are like little oases, often remarkably lush, and each one is entirely different from any other. The Seine-Maritime is the garden capital of France, and clustered around Dieppe are some of the most luxuriant, unusual and inventive examples in the whole country.

In culinary matters, Dieppe is most famous, as you would expect, for fish and seafood – especially served with the classic *dieppoise* sauce combining Norman cream with white wine and mushrooms. In the beautiful village of Varengeville there is in **La Buissonnière**, a restaurant that for stylish originality and sophisticated, light, modern food stands out very much from the crowd.

Getting There

Ferries arrive at the new terminal on the east side of Dieppe harbour; from there follow signs for *centre-ville*. Parking is free on the fish quay and on the seafront, and pretty cheap everywhere else. There are free courtesy buses for ferry foot passengers to the town centre. By car from Calais or the Channel Tunnel, leave the *autoroute* near Abbeville and take the D925 via Eu; as you arrive in Dieppe, follow signs for *centre-ville*.

To get to Varengeville, find the seafront Bd de Verdun and turn left, then left again by the castle to triangular Place des Martyrs. A right turn following signs for Pourville and Varengeville leads to the Route de Pourville (D75), a winding road that runs along the cliffs through Varengeville. Look out for a turning to the right signposted to Cap d'Ailly and the Phare d'Ailly lighthouse. The entrance to La Buissonière is a little way up on the left.

There are still several trains daily from Paris St-Lazare, via Rouen.

Tourist Information

Dieppe: Pont Jehan Ango, t 02 32 14 40 60, f 02 35 06 27 66. 'Impressionist Itineraries' leaflets suggest routes around sites with painterly associations.
Pourville-Varengeville: Maison du Tourisme, Rue des Verts Bois, t 02 35 84 71 06.
St-Aubin-sur-Mer and Vallée du Dun: Mairie, St-Aubin-sur-Mer, t 02 35 83 54 64.
St-Valery-en-Caux: Maison Henri IV, t 02 35 97 00 63, f 02 35 97 32 65.
Veules-les-Roses: 12 Rue du Marché, t 02 35 97 63 05, f 02 35 57 24 51.

La Buissonnière

Route du Phare d'Ailly, Varengeville-sur-Mer, t/f 02 35 83 17 13.
Open Tues–Sat 12–2 and 7–9.30, Sun 12–2; closed Mon and Jan, Feb.
Booking advisable. Menus 175F/€26.68 and 245F/€37.35;
à la carte average 300F/€45.73.

Varengeville-sur-Mer's fame as a beauty spot is due in large part to its special combination of features: its location on top of giant cliffs, with superb views out to sea; a unique mix of fine architecture, from its Norman clifftop church to Edwin Lutyens' Bois des Moutiers house; an exceptional lushness; and the way in which the narrow lanes of the village wind up, down and along steep, snug little valleys full of densely packed woods, only to bring you out suddenly before sweeping views over the sea or the valleys to the south. Varengeville has attracted not only painters like Monet or Braque, but also plenty of well-heeled home-buyers, so that half-hidden among the trees there are some very grand and opulent houses and villas, often with elaborate Belle Epoque details. There are gardens everywhere, several of which are open to visitors. West of the village, towards Cap d'Ailly and its lighthouse, these woods give way to quite wild forest, which is much appreciated by walkers.

La Buissonnière, near the beginning of the Cap d'Ailly road, occupies a 1930s villa that is surrounded by a large garden. Its owner, Marijo Colombel, is incorrigibly chic, with a charming smile and a warm generosity. Her house is the same. The dining room – tastefully decorated in whites and pale greens, and bathed in light through big windows – has a distinctive style (it has been featured in several magazines), but is also utterly comfortable. There are tables on a veranda in summer, and everything has a great deal of charm.

Filets de Soles au Saumon Fumé et Pâtes Fraîches au Basilic (Fillets of Sole with Smoked Salmon, Fresh Pasta and Basil)

Serves 4

2 good-sized Dover soles, skinned and filleted
knob of butter
300g/10oz fresh tagliatelle
splash of olive oil
200g/7oz smoked salmon, finely diced
2 tablespoons finely chopped mild white onion
2 tablespoons finely chopped red onion
handful of basil leaves, torn
snipped chives and thyme leaves
salt and pepper
For the sauce:
200ml/7fl oz full fat crème fraîche
100ml/3½fl oz white wine
100ml/3½fl oz flavourful fish stock
2 bay leaves
2–3 thyme sprigs
40g/1½oz/3½tablespoons cold butter, diced
salt and pepper

To make the sauce, heat the crème fraîche in a small saucepan. Add the wine, bay leaves and thyme and stir. Boil gently to reduce by about one-third. Remove the herbs and stir in the fish stock. Bring back to a gentle boil and vigorously whisk in the butter by bits, until the sauce is smooth and thickened. Remove from the heat, check the seasoning and keep warm.

Bring a large pot of salted water to the boil. Cut the sole fillets in half on the diagonal and season. Melt the butter in a large frying pan over medium heat. When it foams, add the fish and sauté a few minutes on each side until lightly coloured and just cooked through (the flesh is opaque). Meanwhile, boil the tagliatelle for about 2 minutes, or until tender but still a little firm to the bite. Drain and place on a warm serving platter, season with salt and pepper, drizzle with olive oil and mix gently.

To serve, arrange the pieces of sole on the noodles, radiating from the centre. Strew over the smoked salmon and nap with the sauce. Sprinkle with onion, basil, chives and thyme and serve at once.

Mme Colombel used to work in marketing in Paris, but came to live here permanently a few years ago, in what had been a weekend home. She began the 'restaurant' on an informal basis, doing all the cooking herself. Word got around, and as the business grew she took on a chef, Ludovique Amart. The menus combine her ideas and home cooking and his professional restaurant skills. She describes it as *cuisine de femme* – much lighter, more modern and more varied than the traditional local dishes, and with a touch of fantasy to reflect the style of the house and gardens.

The menu is compact but still manages to offer a wide range of choice. The dishes feature strong, clear flavours, and local ingredients are expertly sourced. From the main menu, a starter of pan-fried wild mushrooms with fresh figs is utterly delicious, a perfectly balanced and refreshing dish with apple and an earthy tone of garlic. To follow, *noix de St-Jacques à la fondue de légumes verts* is enormously impressive. Fish and seafood dominate the menu, but another regular is a fine *confit* of duck with apples and garlic.

For the cheese course, the house speciality is roast Neufchâtel with toast, the cooking drawing out the cheese's punchy flavour. Desserts may be light, but this doesn't stop them being both intricate and luxurious, as in an *émincé* of pears with delectably rich chocolate sauce, and a fabulous little profiterole of homemade mixed-fruit ice-cream. Afterwards, walk through the woods by the lighthouse at the end of the road to see more great views from the cliffs out to sea.

Touring Around

If you arrive in **Dieppe** on a Saturday morning, make straight for the centre of town and the ample Place Nationale, the adjacent Place St-Jacques around the church of the same name, and the Grande-Rue, the now-pedestrianised main street that runs through the old town from the harbour quays. All three and many of the smaller streets in between are taken over by Dieppe's wonderful **market**, with a seemingly endless array of fruit, sausages, vegetables – particularly fine garlic and salad greens – fresh flowers, herbs, **terrines**, cheeses, cider and butter, as well as clothes, bargain-basement shoes and other miscellanea. It attracts farm producers from all over the surrounding region, and is one of the best places to find the highest quality, fresh Norman specialities – especially superb Neufchâtel and other cheeses – as well as produce from other parts of France, such as olives, oils and honeys. There is a smaller market on Tuesdays, Wednesdays and Thursdays, especially in summer.

The market thins out after about 1pm, but Dieppe's shops are also impressive, especially – unusually for a town of this size – for luxury foods. Dieppe is known for chocolate and sweets, and the Grande-Rue contains several spectacular *chocolatiers*.

From the market squares, several short, narrow streets connect with the **port**, just to the east. This area was fairly run-down by the 1980s, but in the last decade substantial renovation work has been set in motion. The tall brick or stone buildings that line the harbour side are quite distinctive, most of them built in the 18th century after a great part of the medieval town had been burnt down in an attack by an Anglo-Dutch fleet in 1694. Their stone-colonnaded arcades are a particular feature. The **Quai Henri IV**, the continuation of the Grande-Rue along the north side of the harbour, is now lined by cafés and fish restaurants, with the requisite quayside terrace tables.

Dieppe long had the most impressive approach of any of the Channel ports: from the 1850s until 1994 the Newhaven ferry sailed right into the harbour to dock (the new ferry terminal is just outside the main harbour, on the eastern side). In the absence of ferries part of the outer harbour alongside Quai Henri IV, the **Avant-Port**, has become a yacht marina, but the business of the port – the movement of ships, cargoes and little boats – is still an integral feature of the town centre. If you carry on inland down Quai Duquesne or across to the Quai du Carénage, on the Ile du Pollet in the middle of the harbour, you can walk alongside the **fishing quays**, where most mornings you can see a dazzling array of superbly fresh fish and shellfish being unloaded, and equally dazzling stalls selling the day's catch, especially scallops.

Dieppe's 'deep inlet' was one of the first points on the French coast discovered by the Vikings as they raided southwards, but it really became an important port to the Normans after their conquest of England. It grew to a substantial size during the Middle Ages, both as a port on the road to Santiago and as a stronghold that was fought over several times during the Hundred Years' War. Its greatest expansion, however, came in the 16th and 17th centuries when Dieppe seamen were among the first in northern Europe to join in the vogue for exploration to other continents. In the 1520s, when they sought to join the trade with Africa and the East Indies, they found their way blocked by the Portuguese, who had arrived first. A Dieppe shipbuilder, Jean (or Jehan, in the old Norman spelling) Ango, was authorised by François I of France to raise a fleet of privateers, which battered the Portuguese into submission in a semi-private war. Ango died Dieppe's richest man, and has been a local hero ever since, and his name still crops up all over town.

Its long prominence as a port is an essential part of Dieppe's very individual character. In the 15th century Venetian sailors on voyages between the Mediterranean and Flanders used Dieppe as a haven, and many are said to have settled in the district of Pollet and its island to the east of the port, contributing Italian words to the local dialect. The Dieppois were associated with being unconventional, and a bit chippy and rebellious by comparison with their more traditionalist neighbours inland. In the 16th and 17th centuries Dieppe had a large Protestant community, among them one of the town's greatest mariners, Abraham Duquesne, who became the effective head of Louis XIV's navy, even though as a Protestant he was not able to hold the post officially. Most recently Dieppe's chippiness has been expressed in a growing frustration at the decline of the Newhaven-Dieppe ferry route. In the days when this provided the fastest rail-and-boat connection between London and Paris it was the fashionable route of choice, but the expensive 1994 renovation of Dieppe's ferry port has not been matched by any comparable investment in the now-privatised harbour on the other side. Since 1999, following constant badgering from Dieppe, the Département of the Seine-Maritime has been in the process of actually buying Newhaven ferry harbour to run it themselves, a creeping extension of French sovereignty that has been strangely passed over by the Europhobes in the British press. If – as seems very likely – the plan goes through, year-round ferry sailings will be guaranteed in addition to the current April to October Hoverspeed service.

Returning into town from the port, you will almost inevitably wander back to the market squares and Dieppe's largest church, **St-Jacques**, the pinnacles and buttresses of which loom up at the end of many of the streets and alleys in this area. It's in obvious need of restoration, but is impressive nonetheless. The oldest part is the 13th-century nave, but its greatest feature is the 14th-century rose window on the west front, especially beautiful in the evening light. The line of chapels around the church were mostly built as donations by Dieppe shipowners in the 16th century, including one, the Sacré-Coeur, with very fine late-Gothic vaulting, and another with the tomb of Jehan Ango himself.

From the church, Rue St-Jacques leads off to meet up with the Grande-Rue in the intimate **Place du Puits-Salé**, the centre of Dieppe outside market hours. It is presided over by the **Café des Tribunaux**, one of the truly grand traditional French cafés. First built as a cabaret in the 18th century, it looks like something much more official, and did indeed serve as Dieppe's town hall at one time. As a café, it was an important place to be in the years when Dieppe acquired its artistic community. One of the first painters to come here was the English artist, long resident in France, Richard Bonington, who encouraged his friends Turner and Delacroix to visit Dieppe and paint its sea and sky in the 1820s. Later, Monet painted the church of St-Jacques, and Pissarro street scenes; other artists seen in Dieppe were Whistler, Renoir, Gauguin, William Nicholson, Degas, and especially the latter's friend, Walter Sickert, a near-fixture in the town over 40 years, who did much to introduce Impressionist ideas into English art. In the 20th century Braque, Miró and Barbara Hepworth were also drawn to Dieppe, and virtually all of them passed at some time or other through the Tribunaux. One figure most often associated with the place was Oscar Wilde. He first visited Dieppe in happier circumstances in 1878, invited by Sickert, and came back here, broken and depressed, immediately after his release from prison in 1897. He stayed for several months, spending long hours in cafés, and it is a matter of argument whether he wrote 'The Ballad of Reading Gaol' in the Tribunaux or the competing Café Suisse by the port.

After an aperitif at the Tribunaux, it may be time to go out to Varengeville for lunch. Otherwise, or if you are coming back into town, continue west from Place du Puits-Salé to the end of Rue de la Barre or any of the old streets parallel to it, where all roads immediately begin to climb a steep hill, crowned by the dramatic castle, now the **Château-Musée** (*open June–Sept daily 10–12 and 2–6; Oct–May Mon, Wed–Sat 10–12 and 2–5, Sun 10–12 and 2–6; closed Tues; adm*), which can be seen glowering down at you from many places in Dieppe. Built mainly in the 14th and 15th centuries, it's a rambling complex of ramparts, rooms, turrets and side-towers, with great views over the town and the sea.

The collection inside is an attractive mixture that, apart from a few nautical exhibits and an entertaining display on the history of sea bathing in Dieppe, mostly divides into two halves. One is made up of paintings, especially by artists associated with Dieppe; Renoirs, Boudins, Pissarros, Sickerts and an important collection of prints by Braque. Its greatest treasure, however, is its extraordinary collection of Dieppe ivories. When Dieppe was at its commercial height in the 17th century, its sailors wandered the coast of Africa trading for ivory tusks, which were brought back and worked on here by local carvers renowned throughout Europe for their skill. They produced combs, fans, crucifixes, thimbles, pens, decorative scenes and all kinds of other articles in fine ivory; all are represented here, and, whatever you feel about the fate of the elephants, reveal a quite staggering level of painstaking, sensitive workmanship.

From the castle take the steps down the seaward side of the hill to reach the sea front. At the foot of the hill is **Square du Canada**, which commemorates the 'Canadian Martyrs' –Jesuit missionaries killed by Indians in Quebec in the 17th century – and the terrible military mess of the Dieppe Raid of 19 August 1942, when a predominantly Canadian force of 6,000 men paid an appalling price – three-quarters of them killed, wounded or captured – to demonstrate to the Allied commanders that a frontal assault on a Channel port was not a viable prospect. Just beyond the square, next to the modern casino, there is a massive stone gateway, the **Porte des Tourelles**, which is the only remaining part of Dieppe's 14th-century walls.

In Dieppe the line of hotels and houses looking seawards along the main prome-nade, Boulevard de Verdun, is a considerable distance from the actual sea front; the space between them is occupied by a mini-golf course, a *jardin d'enfants*, a swimming pool, tennis courts and the inevitable thalassotherapy centre. The beach is shingle, but is actually the closest one to Paris, which may have been an important factor in prompting the Duchesse de Berry to introduce the English fad of sea-bathing into France here in 1824. Despite the rise of Deauville and the more ostentatious Côte Fleurie, Dieppe remained fashionable throughout the next century. Nowadays the sea front's grandeur seems a little faded, but like all old seaside resorts it still has plenty going on in summer. It also has a more modern attraction in the **Estran-Cité de la Mer** (*open May–Aug daily 10–7; Sept–April daily 10–12 and 2–6; adm*), at the very eastern end of the front, an aquarium and exhibition on all things to do with the sea.

Of the many attractions around Dieppe, one of the most distinguished is the **Château de Miromesnil** (*open May–15 Oct Mon, Wed–Sun 2–6; closed Tues; adm*), about 10km due south of the town near the N27 Rouen road . Begun in 1589, it's a very elegant example of a Henry IV-style, brick and stone château. The house has had two famous residents: the Marquis de Miromesnil, one of the enlightened ministers of Louis XVI who attempted ineffectually to reform the Ancien Régime in the years leading up to the French Revolution, and Guy de Maupassant, who was born here in 1850. This happened rather by accident, since his father was given to living above his means and rented several châteaux and other residences around the region, and the family moved on from Miromesnil four years later. Particularly impressive, though, are the lush grounds and gardens outside, and especially the approach, an immensely long beech-lined avenue. In the woods of the park there is a lovely 12th-century chapel, with fine 16th-century wood panelling inside. The château can only be visited by taking the sometimes-eccentric guided tours.

Otherwise, follow the D75 coast road west from Dieppe. **Pourville** is a pleasant, relaxed little beach village, in a broader-than-usual gap in the cliffs, which is why it was chosen as one of the main landing beaches for the 1942 Dieppe Raid. In a more peaceful time, it was particularly loved by Claude Monet, who rented a house and painted here with Alice Hoschedé in the 1880s before they made their definitive home in Giverny. In **Varengeville**, the next village along, the closest artistic associa-tions are with Georges Braque, who lived here for 20 years until his death in 1963. He is buried in the little churchyard, the Cimetière Marin, along with a Napoleonic soldier who from his gravestone seems to have been present at an impossible number of battles. It is in an extraordinary location on top of one of the area's tallest cliffs, next to Varengeville's beautiful 12th-century church – carefully shored up to prevent it sliding towards the sea. The church is marvellously peaceful, and has stained glass panels by Braque that combine wonderfully with the early-medieval structure. The view of the coast and the sea, with colours that shift continually from turquoise to grey, green or deep blue, is only one of Varengeville's celebrated features.

Now more of a smart residential community than a rural village, it also has two other special attractions. Just inland is the **Manoir d'Ango** (*open mid-Mar–mid-Nov daily 10–12.30 and 2–6.30; adm*), the grand and never-quite-finished palace that Dieppe's pirate-prince Jehan Ango had built with his ill-gotten and other gains, in another dramatic location atop a hill. It's a remarkable construction: a combination of Loire Valley-style French Renaissance château with finely worked Italian touches and a rustic Norman half-timbered manor house. In the great courtyard there's a giant drum that is France's largest pigeon loft (as symbols of wealth and status big pigeon lofts were the equivalent of a Mercedes and Rolex watches for 16th-century Norman aristocrats). Inside the house there is little to see (most of it is still a private residence), but around it there is now a magnificently colourful, recently created hydrangea garden, taking full advantage of the setting.

Varengeville's most renowned and unusual house and garden, though, is the **Bois des Moutiers** (*open 15 Mar–15 Nov; tickets sold 10–12 and 2–6, gardens open daily 10–8; adm; house tours by appointment*), a unique Anglo-French hybrid. It was built in 1898 for Guillaume Mallet, a wealthy anglophile banker, by the subsequently distinguished English architect Edwin Lutyens and the garden designer Gertrude Jekyll. It is the only English Arts and Crafts house in France, and Jekyll's garden similarly flies in the face of formal French traditions. Architect and garden designer worked closely together, and each part is inseparable from the other. Both are fabulous. The house (*guided tours only*) is not simply a transplanted English building, but includes local Norman features – sometimes quite playfully – and remarkably at times combines a medievalist feel with a futuristic look, such as the wonderfully lofty and elegant music room. The garden, created from nothing and beatifully moulded to the contours of the hillsides, is ravishing, especially in May and June. Guillaume Mallet and his wife were also theosophists, and around house and garden there are occult touches, such as the circle of trees upon a knoll, probably created in imitation of a druidic circle. The house is still owned by the Mallet family, and the very affable Antoine Bouchayer-Mallet takes many of the guided tours.

Beyond Varengeville the road continues a little inland from the clifftops. At **Sotteville**, about 15km further west, a turning seawards comes to an abrupt end above a steep gash in the rock, where a staircase of 230 steps provides the sole access to the beach, a magically atmospheric spot with crashing waves and fabulous views. A little further west again there is another of the area's special places, the spectacularly pretty village of **Veules-les-Roses**, built along 'the smallest river in France', the Veules. This was another of the apparently endless number of places in France that was first brought to the attention of the world at large by Victor Hugo, and later was much appreciated by the Impressionists. Its little river runs for just one kilometre along a steep dip in the cliff, but picks up surprising force, which for centuries has been used to power a series of small mills, as well as to sustain the dainty watercress beds that are another characteristic of the town. Go past Veules along the main road and you may scarcely notice it: it's essential to stop and explore it on foot, along the 'Circuit de la Veules' beside the river. The sheltered valley is extraordinarily lush, and the whole place is almost impossibly pretty, with thatched half-timbered mills and 19th-century villas forming an almost unreal, miniature town. The centre of the village is less *petite* but almost as attractive, and contains a very unusual 16th-century Gothic church, St-Martin, with curious sculptures on its columns that do not represent any recognisable Christian imagery; one theory suggests that they were influenced by pre-Columbian carvings seen by local mariners in the Americas.

St-Valery-en-Caux, capital of the Caux Maritime, was the site of bitter fighting in June 1940, when it was defended by French troops and the British 51st Highland Division, cut off from the main British force which had retreated to Dunkirk – which is why the town is now twinned with Inverness. Much of it had to be completely rebuilt post-war, but the old Quartier des Pénitents by the west bank of the harbour survived, a little knot of narrow alleys with a Gothic church and, by the quay, the giant 1540 half-timbered Maison Henri IV, which now houses the tourist office and a small museum. Otherwise, modern St-Valery is a likeable, busy fishing and yachting port, with plenty of movement in the harbour and a pebble beach at the foot of its cliffs.

Inland from Veules and St-Valery, the Valley of the Dun and the Caux plateau can appear superficially bleak, but anyone wishing to lose themselves in a rural world can easily spend an entertaining afternoon wandering in no particular direction between the villages, past half-timbered cottages, solid grey sandstone churches and village ponds and greens. It's a land of isolated villages glimpsed between clumps of trees in the misty flatness, with its own distinctive traditions, an area that provided much of the material for the rural tales of Maupassant. And in virtually every village there is the glimpse of a baroque château in isolated grandeur at the end of its *allée* of trees, for the Caux seems to have the highest concentration of baronial residences anywhere in Normandy. Villages with striking châteaux or manors include Gonzeville, Crasville-Le-Rocquefort and especially Ermenouville, built almost entirely around its giant 18th-century château (*only open for France's jours du patrimoine, or national heritage weekend, in Sept*). And near Mesnil-Durdent – around 10km from St-Valery and the smallest municipality in the Seine-Maritime, with just 27 inhabitants – there is one of the grandest of the region's mansions, the Château de Mesnil-Geoffroy (*open May–Sept Fri–Sun and hols 2.30–6; adm for château and park, or park only*). It was built in the 17th century in Louis XIII style and greatly extended in the 18th, when it was the residence of one of Louis XV's ministers. The current owners, the Prince and Princess Kayali, have taken great pains to restore both the décor the house wore in its grandest incarnation and the huge Le Nôtre-style gardens, with maze, aviary and a delicious rose garden. Visitors can see the house with a tour, and wander freely around the park. What's more, you can also stay as guests, for Mesnil-Geoffroy is one of France's most opulent *chambre-d'hôte* (*see* below).

Shopping

The Saturday Market is the great target for shoppers in **Dieppe**, but there are some stalls in the town centre mid-week as well. The best shopping streets are the Grande-Rue, Rue St-Jacques and Rue d'Ecosse. There are other attractive markets along the coast in **Veules-les-Roses** (*Wed*), and **St-Valery-en-Caux** (*Fri, and Sun mornings in summer*).

For convenience shopping the big centre in Dieppe is the **Belvédère shopping mall** – easy to find beside the big roundabout on the Rouen road out of town – with a well-stocked Auchan. Two other hypermarkets, Intermarché and Leclerc, are a little further east near the D154, and also very easy to spot.

Dieppe ✉ 76200

Chocolaterie Duvernet, 138 Grande-Rue, **t** 02 35 84 13 87. One of the most opulent of the Grande-Rue's chocolate specialists, with a magnetic display of fine handmade chocolates, fruit sweets, biscuits and pastries.

L'Epicier Olivier, 18 Rue St-Jacques, **t** 02 35 84 22 55. Claude Olivier is the father of Philippe, the near-legendary Boulogne master cheese-merchant, but this marvellous old shop is not as specialised: as well as an excellent selection cheeses maturing in the *caves* beneath the shop – including high-quality local Neufchâtel – there's a great range of coffees, fine wines, ciders, preserves and many other delicacies.

M Pommier, 18–24 Place Nationale, **t** 02 35 84 14 62. A quirky old shop selling fine wines, a range of coffees, teas, biscuits and other fine foods, and a surprising range of liqueurs.

Le Sommelier, 27 Rue des Maillots, **t** 02 35 06 05 20. In a narrow street just off Rue St-Jacques, this attractive fine wine merchant has a well-displayed range of French wines, brandies and liqueurs.

Where to Stay

St-Valery-en-Caux ✉ 76740

L'Albarquel, Côte d'Albatre SARL, Logement Mairie, Pleine Sève, **t/f** 02 35 57 21 58, **t** 06 11 97 56 50 (*doubles 210–250F/ €32.01–38.11, breakfast extra; whole boat: minimum six,* maximum ten, from 4,000F/€609.80 per day). This 80ft former Portuguese sailing barge, based in the harbour at St-Valery-en-Caux, has four comfortably appointed, compact cabins (this is a boat), dining and kitchen areas and two bathrooms that are minor miracles of space organisation. You can stay moored by the quay, or cruise along the Normandy coast and around the Channel. Bespoke trips can be arranged, including coming across to pick people up in England. Reservations must be made at least ten days in advance.

Ermenouville ✉ 76740

Château du Mesnil-Geoffroy, **t** 02 35 57 12 77, **f** 02 35 57 10 24 (*double rooms 380–500F/ €57.93–76.22; suites 550–700F/€83.85–106.71*). For a taste of the Ancien Régime, this is one of the best-maintained of the region's private châteaux, and also the Caux Maritime's most distinguished *chambre-d'hôte*. The rooms combine opulent Louis XVI décor with very good modern bathrooms and other necessities; 'gourmet breakfasts' and dinners featuring 18th-century recipes are available.

Hautot-sur-Mer ✉ 76550

Les Dryades, Rue de Bernouville, **t** 02 35 84 44 30, or **t** 06 12 52 55 17 (*rooms 270F/€41.16 for two; duplexes 350F/€53.36 for two, 60F/ €9.15 per extra person*). An exceptional *chambre-d'hôte* amid woods and winding lanes in a hilly village west of Dieppe, a short distance from the sea. Dominique and François Bloch's giant Norman farmhouse contains four themed rooms: the 'Joker' is like a multi-coloured circus tent, while 'Soleil' is in warm, sunshine orange and golden shades. There's a pleasant breakfast room and a garden with wonderful views.

Dieppe ✉ 76200

Villa des Capucins, 11 Rue des Capucins, **t** 02 35 82 16 52, **f** 02 32 90 97 52, *www.planete-b.fr/villa-des-capucins* (*rooms 320F/€48.78 for two, 450F/€68.60 for four*). Mme Ghislaine Boré's *chambre-d'hôte* is on a workaday street in the old fishermen's quarter of Le Pollet. Inside the gate is a big enclosed garden, and the turreted 19th-century house, formerly a Capuchin convent. The comfortable guest rooms are in former outbuildings either side of the garden.

Hôtel-Restaurant Au Grand Duquesne, 15 Place St-Jacques, **t** 02 32 14 61 10, **f** 02 35 84 29 83, *www.augrandduquesne.fr* (*doubles with shower or bath 250–280F/€38.11–42.69; single without shower 175F/€26.68*). A classic Logis de France hotel, in the heart of Dieppe by St-Jacques, which has been attractively renovated (although there's still no lift). The rooms are cosy and comfortable, and there's an above-average restaurant (*see* below).

Bar-Hôtel de l'Entracte, 39 Rue du Commandant, **t** 02 35 84 26 45 (*rooms 150–190F/€22.87–28.97*). Dieppe's favourite budget choice, right by the castle and the casino. All the rooms have some sort of sea view, and are plain but comfortable. Owners Michel and Jocelyne are very *sympa*, and breakfast is served in the bar downstairs, a real neighbourhood café.

Pourville-sur-Mer ✉ 76550

Mme Colette Marchand, Les Hauts de Pourville, **t** 02 35 84 14 29 (*rooms c. 280F/ €42.69 for two*). Mme Marchand offers B&B in her modern house on the cliffs above Pourville, with fabulous views over the beach and a heated indoor pool. The rooms, decorated with her paintings, are very spacious and comfortable.

La Thébaïde, 577 Rue des Verts Bois, **t** 02 35 84 21 14, or **t** 06 17 78 43 08 (*double room 270F/ €41.16*). A late-19th-century villa on the winding hill road between Dieppe and Pourville, just five minutes from the beach, with a very pretty, sun-filled room with its own entrance at the back of the house, plus its own terrace and fine views.

Veules-les-Roses ✉ 76780

Relais Douce France, 13 Rue du Docteur Girard, **t** 02 35 57 85 30, **f** 02 35 57 85 31 (*double rooms 420–590F/€64.03–89.94*). In the middle of Veules, beside the babbling river, this imposing old coaching inn with semi-fortified gateway has been attractively and comfortably restored. Its unusual and charming rooms have kitchenettes. There's a flower-filled courtyard, with tables outside for summer, and a restaurant (*see* below).

Eating Alternatives

Veules-les-Roses ✉ 76780

L'Assiette, in the Relais Douce France, *see* above (*menus 95–280F/€14.48–42.69*). A timbered dining room with flowers on the tables. Menus generally stick to Norman traditions, but with a light and imaginative approach, making fine use of local products, seafood and interesting seasonings.

Dieppe ✉ 76200

Hôtel-Restaurant Au Grand Duquesne, *see* above (*menus 68–249F/€10.37–37.96*). A restaurant and *traiteur* serving particularly good seafood and a range of sophisticated menus at amenable prices.

A la Marmite Dieppoise, 8 Rue St-Jean, **t** 02 35 84 24 26 (*menus 100F/€15.24, lunchtime only, 150F/€22.87 and 220F/€33.54*). An old-fashioned restaurant near the harbour – *the* place to try the eponymous *marmite dieppoise*: a stew combining fish and seafood in a Norman cream sauce. *Closed Sun eve and Mon, and Oct–May Thurs eve*.

Restaurant du Port, 99 Quai Henri IV, **t** 02 35 84 36 64 (*menus 98–170F/€14.94–25.92*). Near the end of Quai Henri IV – restaurant row – this stylish little restaurant serves imaginative food that's a cut above the harbourside norm. Fish and seafood are, of course, highlights, but there's a wide range of other alternatives. Excellent value.

Le Bistrôt du Pollet, 23 Rue de Tête de Boeuf, **t** 02 35 84 68 57 (*lunchtime menu only 75F/ €11.43*). A pretty, unassuming little restaurant on the Ile du Pollet that is highly regarded by locals. A meal – fish features strongly – need not top 130F/€19.82. Arrive early or book. *Closed Sun and Mon*.

Café Suisse, 19 Arcades de la Bourse, **t** 02 35 84 10 69 (*lunch menu 60F/€9.15*). The other historic café, in the arcades by the corner of the Grande-Rue. The new owners have opened it up to global influences with a good range of vegetarian dishes and organic foods and drinks.

Café des Tribunaux, 1 Place Puits-Salé, **t** 02 32 14 44 65. The legendary Tribunaux (*see* p.147) has a brasserie menu plus seafood dishes and snacks. Its outside tables are a great vantage point on Dieppe's street life.

Benedictine Luxuries:

Fécamp and Etretat

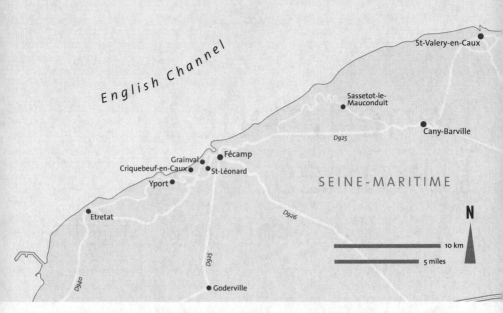

Some towns are conventionally pretty, all scenery and fine architecture, or have distinctive museums or cultural monuments; some may be no beauties but are strong on life and atmosphere. Others manage to combine a little of all these qualities in different measures. One such is Fécamp. Like Dieppe and the other ports of northern Normandy it sits in a gash in the long chalk cliff that lines this coast, dubbed the Côte d'Albâtre (Alabaster). At Fécamp the break in the cliffs is especially narrow, so that they stand huge, white and impressive above the town, squeezing most of it into a snug valley running inland. Its harbour is similarly an inlet much longer than it is wide, still very much a working port with a fishing fleet, but now shared by an increasing number of yachts. At the end of the harbour, beneath the cliffs, is the giant shingle bank of the beach, backed by a traditional seaside prom, where if you don't fancy windsurfing you can stroll and watch the gulls soaring against the wind.

In the year 1001 Duke Richard II of Normandy established one of the largest Benedictine abbeys in France in Fécamp, and during the Middle Ages it was among the most important pilgrimage centres in Europe, thanks to its shrine of the Precious Blood of Christ, believed to have been deposited here by Joseph of Arimathea. Fécamp was also one of the favoured capitals of the Norman dukes, and William the Conqueror threw lavish revels here at Easter 1067 to celebrate his conquest of England. Much later, it became a gritty deep-sea fishing port. From the 1830s on it also followed in the footsteps of Brighton and Dieppe and became one of the first seaside resorts, but Fécamp is marked out from all other towns along this coast by one unique feature, the result of the epic fancy of one man: the neo-Renaissance-Gothic-Baroque palace, museum and distillery that is the home of Bénédictine liqueur.

Getting There

Fécamp is about a 40min drive from Le Havre on the D925 via Goderville (or longer on the more attractive D940 coast road through Etretat), slightly further from Dieppe. From Calais and the north on the A29 *autoroute*, exit just west of Yvetot on to the D926.

The Auberge de la Rouge is in St-Léonard, about 2km south of Fécamp town. From the centre of Fécamp follow the signs for the Le Havre road (D925), which begins as Rue Charles-le-Borgne. Climb the hill and after a few bends you will arrive in St-Léonard, where the Auberge is unmissable on the left, shrouded by a few trees, with its own car park. From Le Havre, via Goderville, the Auberge will be on your right before you reach Fécamp.

Fécamp has train connections in two directions, from Le Havre and from Rouen and Paris. From the station in the middle of town the best way to get to St-Léonard is by cab.

Tourist Information

Fécamp: Maison du Tourisme, 113 Rue Alexandre Le Grand, t 02 35 28 51 01, f 02 35 27 07 77, *www.fecamp.com*. There's also an information kiosk on the seafront (*July and Aug*). The Seine-Maritime's 'Impressionist Itineraries' leaflets provide interesting information on Fécamp and Etretat.

Etretat: Place Maurice Guillard, t 02 35 27 05 21, f 02 35 28 87 20, *www.etretat.net*.

Yport: Place J.P. Laurens, t 02 35 29 77 31.

The coast west of Fécamp is also the most celebratedly beautiful part of the whole Côte d'Albâtre, above all Etretat, 20km away along the shore. Of all the many places on the north Normandy coast associated with the Impressionists, none was perhaps more important for painters like Monet and Boudin than this little oasis-town and its cliffs, with their ravishing light and spectacular rock formations; in the same era it also became a very singular and raffish resort for the upper crusts of France and Europe. This combination has left Etretat with a very individual, delicately cranky atmosphere that can still be felt today.

When the Fécampois wish to celebrate or tackle Sunday lunch in style, they commonly head for the **Auberge de la Rouge**, just outside town. It's an impressive, half-timbered Norman inn, a century old and supposedly named after the first owner and her red hair. Recently a new young chef has added some culinary innovations to the Auberge's established repertoire of superior, sophisticated variations on classic Norman and French cuisine. If you're feeling a desire to be pleasantly pampered, La Rouge is ideal.

Auberge de la Rouge

Route du Havre, St-Léonard, t 02 35 28 07 59, f 02 35 28 70 55, www.auberge-rouge.com. Open Tues–Sat 12–2.30 and 7–9.30, Sun 12–2.30; closed Mon and three weeks Jan and Feb. Booking advisable, and essential Sun. Menus 105F/€16.01, 165F/€25.15, 198F/€30.18 and 300F/€45.73; children's menu 65F/€9.91; à la carte average 300F/€45.73.

You enter the Auberge via a large gateway and an especially pretty leafy garden, with a pond, a fountain and loungers, chairs and tables where you can sit outside to eat or drink in summer. The same comfortable degree of luxury is continued inside.

The old inn has been elegantly renovated throughout: in the dining room, there are model boats and nautical prints which recall Fécamp's maritime traditions, fine silver and enough carpeting to create a satisfying hush. The waistcoated waiters exude traditional professionalism, but the atmosphere is friendly and charming, and few other restaurants at this level have better facilities for families with small children.

All French towns tend to have one restaurant that is generally considered the best in the area, and in Fécamp for many years this accolade has gone to the Auberge de la Rouge. For just as long the restaurant was inseparable from the figure of its ebullient chef-proprietor Claude Guyot who, as well as preparing superb Norman cuisine, ran marathons, gave cookery courses, held special lunches for Fécamp's football club and contributed in many other ways to local life. In spring 2000, however, M Guyot announced his retirement, and a new young chef, Thierry Enderlin, and his wife Anneke began work, having been carefully selected by Claude Guyot as the right people to take over his inheritance.

M Guyot was a hard act to follow, a supreme expert in traditional, buttery Norman sauces without a trace of heaviness. A faithful clientele like that of La Rouge also has very high expectations, and their own favourites. Thierry Enderlin is from the south and has his own style, with more use of olive oil and reductions rather than butter and *roux*. He has retained the lynchpins of the menu, such as the range of duck dishes and, naturally, the use of the finest local ingredients such as superb Fécamp fish, but is introducing his own imprint bit by bit. To some extent he is still finding his feet, but he's clearly a chef of flair from whom a lot can be expected.

His own dishes are light and intricate – sometimes a little overly so – and often feature radical combinations of foods and flavours (meat and fish, sweet and savoury) in Pacific-rim style, but still using entirely local ingredients. A wild duck *pâté en croûte* with foie gras is subtly smooth, and served with a multi-flavoured mixed-game *gelée*; in a main course *coquille St-Jacques* comes in a strong veal jus with caramelised chicory and leeks, a daring mix that succeeds wonderfully, with an entirely original flavour. More traditional regulars on the menu include the delicious Rouennais-style duck, with an addictive rich, dark sauce, and often served with fresh pasta; and the fabulous fresh fish dishes making the most of the local catch, such as simply grilled sea bass with a shellfish coulis and pan-fried tomatoes.

To go with these luxurious dishes there's an equally luxurious wine cellar, with a particularly good choice of fine rosés, and one tradition of the Rouge that has not been challenged is that of the *trou normand*, the sybaritic little bowl of apple sorbet in calvados that comes between first and main courses (except on the 105F menu). The cheese course is a great showcase for Normandy cheeses, but save some room for the Auberge's other speciality, its wonderful, rich desserts. A *gratin* of seasonal fruits with an orange *sabayon* makes a lovely warm pudding that explodes with goodness, the refined orange flavour cutting delicately across those of apples and berries, while another regular retained from the Guyot régime is a decadent warm soufflé with Bénédictine. As a final touch, the *petits-fours* served with coffee might be little tarts of woodland fruits, in fine, crumbly pastry.

Touring Around

In Fécamp, visitors' eyes tend to be drawn towards the town's most spectacular attraction. The **Palais Bénédictine** (*1½hr guided tours Feb–mid-Mar and mid-Nov–Dec daily 10–11.15 and 2–5; mid-Mar–June and Sept–mid-Nov daily 10–12 and 2–5.30; July and Aug daily 9.30–6; closed Jan; adm*) has pinnacle towers, baronial staircases and fine stained glass, and must be the world's grandest distillery. It was built for the founder of the company, Alexandre Le Grand, and stands comparison with William Randolph Hearst's San Simeon as one of the most extravagant creations of the pirate-prince era of capitalism.

The recipe for Bénédictine liqueur was invented by an Italian monk at Fécamp Abbey in about 1510, and for centuries it was made only by the monks for medicinal purposes. The Le Grands were a local family of beer and wine merchants and, when the abbey was dissolved during the French Revolution, an erudite Le Grand forebear bought up many relics and monastic documents, to prevent them being destroyed. In 1863 Alexandre, then aged 33, was browsing through these old papers when he came across the recipe, and a new life opened up before him. Not content just to tinker with the liqueur a little and put it on sale in the family shop, he chose to advertise his product aggressively, using some of the best poster artists of the great age of French graphic art, and to target the export market. The French had only a certain capacity for a sweet liqueur, and right from the start Bénédictine's market was the world.

The results were immediate. Le Grand also sought very deliberately to create a prestigious image for his brand, and to root it in history; providing a palace for his distillery naturally added to the mystique around the liqueur, and suggested a continuity with the ancient abbey. There was a shrewd commercial element in his plan, but looking at the Palais it's impossible not to think that Le Grand's personal ambition, romantic fantasy and antiquarianism played a major part as well. No expense was spared; then, in January 1892, the recently finished Palais burnt down. Undismayed, Le Grand rebuilt it on an even bigger scale. He did not live to see it all completed, dying in 1898, two years before its final inauguration.

The Palais Bénédictine has often been dismissed as pure kitsch, but more recent opinion has been more generous. Le Grand employed an otherwise obscure local architect, Camille Albert, who was thought to be influenced mainly by Viollet-le-Duc, the godfather of the Gothic revival in France. But so eclectic is the Palais that Albert's imagination seems just as close to that of Charles Garnier, creator of the Paris Opéra and prime exponent of pure extravagance in French architecture. In stone and red brick, the Palais appears neo-Gothic from a distance, but has windows and arches that would suit a Loire Valley Renaissance château; inside, there are rooms in operatic baroque. The standard of workmanship in details such as the stained glass and ironwork is extremely high.

The grandest parts of the Palais were built as a **museum** to house the collection of artefacts, mostly medieval and Renaissance, amassed by Le Grand – religious statuary, paintings, carved wooden chests, English alabaster altarpieces, Limoges enamels, furniture and magnificent 15th-century illuminated manuscripts. As a private collection it's hugely opulent, but also engagingly quirky and personal; there is a whole room, for example, full of 16th–18th-century doorknobs, locks, keys and door-knockers. After the museum rooms the tour takes in the distillery and cellars, with an imaginative display on the many herbs used in Bénédictine, although the famous recipe is of course not divulged. There is also a gallery that hosts temporary shows of contemporary art. Free tastings are offered in the stylish bar, before the tour ends in the shop. Bénédictine is now part of the Bacardi empire, which, conscious that it has not exactly been a hip tipple in recent years, is promoting it as a cocktail mixer in concoctions such as the Rainbow (Bénédictine, rum, orange juice, peach nectar and grenadine).

Opposite the main entrance is the tourist office; from there, take the street downhill beside the Palais, Rue du Domaine, to reach Rue de la Mer, and turn right for the centre of town. Early Fécamp and the abbey that once exercised control over a large part of the surrounding area grew up on higher ground some way inland, and the fishing community by the port was almost a separate village until the 19th century. Rue de la Mer becomes Rue St-Etienne and then runs out into Fécamp's two main squares, Place St-Etienne, to the left and dominated by the fine 16th-century church of St-Etienne, and the larger Place Charles-de-Gaulle on the right, which, if it's Saturday, will be filled by the market. The main shopping streets are also close by, around Rues Jacques-Huet and Alexandre-Legros. The **Musée des Arts et de l'Enfance** (*21 Rue A-Legros; open Sept–June Mon, Wed–Sun 10–12 and 2–5.30; closed Tues; July and Aug daily 10–12 and 2–5.30; adm; same ticket also admits to Musée des Terre-Neuvas*) is a very charming museum in an 18th-century *hôtel* with an original display of local ceramics, carved ivories, painting, furniture, archaeological finds and especially items related to childhood, including a rare and remarkable collection of antique babies' bottles.

From the landward end of Rue A-Legros, Rue Leroux leads into the oldest part of Fécamp, and to the **abbey**. The main surviving monastic buildings, rebuilt in the 17th and 18th centuries and classical-baroque in style, now form the **Hôtel de Ville**. Alongside them is the abbey church, the **Eglise de la Trinité**, which is larger than many cathedrals. Like the rest of the abbey it was given a rather jarring 18th-century façade, but behind it the church is a beautiful example of early Gothic in plain, light-coloured stone, an interesting contrast to the Bénédictine's decorative overkill.

Its visual impact stems especially from the fact that it's unusually long (127m) for its width. This is the fourth church on this site. The legend that some of the **Precious Blood** had made its way to Fécamp was known in the 7th century, and a small women's convent and chapel grew up at the shrine. At the end of the 10th century, in fulfilment of a vow to his father, Richard I of Normandy, and to mark the first millennium, Duke Richard II built a far grander church and attracted the Benedictines to found a men's abbey. The tombs of both Richards are now in the south transept. So many pilgrims came to Fécamp, though, that this church too became inadequate, and it was entirely rebuilt in Romanesque style in 1106. This third church was then destroyed by fire in 1168, and replaced by the present, Gothic, church, most of which was completed by 1220.

The Precious Blood is still there, in a reliquary on the marble altar from 1510, by the Italian Renaissance sculptor Viscardo. More striking, though, and in front of the altar is a rare Romanesque reliquary chest, believed to have been used for the transfer of the remains of Richards I and II. Elsewhere in the church there is a delicate Renaissance carved chancel screen, behind which, in the side chapels, there are superb medieval carved tombs and stained glass. In the south transept there is an exquisite, vivid carving of the *Entombment of the Virgin* in polychrome stone (1495), but most unique is the giant, ornate 1667 clock in the north transept, which indicates the time, months, seasons and even the tides. Outside, opposite the church's main entrance, some ruins remain of the **Palais Ducal**, the palace of the dukes of Normandy; in the streets off to the left, such as Rue Arquaise, there are still several medieval houses.

From the abbey a walk seawards, veering to the right through Rue Jacques-Huet and the shopping streets around the market, will bring you eventually to Quai Bérigny and the **harbour**. Commercial and fishing traffic is now largely confined to the inner basin; the outer harbour is mainly a *port de plaisance* for yachts. The break-waters of the outer harbour are lined with wooden walkways, called *estacades*, on wooden piers above the water, and a stroll along them is a very pleasant way to see the port. Alternatively, in **Place Nicolas Selle**, where Quai Bérigny meets Rue de la Mer, there are several outdoor cafés in which to have a drink while engaging in the time-honoured custom of watching boats go up and down.

It was the building of the port in the 19th century that made old Fécamp and the **fishing community** into one town. Fécamp had a high-seas fishing fleet, especially dedicated to fishing for cod on the Newfoundland (Terre-Neuve) Banks, and for decades a large proportion of the town's menfolk disappeared for months each year on these perilous Atlantic voyages, in sailing ships known as Terre-Neuvas, while others worked in shipyards and fish-smokers. This was the town known to Maupassant, 'ever pervaded by the smell of fish'. The streets alongside the port and, oddly, around the Palais Bénédictine still have some of the look of a 19th-century industrial town, with rows of small terraced houses. At the end of the harbour, just around the corner on the sea front (called Boulevard Albert I), there's an imaginatively presented modern museum, the **Musée des Terre-Neuvas et de la Pêche** (*open Sept–June Mon, Wed–Sun 10–12 and 2–5.30; closed Tues; July–Aug daily 10–7; adm; same ticket also admits to Musée des Arts et de l'Enfance*), dedicated to Fécamp's maritime traditions. Of great interest to anyone with nautical leanings, it also covers a good deal of social history, including the development of Fécamp as a seaside resort.

The **seafront** was the other major 19th-century addition to the town, running along the beach to end at the casino and a footpath up to the cliffs. The beach is all pebbles and not much good for swimming, but fine for windsurfing or a paddle. Alternatively, if you're feeling energetic, make your way right back across the quays to the north side of the port, from where there is a steep but enjoyable climb up the giant cliff via a historic pilgrims' path, the **Côte de la Vierge**, to reach the chapel of **Notre-Dame-de-Salut**, where Fécamp fishermen traditionally gave thanks for a safe return. There are also some old German blockhouses, and wonderful views over the town and out to sea.

West of Fécamp the D940 to Etretat curves slightly inland, but several turnings head back to the sea, and the narrow winding lane of the D211 (and the GR21 long-distance footpath) stays close to the cliff edge. About 8km from Fécamp is **Yport**, one of the coast's curiosities. It's like other breaks in the cliff along this coast, only in miniature: in a deep little valley that almost seems hidden from the world by its sea cliffs, with a small beach, small casino and a village instead of a town. Its charm and beauty made its name in the 19th century, and Boudin, Maupassant, Corot and André Gide all visited at different times. Today, it has some curiously elegant shops for such a small place, and a very placid atmosphere. **Grainval**, between Yport and Fécamp, is an even smaller beach village.

One of the most distinctive features that make up both Yport and Etretat is their special climatic conditions. The steep valleys in which they sit are sheltered from the Atlantic winds, creating lush, almost sub-tropical microclimates that contrast strikingly with the flat plateau just above them. **Etretat** also has the most dramatic **cliffs** on the whole coast, standing like massive gateways to the beach and battered by the sea into giant arches that look eerily as if they must have been the product of human intervention, with a solitary pinnacle of rock, **L'Aiguille** or Needle, just offshore. Monet did a whole series of paintings of these cliffs at different times of day, and Boudin, Corot, Courbet and innumerable other artists were drawn to them as well. At about the same time, Etretat's combination of sea air, famously clear light and balmy temperatures led to it being recommended as an especially healthy place to spend the summer, and it became a fashionable resort favoured by high society and minor European royalty. Offenbach took a villa here, when he was the most popular composer in France. It was this combination of artists and aristocracy that led to the sides of the valley being taken over by rather grand villas, in a style that could be called Second Empire-fairytale.

Etretat's collection of the French equivalent of over-the-top Victoriana – turrets, pinnacles, curving balconies, hidden gardens – is one more essential part of its whimsical individuality. One of the writers most associated with the town was **Maurice Leblanc**, whose stories of the 'gentleman burglar' Arsène Lupin rivalled Sherlock Holmes in popularity in France. Leblanc's own fantasy cottage, **Le Clos Lupin** (*open April–Sept daily 10–7, night sessions 7–10; Oct–Mar Mon, Fri–Sun 11–5; adm*), now hosts a kind of 'performance-museum' that makes the most of the house's mysteriousness, and can be enjoyed even if you're not familiar with the Lupin stories.

There is much that is 'mock' in Etretat (as well as some rather drab 1960s buildings by the beach, put up when the 19th century was less appreciated). In the centre of the town there is an imposing timber-frame Norman **market hall** which, despite appearances, was only built in 1926, albeit using the very best-quality timbers from the Eure, from where the style was copied. Today, the hall houses some twee knick-knack shops. As a renowned beauty spot, without the workaday concerns of Fécamp, Etretat fills up on summer weekends, but it retains a great deal of quirky, small-town charm. There are superb walks along the clifftops to the west (the *falaise d'aval*) and to the east (*amont*); the tourist office has free maps, but the paths are also well marked-out. The view from the east back across to the *falaise d'aval* at sunset is one of the Côte d'Albâtre's greatest pleasures.

Shopping

Fécamp's large market fills the town centre on Saturdays; the most attractive shops are in the streets around the market square, especially Rue Jacques-Huet. In **Etretat**, the market is on Thursdays, in **Yport** on Wednesdays.

Fécamp ✉ 76400

Brûlerie Fécampoise, 26 Rue Jacques-Huet, t 02 35 27 68 21. A delightful little shop specialising in fine coffees (and teas). There's also a little *café-salon*.

Caves Bérigny, 91 Quai Bérigny, t/f 02 35 27 19 79. A compact wine merchant on the harbour quay. The French wines are expertly selected and of high quality. Prices are competitive, and the staff are helpful.

Epicerie Fromentin, 52 Rue Jacques-Huet, t 02 35 28 58 88, f 02 35 28 95 23. A cross between a traditional luxury *épicerie* and a very high-quality supermarket, selling fine wines, teas, coffees (beans or ground), jams, oils, excellent *charcuterie* and fresh veg.

Etretat ✉ 76790

Fromagerie Le Valaine, Manoir du Cateuil, Route du Havre, t 02 35 27 14 02, f 02 35 29 23 92. A goat farm just west of Etretat, well-signposted on the D940, that produces fine *chèvre*, as well as ice-cream, chocolates, goat pâté with calvados, and farm cider. *Shop open Mar–Nov daily, closed 12.30–2. Guided tours in French, English and German, Easter–11 Nov Sun 11am; July and Aug also Mon–Wed 11am and Sat 3.30pm.*

Maison Tranchard, 10 Av George V, t 02 35 27 01 56, f 02 35 29 89 82, and 2 Rue Alphonse Karr, t 02 35 27 01 56. The first-choice local purveyors of gourmet goodies. The George V shop is the main *épicerie*, with wonderful honeys, terrines, chocolates, coffees and foie gras, and a superior choice of wines, Normandy ciders and calvados. Around the corner is the excellent *fromagerie*.

Yport ✉ 76111

Pierre, 38 Rue Alfred Nunès, t 02 35 27 30 21. A beautifully neat and ornate *confiseur-chocolatier*, with a superb display of rich handmade chocolates, slabs of praline, fresh pastries and other irresistible delights.

Where to Stay

Fécamp ✉ 76400

Auberge de la Rouge, *see above* (*double rooms 350–420F/€53.36–64.03*). Most of the compact, comfortable guest rooms have a bathroom and single bed on a lower level and a double bed on a platform above. They open on to the lovely garden behind the inn.

Hôtel d'Angleterre, 91–93 Rue de la Plage, t 02 35 28 01 60, f 02 35 28 62 95, *www.hotel angleterre.com* (*double rooms 250–390F/ €38.11–59.46*). One street back from the beach, this is an archetypical French 19th-century hotel, but with a youthful feel (in part due to the laidback 'Pub Anglais' on the ground floor). The rooms are bright and airy, and include a family room and a suite. The **Restaurant de la Manche**, downstairs, has a bargain lunch menu (*60F/€9.15*).

Hôtel-Restaurant Le Martin, 18 Place St-Etienne, t 02 35 28 23 82, f 02 35 28 61 21 (*rooms 185–205F/€28.20–31.25*). The best budget hotel: a piece of old France, with simple, well-kept rooms and friendly staff. It has an excellent restaurant, *see below*.

Etretat ✉ 76790

Château des Aygues, Route de Fécamp, t 02 35 28 92 77 (*'Oriental Room' 650F/€99.09, breakfast 70F/€10.67; 'Suite de la Reine' 1,250F/ €190.56*). One of Etretat's rarer attractions: a 19th-century fantasy house, with grand staircases, pointed turrets and ornamental brickwork. It has been lovingly restored and filled with a dazzling collection of antiques. The two guest rooms are extraordinary: the 'Oriental Room' has superb Chinese fittings, twin beds and a circular shower room in one of the towers; the Suite de la Reine is in Napoleon III-style with two double beds and a separate bathroom. The palatial breakfast room has lovely views over the wooded garden. *Rooms available Easter–1 Nov, and out of season by request. No children.*

Le Donjon, Chemin de St-Clair, t 02 35 27 08 23, f 02 35 29 92 24, *www.le-donjon.com* (*rooms 580F/€88.42 in winter, from 880F/€134.16 April–Nov; demi-pension obligatory at weekends*). An ivy-clad 1860s mock-château in a superb location, surrounded by cedars on the heights behind the town with views down to the cliffs and the sea. It's undeniably touristy, but extremely luxurious and comfortable. Some of the rooms have balconies, there's a heated open-air pool, and a high-standard restaurant (*see* below).

Hôtel La Résidence, 4 Bd René Coty, **t** 02 35 27 02 87 (*rooms 170–690F/€25.92–105.19*). The building, better known as the Manoir de la Salamandre, looks the very essence of ancient Norman half-timbering, but is in fact a reconstruction of two 15th–16th-century houses from Lisieux, brought here in the 1920s. The interior has a cranky charm. The 15 rooms have all modern comforts, although they vary a lot in size.

Villa les Charmettes, Allée des Pervenches, **t** 02 35 27 05 54, **f** 02 35 28 45 05 (*450F/ €68.60 for two*). Three *chambres-d'hôtes* rooms in a classic villa on one of the wooded *allées* behind the town. The Renards seek to maintain the house and gardens in keeping with their original style. The spacious, high-ceilinged guest rooms have a Belle Epoque feel, punctuated by a collection of contemporary art; all have wonderful views over Etretat and the sea.

Sassetot-Le-Mauconduit ✉ 76540

Château de Sassetot-Le-Mauconduit, **t** 02 35 28 00 11, **f** 02 35 28 50 00, *www.chateau-de-sassetot.com* (*rooms 520–950F/€79.27– 144.83; suites from 1,200F/€182.94; 'Sissi Suite' c. 1,900F/ €289.65 per night, book well ahead*). This elegant, 18th-century château, in its own park 15km east of Fécamp, is now a lovely country-house hotel. Empress Elizabeth of Austria, known as Sissi, stayed here in the 1870s, and the regal 'Sissi Suite' is the hotel's star accommodation. The basic rooms are a little small; go for a *chambres charme* or junior suite if you can.

Criquebeuf-en-Caux ✉ 76111

Ferme-Auberge de la Côte d'Albâtre, **t/f** 02 35 28 01 32 (*rooms 250F/€38.11 for two, 400F/ €60.98 for four*). A Caux-style brick farmhouse with two cosy B&B rooms, with antique country furniture. M and Mme Basille are warm and welcoming, and you can of course order meals in the *auberge* downstairs (*see* below). It's easy to locate in the village by the Gîtes de France signs.

Eating Alternatives

Sassetot-Le-Mauconduit ✉ 76540

Château de Sassetot-Le-Mauconduit, *see* above (*menus from c. 180F/€27.44*). The hotel's pretty dining room has 18th-century panelling, big fireplaces and vases of fresh flowers; in good weather there are also tables on the terrace. The menu often features refined versions of local dishes. Save room for the decadent desserts, such as *nougat glacé à la Bénédictine*.

Etretat ✉ 76790

Le Donjon, *see* above (*menus from 130F/ €19.82*). A comfortable, pretty restaurant with seasonal menus based on local mainstays: wild mushrooms, lamb, duck, seafood, local cheeses. Dishes are luxuriously rich, and a few globetrotting touches creep in.

Criquebeuf-en-Caux ✉ 76111

Ferme-Auberge de la Côte d'Albâtre, *see* above (*four-course feasts 115F/€17.53 or 147F/€22.41*). Mme Odile Basille prepares ample meals of traditional Norman cooking using produce straight from the farm. The wide range of dishes includes a great Pont-l'Evêque cheese brioche, onion or leek tarts, her own terrines and pâtés, *coq au cidre*, and classic fruit tarts. Reservations essential. *Closed Wed and Sun eves.*

Fécamp ✉ 76400

Le Maritime, 2 Place Nicolas Selles, **t** 02 35 28 21 71 (*menus 99–210F/ €15.09–32.01*). A bustling seafood brasserie on the quayside, with a *salle panoramique* looking over the harbour, serving good-value local favourites: *moules*, *sole à la normande*, simple fish grills, platters of *fruits de mer*, oysters, lobsters and fish-and-seafood stews.

Restaurant Le Martin, *see* above (*menu gastronomique only 160F/€24.39*). A snug café-restaurant on one of Fécamp's main squares, with check tablecloths and exposed beams. Bluff chef-proprietor Jean Martin is a master of classic Norman dishes: chicken in cider, *moules à la crème*, sole with vermouth and cream sauces. *Closed Sun eve and Mon.*

Deep in France:
the Pays de Bray

17

Long, rolling ridges rise and fall between steep-sided valleys in the Pays de Bray, the long rift that runs from just below Dieppe diagonally southeast towards Beauvais and Paris. It's a geological oddity, known as the Boutonnière or 'Buttonhole' – a cleft of clay and sandstone between two great slabs of chalk which has created a pocket of hilly, often lush landscape, small rivers and long stretches of woodland in between the flat and monotonous plateaux of Caux and Picardy.

The clay soil makes excellent pasture, and the region's sheep and brown-and-white dairy cattle are often its most visible inhabitants. This is the home of Neufchâtel cheese, by far the oldest of the classic Normandy cheeses, already known before William the Conqueror first set foot in England. Since the coming of railways in the 1850s the fortunes of the Pays de Bray have been tied to the markets of Paris, as one of the capital's favourite sources of butter, cheese and every other kind of dairy product. In 1850 in Gournay-en-Bray, Charles Gervais, an enterprising local businessman with a shop in Paris, began to manufacture Petit-Suisse, supposedly invented in a happy collaboration between an itinerant Swiss farmhand and a Norman milkmaid. Today, Gervais produce huge quantities of Petits-Suisses, yogurts and cheeses. The Bray valleys are also known for their duck, geese and the products made from them, and, not surprisingly, for their apples and ciders.

And yet the overall impression given by the Pays de Bray, especially in the north, is not one of an area given over to large-scale agribusiness. Instead the farms are small and discreet, often built in a distinctive brick-chalet style with low-hanging roofs. Nor, despite its range of traditional produce, is this a part of Normandy where agri-tourism is intensively developed. It has its special destinations – including three spectacular gardens – but the local tourist authorities have adopted the slogan of *Normand tout simplement*, 'Simply Norman', perhaps a shy way of admitting that its villages, speciality food producers and local museums are engagingly low-key rather than postcard-pretty. It's a genuine piece of rural France, one of the most attractive, characterful and peaceful stretches of countryside between Paris and the Channel coast.

Getting There

The main trunk road into the Pays de Bray is now the A28 Abbeville–Rouen *autoroute*, which branches off the A16 from Calais and runs just south of Neufchâtel-en-Bray, parallel to the more peaceful N28. From Calais to Neufchâtel is about a 2hr drive. From Dieppe two relatively tranquil roads lead into the Pays de Bray, the D1 to Neufchâtel and the D915 to Forges-les-Eaux and take *c.* 45mins or less.

In Forges-les-Eaux, all roads converge on the main square, Place de la République, and the smaller Place Brévière to one side. The Hôtel de la Paix very nearly overlooks the latter. If you come into Forges from Neufchâtel and the north on the D1314, you will see the hotel on your right on the same road just before you enter the square. Entering from Dieppe or Rouen on the D915 you will arrive at Place Brévière; turn left and the hotel is on the left. The Amiens and Paris roads also enter the same square, on the eastern side. There is a car park at the back of the hotel.

Local trains on the Paris–Dieppe line stop at Forges and Neufchâtel, and the Rouen–Amiens line passes through Forges.

Tourist Information

Forges-les-Eaux: Rue du Maréchal Leclerc, t 02 35 90 52 10, f 02 35 90 34 80. The office is just off the central Place de la République.
Neufchâtel-en-Bray: 6 Place Notre-Dame, t 02 35 93 22 96, f 02 32 97 00 62. The office is next to the church of Notre-Dame in the town centre.
St-Saëns and **Forêt d'Eawy**: Place Maintenon, St-Saëns, t 02 35 34 57 75.

The Pays de Bray was also once a border area, the eastern frontier of the independent Duchy of Normandy. It was settled relatively late, much of it in the 12th century, and many of the villages have small, plain Romanesque churches from that time. The towns, similarly small-scale, mostly grew up as markets for the surrounding farms. An exception is Forges-les-Eaux, which has a rather grander past as a spa, 'discovered' in the 17th century. And at the centre of Forges is the **Hôtel de la Paix**, a classic small-town Logis hotel, where M Rémy Michel has won an enviable reputation throughout the valleys with his satisfying, traditional Norman cooking.

Hôtel de la Paix

*15 Rue de Neufchâtel, Forges-les-Eaux, t 02 35 90 51 22,
f 02 35 09 83 62. Open Oct–May Mon 7.15–9.30, Tues–Sat 12–2
and 7.15–9.30, Sun 12–2; June–Sept Mon 7.15–9.30, Tues–Sun 12–2
and 7.15–9.30. Book weekends. Menus 92F/€14.03, 110F/€16.77,
147F/€22.47 and 198F/€30.18; children's menu 60F/€9.15;
à la carte average 170F/€25.92.*

M Michel reckons – and this is a considered observation, not a casual remark – that in the 23 years since he took over the hotel 80 per cent of the inhabitants of Forges-les-Eaux and the vicinity have eaten there at some point; many return at least once a month. Around the tables you will see family groups, young couples, men in denims, ladies with dogs, men in suits, men in sweaters and every other element of local society.

As usual in the French countryside, the décor is not self-consciously rustic: the dining room is bright and comfortable, substantially renovated like the hotel, and decorated with local painted ceramics. Front-of-house is presided over by Mme Régine

Poulet au Cidre Fermier

Serves 4

1 free-range chicken, about 1.8kg/3lb
1 carrot, finely diced
1 onion, finely diced
1 tablespoon plain flour, plus more for dusting
1 tablespoon tomato purée
1 garlic clove, crushed or chopped
bouquet garni (thyme, bay leaf and parsley stems, tied)
40g/1½oz butter
100g/3½oz lardons, blanched
250g/9oz mushrooms, sliced
1 shallot, finely chopped
2–3 tablespoons calvados
250ml/9fl oz dry cider
3 tablespoons double cream or crème fraîche
salt and pepper

Joint the chicken and reserve the pieces in the fridge.

Roughly chop the carcass and brown it in a heavy casserole with the carrot and onion, either in a hot oven or on the hob. Sprinkle with the flour, stir to blend and continue cooking until the mixture is lightly browned, stirring occasionally. Cover with cold water and add the tomato purée, the garlic and bouquet garni. Bring to a boil, reduce the heat and simmer gently for ½hour, skimming off the foam as needed. Sieve the stock, discarding the solids, and reserve.

Dust the chicken pieces lightly with flour; season with salt and pepper. Heat the butter in a sauté or frying pan over a medium heat until it foams. Add the chicken, skin-side down, and sauté until lightly browned. Turn the pieces and brown the other side. Add the lardons, mushrooms and shallot, reduce the heat, cover and cook for about ½hour, stirring occasionally, until the chicken is just cooked through. Remove the chicken, mushrooms and lardons and skim off the fat from the pan.

Add the calvados to the pan and flame. Add the cider and boil until it is almost all evaporated. Add the reserved stock and boil 2–3 minutes until slightly reduced, stir in the cream and return the chicken to the pan to reheat. Taste for seasoning and serve on warm plates, the chicken in the centre, surrounded by lardons and mushrooms. Pour over the sauce, dividing it evenly.

Michel, and service is provided by a young staff who are well schooled in the traditional arts of waitering *comme il faut*. M Michel's cooking is firmly based in the classic Norman repertoire – plenty of duck, ham, chicken and steaks, fish such as cod, sole and salmon, and cream, cheese and cider sauces – turned into creative dishes such as his *croustades* (pastry cases) of *coquilles St-Jacques* with *pommeau* or *suprême de barbue* (brill) *au cidre*, skilful variations on traditional styles and ingredients.

There are four exceptional set menus, handily labelled A to D. They change a little from time to time, but each offers an excellent and generous choice of quality Norman cooking at very reasonable prices. The B menu includes a fabulous savoury salad with a beef vinaigrette; mains include *poulet au cidre* and lamb with a tarragon sauce. The most truly local dishes are on C, the *menu du terroir*, such as the meaty-but-subtle homemade terrine of *canard à la Rouennaise*, maybe followed by a flavour-rich *magret de canard aux cerises à l'aigre doux*, skate wings in sorrel cream or *paupiettes* (rolled slices) of veal with girolles mushrooms.

All but the A menu include a cheese course: you obviously have to try the Neufchâtel, which is as good it can be. Just as excellent is the Camembert. Finish off with a dessert. A recent speciality is a *tourte aux poires de Fisé*, a deceptively simple-looking but intricately prepared pear tart.

The excellent cellar is well above the norm for a small-town hotel. There's nothing on the wine list that isn't French – the very idea – but there's a fine representation of classic French regions, and especially Bordeaux. You can venture into grand bottles such as an Amiral de Beychevelle Haut-Médoc or *premier cru* red Burgundies, but even if you stay at the more accessible end with wines like St-Nicolas-de-Bourgueil or Gigondas from the Loire, you'll find that they too have been carefully selected.

Touring Around

Neufchâtel-en-Bray, at the junction of the roads from Dieppe and Abbeville, is the traditional capital of the Pays de Bray, although no longer its largest town. It's also one of the best places to buy Neufchâtel cheese, most of all at the **market**, which every Saturday fills both the square around the church of Notre-Dame, halfway up the hill of the Grande-Rue, and Place 11 Novembre further up. This being a country market it's best to get there in good time, for many stalls start packing up soon after midday; the best cheese displays are generally inside the covered market in Place 11 Novembre. In addition to the local cheese you can find fine *chèvre*, as well as the usual stalls offering excellent terrines, spit-roasted chickens, wonderful fresh vegetables and a huge number of leather jackets. Around them you can watch what seems like nearly half the population of the Pays de Bray, chatting and mingling.

Neufchâtel cheese is mentioned in a document from 1035, and some was already being shipped to England in its current form in the 16th century, but it was not given an *appellation contrôlée* until 1977. It still comes entirely from local farms, for there are no large-scale producers. The cheese is made in a variety of shapes: cylinders (*bondes*), rectangles (*briquettes* and *carrés*) and, most distinctively, hearts (*coeurs*). This doesn't affect the flavour, which depends on whether it's *jeune* (up to twelve days old), *demi-affiné* (one to three weeks) or *affiné* (one to three months), the last of which has a pretty gnarled appearance. The story goes that the heart shape was first made by Norman milkmaids during the Hundred Years' War, in an effort to 'soften the hearts' of the depraved English soldiery.

When the market is not in session Neufchâtel is a quiet country town. Several build-ings along the Grande-Rue have the plain, functional lines of late-1940s reconstruction architecture, an indication that Neufchâtel was badly damaged during the Second World War and then rebuilt. The church of **Notre-Dame**, at the hub of one of the market squares, was begun in 1126 and has a fine 13th-century Gothic choir. It too, though, was severely hit by German bombing in 1940, and a good deal of the present building is a reconstruction. Remarkably unharmed, however, was its most beautiful possession, a delicate 16th-century carved *Entombment of Christ*, in one of the side chapels. At the foot of the hill of the Grande-Rue, in a pretty 16th-century merchants' house, there is a charming local museum dedicated to rural traditions and crafts, the **Musée Mathon-Durand** (*open Sept–June Sat and Sun 3–6; July and Aug Tues–Sun 3–6; adm*), with an attractive collection of local glass and pottery and a monumental 1837 cider press.

South of Neufchâtel the D1314 valley road passes under the A28 *autoroute* and immediately re-enters open downland. European regulations mean that it's now diffi-cult to visit farms to see cheese being made, but there are several around the area that offer their Neufchâtel cheeses for direct sale, indicated on the tourist offices' Route du Fromage de Neufchâtel leaflet. One place that is organised for visitors is the Brianchon family's Ferme des Fontaines, near the tiny village of Nesle-Hodeng (*see* p.171). From there it's possible to meander on southwards away from the main routes, through tiny lanes and villages such as Mesnil-Mauger, where massive old farm-houses and a tumble-down château stand between much smaller cottages, all with a pleasant air of quaint remoteness. This will bring you into **Forges-les-Eaux** on the north side, from where it looks just like another straightforward country town, with the main cafés and the Hôtel de la Paix arranged around the central squares. A walk down Rue de la République after lunch will reveal its smarter aspect.

The town's hot springs, the Eaux, were discovered in the 16th century, but they were not widely known until 1633, when Louis XIII, his queen Anne of Austria and Cardinal Richelieu arrived here together to try the waters. Forges was quickly transformed into a fashionable spa, and remained so throughout the Ancien Régime, numbering Voltaire and many other distinguished names among its visitors. In the 19th century, however, when the most famous waterholes of Europe were doing their best busi-ness, the town was largely forgotten. The spa was not really redeveloped until the 1950s, when the bulky modern **Grand Casino** was built amid neat gardens on the western side of town by the Andelle river, fronted by a neoclassical gate that came from a convent in Gisors destroyed during the war, and which was bought and installed here by the casino promoters to add a touch of grandeur. More recently casino and spa have been taken over by Club Med, which has made them into one of France's premier health-and-leisure farms.

The casino stands beside **Avenue des Sources**, a broad and elegant stretch of the Rue de la République–Dieppe road that seems strikingly out of sorts with the humble main part of town just to the east. On the north side of the avenue the river widens into two pretty lakes with pedalos for hire, and in between them there is a formal French-style park that was originally laid out in the spa's most fashionable era in the

18th century. Walk through this park and you will come to the **Bois d'Epinay**, an unspoilt forest with well-marked paths where you could wander for miles.

While the spa was declining in the 19th century, one business that was doing well in Forges was the manufacture of painted earthenware using local clay, introduced by an Englishman, George Wood, in 1797. A good collection of the simple but decorative Forges earthenware is on show in the **Musée de la Faïence** (*admission via tourist office; adm*) on the main square. This industry too fell into decline in the 20th century, but recently some attempts have been made to revive it.

The most interesting museum in the area is a wonderful 'farm-museum', the **Ferme de Bray** (*open Easter–June and Sept–Nov Sat, Sun and public hols 2–6; July and Aug daily 2–6; adm*), well-signposted on the D915, about 7km north of Forges near Sommery. Its owner Patrice Perrier, an engaging combination of Norman farmer and middle-aged hippy, has a document in his possession that shows that his family have been on this property since 1452. He ran it as a dairy farm until the 1980s, when he realised that in the age of quotas the farm itself was more of an asset than anything it could produce. The main farmhouse is 16th-century, and nearby there's a 15th-century watermill, a *laiterie* (dairy) built and altered from 1400 to 1800, and a 15th-century brick bread-oven and 17th-century horse-driven cider press, both still regularly in use. Running through the middle of the farm is what was for centuries the main road between Dieppe and Paris, until the line of the present-day D915 was laid out in Napoleon's time. It all seems implausibly ancient, especially since no conscious effort has ever been made to bring it all together.

The farm also has *chambre-d'hôte* (*see* below), a large trout fishing pond, a picnic area, meals (for groups) and courses in such things as cider-making and restoring the local wattle-and-daub style buildings, cleverly orientated towards urbanites who buy up old properties and find them to be crumbling away. An explanatory leaflet is provided in English. This is not a synthetic heritage site, but a fascinating repository of rural traditions, and very amiably run. A series of special events is held at the farm through the season, and it also hosts farmers' markets.

From Sommery, anyone going on south should backtrack towards Forges-les-Eaux for the roads to Rouen or Paris; otherwise, continue on a circuit northwards on the same road, the D915. Back to the north of Neufchâtel is the Pays de Bray's grandest monument, the Renaissance **château of Mesnières-en-Bray** (*guided tours only Easter–June and Sept–Nov Sat, Sun and public hols 2.30–6.30; July and Aug daily 2.30–6.30; adm*), built between 1520 and 1550 for the De Boissay family. The white and grey exterior is dramatic and imposing, especially if you approach it as once intended, head-on to the main façade on the little road from the D915 via Fresles, rather than on the D1 from Neufchâtel. It has massive round drum towers with pinnacle tops on either side, and steeply raked roofs and ornamented dormer windows in the central building; between the towers is a superb peacock-tail-shaped staircase, added in the 18th century and designed to be ridden up on horseback. It's rather like a smaller version of the contemporary châteaux in the Loire Valley, a connection explained by the fact that the De Boissays were closely associated with the Amboises, lords of Chaumont, one of the grandest Loire mansions.

The interior, on the other hand, is very much a mixed bag. Mesnières' last aristo-cratic owners, the De Biencourts, reclaimed it after the Revolution but then ruined themselves restoring it, and in 1835 they sold it to a Catholic order as an orphanage. Today, most of it is an agricultural college and school, still run by the same order. Parts of it are beautiful, especially the **Galerie des Cerfs** (Stags), with seven life-sized statues of stags installed by a hunting-mad *seigneur* in 1660, and the superb original chapel, with some magnificent Renaissance stained glass and Baroque woodwork. Other rooms have the shabby look of a distinctly under-heated boarding school, and there is a huge, gloomy neo-Gothic additional **chapel**, built for the orphanage in the 1860s. The guided tours, given by sweet but harassed students, take you indiscriminately round all of them (in French only; a leaflet is provided in English).

The western flank of the Pays de Bray contains the most lushly wooded and densely green part of all the Bray valleys. Look to the left along the D915 going north and you'll see the **Forêt d'Eawy**, 20km of dense and beautiful beech forest. Several roads run into the forest, and tourist offices have maps of the many foot- and bridle paths such as the Allée des Limousins, a renowned 14km track that's a riders' favourite. A number of riding centres around the area have horses for hire, especially around Pommeréval, Les Grandes-Ventes and St-Saëns, and generally offer guided trekking trips as well. On the western side of the forest in St-Saëns, ancestral home of the composer, there's a particularly luxuriant golf course, with a genuine château for a clubhouse. And a little further west again is a remarkable 'triangle' of three of the Seine-Maritime's, and France's, most impressive recently created private gardens.

In Grigneuseville, about 6km from St-Saëns south of the N29 road towards Tôtes, is **Agapanthe** (*t 02 35 33 32 05; open Easter–Oct Fri–Sun 2–6; adm*), an intimate, slightly formal garden dedicated above all, as the name suggests, to agapanthus. A couple of kilometres west of there in Etampuis is the **Clos du Coudray** (*t 02 35 34 96 85; open Easter–1 Nov Mon, Thurs–Sun 10–7; closed Tues and Wed exc public hols; adm; garden centre open Mar–Nov Mon, Thurs–Sun 10–5.30*), a much bigger and more luxuriant organic garden with over 6,000 species from around the world, especially poppies, dahlias and flowering maples. Other highlights include areas arranged by colour (a yellow garden, a white garden), a giant rock garden of alpine plants and a rose garden that is fabulously colourful in June and July.

Most spectacular of all, though, are the **Jardins de Bellevue** (*t 02 35 33 31 37; open daily 10–6; adm*), in Beaumont-le-Hareng, reached by turning back towards St-Saëns. Created from nothing since the 1980s by Martine Lemonnier and her family, this extraordinary hillside shangri-la is as much a botanical reserve as a conventional garden. Around the six-hectare estate there are hundreds of rare and strange trees and plants from across the world, especially Asia, particularly high-altitude species: Himalayan plums, Japanese maples, pure-white trees from China, giant lilies, and Europe's largest collection of Christmas roses. Colours are superbly combined, and there is something in flower every month of the year, although the garden is, naturally, at its best in early summer. There is a small café, and you can even stay in a cottage in the garden (*see* p.172). You can wander around independently, or book a tour (in English) with an enthusiastic member of the Lemonnier family.

Shopping

The Saturday market in **Neufchâtel** is the best place to find fine-quality Pays de Bray specialities all in one space. Other good markets in the area are those in **Forges-les-Eaux** (*Thurs and Sun*), in **St-Saëns** (*Thurs*) and in **Bellencombre** (*Tues*). A series of informal farmers' markets are held on farms around the region throughout the year, especially on summer Sundays; local tourist offices will have information. They also sell a little book of recipes for cooking with Neufchâtel cheese.

St-Saire ✉ 76270

Le Clos du Bourg, t/f 02 32 97 10 74. Etienne Lurois' fine organic ciders are some of the most highly regarded in the Seine-Maritime, and are used by many of the region's best chefs. There's also fine calvados, *pommeau* and fresh apple juice. *Shop open daily exc Sun 10–6; tours of the farm available.*

Nesle-Hodeng ✉ 76270

La Ferme des Fontaines, t 02 32 97 06 46. Alex and Françoise Brianchon make *appellation contrôlée* Neufchâtel cheese and sell it direct. Mme Brianchon also gives tours of the *caves*, with a demonstration of cheese-making (*by reservation, April–Oct, mornings only*). The farm is about 6km south of Neufchâtel, just north of the turning off the D1314 for Nesle-Hodeng.

Frichemesnil ✉ 76690

Ferme du Val au Bouvier, t 02 35 33 41 44. A sprawling old farm where Philippe and Valérie Levigneux make their own Camembert, a Frichon white cheese, and butter. They also offer tours of the farm at weekends or by reservation.

St-Michel-d'Halescourt ✉ 76440

M and Mme Fougeray-Duclos, t/f 02 35 90 61 39. Denise and Hervé Fougeray-Duclos raise sheep and produce high-quality cider, calvados, *pommeau* and apple juice on their historic old farm in this tranquil village about 5km east of Forges-les-Eaux. The most attractive route from Forges is via the winding road through La Bellière, which turns off the D915. It's best to phone ahead.

Where to Stay

Neufchâtel-en-Bray ✉ 76270

Le Cellier du Val Boury, t 02 35 93 26 95, f 02 32 97 12 30, *www.cellier-val-boury.com* (*rooms 260F/€39.64 for two, 420F/€64.03 for four*). A beautiful B&B in a giant farm on the outskirts of Neufchâtel. The four rooms are across the courtyard in a spectacular restored 17th-century wine store. In the middle of the courtyard there are tables and a kids' play area, and elsewhere on the farm there are two self-contained *gîtes*. The centre of Neufchâtel is within easy walking distance, but it feels very rural.

Hôtel du Grand Cerf, 9 Grande-Rue-Fausse-Porte, t 02 35 93 00 02, f 02 35 94 14 92 (*double rooms 240–360F/€36.59–54.88*). The traditional 'main hotel' of Neufchâtel, a Logis de France in a post-war building on the main street by the Saturday market. The rooms are well-maintained and comfortable.

Sommery ✉ 76440

La Ferme de Bray, t 02 35 90 57 27, *www.ferme-de-bray.free.fr* (*rooms 260F/€39.64 for two, 360F/€54.88 for four*). The extraordinary Ferme de Bray (*see p.169*) also contains five delightful B&B rooms in one of the many outhouses – cosy showcases of Norman country style with hefty carved-wood furniture. A special place to stay.

Forges-les-Eaux ✉ 76440

La Folie du Bois des Fontaines, Av des Sources, t 02 32 89 50 68, f 02 32 89 50 67 (*standard rooms 900F/€137.20, suites 1,500F/€228.67, duplexes 2,500F/€381.12, Suites Royales 2,900F/€442.10*). The luxury option in the Pays de Bray, aimed squarely at the romantic hideaway market, with ten emphatically opulent rooms with things like two-seater jacuzzis with gold taps surrounded by classical statuary. It's in a former château in a prominent position by the avenue through the smart side of Forges-les-Eaux, so you can nip across to the Club Med spa for a workout and some health treatments. After which, you can return to romantic mode in the hotel's gourmet restaurant (*see below*).

Hôtel de la Paix, 15 Rue de Neufchâtel, t 02 35 90 51 22, f 02 35 09 83 62 (*double rooms*

280–400F/€42.69–60.98). The 18 rooms were all renovated during the 1990s, and are very comfortable with excellent bathrooms and other facilities. The décor is pretty enough, but the character is provided by the hotel's relaxed and welcoming small-town feel. It's very popular, and often necessary to book ahead, especially for weekends.

Beaumont-le-Hareng ✉ 76850

Les Jardins de Bellevue, t 02 35 33 31 37, f 02 35 33 29 44 (*rooms 280F/€42.69 for two, or 520F/€79.27 for five in the apartment*). Right inside the spectacular gardens at Bellevue is one of France's most special *chambre-d'hôte*. Among the trees there is an old carters' cottage where two rooms are available; upstairs there is a large room with space for up to four, while the ground floor is more like an apartment, with more space and a kitchenette. Both floors have their own showers, etc., but it's fairly basic. The location, however, is magical. The cottage stands on its own in the garden, but one of the Lemonnier family will bring you breakfast every day from their nearby house.

Saumont-la-Poterie ✉ 76440

La Ramée, Rue d'Auvergne, t 02 35 09 20 17 (*rooms 250F/€38.11 for two; extra beds available*). A classic Pays de Bray farmhouse – in brick, and long and narrow, with the rooms arranged in line – with three B&B rooms. The conversion is attractive, and the rooms are extremely comfortable. Around the house there is a huge garden, with a duck pond. Breakfasts are abundant, and **evening meals** can be provided with prior notice (*85F/€12.96*). The villlage is deep in the countryside, 7km south of Forges-les-Eaux.

Frichemesnil ✉ 76690

Au Souper Fin, Place de l'Eglise, t 02 35 33 33 38, f 02 35 33 50 42 (*rooms 400F/€60.98 for two; extra beds available*). The excellent Souper Fin restaurant (*see below*) also has three bright and comfortable rooms, next to a small garden. Although this is a member of Logis de France, they are more like *chambre-d'hôte* semi-self-contained suites, and Mme Buisset offers them on a B&B basis.

Eating Alternatives

St-Martin-Osmonville ✉ 76680

Auberge de la Varenne, 2 Route de la Libération, t 02 35 34 13 80 (*menus 105F/€16.01 (Mon–Fri), 125–220F/€19.06–33.54*). A pleasant roadside village inn in a great hilltop location, with beautiful views. The good-value menus are strong on traditional Norman cooking: homemade rabbit pâté, delicious local cheeses and calvados-rich desserts. *Closed Sun eve and Mon.*

Forges-les-Eaux ✉ 76440

La Folie du Bois des Fontaines, *see* above (*menus 190–390F/€28.97–59.46*). The restaurant has grand chandeliers and Louis XVI décor, and a gourmet menu of extravagant dishes, to match the hotel. The *tour de force* of highly regarded chef Jean-Luc Tartarin is a ten-course menu, designed to showcase a range of fine produce. The wine list goes straight for the *grands crus*. *Closed Wed.*

Crêperie aux Trois Pommes, 9 Place Brevière, t 02 35 09 87 86. A likeable crêperie and grill right on the main square, offering a whole range of light meals: an assortment of mixed salads (*from 38F/€5.79*), savoury galettes (*c. 20–60F/ €3.05–9.15*) and sweet crêpes (*under 40F/ €6.10*), as well as a few larger things like steaks. Several dishes make use of local cider and Neufchâtel cheese.

Neufchâtel-en-Bray ✉ 76270

Hôtel du Grand Cerf, *see* above (*weekday lunch menu 77F/€11.74, other menus 95–165F/€14.48–25.15*). Even more of an institution in local life than the hotel. The hearty Norman cooking is very satisfying – homemade terrines, *lapin au cidre*, Caen-style tripe, and trout with almonds – and it is renowned for its big portions and remarkable value.

Frichemesnil ✉ 76690

Au Souper Fin, *see* above (*menus 98–230F/€14.94–35.06*). A tiny village with a delightful little restaurant serving sophisticated cuisine: *pavé* of venison with potato *gratin* and a bilberry sauce. Local duck features strongly, as well as a range of other, imaginative dishes; the set menus are exceptional value. *Closed Wed eve and Thurs.*

The Half-timbered City:
Rouen

18

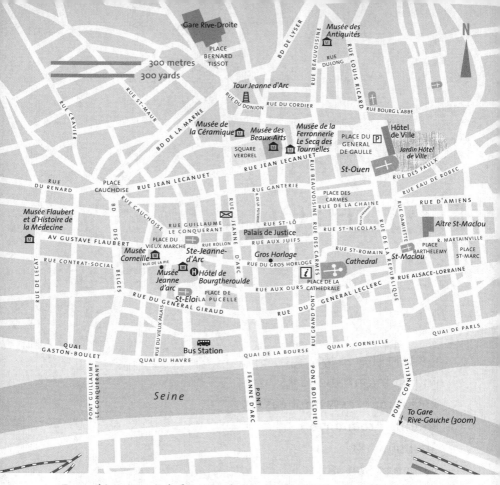

Rouen, historic capital of Normandy, is a city characterised by a dense intertwining of old and new. It is a thriving city: an industrial hub, a business and transport centre and, despite being so far from the sea, a major port. It was terribly ravaged in the Second World War, and large parts of it have had to be rebuilt, but throughout the centre of Rouen there are medieval streets and squares, delicate Renaissance carvings and grand 18th-century monuments – to such an extent that it has been labelled *la ville-musée*. In particular, there are whole rows of half-timbering: old Rouen was one of the largest communities ever built in this style.

Rouen is also a Gothic city. The period of its greatest wealth and energy at the end of the Middle Ages coincided with the apogee of French Flamboyant Gothic, favouring the most elaborate lacework carvings and the most intricate decoration. The great cathedral painted so many times by Monet is one of a trinity of magnificent major Gothic religious buildings in Rouen, with the abbey of St-Ouen and the church of St-Maclou. Around them there are many more Gothic churches with superb stained glass – for which the city is renowned. The city of Flaubert and Marcel Duchamp also has a vibrant contemporary life, and one of the best French regional art museums. And running through the middle of Rouen – along the attractive

Getting There

Driving into Rouen is slightly complicated by the fact that it does not have a ring road to filter the traffic, which can be atrocious. All three main routes into the city – the A28 *autoroute* from Calais, Dieppe and the north, the A29 and A15 from Le Havre, and the Avenue de Caen which leads in from the A13 from Caen or Paris, several kilometres south of the city – tend to bring you via *centre-ville* signs to the long quays along the north bank of the Seine. The best way to get off them and into town is to turn up Rue de la République, which runs through the east side of the city centre. There are useful car parks at Vieille Tour, off Rue du Général Leclerc, and beneath the square in front of the Hôtel de Ville and St-Ouen. There are pay-and-display parking spaces in many streets, but it is generally easier to use an underground car park.

Rouen has frequent train connections to Paris (Gare St-Lazare) and many other parts of France. The station is at the north side of the city centre, at the top end of Rue Jeanne d'Arc. The bus station (Gare Routière) is near the opposite end of the same street, on Rue des Charettes, by the river. Rouen's Boos airport, 10km to the east, mainly has French domestic services.

Central Rouen is easily walkable, but there are plenty of buses and taxis, and a Découverte ticket can be bought at the tourist office giving unlimited travel on public transport. The Métrobus line that goes up and down Rue Jeanne d'Arc (actually a modern tram) is not usually of much use unless you wish to get to somewhere south of the river, such as the Place des Emmurées flea market.

Les Nymphéas restaurant can best be located by first finding Place du Vieux Marché, on the west side of the city centre (which also has an underground car park). Although its address is officially in Rue de la Pie, the entrance is on the south side of the square.

Tourist Information

Rouen: Hôtel des Finances, 25 Place de la Cathédrale, **t** 02 32 08 32 40, **f** 02 32 08 32 44, *www.mairie-rouen.fr (open May–Sept Mon–Sat 9–7, Sun and hols 9.30–12.30 and 2.30–6; Oct–April Mon–Sat 9–6, Sun 10–1).*

pedestrianised streets – are the shops, cafés and restaurants, characteristic of a modern French city.

Rouen has long been established as one of the gastronomic capitals of France. Its distinctive style has been characterised by a combination of loyalty to certain local, Norman traditions – especially duck – with a very urbane refinement. One of the most admired chefs in Rouen is M Patrice Kukurudz, whose restaurant **Les Nymphéas** is just off the Place du Vieux Marché, the old market square.

Les Nymphéas

*7–9 Rue de la Pie, **t** 02 35 89 26 69, **f** 02 35 70 98 81.*
Open Tues–Sat 12–2 and 8–10, Sun 12–2. Book always.
Menus 165F/€25.15, 200F/€30.49, 260F/€39.63, 270F/€41.16
and 380F/€57.93; à la carte average 400F/€60.98.

The Place du Vieux Marché has been one of Rouen's busiest, most bustling squares since the early Middle Ages. Pass through the discreet entrance to Les Nymphéas, however, just off the square in a beautifully restored half-timbered building, and you enter a snug little haven of luxury: opulent curtains, abundant flowers, and a tastefully pretty garden terrace at the back, where you can eat outside in summer.

Presiding over the restaurant is M Patrice Kukurudz, who has been a chef for 25 years, and took over Les Nymphéas in 1991. He believes that in cooking you need to be aware of traditions – which in Rouen means Norman tradition – and to preserve the roots of a cuisine, because you need to have a base upon which you can create and experiment. He also thinks that it's quite acceptable, and may be increasingly necessary, for restaurants to act slightly as 'temples of tradition', holding up ideals of good practice. In his own cooking he makes great use of local staples such as duck and turbot – one of his specialities is *sauvageon à la Rouennaise* (with wild instead of farm duck) – but each of them is used in original ways. Nor is Les Nymphéas over-formal: it's a comfortable restaurant where customers make the effort to dress for dinner.

The dominant impression given by M Kukurudz' cooking is of a tremendous refinement. It begins with the *mises-en-bouche*, maybe a subtle *vol-au-vent* of warm duck mousse. One of his trademark first courses is an escalope of duck foie gras with a cider vinegar jus; a salad of fresh asparagus with *langoustines* in a delicate balsamic and herb vinaigrette is almost fashionably Mediterranean. Between courses comes an exquisite sorbet and calvados *trou normand*. Main courses might make use of seasonal produce, as in turbot with an assortment of forest mushrooms in autumn, but one of M Kukurudz' most celebrated specialities is permanent – his superb *civet de homard* (lobster stew), made with fine sauternes.

The cheese course is innovative, served with fruit breads, while desserts continue the delicate style, as in a *croquant* of almonds and apples with a very smooth, fresh cinnamon ice-cream. The wine list is encyclopaedic.

Touring Around

Claude Monet painted the west front of **Rouen Cathedral** over 30 times, forever trying to capture the changing play of light over its complex surfaces. He did so from three different vantage points, all of them indoors, convincing shopkeepers to let him use their upstairs rooms. His final location was above a drapers' shop in the south-west corner of the cathedral square, from where he painted his most famous series of the great west portal. In a moment of inspiration the local tourist authorities, as part of their 'Impressionist Itineraries' (leaflets on which are available at the tourist office), have placed a plaque as near as possible to the site of the room, to allow you to compare image and reality. The actual building was destroyed in the Second World War, which left the square a good deal larger than it was in Monet's time.

William the Conqueror presided over the consecration of the first Rouen Cathedral in 1063. This plain Norman building was severely damaged by fire at the beginning of the 13th century, which conveniently provided an opportunity for comprehensive rebuilding in Gothic style. The west façade itself is almost a display case of medieval architecture. The relatively simple tower to the left, the north side, the **Tour St-Romain**, is a 12th-century survivor from the Norman cathedral, although topped by a much more elaborate upper level and roof added in the 1470s; on the other, south side is the Flamboyant **Tour de Beurre** (Butter Tower), built at the end of the 15th century – paid for with a special tax to avoid having to give up butter for Lent. Between them, the two smaller portals, one on the left with scenes of the life of St John the Baptist and the other of St Stephen, are from the first, 13th-century Gothic reconstruction; the soaring screens above them were added in the 14th century, while the extraordinary central portal, rising up to a 'Tree of Jesse', was built by the greatest of Rouen's Flamboyant Gothic architects Roulland le Roux (1509–21). If you walk all the way around the outside of the cathedral you can see many more of the Flamboyant details that were added around the same period, especially the rhythmic lines of triangular gables along the side, the remarkable portals of the transepts, and the magnificent gateway to 'Bookseller's Court', the passageway by the North Transept.

Inside, the main structure of the cathedral is much simpler, with an exquisitely lofty, plain 13th-century early Gothic nave. The interior is very dark, which makes all the more breathtaking the cathedral's superb glass, a great deal of which dates from around 1230. Much of the stained glass had fortunately been stored away at the beginning of the Second World War and so escaped later bombing, but it is inter-spersed with many windows of plain clear glass, which gives the building a strangely ghostly feel. The Choir is fabulous, both for its glass and the elegance of its early-Gothic arches.

Another feature of the cathedral is that it is visibly battered, many of its carvings gnarled and pitted by bomb damage. It used to be much more so, for restoration work has been going on more or less since the last war, when Rouen was probably more ravaged than any other city in France. It was devastated by German attacks in 1940 – which set off instant fires in a city with so much wood – and then hit again by Allied bombing in 1944, including one misconceived British night raid on 19 April when many aircraft, targeted to hit the railway yards south of the river, got lost and dropped their bombs on the city instead. The restoration effort has been extraordi-nary, to the extent that it is often genuinely difficult to distinguish between real survivors and restored buildings. However, some parts – like the quays and much of the area between the cathedral and the Seine – were unfortunately rebuilt in the usual functional post-war reconstruction style.

Immediately opposite the cathedral in Place de la Cathédrale, the tourist office enjoys a very grand setting inside the 1509 **Hôtel des Finances**, so-called because it was built for the chief tax-collector of the time. It was also designed by Roulland le Roux, and is one of his most interesting buildings, with fine proportions combined with his usual ornate decoration reflecting a move from pure Flamboyant Gothic to a more restrained approach influenced by the Italian Renaissance. The square also makes a natural starting point for exploring Rouen. To the north, Rue des Carmes leads to the main shopping area and the museums; beside the tourist office, Rue du Gros Horloge leads to the famous 'great clock' and the old market area; while to the left of the cathedral, Rue St-Romain, half-timbered from end to end and full of inter-esting shops, takes you into one of the most characterful areas of old Rouen.

Rouen began life as a Roman city called Rotomagus, but its development really gathered pace after 911, when the Norse chieftain Rollo made it his capital. Like the rest of Normandy it had a major role in the Hundred Years' War, and was besieged and taken by Henry V of England in 1418. It was because the city was the main hub of English power in France that the captured Joan of Arc was brought here, to be tried in the abbey of St-Ouen before she was burnt at the stake in Place du Vieux Marché on 30 May 1431. Once French power revived, the city entered a virtual golden age, lasting over a century and a half. Trade expanded rapidly, and Rouen enjoyed considerable power, with a wealthy local merchant class. It was especially favoured by Cardinal d'Amboise, first of France's great Cardinal-Ministers and Archbishop of Rouen, who at the beginning of the 16th century sponsored all kinds of buildings around the city, many by his favourite architect Roulland le Roux.

Across Rue de la République from the cathedral, Place Barthélémy is a gem of a half-timbered square arranged around the church of **St-Maclou**, the second point in Rouen's Gothic church triangle. Dedicated to the same Welsh/Breton saint as the city of St-Malo, it's much smaller than the cathedral, and much more abruptly vertical, but still awe-inspiring. Instead of an architectural mishmash, it's an integral work of Flamboyant Gothic, built between 1437 and 1517. The west portal, facing you, is astonishing, as much like a Gothic fantasy as a real Gothic structure, with stone carvings of the *Last Judgement* and massive carved timber doors that have remarkably survived from the 16th century. It's a sombre, blackened church; it was severely damaged in 1944, and the effects of bombing are still plain to see: there are many windows that are now clear as well as some marvellous stained glass.

From the back of the church, head a little way up Rue Martainville and look out for a tiny (signposted) entry to the left. This will take you via a low-ceilinged passageway into the **Aître St-Maclou** (*open daily 8am–8pm*), a large, complete 16th-century half-timbered courtyard, with precariously sloping upper galleries and erratically angled timbers, carved with death's heads, crossed bones and skeletons. The Aître was first created as a cemetery for plague victims during the Black Death, in 1348; later, it became a general cemetery for the poor of Rouen, and the current buildings were erected in the 1520s, as ossuaries to contain the bones from re-used graves. Today it houses Rouen's School of Fine Arts, which only makes it more bizarre: there are fashion workshops in some of the old bone-halls, and the students seem oblivous to the strangeness of their surroundings.

If you're in this area on a Sunday, continue along Rue Martainville to reach Place St-Marc, site of the weekly flea market. Otherwise, cut back to St-Maclou and turn right up Rue Damiette, towards Rouen's third great Gothic temple, the **Abbatiale St-Ouen** (*open mid-Mar–Oct Mon, Wed–Sun 10–12.30 and 2–6; Nov–mid-Dec and mid-Jan–mid-Mar Wed, Sat and Sun 10–12.30 and 2–4.30; closed mid-Dec–mid-Jan; adm*), rivalled by the huge 19th-century Hôtel de Ville, built on former abbey land next to it.

Enter the abbey church through the spectacular Gothic portal on the south side, known as the 'Porch of the Marmosets' because some of the strange little figures in its intricate carvings were long thought to represent monkeys. The abbey dates from the pre-Norman era, for it was founded in about 750, in commemoration of the local saint Ouen who had been Bishop of Rouen for over 40 years in the previous century. At the beginning of the 14th century, however, Abbot Jean Roussel announced his attention to build a new 'Celestial Jerusalem' and commissioned the great church we can see today, built in the simpler, mid-Gothic style known in French as Rayonnant. Inside, the overriding impression given by the great nave is of soaring immensity. It is much lighter and appears much larger than the cathedral, because it is less cluttered but also because of the beautiful purity of its lines. It also has dazzling stained glass, which has survived better than that in any other of the Rouen churches, some of it from the 14th-century rebuilding of the abbey but most added in a more Renaissance style between 1500 and 1550. Among the most astonishing is the 15th-century rose window in the North Transept, in a modern-looking star pattern.

From Place du Général de Gaulle, busy Rue Jean Lecanuet runs directly to Rouen's 'museum quarter'. The august-looking **Musée des Beaux Arts** (*open Mon, Wed–Sun 10–6; closed Tues and most public hols; adm*) has one of the liveliest of French regional museum collections, with far more variety and fewer local painters than is sometimes the case. It has its great masterpieces, above all Caravaggio's *Flagellation of Christ on the Cross*, and *Demócrito*, a penetrating portrait of the Spanish court jester by Velázquez. There are also very fine works by Perugino and Gérard David, and a whole room of giant canvases by Veronese, originally painted for the church of San Rocco in Rome. From closer to home there are dramatic small paintings by the Rouen-born Géricault, and a good Impressionist collection, including (of course) a Monet of *Rouen Cathedral*. Later attractions include several excellent Sickerts and a room dedicated to the region's great contribution to modern art: Marcel Duchamp, born at Blainville-Crevon, near Ry (see p.188), in 1887. The museum also contains many engaging surprises: eccentric Symbolists like Alfred Agache, and a rare piece of 17th-century English Catholic art, *Lord Arundel of Wardour and his wife Cecily at the Foot of the Cross* by John Michael Wright, painted for the Convent of the English Poor Clares in Rouen, which was endowed by the Arundel family. The Beaux-Arts also hosts a very dynamic series of temporary shows.

The **Musée de la Céramique** (*open Mon, Wed–Sun 10–1 and 2–6; closed Tues and most public hols; adm*), in a distinguished 1650s *hôtel particulier* across the square, is dedicated primarily to the distinctive style of decorated porcelain produced in Rouen from the 16th to the 18th centuries, but also has Italian and Delftware, with many beautiful pieces; the **Musée de la Ferronerie-Le Secq des Tournelles** (*open Mon, Wed–Sun 10–1 and 2–6; closed Tues and most public hols; adm*), in the former church of St-Laurent behind the Beaux-Arts, contains an often bizarre collection of historic ironwork – keys, lamps, ornaments, remarkably fine gates and so on. A few streets further north is the **Tour Jeanne d'Arc** (*open May–Sept Mon, Wed–Sat 10–12.30 and 2–6, Sun 2–6.30; Oct–April Mon, Wed–Sat 10–12.30 and 2–5, Sun 2–5.30; closed Tues; adm*), so-called because it has been traditionally been believed that Joan of Arc was imprisoned and tortured there, although this has been questioned. The massive tower, the only remaining part of Philippe Auguste's 13th-century castle, contains a small exhibition on the history of Rouen.

From the Beaux-Arts, cross Rue Lecanuet and go down the wide Allée Délacroix to Rue Ganterie, Rouen's most attractive shopping street. Wander back towards the cathedral along Rue des Carmes; just to the east in pretty Place des Carmes is Rouen's statue of Flaubert. At the tourist office, turn up Rue du Gros Horloge. Looming up ever larger in front of you is one of the city's most celebrated monuments, the **Gros Horloge**, an extraordinarily lavish, gilt-detailed Renaissance clock built over the street in the 16th century. One of the oldest streets in the city, Rue du Gros Horloge is still busy, full of shops and bars. Turn right (north) up one of the alleys either side of the clock and you will see the magnificent courtyard and façade of the **Palais de Justice**, the greatest Flamboyant Gothic civil building in Rouen. Its restoration was one of the most painstaking tasks undertaken after 1945. The palace was built from 1499 to 1526 to house the Parlement and Exchequer of Normandy, and the most intricate sections were by Roulland le Roux. After the Revolution, it was taken over by Rouen's law courts. The street on which it stands, Rue aux Juifs, was at the centre of one of the oldest Jewish communities in France before their expulsion by royal dictat in 1306. During the restoration a room was discovered beneath part of the Palais, now called the Monument Juif, built around 1100 and believed to be part of a synagogue – the oldest relic of Jewish life in France (*guided tours usually on Saturday afternoons; book well in advance via the tourist office*).

Cross noisy Rue Jeanne d'Arc and continue in the same direction to reach Place du Vieux Marché, ringed by exquisite restaurants (like Les Nymphéas) and budget cafés. The old church of St-Vincent was destroyed in 1944, and in its place is the striking 1970s church of Ste-Jeanne-d'Arc, with a swooping, bird-like roof. Imaginatively integrated into the church's structure is the brilliantly coloured glass from St-Vincent, which was protected during the war. The tacky **Musée Jeanne d'Arc** (*open May–mid-Sept daily 9.30–7; mid-Sept–April daily 10–12 and 2–6.30; adm*) on the south side of the square does its heroine no favours; the waxwork tableau of Joan at the stake, especially, is a hoot. From the southeast corner of the market square, to the left of the museum, walk down Rue Panneret to enter the Place de la Pucelle, another lovely, small medieval square. On it there stands the 16th-century **Hôtel de Bourgtheroulde** (*open Mon–Fri 9–12.30 and 1.30–5.15, Sat, Sun and hols 2.30–5.30*), a fascinatingly transitional building: the initial structure is pure Flamboyant Gothic, with characteristic lacework carvings and decoration, but the later stages were built more spaciously under Renaissance influence.

Boulevard des Belges more or less marks the western limit of central Rouen, but carry on across it down Avenue Flaubert to one of France's most intriguing museums, the **Musée Flaubert et d'Histoire de la Médicine** (*open Tues 10–6, Wed–Sat 10–12 and 2–6; closed Sun, Mon and hols; adm*). It is, first of all, the birthplace of France's greatest novelist, born here in 1821 when his father was the Chief Surgeon of the Hôtel-Dieu, next door. The Flaubert exhibits – the room where he was born, the medical books he consulted in researching his novels – are fascinating. They share the house, though, with the historical collection of one of France's oldest and most distinguished public hospitals. There's a hospital bed that slept six, an altarpiece from a plague chapel, the 'cabinet of curiosities' of the renowned Dr Le Cat, an 18th-century predecessor of Dr Flaubert, including mummified bodies, and an astonishing collection on childbirth. And in one room there's also Flaubert's parrot, the stuffed parakeet borrowed by Flaubert, never returned, and made famous by Julian Barnes' novel.

Shopping

Rue des Carmes, Rue Beauvoisine and espe-cially Rue Ganterie and Rue St-Lô, have the biggest concentration of chic fashion shops. There are also a large number of shops on or around Rue Jeanne d'Arc, but they're bigger and more everyday, and it's a much less attrac-tive street. There's a little clutch of fine food shops around the Vieux Marché, especially on Rue Rollon.

The main market is in Place du Vieux Marché (*every morning exc Mon*), and is particularly good for fresh fruit. There are flea markets twice a week in Place St-Marc, east of Rue de la République, the better of the two (*every Sun morning*), and in Place des Emmurées, south of the river (*all day Thurs*). There are also general food markets in Place St-Marc (*Tues, Fri and Sat*) and Place des Emmurées (*Tues and Sat*). For Place des Emmurées it's worth taking the tram from Rue Jeanne d'Arc to Place Joffre.

Rouen ✉ 76000

Caves Berigny, 7 Rue Rollon, **t** 02 35 07 57 54. An attractive fine wine merchant near the Vieux Marché. Its stock of modern French wines is carefully selected, and there's a superior range of fine calvados, and some of the best Normandy ciders.

Fayencerie Augy, 26 Rue St-Romain, **t** 02 35 88 77 47. Dedicated to maintaining Rouen's own tradition of decorated porcelain. As well as reproducing historic styles they create orig-inal designs, and can make personalised pieces. It's possible to visit the workshop, by appointment. *Closed Mon.*

Fromagerie du Vieux Marché, 18 Rue Rollon, **t** 02 35 71 11 00. A busy cheese merchant by the corner of Place du Vieux Marché, with a comprehensive selection of fine Normandy cheeses – especially good Neufchâtel – plus others from other parts of France. There are a few other things, such as apple preserves.

Where to Stay

Rouen ✉ 76000

Hôtel de Dieppe, Place Bernard Tissot, **t** 02 35 71 96 00, **f** 02 35 89 65 21 (*rooms from 530F/€80.79*). This classic hotel is now affili-ated to Best Western, but it has been run by one branch or other of the Guéret-Le Grand family ever since it opened opposite the railway station in the 1880s, and the fifth generation is now in charge. It's run with a distinctive charm and brio. The 41 rooms are large, traditional, well equipped and very comfortable. There's a smart, popular cock-tail bar, and the restaurant (*see* below) is a prime temple of traditional Rouen cuisine.

Hôtel Le Cardinal, 1 Place de la Cathédrale, **t** 02 35 70 24 42, **f** 02 35 89 75 14 (*double rooms 300–410F/€45.73–62.5*). The hotel with the best location in Rouen. Around three-quarters of its 18 rooms have views of the cathedral; the very best on the top floors have balconies. The rooms are comfortable but functional; character is provided by the owner and her staff, who are friendly in a slightly cranky way.

Hôtel Le Vieux Carré, 34 Rue Ganterie, **t** 02 35 71 67 70, **f** 02 35 71 19 17, vieux-carre@mcom.fr (*double rooms 330 360F/€50.3–54.88*). Recently opened by Patrick Beaumont, who also owns the Hôtel des Carmes, this 14-room hotel has a similar style: the staff are young and relaxed, and rooms are quite simple but comfortable, and decorated with a touch of contemporary flair. It's in an old timberframe building around a courtyard – where breakfast is served outside in summer – and down below there's a contemporary restaurant (*see* below). There's still no lift.

M Philippe Aunay, 45 Rue aux Ours, **t** 02 35 70 99 68 (*rooms 300F/€45.73 for two, 150F/ €22.87 per extra person*). This lofty half-timbered townhouse is a remarkable survivor: despite being in one of the narrow streets near the cathedral it was miracu-lously little damaged in the Second World War. It is entered via a stone passageway dating from 1424. Philippe Aunay's family have lived in the house ever since his great-grandfather had a fabric shop on the ground floor. Inside, it is packed with a collection of antiques and curios that outdoes many museums. There are three B&B rooms which have enormous character and are very comfortable. M Aunay speaks English and is a fountain of knowledge about Rouen and Normandy.

Hôtel des Carmes, 33 Place des Carmes, **t** 02 35 71 92 31, **f** 02 35 71 76 96, *H.des.carmes@ mcom.fr* (*rooms 210–250F/ €32.01–38.11*). In 1996 Patrick Beaumont took over this old hotel with its art nouveau façade, did up the 12 rooms with bright, modern colours and installed a pretty breakfast room on the ground floor – creating a hotel with a distinctive, fresh style. Rooms at the front have views over the square. Note that there are a lot of stairs and no lift.

Hôtel des Arcades, 52 Rue des Carmes, **t** 02 35 70 10 30, **f** 02 35 70 08 91, *hotel-des-arcades@wanadoo.fr* (*rooms 150–250F/ €22.87–38.11*). A warm and friendly hotel in one of the duller 1950s–60s blocks in the town centre, and by far the best budget option in central Rouen. The rooms are pleasant and well-kept, and there's a charming little breakfast bar.

Eating Alternatives

Rouen ✉ 76000

Hôtel de Dieppe-Restaurant Les Quatre Saisons, *see above* (*menus 178–218F/ €27.13–33.23*). The smart, comfortable restaurant in the Dieppe hotel has full and varied menus of Norman-based cuisine, but the thing to have here is traditional Rouennais duck (*175F/€26.68 per person, minimum two*), of which the Guéret family are prime exponents. Other dishes feature uninhibited modern cuisine, with a notably luxurious touch, as in a meaty oxtail ravioli, or richly chocolatey desserts.

Le Petit Zinc, 20 Place du Vieux Marché, **t** 02 35 89 39 69 (*menus from 130F/€19.82*). A busy, lively bar-bistro with retro-style French bar décor and some outside tables, right on the Vieux Marché square, which has won favour with a youngish crowd. The chalked-up menus offer a good range of choices, from traditional grilled fish and maybe *andouille*, to lighter seafood and salads, and great use is made of fresh produce from the market right across the street. *Closed Sun.*

Brasserie Paul, 1 Place de la Cathédrale, **t** 02 35 71 86 07, **f** 02 35 15 14 43 (*menus c. 130F/€19.82*). A classic brasserie, opposite the cathedral, which opens every day from bright and early

till 2am, for breakfast, coffee, excellent lunches, quick snacks, late-night drinks or warmers of French onion soup, and the terrace outside offers about the nearest seat you'll get to Monet's view of the cathedral. Apollinaire ate here, Marcel Duchamp came here often during a time when he gave up art for chess, and Simone de Beauvoir came in for breakfast every day when she taught in Rouen during the 1930s.

Taverne St-Amand, 11 Rue St-Amand, **t** 02 35 88 51 34 (*menus 80–95F/€12.2–14.48*). In a slightly off-vertical, half-timbered building in one of the picturesque narrow alleys between the cathedral and St-Ouen, this laidback tavern, very popular with students, offers plenty of hearty, cidery Norman dishes such as *poulet vallée d'Auge*, as well as a few salads and lighter choices. To drink, there's a select range of French, Belgian and other beers as well as ciders and wines.

Pascaline, 5 Rue de la Poterne, **t** 02 35 89 67 44, **f** 02 35 71 18 30 (*menus 69–99F/€10.52–15.09, children's menu 39F/€5.95*). Run by the same family that owns the Hôtel de Dieppe, Pascaline offers more of a bistro style of cooking, still using fine-quality ingredients. It offers a range of good-value options – steaks and brasserie staples like classic fish dishes and St-Vaast oysters – and, very unusually in France, there are self-service salad and dessert bars, which are very well stocked. *Open daily till 11.30pm.*

Le Vieux Carré, *see above*. A pretty and relaxing restaurant, with décor that stylishly combines old and new, a few leather armchairs and usually some cool music in the background. It's called a 'Gourmet Salon de Thé', and it specializes in the kind of light, fresh lunches that are increasingly popular with young French urban diners. The excellent-value lunch formula offers a main course, dessert and a glass of wine for 75F/€11.43: favourite dishes are one-course *assiettes* such as mixed salads and pasta combinations, and ingredients are consistently high-standard. There are always some vegetarian options: perhaps a delicious omelette with *girolles* mushrooms, or a classic leek *flamiche*. It's also open for teas, coffees and snacks during the afternoon.

Bovaryland:
Ry and the
Forêt de Lyons

19

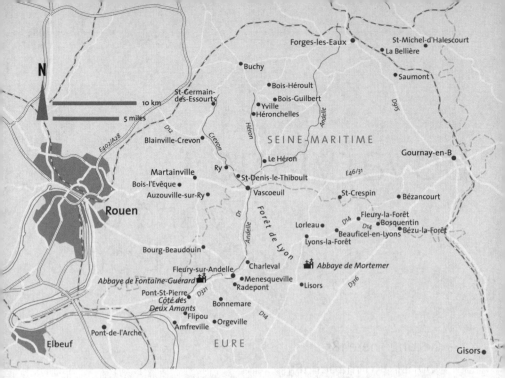

Flaubert never admitted that the fictional town of 'Yonville-l'Abbaye' in *Mme Bovary* was related to any one place in particular, but a great deal of the action and geography of the book can be identified in the country town of Ry, some 20km east of Rouen, and Ry was moreover the scene of the incident that inspired *Mme Bovary* in the first place. Today, Ry is pervaded by imaginary memories of Yonville, and an exploration of the town and its surrounding villages allows anyone to try a little of the kind of literary reconstruction undertaken by Julian Barnes in *Flaubert's Parrot*.

Away from its Flaubertian associations, and without the aura of autumnal gloom and backwardness with which Flaubert surrounded it, the countryside north of Ry that some tourist leaflets now pertly refer to as the Pays d'Emma has other notable features: it runs up the valleys of two fast-flowing, gleaming rivers, the Crevon and the Héron, with many beautifully individual villages with crumbling châteaux and historic churches towering up above the trees. And to the south is the Forêt de Lyons, the largest native beechwood in France (and possibly Europe), a superb stretch of dense woodland criss-crossed by paths and with wonderful vistas from its many hills. At its centre is Lyons-la-Forêt, one of the most extravagantly pretty half-timbered towns in Normandy. Just to the west, minor rivers, roads and forest all meet up in the narrow valley of the Andelle, another quick, lively river, lined by lush forest and engaging villages as it runs down to meet the Seine. Scattered all through this area is a remarkable collection of châteaux – it can look like one in every village – from France's golden era between the 16th and 18th centuries.

In its restaurants, this area offers a mixture of Norman country tradition and the more refined, contemporary cuisine you might expect in a region not too far from a city like Rouen, or even Paris. Both these elements – and a superlative wine selection

Getting There

From Calais and the north, or Dieppe, the most direct route into this region is to take the A28 *autoroute* south towards Rouen; leave it at exit 12, near Buchy, and cut across minor lanes to Ry, or follow the A28 to its end outside Rouen and then instead of going into the city look for a turning east on to the N31 for Beauvais, which passes just south of Ry. From Le Havre, cut across on the A29 to meet the A28 and loop around Rouen, or leave the A29 at Yvetot to cross the Seine by the Pont de Brotonne and get on the A13 *autoroute*.

To get to Pont-St-Pierre, leave the A13 at exit 20, Pont de l'Arche, cross the Seine to the north bank and take the D321 eastwards to Pont-St-Pierre. The Bonne Marmite is easy to find on the main street. To reach Pont-St-Pierre or the Forêt de Lyons from the north via Ry, follow the road signposted to Vascoeuil and Fleury-sur-Andelle, a slow but pretty route.

There are no rail services to this area; the nearest stations are Rouen and Gisors. There are buses from Rouen to Ry and Lyons-la-Forêt.

Tourist Information

Charleval: Grande Rue, **t** 02 32 48 19 59.
Lyons-la-Forêt: 20 Rue de l'Hôtel de Ville,
  t 02 32 49 31 65, **f** 02 32 49 29 79.
Pont-St-Pierre: Piscine Intercommunale,
  t 02 32 49 70 90.
Ry: Maison de l'Abreuvoir, **t** 02 35 23 19 90.

– can be found under one roof at the **Hostellerie La Bonne Marmite**, a magnificent old inn in Pont-St-Pierre, at the southern end of the Andelle valley.

Hostellerie La Bonne Marmite

*10 Rue René Raban, Pont-St-Pierre, **t** 02 32 49 70 24,*
f 02 32 48 12 41, www.la-bonne-marmite.com. Open Tues–Sat
12–2.30 and 7.30–9, Sun 12–2.30. Closed two weeks Feb–Mar
and two weeks July–Aug. Menus 99.7F/€15.2 (Tues–Sat midday only),
147.6F/€22.50, 196.8F/€30, 236.1F/€36, 314.9F/€48, 492F/€75;
à la carte average 327.9F/€50.

Pont-St-Pierre is a large, quite bustling village, at least on some days of the week. It is centred on the much-reduced remains of its old Norman motte-and-bailey castle, but the most striking building in town has to be its historic inn, the Bonne Marmite, presiding over a curve in the main road as it runs down to the Andelle. It has one of the most imposing of Norman half-timbered façades, eight windows long; through the coach-and-four-sized gateway is a lovely flower-and-ivy-clad courtyard, with a large, stone building further back. Like many similar old *auberges* and *hostelleries* it began life as an 18th-century *relais de poste*, or coaching inn. Since 1966 it has also been tended with devotion by M Maurice Amiot and his wife Denise. Their very personal care is visible in all kinds of details: the elegantly manorial décor in the timber-ceilinged dining room, the wonderfully snug and comfortable bar; they also designed the whimsical 'coat of arms' on the baronial-looking plates, combining the lions of Normandy, the keys of St Peter, Bacchus and a little *marmite* or cooking pot.

In his time at the Bonne Marmite M Amiot has also won a whole string of awards for his cooking. Although he has been at his craft many years, he is the kind of chef who can always teach young contemporary cooks new tricks: his style combines a sense of tradition with inventiveness, a timeless use of strong, unmasked flavours and superb ingredients with original combinations and a light touch. A first course of *crêpinières* (small pancakes) of *fruits de mer* is extravagantly fishy; to follow, *magret* of duck served with a cherry sauce and a delicately herby omelette is deliciously hearty but subtle at the same time. Very fine fish and seafood dishes such as lobster ravioli or his own *civet de homard* (lobster stew) are also house specialities.

The traditional cheese course includes, as well as all the proper Norman cheeses, a more modern mix of warm *chèvre* with fruit. This provides a suitable pause before another of the highlights, the desserts, above all those that include fruit, from original inventions such as *galettes* with woodland berries or the perfect versions of local classics like *tarte aux pommes*. Everything is beautifully done, right down to the melt-in-your-mouth shortbread *petits-fours* and superior coffee.

M and Mme Amiot are warm, attentive and charming hosts, which, with the comfort of the setting and the satisfying food (and the similarly opulent guest rooms, *see* p.193), gives the Bonne Marmite a distinctly cosy-but-sybaritic feel. This is rounded off by one other major feature, the wine cellar, which is as much the Amiots' pride and joy as the products of the kitchen. It too has won many awards, and is one of the finest in Normandy: there are over 500 reds on the list, and around 240 whites. Among them there is a magnificent selection of French *grands crus* and rare bottles dating back to 1858, but the Amiots are also – rare in France – open-minded oenophiles, and have included in their cellars a variety of New World wines, and even sent their daughter on a wine course in Australia.

Touring Around

In his novel *Mme Bovary*, Flaubert not only insults the Neufchâtel cheese produced in Yonville, but goes on to present the town as a symbol of banality and small-town tedium. The novel being a story of everyday tragedy, imbued with sadness, you might think that anywhere would back away from being identified with such an image, but such is the power of Mme Bovary as a French cultural icon that people have long come to Ry looking for a scent of Emma, ever since the scandal caused by its first publication faded away, while the town for its part – although still an ordinary country town – has embraced its fate so that reality and its literary identity seem constantly to blend into one another.

Some of the details given by Flaubert in his description of Yonville don't quite fit with Ry, and some might rather suggest Forges-les-Eaux, but there is no doubt that Yonville is based on Ry. For one thing, Ry provided the storyline of *Mme Bovary*. In 1848 the attention of Rouen and its region was seized by a scandal in which Delphine Delamare (or Couturier, her maiden name), the young wife of a country doctor in Ry called Eugène Delamare, poisoned herself; it quickly emerged that she had run up huge debts, and had had a lover, or lovers. Eugène Delamare, destroyed by despair, poisoned himself in turn the following year. The story was suggested to Flaubert as a basis for a novel in 1851 by his friend Louis Bouilhet, who had known Eugène Delamare in Rouen, 'a poor devil of an officier de santé', like Charles Bovary. Flaubert knew Delamare too, for he had studied under Flaubert's father at the hospital in Rouen, and Flaubert's mother had helped Delamare's mother after her son's death. Another of his friends, Maxime du Camp, wrote that he had also met Delphine, and recalled that she had a soft voice 'dishonoured' by a strong Norman country accent. Flaubert initially rejected the idea of writing about the events in Ry: in his earlier writings he had tried to deal with grander subjects, and he thought the Delamare case was too banal; oddly for a writer considered so provocative he also didn't like the idea of offending the Delamares and other people in Rouen. However, Bouilhet convinced him.

When you arrive in Ry today the most remarkable thing is the precision with which Flaubert followed the layout of Ry in creating Yonville, almost as if, having got over his reservations he had set out to reconstruct the incident, in a Truman Capote-Norman Mailer factoid style. This is what makes Ry and Yonville so difficult to tell apart. The main street or Grande Rue, 'about a gunshot in length, with a few shops on each side', is still there, so short and stubby that, if you imagine it without the few cars and trucks that pass by, you can still get a wistful sense of the claustrophobia that is so palpable in the book. The Crédit Agricole savings bank on one side occupies the (much altered) building that in Flaubert's day was the Hôtel de Rouen, or the Hôtel Lion d'Or in the book; the curious half-timbered building that is now the Bovary restaurant, by the little square at the western end of the street, was in the 1840s the Hôtel de France, which features in *Mme Bovary* as the Café Français, the Lion d'Or's new-fangled rival. Next to it, the old timber Halles or market is now the Mairie; across the street at no.32, the souvenir shop that's now just called 'Emma' was long ago the Pharmacie Jouanne, the precise model for the shop of the legendary busybody M Homais. The two houses that were lived in successively by the Delamares were the big half-timbered house on the corner of the D12 to Blainville (which did not exist at that time) and the smaller no.60, above the modern pharmacy. All around there are cute references: even the local *épicerie* is called Au Marché d'Emma, and on some of the literature around the town the Delamares are referred to as the Delamare-Bovarys, as if any idea that Delphine ever had an identity of her own has disappeared into the woods.

A turn off the Grande Rue will take you to the **church**, where Eugène Delamare and his daughter, also called Delphine, are buried. The church dates from the 12th to the 17th centuries, and is fronted by a superb Renaissance portico in carved wood that's a remarkably elaborate feature to find in such a small and insignificant place. The old farm next to the church was the home of the wet nurse employed by Delphine Delamare for her child, the model for Emma Bovary's nurse Mère Rollet. Right at the other end of the Grande Rue, by the River Crevon and the tourist office, elevated literary thoughts are brought down to earth with a bump by Ry's main 'attraction', the **Galerie Bovary** (*open Easter–June, Sept and Oct Mon, Sat, Sun and hols 11–12 and 2–7; July and Aug Mon, Sat, Sun and hols 11–12 and 2–7, Tues–Fri 3–6; adm*), installed in an old cider press, in which scenes from the book are brought to life by ... automated puppets. Flaubert would presumably have taken a hammer to it, or roared with laughter. By a strange piece of serendipity, opposite the Galerie there is a sombre

19th-century brick building with an old-fashioned brass plaque with the words Médecin de Garde and the names of the two men currently in charge, which looks more like a part of *Mme Bovary* than most of the specifically Bovarian sites. Being a local doctor in Ry must be a heavy burden to bear, forever wondering whether you're always trying your best like poor Charles Bovary without actually getting anything right, and when your wife is going to start becoming chronically dissatisfied.

Outside of Ry, the **Circuit Bovary** signposted on the lanes and indicated on leaflets available at local tourist offices is, like the Routes du Cidre and similar routes worked out by French tourist offices elsewhere, an interesting means to getting to know the countryside, Bovary connections aside. South of Ry a lovely road leads over a crest to the village of St-Denis-le-Thiboult, just southwest of which is the hamlet of **Villers**, where there is an essential reference point for those most in love with our tragic heroine, the little manor house where she had her meetings with her aristocratic lover Rodolphe. It's not open to visitors, but is clearly visible from the N31 Rouen road, set back among trees. Again, Flaubert didn't make much up: this was the house where Delphine Delamare went to meet her lover Louis Campion, a spendthrift local gentleman who had come to live on his country estate here to avoid the debts he had incurred in Paris and Rouen. And, in a further confusion of realities, the house is now near-universally known as La Huchette, as it is in the book, instead of by its correct name of Gratianville.

In the opposite direction, following the D12 north from Ry along the green valley of the Crevon will take you to **Blainville-Crevon**, a very attractive, large village with the moodily impressive ruins of a medieval castle and a fine Flamboyant Gothic **church**, commissioned in 1488 by a local lord, Jean d'Estouteville, for the good of his soul. Eugène and Delphine Delamare were married here in 1839; inside, there is some very refined 15th-century carving in wood. Blainville was also the birthplace in 1887 of Marcel Duchamp. The Dadaist's dadda had the very respectable occupation of local notary, and served several times as Blainville's mayor. From there, a still smaller lane leads alongside the vivid little Crevon to **St-Germain-des-Essourts**, the birthplace of Delphine Couturier-Delamare. It's also an exceptionally pretty place: the name 'des-Essourts' comes from its large number of small springs, which are used to support the growing of watercress, in little beds alongside the river.

The main Circuit Bovary reaches its northernmost point at the old Pays de Bray town of Buchy – with its spectacular timber-roofed market hall – but there are many roads that cut across between the Crevon and the still prettier, narrower valley of the Héronchelles, a name that originated in the number of herons seen along it. **Bois-Héroult**, in a much more forbidding location on the plateau above the valley, is a village around a small château, built for a gentleman of Buchy in 1721, and a manor farm that's almost bigger than the main house. This is also an area with many horses, and **Bois-Guilbert** is known for its *ferme-equestre* and riding centre, one of the most important in the area (information, **t** 02 35 34 42 51). It occupies the elegant 17th-century château of the Domaine de Bois-Guilbert, once the home of the early economist and savant Pierre le Pesant de Boisguilbert, a friend of the dramatist Corneille, who stayed here several times. Back down in the valley, **Héronchelles** village and tiny **Yville** are two of the loveliest places in the area, at a point where the little river is at its liveliest and clearest; on any decent day, the landscape seems exuberant and welcoming. Héronchelles also contains an august 16th-century French-Renaissance manor, and the villages all along the valley present an impressive array of churches, mostly with grey-slate spires like giant pots. At **Le Héron** the ivy-clad ruins of the medieval village church stand by the roadside, with geese and ducks scrabbling beneath them, like a romantic folly; it was destroyed by fire in 1879. Le Héron also has a Flaubert connection as the site of the château of the Marquis de Pomereu, where the future writer attended a ball when aged 15 that gave him one of his first tastes of aristocratic living; he is said to have used it as a model for the ball at the château of La Vaubyessard, which so feeds the fantasies of Emma Bovary. The château of Le Héron was destroyed during the Second World War, but much of its Le Nôtre-style formal gardens still exists.

Nearby there are some more intact châteaux to visit. A short way west of Ry in Martainville-Epreville is the **Château de Martainville**. Begun in 1485 for a wealthy and powerful Rouen merchant, Jacques Le Pelletier, it is one of the earliest creations of the French Renaissance style, in brick with soaring slate roofs and massive pepperpot towers, and of a very different order of comfort and opulence from the medieval castles that preceded it. It now houses the **Musée des Traditions et Arts Normands** (*open Oct–Mar Mon, Wed–Sat 10–12.30 and 2–5, Sun 2–5.30; April–Sept Mon, Wed–Sat 10–12.30 and 2–6, Sun 2–6.30; closed Tues; adm*), an interesting and comprehensive folk museum with traditional costume, lace, embroideries, carved furniture, table-ware and other artefacts of everyday life from around Upper Normandy and especially the Seine Maritime, which combines well with surviving sections of the château interiors like the massive 15th-century kitchen. Some 6km southeast of here is the **Château de Vascoeuil** (*open April–June, Sept and Oct Mon–Sat 2.30–6.30, Sun 11–7; July and Aug daily 11–7; adm*). This is less distinguished as a building: a much more rugged stone pile built and altered many times from the 12th to the 16th centuries, with a great drum-like 16th-century pigeon-loft in the garden alongside. It is known, though, as the home of the 19th-century historian Jules Michelet, and has a museum dedicated to him. Probably of more interest to non-French visitors is the arts centre that Vascoeuil also contains, with a **sculpture garden** that includes work by major names in French contemporary art and international figures such as Dalí. A series of exhibitions is also held each summer – Léger, Delvaux and Cocteau have all featured – together with concerts. The château also has an unusually lovely café.

To the east of the River Andelle and the parallel D1 as they run south from Vascoeuil is the **Forêt de Lyons**, extending for over 10,000 hectares, or 40 square miles. This was one of the favourite hunting-grounds of the Anglo-Norman dukes, and later other kings and aristocrats, which is a major reason why it has survived. The forest has been much reduced from its original medieval extent, and there are large gaps and clear-ings around the villages within it, but it remains one of the largest stretches of native deciduous forest in northern Europe, a giant wild woodland of towering beeches with, in many sections, only limited human interruptions between the rolling crests and deep little valleys. It's especially lovely to come here in autumn, when the trees are golden in the clear light. The forest is still very dense in parts, and the shelter it provided meant that this became a major focus of Maquis Resistance activity during the Second World War. There are many routes and paths into the woods, but the best way to begin is to head to its main village, **Lyons-la-Forêt**, and pick up a map at the tourist office.

Ry may have the 'real' Flaubert connections but the two French film adaptations of *Mme Bovary*, by Jean Renoir in 1934 and Claude Chabrol in 1991, have both used Lyons-la-Forêt as a location, perhaps because poor Ry just didn't look 'historic' enough. Lyons is also one of that select bunch of communities accoladed with being one of the Plus Beaux Villages de France. And it's true: Lyons is ravishingly pretty, almost entirely made up of half-timbered houses built from the 16th to the 18th centuries. Genuinely modern structures can be counted on the fingers of one hand: none would be allowed today. Lyons predictably draws the crowds on summer weekends, but in spring and autumn, especially during the week, it's often surprisingly left to itself, and the atmosphere in the cafés around its superb main square is unfussy and relaxed.

Lyons is unusual in that the Norman castle around which the village developed has almost entirely disappeared. The castle reached its greatest size under Henry I, King of England and Duke of Normandy and youngest son of William the Conqueror, for whom it was one of his favourite residences, and who died here in 1135. As the old castle crumbled into disuse in the 16th century the current village was actually built on top of its remains, thus covering most traces of it. If, however, you walk from the foot of Rue de l'Hôtel de Ville across the D32 and down the path toward the River Lieure and the 'Trois Moulins', an idyllically pretty set of three tiny watermills next to small ponds, and then look back at Lyons you can see clearly the way in which the 1652 **Benedictine Convent**, just to the left, was built on the base of the old Norman masonry. The convent was one of several religious houses established in Lyons during the 17th century, mostly along the road through the village beside the river, now the D32; all of them closed with the Revolution. Because of Lyons' curious growth, though, the village **church of St-Denis** is unusually isolated outside the village, a five-minute walk along the D32 to the west, since it was founded outside the castle walls in the 12th century. It was given a Gothic transformation in the 15th–16th centuries, and contains fine carvings of figures of saints, in wood from the forest.

The steep **Rue d'Enfer** or 'Hell Street', half-timbered from end to end, is the most attractive way up from the through road to the centre of the village. On the left at no.4 is the little house, now with a plaque, where Maurice Ravel stayed several times in the 1920s, when he came here to compose amid the rural calm. The main square at the top is the heart of Lyons and an astonishing Norman monument, especially the south side, facing you, an array of different patterns in half-timbering. With its bars and local shops as well as antique emporia, it's also pleasantly lively. One of the most time-worn looking houses on the square was the birthplace, in 1612, of the poet of Jewish descent Isaac de Bensérade, an important figure at the court of Louis XIV, after whom the square is officially named. Dominating the scene in the middle of the square are the **Halles**, the tiled-roofed, open-sided market hall, which was built in the 18th century for the powerful Ancien Régime aristocrat and benefactor of Lyons the

Duke of Penthièvre, who also commissioned the surprisingly plain Hôtel de Ville around the corner.

From Lyons paths lead off into the woods in all directions (one of the most attractive easy walks is just to carry on along the path beyond the Trois Moulins, into the woods across the river). Other paths are indicated on maps available from the tourist office (next to the Hôtel de Ville), which also organises **guided walks** with a forester (*usually in French only; April–Sept weekends only*). Otherwise, there are many more places to explore in the forest around Lyons, especially along the lane to the northeast through Lorleau. Directly eastwards, the little D14 runs through Beauficel, which has a magnificent church with a giant wooden porch, to **Fleury-la-Forêt**, a village with a curiously remote feel widely dispersed around its grand Louis XIII-style **château**, which now provides some of Normandy's most memorable B&B rooms (*see p.193*). Fleury château is also open to visitors; guided tours take you around the house's main rooms with their scarcely altered 18th-century décor, and a small but engaging doll museum, and you are free to wander around the rambling **park** (*open Easter–Sept daily 2–6; Oct–Easter Sun and hols 2–6; adm*). For something more rustic, just to the east **Bosquentin** (*open Easter–Oct Sat, Sun and hols 2–6; adm*) and **Bézu-la-Forêt** contain a homely but charming pair of locally run farm museums, with all sorts of artefacts relating to the traditional life of the forest villages; the farm in Bézu, **La Ferme de Rome** (*open May, June, Sept and Oct Sat, Sun and hols 2–6; July and Aug daily 2–6; adm*) also has a shop with local produce for sale. Directly south of Lyons-la-Forêt near Lisors are the remains of the Cistercian **Abbaye de Mortemer**, another institution that in the 12th century was greatly favoured by Henry I and by his daughter Matilda (*park open daily 1–6.30; abbey and museum open Easter–Sept daily 2–6.30; Oct–Easter Sat, Sun and hols 2–6; adm*). It is surrounded by a huge forested park, with three small lakes and St Catherine's Spring, where the young women of the region once went to pray for a husband. Still visible from the medieval abbey are the castle-like 12th-century walls, part of the solid Norman chapterhouse and the 15th-century pigeon-loft. Mortemer is now a well-developed tourist attraction: the main abbey buildings, rebuilt in the 17th century, contain – as well as some more religious relics – a museum of 'Fantômes et Legendes', ghosts and legends, designed to evoke things that go bump in the night, and medieval pageants are staged in the ruins every Saturday night during August.

Outside the forest to the west and south is the **Valley of the Andelle**, one of the most attractive of the valleys that run down to join the Seine, even though its traffic now gets a little busier as you approach the great river. Fleury-sur-Andelle is a quiet, straightforward country town. The valley below it is delightful: the division, found in all the Seine-Maritime valleys, is particularly marked between the sombre plateaux on either side of brown, open fields and huge horizons and the soft valley of woods and meadows below, where everything is greenness and running water. A good way of avoiding whatever traffic there might be on the D321 down the left bank is to cross over on to the parallel D149 down the right, a very quiet country road.

About 3km south of Fleury-sur-Andelle at Radepont you are presented with a choice of monuments. A turn left, southwards, up a very narrow lane will take you to the very grand and slightly mysterious **Château de Bonnemare** (*open to 'individual' visitors only in summer on certain weekend afternoons, but 'group' visits by reservation are allowed April–mid-Oct on any weekend, so it can be worth calling ahead or checking with local tourist offices; Bonnemare,* **t** *02 32 49 03 73*), built in 1570 in late French-Renaissance style for Nicolas Leconte de Daqueville, President of the Parlement of Rouen. Its glowering perimeter walls completely dominate the tiny hamlet of Bonnemare; to get the full effect of the château you have to go around it to the south side, intended as the main approach, where the giant slate-roofed *châtelet* or gatehouse stares down an extraordinarily long, straight *allée* of lime trees. Inside the walls are large gardens, a manor farm with bakery and 17th-century cider press and, in the house itself, several rooms with their original decoration. In contrast, a short journey back across the river and along the road down the right bank will lead to the ruins of the Cistercian **Abbaye de Fontaine-Guérard** (*open April–Oct Tues–Sun 2–6; adm*), nestling in the woods. A nuns' convent, it was founded in the 12th century, and the now-ruined abbey church was completed in 1281. The nuns' parlour, a dormitory with a massive timber roof, the early Gothic work chamber and a much later chapel are all fairly intact, and the superb vaulted chapterhouse is one of the finest surviving examples of Norman monastic architecture. Above all, it's a wonderfully serene place, with the river alongside and the white stone chapterhouse sheltered by trees as if in its own bower.

Little more than a kilometre further south along the D149 another, still larger set of towers rises up above the trees, part of a monument from the Industrial Revolution, although anyone could be forgiven for not recognising it. These are the extraordinary remains of the **Anciens Filatures Levavasseur**, a textile mill built here in the 1850s by an ambitious local landowner to make use of the current of the Andelle. As a 'cathedral of industry' it was built in the English neo-Gothic style, with a scale and lavishness that seems completely out of proportion to its purpose; moreover, most of it burnt down only 20 years later, although parts of the factory were still in use until the Second World War. Today, its ruins loom up through the woods as atmospherically as those of any ruined medieval cathedral.

The roads either side of the river meet up at **Pont-St-Pierre**. In the centre of the village there are the ruins of another medieval fortress, surrounded by an unusually wild park, and there is a very fine 12th-century church, St-Nicholas, which contains an exceptional wealth of medieval wood carvings and some relics saved from Fontaine-Guérard. To the south a road winds round via Amfreville to the top of the **Côte des Deux Amants**, a massive rock escarpment overlooking the point where the Andelle joins the Seine. Its name refers to a medieval legend in which a jealous king, not wishing to relinquish his daughter Caliste, declared that no man could marry her unless he could run non-stop to the top of the great rock with her in his arms. Her noble beloved Raoul duly undertook to do it, but collapsed and died just as he reached the summit, whereupon she died as well in sympathy. Caliste and Raoul, the 'two lovers', are said to be buried at the top (to which there's also a footpath from Pont-St-Pierre, for anyone wishing to follow their route). Below at Amfreville are the last set of locks on the Seine going seawards, and from the top of the Côte there are fabulous views over the Andelle and up and down the Seine valley.

Shopping

The largest market in this area is in **Buchy** on Mondays; **Ry** has a market on Saturdays, **Lyons-la-Forêt** on Thursdays; its Halles also hosts occasional exhibitions and antiques fairs in summer. There is a market in **Pont-St-Pierre** on Saturdays.

Bois-l'Evêque ✉ 76160

Ferme de Beaulieu, t 02 33 23 57 43. A goat farm, which sells *chèvre* and does tours by reservation. It is signposted on the N31, just west of Martainville. *Closed Mon and Tues.*

Lisors ✉ 27440

La Ferme du Logis, 10 Rue de l'Eglise, **t** 02 32 49 11 23, **f** 02 32 49 57 11. The Ouine family make traditional *charcuterie* from their own pigs, which they sell direct from their farm – near the entrance to the Abbaye de Mortemer, north of Lisors. *Open Fri and Sat.*

Orgeville-Flipou ✉ 27380

Les Vergers d'Orgeville, t 02 32 49 72 31, **f** 02 32 49 34 54. A big traditional cider farm on the D508 *c.* 3km south of Pont-St-Pierre, selling high-quality corked cider – no calvados – plus fresh apples, in season, and honey.

Where to Stay

Pont-St-Pierre ✉ 27360

Hostellerie La Bonne Marmite, *see above* (*double rooms 373.9–557.6F/€56–85*). The Bonne Marmite is a Logis de France hotel, but its nine spacious guest rooms are a cut above the norm. To go with the historic building they're decorated in more-or-less Louis XIII or Louis XVI styles (with modern fittings); the largest are very grand, and some have four-poster beds. It's a tad over the top, but service is exceptional. *Closed two weeks Feb–Mar and two weeks July–Aug.*

Le Cardonnet, Route de Radepont, **t/f** 02 35 79 88 91 (*rooms 240–270F/€36.59–41.16 for two, 360F/€54.88 for four*). A B&B in a great location, high on a hill above Radepont in the Andelle valley, with great views. It's part of a large farm that also has a separately run riding stables (**t** 02 35 79 03 12). The guest rooms are in a separate building, there's a comfy living room with fireplace, and **evening meals** are available with prior notice (*85F/€12.96 per person*).

Fleury-la-Forêt ✉ 27480

Château de Fleury-la-Forêt, t 02 32 49 54 34, **f** 02 32 49 46 39 (*double room 500F/€76.22, suite 700F/€106.71*). This is a very special château with *chambre-d'hôte* rooms: you'll think you've just walked into a scene from the Ancien Régime (with plumbing): from the giant gates in front of the house to the Louis XVI décor in the rooms. Breakfast is served in an astonishing 18th-century kitchen. Guests also have free access to the other parts of the château and the doll museum (*see* p.191). Don't worry: the guided tours don't enter your bedroom.

Bézancourt ✉ 76220

Château du Landel, t 02 35 90 16 01, **f** 02 35 90 62 47, *contact@chateau-de-landel.fr* (*rooms 490–800F/€74.7–121.95*). An elegant 17th-century château, now a luxurious country house hotel. Some of its rooms have been redecorated in period style, others are more contemporary. There's a fine **restaurant** (*menus from 160F/€24.39*), and in the grounds there are tennis courts and a pool. Bézancourt is on the east side of the Forêt de Lyons, far from the madding crowd. *Closed mid-Nov–mid-Mar.*

Bourg-Beaudouin ✉ 27380

Ferme du Coquetot, 46 Rue du Coq, **t/f** 02 32 49 09 91 (*rooms 220F/€33.54 for two, 300F/€45.73 for three*). This big old Norman farm is owned by a friendly young couple, Bénédicte and Jean-Luc Delavoye. The rooms are lovely, with excellent facilities, a sitting room, and access to a kitchenette. There's also a wonderful, romantic self-contained *gîte* in a converted dovecot, with room for up to four.

Auzouville-sur-Ry ✉ 76116

Le Gentilhommière, t 02 35 23 40 74 (*rooms 200F/€30.49 for two, 250F/€38.11 for three*). An impressive 17th-century house, once the residence of a country *gentilhomme* in a little village 3km south of Ry. Guests have the use of a living room and a small kitchen.

The house is surrounded by a lush garden full of fruit trees.

Lyons-la-Forêt ✉ 27480

Hostellerie de La Licorne, 27 Place Isaac de Bensérade, **t** 02 32 49 62 02, **f** 02 32 49 80 09 (*rooms 450–850F/€68.6–129.57*). This been an inn since 1610, with one of the most imposing half-timbered frontages on the main square. There are plenty of creaking timbers inside, including a wonderful old carved staircase, while at the back there's a delightful garden courtyard. The comfortable rooms have rather old-fashioned plush décor, and are quite expensive, but you pay for the history. There's a great bar, and a fine **restaurant** serving opulent *haute cuisine* (*menu 195F/€29.73*). *Closed Dec and Jan.*

Lorleau ✉ 27480

Mme Marie-Christine Paris, 3 Hameau St-Crespin, **t/f** 02 32 49 62 22 (*rooms 250F/€38.11 for two, 380F/€57.93 for four*). M and Mme Paris' modernised farm is in a wonderful location on a hill, surrounded by fields, well within the Forêt de Lyons. The two very comfortable B&B rooms are in a converted stables. Both are really more like suites, and one has a superb view. Mme Paris is quietly charming, and serves up fine breakfasts; she can also point you towards the best walks nearby and has bikes for rent. St-Crespin is a tiny collection of farms off the meandering lane that leads northeast from Lyons, beyond the village of Lorleau.

Eating Alternatives

Ry ✉ 76116

Le Bovary, Grande Rue, **t** 02 35 23 61 46 (*menus 95–170F/€14.48–25.91; weekday lunch menu 60F/€9.15*). In the former Hôtel de France – or the Café Français as it appears in *Mme Bovary* – this is one of the most charming half-timbered buildings on Ry's main street. The restaurant has its touristy side, but it's also a good-value local. Classics – home-made terrines and duck dishes – feature strongly, together with some fish and seafood choices, and a sizeable range of salads and snacks. *Closed Mon eve and Tues.*

L'Hirondelle, Grande Rue, **t** 02 35 02 01 46 (*menus 85–155F/€12.96–23.63*). Something of a radical alternative in Ry, but one of the most attractive places to eat, with a pleasant outside terrace; the décor is semi-contemporary and the menu highlights the food of southwest France, with dishes such as Bayonne ham and *cassoulet*. There's also a large choice of salads, crêpes, omelettes and other one-course dishes (*c. 40–60F/€6.1–9.15*). *Closed Sun eve and Mon.*

Fleury-sur-Andelle ✉ 27380

La Potinière, Place de l'Hôtel de Ville, **t** 02 32 49 00 55 (*menus 78–170F/€11.89–25.91*). A charming local restaurant on Fleury's broad main square, serving careful versions of French standards – *boeuf bourguignonne* – and Norman favourites – a *duo de poissons* in a creamy *sauce normande*.

Ménesqueville ✉ 27850

Le Relais de la Lieure, 1 Rue Général de Gaulle, **t** 02 32 49 60 44 (*menus 90–220F/€13.72–33.54*). This cosy inn in an attractive location next to the River Lieure has a real French-countryside feel: pullovered farmers come in looking for satisfying food. It's pretty much classic local fare, with plenty of meat with rich, cheesy and mushroomy sauces. This is also a Logis hotel, with 16 pleasant **guest rooms** (*rooms 290–350F/€44.21–53.35*), some looking out on to a beautifully flowery garden.

Lyons-la-Forêt ✉ 27480

Restaurant de La Halle, 6 Place Isaac de Bensérade, **t** 02 32 49 49 92 (*menus 65–130F/€9.91–19.82*). A great little country-bistro style restaurant in an ideal situation right on Lyons' ravishing main square. With half-timbering inside and out and masses of geraniums beneath the windows, it has plenty of the proper local features, but the friendly young staff give it a likeably fresh atmosphere. The excellent-value menus served in the upstairs restaurant feature fresh-flavoured dishes, such as a tangy seafood tagliatelle. Varied salads, omelettes and other light dishes can be had in the bar downstairs, in front of which there are terrace tables from spring to autumn.

Monet's Paradise:
Giverny and the Seine Valley

20

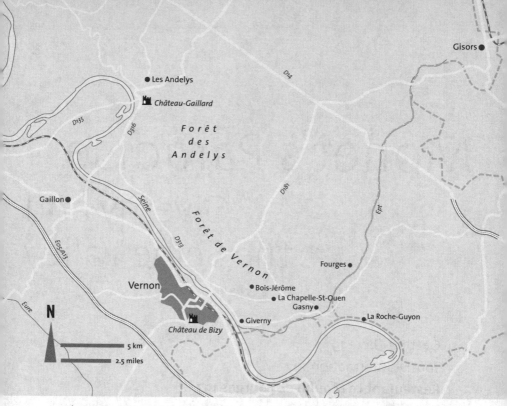

The Impressionists have provided us with familiar images of France – fields with swathes of poppies and irises, bright dresses and dappled sunlight glimpsed through trees – and Normandy has a reasonable claim to have been its birthplace. Painters have been attached to particular places: Boudin, a precursor of the movement, rarely strayed far from Honfleur, and Trouville and Etretat, among other places along the coast, provided inspiration for many artists. Nowhere, though, is more inextricably linked to a specific painter than Giverny, beside the Seine, where Claude Monet lived from 1883 until his death in 1926.

Monet discovered Giverny by accident from the window of a train, and the Seine between Paris and Rouen also attracted other artists seeking light and nature. The river wanders quietly through bends and long meanders. In midstream there is a line of small islands, with the odd boathouse and thickets of trees, woods are scattered along the banks, often climbing up steep hills and cliffs that at times make the valley almost like a gorge. Barges still chug upstream towards Paris.

History has been marching along the Seine Valley since Roman times. Along the river are towns such as Les Andelys and Vernon, with Romanesque and Gothic churches, and Renaissance and neoclassical châteaux. This was also the route chosen at the end of the 12th century by Philippe Auguste of France when he began his drive to subdue his over-mighty vassals, the dukes of Normandy and kings of England. To resist him, Richard the Lionheart built a massive castle, Château-Gaillard, on a crag above Les Andelys, now one of the most atmospheric of medieval ruins.

Getting There

This area is easily accessible from Caen, Le Havre or Paris via the A13 *autoroute*: exit at junction 18 (Louviers) and take the D135 east for Les Andelys, or junction 16 for the most direct route to Vernon and Giverny. From Dieppe, the quickest route is usually the D915 through Forges-les-Eaux to Gournay, and then the D316 to Les Andelys (*c. 1½hrs*); from Calais and the north, turn off the A16 *autoroute* at Beauvais on to the D981 for Gisors, from where the D181 leads to Vernon (*c. 3hrs*).

To get to the Moulin de Fourges from Giverny (*c. 9km*), follow the D5 below the Fondation Monet eastward as far as Gasny, from where Fourges is signposted. In Fourges a sign indicates the way to the mill.

Several trains a day on the Paris (St-Lazare)–Rouen line stop at Vernon and Gaillon, the nearest station to Les Andelys. From Vernon local buses run to Giverny.

Tourist Information

Very little is open in Giverny when the Fondation Monet is closed (*Nov–Mar*). Tourist offices have details of cycle and walking routes in the area.

Les Andelys: Rue Philippe Auguste, Le Petit-Andely, **t** 02 32 54 41 93 (*open April–Oct only*).
Gaillon: 1 Place de l'Eglise, **t/f** 02 32 53 08 25 (*open April–Oct only*).
Vernon: 36 Rue Carnot, **t** 02 32 51 39 60, **f** 02 32 51 86 55, *tourisme.vernon@wanadoo.fr*.

In a place so famed for its beauty, it's only natural to want to eat in a setting to match. This can be done in some style at the **Moulin de Fourges**, in an almost impossibly picturesque historic watermill, a few kilometres east of Giverny along the valley of the River Epte.

Le Moulin de Fourges

*38 Rue du Moulin, Fourges ✉ 27630, **t** 02 32 52 12 12, **f** 02 32 52 92 56, www.moulin-de-fourges.com. Open late Mar–June, Sept and Oct Tues–Sat 12–2.30 and 7.30–10, Sun 12–2.30; July and Aug Mon–Sat 12–2.30 and 7.30–10, Sun 12–2.30; closed Nov–late Mar. Book weekends. Menus 165F/€25.15, 255F/€38.87 and 355F/€54.12; à la carte average 350F/€53.36.*

The Epte is one of the smaller, faster-flowing tributaries of the Seine, beside which a narrow lane runs from Gasny up to Fourges. From the village, a still narrower lane rolls and bends down to the river through thick clumps of trees to bring you to the celebrated mill, initially half-hidden among the greenery. Behind the curving outer wall and gateway you come to a pretty garden terrace, and, first of all, a large cottage-like building with small wood-framed windows, roses climbing up the façade and a massive timber porch. It isn't instantly clear just where the building begins and ends. To get the full effect you have to walk round to the other side and cross over the mill-race by a little bridge, to look back on the Moulin from across the Epte. Parts of the wall are half-timbered, others are clad in stucco in a gentle shade of ochre, and up them climb ivy and dazzling flashes of flowering plants. And in the middle is the giant old mill-wheel, beneath a delicately carved, tiled-roof canopy that wouldn't be out of place on a church, with alongside it the bright little waterfall of the mill race.

Rosace de Magret de Canard, sur Pommes Ecrasées Parfumées aux Olives (Rosette of Duck Breast with Potato and Olive Mash)

Serves 4

4 boneless duck breasts, 200–250g/7–9oz each (with skin)
200g/7oz black olives, stoned
extra virgin olive oil
1kg/2¼lb potatoes, peeled and cut in large pieces
200ml/7fl oz double cream
salt and pepper
For the sauce:
100g/3½oz caster sugar
250ml/9fl oz port
1 tablespoon runny honey
1 tablespoon crème de cassis (blackcurrant liqueur)
juice of half a lemon
pinch of cinnamon

To make the sauce, combine the sugar, honey and port in a small saucepan and boil gently until it reduces to a caramel-like syrup. Add the crème de cassis, lemon juice and cinnamon, and season with salt and pepper. It can be reheated before serving.

Trim any fat from the sides of the duck breasts and score the skin. Season on both sides. Preheat the oven to 180°C/350°F/Gas mark 4.

Put the olives in a food processor and reduce to a coarse purée, adding 2–3 tablespoons of olive oil to make it looser. Cook the potatoes in boiling salted water until very tender. Drain the potatoes, return them to the pan and mash roughly with a fork. Beat in the olive purée, then the cream (you may not need it all), retaining the coarse texture. Season to taste with salt and pepper, cover and keep warm.

Set an ovenproof sauté pan over high heat until hot. Add the duck breasts, skin-side down, and sauté for about 2 minutes until the skin is lightly coloured. Turn and cook for 1 minute, skin-side up, and transfer to the oven to finish cooking, 10–15 minutes, depending on how you like them done.

To serve, carve the duck breasts into slices, mound the potatoes on warm plates, arrange the duck slices around them and pour over the sauce.

The mill was built in the 1750s, and is unusually large for a mill of that time. It was abandoned and derelict by the end of the Second World War, when a local farmer bought it and turned it into a fairly modest inn. The mill's next transformation came in 1993, when the current owners Jérôme and Cathy Crepatte installed a ravishingly pretty, high-quality restaurant beneath the eaves. Some of the tables in the dining room have a view of the creaking mill-wheel. Outside there are tables in the lush riverside garden, and a separate, stable-like building that's in great demand for family parties and weddings.

The Moulin's cuisine emphasizes the true flavours of the ingredients, often with radical, modern contrasts, as in a lobster salad cleverly offset by a punchy, earthy walnut vinaigrette. Other hallmarks are delicate reductions and marinades, and an inventive use of spices, herbs and mushrooms. A fillet of pike comes with a deliciously fragrant fennel butter and a superb stir-fry of mixed mushrooms. More classically French are the four luxuriously elaborate options with foie gras (such as foie gras marinated in spices and lavender). Other dishes are vigorous variations on standards, as with the richly flavoured *magret* of duck that's served with arguably the world's best potato and olive mash (*see* above).

The Moulin is only a few metres into Normandy (the Epte being the border), and the excellent cheese selection includes very fine Chaource and other cheeses from nearby regions as well as the famous Normandy varieties. Desserts might include a *gratin* of summer fruits, or a beautifully subtle nougat ice-cream with red berries. Afterwards, a stroll by the river among the flowers is near-obligatory. Note that the Moulin gets very busy on summer weekends.

Touring Around

Les Andelys make up the most attractive of the riverside towns between Paris and Rouen. There are two of them: Le Petit-Andely, built next to the river to provide supplies for Richard the Lionheart's castle, and the much older Le Grand-Andely, founded by the Romans, and a little way from the Seine up a narrow valley. Since the 19th century they have been joined into one town by a long, straight main street. For an overview of the town and for magnificent views over the Seine Valley and the surrounding countryside, go immediately up to Château-Gaillard. From Le Petit-Andely there's an invigoratingly steep walk up to the castle, beginning by the tourist office; by car, you must follow a well-signposted one-way system all the way through Grand-Andely and round via a fairly precipitous track to come upon it from behind.

When Richard the Lionheart returned from his famous imprisonment in Austria after the Third Crusade, he found that his former childhood friend, fellow Crusader and (it has always been rumoured) lover Philippe Auguste of France was planning to end the effective independence of the Duchy of Normandy. To stop him, Richard resolved to build the most advanced fortification yet seen in Europe, incorporating all the lessons he had learned from Crusader and Arab castles.

In a prodigious effort **Château-Gaillard** was built in only one year, from 1196 to 1197. Philippe was deterred for a few years, but after the Lionheart's death his hapless brother John seemed an easier adversary, and in 1203 a French army besieged the castle. It resisted them, as it was supposed to do for several months, until some of Philippe's troops gained entry by stealth, through the latrines. The castle fell in March 1204, and with it the dual Anglo-Norman monarchy came to an end. Château-Gaillard, though, continued to be an important stronghold through the wars of the later Middle Ages and into the French Wars of Religion of the 1560s to 1590s, so much so that in the 17th century Henri IV and later Richelieu ordered that it be demolished so that it could never bother them again.

Their demolition work and centuries of pilfering by local builders have taken their toll on the castle, but the sections that remain – the keep, part of an outer bastion, parts of the walls – are still massive and awe-inspiring. The keep's giant, 16ft-thick walls seem to grow out of the rock, and, visible for miles, look as if they could still at least partly fulfil their original purpose. Recently, the local authorities have installed a totally unnecessary concrete viewing platform (in the market in Les Andelys you can sign a petition asking for this eyesore to be removed), and in future it is possible that access to the whole castle may only be possible during the official opening times. For the moment, though, they only apply to the **keep** (*open 15 Mar–15 Nov Mon, Thurs–Sun 9–12 and 2–6, Wed 2–6 only; closed Tues; adm*), around which there are hourly guided tours. You are free at all times to wander around the other parts of what so far is still a very wild ruin, and enjoy the views over the river, its islands and the plains beyond. They are especially spectacular at sunset.

Le Petit-Andely is an attractive quarter of little narrow streets with some half-timbered old buildings, and an open-air swimming pool by the river in summer. **Le Grand-Andely** has an ample central square where the market is held on Saturdays. Not far away is the Collegiate Church of Notre-Dame, standing on the site of a monastery founded in the 6th century by Ste-Clothilde, wife of Clovis, first of France's Frankish kings. The present church is a classic assemblage of architectural periods: the main nave is plain, 13th-century Gothic, but on either side there are transepts in elaborate, 15th-century Flamboyant and later Renaissance styles, with finely worked rose windows. Inside, there is some beautiful 16th-century stained glass, and, in the chapels, two fine altar paintings by a local painter of some renown, Quentin Varin. He was the first teacher of Les Andelys' most famous son, Nicolas Poussin, the greatest of all French Baroque painters, born nearby in 1594. Poussin seems to have felt very little devotion to his *terroir*; he scarcely returned after leaving to study in Paris in his twenties, and did most of his major work in Rome. However, there is a small **Musée Nicolas Poussin** (*open Mon, Wed–Sun 2–6; closed Tues; adm*), not far from the market square (actually Place Nicolas Poussin), which has one of his major paintings, *Coriolanus answering the tears of his mother*, together with a few articles associated with him and an eccentric collection of unrelated artefacts and pictures by other local artists.

From Les Andelys follow the D313 south beneath Château-Gaillard and along the river, through small villages and long clumps of woodland, and then turn right on to the D316, signed to Evreux, to cross over to the west bank of the Seine and **Gaillon**, a little, half-timbered town with the finest Renaissance château in Normandy, **Château-Gaillon** (*open July and Aug Mon, Wed–Sun 10–12 and 2–6; closed Tues; adm*), built at the beginning of the 16th century for Cardinal d'Amboise, in imitation of the Renaissance mansions he had seen in Italy. The interior was severely damaged during the Revolution, but the elegantly ornate exterior, one of the first examples of Italianate influence in France, is by far the château's most important feature. From Gaillon, the N15 runs on down the river bank to Vernon.

Today **Vernon** is a lively place, one of the main centres of France's high-tech industries and associated with the Ariane space rocket programme. At its heart is still the old riverside town, and the knot of narrow streets around the giant Gothic church of the Collégiale has a Victor Hugo-esque air, all wild gables, sloping roofs and leaning half-timbering. The local tourist office is installed in the most spectacular building in town, the **Maison du Temps Jadis** or 'House of Time Gone By', next to the church. The church itself has a superb 15th-century façade with a spectacular rose window, while inside there is a rare 17th-century organ. There is a pleasant walk along the riverbank to the south, while just across on the east bank, to the left of the modern bridge, is the **Vieux Moulin**, a half-timbered mill-cottage on top of the last three surviving arches of the medieval bridge that carried traffic across the Seine until the 18th century. As an important river crossing Vernon also acquired all sorts of fortifications: next to the Vieux Moulin is the **Château des Tourelles**, a dramatic 12th-century keep built to protect the bridge, while in the middle of the old town is a massive round tower from the same era, the **Tour des Archives**.

Vernon's most grandiose monument, though, is the **Château de Bizy** (*open April–Oct Tues–Sun 10–12 and 2–6; Nov, Feb–Mar Sat and Sun 2–5; guided tours only; closed Dec and Jan; adm*), in its own large park on the hill on the western side of the town. Bizy – sometimes called the 'Little Versailles' – is pure Ancien Régime, built in 1741 by the fashionable architect Constant d'Ivry for the Duc de Belle-Isle, one of the most important figures of the reign of Louis XV. Its most impressive feature is the remarkably intricate visual coordination between rooms, windows, archways, gates and the paths in the grounds, to create surprise vistas that run from room to room and out into the courtyards and the park. The château's contents are a bit of a mixture, reflecting its complicated history. It passed to another aristocratic family before the Revolution, and then to Louis-Philippe; since the 1900s it has been owned by the Dukes of Albufera, descendants of Marshal Suchet, one of the generals who rose with Napoleon. It has uniforms, portraits and other memorabilia associated with the founder of the clan, and the guided tours deal with the Napoleonic era with a patriotic reverence, even though Suchet was one of the Marshals who dumped the Emperor and went over to the restored Louis XVIII in 1814.

Cross the Seine by the new bridge in Vernon and turn right to reach **Giverny**, where all eyes naturally turn to the **Fondation Claude Monet** (*open April–Oct Tues–Sun 10–6; closed Mon; adm*). It's only about 70km from Paris, and the house and gardens are often full of coach tours, especially in mid-summer, so it's worth trying to visit towards the beginning or the end of the season, and on a weekday. Monet's images of his garden are as widely commercialised as the *Mona Lisa* – reproduced on thousands of birthday cards and tea towels – but it is so beautiful in real life that nothing can spoil it, and it is still a truly wonderful place to visit.

Monet moved here in 1883 with Alice Hoschedé, a friend of his first wife who had been abandoned by her husband, and their several children by their respective first marriages. They later married. When he first arrived Monet, then 43, rented the house and its main garden, called the **Clos Normand**; as he became more successful, he was able to buy them and remodel the garden exactly to his liking; in 1895 he added an additional plot in which to create, from nothing, his **Japanese Water Garden** and lily pond. At that time the Water Garden was separated from the main plot by a railway line and a dusty track. This track is now a main road, but access from one side to the other is made easy by a pedestrian underpass paid for by the Texan millionaire and sometime diplomat Walter Annenberg. The current immaculate condition of the house and gardens, in fact, is due in great part to American benefactors.

Each of the gardens has a different character. The Clos Normand was originally a traditional French garden with neat, formal paths, but Monet's love for colours soon overcame these limitations. These gardens are all about abundance, exuberance and explosions of colour. There are great flashes of azaleas, foxgloves, crocuses and – Monet's particular favourite – irises; begonias and roses climb over frames and metal arches, and there is an astonishing alley carpeted with dazzling orange nasturtiums. Each season, each month, produces its special colours. The Water Garden meanwhile is leafy and focused on the pond, often surrounded by white wisteria. This naturally attracts the biggest crowds, especially the Japanese bridge, but one of the best features of Giverny is that you are free to wander as you like.

The **house** is almost as pretty as the gardens, beautifully light and, remarkably, still possessed of a cosy and almost lived-in feel. Most striking and surprising in a house of that time are the colours: summery yellows in the dining room, blue tiles and duck-egg woodwork in the kitchen. Decorating virtually every wall is one of the world's finest collections of **Japanese prints**, including superb works by Hokusai and Utamaro. They are the original examples acquired by Monet, arranged exactly as he hung them. Monet had his warehouse-like **studio** built in order to work on his giant near-abstract water-lily paintings, the *Nymphéas*, in the years before his death. Today, it contains reproductions of his and other artists' work, and a well-stocked souvenir shop.

Outside, along Giverny's main street – Rue Claude Monet – several of the pretty old houses are now occupied by painters offering Monet-like flower paintings, a little neo-Impressionist industry. On the other side of the road is the lavishly appointed **Musée d'Art Américain** (*open April–Oct Tues–Sun 10–6; adm*). In the 1890s several young painters, mostly Americans, arrived in Giverny to follow the master's example, and this museum, founded by a former US Ambassador to France and his wife, is intended to showcase their work and that of other American artists living in France around that time. Monet's reactions to his fan club were mixed; some became his friends and one, Theodore Butler, married his stepdaughter and is buried in the Monet family grave in Giverny; others he just found irritating. Much of the work in the museum prompts a similar response, but there are some very fine pictures by artists such as Mary Cassatt.

The best time to see Giverny village is after about five in the evening, when the tour buses have gone back to Paris. It can to an extraordinary extent still look much as it must have first appeared to Monet, as a tranquil, pretty Norman village strung out along its long main street, with just a few boys idling on bicycles amid lengthening shadows while the sun glances softly off the rooftops. Some way past the Musée d'Art Américain is the old **Hôtel Baudy**, where most of the young Americans, and more familiar figures such as Renoir and Pissarro, stayed during their visits here, and which is now a likeable 'museum-café-restaurant' that's a good place in which to spend some time (*see* below). Further on is the simple village **church**, where Claude Monet is buried, with the rest of his family.

Shopping

The best traditional market in this part of the Seine Valley is in **Les Andelys** (*Sat mornings*). Vernon has an open-air market (*Sun*), and a covered market (*Mon–Fri*).

Vernon ✉ 27200

La Fromagerie, 82 Rue d'Albufera, **t** 02 32 51 55 94. Part of a chain of fine *fromageries*, which began here and has shops in Paris and other parts of France. There's a beautiful display of carefully matured cheeses from France, Italy and elsewhere. There is also a branch at 14 Rue St-Jacques.

Guérard & Floc'h, 2 and 7 Rue Ste-Geneviève, **t** 02 32 21 50 16. Vernon's leading combination wine shop, *fruiterie* and *épicerie*, with a range worthy of a major city. Excellent fine wines and liqueurs, *charcuterie*, preserves and most other types of delicacy are found at no.2; superb, high-quality fruits, salad vegetables and more liqueurs are across the street at no.7. There is a 'daily selection' of fine wines at special-offer prices.

Bois-Jérôme ✉ 27620

Les Vergers de Giverny, 1 Rue Ste Geneviève, La Chapelle St-Ouen, **t** 02 32 51 29 36. On the flat 'plateau' above Giverny (follow the road uphill from Giverny, from Rue Hoschedé-Monet), this beautiful old cider farm produces an exceptional dry cider and fine fresh apple juice. The shop also sells *chèvre*, terrines, honey, jams and fruit tarts from nearby farms, and in the massive barn there is a pretty café. *Shop open daily exc Mon and Tues; café open April–Oct Thurs–Sun and hols.*

Where to Stay

Giverny ✉ 27620

Note that in Giverny most hotels and restaurants are closed from November to March.

La Réserve, **t/f** 02 32 21 99 09 (*rooms 650–850F/€99.09–129.58*). A luxurious *chambre-d'hôte* in a modern house that looks like a grand old manor, and is furnished throughout with antiques. The rooms are positively palatial. One room on the ground floor is fully adapted for disabled

use. The owners, Didier and Marie-Lorraine Brunet, have been described as 'the best hosts imaginable': they're especially charming and attentive, speak excellent English and can provide an ample list of local restaurants and other information. The house is on the plateau above Giverny to the east; follow the uphill turn from Giverny village towards Chapelle-St-Ouen and look for some discreet white signs. *Usually open April–Nov; usually two-night minimum stay.*

La Musardière, 123 Rue Claude Monet, **t** 02 31 21 03 18, **f** 02 31 21 60 00 (*rooms 300–400F/ €45.73–60.98, breakfast 35F/€5.34*). A big, utterly French 19th-century house with pricey, this being Giverny, and old-fashioned rooms, with red plush décor and metal bedsteads which add to the hotel's Belle Epoque-fantasy flavour. Rooms are comfortable – several have pretty views – and there's a lovely garden terrace, and **dining room** (*menus 145F/€22.11 and 220F/€33.54*) where crêpes are served as well as a full menu. *Open April–Oct; at other times by reservation.*

Les Agapanthes, 65 Rue Claude Monet, **t** 02 32 21 01 58, or **t** 06 14 08 56 80 (*rooms 260F/ €39.64 for two*). A B&B in a former restaurant on Giverny's main street, run in amiably Bohemian style by painter Alain Cournuejols who bought the place intending to use it as an art workshop, and set up the *chambre-d'hôtes* to help keep it going. The rooms are the best value in Giverny – brightly painted, decorated with original paintings and cosily comfortable. It's one of the very few places to stay in winter, when Alain also offers **meals** (*85F/€12.96*), as nowhere else is open. He still runs painting courses, and is a mine of information on the surrounding area.

Les Andelys ✉ 27700

La Chaîne d'Or, 25–27 Rue Grande, Le Petit-Andely, **t** 02 32 54 00 31, **f** 02 32 54 05 68, *www.planete-b.fr/la-chaine-d-or* (*rooms 420–600F/€80.80–91.47; suites 760F/ €115.86*). This much admired hotel, in an inn that has been welcoming guests since 1751, is famed above all for its ravishing terrace by the Seine and wonderful views of the river. The traditional rooms are extremely comfortable, the staff are charming, and there's a celebrated **restaurant** (*see* below).

Hôtel de Normandie, 1 Rue Grande, Le Petit-Andely, **t** 02 32 54 10 52, **f** 02 32 54 25 84, *www.hotelnormandie-andelys.com* (*rooms 285–330F/€43.45–50.31*). Another historic inn beside the old Paris-Rouen road, with a riverside garden. It's a distinguished old building, run for years by the Bourguignon family as a small-town hotel with old-fashioned comforts, including a very high-standard **restaurant** (*see* below).

Vernon ✉ 27200

Hôtel d'Evreux-Restaurant Le Relais Normand, 11 Place d'Evreux, **t** 02 32 21 16 12, **f** 02 32 21 32 73 (*rooms 210–350F/€32.01–53.36*). A popular Logis hotel with an art-nouveau sign and Norman-Belle Epoque façade. The rooms have been well renovated and are reliably comfortable. There's a pretty interior courtyard, and the **restaurant** is a local favourite (*see* below). It's in the middle of the town, but the rooms are quiet at night.

Eating Alternatives

Gasny ✉ 27620

Auberge du Prieuré Normand, 1 Place de la République, **t** 02 32 52 10 01 (*menus 135F/ €20.58 and 195F/€29.73*). An unassuming, attractive restaurant slightly off the main visitor trail. A locals' favourite, with one of the area's most able and respected chefs, and some of the best food in the region at reasonable prices. The ambitious menus might include petals of monkfish in balsamic vinegar with a shellfish sauce and fried leeks, and original takes on traditional Norman dishes. *Closed Tues eve and Wed.*

Les Andelys ✉ 27700

La Chaîne d'Or, *see above* (*menus 150F/€22.87 (Mon–Sat only), 245F/€37.35 and 330F/€50.37; à la carte average over 400F/€60.98*). Under chef Christophe Bouche the Chaîne d'Or is as established as a gourmet destination as it is as an hotel. There are refined dishes such as roast guinea fowl with a red pepper coulis and fresh pasta, or red mullet with an anchovy butter and celery fondue, and exquisite desserts. Service is as classically correct as the traditional décor, and there

are tables on a terrace by the gleaming waters of the Seine. *Closed Sun eve and Mon.*

Hôtel de Normandie, *see above* (*menus 105–280F/€16.01–42.69; à la carte c. 250F/ €38.11*). A typical family-run, small-town restaurant *bourgeois*, which serves classic French and Norman cuisine: homemade terrines, seafood salads, excellent lamb and beautiful, traditional desserts. Ask for a table on the terrace, or a table in the dining room with river view.

Vernon ✉ 27200

Hôtel d'Evreux-Restaurant Le Relais Normand, *see above* (*menus 130F/€19.82 and 165F/ €25.15*). Bright and charming restaurant – one of the best in the area for satisfying traditional Norman staples with lots of duck and apples, alongside more unusual specialities such as a warm, homemade sausage of pigs' trotters with truffles. *Closed Sun eve.*

Les Fleurs, 73 Rue Carnot, **t** 02 32 21 29 19 (*menu 88F/€13.42*). A popular, easygoing little bistro in the middle of Vernon with a truly bargain *plat du jour* (*50F/€7.62*) and straightforward dishes: ham in cider, rabbit with puy lentils, grilled fish, salads and quiches. *Closed Sun and Mon eve.*

Giverny ✉ 27620

Les Jardins de Giverny, Rue du Roy, **t** 02 32 21 60 80, **f** 02 32 51 93 77 (*menus 130–230F/ €19.82–35.06; à la carte c. 300F/€45.73*). In a Belle Epoque mansion surrounded by a rose garden, with a terrace. The cuisine of chef-owner Serge Pirault is refined and quite ambitious: game terrine and *fruits de mer*, or a *croustillant* of cod garnished with seaweed. There's a highly regarded wine list. *Open April–Oct; closed Sun eve and Mon.*

Musée-Hôtel Baudy, 81 Rue Claude Monet, **t** 02 32 21 10 03 (*menu 115F/€17.53; dishes 40–78F/€6.10–11.89*). Now a laid-back café-restaurant that retains a decent dose of the village's bohemian feel and serves its best-value food: a daily *plat du jour* such as grilled fish in a shallot sauce with *frites* and salad, and of course coffee served all day. The dining room is lined with pictures and there are occasional temporary art exhibitions and painting courses. *Open April–Oct Tues–Sat all day , Sun till 4pm; closed Mon.*

Explorers and Eccentrics:
Honfleur

21

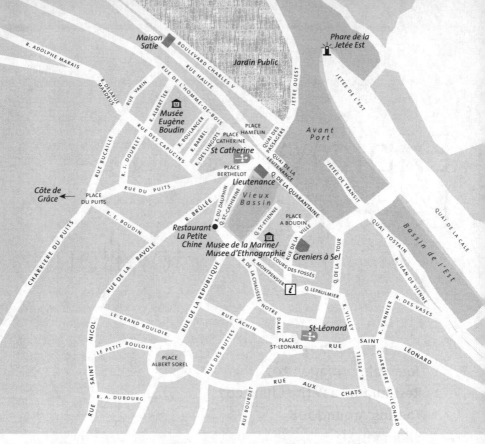

Honfleur is a town unlike any other on the French coast, clustered around its little harbour, which is ringed by an erratic line of 17th-century grey slate and timber-fronted skyscrapers. Around it there is the idyllic rural heartland of the Pays d'Auge, Deauville, Trouville and the other resorts of the Côte Fleurie, and the very visible industries of Le Havre, but Honfleur doesn't seem to have that much to do with any of them. It stands on its own within its curious little circle of hills, apparently tied more to the sea than to the land.

Honfleur has played its part in French maritime, military, economic and cultural life, and produced a range of famous offspring out of all proportion to its size (it still has fewer than 9,000 inhabitants). It was fought over many times in the Hundred Years' War, and there were times when Honfleur appeared to carry on the fight more or less on its own while the rest of France was occupied with other things. Honfleur disputes with St-Malo the paternity of French Canada (the Malouin Cartier discovered the St Lawrence river, but it was from Honfleur that Champlain set out to found the Quebec colony in 1608). As well as shiploads of hardy mariners, Honfleur has also been home to Frédéric Le Play, one of the founders of modern sociology and economics, and the historian Albert Sorel. Eugène Boudin, the painter often considered the forefather of Impressionism, was born in Honfleur in 1824 and founded a whole school of 'Seine estuary' painters, teaching the young Monet and inspiring

Getting There

The closest entry port to Honfleur from Britain is Le Havre, about 30 minutes' drive away via the A29 *autoroute* and the Pont de Normandie (a toll bridge). From Caen-Ouistreham, take the A13 *autoroute* past Pont-l'Evêque and then the A29 north, which will take about an hour; a prettier and more leisurely alternative is the D513 coast road via Cabourg and Deauville. From Calais, the Tunnel or Dieppe, the best route is to take the A16, A28 and A29 *autoroutes* towards Le Havre and cross the Pont de Normandie, avoiding Rouen. From Paris, follow the A13 to Pont-l'Evêque.

Inside Honfleur parking is restricted, especially in summer; the most convenient car parks are around the east side of the harbour. From there, walk back to the Vieux Bassin, and the junction with the long Rue de la République that runs inland. Walk a short way up this street and turn first right into Rue du Dauphin to find the Petit Chine restaurant.

The nearest station is at Deauville (*see* p.217), from where Bus Verts no.20 runs to Honfleur.

Tourist Information

Honfleur: Quai Lepaulmier, **t** 02 31 89 23 30, **f** 02 31 89 31 82, *www.ville-honfleur.fr*. The new tourist office is on the main through-street around the south side of the Enclos. Among other services, it offers a Carte d'Hôte, which gives holders discounts at a range of local attractions, and a Pass-Musées, for museums only. It also organises guided tours, some available in English.

many of his friends such as Renoir and Bazille. Honfleur also produced two of France's greatest eccentrics, the wonderfully off-the-wall humorist Alphonse Allais and the completely unique mind of Erik Satie.

Honfleur is a place of enormous charm. The old port, or Vieux Bassin, is still alive with yachts and old sailing ships, and behind its towering façades Honfleur is a town of narrow lanes, unexpected architecture and tiny alleys. Beautiful in summer, it's also a wonderfully atmospheric place to wander around on a dark, damp evening, mistily quiet, full of strange shadows and surprising corners. To see it without hordes of visitors avoid July and August, and weekends if possible. However, despite the tourists, Honfleur somehow manages to retain a strong tang of real life.

Honfleur also has about one restaurant for every 80 permanent inhabitants: it's a place that people go to for lunch, especially on summer Sundays, descending upon it from Paris and all over Normandy and beyond. In this food-lover's haven, choice is not a problem. One of the most distinctive places to eat among the many is **La Petite Chine**, a very stylish little *salon de thé*.

La Petite Chine

14–16 Rue du Dauphin, t 02 31 89 36 52, f 02 31 89 18 94.
Open Tues–Fri 11–7, Sat and Sun 10–7. Closed Mon, two weeks
in June, and two weeks from 11 Nov. A la carte average 100F/€15.24.

Honfleur may be known for seafood restaurants, but La Petite Chine offers a radical contrast. It occupies one of the old town's most idiosyncratic buildings, one of the tall thin towers on Quai Ste-Catherine: the entrance is actually on the bend of Rue du Dauphin. As you climb the winding staircases to the floors above, you get more light, and better and better views over the old harbour. Some of the best views of all are actually from the lavatory right on the top floor. The décor throughout is extremely pretty, in a very neat, very French kind of way: yellow walls and cushions in carefully coordinated colours, little wooden tables, lots of modern bric-à-brac – ceramic dogs and elephants, all kinds of unusual tea services, bowls of artificial fruit, and plenty of fresh flowers. It's undoubtedly twee, but also rather chic, in a very French sort of way.

La Petite Chine is a *salon de thé*, which in France can mean various things. It does, of course, serve teas – a very superior list of over 100 varieties. It also presents light lunches and coffees for Honfleur's 'ladies who lunch' and a fairly fashionable crowd. The atmosphere is calm and easygoing. Sophie Marceau and various other actors drop in fairly regularly, but it wouldn't do to make a fuss.

The owner, Fan, is a character: vibrant and friendly, with close-cropped, bright yellow hair and a penchant for wearing strong colours. She first opened La Petite Chine as a shop selling gifts and curios – hence the unusual ceramics – and only preparing food as a sideline, but it gradually took over. She is responsible for most of the savoury dishes, while partner Jean-Claude makes the salon's renowned cakes and ice-creams. La Petite Chine opens for leisurely weekend breakfasts and brunches, with excellent freshly squeezed orange juice; the chalked-up lunch menu might feature five or six options, as well as a few fixtures such as homemade vegetable potage. Among them might be a leek and smoked salmon tart with salad, or a *crêpe complet* (with ham and cheese), and there are also all-vegetarian choices. Ingredients are deliciously fresh: a *tarte de chèvre* has a nice onion tang combined with the goats' cheese and ideally crumbly pastry, and comes with homemade pickle; a vaguely traditional *assiette normande* is more substantial, with salad, ham, eggs and warm Camembert, beautifully complemented by apple mayonnaise and a delicate vinaigrette. To drink, as alternatives to teas and water there are beers, local cider and a fine range of fresh fruit juices and fruit cocktails.

Few people manage to resist Jean-Claude's cakes and desserts, especially the tarts and small pies oozing with spectacularly fresh fruit, maybe with a ball of his homemade ice-cream on the side. Afterwards, take a look around the shop, where you will see some of Jean-Claude's fine photographs of Honfleur.

Touring Around

The **Vieux Bassin**, the inner harbour, is the natural centre of Honfleur and one of France's most special ports. All around it there are café and restaurant terraces from which to take in the scene. It still usually contains a few fishing boats, although the greater part of its moorings are taken up by yachts, and an assortment of historic sailing boats such as the old *chalutière* sailing boats once typical of the Seine estuary, which are given special facilities in Honfleur. The main business of fishing has shifted to the much larger Avant-Port outside the Vieux Bassin, although on most evenings you can see some fishing boats come up to the Quai de la Lieutenance, the quay and bridge across the mouth of the old harbour, to unload their catch – especially

Honfleur's prized *crevettes* or prawns, which can only be sold direct there by fishermen's wives, a historic right that is jealously guarded.

The landmark on this quay is the **Lieutenance** itself, the four-square stone 16th-century former residence of the Lieutenant-Governors of Honfleur. Attached to it is the Porte de Caen, the last remaining part of the town ramparts built in the same period, inside which there is a plaque commemorating Champlain's departure for Quebec from this same spot. If you look back from the Lieutenance across the Vieux Bassin you see an emphatic contrast between the two sides of the harbour. The Quai St-Etienne, to the left along the southeast side, contains a charming but fairly normal line of old French three-to-four-storey harbourside houses, some half-timbered and some in stucco. The really extraordinary sight is along the Quai Ste-Catherine to the right, Honfleur's sheer curtain wall of slate and timber blocks, seven, eight or even ten storeys high, sometimes inexplicably narrow for their height, none of them with a roof at the same level as its neighbour and looking a little as if at any moment they might all knock each other over like a pack of cards.

The two sides of the Vieux Bassin correspond to the two parts of historic Honfleur. The area behind the Quai St-Etienne, known as L'Enclos, is the very oldest part – once the original, tiny walled town. First heard of in the 11th century, it became increasingly important after the French takeover of Normandy in 1204, as the primary maritime stronghold at the mouth of the Seine. The Faubourg Ste-Catherine to the northwest grew up outside the initial fortified area, separated from the Enclos by streams and a large pool, where the Vieux Bassin is today. Many of its early-medieval buildings were destroyed during the Hundred Years' War, but the years that followed were some of the most dynamic and expansive in the town's history. In the early 1500s Honfleur sailors explored the coasts of Brazil and Canada, and traded around the coasts of Europe. Later in the same century a new set of fortifications was built around the Enclos and the port, and in 1608 Samuel Champlain used Honfleur as his base for the foundation of Quebec.

A major transformation came in the 1660s, when Louis XIV's great minister Colbert ordered the demolition of virtually all of the town's walls, and the building of one of France's first all-weather harbours, giving the Vieux Bassin the solid form it has today. The tower-houses of Quai Ste-Catherine were mostly built in the years immediately afterwards, their unique form dictated by the need to adapt to the steep incline west of the harbour and to maximise space. Honfleur was the main port of departure for migrants to Canada, who were drawn predominantly from the Norman countryside. Among them were several thousand young women, labelled the *filles du roi*, the king's daughters. These were poor, single girls from around Normandy who were shipped off to Canada to marry the settlers. Later, Honfleur ships took part in the slave trade (something that's rarely mentioned nowadays). In the 19th century fishing took over from trade and exploration as the town's major occupation.

L'Enclos is a charming area, a little knot of low, partly medieval buildings, neatly square in shape, and arranged between tiny streets, alleys and even smaller courtyards, with the historic main throughfare, Rue de la Ville, running through its centre. Quai de la Quarantaine is Honfleur's cheap restaurant row, with a line of boisterous bistros with big outdoor terraces, mostly specialising in seafood. The food isn't always all that great, and the Quai can get busy, but these are fun places to spend an afternoon. Rue de la Ville is dominated by the giant **Greniers à Sel**, the royal salt warehouses, built on the orders of Colbert in 1670. Royal control over the sale and supply of salt was one of the most characteristic and rigorously enforced features of Ancien Régime France (and one of the most widely hated, which contributed directly to the Revolution of 1789). Honfleur was a major importer of salt, and needed a great deal of it for the preparation of salt cod. The Greniers are massive stone halls, with spectacular timber roofs that have recently been restored; they are now used for exhibitions, concerts and various other events.

The Enclos also contains Honfleur's two most traditional museums. On Quai St-Etienne itself is the **Musée de la Marine** (*open mid-Feb–Mar and Oct–mid-Nov Tues–Fri 2–5.30, Sat and Sun 10–12 and 2–5.30; closed Mon; April–June and Sept Tues–Sun 10–12 and 2–6; closed Mon; July and Aug daily 10–1 and 2–6.30; adm, joint ticket with Musée d'Ethnographie*), which occupies the former church of St-Etienne. The museum display is a quaint collection of relics of the days of sail – shipbuilders' models, figureheads, charts, sea chests, and intriguing instructions to 17th-century boat-builders.

The **Musée d'Ethnographie et d'Art Populaire Normand** (*joint ticket with Musée de la Marine*), just around the corner up tiny Rue de la Prison, is entered by what looks like a centuries-old courtyard, but is actually a combination of existing buildings with others brought here from elsewhere. The wall at the far end of the righthand side of the courtyard is the only remaining part of the 14th-century wall of the Enclos, while next to it is the prison of the 16th-century Vicomte de Rocheville. The main museum is a real mishmash. Its main features are reconstructions of Norman interiors from the 17th to the 19th centuries.

The Enclos comes to an end at Quai Lepaulmier. Immediately to the south is the **Faubourg St-Léonard**, whose main monument is the church of St-Léonard, built at the end of the 15th century, with a fine Flamboyant Gothic portal, and an octagonal bell tower added in 1760 that is completely out of style with the rest of the building. An organic food market is now held in front of the church every Wednesday morning.

From Quai Lepaulmier a walk around the landward end of the Vieux Bassin will take you toward the **Faubourg Ste-Catherine**. The district's big, sloping twin main squares, Place Berthelot and Place Ste-Catherine, are another of the town's highlights, the site of the main market every Saturday, and lined by a lively variety of cafés and restaurants. In the middle, theoretically dividing the two squares from each other, is the church of **Ste-Catherine**, Honfleur's extraordinary half-timbered wooden 'cathedral', rebuilt by Honfleur's master shipbuilders at the end of the 1460s, to celebrate the English departure. The two parallel naves are in effect giant, upturned ship's hulls. Inside, there is a wonderful sense of space, and carving of a staggering quality.

The Ste-Catherine district was the classic fishing quarter of Honfleur, and is endlessly fascinating to explore. It's made up of long streets running along the hillside, linked by passages and stairways that appear in tiny gaps in the main streets. Rue Haute, Upper Street, the district's main thoroughfare, is, with suitable Honfleur eccentricity, near the bottom. All along these streets there's a fascinating jumble of half-timbering, slate-fronting and other styles – no.30 Rue Haute is a great example, its timbers apparently sinking into the street; elsewhere, there are glimpses of half-timbered courtyards decked in brilliant arrays of flowers. This area – especially the lower end of Rue de l'Homme-de-Bois – is also one of the best places in Honfleur in which to find fine art and craft galleries.

Rue de l'Homme-de-Bois and Rue Haute meet near the harbour in **Place Hamelin**, an attractive small square lined with yet more restaurants, named for Rear-Admiral Hamelin, one of the commanders of Napoleon's navy, who was born here in 1768. Above no.6 there is a plaque recording that this was also the birthplace of **Alphonse Allais**, France's greatest comic writer. His marvellously loopy imagination produced, among many other things, the world's first entirely abstract art show, with paintings such as an all-red canvas titled **Apoplectic Cardinals Harvesting Tomatoes by the Red Sea**; he also came up with the great French philosophical aphorism 'I think, therefore I forget'. His only foray into English so far has been in a sadly now out-of-print anthology translated by Miles Kington in the 1970s, but his writings, undoubted precursors of 20th-century surreal humour, are well due for more recognition.

A walk up Rue de l'Homme-de-Bois will take you to the **Musée Eugène Boudin** (*open mid-Mar–Sept Mon, Wed–Sun 10–12 and 2–6; Oct–mid-Mar Mon, Wed–Fri 2.30–5, Sat and Sun 10–12 and 2.30–5; closed Tues; adm*), which was actually established by Boudin himself, in 1868, together with another Honfleur-born painter, Louis-Alexandre Dubourg. The interior is modern, but the museum stays true to its founders' intentions as a showcase for the 19th-century 'Seine estuary' or 'Honfleur school' of painters, including Corot, Isabey, the Englishman Richard Bonington and Jongkind from Holland. Boudin took on the young Claude Monet, then only 15, as his pupil in 1855, and also encouraged other young painters such as Renoir, Sisley and Pissarro. The museum is, naturally, very strong in works by Boudin himself, including small drawings and pastel roughs. Other artists represented include Jongkind, Courbet and Monet, and 20th-century artists such as Vallotin, Hebdo and above all Raoul Dufy, who was born in Le Havre.

From the Boudin museum, head further up Rue de l'Homme-de-Bois and then go down any of the suitably surreal-looking stairways to the right to descend to Rue Haute and Honfleur's newest and now most must-see museum, the **Maison Satie** (*open June–Sept Mon, Wed–Sun 10–7; Oct–May Mon, Wed–Sun 10.30–6; closed Tues; adm*), in the rambling old half-timbered house where the town's greatest eccentric of all, Erik Satie, was born in 1866. Satie – who was a friend of Alphonse Allais – left this house when he was 12, and it subsequently went through many other owners before it was left to the town and opened as a museum in 1998, so that there was little in it directly connected to him. Rather than just open up empty rooms with a few scarcely related artefacts, the adventurous decision was taken to fill the house with inventively designed scenes evoking the many different aspects of the very unique world of Satie, supported by videos and interactive and optical effects. You go round the museum with earphones and a tape – the English version is excellent – which moves to the right place automatically as you enter different rooms, so that you can go back and forth if you wish. It works wonderfully well in opening up the Satie universe: his appointment as 'Chapel Master' to the esoteric cult of the Rosicrucians while simultaneously working as a cabaret pianist, his (now fashionable) insistence on wearing only black clothes and eating only white food. And above all there is music: not only the delightful well-known Satie pieces like *Gymnopédies* and *Gnossiennes*, but a huge variety of other work, from awesome oratorios and bizarre religious works to 'Furniture Music', designed to be as bland as possible, and *Bonjour Biqui*, a 25-second piece with which Satie commemorated his very short love affair with the painter Suzanne Valadon, known as Biqui. At the end of the tour you have a chance to ride on the 'pedalo quaver', a mad music machine on which you pedal round a kind of merry-go-round generating different sounds as you go. It's a 'museum' that suits its subject exactly: illuminating, enjoyable and, Satie being Satie, with a great sense of unpredictable humour. The shop sells Satie CDs, including a great anthology of the music heard on the tour that is only available here.

One other aspect of the museum has nothing directly to do with Satie, but also seems to fit in curiously well. During the restoration of the house the discovery was made behind the plaster of a whole wall of ancient graffiti, with one scene dated 1543 and several dating back to the 15th century. Most are of ships and boats – sometimes well-drawn – and one can well imagine bored youths sitting on the stairs, dreaming of sailing away.

As you leave the Maison Satie, a walk across Boulevard Charles V will take you to Honfleur's main park, the **Jardin Public**, and eventually the beach, although anyone looking for a beach is usually better advised to go on to Trouville. A better brief excursion out of town is the climb – very steep, if you're walking – to the top of the giant cliff-escarpment of the **Côte-de-Grâce**, just west of Honfleur at the back of the Faubourg Ste-Catherine. The summit of the hill above the sea has been a look-out point and local pilgrimage centre for over a thousand years. A chapel was built here by Duke Richard II of Normandy in 1023, but it collapsed in the 1530s due to erosion of the cliff. The current chapel of **Notre-Dame-de-Grâce**, nestling between lofty trees, was built in 1600–15 in a plain early baroque style. For a similar number of centuries it has been traditional for Honfleur's mariners to pray at Notre-Dame-de-Grâce before and after voyages and to give thanks here for the saving of lives at sea, and the interior is literally lined with ex-voto plaques of thanks to Our Lady of Mercy, many from the 19th century, which add to the atmospheric darkness of the chapel and a notable atmosphere of religious intensity.

The limitless view from the Côte-de-Grâce was one of those that most inspired Boudin and the young Impressionists. However, certain things have happened since then. Across the Seine, Le Havre was pulverised in the Second World War, and since then has been massively rebuilt, while stretching along the north bank of the river there are oil refineries, factories, a huge Renault export depot. East of old Honfleur is the town's new industrial area, looming above which is the awesome stretch of the Pont de Normandie, the longest single-span suspension bridge in Europe. Between them sits historic Honfleur, apparently unaware of the changes that have taken place all around.

Shopping

Honfleur is full of art and antique shops and artists' studios, especially on or around Rue Haute and Rue de l'Homme-de-Bois. It also hosts an antiques market in Place St-Léonard and Rue Cachin (*2nd Sun of the month*).

Honfleur's regular market is held in Place Ste-Catherine (*Sat am*), and is one of the region's best, with wonderful cheeses, breads, terrines, fruit and veg, and other produce from the Pays d'Auge and the rest of Normandy. A smaller bio (organic) market is held in Place St-Léonard (*Wed am*).

Honfleur ✉ 14600

Compagnie des Calvados, 19 Rue de la Ville, **t** 02 31 89 57 56. A wonderful source of the very best of Normandy's distinctive drinks – cider, *pommeau, poiré* – including a fabulous array of 80 different bottles of calvados, and almost as many ciders.

Galerie Hamelin, 32 Place Hamelin, **t/f** 02 31 98 88 42, mobile 06 82 38 68 44. A cool, attractive gallery that shows beautiful contemporary ceramics. Owner François Dutoit lives nearby and is often happy to open up on his closed days. *Open Mon, Thurs–Sun or by request (call mobile)*.

Goutte de Pluie, 18 Rue de l'Homme-de-Bois, **t** 02 31 89 09 08. A striking contemporary glass and jewellery gallery, which frequently features understated modern work. *Usually open Sat, Sun and hols, or by appointment*.

Gribouille, 16 Rue de l'Homme-de-Bois, **t** 02 31 89 29 54. A delightful little grocery shop specialising in *produits régionaux*: an excellent range of fine calvados, *pommeau* and ciders, an unusually wide choice of cider vinegars, jams, biscuits, terrines and cheeses.

Gris Pomme, 32 Rue de la Ville, **t** 02 31 89 39 99. At the landward end of Rue de la Ville, an attractive little craft and household-items shop selling original ceramics, and similarly eye-catching cushions and textiles, etc.

L'Oeil du Chat, 5 Rue des Lingots, **t** 02 31 89 42 70. An old curiosity shop near Place Ste-Catherine stocking Japanese swords, old toys, chic little miniature mannequins in exquisitely made copies of real couture dresses (*250F/€38.11*), miniature shoes, books and many other surprises.

Where to Stay

Honfleur ✉ 14600

Ferme St-Siméon, Rue Adolphe Marais, **t** 02 31 81 78 00, **f** 02 31 89 48 48, *www.saint-simeon.com* (*rooms from 790F/€120.43, suites c. 5,000F/€762.2; weekend lunch c. 500F/€76.22*). Honfleur's undisputed top hotel, in its own grounds on a lofty ridge overlooking the Seine just west of town. It's famed for its associations with the Impressionists, who used to stay and paint here. Now a Relais-et-Châteaux hotel with opulent rooms, a gourmet restaurant, terrace, indoor pool and lavish health and beauty facilities.

Hôtel L'Ecrin, 19 Rue Eugène Boudin, **t** 02 31 14 43 45, **f** 02 31 89 24 41, *www.honfleur.net* (*rooms 420–950F/€64.02–144.82*). An 18th-century *hôtel particulier* in a quiet part of the town centre, extravagantly restored with antique mirrors, furniture, chandeliers, carpets and even some original paintings. The rooms have every modern comfort with lavish bathrooms, and there's a garden and very pretty conservatory for breakfast. The main salon with grand piano is straight out of a Victorian fantasy.

L'Absinthe, 1 Rue de la Ville, **t** 02 31 89 23 23, **f** 02 31 89 53 60, *antoine.ceffrey@wanadoo.fr* (*double rooms 550–750F/€83.84–114.33, suite 1,350F/€205.79*). One of Honfleur's most special hotels, in a 16th-century former presbytery. Owner Antoine Ceffrey has restored it with real flair, respecting the charm and structure of the building while adding elegant, stylishly modern details. There's a delightful lounge with giant fireplace; the rooms have a distinct touch of luxury, and the suite is fabulous. Service is special, and rooms are in great demand. The equally striking Absinthe restaurant (*see* below) is across the street.

Hôtel Le Cheval Blanc, 2 Quai des Passagers, **t** 02 31 81 65 00, **f** 02 31 89 52 80 (*double rooms from 514F/€78.35*). A traditional hotel right on the port: smart but relaxed, and now shared with the Assiette Gourmande restaurant (*see* below). The rooms are conventional but very comfortable, and all have fine views of the old port or out to sea; there's one studio-suite with jacuzzi.

Hôtel du Dauphin, 10 Place Berthelot, **t** 02 31 89 15 53, **f** 02 31 89 92 06 (*double rooms c. 300–450F/€45.73–68.6, breakfast 40F/€6.1*). A popular hotel with comfortable, pretty rooms, combining old-world style with good modern fittings. The best are in the older 'annexe', several of which have superb views of the church of Ste-Catherine.

Hôtel Le Belvédère, 36 Rue Emile Renouf, **t** 02 31 89 08 13, **f** 02 31 89 51 40 (*doubles 320–390F/€48.78–59.45; half-board preferred July and Aug*). A Logis hotel, about a 15-minute walk from the Vieux Bassin east of town, with an eccentric little watchtower and lovely garden with tables and sunshades. Four of the nine rooms are in a summerhouse at the foot of the garden, in a little world of their own. The **restaurant** (*menus 105F/€16.01 and 148F/€22.56*) enjoys a high reputation, and serves creative dishes.

Le Haut Butin, Chemin des Bruyères, Côte-de-Grâce, Vasouy-sur-Honfleur, **t** 02 31 89 38 28 (*rooms 230F/€35.06 for two, 300F/€45.73 for three*). A converted half-timbered farm on one of the narrow roads along the cliffs about 2km west of Honfleur, a little beyond the Côte-de-Grâce, with three B&B rooms. There's a great walk down to the town, but it's pretty steep coming back up.

Eating Alternatives

Honfleur ✉ 14600

L'Assiette Gourmande, 2 Quai des Passagers, **t** 02 31 89 24 88 (*menus c. 170F/€25.91, menu dégustation 450F/€68.6*). Honfleur's premier restaurant, and Michelin-starred, with a relaxed atmosphere. Chef Gérard Bonnefoy is known as a master of classic French sauces, but he also likes to experiment: try lobster gazpacho or *poitrine de pigeon rôti avec son jus aux arômes de cacao*. M Bonnefoy also owns *La Terrasse de l'Assiette*, 8 Place Ste-Catherine, **t** 02 31 89 31 33, which has tables on the square and rather simpler but still wonderful dishes at lower prices. *Closed Mon evenings and Tues*.

L'Absinthe, 10 Quai de la Quarantaine, **t** 02 31 89 39 00 (*menus 175F/€26.68, 298F/€45.43 and 380F/€57.93*). Standing out amid the bargain bistros, this is a very attractive restaurant in an old heavy-timbered building with chic modern décor, a pretty, plant-clad terrace, and an unconventional menu, presenting fine local produce in innovative dishes with international touches. A sister to L'Absinthe hotel across the street (*see* above).

Au Vieux Honfleur, 13 Quai St-Etienne, **t** 02 31 89 15 31 (*menu 175F/€26.68, menu du terroir 305F/€46.5*). One of Honfleur's classic restaurants, with terrace tables overlooking the Vieux Bassin. Old-fashioned, but highly regarded. The *menu du terroir* includes grilled lobster and *langoustines* with tarragon.

La Tortue, 36 Rue de l'Homme-de-Bois, **t** 02 31 89 04 93 (*vegetarian menu 77F/€11.74, other menus 100–183F/€15.24–27.9*). A pretty, small bistro-style restaurant with, unusually, a full vegetarian menu as well as more conventional dishes such as cod in cider, or a fine *salade paysanne* with cold meats. Several of the menus include a *trou normand*. The restaurant also has some B&B **rooms** (*c. 250F/€38.11*). *Closed Oct–May Tues, and Jan.*

Le Bistrot du Port, 14 Quai de la Quarantaine, **t** 02 31 89 21 84 (*menus 100–150F/ €15.24–22.87*). A little rough and ready, but perennially popular for bargain *moules-frites*, local *crevettes*, or just a snack on its giant terrace.

Au Gars Normand, 8 Quai des Passagers, **t** 02 31 89 05 28 (*menus 125F/€19.05 and 148F/€22.56*). A friendly restaurant with a pretty dining room and rustic exterior. *Fruits de mer* are the speciality, but there are also fine Norman fish and meat dishes: *poulet vallée d'auge* or turbot in a *sauce normande*.

Au P'tit Mareyeur, 4 Rue Haute, **t** 02 31 98 84 23 (*menu 125F/€19.05*). Many people's favourite, a very pretty, welcoming place where chef Christian Chaillou offers a combination of traditional Norman cuisine with his own imaginative creations, mainly using prime-quality fish, seafood and duck. Extravagant desserts are another speciality.

La Maison du Gouverneur, 15 Rue Haute, **t** 02 31 89 42 42 (*menus 59F/€8.99, 80F/€12.2 and 129F/€19.66*). In a marvellously time-worn 17th-century house, with tables crammed in between its timbers. Good for an easygoing lunch, with plenty of light dishes or a more substantial seafood stew and other fish choices *à la crème*.

Moules, Movers and Shakers:

Trouville and Deauville

22

Fleeting glimpses of French actresses and Euro-celebrities, sharply preserved matrons promenading with little dogs, Belle Epoque *roués* staggering ruined from the casino, men and women with flawless skin lolling in unbelievably comfortable chairs at beachfront cafés, a precise sense of chic and luxury: these are the images and ideas conjured up by Deauville, legendary capital of the Côte Fleurie. This stretch of coast at the mouth of the Seine has been the seaside of affluent Paris since the mid-19th century, when Deauville, above all, became the capital's self-styled 21st *arrondissement*, and in the 1900s anyone who was anyone could be found at some time each summer on parade along its neatly clipped seafront. More recently, its position has been challenged by the more reliable weather of other resorts further south, but Deauville has fought to maintain its status, promoting its overall ritziness and its role as a venue for prestige events.

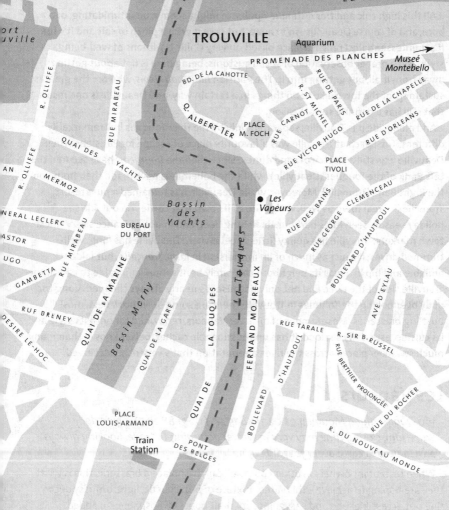

La Manche

TROUVILLE

Aquarium

PROMENADE DES PLANCHES

Museé Montebello

BD. DE LA CAHOTTE

Q. ALBERT 1ER

R. OLLIFFE

RUE MIRABEAU

QUAI DES YACHTS

R. OLLIFFE

MERMOZ

AN

NERAL LECLERC

ASTOR

UGO

GAMBETTA

RUE MIRABEAU

RUF DRENEY

DESIRE LE-HOC

PLACE
M. FOCH

RUE CARNOT

R. ST MICHEL

RUE DE PARIS

RUE VICTOR HUGO

RUE DE LA CHAPELLE

RUE D'ORLEANS

PLACE
TIVOLI

Les
Vapeurs

RUE DES BAINS

RUE GEORGE CLEMENCEAU

BOULEVARD D'HAUTPOUL

AVE D'EYLAU

Bassin
des
Yachts

BUREAU
DU PORT

QUAI DE LA MARINE

Bassin Morny

QUAI DE LA GARE

LA TOUQUES

La Touques

FERNAND MOUREAUX

RUE TARALE

D'HAUTPOUL

BOULEVARD

R. SIR B. RUSSEL

RUE BERTHIER PROLONGÉE

RUE DU ROCHER

QUAI DE

PLACE
LOUIS-ARMAND

Train
Station

PONT
DES BELGES

R. DU NOUVEAU MONDE

ort
uville

Port
Deauville

Getting There

Approach Deauville/Trouville on the N177 in from Caen, Rouen and the A13 *autoroute* and you will enter the towns on the Deauville side, and shortly come to Pont des Belges, the only bridge between them. Cross the bridge, and Quai Fernand Moureaux runs off towards the sea on the left, beside the river. About halfway up there is a bank of bars and brasseries, and Les Vapeurs is right in the middle. If you are coming from the east and Honfleur on the D513, you will arrive at the Trouville end of the bridge, in which case you should turn right along the quay.

There are quite frequent train services to Deauville from Gare St-Lazare in Paris, via Lisieux. The station is next to Pont des Belges.

Tourist Information

Deauville: Place de la Mairie, **t** 02 31 14 40 00, **f** 02 31 88 78 88, *www.deauville.org*.
Trouville: 32 Quai Fernand Moureaux, **t** 02 31 14 60 70, **f** 02 31 14 60 71, *o.t.trouville@ wanadoo.fr*.

All this high chic and *très distingué* opulence might seem a bit intimidating, or a bore, and of course Deauville isn't cheap, but take it with a pinch of salt and it's fun. It's quintessentially French: a place based on very Gallic traditions of well-being, style, and a proper observation of social customs; being here is not about getting away from it all, but getting into it. The Parisian *haut-bourgeois*, who are the greatest sustainers of the town, like to do things in a certain way, and Deauville is one resort that still has a definite social Season.

And alongside it is Trouville, separated only by the river Touques but remarkably different. The beach at Trouville was a favourite place of escape for Parisians when Deauville was still a stretch of sand dunes. Since then the *bourgeois* have secured the Left Bank of the Touques (Deauville), while the bohemians have made their home on the Right Bank (Trouville). Moreover, while Deauville has remained a pure resort, Trouville is a real town as well, with a life of its own that carries on outside the holiday season, seen in its harbour, its fishing fleet, and in one of France's very finest town markets. Trouville has quirky little streets where Deauville has long, well-trimmed drives; it's just as much of an immersion in *la vie française*, but laidback, amiable and hip in a way its neighbour can rarely be. It's more enjoyable to eat on the Trouville side of the river, and not only because it's nearly always cheaper. Along the quay overlooking the Touques in Trouville there are some of France's best, most bustling brasseries. Most famous of all is **Les Vapeurs**, renowned for both its style and its cuisine, especially seafood. It has unquestionable cachet, better known than many much swankier places across the river, a reputation that's very richly deserved.

Les Vapeurs ╱Trouville╱

160 Quai Fernand Moureaux, t 02 31 88 15 24, f 02 31 88 20 58. Open daily 8am–1am, closing time may vary in winter according to trade. Booking always advisable; à la carte average 170F/€25.92.

When restaurant owners in other countries call their place a brasserie, this is what they are hoping to achieve – this same mixture of buzz, bustle, light, unfussy décor, fine but accessible food and easygoing, open-all-hours atmosphere. An added element is the special care, seen in the exceptional quality of ingredients and touches such as the plentiful fresh flowers, that is needed to sustain a place like this over many years. It has been through a few changes in ownership since it opened in 1927; Gilbert and Ghislaine Meslin have been in charge since 1997, but have scarcely changed a thing, probably because neither the regulars nor the staff would ever allow them to. Throughout, and despite its growth in reputation, it has retained more or less the same art deco fittings, with curious 1930s accessories and mirrors that are now adorned with an accumulation of souvenirs and signed photographs. It seems quite small from the entrance, long and narrow with tables intimately packed down each side (and note that the clientele tend to smoke), but it's positively labyrinthine inside, with several rooms upstairs. One change has been the over-the-top flashing neon sign installed outside for the 70th anniversary in 1997, but this only adds to the brasserie's vibrant style.

Moules à la Crème Normande

Serves 4

2.25kg/5lbs mussels (*buchots*)

500ml/17fl oz dry white wine

2 onions, finely chopped

500ml/17fl oz crème fraîche

2 tablespoons chopped fresh parsley

salt and pepper

Discard any broken mussels and those with open shells that refuse to close when tapped. Under cold running water, scrape the mussel shells with a knife to remove any barnacles and pull out stringy beards.

In a large heavy flameproof casserole combine the wine, onions and a little pepper. Bring to a boil over a medium heat and cook for 2 minutes. Add the mussels and cook, tightly covered, for 5 minutes, or until mussels open, shaking and tossing the pan occasionally. Remove mussels to a bowl and cover to keep warm.

Pour off the cooking liquid into a large saucepan, leaving behind the gritty bit at the bottom, add the cream, and boil to reduce by half, about 7–10 minutes. Add the mussels and parsley. Cook for about a minute more to reheat the mussels. Divide mussels and creamy liquid among warm soup plates and serve.

Antoine de Caunes is a devoted regular, Gérard Depardieu pops in when he's in town, and over the years virtually every French entertainment star anyone has ever heard of – as well as many Hollywood and international names – have signed the Livre d'Or, among them the director of *Diner* and much else besides, Barry Levinson, who wrote that you can eat here better than in any diner. In high season there are also obscure fashion types, and people who work somewhere in French TV, vying for the best tables alongside the zinc bar or on the pavement outside. But despite all this celebrity hubbub, the place still manages to generate a comfortable warmth, with locals coming in just to eat a quick lunch alone, and plenty of ordinary punters among the *poseurs*.

Mutterings have been made about the service at Les Vapeurs. The squad of men in white shirts and black bow ties are certainly the kind of Frenchmen for whom going 'bof!' and shrugging their shoulders is second nature, but my own experience is that the waiters here are genuinely friendly in a quick-fire way. The restaurant is usually busy, and they don't hang about – the zippiness of the staff and their agility in nego-tiating the tables are essential to the ambience – but requests for changes or extras are met with professional aplomb, and they'll never harass you to hurry your coffee.

Since this is a brasserie, there is only an *à la carte* menu, and eating a full meal can be expensive, but it's perfectly acceptable to have just one or two plainer dishes. Starters are straightforward, with a sizeable selection of simple, fresh salads. There's also plenty of food for people who like to use their fingers, such as one of the great specialities, *crevettes grises* – shrimps, swiftly boiled in salt and pepper. Eat them in their shells, minus only heads and tails. Real aficionados eat the tails too.

Main courses include steaks, and above all many varieties of superbly fresh fish, all landed right in Trouville. Some are fixtures on the menu, like sole, while others are seasonal market specials such as sea bream, plainly grilled or served in a classic sauce. Les Vapeurs is above all home to what is probably the definitive *moules marinières*, a superlative concatenation of subtle flavours that contrives to explode and melt in the mouth simultaneously. If you want your mussels with more traditional Norman richness, try them *à la crème normande*, an equally delicious combination of seafood, wine and cream. The chips are excellent too, and the brasserie's steady supply of perfectly chilled muscadet is an ideal accompaniment.

Don't pass on the classic desserts. A *crêpe suzette* with Grand Marnier is wonderfully boozy, and the pear *Belle Helène* and *tarte tatin* are beautifully made and packed with fresh fruit – and with them appears a whole earthenware tub of crème fraîche. Round off your meal with a shot of calvados, and you'll truly be set up for the day.

As an alternative, next door is another attractive restaurant, **Les Voiles, t** 02 31 88 45 85 – attached to Les Vapeurs – which has more restricted hours but is cheaper and rather more spacious (*menus 70F/€10.67 and 119F/€18.14; children's menu 59F/€8.99*).

Touring Around

Dieppe may have beaten it as France's first seaside resort, but thanks to a better beach and its good connections with Paris, **Trouville** quickly became more popular. The first beach huts appeared in the 1840s, and when Napoleon III began to bring his court here in the following decade its popularity was assured. The great forerunner of Impressionism Eugène Boudin, and later Monet and Renoir, all painted here, and the view along the wooden boardwalk or *planches*, with flags fluttering in the wind, must be one of the most familiar images in 19th-century French painting. After the élite had transferred their allegiance to Deauville, Trouville continued to draw in the crowds. Maupassant, in his 1888 novel *Pierre et Jean*, described the beach as looking like 'a long garden full of brilliantly coloured flowers', covered in 'sunshades of all colours, hats of all shapes, dresses of all shades'.

Trouville's **beach** has been its fortune, a sweep of soft sand running away to the cliffs in the far distance to the east, fine for frolicking in the waves even though it can be a hike to reach the water at low tide, and backed by the *planches* for all of its length. It's a relaxing, old-style seafront, with bars, ice-cream stands and some grand old 19th-century beach villas along the *planches*, and still fills up on summer weekends. Part-way along there is an **aquarium** (*open Easter–June and Sept–Oct daily 10–12 and 2–7; July and Aug daily 10–12 and 2–7.30; Nov–Easter daily 2–6.30; adm*), for a rainy day, with displays of all kinds of marine life. Even Trouville's casino, at the point where the seafront meets the river Touques, and home for some years now to the 'Louisiana Follies', has more of an end-of-the-pier than a jet-set look to it.

Away from the beach Trouville is an engaging, idiosyncratic town, with little narrow streets intersecting and winding up suddenly steep hillsides, and a good deal of bizarre Norman holiday-town architecture combining half-timbering and pebble dash: 19th-century churches sport neo-Byzantine flourishes, and even prosaic public buildings like the post office have a certain mad seaside grandeur about them. The town's bohemian aura is reflected in its bar and bistro life, with a string of suitably relaxed hang-outs along the charming pedestrianised main street of Rue des Bains, in the presence nearby of some interesting antique, fashion and curio shops. On Rue Général Leclerc, the long street that runs eastward parallel to the beach, there is the **Musée Montebello** (*open mid-April–Sept Mon, Wed–Sun 2–6; closed Tues; adm; free on Wed*), a small museum with some charming works by Boudin and other Trouville painters, and some exhibits on other aspects of the history of the town.

Trouville has another major focus of activity, the long quay along the Touques, where fishing boats are moored in line to unload their catch, and also the location of Les Vapeurs and other good bars and restaurants. The best times to come here are on Wednesday and Sunday mornings, when the tree-shaded space along the quays is also the site of Trouville's wonderful **market** (*July–Sept some stalls are also there virtually every day*). It's a fascinating combination of luxury food display and jumble sale. Because Trouville and Deauville together offer a large number of, generally free-spending, customers, many of Normandy's finest producers of traditional foods bring their wares here: farmhouse cheeses, terrines, pâtés and *confits* of duck, *andouilles* and other gutsy products, ciders and calvados, honey, cakes and traditional breads. The only permanent building is the **fish market**, where the day's catch is put on sale just a few feet from where it is landed. The displays of *tourteaux*, sea bass, mussels, prawns, *bigorneaux* and other less familiar sea creatures are utterly spectacular, and the lack of any fishy odours is a vivid testament to their freshness. This is also a market that thoroughly demonstrates Trouville's quirky, small-town identity, for as you wander around you'll find, alongside the gourmet delicacies, stalls selling anything from scarves featuring Johnny Halliday or Britney Spears, unidentified stretches of elastic, extremely tacky cardigans, plastic bags, bargain overcoats and a huge selection of trilby hats to American quilts, fire extinguishers, rare books and vaguely baroque furniture. It's wonderfully vibrant and rough-and-ready, and nothing to do with the supposed stuffiness of the Côte Fleurie.

The market ends at the bridge across the river, called **Pont des Belges** because of the curious fact that Deauville and Trouville were liberated in August 1944 by a Belgian Brigade operating with the Canadian Army. On the other side, you can walk down the neat, shaded path along the Touques, or stroll into the broad avenues of **Deauville**. The town is a product of the decadent Second Empire. In 1860 Napoleon III's half-brother the Duc de Morny strayed across from Trouville and decided to develop the empty dunes on the left bank of the river, as a much more exclusive, and so more profitable, resort. Another major contributor to its development was a speculator called Eugène Cornuché, who at the turn of the 20th century built the current seafront and the casino. Deauville's two great heydays were either side of the First World War, and in the Jazz Age flappers danced the night away at parties in the town's extravagant villas, and entertainers such as Mistinguett and Maurice Chevalier were obligatorily snapped in photo opportunities on the seafront every year.

Since Deauville is an artificial town, its promoters were able to control building and impose particular styles, and above all the one known locally as 'Anglo-Normand', with much use of mock-traditional half-timbering in giant mansions several storeys high, giving the impression of a Pays d'Auge manor house after a severe dose of steroids. Walk around the quiet, neatly kept streets of the town and you find a fascinating variety of such creations, with pepperpot towers, turrets, Swiss-chalet roofs, ginger-bread-house windows, elaborate pagoda cornices and all kinds of other fanciful details, all within smart gardens surrounded by tightly clipped hedges. It's the presence of so much mock architecture in Deauville that gives the place its distinctly Beverly Hills, slightly dotty look. There are relatively few shops, and probably as many *esthéticiennes* as food stores.

Right next to Pont des Belges is one of the most engagingly silly of the Anglo-Normand edifices, the half-timbered **railway station**. Carry on past it and veer to the right, and you will come to the heart of town. Away to your right again are Deauville's two large yachting marinas. At the centre of town is the shiny white casino, over-looking the beach, looking a bit like the White House with the upper floors missing. On either side of it are two of the three Empress-Dowagers of Deauville hotels, the Normandy and the Royal. The third, the Hôtel du Golf, perhaps the largest half-timbered cottage ever built, is on Mont Canisy at the back of the town, next to its golf holes, one of the finest courses in France.

The casino and the grand hotels are separated from the beachfront by a flat, open area, lined with flowerbeds, that now contains such services as tennis courts, an indoor swimming pool and the esplanade of the **Centre International de Deauville** (CID), the venue for exhibitions, festivals and conferences. Beyond that, finally, is the beach, lined with more wooden *planches* that form Deauville's historic **promenade**. The bars along the front – Le Ciro's, the Bar du Soleil, the Bar de la Mer – are perhaps the original beach cafés; they still draw in the visiting glamour today, busily air-kissing across the tables. You also see Deauville's more regular clientele along the prome-nade, participating in their daily rituals. The French middle classes have a persistent fondness for little dogs, and parts of Deauville could be considered a preserve where all the poodles and pekinese that have disappeared from the rest of the world have been taken for safety. There are clusters of *bc-bg* (*bon chic-bon gens*), those wealthy young French people best identified by their complete domination of the art of wearing a pullover, and every so often pretty girls and boys may appear on roller blades and push a piece of paper towards you, promoting something. After the bars come to an end there are lines of rather elaborate, well-kept beach cabins, the little fences between them painted in imitation Hollywood Boulevard style with the names of all sorts of international film figures who presumably have passed through.

Next to the esplanade by the casino there is a large centre for **thalassotherapy**: bombardment with sea water through a high-pressure hose. *Thalasso* fits all the requirements of a French middle-class health fad: you don't have to do anything, it's all done to you, and it's as much about looking good as it is about health. It's also supposed to be very good for *le stress*, and basic treatments can be had in Deauville from around 1,200F/€182.93 a day. There are *thalasso* centres all round the French coast, but the Deauville establishment is one of the most luxuriously equipped.

Deauville's Season runs essentially through July and August. In the last 20 years, though, since the town has had to work much harder to keep up its prestige, this has been extended on either side, into early summer and autumn. Programmes listing all the events organised each year are available from the tourist office.

Deauville is also one of the most important centres of the French horse world. There are two tracks, La Touques for flat racing and the more casual Clairefontaine, which hosts some flat races but is mainly used for steeplechases and trotting. Both have lavishly equipped, beautifully maintained buildings in Anglo-Normand manor house style, and hold regular meetings through the summer season, with some additional races and thoroughbred sales at La Touques in mid-October. Clairefontaine also offers free guided tours, every day in season at 10.30am.

Some events are especially sniffy, definitely the kind of occasions where you would not want to turn up wearing the wrong hat. These include the August polo tournament at La Touques, and the Grand Prix de Deauville – the traditional end to the season at the same track at the end of August. Others are much less so, and Deauville most lets its hair down during the Festival du Cinéma Américain in early September, which generally previews American movies before their European release dates, and always ensures that some major Hollywood figures such as Clint Eastwood, Johnny Depp or Robert de Niro put in an appearance, amid much flashing of lights and rippling crowds. Oddly enough, it's also much easier to get into than other trade-orientated festivals such as Cannes.

From November to mid-spring, while Trouville stays alive, Deauville largely closes down. A few people still come up for weekends to catch the sea air, but many of the grand houses are tightly shuttered, the lines of beach umbrellas are tied up like so many coloured pillars, and the streets are oddly but atmospherically quiet.

If you've had enough of Deauville, then the D513 back across the river through Trouville will lead you after 15 kms to Honfleur. Alternatively, follow the same road west from Deauville, through the neat, orderly little seaside towns that make up the rest of the Côte Fleurie. Part-way along, the road stands back from the coast to avoid the cliffs of the **Vaches Noires**, beneath which there's a great walk at low tide. Almost hidden in amongst these precise resorts is the ancient town of **Dives-sur-Mer**, from where William the Conqueror's main fleet set sail for Hastings. Its port has since largely silted up, but it still has a fine Romanesque and Gothic church and a superb 15th-century covered market hall, which hosts another vibrant market on Saturdays.

Deauville may have reinvented itself a little for the modern era, but the Belle Epoque still lives on in **Cabourg**, just across the Dives river from Dives-sur-Mer, where Marcel Proust came for his adolescent holidays, and which he immortalised as 'Balbek' in *Within a Budding Grove*. All roads in Cabourg lead to the Grand Hotel, around which the town was created. It looks exactly like the kind of hotel that would have been patronised by the Margaret Dumont character in the Marx Brothers movies, but now trades shamelessly on its Proustian associations by offering wildly expensive teas in its *salon de thé*.

Shopping

Shopping is made especially easy in **Trouville**: the market fills the quays along the right bank of the Touques every Wednesday and Sunday, and the fish market, unmissable in the centre of the quay, is open every day; the town's interesting specialist shops, meanwhile, are all concentrated along the quay: Boulevard Fernand Moureaux, the charming pedestrianised alley of Rue des Bains, which runs away from Boulevard Moureaux by the Hôtel Le Central, or on Rue d'Orléans, which runs on from the end of Rue des Bains.

In **Deauville**, the main area for luxury shopping is around the circular, flower-decked Place Morny, between Pont des Belges and the beach, with the tourist office nearby; for foods, especially, Rue Désiré-le-Hoc, between Place Morny and the railway station, is Deauville's street of gourmet goodies.

Trouville ✉ 14360

La Cave Trouvillaise, 34–36 Rue des Bains, **t** 02 31 88 87 49. A fine wine merchant in a characterful old 19th-century shop in the heart of Trouville, looking like a piece of the Impressionist era itself, with excellently varied stock, and a particularly impressive collection of fine calvados and local ciders.

Aux Ducs de Normandie, 85 Rue des Bains, **t** 02 31 88 96 10. An eye-catching *confiserie artisanale*, with a delicious range of homemade chocolates, sweets, twee little fancy cakes and other goodies.

Le Fromager, 50 Rue des Bains, **t** 02 31 98 28 14. As well as an excellent selection of local cheeses – wonderful Pont-l'Evêque, Livarot and fresh Camembert – this little shop also stocks farmhouse ciders, meaty and mushroomy terrines, and other Norman produce.

Pain et Tradition–Pascale et Jean-Pierre Boullen, 134 Quai Fernand Moureaux, **t** 02 31 88 13 82. As dedicated to maintaining the culinary arts as the name suggests, Maison Boullen on the quay in Trouville offers over 20 wonderfully fresh traditional breads on any given day – including an apparently un-French variety of brown loaves and rolls. The breads are really the stars of the show, but

around them there's a delicious range of *pâtisserie* and homemade chocolates, which you can take away or sample in the little tea-room alongside.

Deauville ✉ 14800

Charcuterie Bernard, 31 Rue Désiré-le-Hoc, **t** 02 31 88 22 30. One of the more discreet and unassuming of Deauville's luxury food outlets, Bernard nevertheless has a wonderful range of fine sausages, meats, hams, cheeses and other delicacies. Staff are also unfussily charming.

Aux Délices de l'Etoile, 35 Rue Désiré-le-Hoc, **t** 02 31 88 22 15, **f** 02 31 88 89 95. The kind of shop that France (or rather Paris) invented, and has never been done quite as well anywhere else: a gleaming combination of *pâtisserie*, *confiserie* and *boulangerie*, with delectable cakes, exquisite little sculptures in chocolate, and fine breads, all presented beautifully *comme il faut*. Even if you can't decide what to buy, the display is magnetic.

La Halle aux Vins, 10 Quai de la Touques, **t** 02 31 98 33 85, **f** 02 31 98 75 21. On the quay facing across the river to Trouville, this big wine store has an un-Deauville-like casual style, based as it is in a former warehouse. The ample stock covers all the French regions, and the staff are very knowledgeable.

Where to Stay

Trouville ✉ 14360

Hôtel-Restaurant Carmen, 24 Rue Carnot, **t** 02 31 88 35 43, **f** 02 31 88 08 03 (*double rooms 380–460F/€57.93–70.13, family rooms 530–610F/€80.80–92.99, breakfast 37F/€5.64*). A long-running, traditional family-run Logis de France hotel in Trouville. The stairs (with no lift) creak a little, but the 17 attractive, comfortable rooms have all been recently renovated, and are good value. Although only a couple of streets away from both the beach and the port, the rooms don't actually have a view of either, but the hotel is extra cosy, and the helpful staff give a warm welcome. The **restaurant** (*menus 135–190F/€20.58–28.97*) offers reliable, classic Norman cuisine.

Hôtel Le Central, 5–7 Rue des Bains, t 02 31 88 80 84, f 02 31 88 42 22, *www.hotel-le-central.com (double rooms with port view 450F/€68.60, without 330F/€50.31, suites from 450F/€68.8)*. One of Trouville's best-known and most popular hotels, in a stately Belle Epoque building fronted by 1930s-style signs rising up out of the quayside alongside Les Vapeurs. Truth to tell, the 25 rooms are more functional than characterful, but the location, with harbour views from some rooms, is the best in town, and the hotel has a distinctive brio. There is a brasserie on the ground floor, for late-night meals (*see below*). The garage quickly fills up, and the entrance is very narrow, so you might well prefer to park in the street.

Hôtel La Calèche, 87 Rue des Bains, t 02 31 88 74 04, f 02 31 88 32 17, *La.Caleche@wanadoo.fr (single rooms 250F/ €38.11, double rooms 300F/€45.73, family rooms 500F/€76.22, breakfast 40F/€6.10)* A likeable hotel in the middle of Trouville with a friendly, youthful feel – and one of the best-value options in this expensive area. The ten rooms, all recently renovated with good bathrooms or showers and other comforts, vary a good deal in size, from very ample family rooms to tiny garret-like rooms in the roof (no lift). On the ground floor there's a very comfy, suitably laidback bar, with food such as *moules-frites (60F/€9.15)*.

Deauville ✉ 14800

Hôtel Normandy, 38 Rue Jean Mermoz, t 02 31 98 66 22, f 02 31 98 66 23, *normandy@lucien-barriere.com (double rooms from 1,250F/ €190.56; packages can include golf, admission to shows at the casinos or beauty treatments)*. Once in a while, driven by an anthropological desire to get to the heart of French luxury culture or just an itch for an all-out splurge, you might want to take the Deauville experience head-on. If so, then you need to stay in one of the town's extraordinary grand hotels. All three of the town's extraordinary grand hotels. All three battleships – the Normandy, the Royal and the Golf – are now owned, with the casino, by the same Lucien Barrière organisation, and information is available on a joint

website (*www.lucienbarriere.com*). The Normandy, a mad half-timbered fantasy mansion from 1912, to the right of the casino looking seawards, is the largest of all, with 290 rooms and suites, and is the only one open all year round; the 176-room **Golf** is in manicured grounds on top of Mont Canisy and naturally next to its magnificent golf course (*open Christmas and Mar–Oct only*). The comforts and service offered by all three are, of course, fabulous, and specific facilities at the Normandy include a choice of gourmet restaurants, an indoor pool, tennis courts, live entertainment and a health and beauty centre worthy of a health farm.

Hôtel Le Trophée, 81 Rue du Général Leclerc, t 02 31 88 45 86, f 02 31 88 07 94 (*double rooms 340–540F/€51.83– 82.32*). A good option for those who wish to try out Deauville without paying the prices of the *grandes-dames* hotels, the Trophée is a smart, comfortable hotel in the centre of town, with 24 rooms and two suites, in a building that's quite modern but is disguised, Deauville-style, by half-timbering. There's also a traditionally elegant restaurant, **Le Flambée** (*menus from 150F/€22.87, weekday lunch menu 85F/€12.96*), with smartly presented Norman cuisine.

Eating Alternatives

Trouville ✉ 14360

Bistrot Les Quatre Chats, 8 Rue d'Orléans, t 02 31 88 94 94 (*dishes c. 40–95F/ €6.10–14.48*). An intimate Trouville-bohemian bistro, often popular with fashionable visitors to town, with an old-world circa-1900 look provided by heavy wooden tables, a mass of old prints, books, posters and other bits and bobs around the walls, and a truly spectacular antique metal coffee machine gleaming on the bar. On offer are a fine wine selection, cocktails, homebaked bread and small dishes described as 'tapas': there's no set menu, but the possibilities on the chalked-up à la carte menu might include lighter dishes such as a *tarte aux légumes confits* and inventive salads or local classics like *daube de bœuf*, often with innovative seasonings. Another speciality is hefty roast lamb. *Closed Wed, Thurs exc July and Aug, and Jan.*

La Petite Auberge, 7 Rue Carnot, **t** 02 31 88 11 07 (*menus 136–195F/€20.73– 29.73*). In contrast to the usual brasserie-and-bistro style of Trouville's eating places, the Petite Auberge is a neat, restrained, rather intimate restaurant with pretty décor and sophisticated food that combines local traditions with notably refined original touches. The *menu du terroir* might feature a delicate *tarte* of young mackerel with apple vinegar compote, or a *papillote* of rabbit with sorrel cream (a house speciality) and wild garlic. Market freshness is naturally a touchstone, and the 195F/€29.73 menu is a *panier du mois*, a 'monthly basket', highlighting the best products of the season. *Closed Tues and Wed.*

Cocotte Café, 58 Rue des Bains, **t** 02 31 88 89 69 (*menus 72–139F/€10.98–21.19*). A very popular, convivial little bistro in the middle of Trouville that's much appreciated by locals and regular visitors to the coast for its relaxed, neighbourhood-bohemian café atmosphere and excellent quality at reasonable prices. Amiable chef-host Hervé prepares his menus with an admirable eye to whatever's best in the market that day, and they might include interesting offerings such as snails in Camembert, a traditional Norman *poulet vallée d'auge* or great fish and seafood brochettes. *Closed Mon and Tues.*

La Maison, 66 Rue des Bains, **t** 02 31 81 43 10, **f** 02 31 14 96 46 (*dishes c. 30–60F/€4.57–9.15*). This is the proper name of this newish (opened 1999) Trouville wine bar-bistro, although what you're likely to notice first is 'Du Coq Hardi' written on the window, from the brewery near Lille whose products are among the high-quality beers the Maison has in stock. It's a hip, dark little bar, with décor that's a mix of mock-old and stylish new, and as well as beers has a very good, imaginative list of fine wines. To eat there are *collations* – an enjoyable range of light dishes, salads, soups, desserts and *tartines* – open sandwiches with different toppings – plus a *plat du jour*. Run by a friendly crew.

Brasserie Le Central, 158 Quai Fernand Moureaux, **t** 02 31 88 13 68. Although it's right alongside Les Vapeurs (to the extent that it's not easy to see where the outdoor tables of one bar end and the others' begin), the big brasserie in the Hôtel Le Central (*see* above) is condemned never to have the history or quite the cachet of its neighbour. However, it too is a classic of sorts, with 1930s décor, and it makes a perfectly good alternative whenever Les Vapeurs is full, or if you feel a need to stretch out while eating (the Central is by some way the less cramped of the two). The menu features all the brasserie classics, naturally highlighting *moules* and grilled fish, but with a huge choice of other dishes, large and small, which are cheerfully served through the day and late into the night.

Deauville ✉ 14800

Le Ciro's, Bd de la Mer, **t** 02 31 14 31 31 (*menu 205F/€31.25*). If you're doing Deauville properly then you have at least to call in at Ciro's, for years the number-one place to see and be seen, and one of France's definitive beachfront bar-restaurants. Its mainly seafood cuisine has an august reputation, with refined options such as *moules au safran* and tournedos of salmon in calvados, but it's best known for its menu of superb seafood such *as langoustines*, lobster *à l'armoricaine* (flambéd in cognac and with a cream and wine sauce) or the utterly lavish *plateaux des fruits de mer* (240F/€26.59). If you're concerned about the price, then you probably shouldn't be here: for a sampler, have a lighter dish or an *apéritif* on the terrace. Dress: smart casual, and be sure to pay equal attention to both.

Chez Miocque, 81 Rue Eugène Colas, **t** 02 31 88 09 52. The classic Deauville restaurants are the *haute gamme* establishments in the *grands hôtels*, but the Miocque is a more easygoing bar-brasserie, with satisfying seafood (*moules-frites c.* 80F/€12.20), grills and lighter dishes such as assorted salads, at decent prices. The terrace tables make a good place from which to watch the Deauville world go by.

Cider and Flowers:
the Northern Pays d'Auge

23

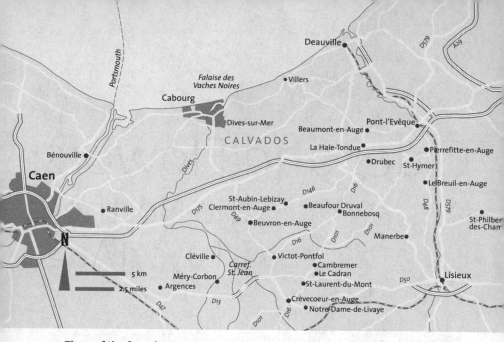

Three of the four classic Norman cheeses – Camembert, Livarot and Pont-l'Evêque – and the ciders traditionally considered the best in all Normandy all come from the Pays d'Auge, the vaguely defined area of rambling, intertwined valleys that spreads roughly from east of Caen across towards the River Risle, and from near the coast at Honfleur down beyond Vimoutiers in the south. Known as a region of agricultural abundance since the early Middle Ages, it also provides the classic image of the Normandy countryside: half-timbered, thatched-roofed farms and manor houses with roses climbing up the walls, scattered between apple orchards, woods and open fields across green valleys. At times the landscape seems almost impossibly lush, with a perfect prettiness that can be hard to credit.

This is also the best area in the region in which to search out and sample the local specialities. Meander along the narrow lanes, some of them almost tunnel-like between ranks of giant, wildly beautiful beeches, and there are any number of farms to be discovered that sell their own cider, calvados and other delicacies, while fine cheeses and dairy produce can be found at the spectacular local town markets.

The Pays d'Auge divides more or less in two halves, north and south, roughly along the line of the N13 Caen–Lisieux road (for the southern half, *see* Chapter 21). To the north is the most important area for ciders, while in the south cheese is king. The northern Pays d'Auge also has the leafiest, most intimate and sheltered valleys, the narrowest and most intriguingly tortuous lanes, the prettiest villages apparently hidden away up green hillsides. There are relatively few major monuments, but the landscape itself is a monument, making this little arcadia a delightful place to experience with no fixed destination, wandering up the deserted little roads that criss-cross each other through the valleys to find more magnificent old farms. Follow your nose – sometimes literally, for the air often carries a fragrant but noticeable scent of

Getting There

The main fast road through this area is the A13 Paris–Caen *autoroute*, which passes very close to Pont-l'Evêque, and meets the A28 from Calais and the north near Rouen. Parallel to the A13, for those who want to take things a little more gently and/or don't want to pay *autoroute* tolls, there is the old N175. Caen/Ouistreham to Pont-l'Evêque takes about 45mins by the A13, an hour by the N175. Le Havre is about an hour from Pont-l'Evêque, via the A29 and the Pont de Normandie bridge (toll), which crosses the Seine just east of Honfleur.

Pierrefitte-en-Auge is a few kilometres south of Pont-l'Evêque: from the A13, take the exit for Pont-l'Evêque to meet the N175 at the crossroads in the middle of town, and turn left towards Caen. If you approach Pont-l'Evêque from the north, from Deauville, Honfleur or the Pont de Normandie on the N177/D579, turn right at the same crossroads. On the west side of Pont-l'Evêque there is a turn south off the N175 on to the D48, signposted to Lisieux, and a short way down this road, past the *autoroute*, there is a right turn for the D280A to Pierrefitte-en-Auge. The Auberge is unmistakable in the centre of the village.

Pont-l'Evêque has a train station and is a stop on the Paris–Lisieux–Deauville line. Calvados Bus Verts run from outside the station to many villages, but to explore them at all a car or bike is indispensable.

Tourist Information

Cambremer: Rue Pasteur, t 02 31 63 08 87, f 02 31 63 08 21. There are usually temporary information points open in Bonnebosq and Beuvron-en-Auge (*June–Sept, especially weekends*).

Pont-l'Evêque: 16 bis Rue St-Michel, t 02 31 64 12 77, f 02 31 64 76 96, *pontleveque-tourism@wanadoo.fr*

apples. If the fragrance brings on hunger pangs, an ideal place in which to get further immersed in the atmosphere of rural calm is the wonderful **Deux Tonneaux** (Two Barrels) in Pierrefitte-en-Auge. With a barrel for a sign, creaking timbered walls, a garden alongside with tables beneath apple trees and a fabulous view, it's a traditional Norman village inn and bar-*tabac* that even locals are surprised to find still exists, serving cider from the barrel and traditional country dishes made with the best local produce.

L'Auberge des Deux Tonneaux

Pierrefitte-en-Auge, t 02 31 64 09 31, f 02 31 64 69 69.
Open Sept–Nov and Feb–June Tues–Sat 12–9, Sun 12–4;
July and Aug also open Mon 12–9. Closed 12 Nov–1 Feb.
A la carte average 160F/€24.39.

Pierrefitte-en-Auge is not that far from the *autoroute* and the busy N175, and yet seems entirely oblivious of them in its tranquillity. A scattering of farms and barns up and down a steep hillside overlooking the broad valley of the River Touques, the whole village is *protégé*, and just about every building is half-timbered except the church. The Auberge des Deux Tonneaux stands by the roadside opposite the latter. Built in the 17th century, it looks very much the kind of place a musketeer might have chased a serving wench around in its early days. Outside, its brown-timbered walls lean and bulge at odd angles beneath the dense eaves of thatch, and out of each

Lapin Façon Grand-mère au Cidre et au Pommeau

Serves 3–4

1 rabbit, jointed
1 heaped tablespoon seasoned flour
75g/3oz butter
2 onions, sliced
2 carrots, sliced
250g/9oz mushrooms, cut into quarters
4 tablespoons *pommeau*
1 tablespoon chopped thyme
1 bay leaf
500ml/1 pint Normandy cider
chopped parsley to garnish
salt and pepper

Dust the rabbit pieces in the seasoned flour, shaking off any excess. Heat the butter in a large pan, add the rabbit and brown well on all sides. Remove from the pan.

Add the onions, carrots and mushrooms to the pan and cook gently until lightly coloured, then add the *pommeau* and bring to the boil, stirring to scrape up the sediment from the bottom of the pan.

Return the rabbit to the pan, then stir in the thyme, bay leaf, cider and salt and pepper. Simmer for about 1 hour or until the rabbit is tender. If the sauce is too thin, you can remove the rabbit from the pan and boil the liquid until reduced and thickened. Return the rabbit to the pan, adjust the seasoning if necessary, and serve sprinkled with chopped parsley.

window spill great clumps of potted geraniums. The garden is on a raised terrace at one side; it's at its best in May, when the apple blossom enhances the great vista over the green valley spread out beneath you. At the back of the garden there's an additional dining room with long tables and pews for seating, where red-faced farmers come for lunch in big noisy groups.

Inside, the snug main dining room has oak beams, a massive oak bar, oak tables neatly covered in checked oilcloth, and a fascinatingly ornate gold-plated grandfather clock in one corner. The windows sport little embroideries and a collection of coffee pots, and through the glass beyond them the view over the Touques is framed by those red geraniums. Mme Jacqueline Rayer and her charming young staff run it as a local restaurant and, despite the 'official' opening times, they may sometimes close mid-afternoon on quiet days.

The Deux Tonneaux offers *'plats authentiques du terroir'*, and straightforward Norman cooking is what you get: omelettes, salads, hams, sausages of various kinds, *lapin grand mère*, chicken and so on, with apples, cider and mushrooms turning up in several dishes. There are no set menus, but possible starters include platters of ham or *charcuterie*, or just a plain green salad in a tasty mustard vinaigrette; to follow, there are some daily specials chalked up on a blackboard, such as a *mijoté* of veal in a rich sauce with wild mushrooms (*c. 95F/€14.48*). But the simplest things on the menu – the omelettes, salads and local dishes – are the best.

What makes these apparently everyday offerings spectacular is the sheer quality of the local ingredients: the gutsy terrines are made at the Auberge itself, and you can taste the sheer goodness of the tomatoes or the deep-yellow eggs used in the omelettes. An *omelette campagnarde* comes filled with potatoes and their own home-dried bacon and seasoned with woodland herbs, while the meaty *andouillette* bursts open when you cut it and is full of strong, varied, earthy flavours; a *salade paysanne* of chicken, tomato, egg, lettuce and chives, with a smooth cider vinegar dressing, makes a perfect light lunch. If you come forewarned and are ready for a larger meal, then another of the Deux Tonneaux's renowned specialities is its succulent whole roast farm chickens, served absolutely simply with sautéd potatoes and salad. Chickens must be ordered at least four hours in advance, and for a minimum of four people (*98F/€14.94 per head*).

To drink, there are wines, beers and the usual alternatives, but it's only natural in this setting to have one or two of the earthenware jugs of farm cider, dry or sweet – the dry cider from the barrel is fruity, but still very refreshing. For something a bit more smooth and refined, there's also local corked cider (*cidre bouché*).

After the main course, you can naturally try some creamy Pont-l'Evêque, or there's a classic Norman *douillon de pomme*. It's worth inquiring, too, after the special dessert of the day, which in autumn might be a fabulously smooth *gratin* of deliciously fresh blackberries. Another speciality of the house, however, are the *crêpes*: they come in a range of fruity and alcoholic combinations, and even the innocently named '*crêpe au chocolat*' arrives powerfully doused in calvados as well as a thick, aromatic chocolate sauce. As you leave, you might be tempted to buy a bottle of Mme Rayer's own cider and *pommeau*, lined up behind the bar, to take away with you.

Touring Around

Together with greenness and the thick leaf-coverage from the beech trees, the third great abiding image of the northern Pays d'Auge is half-timbering. Once you get away from the main trunk routes virtually every small town and village is made up predominantly of **maisons de colombage** or half-timbered houses. Norman half-timbering uses more and thinner uprights than its English equivalent, giving a more stripey look, but the three basic elements of the technique – the *poteaux* (structural timbers), *écharpes* (diagonals) and *colombages* (the thinner pieces between the main timbers) – provide an apparently infinite variety of design possibilities, with intricate zig-zags, buttresses and counter-posed panels creating a fascinating diversity. The steep, fairytale-house roofs are sometimes of thatch, but more often of red tile. The farms tend to sprawl into several equally impressive buildings, for it has been the practice for the original house to become a barn or cowshed once a larger one could be built.

Apples, cider and calvados are the Auge farms' most inescapable products. Farmers in the Bessin and the Cotentin *bocage* might not agree, but the Pays d'Auge ciders have traditionally been the most highly regarded in the whole of Normandy, and this is the only area with the hallowed accolade of an *appellation d'origine contrôlée* for its ciders (as opposed to calvados, which has always been subject to more official controls). Normandy ciders are infinitely variable (from place to place and year to year, much more even than wines), but the Auge ciders are often slightly fruitier than those from other areas, with a round, full-ish, warm body and a denser, golden colour: lovers of dry ciders may prefer those from stonier soils further west. Auge calvados, similarly, is relatively full-bodied, but marvellously subtle. Locating good cider farms is made very easy by the official **Route du Cidre**, which is well signposted along the roads. Farms that meet the exacting demands of the *appellation contrôlée* for Auge ciders and offer direct sales to the public are indicated by small signs with an apple and the words Cru de Cambremer by their gates. The local cider authorities also set a recommended price for direct-sale ciders. All local tourist offices have leaflets on the Route and cider producers in the area, and on the special farm open days that are often held between spring and early autumn. Food and drink aside, this is also naturally a wonderful area for walking and horse riding, and tourist offices also have route maps and information on local riding centres.

Pont-l'Evêque is the most important town in the northern Pays d'Auge and is immortalised in the name of one of its finest cheeses, first produced some time in the 13th century. The town, unfortunately, is a little disappointing: it suffered greatly in the Second World War, and suffers today from its role as a major road junction, even though the *autoroute* has drained off much of the long-distance traffic. At its centre, though, there is still a characterful old heart that's interesting to stroll around, especially the Rue de Vaucelles and the streets around it, with several 15th–17th-century half-timbered houses. The church of St-Michel, begun in the 13th century and rebuilt in Flamboyant Gothic style in the 15th, is grandly impressive, with a very odd square tower. Just west of Pont-l'Evêque, a detour of a few kilometres down a quiet road will take you to **Beaumont-en-Auge**. A large, placid village, it's a place of homage for scientists as the birthplace of the 18th-century mathematician Laplace, but its most remarkable feature is its wonderful location at the top of a precipitous escarpment, with hypnotic views down to Deauville and out to sea.

Head south from Pont-l'Evêque and you will really enter the Pays d'Auge landscape. As soon as you pass under the *autoroute* on the D48, on the way to the turn-off for Pierrefitte-en-Auge, the road becomes quiet, green and rural, between orchards and hedges, with an open view eastwards across the lush expanse of the Touques valley. From Pierrefitte, instead of returning to the D48 carry on along the village lane over the top of the next hill to **St-Hymer**, a dazzlingly pretty village in its own tiny valley with a bubbling little river. This same lane eventually leads via hills and gulleys to Drubec, where it meets the main 'artery' of the northern Pays d'Auge, the D16. Turn left (south), and about 5km further on, north of the village of Bonnebosq, you will see signs off to the left for the 16th-century **Manoir du Champ Versant** (*open April–June and Sept Wed–Sun 2.30–6; July and Aug Tues–Sun 2.30–6; adm*), a classic Pays d'Auge manor house. As with a great many Norman manors, one of its most engaging features is its combination of rusticity (the half-timbered façade, the drooping tile roof) with more ornate touches to fit the status of the country gentry for whom it was built, such as the fine ornamental brickwork supporting the chimneys. Inside, there is a small museum of traditional furniture and ceramics of the Pays d'Auge, and visitors can also see all the other parts of the rambling manor – the stables, barns, cider-press, bakery, calvados distillery and more.

From Bonnebosq, carry on south along the D16, ignoring other turnings, until you see a turn right on to the D49 for Victot-Pontfol and Beuvron, to enter perhaps the very prettiest part of the entire Pays d'Auge. Very shortly the countryside begins to resemble a small-scale Kentucky. As well as apple country, this is also prime horse-breeding territory, generally for *le Trot* – trotting races – rather than flat racing, and between the orchards there are plenty of lushly carpeted meadows containing some very sleek, elegant horses behind white-painted fences.

Beuvron-en-Auge describes itself as one of the *'plus beaux villages de France'*, and few people would argue. It's a remarkable ensemble of traditional Norman houses, mostly built between the 16th and 18th centuries. The delightful main square, where the timbers form crosses, arrowheads and other intricate patterns against a gentle background of clay wash, is a wonderful demonstration of the ingenuity and imagi-nation of the region's anonymous builders. One of the highlights is the grand 16th-century Vieux Manoir, on the south side of the *place*, with some fine, gargoyle-like carvings, but really the whole village is the attraction. As one of the most beautiful of all the Auge's many beauty spots, Beuvron inevitably gets congested on summer Sundays, but it's very hard to take away its charm. The little timber market hall in the middle of the square now contains a restaurant and shops, and the village also has plenty of craft and souvenir shops and others selling local produce and similar delicacies. Most are a little expensive, but seek out the **Ferme de Beuvron**, a farm cooperative that takes over one of the few brick buildings on the north road out of the village with a farmers' market of fine produce (*most weekends throughout the year, and some other days in July and Aug*).

Leaving Beuvron to the north, turn right on to the tiny D146 for Clermont, one of the leafiest of country lanes. Don't miss the sign to the left for the **Chapelle de Clermont**. A footpath leads through a canopy of dense beeches to the chapel, on a precipitous crag where you suddenly emerge to find sweeping views over the Dives valley to the west, and sometimes a strong, gusting wind to wake you up. Believed to have been founded in the 12th century or even earlier, and then rebuilt in the 15th, the chapel is wonderfully simple: it is whitewashed inside, with some fine locally carved statues of saints around the walls, including an oddly cute *Virgin and Child*.

Clermont is also a good place to pick up the Route du Cidre and begin cider hunting. Even if you've already bought enough cider to last you a year, following the route through the maze of lanes east of Beuvron is one of the most enjoyable ways of exploring the area and getting to know its idiosyncrasies. The backroads of the Pays d'Auge can often seem deliberately confusing, and sometimes look like ending in a solid green wall, but – just when you think all hope is lost – a Route du Cidre sign will turn up to help out.

The **apple harvest** runs from late September to November, and the dryness of the cider depends on how long it is left to ferment in the barrel. Once bottled, cider, unlike calvados, does not change significantly with age. A few farms produce some very sweet *cidre nouveau* for Christmas, but more normal *demi* and *brut* (dry) ciders do not become available until February or March, and so the best time for tasting and buying is from spring to summer. By October, the smallest farms may have sold their production for the year, but the large producers will still have ciders on sale. The cider producers of the Pays d'Auge cover both of the two main 'categories' found in Normandy. Some are basic farms where, having been attracted in by the apple sign and 'Cidre-Calvados-Vente Directe-OUVERTE', not even the dog takes much notice of you, but someone will eventually appear and unbolt the large half-timbered sheds where the cider is kept. Others are much more sophisticated operations, often around large manor houses, and with separate farm shops. Whether producers are one or the other seems to have no relevance to quality, and in all cases it's advisable not to call during the sacred hours of lunch (*12.30–2*) or too late in the evening.

As you wander around the countryside, through lovely, leaf-shrouded villages like Beaufour-Druval, you periodically emerge back on to the D16, which serves as a handy reference point (another is the Carrefour St-Jean, the wide crossroads where the D16 meets the N13 Caen–Lisieux road).

East and south of the D16 the lanes tend to converge on **Cambremer**, the other main town (or larger village) in the area. It's a pleasant, likeable place, not as postcard-pretty as Beuvron and therefore less touristy. Cambremer also has a very attractive main square, with enjoyable cafés and restaurants, built on a steep hill, so that you get different perspectives from one side or the other.

The road continues south to St-Laurent-du-Mont, from where it's not far down a lovely road to the crossroads village of **Crèvecoeur-en-Auge** with, just to the west, its **château** (*open April–June and Sept Mon, Wed–Sun 11–6; July and Aug daily 11–7; Oct Sun 2–6; adm*). Crèvecoeur immediately suggests a picture-book illustration of a Norman motte-and-bailey castle; its oldest ramparts were built before its lord joined Duke William in invading England, while the other, half-timbered buildings around the grassed-over courtyard were built and rebuilt over the following centuries. Most impressive is the giant dovecote – built shortly after the castle was sacked by an English army in 1449 – an indication of the status of Crèvecoeur's owners, since only the aristocracy were allowed such buildings in medieval Normandy. Curiously, Crèvecoeur has since the 1970s been owned by a foundation created by the Alsatian Schlumberger engineering family, who have lovingly restored it to house a museum on oil exploration, the interest of which is very much a matter of taste. However, the castle also contains semi-permanent 'temporary' exhibitions of more direct Norman interest on traditional building techniques, medieval music, local customs, and so on, which are often fascinating. In July and August there are occasional medieval music performances, pageants and similar events.

Shopping

There are regular weekly markets all year in **Pont-l'Evêque** (*Mon; plus a farmers' market July and Aug Sun*), **Bonnebosq** (Wednesdays), **Cambremer** (*Fri*) and **Beuvron** (*Sat*). Many of the area's best farm producers also set up stalls at the Marché à l'Ancienne in Cambremer (*July and Aug Sun am*).

The Pays d'Auge has the largest concentration in Normandy of small producers who sell direct to the public. The Route du Cidre and Produits Fermiers et Artisanaux leaflets are very helpful, or just look for signs along the roads. Many farms also host open days and offer tours, especially in summer, or in October and November, during the apple harvest.

Beaufour-Druval ✉ 14340

Albert Biron, t 02 31 65 11 76. A small, peaceful farm-based producer of fine cider and calvados, north of Bonnebosq.

Cambremer ✉ 14340

Calvados Pierre Huet, Manoir La Brière des Fontaines, t 02 31 63 01 09. One of the grand names in the world of calvados, based in a distinguished manor house on the road towards Crèvecoeur. They also produce delicious ciders, *pommeau* and other apple products. The tours (*in English as required*) are entertaining and informative.

St-Aubin-Lebizay ✉ 14430

Mme Denis, t/f 02 31 65 13 39. A low-key little farm producing good ciders and calvados, and particularly *poiré* (perry).

Gerard Desvoyé, Le Lieu Gris, t/f 02 31 65 11 94. M Desvoyé's award-winning *demi-sec* and *brut* ciders are supplied to smart wine and spirits merchants in Rouen and Paris. Bought here, they're a real bargain, and he also has fine calvados, *pommeau*, jams and truly exceptional cider vinegar. There are also two basic, cosy *gîtes*: there are no shops nearby, but you won't run out of cider.

Cambremer ✉ 14340

Ferme de la Mimarnel, t/f 02 31 63 00 50. Jacques-Antoine Motte produces superb *chèvre* – plain or with herbs – and offers tours of the farm and *fromagerie* (by reserva-

tion, *daily exc Thurs*). The entrance is on the D50, just east of the crossroads with the D101 from Cambremer; there is usually a sign, but it's sometimes hard to see.

Mery-Corbon ✉ 14370

Mme Odile Gasson, t 02 31 23 66 21. A dairy farm in the Dives valley, west of Carrefour St-Jean, selling delicious butter, crème fraîche and *confiture de lait*, a kind of light toffee spread. *Open daily exc Sun and Thurs am, when she sells at the market in Argences.*

Where to Stay

Cambremer ✉ 14340

Château Les Bruyères, Route du Cadran, t 02 31 32 22 45, f 02 31 32 22 58 (*rooms 390–960F/ €59.45–146.34*). A very comfortable country-house hotel in a delightful setting north of Cambremer. Its rooms vary a good deal in size (and price), but all are plushly pretty, and around the house there is a large, very well tended garden with a swimming pool. There's also a good **restaurant** (*menus from 140F/€21.34*). Closed Jan–Mar.

Manoir de Cantepie, Le Cadran, t 02 31 62 87 27 (*rooms 300F/€45.73 for two*). Distinctly grand *chambre-d'hôte* in an extraordinary 16th-century manor house, with wood panelling and mock-medieval paintings. M Gherrak and his wife are attentive hosts. The driveway is on the D50, a few kilometres east of Cambremer.

St-Laurent-du-Mont ✉ 14340

Le Clos de St-Laurent, t 02 31 63 47 04 (*rooms 250F/€38.11 for two, 380F/€57.93 for three*). An old house in a truly spectacular location off the D50 just west of St-Laurent-du-Mont, surrounded by rambling lawns and with fabulous views over the Dives valley. Its rooms are simple and cosy and it is very popular. It's quite isolated, but evening meals can be provided (*90F/€13.72*).

St-Philibert-des-Champs ✉ 14130

La Ferme des Poiriers Roses, t 02 31 64 72 14, f 02 31 64 19 55 (*rooms 350–600F/ €53.35–91.46; suite 500F/€76.22*). Almost too pretty to be true: a 17th-century half-timbered cottage with gabled roof in a lush garden, usually surrounded by a colourful array of flower beds, window boxes and hanging baskets. Inside, the house is full of all the bits and bobs that the French refer to as *bibelots*. The 'gourmet breakfasts' (*52F/€7.93*) are an experience in themselves.

Beuvron-en-Auge ✉ 14430

Mme Monique Hamelin, La Place de Beuvron, **t** 02 31 39 00 62 (*rooms 280F/€42.68 for two, 440F/€67.07 for four; cheaper for more than two nights*). A perfect, 17th-century Pays d'Auge black-and-white half-timbered house with two B&B rooms. *Closed Nov–Easter.*

Manoir de Sens, **t** 02 31 79 23 05, **f** 02 31 79 45 20 (*rooms 350F/€53.35 for two; suite 650F/€99.09*). Another grand black-and-white timbered Auge mansion, in neat grounds beside the road north of Beuvron. This is also a stud farm and cider farm. The rooms are old-fashioned French manorial in style. The David family who own the manor are more down-to-earth and friendly than the house might suggest, and all sorts of activities are available nearby.

Notre-Dame-de-Livaye ✉ 14340

Aux Pommiers de Livaye, **t** 02 31 63 01 28, **f** 02 31 63 73 63, www.banb.normandy.free.fr (*rooms 420–650F/€64.02–99.09; suite 740F/€112.8*). A delightful old half-timbered house near the N13 just east of Crèvecoeur. There are four rooms in a separate little cottage, and a three-room 'family suite' in a tower of the main house. Decoration is pretty twee, but the room are comfy and well cared for. **Dinner** is served for guests (*125F/€19.05*), full of good Norman things like *escalope au cidre avec crème fraîche*, or *pommes de terre farcies au fromage blanc*.

Eating Alternatives

Beuvron-en-Auge ✉ 14430

Auberge de la Boule d'Or, **t** 02 31 79 78 78, **f** 02 31 39 61 50 (*menus 99F/€15.09, 133F/€20.27 and 180F/€27.44*). In a bulging old half-timbered house on Beuvron's square, with an intimate dining room, where you can try satisfying versions of local classics –

andouilles, rabbit in cider – along with some French standards like *sole meunière*.

La Forge, **t** 02 31 79 29 74 (*menus 82F/€12.5, 102F/€15.55 and 139F/€21.19*). An alternative choice, with a pretty dining room and an atmospheric little bar. The menu features good versions of meat-and-cider *terroir* specialities, and an extensive brasserie-style range of lighter dishes and snacks.

Auberge de Laizon, Cléville, **t** 02 31 23 64 67 (*menus c. 150F/€22.87*). Almost impossibly remote, in the woods southwest of Beuvron, but with its own signs by the relevant turn-off from the D49. This farmhouse *auberge* offers the full Norman country culinary experience – terrines to start, followed by vegetables, then a proper *calvados trou normand*, and a choice of meaty main courses – *côte de porc*, *lapin à la normande*, *côte de boeuf* – with salad, cheese and apple desserts. Reservations essential.

Drubec ✉ 14130

La Haie Tondue, **t** 02 31 64 85 00 (*menus 120–210F/€18.29–32.01*). A massive 18th-century coaching inn on the N175, ivy-clad outside and heavily timbered within. Menus feature classic Norman dishes with some adventurous touches such as the use of balsamic vinegar and delicate fruit sauces. It gets very full on summer weekends. *Closed Mon eve and Tues exc public hols and Aug; also one week Feb–Mar, one week June, and most of Oct.*

Cambremer ✉ 14340

Au P'tit Normand, Rue Pasteur, **t** 02 31 32 03 20 (*menus 42–97F/€6.40–14.79*). A bright little restaurant and *saladerie* on the main square, right opposite the tourist office. As well as the set menus, there is an excellent range of omelettes, snacks and mixed salads.

Beaufour-Druval ✉ 14340

Les Puces Gourmandes, **t** 02 31 65 12 91 (*lunch menu 90F/€13.72*). A curious little restaurant and *salon de thé*, in a tiny village apparently in the middle of nowhere, which serves a bohemian mix of salads and other light dishes, at bargain prices (*c. 35F/€5.43*); there's also a more substantial lunch menu, and a big selection of teas.

Camembert and *Grands Châteaux*:
the Southern Pays d'Auge and Falaise

24

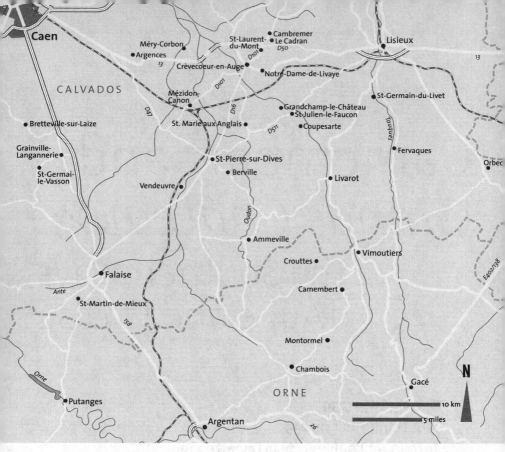

In the southern half of the Pays d'Auge, roughly below Crèvecoeur and the N13, the fields are larger, the landscape a bit more open, than to the north, although there are still plenty of cider farms and half-timbered cottages. To the southwest, the Auge fields blend into the still more open countryside of the Pays de Falaise, a more windswept, glowering landscape of rolling plains. Falaise is also a significant point of transition within Normandy, from the brick and wood, half-timbered traditional houses to the east to the beginnings of the four-square stone cottages, manors and farms that are increasingly frequent as you head west towards the Cotentin.

The southern Pays d'Auge is one of the foremost cheese-producing regions in France (and the world), with famous names like Camembert, Livarot and Pont-l'Evêque, and lesser-known varieties like Petit-Lisieux and Pavé d'Auge. Most of it is still produced on small family farms dotted across the very tranquil countryside. This is still one of the most genuinely rural areas of France, a place where the traditions of the *terroir* retain a strength that is hard to credit in industrial northern Europe.

As in the north, this is an area where it's most enjoyable just to wander around, discovering unexpected places. There are early Norman churches, and a spectacular range of historic houses: from battered medieval castles to opulent Ancien Régime châteaux. Falaise, as well as being the site of some of the most decisive struggles in the 1944 battle for Normandy, was also the home of William the Conqueror.

Getting There

From Ouistreham and the Caen ring-road, two main roads lead into this area: the N13 to Lisieux, and the N158 for Falaise. From Paris, Le Havre or the north on the A13 *autoroute*; exit at Pont-l'Evêque, head due south on the D579, and cut westwards at Le Breuil-en-Auge to Manerbe, to get on to the N13 avoiding the traffic bottleneck of Lisieux.

St-Julien-le-Fauçon sits across the historic Lisieux–St-Pierre-sur-Dives road, now the D511, which is connected to the N13 by a series of winding northward lanes. The Auberge de la Levrette is located beside the main square.

There are stations at St-Pierre-sur-Dives, Mezidon-Canon and Falaise with connections to Caen, Lisieux, Paris and further afield, but exploration is difficult without a car. Calvados Bus Verts run to many of the larger villages, especially from Caen and Lisieux.

Tourist Information

Falaise: Le Forum, Bd de la Libération, **t** 02 31 90 17 26, **f** 02 31 90 98 70.

Livarot: Place Georges Bisson, **t** 02 31 63 47 39, **f** 02 31 63 18 19.

Orbec-en-Auge: Rue Guillonière, **t** 02 31 61 12 35, **f** 02 31 61 22 09.

St-Pierre-sur-Dives: 23 Rue St-Benoît, **t** 02 31 20 97 90, **f** 02 31 20 36 02.

Vimoutiers: 10 Av du Général de Gaulle, **t** 02 33 39 30 29, **f** 02 33 67 66 11.

The basis of the region's food is, naturally, the superb, fresh produce of its farms. Its presentation combines the pure and hearty Norman cream-and-cider tradition with those spectacular little shoots of culinary invention and refinement that in France turn up even in the most out-of-the-way places: such as the **Auberge de la Levrette** in St-Julien-le-Fauçon, a village inn serving creative cooking.

L'Auberge de la Levrette

*St-Julien-le-Fauçon, **t** 02 31 63 81 20, **f** 02 31 63 97 05.*
Open Tues–Sat 12–2.30 and 7.30–9, Sun 12–2.30. Closed Mon,
one week Oct and Christmas. Booking advisable weekends.
Menus 100F/€15.24, 150F/€22.87 and 195F/€29.73, children's
menu 55F/€8.38; à la carte average 200F/€30.49.

The current chef-proprietor, Georges Fayet, has a copy of a document indicating that its building was begun in 1752, as a *relais de chasse* (hunting lodge) for the Marquis de Grandchamp, lord of the château of Grandchamp just to the north and of much else besides. He was particularly fond of hunting hares, hence the name, La Levrette. After the Revolution it became a *relais de poste* (a mail and coaching inn). The *auberge* and the little house across the road are the oldest buildings after the church.

This is a classic Pays d'Auge inn, with half-timbering for most of its length and a brick extension casually added at one end. At the back there's an unusually large hall, which was used as a barracks in the Second World War by German soldiers, who left the marks of their target practice in the old coaching yard alongside. In the 1950s the hall served as the village cinema, and today it's used for weddings and other feasts, and also occasional concerts by local bands. Inside the main *auberge*, the lovely dining room has low ceilings, a mass of heavy old timbers and magnificent 1750s fire-places, and it's extremely comfortable. La Levrette is phenomenally good value, even

Variation sur le Thème de la Pomme (Variations on the Theme of an Apple)

Serves 4

Most of the components of this entrancing dessert can be made ahead, so when the baked apples are done, it is easy to assemble. If you wish, omit the caramel and drizzle a little calvados over each serving. There will be some biscuits left over.

5 golden delicious apples
lemon juice
runny honey
150g/5oz caster sugar
3 tablespoons calvados
300ml/½pint custard sauce
apple sorbet

For the biscuit base:
100g/3½oz ground almonds
100g/3½oz plain flour
100g/3½oz butter
100g/3½oz golden caster sugar
1 eating apple, peeled, cored and finely chopped

in an area where dining is scarcely ever expensive. It's also likely to be as tranquil as the countryside around it, and other diners will mostly be local.

M and Mme Fayet are originally from Clermont-Ferrand, but have worked in Normandy for some 15 years, and M Fayet likes to be creative with local produce. His *andouilles de Vire* with a *crème de Livarot* sauce and leek flan, is a wonderfully subtle starter. For a main course, there might be a *faux-filet à la crème de calvados*, escalope of salmon with vermouth and dill, or sole fillets with ratatouille in saffron butter.

The cheese board is as good as it should be, but save room for the desserts: Georges Fayet is a superb *pâtissier*, and often creates a *dessert du jour* as well as new flavours of homemade ice-cream. His *variation sur le thème de la pomme* is a fabulous, intricate combination of apple dishes on the same plate. After that, a fragrant calvados is the natural way to end your meal, along with the chocolatey, homemade *petit-fours*.

Touring Around

If you can be in this area on a Monday, make every effort to get to the Pays d'Auge's largest market in **St-Pierre-sur-Dives**. It has been held here virtually every Monday morning since the early Middle Ages, and the town largely developed around it. The Halles, the giant covered market hall at its centre, was first built in the 11th century, and has been altered and faithfully rebuilt several times since after fires and other

For the biscuits, preheat the oven to 170°C/325°F/Gas mark 3. Combine the ground almonds, flour, butter, sugar and chopped apple in a food processor and pulse until well combined and a soft dough forms. Roll or press out fairly thinly on baking parchment and cut out 8–10cm/3½–4in rounds. Arrange on a greased baking tray and bake until golden, about 20 minutes.

Preheat the oven to 110°C/225°F/Gas mark ¼. Peel 1 of the apples and rub with lemon juice. Using a vegetable peeler, cut off long strips, working in a spiral. Slice these lengthways into 'shoestrings'. Place on a non-stick baking tray, coiled into loose spirals, and bake for about half an hour, until dried.

Raise the oven temperature to 170°C/325°F/Gas mark 3. Peel the remaining 4 apples and core, leaving them whole. Rub all over with lemon juice. Put them into a baking dish and drizzle with honey to coat. Bake until coloured and cooked, but still retaining some firmness, about 30 minutes, basting with honey once or twice.

Just before serving, make a caramel: put the caster sugar in a small, heavy saucepan with 3 tablespoons of water. Bring to a boil over high heat, swirling the pan to dissolve the sugar. Boil, without stirring, until the syrup turns a medium caramel colour, 3–4 minutes. Remove from the heat, stir until the bubbles diminish (protect your hand if using a metal spoon) and add 1 tablespoon of calvados. Flavour the custard with the remaining calvados.

To serve, put a biscuit on each plate, top with a baked apple, spooning over any cooking juices. Place a small scoop of apple sorbet on top and drape dried apple spirals over it. Pour custard around the edge and drizzle the caramel over the top.

disasters, the last in 1944. It is a powerful reminder that the Pays d'Auge remains very much a rural, small-farm area: inside the Halles there are geese, ducks, chickens, rabbits and any other small farmyard animal you can think of – all of them alive. Outside the market also sprawls over two very large, open squares. Close to the Halles, there are stalls with superb local meat and *charcuterie*, great fruit and vegetables, and some of the very best Camembert, Livarot and other local cheeses. At others you can buy all-weather jackets, toys, machinery and leather bags. The market, according to tradition, begins to pack up around half noon. Antique shows are also held in the Halles on the first Sunday of each month.

Once the market crowds have gone back to their villages, St-Pierre is a slow-moving, peaceful town, spread out along a long, straight street, called **Route de Falaise** for most of its length, which runs roughly north-south. With its huge market squares, the town seems a little too big for its permanent population. Next to the Mairie on the west side of Route de Falaise is the church of the **Abbatiale**, one of very few surviving parts of what was (under the Anglo-Norman monarchy) one of the largest abbeys in Normandy. Converted into St-Pierre's parish church after the dissolution of the abbey during the Revolution, it's one of the most impressive and calmly atmospheric of Norman town churches, with a delicate 14th-century Gothic façade added to the massively solid 12th–13th-century nave, transepts and main tower.

St-Pierre also contains, above the very helpful tourist office one street south of the church, the most important of the Pays d'Auge's cheese museums. The **Musée des**

Techniques Fromagères (*open April–mid-June and mid-Sept–Oct daily 9.30–12.30 and 2–6; mid-June–mid-Sept daily 9.30–6; Nov–Mar Mon–Sat 10–12 and 2–5; adm*) tells you a huge amount about cheese-making in truly French didactic style. More engaging (and more accessible to English-speakers) are the older little **Musée du Fromage** in Livarot (*open Mar–Oct daily 10–12 and 2–6; adm*), and the **Musée du Camembert** in Vimoutiers (*open Mar–Oct Mon 2–6, Tues–Sun 9–12 and 2–6; Nov and Dec Mon 2.30–6, Tues–Fri 10–12 and 2.30–6, Sat 10–12; closed Jan and Feb; adm*). Both museums have oddly fascinating (no, really) collections of cheese labels. They also have shops.

Vimoutiers' best-known monument is a statue in the main square of **Marie Harel**, the milkmaid credited with the 'invention' of Camembert. As the legend goes, in the years following the Revolution Marie gave shelter to a fugitive priest, who in return gave her a special cheese recipe, and so a new *grand fromage* was born. Her home village of Camembert itself is a few kilometres to the south. Spread over a crest in a hilly valley, it's an idyllic place – despite the tacky souvenir-overkill that surrounds the **Maison du Camembert** museum, shop and visitor centre (*open April–Nov daily 10–7*).

About two kilometres north of St-Julien-le-Fauçon is the **château of Grandchamp**. It's closed to visitors, but from the road it's possible to see, beyond the half-timbered gatehouse, the brick and stone façade of the house, built in two stages in the 16th and 17th centuries, with four strangely oriental-looking turrets. South of St-Julien there is the remarkable 15th-century **Manoir de Coupesarte**, one of the loveliest of the area's half-timbered manors, with a placid moat on three sides and half-timbered turrets on all four corners. It is not open to visitors, but it hosts a farmers' market in summer (*see* p.245). A little to the west is the peaceful village of **Ste-Marie-aux-Anglais**, which has a remarkable, tiny 11th-century church, one of the oldest in Normandy never to have been substantially altered since it was built. The church is often kept closed, but it's worth trying to visit on a Sunday to see the rare ceiling paintings inside; easily visible outside are its beautiful early medieval carvings.

Some 15km to the east is the grandest 16th-century, French-Renaissance style château in the Pays d'Auge, at **St-Germain-de-Livet** (*guided tours April–Sept Mon, Wed–Sun 10–12 and 2–7; Oct–Mar Mon, Wed–Sun 10–12 and 2–5; closed Tues, 1–15 Oct, Dec and Jan; last admission 1hr before closing; adm*), just beyond the D579 in a striking setting, nestling at the bottom of a valley and fronted by a garden ablaze with dahlias. It is renowned above all for its façade, with giant pepperpot turrets and walls in an almost playful checkerboard pattern of stone and differently coloured bricks, combined with an earlier, half-timbered house at one side. Inside, the castle has stone-walled rooms giving way to others with plain, dark décor added in the 1900s. There are many original details, such as the beautiful tiling, and some very rare 16th-century frescoes of biblical scenes in the Guardroom.

For a complete contrast in style and era, cut back west of the D511 to the **Château de Canon** at Mezidon-Canon (*gardens open Easter–30 June Sat, Sun and hols 2–6; July–Sept Mon, Wed–Sun 2–7; adm*). The house was first built in the 1720s, and then greatly altered and extended from the 1760s to the 1780s for Jean-Baptiste Elie de Beaumont, a noted lawyer, friend of Voltaire and follower of the advanced ideas of his day. The château itself is closed to visitors, but Canon is most famous for its remarkable gardens, which were laid out over many years by Elie de Beaumont in line with Enlightenment philosophical ideas. They are full of little follies, sculptures, artificial groves and other curious features: among the highlights are a Chinese summer house, an exquisite pond, the Greek-style 'Temple of the Weeping Woman', and above all the Chartreuses, a series of interconnected walled gardens and orchards which fill with luminous arrays of flowers each summer. A separate building in the grounds was used as the site of the Fêtes des Bonnes Gens, the 'Feasts of Good People', begun by the equally liberal-minded Mme Elie de Beaumont in 1775, in which deserving local villagers were given a series of prizes for services to the community.

Just south of St-Pierre-sur-Dives is the **Château de Vendeuvre** (*open Mar–April and Oct–11 Nov Sun and hols 2–6; May–Sept daily 10–6; closed Dec–Feb; adm exp*), a Louis-Quinze *bonbon* of a stately home that is a revelation to anyone who thought the French aristocracy had been on hard times since 1789. Gutted in 1944, it has been lavishly and beautifully restored by the Comtes de Vendeuvre with all of its original, pastel-shaded décor, plus a remarkable collection of furniture and bric-à-brac. In each room there are also life-size automata, which start up as you come in: especially entertaining is the kitchen, where the automaton appears to talk manically as it shows off the different pots and pans. In the Orangerie the Comtesse has the world's largest collection of miniature furniture – some made as toys, others as curiosities, others as demonstration pieces by craftsmen – a whimsical display of extraordinary skills. Outside are the Jardins d'Eau-Surprises, a fanciful water garden with elaborate concealed fountains set off by electric sensors as you walk by. It's all a bit twee, but very entertaining.

South of Vendeuvre the D511 leads across a flat plain to **Falaise**. Virtually nowhere in Normandy was completely unscathed by the Second World War, but Falaise formed one of the great anvils of the battle. In August 1944, as the British and Canadian armies pushed southwards from Caen, the Americans broke out from the Normandy bridgehead at Avranches, cut across Brittany to Nantes and then swung east to Alençon and Argentan, almost encircling the German armies in Normandy in the 'Falaise Pocket', the only exit from which was the 'Falaise Gap' between Falaise and Argentan. The German defence of Falaise against allied efforts to close the Gap was the final, deciding battle of the Normandy campaign, as the German generals struggled to extricate their armies (in the face of increasingly deranged orders from Hitler). Falaise and its surrounding villages were pounded into rubble before the Gap was finally shut off, when Polish and US troops met at Chambois, to the southeast, on 19 and 20 August.

Post-war, much of Falaise was rebuilt in straightforward reconstruction style, which rather fails to match its spectacular location on a gorge in a valley of the River Ante, still dominated by one of the grandest of Norman castles, built like all good Norman strongholds on the highest point for miles around and with massive masonry that resisted 20th-century bombs and artillery better than anything else in the area. It is a likeable, untouristy town – with a good market – which still has some characterful old corners, especially in the steep, narrow streets along the gorge. The war museum, the **Musée Août 44** (*open April–May and Sept–11 Nov Mon, Wed–Sun 10–12.30 and 2–6;*

June–Aug daily 10–6; adm), gives full information about the battle of the Pocket. Locals, though, are less given to recalling the painful events of 1944 than to commemorating Falaise's role as the birthplace of **William the Conqueror**, and still more the home of his mother, Arlette, a livelier local heroine than little Marie, the cheese girl. As the legend goes: one day in 1027 Robert, younger son of the Duke of Normandy, was returning from hunting to Falaise castle when he caught sight of the humble tanner's daughter, Arlette, just sweet 17 and doing the family wash in the river, and was smitten. He exercised his *droit de seigneur*, but the feisty Arlette refused to accept any furtive affair and took up residence in the castle by the main gate, while Robert succeeded his brother to become Robert 'the Magnificent', Duke of Normandy. Their son grew up in Falaise castle, but, never formally legitimised, would be known as William the Bastard until he became King of England and acquired the rather more dignified title of 'Conqueror'.

A very belligerent 19th-century statue of William dominates the square, predictably Place Guillaume-le-Conquérant, which leads up to the **Château Guillaume-le-Conquérant** (*open daily 9.30–6; adm*). Its current name is a little bit misleading, for not much of the castle William knew survives: the massive Great Keep was rebuilt for his youngest son, Henry I, in the 1120s, a smaller keep was added by Henry II in the 1150s and the round 'Talbot Tower' was actually built for Philippe Auguste of France, after he had successfully ended the independence of William's descendants in Normandy in 1204. It remains, though, one of the most dramatic of Norman castles, with its keeps and buildings standing out on rocky crags, surrounded by a vast walled bailey courtyard. Visitors to the castle today, however, may appreciate a little advance warning. Besieged by Henry V of England in 1417, Falaise castle was last used in war in the 16th century and was already a ruin by the 19th, when some restoration work was done, which was largely undone in 1944. Things have changed since the 1980s, as the castle has been the object of a radical renovation programme masterminded by Bruno Decaris, chief architect of France's Department of Historic Monuments: a leaflet explains, perhaps to pacify those whose jaws drop when they see it, that it has been conceived in line with recent international agreements that in any restoration of a monument there should be no confusion between the remnants of the original and the restoration work, or in other words, it's all right not to make things look old. Whole floors have been added within the previously empty walls of the keeps: in parts it looks as if the new sections have been added to make it easier to appreciate the original structure, in others it appears more that the medieval masonry has just been used as a base for a striking contemporary building, including lifts taken from a Mad Max-style sci-fi film alongside the Great Keep. The new rooms are used to host interesting historical exhibitions, concerts of early music and other events each summer. And the restoration of the towers allows you to get right to the top, from where there are wonderful views over the town, the gorge and the plain. You can also look down to the **Fontaine d'Arlette**, the place where the tanner's daughter first flirted with the Duke's son. A pleasant path leads down the grassy flanks of the castle to this little spring by the river, now surrounded by a monument, where the seeds of the English monarchy, as it were, were sown.

Shopping

The Monday market in **St-Pierre-sur-Dives** is by far the most important in the Pays d'Auge, but there are also markets in **Orbec** (*Wed*), **Livarot** (*Thurs*), **Falaise** (*Sat*), and **Vimoutiers** (*Mon*). In July and August there is also a special farmers' market every Sunday in Orbec, while St-Pierre-sur-Dives hosts an extra market every Friday afternoon (*till 8pm*).

A good aid to finding more of the individual small food producers is the Produits Fermiers et Artisanaux leaflet from most tourist offices.

St-Germain-de-Livet ✉ 14100
Ferme de la Cour Fleurie, t 02 31 31 18 24. This modernised cider farm produces excellent ciders and *pommeau*, and fine *poiré* (perry) and cider vinegar. *Farm shop open daily 10–12 and 2.30–6.*

Coupesarte ✉ 14140
Ferme du Manoir de Coupesarte, t 02 31 63 82 84. Every weekend from Easter to the end of October the farm hosts a shop-market with a wide range of products from local farms – ciders, calvados, cheeses, meat products. *Also open daily mid-June–mid-Sept.*

St-Germain-le-Vasson ✉ 14190
Ferme des Massinots, t 02 31 90 54 22. As well as running their *ferme-auberge* (*see* below) the Tocheports produce prize-winning duck and goose foie gras and *rillettes*, and fine ciders, *pommeau* and calvados, all available from the farm shop. The farm is a little to the west of the Caen–Falaise road, reached via a turning in Grainville-Langannerie. *Tours of the farm, by reservation.*

Fervaques ✉ 14140
Ferme de la Moissonière, t 02 31 32 31 23. The Lallier family produces classic Pays d'Auge cheeses on their farm on the south side of Fervaques, due south of Lisieux on the D64. *Open every afternoon (exc Sun) until c. 4pm.*

St-Pierre-sur-Dives ✉ 14170
Parc du Moulin, Ammeville-l'Oudon, **t** 02 31 20 62 67. An impressive farm near Ammeville, c. 10km southeast of St-Pierre, where René-Philippe Denoly produces a full range of ciders and similar products. His speciality is fine *pommeau*. There are tours of the *caves*.

Where to Stay

Bretteville-sur-Laize ✉ 14680
Château des Riffets, t 02 31 23 53 21, **f** 02 31 23 75 14 (*rooms 550F/€83.84 for two, 890F/ €135.67 for four*). A small château on a hill within 15 hectares of wooded grounds, about 15km south of Caen west of the Falaise road. Some of its spacious rooms have – as well as gilt mirrors and antiques – jacuzzis and hydromassage showers, and there's a pool. The hosts, M and Mme Cantel, are very affable, speak English and German, and can also provide expansive **evening meals** with advance notice (*240F/€36.59*).

Falaise ✉ 14700
Le Château du Tertre, Rte de Fourneaux-le-Val, St-Martin-de-Mieux, **t** 02 31 90 01 04, **f** 02 31 90 33 16 (*rooms 490–970F/€74.7–147.87; suites 880–1,400F/€134.15–213.41*). Country-house comforts in a beautifully restored early 18th-century château in the countryside southwest of Falaise. All the rooms have lovely views over the grounds and the fields beyond. The **dining room** (*menus c. 200F/€30.49*) is also of a high standard. Riding, tennis, golf, rock-climbing, etc. can be arranged, nearby. *Closed mid-Nov–Feb.*

St-Pierre-sur-Dives ✉ 14170
Hôtel Les Agriculteurs, 118 Rue de Falaise, **t** 02 31 20 72 78, **f** 02 31 20 62 74 (*rooms 170–250F/€25.91–38.11*). A long-established Logis hotel with lots of character. It's better known as a restaurant (*see* below), but its rooms are light, well-kept and good value.

Falaise ✉ 14700
Hôtel de Souza, 26 Rue du Camp Fermé, **t/f** 02 31 40 84 25 (*twin room 380F/€57.93; suite 600F/€91.46*). A classic 18th-century *hôtel particulier* in the middle of Falaise, superbly restored by owner Patrick Lapre, who takes guided tours around it (*June–Sept afternoons*). The two rooms are exquisitely decorated with antiques. *Open April–Oct, and at other times by arrangement.*

Hôtel de la Poste, 38 Rue Georges Clémenceau, t 02 31 90 13 14, f 02 31 90 01 81 (*rooms 200–390F/€30.49–59.45*). A pleasant, comfortable Logis hotel on the main street, rebuilt after the Second World War, with attractive, modern rooms. The **restaurant** (*menus 88–260F/€13.41–39.63*) serves mainly Norman fare. *Closed Sun eve and Mon.*

Berville-L'Oudon ✉ 14170

Le Pressoir, Route de l'Eglise, t 02 31 20 51 26, f 02 31 20 03 03 (*rooms 270F/€41.16 for two, 320F/€48.78 for three*). Mme Annick Duhamel's three charming *chambre-d'hôte* rooms are in a restored cider-press built in 1462, with giant timber beams. Outside, there is an extensive, pretty garden and a placid pond. Berville is a lovely, quiet village 3km southeast of St-Pierre-sur-Dives.

Bretteville-sur-Dives ✉ 14170

Le Pressoir de Glatigny, t 02 31 20 68 93 (*rooms 250F/€38.11 for two, 400F/€60.98 for three*). A peaceful B&B in an 18th-century farmhouse with rambling outbuildings and an old cider-press (*pressoir*). There are three pretty rooms, a lounge, and access to a kitchen.

Crouttes ✉ 61120

Le Prieuré St-Michel, t 02 33 39 15 15, f 02 33 36 15 16 (*double rooms 400–600F/€60.98–91.46; breakfast 60F/€9.15*). A former Benedictine priory (13th–18th-century), run as the Centre Edgar Chahine, hosting concerts, exhibitions and other activities in summer. There's an exquisite park, including a rose garden and an aromatic herb garden. There are three distinctive guest rooms in half-timbered cottages. In summer meals are available in a separate **restaurant** (*c. 240F/€36.59*). The priory is in tranquil countryside east of Crouttes, *c.* 7km from Vimoutiers in the direction of St-Pierre-sur-Dives. *Rooms normally available April–Oct; check for other times.*

Eating Alternatives

Falaise ✉ 14700

L'Attache, Route de Caen, t 02 31 90 05 38, f 02 31 90 57 19 (*menus 95–320F/€14.48–48.78*). Chef Alain Hastain combines wild herbs, woodland mushrooms and edible flowers with fine local meats and fresh seafood in enormously inventive dishes which are lighter than much of the local fare. Booking is absolutely necessary. It's on the way out of Falaise on the Caen road. *Closed Mon and late Sept–early Oct.*

La Fine Fourchette, 52 Rue Georges Clémenceau, t 02 31 90 08 59, f 02 31 90 00 83 (*menus 88–178F/€13.41–27.13*). A popular, small restaurant. The menus of chef Gilbert Costil feature light, subtle touches, as in his use of citrus zest with grilled fish. Excellent value. *Closed Tues eve and early Feb.*

Mezidon ✉ 14270

L'Auberge du Doux Marais, Ste-Marie-aux-Anglais, t 02 31 63 82 81, f 02 31 63 96 33 (*menus 110F/€16.77 for four courses, 140F/€21.34 for five; 'gastronomic' menus 140–180F/€21.34–27.44*). A farm inn deep in the countryside (head east from the tiny village of Ste-Marie-aux-Anglais, then more or less south looking for signs to Doux Marais), popular with locals. The menus of inventive Norman country cooking are spectacularly good value: *galettes* in Camembert sauce, meats grilled over a wood fire, guinea fowl in *pommeau*, and apple desserts. Booking obligatory. *Closed last Sun of each month and usually Sun eve, and Mon–Wed.*

St-Germain-le-Vasson ✉ 14190

Ferme-Auberge des Massinots, *see above* (*menus 98–189F/€14.94–28.81, children's menu 50F/€7.62*). Anne-Marie Tocheport and her family prepare fine meals using the farm's own produce. Dishes include roast chicken in *pommeau*, smoked duck salad with prize-winning foie gras, goose roast with apples, and fruit tarts; to drink, there's the farm's own cider and calvados, and wines and liqueurs. It's best to book. *Closed Sun eve and mid-Dec–mid-Jan.*

St-Pierre-sur-Dives ✉ 14170

Hôtel Les Agriculteurs, *see above* (*menus 79–145F/€12.04–22.10, menu du terroir 119F/€18.14*). No-nonsense Norman cooking – *jambon au cidre*, chicken *vallée d'auge*, apple desserts – made with superb local ingredients. *Closed Fri eve, Sat lunch and Sun eve.*

Long Memories:
Normandy Beaches

25

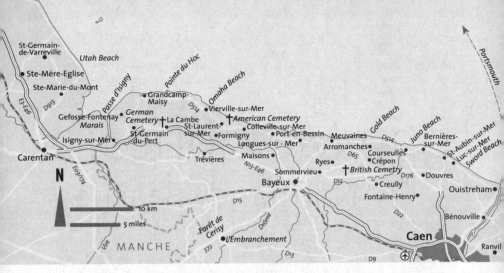

The wide arc of the Lower Normandy coast, stretching west from the Bay of the Seine and the River Orne to the Cotentin Peninsula, is a fine, open coastline, gentle in parts and more rocky and abrupt in others. Today it's hard to disassociate this coast from the events of summer 1944. Even on French maps this area is marked as the Plages du Débarquement and, since the 50th anniversary in 1994, every point of historical significance has been smartly signposted, with an abundance of information for anyone wishing to retrace any part of the Normandy campaign.

Surprising, perhaps, to first-time visitors is the sheer length of the stretch of coast covered by the D-Day invasion beaches, close to 60 miles from end to end. The eastern section from Ouistreham to Arromanches, corresponding to the British and Canadian beaches of Gold, Juno and Sword, is otherwise known as the Côte de Nacre, a near-continuous, quite narrow beach fronted by a line of old-fashioned French seaside towns. For the machine-guns to have sliced up the sand and the flail tanks to have crashed ashore here seems particularly bizarre. Further west the towns fade away, and the lush farmland of the Bessin plain comes down almost to the sea's edge. The coastline is broken up by sandstone cliffs, punctuated by wide, open beaches, the largest of them Omaha, where the main US invasion force so nearly came to disaster. Finally, Utah Beach is further west again, on the Cotentin peninsula.

The D-Day sites and museums may be an obvious centre of attention in this area, but its more conventional attractions shouldn't be ignored. The Bessin is actually one of the best farming areas in Normandy, the tranquil home of *crème fraîche*. Its old stone villages are truly rural, with massive Norman churches, and the region's most distinctive feature of all is its extraordinary grand medieval farms, which stand out like great stone towers across the countryside. Most are still working farms, and several also contain unforgettable places to stay. The area also contains several very distinguished full-blown châteaux.

A few kilometres inland from the beaches, its few streets normally patrolled only by tractors, is Crépon, population 203. However, in one of its fortified manor houses is **La Rançonnière**, offering some of the most sophisticated food in the area.

Getting There

The most direct route to this area from Britain is by the Portsmouth–Caen ferry, the harbour for which is actually in Ouistreham: from the ferry terminal, turn immediately right to get on to the coast road. Ouistreham is about an hour from Le Havre, via the Pont de la Normandie bridge over the Seine and the A13 *autoroute*, which is also the main road from Paris (Paris to Caen takes about 2½–3hrs by car). At the other end of the beaches, Utah Beach is *c.* 45mins from Cherbourg on the N13.

Crépon village is a crossroads of several country lanes. From Arromanches, take the main Ouistreham road, and then half-way up the steep hill at the back of town take a sharp right turn on to the D65, signposted for Creully. After rolling though the fields and another village, Meuvaines, this will bring you into Crépon. Go straight through the village, and on the south exit, round a sharp left bend, is la Rançonnière. The gateway through its turreted walls is quite narrow, and it's advisable to take a wide turn to breach them. From Bayeux, take the D12 for Douvres, and in Sommervieu continue on to the D112 (actually straight on) instead of following the main road to the right. This will bring you into Crépon from the west. From Caen, take the D22, signposted to Creully and Arromanches.

The Paris-Cherbourg railway line runs a little inland from the coast, with main stops at Caen, Bayeux and Carentan. The Calvados Département has a good local bus service, Les Bus Verts, with connecting services by which – with a little time and patience – it's possible to get all the way along the Invasion coast from Ouistreham to Isigny (for information, within France, t 0801 214 214). In the Manche (around Utah Beach), services are a bit less frequent, but there are buses from Carentan to Ste-Marie-du-Mont and Utah Beach.

Tourist Information

Ouistreham-Riva Bella: Jardins du Casino, t 02 31 97 18 63, f 02 31 96 87 33, *www.ot-ouistreham.fr*. The largest and best-supplied tourist office on this coast. There is also a smaller information point in Place Charles-de-Gaulle, near the ferry terminal.

Arromanches: 4 Rue du Maréchal Joffre, t 02 31 21 47 56, f 02 31 22 92 06.

Courseulles-sur-Mer: Rue de la Mer, t 02 31 37 46 80.

Grandcamp-Maisy: 118 Rue Aristide Briand, t 02 31 22 62 44, f 02 31 22 99 95.

Port-en-Bessin: 2 Rue du Croiseur-Montcalm, t 02 31 21 92 33, f 02 31 22 08 40.

Ferme de la Rançonnière

Route d'Arromanches, Crépon, t 02 31 22 21 73, f 02 31 22 98 39.
Open daily 12–2 and 7–9; June–Sept daily 12–2 and 7–9.30).
Book at least a day in advance. Menus 98F/€14.94, 138F/€21.04,
168F/€25.61 and 240F/€36.59; children's menu 55F/€8.38;
à la carte average 250F/€38.11.

The oldest part of La Rançonnière, a tower on one side of the courtyard, is 15th-century. Within a massive, sandstone outer wall the farm buildings shelter the watchtowers, crenellations and other fortifications which were still being added to until the 18th century, such was the fear in these parts of the English and other marauders. Today, though, the courtyard contains lawns, flower-beds and some café-style tables. The father of Mme Agnès Vereecke, the present owner, bought the place as a farm shortly after the war, and the family first opened it as a hotel in the 1970s. It's now mainly run by Mme Vereecke's daughter, Isabelle Sileghem, and her husband. The Rançonnière's superb hotel rooms occupy the magnificent 17th-century main farmhouse, while the dining room is in a former stables opposite the main gate.

Suprême de Pintadeau à la Fondue de Poireaux
(Breast of Guinea Fowl in a Creamy Leek Sauce)

Serves 4

2 leeks, finely chopped

125g/4½oz chilled unsalted butter

4 boned guinea fowl breasts

3 tablespoons port

5 shallots, chopped

500ml/1 pint crème fraîche

salt and pepper

Sweat the leeks in 25g of the butter until very soft, and set on one side. Then, brown the guinea fowl breasts briefly on both sides in a pan. Pour in the port and flambé. When the flames have died down, remove the breasts, put in an ovenproof dish, season and cook in an oven at 200°C/400°F/Gas Mark 6 for about 15 minutes.

To make the sauce, add the shallots and crème fraîche to the pan and allow the mixture to reduce by half or until it reaches the desired consistency. Add the leeks to this sauce, dice the remaining butter and whisk in, a few pieces at a time, until the sauce is glossy. Season to taste, and serve with the guinea fowl.

The restaurant is big and barn-like, with thick stone walls, a stone fireplace, oak beams and long tables clad in white linen with bouquets of pinks on each one. It fills up at weekends but will generally be much quieter at other times.

Diners will very possibly be tucking into some form of poultry or similar game, which is spectacularly good here: perhaps a wonderful *salade champêtre* of smoked *magret* of duck, foie gras and roast quail in the same platter. The daily special might be chicken or duck with a *sucré* of pears, or a traditional Norman cider sauce. Sauces are rich, often fruity, but made with a fine light touch, and suit the meat perfectly: pine kernels and hazelnuts with the quail, a sauce of *pommeau*, the calvados-and-cider liqueur, and baked potato stuffed with Livarot cheese with farm chicken.

There's a reason why the poultry here is so good. Although no longer a working farm, La Rançonnière still takes in quality domestic poultry and other fowl from around the district for slaughtering and dressing, for its own use, for making terrines and other related products, and for selling at local markets. For the French this close-ness to source is a major selling point – while here you'll probably see a regular stream of people drive up to the little farm shop by the gate, having come here from Bayeux or further away just to buy farmhouse terrines and cheeses.

There are of course alternatives to poultry: one of the first-course specialities is a terrine of pavé d'Isigny cheese (similar to pavé d'Auge) with calvados. Among the fine fish dishes is a luxurious *marmite* of mixed fish and shellfish with leeks and shallots, and other meat choices include excellent lamb with aubergines and a garlic sauce. Wines are served from an ample list, and La Rançonnière is one place that maintains the tradition of the *trou Normand*, with a superb little bowl of calvados and homemade apple sorbet to punctuate your meal. Cheese is another house speciality, and of those on the board several are their own, and all are local; particularly enjoyable are the *chèvre* and *pavés* from nearby farms.

Desserts similarly combine country traditions and more urbane delights. Warmly satisfying *teurgoules*, the crusty Norman rice pudding, are made by Mme Vereecke herself (and can also be bought from the farm shop). Other, perhaps lighter, *pâtisserie* pleasures might include a vanilla custard exploding with real vanilla, a traditional apple tart full of fresh goodness or a great, gooey coffee and chocolate mousse. After that, and maybe a calvados to accompany coffee and *petits fours*, a wander into the field of clover at the back of the farm is in order to round out the contentment.

Touring Around

Crépon itself is an attractive, peaceful place, with a traditional *bar-tabac* as well as its noble ensemble of yellow sandstone Bessin manors. At the centre of the village is the 12th-century Romanesque church, with a huge, typically solid Norman tower, and in the dark interior some exceptional 17th- and 18th-century Baroque woodwork. About 4km south of Crépon is the dramatic romantic pile that is the **Château of Creully** (*guided tours July–mid-Sept Tues, Thurs and Fri 10–12 and 3–6; adm*), a remarkable mix of medieval base, looming 16th-century towers and Louis XIII additions. In 1944 Creully had the distinction of housing the first BBC radio station in Normandy after the landings, and inside there is also a small radio museum. Creully village is another that has a very fine 12th–15th-century church, within which is the tomb of Antoine de Sillans (*d.* 1641), the Seigneur of Creully who was responsible for many alterations to the castle.

Another 6km or so east of Creully is the grandest of all Bessin mansions, the spectacular 16th-century **Château of Fontaine-Henry** (*guided tours Easter–mid-June and mid-Sept–Oct Sat, Sun and hols 2.30–6.30; mid-June–mid-Sept Mon and Wed–Sun 2.30–6.30; adm*). Surrounded by lush gardens, it is still privately owned by descendants of the family for whom it was built. Above the ornate carved façade is one of the tallest French Renaissance-style roofs, a magnificent slate peak that's the same height as the building below it; other parts are much older, and there is a beautiful mainly 13th-century chapel. Inside, as well as very elegant rooms mostly in 19th-century style, there are some fine paintings, by Correggio, Rigaud and Géricault.

For most visitors to this area, though, the Bessin's historic châteaux are secondary to the war sites along the coast. There are war museums of all sizes and for all tastes in Normandy – a full list can be found on leaflets provided at tourist offices covering the whole area of the campaign, and there is a scheme by which, if you buy a full-price ticket at any of the publicly owned 1944 museums, you are entitled to discounts at all the others for the next 30 days. To make a start it's worth getting an overview, which can be provided by either of the two largest museums.

The **Caen Mémorial–Musée pour la Paix** (*open Sept–May daily 9–7; July–Aug daily 9–9; closed 20 Mar, 25 Dec, 1–15 Jan; adm exp, free for under-10s and Second World War* *veterans*) is a state-of-the-art facility opened in 1988, a sculptural slab of a building with a gash for an entrance to recall the violence of war, in a beautifully landscaped park on the north side of the Caen Périphérique ring road (so that it's not necessary to go into the city to visit it). Its different sections are highly imaginative, strongly visual mixed-media displays as much as traditional museum exhibits, with a strong sense of drama – there is a powerfully emotional room on the Holocaust – and the visit culminates with an hour-long, three-screen film centred on the Normandy battles. The Mémorial also seeks to present a global picture of the causes of the war from 1918, the political and social background and life at the time, and, since this is a peace not a war museum, there is a separate exhibit on the Nobel Peace Prize. There are also plenty more museum-like exhibits, such as wartime aircraft hanging from the roof, and what must be the most comprehensive D-Day book and souvenir shop in existence. A full visit to the Mémorial including the film requires over two hours.

Conventional militaria enthusiasts, and those with a more immediate interest in the Normandy campaign itself, tend to prefer the **Musée-Mémorial de la Bataille de Normandie** (*open May–mid-Sept daily 9.30–6.30; mid-Sept–April daily 10–12.30 and 2–6; closed 15–31 Jan; adm*), opposite the largest British war cemetery in Normandy at Bayeux. This one has tanks, trucks, artillery, aeroplanes, all kinds of other equipment and any number of uniforms, arranged on sometimes slightly wobbly shop dummies, plus a hugely comprehensive display of newspaper cuttings and other material that, if you take time to read it all, enables you to follow the campaign almost day-by-day, or to home in on particular incidents. As in many of the similarly traditional smaller museums, all these military accessories can fade into a blur to the uninitiated, although in amongst it all there are still personal details and items that cut through to the quick, such as the various pieces of paper which informed the family of Canadian airman James Lanfranchi that he wouldn't be coming home. Again, a visit to the museum can easily take two hours.

To see the D-Day coast itself, maybe after visiting one of the main museums, it's best to start at one end. Just off the Caen-Ouistreham road at Bénouville is the **Pegasus Bridge** over the Caen Canal, taken by the British 6th Airborne Division at midnight on 5 June 1944. Like many Normandy sites it all seems very peaceful, especially with a gentle breeze across the water and the canal dredger quietly chugging away. In a scrubby, brambly field at the Ranville end of the bridge the places where the paratroops' gliders landed, remarkably close to the target, are precisely marked; across the bridge is the **Café Gondrée**, the 'First House Liberated in France', where the Gondrée family have been dispensing hospitality to British veterans ever since, and which is now itself almost as much a museum as a bar. Next to the bridge on the eastern, Ranville, bank there is a glossy new museum, the **Mémorial Pegasus** (*open May–Sept daily 9–6.30; Oct–Nov and Feb–April daily 10–1 and 2–5; closed mid-Nov–Jan; adm*), which opened in June 2000, and which has replaced the modest museum that for years stood on the Bénouville side. Like others of its kind the Mémorial is state of the art, with a film and loads of information, but doesn't have the intimacy of the old exhibition. The bridge that currently spans the canal is not actually the one that was fought over in 1944, but a more modern, wider model that was installed a few years ago; the otherwise very similar old bridge now sits in a field alongside the Mémorial, oddly 'beached' and surrounded by artillery. In summer a *son-et-lumière* is presented at the Bénouville Bridge (*May–Sept every night exc Mon*).

Ouistreham is a pleasant harbour and seaside town that has gained a good many restaurants, cafés and so on since the opening of the Portsmouth ferry route in the 1980s. A few streets inland, and ignored by most visitors, it also has one of the finest of all classic Norman churches, from the 12th century. From Ouistreham the road turns west along the beaches of the **Côte de Nacre**, now popular with windsurfers and lined with holiday homes, some quite grand, others much more modest, between the centres of the small seaside towns. In summer, sand spreads inland along the sides of the streets, kids pad around barefoot, and there are plenty of bars and snack stands with *moules-frites* and shops offering freshly caught *tourteaux* and *homards*. Every so often the seafront is interrupted by a tank set in concrete, with a plaque. **Luc-sur-Mer** is a bit more substantial than most of the other towns, with a large, glossy, modernised casino dominating the front, and a thalassotherapy centre that's a lot cheaper than Deauville's; at **St-Aubin-sur-Mer** the casino is more modest, but has a striking art deco mosaic façade, perhaps a sign of former glory. **Courseulles** meanwhile is a more modern resort, with a pretty yacht marina surrounded by recently built holiday apartments. It also has monuments recording that this was the place where Churchill and De Gaulle first came ashore on their visits to the beachhead after D-Day. From here, it's a quick drive inland to Crépon.

Beyond Courseulles the holiday cottages thin out, and lush meadows with quietly grazing brown-and-white Normandy cows come down to meet the beaches. A few kilometres further on, though, is one of the most visited points along the coast, **Arromanches**, still ringed, like so many giant, peculiarly angular beached whales, by several of the huge concrete-and-iron blocks of the Mulberry harbour, the entirely artificial port created here to supply the landing forces. For a few weeks the busiest port in the world, Arromanches is otherwise an attractive small beach town, with two main war-related exhibits, the **Musée du Débarquement** (*open Sept–May daily 9.30–1.30 and 2.30–5.30; June–Aug daily 9–7; closed Jan; adm*), with an interesting film on the immense engineering effort the Mulberry represented; and **Arromanches 360**, a high-impact film show using a 360° wrap-around screen (*shows Feb–April and Oct–Dec daily 10.10–4.40; May and Sept daily 10.10–5.40; June–Aug daily 9.10–6.40; closed Jan; adm*).

West of here the cliffs rise rapidly, while the main coast road cuts inland through hedgerows and small, quiet villages that don't feel as if they are near the sea, although for walkers the GR261 footpath keeps mainly to the cliff edge. Atop the cliffs at **Longues-sur-Mer** are the bunkers of the last of the German batteries along this coast that still has its guns in place, battered and rusting and pointing impotently into the sky. It's also rather beautiful, with paths surrounded by heather and blackberries, and superb views out to sea and along the shoreline.

Port-en-Bessin is, unlike most towns in this area, a busy working fishing port, with a charming, relaxed harbour, a great range of seafood restaurants and a good market on Sundays; it's also the location of one of the oddest of the Normandy museums, the private **Musée des Epaves Sous-marines du Débarquement** (*open May Sat, Sun and hols 10–12 and 2–6; June–Sept daily 10–12 and 2–6; closed Oct–April; adm*). Since 1968 owner Jacques Lemonchois has had the sole concession from the French government to salvage all the various kinds of scrap metal sunk off the Normandy coast, and the 'Museum of Wrecks from the Landings' is in effect his yard. There are whole tanks, ships' turbines, guns, plates and all kinds of smaller items such as coat hooks, razors and old pennies from sunken ships, all rusted a uniform brown. It has a strangely ghoulish feel, more so than the other museums; in answer to persistent demand from visitors, there are also cartridges, old engine parts and other bits and pieces for sale. Beyond Port-en-Bessin the road reaches Colleville, St-Laurent and Vierville (all 'sur-Mer'), now signposted to the world as **Omaha Beach**. The US invasion force lost over 1,000 men here, more than on any of the other beaches. It's actually a fine, open stretch of sand, lined with just a few bars and beach houses, although not many people seem to use it as such. The **Musée Omaha** (*open mid-Feb–mid-Mar daily 10–12.30 and 2.30–6; mid-Mar–mid-May and Oct–mid-Nov daily 9.30–6.30; mid-May–June and Sept daily 9.30–7; July and Aug daily 9.30–7.30; closed mid-Nov–mid-Feb; adm*) is privately run and a little tatty, but gains in intimacy with details such as toothbrushes, pay books, letters, Army-issue condoms and the US Soldier's Guide to France, totalling all of 40 pages.

The numbers of US visitors to Omaha and the other beaches were, surprisingly, quite low a few years ago, but have increased hugely on the back of Steven Spielberg's film, *Saving Private Ryan*. On the cliffs above the beach is the **American Cemetery** (*open Oct–mid-April daily 9–5; mid-April–Sept daily 9–6*), a transplanted piece of American monumental architecture, finely landscaped and with some of the most sharply trimmed lawns and flower beds you'll ever see. Nearly 10,000 of the US dead from France and Belgium were brought together in this one huge plot: the precisely aligned white crosses and stars of David carry only a minimum of information and have a distinct anonymity, demonstrating the depth of loss by sheer scale. There are marked differences between the war cemeteries of different countries in Normandy. The British and Canadian dead, in contrast, are divided following Commonwealth War Graves Commission practice between several smaller, more intimate cemeteries; particularly simple and tranquil is the **British cemetery** on a hillside at Ryes-Bazenville, between Crépon and Bayeux. The other difference stems from the work of the Commission in enabling families to place personal messages on gravestones, small, simple epitaphs that make each man a missed individual, a painstaking task of enormous kindness. The huge **German cemeteries**, such as the one at La Cambe southwest of Omaha, are different again: sombre, devoid of any kind of military insignia and imbued with an immense sadness.

A little further west from Omaha is **Pointe-du-Hoc**, where Colonel James Rudder and his US 2nd Ranger Battalion scaled the cliffs in a few minutes flat on the morning of D-Day in an attempt to silence a German battery on top. This is now American territory, ceded as a memorial (to the extent that even the fencing is Made in USA, presumably brought here out of distrust for any comparable French product). Although grassed over by time, the land behind the point has been left pitted and cratered, a torn-up landscape that gives a clear idea of the ferocity of the fighting. But this is nevertheless a beautiful, tranquil place, with the grassy, yellow sandstone cliffs the Rangers improbably climbed above a small rocky beach where gulls and waders pick for shellfish. And, if you arrive in the early evening, you can watch a fine sunset over the Cotentin.

About 3km from the point is **Grandcamp-Maisy**, another attractive small fishing port, with good cafés along the harbourside, and the **Musée des Rangers** (*open April, May, Sept and Oct Tues–Sun 10–1 and 3–6; June–Aug Mon 3–7, Tues–Sun 10–7; closed Nov–Mar; adm*), which tells the full story of Pointe-du-Hoc. At Grandcamp the main D514 coast road turns south, for Utah Beach is separated from the rest of the landing beaches by the *marais* or marshland at the mouths of the Rivers Vire and Douve, which is now a nature reserve. The narrow lanes that lead off westwards from the D514, through the beautifully tranquil village of Géfosse-Fontenay, peter out on the shores of the **Baie des Veys**, an atmospheric expanse of giant mud flats and oyster beds. The wetlands contain an abundance of birdlife, including rare white storks, buzzards and, in the bay, the red-breasted merganser. There is a particularly good and accessible walk through part of the inland wetlands from St-Germain-du-Pert, with a well-marked path.

The D514 meanwhile leads down to meet the main N13 and carry on west through Isigny, a town dedicated 250 per cent and more to the production of *crème fraîche*, and Carentan, a plainish country market centre. Just beyond, the D913 turns off back towards the coast and the village of Ste-Marie-du-Mont and **Utah Beach**. Utah is a long, windswept stretch of dunes, with a big tidal reach and open horizons backed by flat marsh fields – with none of the steep terrain that caused so many problems at Omaha. It also has a much more 'professional'-looking, public museum, the **Musée du Débarquement-Utah Beach** (*open Dec–Mar Sat, Sun and hols 10–6; April–Nov daily 10–6; adm*), with a panoramic viewing room overlooking the beach. About 10km inland, however, is one of the most popular of all the Normandy Invasion sites, at **Ste-Mère-Eglise**, the little town (otherwise known as the site of Normandy's largest livestock market) that was at the centre of the US paratroop drops on the night of 5–6 June. It has one of the most-visited museums, the **Musée des Troupes Aéroportées** or **US Airborne Museum** (*open Feb, Mar, Oct and Nov daily 10–12 and 2–6; April, May and Sept daily 9–12 and 2–6.45; June–Aug daily 9–6.45; closed Dec and Jan; adm*), with a genuine Douglas C47 Dakota in the yard. Around the town there are also information boards with photos taken of the same streets during the battle, which give a clear step-by-step idea of what happened here.

Ste-Mère also has perhaps the oddest of Normandy war memorials. Hanging down one side of the 13th-century Norman **church tower** in the middle of town is a dummy dressed as a US soldier, dangling from a parachute. This commemorates the exploit of paratrooper John Steele, who, as anyone who has seen the 1960s film *The Longest Day* already knows, was caught by his parachute on the tower as he fell and hung there throughout the night and much of the next day, ignored by the Germans around the church who assumed he was dead. Mr Steele died a few years ago but used to revisit Ste-Mère quite regularly, and now looks likely to stay there in effigy forever.

Shopping

The best traditional markets along this coast are in **Arromanches** (*Sat, and Wed in summer*), **Port-en-Bessin** (*Sun*), and **Isigny** (*Wed and Sat*), but all the small towns have a street-sale of some kind one day a week.

The Bessin produces very fine ciders and calvados, with a distinctive style: quite dry and astringent, less fruity and full-bodied than the Auge ciders but with a greater freshness than the driest ciders of the Cotentin. Because of the semi-flatness of the Bessin plain the cider farms are relatively large and easy to find, and are often well-organised to receive visitors.

Colleville-sur-Mer ✉ 14710

Ferme du Clos Tassin, **t** 02 31 22 41 51, **f** 02 31 22 29 46. This cider farm is relatively small for the Bessin area, but still has a well-organised farm shop with apple jam and vinegars as well as a good stock of calvados, *pommeau* and ciders. The Picquenard family also have five simple B&B rooms (*double rooms from 170F/€25.92*). The farm is on the east side of Colleville on the road towards Port-en-Bessin, not far from Omaha Beach.

St-Laurent-sur-Mer ✉ 14710

Ferme de la Sapinière, **t** 02 31 22 40 51, **f** 02 31 21 48 43. An impressively large and manorial-looking cider farm in the middle of the village, right behind Omaha Beach. The range of products available for sale includes ciders, *pommeau*, a select variety of calvados of different ages, and pure apple juice.

Formigny ✉ 14710

Les Jardins, **t/f** 02 31 22 48 99. A dairy farm in Formigny, just inland from Omaha Beach on the road towards Trevières, where the Gaullier family sell their own *crème fraîche*, butter, cheeses and *confiture du lait*. Call ahead and you can also order a fresh farm chicken. *Open Mon–Sat afternoons only.*

Isigny-sur-Mer ✉ 14230

UCL Isigny, 2 Rue du Dr Boutrois, **t** 02 31 51 33 88, **f** 02 31 51 33 44 (*guided tours July and Aug Mon–Sat 10, 11, 2, 3 and 4; Sept and Oct Mon–Sat 11 and 3; reservations advisable; shop open all year*). With its *appellation d'origine contrôlée*, Isigny (an area which for culinary purposes runs up to Ste-Mère-Eglise) is the capital of *crème fraîche* for the entire known universe, and this is the co-operative's official visitor centre. There's also a shop, where you can stock up on AOC butter, Camembert, Pont-l'Evêque and other cheeses, as well as the essential *crème cru*.

St-Germain-du-Pert ✉ 14230

Les Vergers de Romilly, **t** 02 31 22 71 77, **f** 02 31 22 05 83 (*tours Wed c. 2.30; reservation advisable*). A large, well-organised cider farm of beautiful orchards around a majestic Bessin stone farmhouse. One of the best producers in the area, it has dry and sweet ciders, *pommeau*, cider vinegar, wonderful fresh apple juice and a complete range of superior calvados; the charming Mme Renaud, who speaks English, takes the entertaining tours (with accompanying slides) which are much better than many cider-visits, giving a very good idea of the work of the farm and how both cider and calvados are made. The farm is just south of the N13 near St-Germain-du-Pert, and quite well-signposted.

Where to Stay

Chambre-d'hôte (B&B) rooms are plentiful along this coast. The fullest listing is in the annual Chambres-d'Hôtes et Auberges guide for Normandy, published by Gîtes de France and available in French tourist offices and many bookshops.

Bayeux ✉ 14400

Château de Sully, Route de Port-en-Bessin, **t** 02 31 22 29 48, **f** 02 31 22 64 77, *chsully@club-internet.fr* (*standard rooms 570–620F/€86.90–94.52; superior rooms 640–690F/€97.57–105.19; suites 850–950F/€129.58–144.83, according to season*). A 22-room château-hotel prominently located on the road between Bayeux and Port-en-Bessin in 6 hectares of grounds. The rather austere 18th-century mansion is approached along a neat drive between lawns, alongside which there are two 16th-century towers. The house was damaged in 1944 and extensively restored, and has been a hotel since

1990. Inside things are noticeably plainer, although the traditionally styled rooms still have all the requisite country-house comforts. The superior rooms and suites are much more attractive than the standard rooms. The lounges and public areas are smartly cosy, and the dining room of the high-standard **restaurant** overlooks the flower-filled garden. There's a conservatory-style swimming pool, which can be indoor or pretty much open-air according to the weather. *Closed Dec–Feb.*

Manoir du Carel Maisons, t 02 31 22 37 00, **f** 02 31 21 57 00 (*double rooms 400–600F/ €60.98–91.47; gîte from 850F/€129.58 per night*). One of the largest of the Bessin's fortified manors, with a castle-like tower at its centre, this very imposing farm dominates the view in the tiny village of Maisons, half-way between Bayeux and Port-en-Bessin. As well as being a working farm (with some very fine horses), it contains three manorial B&B rooms, combining stone floors, antique furniture and tasteful renovation with luxury comforts. There is also a self-contained *gîte* in a separate house in the grounds, with its own small garden.

Crépon ✉ 14480

Ferme de la Rançonnière, Route d'Arromanches (Creully), **t** 02 31 22 21 73, **f** 02 31 22 98 39 (*rooms 295–680F/ €44.97–103.67 for two*). The rooms at the Rançonnière are perhaps still more impressive than the rest of the grand old farm. There are 35 in the main house and 12 in a smaller manorhouse, the Ferme de Mathan, a few hundred metres away. All are in a wonderfully baronial style: with giant carved wardrobes, grand oak chairs, massive beams even in the (modern) bathrooms and an amazing double-decker family room with a spiral staircase. The rooms in the Ferme de Mathan are a little less distinctive, but still attractive, and might be preferred by those who like a lot of light and space.

St-Germain-du-Pert ✉ 14230

Ferme de la Rivière, t 02 31 22 72 92, **f** 02 31 22 01 63 (*rooms 260F/€39.64 for two, 360F/ €54.88 for three*). A *chambre-d'hôte* in an apparently impossibly huge 16th-century

fortified stone farmhouse. It is a *gîte-panda*, which means that extra information and facilities – such as loan of binoculars – are provided for guests interested in the area's nature and wildlife. It's on the borders of the Cotentin Marais, and the owners can show you the way to all the good walks, and the best places for birdwatching. The rooms are simply decorated, with an abundance of historic character. *Open Easter–1 Nov.*

Arromanches ✉ 14117

Hôtel de la Marine, Quai du Canada, **t** 02 31 22 34 19, **f** 02 31 22 98 80 (*rooms 270–390F/ €41.16–59.46*). This classic Logis de France hotel has been welcoming British veterans and others virtually ever since 1945. It has the best location in town, dominating the middle of the seafront and with a 180° view of the beach and the Mulberry harbour. It has retained the loyalty of its customers by keeping up a high level of comfort and personal service. There are 30 straightforwardly decorated rooms, and a restaurant, *see* below. *Closed Nov–mid-Feb.*

Ouistreham ✉ 14150

Hôtel-Restaurant Le Normandie-Le Chalut, 71 Av Michel Cabieu, **t** 02 31 97 19 57, **f** 02 31 97 20 07, *hotel@lenormandie.com* (*double rooms 250–350F/€38.11–53.36*). Conveniently located near the ferry port, the Normandie has 22 rooms, plus 10 more in Le Chalut, at no.100 across the street, run by the same owners. They are not as striking as the impressive restaurant (*see* below), and some, given the original design of the 19th-century hotels, are rather snug (if not downright small), but they've all been well renovated and are comfortably equipped.

Géfosse-Fontenay ✉ 14230

Manoir de la Rivière, t 02 31 22 64 45, **f** 02 31 22 01 18, *www.chez.com/manoirdelariviere* (*rooms 285F/€43.45 for two, 365F/€55.64 for three; apartment from 1,000F/€152.45 per night; double room in gîte from 850F/€129.58 per night*). A spectacularly lovely B&B in one of the most massive of the Bessin's medieval fortress-farmhouses, amid quiet fields on the edge of the Marais at the mouth of the Vire, between Omaha and Utah beaches. The three guest rooms have high ceilings, antique country furniture, modern bathrooms and views. Breakfast is served in a lordly room with giant fireplace, and **evening meals** can also be provided with prior notice (*100F/€15.24*). The farm also has two equally special, fully self-contained *gîtes*, where you can stay on a B&B basis. In the main house there is a four-room apartment, while the other is an extraordinary double with all its own facilities (including a wood fireplace) in a 13th-century watchtower in the garden – one of the star rural-romantic retreats of all time. M and Mme Leharivel, who still run La Rivière as a dairy farm, are charm itself.

Eating Alternatives

Bernières-sur-Mer ✉ 14490
L'As de Trèfle, 420 Rue Léopold Hettier, **t** 02 31 97 22 60 (*menus 90F/€13.72, 125F/€19.06 and 140F/€21.34*). An attractive restaurant in a small house that its young owners, Gilles and Sandrine Poudras, renovated themselves a few streets inland in Bernières (aka Juno Beach). They have won great praise for their commitment to quality and fresh approach to Norman cooking. Ingredients – local lobster, *andouille* sausages, duck and cheeses – are painstakingly selected; dishes, whether innovations like a *gratin* of fish and shellfish in Neufchâtel cheese, or classics like a *tarte tatin*, explode with flavour. Prices are very reasonable, the dining room is brightly decorated, and there are a few tables on a terrace. *Closed Sun eve (Oct–May) and Mon.*

Port-en-Bessin ✉ 14520
Le Bistrot d'à Côté, 18 Rue Michel Lefournier, **t/f** 02 31 51 79 12 (*menus 95F/€14.48, 125F/€19.06 and 149F/€22.71*). A likeable seafood restaurant just off the little harbour is very popular with locals. The menu features all the classics, from *moules-frites* (*59F/€8.99*) to a really exceptional platter of *fruits de mer* (*295F/€44.97 for two*), and the fish and seafood are as fresh as they could be. The menus feature refined choices such as a fine red mullet fillet in a shellfish sauce. There's an English menu. *Closed Tues eve and Wed.*

Grandcamp-Maisy ✉ 14450
Ferme du Colombier, **t** 02 31 22 68 46, **f** 02 31 22 14 33 (*menus 89F/€13.57 and 120F/€18.29; 'summer menu' 65F/€9.91*). Another massive stone farmhouse, on the Isigny road just outside Grandcamp-Maisy, which now contains an *auberge du terroir*, presenting dishes made only with fresh produce from farms in the immediate locality: farmhouse rabbit and duck terrines, smoked ham, chicken in cider, roast veal, and superb fruit tarts. Booking is always advisable, and essential between October and March.

Arromanches ✉ 14117
Hôtel de la Marine, *see* above (*menus 99–185F/€15.09–28.20*). The restaurant at La Marine also has a loyal following for its reliably high standard and its speciality seafood dishes: grilled lobster, *moules marinières*, *sole à la normande*, and so on. The panoramic windows have the best view in town of Arromanches bay and the Mulberry harbour. *Closed Nov-mid-Feb.*

Ouistreham ✉ 14150
Hôtel-Restaurant Le Normandie-Le Chalut, *see* above (*menus 95F/€14.48, 159F/€24.24 and 'gourmande', 359F/€54.73*). Ouistreham's highly regarded Belle Epoque hotel-restaurant has been thoroughly renovated in the last few years, and the dining room has a smart look; the food is refined, with sophisticated Norman dishes such as seafood quiches, lobster with lentils and other vegetables, and excellent versions of classics like chicken in cider. *Closed Nov–Mar Sun eve and Mon.*

Ste-Marie-du-Mont ✉ 50480
Restaurant Le Roosevelt, Utah Beach, **t** 02 33 71 53 47, **f** 02 33 71 63 37 (*plats du jour c. 60F/€9.15*). The restaurant among the dunes on Utah Beach is also a cluttered and fairly tacky souvenir shop. The rest of it is the nearest to a French equivalent to a roadside diner, handy for anyone visiting this rather isolated beach. The fare on offer includes decent snacks and salads, as well as local standards like *moules-frites*, and the occasional larger *plats du jour*.

Bishop Odo's Town:
Bayeux

26

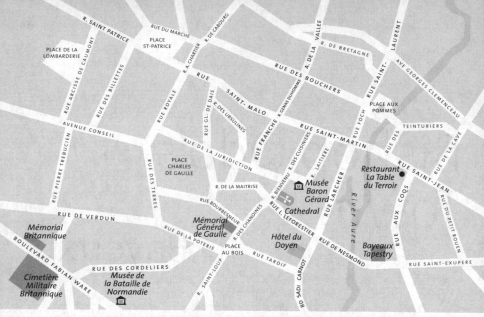

Bayeux is a small town where everything fits together. Its great treasure, the Bayeux Tapestry, which recounts the story of the Norman conquest of England, is complemented perfectly by the magnificent cathedral for which it was made. Around are winding streets, medieval stone courtyards, elegant Ancien Régime townhouses and quiet gardens. The town owes its completeness to a remarkable piece of good fortune. On the morning of 7 June 1944 Bayeux was taken by British troops, only one day after the great invasion, as the first substantial town in France to be liberated and probably the one taken with the least serious fighting. It was thus spared terrible devastation, and stands today as an intact survivor of pre-war Normandy.

The capital of the distinctive region of the Bessin, a lush green plain of cattle, cheese, cider, massive stone fortified farmhouses from the Middle Ages and superb Norman churches, Bayeux has a curious feel somewhere between a town and a big village. In food, it's a stronghold of Norman tradition in cuisine: apples, crème fraîche, fine beef, cider, meaty terrines, excellent fresh seafood from the coast nearby. One of the best and most enjoyable places to find local cuisine at its very best is M Louis Bisson's aptly named **La Table du Terroir**, in the middle of old Bayeux.

La Table du Terroir

*42 Rue St-Jean, **t/f** 02 31 92 05 53. Open Oct–April Tues–Thurs and Sun 12–2.30, Fri and Sat 12–2.30 and 7.30–9.30; May–Sept Tues–Sat 12–2.30 and 7.30–9.30, Sun 12–2.30. Menus 50F/€7.62 (midday only), 60F/€9.15 (Tues–Fri and midday Sat only), 98F/€14.94, 115F/€17.53 and 155F/€23.63; children's menu 45F/€6.86; à la carte average 190F/€28.96.*

If you approach La Table du Terroir from Rue St-Jean, as most people do, you will first pass M Louis Bisson's gleaming butcher's shop on the corner of Rue de l'Orangerie. This is only fitting, as the shop preceded the restaurant. M Bisson is a master butcher,

Getting There

The main road from Caen or Cherbourg (the N13) and all other roads into Bayeux all meet the *périphérique* ring road that runs all the way around the town. A good place to leave the ring road is Bd Sadi Carnot, just east of the railway station on the south side, which leads very quickly to the centre via Rue Larcher, passing a free car park. (Or it's not expensive to park nearer the centre.) The central axis of Bayeux is the crossroads at the end of Rue Larcher (where all the streets also change names). Rue St-Jean leads off to the east, to the right if you're coming up Rue Larcher, with the tourist office the first building you come to on your left. La Table du Terroir is very easy to find a short way along Rue St-Jean on the right: the butcher's shop is actually on the main street, and the restaurant is just behind it down the little alley of Rue de l'Orangerie.

Bayeux is on the Paris-St-Lazare–Caen–Cherbourg rail line, and so has good train connections. The station is on the south side of the *périphérique* ring road, from where it's not too far of a walk into town, although there are also buses. Several small agencies in Bayeux run minibus tours to the invasion beaches and other places around the region: the tourist office has information.

Tourist Information

Bayeux: Pont St-Jean, t 02 31 51 28 28, f 02 31 51 28 59, *www.bayeux-tourism.com*. The Bayeux office is one of the biggest tourist offices in the region, and provides a wide range of services including (expensive) Internet access. Note that the tickets for the Bayeux Tapestry also admit you to the Musée Baron Gérard and Hôtel du Doyen, and vice versa.

recognised as one of the finest producers of Norman meat specialities such as *boudin noir*, terrines, smoked hams, sausages and, above all, fine beef and steaks. His restaurant, naturally, is a meat-eater's haven. He is a great believer in taking proper care with food, and maintaining quality and traditional foods in the face of global 'conglomeratisation' and convenience cooking. He also couldn't be more Norman, more part of his *terroir*: his father had the very Norman occupation of itinerant master distiller, going round the region's small farms as their apple harvest matured to add the touch of skill needed in the making of calvados. In the late 1980s M Bisson decided to add a restaurant to his shop, to make the very best use of his own meat and to showcase the food of the Bayeux region. Most of the meat used still comes from his own shop, and the things he doesn't produce himself – such as the *andouille* sausages – come from Normandy's best producers, in the Vire to the southwest.

Unless you have been living on Mars for the last few years, you will know that times have not been kind for a beef specialist in Europe. M Bisson has his own strong opinions on BSE and other food crises (which do not consist of blaming it all on the British). On a practical level, he is involved in a labelling scheme for quality beef, as a guarantee of the best sources and standards for safety in organically raised cattle.

La Table du Terroir is a cavernous little space in one of Bayeux's old stone buildings, with plain stone walls and exposed beams across the ceiling. The big wooden tables sit six, eight or more people, and you shuffle on at one end to be politely acknowledged by your fellow diners. They might be groups of lunchers from local shops and offices, young couples, some elderly gentlemen on their own, a few tourists, who all appreciate an excellent-quality lunch at very reasonable prices (note that from October to April it is usually only open for lunch). The atmosphere is warm, *sympa* and comfortable, and anyone who feels like a rest from the formality of classic French restaurants will love it.

The restaurant's dishes, as its name implies, are based in Norman country cooking, presented here with a real touch of refinement. A speciality among the starters is *feuilleté bayeusain* from Bayeux itself, a delicious flaky puff-pastry case filled with M Bisson's own utterly smooth black pudding in a rich, mushroomy sauce. As an alternative, a *millefeuilles de légumes* features more fine pastry with crisp vegetables and flakes of ham (scarcely any of the dishes before dessert are 100 per cent meat-free), or there are salads and a wide range of traditional *charcuterie*. To follow, the *plat fort* is naturally beef, steak and veal, in many different cuts and served in many different ways. The superb quality of the meat, cooked precisely as ordered, raises simple dishes into something special: try it rare, as this kind of meat needs very little cooking. Veal especially is also often served *à la Normande*, with a cider and mushroom sauce. Other main dishes might include lamb chops and roast pork with *pommeau*.

There's a short, practical wine list that still includes a good choice of full-flavoured Loire reds that go perfectly with this kind of food, but if you want to stay with the *terroir* there is also very refreshing cider, *poiré* or straight apple juice. With the cheaper menus you have to choose between a cheese course or dessert; the cheeseboard of course offers superior Livarot and Pavé d'Auge. For dessert, try a *teurgoule*, the old Norman rice pudding: beautifully cinnamony and smooth, with a deliciously biscuit-like crust. The natural way to round off the balmy glow at the end of your meal is with a shot of fine calvados.

Touring Around

The origins of Bayeux fade off into prehistory. It was the capital of a Gaulish tribe called the Bajocasses, and became a significant Roman town. It was still a sizeable community in the 9th century, and attracted the attention of the raiding Vikings. The near-legendary Viking chieftain and founder of Normandy Rollo (or Rollon, in French) married Popa, the daughter of the Frankish Count of Bayeux, and their son, who would become William Longsword, second Duke of Normandy, was born here in 905. Bayeux can thus claim to be the true home of the remarkable dynasty of Norman Dukes. It was also one of the last towns in Normandy where Norse was regularly spoken into the 11th century. Bayeux reached its greatest importance around the time of the Norman conquest of England, when it was the main power base of Odo de Conteville, Bishop of Bayeux but also William the Conqueror's half-brother, comrade-in-arms (despite being a priest) and turbulent and often troublesome minister. In the same period, however, William – partly because of his quarrel with the disloyal Odo, whom he imprisoned in 1082 – decisively turned his attention to his own favourite town, Caen, which would eventually lead to Bayeux's decline. It and the Bessin would still be fought over at many stages of the Hundred Years' War, which is when their fortified townhouses, manors and farms were built. Later, though, Bayeux would settle back into being a quieter, more provincial market town.

The spine of Bayeux is the long, more-or-less straight street that runs northwest to southeast, with different names in different sections (which happens a lot in Bayeux):

Rue St-Martin, Rue St-Malo, and Rue St-Jean. The main street is the one street that's often quite busy, with a fair amount of traffic and crowds of shoppers on Saturday afternoons; walk up any of the side streets and very soon stillness prevails.

From the 16th to 18th centuries Bayeux was a prosperous little town, and its merchants and gentlemen were able to build themselves many *hôtels particuliers* or town mansions. On the corner of Rue St-Martin and Rue des Cuisiniers is the oldest completely intact house in Bayeux, a wonderfully massive 14th-century house, a mixture of Bessin stone and half-timbering, that rises up to its erratic roof line thorough three tiers and in different sections, with a wonderful combination of the vertical and the horizontal. At 4 Rue St-Malo is the **Grand Hôtel d'Argouges**, a 15th–16th-century mainly stone mansion, much altered in its upper floors, but still with an imposing courtyard. Remnants of Viking Bayeux are, naturally, a matter of archaeology, but poking up all over the old town, often half-unnoticed behind much later houses and yards, are soaring 14th-century stone watchtowers, built to warn of the approach of the English or other troublemakers. **Rue Franche**, the turning to the south where Rue St-Martin becomnes Rue St-Malo, contains almost a compendium of the history of Bayeux since about 1300. The Hôtel de Rubercy, at no.5, has a plainish 19th-century façade, but if you stand back and look above you can see a turreted 15th-century watchtower; no.7, the Hôtel de la Crespillière, is a classically elegant French 18th-century townhouse; no.13, the Manoir de St-Manvieu, is a 16th-century residence concealed behind another simple 19th-century front; while no.18 is the 15th-century Manoir Gilles Buhot, where you can still pick out the medieval structure despite all the later alterations.

Across Rues St-Martin/St-Malo from Rue Franche in Rue Genas Duhomme, even the Méliès cinema is housed behind the columns of an 18th-century *hôtel*. This street is crossed by Rue des Bouchers, a long, charming old street. To the left Rue des Bouchers runs up parallel to Rue St-Malo to **Place St-Patrice**, the main market square (also known as Place du Marché), a big, 19th-century space with several pleasant, entirely untouristy bars and restaurants around it. The market takes over every Saturday.

Back at the central crossroads, the main street continues eastwards via the Pont St-Jean (with the tourist office on top of it) over the Aure, a lovely, lively little river that's lined by a mix of buildings from all sorts of eras. Behind the tourist office is the court-yard-like **Place aux Pommes**, with a Norman craft centre. **Rue St-Jean** across the bridge is pedestrianised and forms one of the most picturesque parts of old Bayeux, with a line of cafés and brasseries with pavement terraces. Part way up on the opposite side is the Bisson butcher's shop, in front of La Table du Terroir. At 51 Rue St-Jean a passageway leads to the 16th-century Hôtel du Croissant, a superb stone house on an intimate courtyard with a rocket-like six-storey watchtower. Rue des Teinturiers, which turns off Rue St-Jean to the north, is a quiet little street that contains, at no.45, Bayeux's smallest house. It's a truly tiny little structure that looks like an insert put in to prop up the two houses either side of it, and it's hard to think it was ever really a separate building. Balzac also lived in this street for a few months in 1822.

Bayeux's main monuments are in the compact little knot of streets south of St-Malo–St-Martin–St-Jean. A short walk down Rue des Cuisiniers (which turns into

Rue Bienvenu) is the spectacular west front and main entrance of the **cathedral**. Begun in the mid-11th century, it was completed rapidly under the patronage of Odo de Conteville, and consecrated in 1077. Odo also commissioned the Bayeux Tapestry to hang inside. The building was damaged by a fire in the next century – which the tapestry remarkably escaped – and was subsequently rebuilt and altered at several different times, and so, like so many medieval cathedrals, is a mixture of eras and styles, above all its original Norman Romanesque and 13th-century Gothic.

The basis of the west front is the two immense towers on either side, survivors from Odo's cathedral, with Gothic details all around them in the portal in between and the spires on top. If you walk all the way around the back of the cathedral you can also see the dramatic 13th-century Gothic flying buttresses around the apse. One of the last major sections added to the cathedral was the 15th-century central tower, on top of which there is a rather odd 19th-century dome, which is about the only part of the whole building that doesn't really fit. Inside, though, the nave is all tremendous Norman simplicity, a superbly serene space. The majestic main arches and giant pillars of the transept are largely unchanged since Odo's time, while the upper levels and parts of the vaults were added in a harmonious, unelaborate Norman Gothic style in the 13th century. The nave is celebrated for its Norman-Romanesque carving, which is wonderfully simple, including long friezes of intertwined foliage and leaf designs running above the arches. The apse and chancel are a more intricate example of fine Norman Gothic, and contain some restored wall paintings of early Bishops of Bayeux and some beautiful 16th-century glass. The woodwork, in contrast – the high altar, the choir stalls, the giant pulpit – is high Baroque and mostly from the 18th century. One of the most atmospheric parts of the cathedral is the beautifully plain 11th-century crypt, with some curious 15th-century frescoes of angels and the delicately sculpted tomb of a canon from the same era.

As you leave the cathedral, don't miss the grand old 16th-century half-timbered house opposite on Rue Bienvenu (no.6), which has wonderful carvings on its upper storeys, including a very coy-looking Adam and a more provocative Eve either side of the Serpent entwined around a tree. Around the cathedral are Bayeux's main museums. The **Musée Baron Gérard** (*open June–mid-Sept daily 9–7; mid-Sept–May daily 10–12.30 and 2–6; adm; joint ticket with the Tapestry and Hôtel du Doyen*) occupies the former Bishops' Palace, just around the corner down tiny Rue de la Chaîne, entered through a lovely courtyard between the palace and the cathedral. It's one of the oldest of France's local museums, and, like many, a curious, often engaging mixture. The large painting collection on the upper floors includes some minor Renaissance Italian works and a surprising portrait of *Sir Thomas More* from the school of (but not by) Holbein, but the greater part of it consists of lesser-known French, and especially local, painters from the 17th to the 19th centuries. A bit more familiar are the works from the Impressionist era, including a lovely group portrait by Gustave Caillebotte, some nature paintings by the local artist Albert de Balleroy (*see* p.273), a few Boudins and a very small Corot (all French local museums have a Corot). There's also some fine marquetry furniture, and a fascinating cabinet on the introduction of the metric system and the Franc by Revolutionary France in 1795; on the ground floor, there are Gallo-Roman artefacts excavated nearby, 17th-century tomb sculptures, a small display on Bayeux lace and a much bigger one on the work of the factory that produced porcelain here from 1812 until 1951. Outside the museum in the courtyard is the Tree of Liberty, a magnificent plane tree provocatively planted next to the old Bishops' Palace by the Revolutionaries in 1797.

The principal showcase for Bayeux's distinguished lacemaking tradition is on the south side of the cathedral in Rue Leforestier, the **Hôtel du Doyen** (*open Sept–June Mon–Sat 10–12.30 and 2–6; July and Aug daily 10–12.30 and 2–7; adm; joint ticket with the Tapestry and Musée Baron Gérard*), an impressive 18th-century mansion that is also an ex-ecclesiastical building. It is a shrine for pious Catholics because modern Normandy's most venerated religious figure, St Thérèse of Lisieux, went there in 1887 to ask the then Bishop for permission to enter a convent; it now also contains the **Musée Diocésain d'Art Religieux**, with a reconstruction of the room where this took place and a display of vestments, manuscripts, church treasure and other religious items. The greater part of the building, though, is taken up by the **Conservatoire de la Dentelle de Bayeux**, the Lacemaking Conservatory, dedicated to maintaining this (traditionally 100 per cent female) art in the traditional manner, by passing it on from one lacemaker to another. As well as giving courses the Conservatoire has an inform- ative exhibition on the history of lace and a permanent display of exquisite pieces, both historic items and recent work, while In August and September each year there is a special show of new lace and students' creations. Visitors can also watch lace- makers at work, and buy in the shop.

You will find a third museum on Rue des Chanoines: the **Mémorial Général de Gaulle** (*open mid-Mar–mid-Nov daily 9.30–12.30 and 2–6.30; adm*), on the corner of Rue Bourbesneur. De Gaulle came to Bayeux a few days after it was freed from the Germans and made his first speech on liberated French soil here on 14 June 1944, speaking to an ecstatic crowd from the Sous-Préfecture in the large square just to the west. He returned here two years later to make another speech in which he put forward his ideas for the Constitution of the post-war Republic. All these events and others associated with the General are recorded with due reverence in his Bayeux museum, but for non-Gaullists its main interest is usually that it is housed in the **Hôtel du Gouverneur**, the former residence of the Ancien Régime royal governors of Bayeux. Built in the 15th and 16th centuries, it is one of the most grandly baronial of all the town's old stone mansions, with a truly spectacular watchtower that is wider – due to strange little 'annexes' having been added – at the top than it is at the bottom. From the Mémorial or Place de Gaulle a short walk through the streets to the south will take you to Bayeux's 1944 war museum, the **Musée-Mémorial de la Bataille de Normandie** and the British war memorial and cemetery (*see pp.252–3*).

This leaves till last the town's great jewel, the **Bayeux Tapestry** (*open mid-Oct–mid-Mar daily 9.30–12.30 and 2–6; mid-Mar–April and Sept–mid-Oct daily 9–6.30; May–Aug daily 9–7; last admission 45min before closing time; adm; joint ticket with the Musée Baron Gérard and Hôtel du Doyen*). Nowadays it is excellently presented in the Centre Guillaume le Conquérant, a former seminary, just east of Rue Larcher and the river. A decent visit to the tapestry will require at least two and a half hours, and can easily take more. It includes an audiovisual display, a film, shown alternately in French and English, and an extensive exhibition on the historical background, which you can visit before you enter the tapestry room itself. The presentation is pretty much a model of how to illustrate a historical artefact and make it as accessible as possible without trivialising it; only the film, with its sentimental account of William the Conqueror's illegitimate birth and his mother Arlette the tanner's daughter (*see* p.244), is a little silly. The exhibition, based on a timeline, leaves you fully informed by the time you actually reach the tapestry, where an excellent audioguide (available in English and several other languages) will take you through it scene-by-scene. It is kept in dim light for its own preservation, but its colours are still remarkably vivid.

The Bayeux Tapestry is surprisingly – and extremely – impressive when seen close up. Strictly speaking it is an embroidery, not a tapestry. It was commissioned by Bishop Odo for his new cathedral at some time between 1066 and his imprisonment in 1082, and is mentioned in cathedral inventories from the 15th century as still hanging around the nave, above the main arches. In France it has often been referred to as La Tapisserie de la Reine Mathilde, because of a belief that it had been commissioned by William the Conqueror's queen Matilda, but this is no longer given any credit. Little is known with certainty about exactly where and how it was made but because of similarities in style between the tapestry and Saxon embroideries it is now believed that it was made by nuns in England and then brought to Bayeux.

Odo commissioned the tapestry to flatter his half-brother William and as a monumental piece of propaganda, presenting the Normans' justification for their invasion of England. Functioning like an early comic strip, it tells its story with great narrative drive, and a remarkable visual rhythm. The central thrust of the first half is to justify William's claim to the throne of England, above all by putting forward emphatically the Normans' claim that his rival Harold of Wessex had previously agreed to support William's rights himself. Having made clear his claim, the tapestry gets on with recounting the story of the invasion preparations, the voyage and the landing at Pevensey, leading up to the final scenes of the Battle of Hastings, depicted with enormous energy and realism, right down to the peasants stripping the bodies of the dead.

Perhaps the greatest fascination of the tapestry, however, is in all the innumerable incidental details of 11th-century life that appear along the way – the way that ships are built, or the sailors hitching up their tunics as they jump on to the beach. The main narrative panel that runs along the middle of the long cloth strip is flanked at top and bottom by separate lines of panels, which imaginatively become intertwined with the main story towards the end as the conflict becomes more and more intense. In them there are mythological scenes, real and imaginary animals, scenes of peasant life and farming in the different seasons, and all kinds of other details that make it vividly human. There aren't many women in the Bayeux Tapestry: one of them is Eve, shown with Adam and the Serpent, while another is a Saxon woman seen fleeing her house as it is burnt by Norman soldiers, an eternal image of war. The Saxon English are shown with long red moustaches, just as they are in Astérix cartoons.

Shopping

Bayeux's main weekly **market**, in Place St-Patrice (*Sat*), is the place to pick up local produce. There is also a smaller market on Rue St-Jean (*Wed*). Bayeux also has antiques shops, along Rue St-Jean or Rue St-Martin.

Bayeux ✉ 14400

Ateliers de l'Horloge-Ateliers du Bessin, 2 Rue de la Poissonnerie/9 Place aux Pommes, t 02 31 92 70 76, or t 02 31 21 91 93. Behind the tourist office in the middle of town, virtually next to each other despite the difference in addresses, two centres for the maintenance of traditional Bayeux crafts. The Ateliers de l'Horloge provide workshops and courses for the making of embroidery, tapestries and lace, as well as having work on sale. The Ateliers du Bessin have decorated ceramics. *Closed Sun; Ateliers de l'Horloge also closed Sept–June Mon.*

Boucherie Louis Bisson, 42 Rue St-Jean, t 02 31 92 05 53. The shop from which La Table du Terroir developed, and still the place to find the very best Norman meats, traditional *charcuterie* and hams, all expertly selected, together with a delicious range of *traiteur*-style ready prepared dishes. It has won many prizes. The staff don't speak much English.

Cidre et Calvados Les Remparts, 4 Rue Bourbesneur-Place de Gaulle, t/f 02 31 92 50 40, *cidrelecornu@wanadoo.fr*. Proof that Bayeux is a very, very tranquil town is that it contains Normandy's only urban cider farm. The orchards are actually on the edge of town, but M François Lecornu's *caves* are in the centre, in a big 17th-century stone house in one corner of the Place de Gaulle. Tastings are free, and you can also have a tour of the cellars (they are very used to English-speakers). *Open mid-Sept–May Thurs and Fri 3–6; June–mid-Sept Mon, Sat and Sun 9.30–12.30 and 6–8, Thurs and Fri 3–6.*

Terres à Vin, 10 Rue des Cuisiniers, t 02 31 21 38 11, f 02 31 21 38 99. An attractive specialist wine shop, with an excellent selection of fine French wines and also spirits, liqueurs and superior local cider, *pommeau* and calvados. Owner Philippe Pommarède has an expert knowledge of his stock, and speaks very good English.

Where to Stay

Bayeux ✉ 14400

Grand Hôtel de Luxembourg-Hôtel de Brunville, 25 Rue des Bouchers, t 02 31 92 00 04, f 02 31 92 54 26, *hotel.luxembourg@wanadoo.fr* (*rooms 480–630F/€73.17–96.04; suites 850–990F/€129.57–150.91*). Bayeux's historic premier hotel, in an elegant 18th-century *hôtel particulier* on quiet Rue des Bouchers, has in the last few years become part of the Best Western chain, and has expanded to incorporate the almost as distinguished Hôtel de Brunville around the corner in Rue Genas Duhomme (t 02 31 21 18 00). It now has 60 rooms, spread between the two buildings; those in the Brunville are a little smaller. Both buildings have been refurbished: some of the resulting renovation is fairly bland, but facilities are luxury-standard. There are large and conventionally smart restaurants in both.

Hôtel d'Argouges, 21 Rue St-Patrice, t 02 31 92 88 86, f 02 31 92 69 16, *dargouges@aol.com* (*double rooms 300–460F/€45.73–70.12; family rooms 650F/€99.09*). An elegantly comfortable hotel in the 18th-century former mansion of the Argouges family, in its own large garden on the west side of Bayeux near the market square. There are ten rooms in the main house, and another 14 in an also 18th-century but less grand house behind it in the garden. Rooms combine modern comforts with old château style, and the best have views of the garden. The lounges and the breakfast room are palatial, and the staff charming. No restaurant.

Hôtel Nôtre Dame, 44 Rue des Cuisiniers, t 02 31 92 87 24, f 02 31 92 67 11 (*rooms 180–280F/€27.44–42.68; family rooms 450F/€68.6*). An amiable old classic Logis town hotel, built some time in the 19th century, with a maze of narrow staircases (and no lift, but people say this adds to the charm) and loads of character. The six best rooms have wonderful views of the great west front of the cathedral – spectacularly floodlit at night – and of the rooftops of old Bayeux. There are 24 comfortable rooms. The restaurant (*see below*) is also popular: in summer (especially July and Aug) they prefer to take guests on a half-board basis.

Relais de la Liberté, 22–24 Rue des Bouchers, t 02 31 92 67 72 (*double rooms 180–200F/€27.44–30.49; family room 370F/€56.4 for four; breakfast 30F/€4.57*). This pleasant little guest house is on quaint old Rue des Bouchers, which is very tranquil. Its three rooms are a real bargain, there's a little garden at the back of the house, and the owners are charmingly easygoing.

Au Bon Coin, 81 Rue St-Jean, t 02 31 92 06 57 (*rooms 150–200F/€22.87–30.49*). A little way up the hill of Rue St-Jean from the centre of town, this is one of Bayeux's most basic hotels, but is handy for budget travellers, with nine straightforward rooms with showers. Downstairs there's also a little **restaurant** (*menu 57F/€8.69*) that offers an equally no-frills set lunch and dinner menu; *steak au poivre* is pretty much a fixture.

Family Home-Les Sablons, 39 Rue Général de Dais, t 02 31 92 15 22, f 02 31 92 55 72 (*dormitories from 95F/€14.48; double rooms c. 230F/€35.06*). A curious combination, in a pretty old 17th-century house just off Place de Gaulle. Part of it is an official youth hostel, with dormitories. A greater distinction has lately been created between the dorms and the recently renovated individual rooms. Everyone tends to be drawn a little into the hostel atmosphere, especially if you have **evening meals** (*65F/€9.91*), served at a long communal table; during early summer the hostel dorms are often booked by school parties, who can be pretty noisy. Its fans, though, love the place, and M and Mme Lefèvre are enthusiastic hosts who also organise a range of bargain minibus tours around the region for budget travellers.

Eating Alternatives

There is a string of cheapish brasseries, crêperies and bistros along Rue St-Jean and Rue St-Martin.

Bayeux ✉ 14400

Hôtel Nôtre Dame, *see above* (*menus 95–180F/€14.48–27.44*). This hotel restaurant sticks to what it knows best: the dining room is big, quite plush and old-fashioned, and the menu offers a wide choice of enjoyable local favourites such as *fricassée* of rabbit in cider, *choucroute de poisson* or *poulet vallée d'Auge*.

Le Petit Bistrot, 2 Rue Bienvenu, t 02 31 51 85 40 (*menus 98F/€14.94 and 165F/€25.15*). Right opposite the cathedral, this is an atmospheric little restaurant with an unusually varied range of Norman-based dishes. The chef describes himself as an *artisan cuisinier*, and dishes are prepared with care and fresh ingredients: fish is especially good here, and first courses might include a rich fish soup or a delicious mixed *salade gourmande*, followed by fillets of sea-bream or *magret* of duck with light, interesting sauces.

La Taverne des Ducs, 41 Rue St-Patrice, t 02 31 92 09 88 (*menus 79–169F/€12.04–25.76; plat du jour 49F/€7.47*). A big and busy brasserie overlooking Bayeux's main market square, a fine place to call in for Saturday lunch. It's bright and a little brash, but in its booth seats you can sample a full range of brasserie staples like *moules* several different ways, onion soup, or meat and fish grills, and there's a big choice of beers.

Le Pommier, 40 Rue des Cuisiniers, t 02 31 21 52 10 (*menus 76F/€11.59, 105F/€16.01 and 145F/€22.1*). This pretty little place is quite touristy (there is a menu D-Day), but offers an interesting variety of truly Norman dishes using all-local produce.

Le Petit Normand, 35 Rue Larcher, t 02 31 22 88 66 (*dishes 40–50F/€6.1–7.62, menus 78F/€11.89, 98F/€14.94 and 128F/€19.51*). A very likeable, straightforward bistro that's hard to beat on value: there's a big range of satisfying one-course dishes such as omelettes with varied fillings, different mixed salads and steaks. The simplest menu might include *entrecôte au poivre* or salmon in a fruity *vigneronne* grape- and wine-based sauce; to drink, there's local cider as well as a practical range of wines. *Closed Thurs.*

La Cassonade, 35 Rue Bienvenu, t 02 31 92 47 32. A popular small crêperie on a corner next to the cathedral, with all the standards – sweet crêpes with fruit, ice-cream and chocolatey fillings, a good range of savoury *galettes* – and some nicely varied salads and larger dishes (*c. 20–60F/€3.05–9.15*).

Norman
Heartland:
Balleroy and
the *Pre-Bocage*

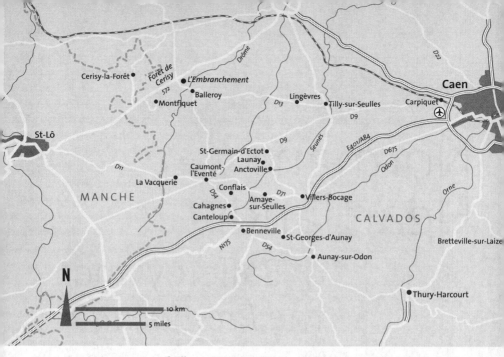

France is a country of villages, French politicians used to say with a rhetorical flourish, of villages and small towns. This isn't nearly as true as it used to be, but a glance at any map will show that there are still enormous areas of the country with no major cities: holes between the main highways occupied by laceworks of lanes and tiny places with curious names. Some are famous as places of beauty, while others have few associations and can come as a complete discovery; and in between the lanes and villages there are patches of almost untouched countryside.

The 50-mile-wide stretch of land between Bayeux, Caen and St-Lô is one such region, with no great centre but a string of engaging small towns and innumerable old Norman villages. In landscape it's a transitional area with plenty of contrasts, from forest and the rolling plain of the Bessin in the north to twisting valleys, hedges and ever-steeper inclines further south. The fields are larger, the hedgerows usually less all-enclosing and the vistas more open than in the true Normandy *bocage* country to the west, and so this area is known as the *Pre-Bocage*. Even so, there are still many villages and farms that seem hidden and lost amid its dips and bends, and a great deal of gentle beauty.

To the north there is an ample stretch of natural beech forest, the Forêt de Cerisy, that's wonderful for walks, next to one of the most impressive but least-known of early Norman abbeys, at Cerisy-la-Forêt. As one of the more lush and garden-like parts of Normandy the area just north of the *Pre-Bocage* was also deemed a suitable place for the aristocracy of the Ancien Régime to build their country residences, and at Balleroy there is one of the most elegant of French 17th-century mansions, now owned by the Forbes family. In 1944 the *Pre-Bocage* was one of the areas that saw the most bitter fighting in Normandy, and places like Tilly-sur-Seulles and Villers-Bocage still carry powerful resonances from that time.

Getting There

From the Caen ring road – meeting point for the road in from Ouistreham and all roads from Paris and further east – the A84 *autoroute* runs southwest, parallel to the old N175, passing just south of Villers-Bocage. A more direct and more placid route to Balleroy itself is to take the Carpiquet airport turn off the ring road and get on the D9-D13 via Tilly-sur-Seulles, from where a left turn will also take you to Villers-Bocage. From Bayeux, the D572 towards St-Lô passes north of Balleroy. A familiar landmark in this area is the Embranchement, the crossroads (with no houses around it) in the Forêt de Cerisy where the D572 and the roads to Balleroy, Le Molay-Littry and Cerisy-la-Forêt all meet.

To get to the Manoir de la Drôme from Bayeux, turn left at the Embranchement, and as you drop into the dip at the entrance to Balleroy the restaurant is on the left. From Caen and Tilly you enter the village on the opposite side, by the main approach: turn right at the castle and the Manoir is at the bottom of the dip on the right.

The nearest mainline station is at Bayeux. Local trains on the Bayeux–Cherbourg line also stop at Le Molay-Littry. Calvados Bus Verts buses run from Bayeux or Caen, but to explore any further you really need a car or bike.

Tourist Information

Aunay-sur-Odon: Place de l'Hôtel de Ville,
  t 02 31 77 60 32.
Caumont-l'Eventé: Mairie, Place St-Clair,
  t 02 31 77 50 29.
Villers-Bocage: Place Général de Gaulle,
  t 02 31 77 16 14.

As a truly rural place the *Pre-Bocage* is also naturally an excellent area for discovering food products of the Norman *terroir*. Before beginning any exploration get a copy of the Route des Traditions leaflet from local tourist offices. Its purpose is ostensibly to guide people to local farm producers, but its real object seems to be to take you down some of the windiest, narrowest and most cavernous lanes in Normandy, and getting you utterly lost. The route winds its way with no obvious rhyme or reason between villages that sometimes seem to be properly named, and sometimes do not, and other places where there are names but no villages. But at the end of the roads you will discover wonderful ciders, breads and honeys.

The modest restaurants and hotels of the *Pre-Bocage* tend to serve straightforward, enjoyable, traditional Norman cooking. This is France, though, where refined cuisine can also turn up even among the woods and fields. And in Balleroy, suitably close to the château, there is one of the premier restaurants in the whole of the Calvados, the **Manoir de la Drôme**, a pretty old stone house in a garden beside the River Drôme.

Manoir de la Drôme

*129 Rue des Forges, Balleroy, **t** 02 31 21 60 94, **f** 02 31 21 88 67.*
Open Tues, Thurs–Sat 12–2.30 and 7.30–9, Wed and Sun 12–2.30;
closed Mon and two weeks end Jan–Feb, one week late Aug.
Menus 180F/€27.44, 250F/€38.11 and 350F/€53.35; à la carte
average 300F/€45.73.

The northern arm of the 'T' that is François Mansart's design for Balleroy village runs away from the château down a long incline towards the River Drôme. The Manoir de la Drôme is to the right just before the river, shrouded by trees and down a short driveway. It isn't really a *manoir*, and looks as much like a large, well done-up country cottage as a restaurant. Around it there is a very pretty, flower-filled garden, with a lawn where some tables are set up in summer. Inside, the dining room also has a certain air of being in somebody's house, combined with other touches that are very much those of a first-class restaurant, such as the utterly smooth service provided by Mme Leclerc and her waiting staff. With a view of the garden through french windows, it's tranquillity itself, and extremely comfortable.

Your eating experience begins with two sets of *mise-en-bouche*, which immediately let you know that M Denis Leclerc is not a chef hesitant about vigorous flavours. On our visit, first came a little bowl of pickled mushrooms, with prunes and cheese on sticks. Following it came some *boudin noir* in a shallot sauce with Jamaica pepper, a tiny but formidable creation featuring some of the best blood sausage ever made. At around the same time, the waiter arrives to present the refined wine list – including an unusually good choice of *fine-cru* half bottles – with a suitably devoted hush.

The menu itself is highly sophisticated, describing a range of intricate dishes: subtle creations with local fish and seafood are particular specialities, as in *langoustines* fried with spices and cocoa liqueur and served with wild rice, or fresh cod with Normandy smoked ham, cream of chives and coarsely mashed potatoes with a touch of *andouille*. However, M Leclerc is also the kind of French chef who seems to make up much of his menu on the hop, according to what's fresh that day. A big, expansive man, he emerges at some point to take the orders himself, which is when he'll tell you about the day's specials.

As a starter you might find lobster in a cream sauce deglazed with madeira, shallots and a little egg yolk, and then served in its shell – very rich and creamy, but also superbly subtle. And as a main course, roast turbot with *girolles*, *trompettes* and other forest mushrooms and a little cake of swede, all with a wild garlic sauce. *Mer et terre* combinations are a real fad in French cooking at the moment, and are on the verge of becoming a cliché, but this dish is of the kind that can justify the whole genre.

The opulent subtleties continue until the end of the meal. After the huge cheese board, which includes an interesting Camembert marinated in-house in cider and calvados, there arrives a pre-dessert of a tiny apple crumble with a little *crème de calvados* ice-cream. The main dessert is another high point. Don't miss the *gratinée* of berries with a *crème de framboises*, with fabulously fresh, hot berries set against a perfectly light, chilled raspberry cream.

Touring Around

Balleroy is different from all the other villages around it. Most Norman villages date back to the early Middle Ages, and coexist with their châteaux with no great sense of organisation or design. Balleroy, on the other hand, was built or rather rebuilt in the 17th century entirely around its château, almost like a model village. If you approach it in the intended way, from Caen and the east, you first see the neat, tall façade of the château away in the distance, facing you at the end of a dead-straight road. On either side of this road are two long lines of stone cottages, set back behind lawns inter-rupted by a few precisely spaced trees, like extras announcing the arrival of the major player. The road continues on between the houses to descend into a steep dip, where it ends at a T-junction with a broad square and, on the opposite side, the ornate gates of the château-proper. It's a remarkable *coup de théâtre*, an eloquent demonstration of the château-builder's wealth and power; enter the village from the north or south and you feel almost as if you're arriving backstage.

The château was built in 1631 by the great François Mansart, one of the most cele-brated architects of the era and credited with the invention of the Mansard roof, for Jean de Choisy, Chancellor to Gaston d'Orléans, brother of Louis XIII. Mansart's recon-struction of the village of Balleroy, a classically French exercise in the remodelling of the world along symmetrical lines, was highly influential in the design of many later projects, including Versailles (much of which was built by his nephew Jules Hardouin-Mansart). The wealthy and powerful Choisys retained the château in an unbroken line until 1704, when it passed by marriage to the Balleroy family, with the title Marquis de Balleroy, who managed to hold on to it through the Revolution and right up until 1970. Their most notable offshoot was **Albert de Balleroy**, a 19th-century painter who was a friend of Manet and other Impressionists. However, he seems condemned to be dismissed as a rich young man who dabbled in painting and could be relied on to bail out his less well-heeled friends rather than ever accepted as an original artist, an impression his most frequent subject matter, animals and hunting scenes painted around his home, has done little to dispel.

So much for history. Balleroy's fortunes took a different turn in 1970, when it was bought by megabucks millionaire Malcolm Forbes, owner of *Forbes Magazine* and much else besides, as one of his several homes around the world. Forbes spent millions on restoring the château, and made it a showcase for one of his special obsessions, ballooning, with a balloon museum and regular international balloon-meets. Malcolm Forbes was also a legendary networker – photos at the château show him pressing flesh with every US President since Truman, Onassis, Henry Kissinger, Elizabeth Taylor and all sorts of other famous faces – and he brought many of his friends and contacts to see his French château. He died in 1990, but his sons Christopher and occasional Presidential hopeful Steve Forbes and the rest of the family still use the house and periodically entertain here lavishly, which gives it a certain buzz uncommon in the more rustic Norman châteaux.

The **Château de Balleroy** (*www.chateau-balleroy.com; open mid-Mar–June and Sept–mid-Oct Mon, Wed–Sun 9–12 and 2–6; July–Aug daily 10–6; tours in French and English, last tours begin 45mins before closing; joint ticket for château and museum adm exp, separate tickets available*) is approached via a precise Le Nôtre-style French garden that leads via a small bridge to a broad courtyard in front of the mansion itself. The house is a pure piece of Louis XIII early French baroque in brick and stone, with a three-storey central block flanked by lower wings, all three beneath Mansard roofs. In a manner that seems exaggerated even for a baroque creation, though, the elegant visual effects are all directed to the approach and the façade, as in a theatre set: look at the château from the side and it appears far less well-proportioned, and too tall for its depth. Inside, there's a mixture of rooms that have been very carefully and authentically restored and touches of pure ostentation, as if Mr Forbes wasn't quite sure whether he really cared for the house or just wanted to play with it.

The entrance *salon* has the genuine look of an old château, with large animal paintings by Albert de Balleroy. The smoking room is dedicated to him, with many more paintings which show him to have been an able, sensuous painter despite his unadventurous themes. The room itself seems very comprehensively restored with Second Empire-Victorian décor, until you look up and see that the ceiling has been painted for Forbes with bright toy-packaging paintings of ... balloons. The ultra-opulent **dining room** has intricately ornate wooden panelling that originally came from a Parisian *hôtel particulier*, while three bedrooms have been decorated by Christopher Forbes, apparently a great Victorian enthusiast, with a rather over-the-top collection of 19th-century artefacts including a bust of the Duke of Wellington. The spectacular **Salon d'Honneur**, on the other hand, has been superbly restored with its original 17th-century Italianate decoration. It has a very fine, high-baroque painted ceiling, by Charles de la Fausse, representing the *Four Seasons*, while around the walls there is a majestic series of portraits by the Flemish painter Juste d'Egmont of *Gaston d'Orléans*, *Louis XIII* and all the other members of the Bourbon royal family in the 1630s.

The Balloon Museum, the **Musée des Ballons**, is in one of the stable blocks beside the entrance garden. It deals with every aspect of ballooning from the Montgolfier brothers onwards, and is an engaging and colourful (and bilingual) display, even though the later sections tend to concentrate disproportionately on the ballooning exploits of Malcolm Forbes himself. The bi-annual Balleroy **International Balloon Meets**, when 20 or more brilliantly coloured balloons float serenely over the château, are popular and spectacular events. They are held in odd-numbered years, nearly always in the third weekend in June, and one is due in June 2001. Behind the château is the large, green **park**, with some 3km of pathways that visitors are free to explore, and the beautifully peaceful church, also designed by François Mansart, in 1651, but in a much plainer, more traditional style. Balleroy **village** is a tranquil, relaxed and characterful little place, apparently unconcerned with any happenings at the big house, and with pleasant small cafés on its grand square.

The road that leaves Balleroy to the north soon enters the **Forêt de Cerisy**, an over-2,000 hectare (5,000 acre) stretch of native deciduous forest (mostly beech) of the kind that's ever harder to find in northern Europe. Within it there are deer and wild boar as well as foxes, badgers and rabbits, and woodcocks, buzzards and various other birds of prey. The forest is not the most organised tourist attraction: contrary to the signs along the D572 there is at present no forest information centre, and the building that used to be one is now a private house (another is promised, but it doesn't look as if it will be open for some time). However, there are signboards at all the turnings off the forest roads, and the paths are well maintained and clearly marked. A good place to use as a jumping-off point for a walk is the **Maison Forestière du Rond-Point**, about 2km north of the Embranchement on the road to Cerisy, a meeting point of several tracks and footpaths, with a parking area. From there, you can walk as far as you like along deliciously quiet, leaf-shrouded paths.

The same road emerges out of the forest into Cerisy-la-Forêt, a quiet village with a broad main street where one motor vehicle seems to pass about every half an hour. A sign indicates the way to one of the least-known but most beautiful sights in Normandy, the **Abbaye de Cerisy-la-Forêt** (*open Easter–mid-Nov daily 9–6.30; guided tours Easter–June Tues–Sun 10.30–12.30 and 2.30–6.30; July–Sept daily 10.30–12.30 and 2.30–6.30; Oct–Nov Sat, Sun and hols 10.30–12.30 and 2.30–6.30; adm*). It is very nearly 1,000 years old: it was founded in 1032 by William the Conqueror's father, Duke Robert the Magnificent, and most of the abbey church had been built by the time William invaded England. It stands in a supremely peaceful location on the edge of the village, with cows and horses grazing in the fields around it and grassy slopes on one side that run down to the lovely *étang*, or pond, that used to supply the monks with water and fresh fish. This is not to say that the abbey has not had its troubles: it was ransacked by Protestants in 1562, and during the long centuries of decline from its early-medieval peak it suffered many alterations and demolitions, even including the destruction of part of the church in the 19th century. The most important parts of it, though, are extraordinarily intact.

Cerisy receives relatively few visitors, so outside of summer weekends you can often have it to yourself. Most of the monastery buildings – the cloister, the refectories, the monks' parlours - were knocked down in the Napoleonic era, but pieces of them and their outline can still be seen in the fields alongside, between the horses. The existing remains consist mainly of the church or **Abbatiale** itself, the **Salle de Justice**, or court-room, and the Gothic **Chapelle de l'Abbé**, added in 1260. If you go around by yourself you can only enter the main church, but with the guided tours you can also see the other rooms and the chapel, via its curiously romantic little colonnaded staircase. Nearby is an enormous grinding-wheel, once used by the monks to prepare their corn. An essential part of any visit is to wander around the outside, on to the green slope, from where you can best appreciate the church's massive perpendicularity and the skill with which its yellow stone walls are buttressed into the hill.

The **interior** of the Abbatiale represents something close to the quintessence of Norman Romanesque architecture, in all its superb simplicity. It is currently covered in a rather odd cream wash, which seems to add to its rather ghostly tranquillity (recordings of Gregorian chant also play semi-permanently). The nave now has only three of its original seven bays, as the others were demolished as unsafe in the 19th century, but what remains is sufficiently impressive. It rises through three tiers of columns, immensely strong and delicate at the same time; look out for some Scandinavian-looking carved heads on the capitals of the middle tier. The brilliantly light apse, beyond the Gothic carved wood choir stalls, is unique in Norman architecture in consisting of three levels of windows, leading up to an exquisite vaulted roof.

The church also contains a permanent exhibition on Norman architecture, in Normandy and England, and the *étang*, which has been beautifully landscaped, is now surrounded by a modern sculpture garden with work drawn from all over the world, a surprising juxtaposition with the old abbey. From across the pond you also get a matchless view of the abbey looming up above you, its grand pepper-pot spire pointing skywards, a magical image of millennial serenity.

Both Cerisy and Balleroy were fortunate in that their serenity was relatively little disturbed in 1944, as both were taken by the Allies quite early in the Normandy campaign. The *Pre-Bocage* further south, though, saw intense fighting as the British army sought to break out of the initial beachhead and take Caen.

Nowhere suffered more than **Tilly-sur-Seulles**. Between 7 and 26 June this little crossroads village was taken and retaken by the British and Germans 23 times, sometimes changing hands more than once in the same day. The local population, meanwhile, took shelter wherever they could, and some 10 per cent of them died. Finally, British bulldozers flattened the remaining ruins of the village, both to prevent them being used as cover in any more German counter-attacks and to stop them hindering advancing traffic, so that Tilly became the only place in Normandy to be all-but obliterated in the conflict. Post-war, a new village was built in plain, reconstruction concrete. The only major structure to be rebuilt was the simple little 12th-century chapel of Notre-Dame-du-Val, which now houses the **Musée de la Bataille de Tilly** (*open May Sat, Sun and hols 2–5; June daily 10–12 and 2–6.30; July and Aug daily 2–6.30; Sept daily 2–5; adm*). This is one of the most affecting of Normandy's war museums, put together mainly by local people: as well as pictures of the lost village of pre-war Tilly it has many items contributed by British veterans, concentrating on individual experiences rather than strategies. Beside the Balleroy road out of Tilly there is a **British war cemetery**, among the 1,224 graves of which is that of the poet Keith Douglas.

South of Tilly the *Pre-Bocage* extends between and over a series of long, roughly southwest-running ridges, the tops of which contain the main towns – none of them really much more than big villages – and are followed by the main roads. **Villers-Bocage** was the scene of one of the most dramatic incidents in the battle on 13 June 1944, when a single German tank across a sunken *bocage* road turned back an entire British Division, a spectacular demonstration of the superiority of Porsche technology that played its part in prolonging the campaign. Villers-Bocage also had to be substantially reconstructed after 1945. It hosts the area's most important market, but apart from that there's no big reason to go there, other than to take a gulp of its small-town Frenchness, and soothe any fears that the Gallic way of life may be in danger. **Caumont-l'Eventé** has retained rather more of its 19th-century architecture, and occupies a spectacular location on top of an especially steep ridge, with wonderful views from the small town squares. Caumont also has a visitor attraction in the **Souterroscope** (*open Oct–Dec and Feb–April Tues–Sun 10–5; May, June and Sept daily 10–5; July and Aug daily 10–7; adm*), a deep limestone cave where guided tours are provided. The biggest attraction in this area, though, has to be the countryside between the towns and major roads, and the way it goes on and on for a surprising distance. In among its lost cold-comfort farms are many small food producers, including those on the Route des Traditions; particularly beautiful among the villages are Anctoville, Cahagnes and St-Georges-d'Aunay, the latter two on the way south towards the third 'big town' of the *Pre-Bocage*, **Aunay-sur-Odon**. It's especially lovely to wander around this area towards evening, when as you top the ridges you're often rewarded with delicious golden sunsets over the woods and hedges.

Shopping

The biggest traditional market in the *Pre-Bocage* is in **Villers-Bocage** (*Wed*). There are also markets in **Caumont-l'Eventé** (*Thurs*) and **Aunay-sur-Odon** (*Sat*), and a small market in **Balleroy** (*Tues*). In summer, look out for the farmers' markets at **Le Clos d'Orval** (*see* below). Many of the farm producers have stalls at one or all of these markets; otherwise, the Route des Traditions leaflet from tourist offices will help you track them down.

Cahagnes ✉ 14240

André Butet, Village de Canteloup, **t** 02 31 77 99 47. Buy home-made *rillettes*, terrines, fresh farm chickens, duck or guinea fowl direct from this farm shop, in a tiny hamlet not far from Cahagnes, signposted off the D54. *Open Mon–Fri am only.*

Ferme du Loterot, Village de Canflais, **t** 02 31 77 54 08. Georges and Claire-France Leveque sell their entirely original, homemade calvados-based liqueurs, along with tastings and light meals (*booking necessary*). The little hamlet of Canflais is just east of Cahagnes off the D54.

St-Germain-d'Ectot ✉ 14240

La Chevretière, Hameau Candon, **t** 02 31 25 00 31. A small goat farm where the Pelcerf family produce their own *chèvre*. It's deep in the country, up an apparently directionless road (vaguely towards Launay) between Anctoville and St-Germain-d'Ectot. *Tours mid-May–mid-Sept Mon–Sat pm only.*

Amayé-sur-Seulles ✉ 14310

Le Clos d'Orval, **t** 02 31 77 02 87, **f** 02 31 77 12 12. A beautiful big old farm, reached via several twists and turns off the D71, producing a superb range of ciders, *pommeau* and extra-dry, very refined calvados. They're among the region's most important producers, and have won many awards. Visitors can sample the product and look around their extensive *caves* and a fascinating little museum of cider making. The Clos d'Orval also hosts a **farmers' market** (*marché à la ferme*) that brings together many independent producers from around the region (*July and Aug every Wed*).

Lingèvres ✉ 14250

Ferme de Bérolle – Dominique Jourdan, **t** 02 31 80 82 56. On the north side of Lingèvres, reached by a well-indicated road off the D13 Balleroy-Tilly road, this is a substantial cider producer with a grand, almost neoclassical manor house inside a massive slate farmyard wall. The farm shop offers tastings and an ample range of dry ciders, *pommeau* and calvados. *Open Mon–Sat 9–12 and 2–6.*

La Vacquerie ✉ 14240

Miel Charozé, Le Haut Hamel, **t** 02 31 77 40 79. Just west of La Vacquerie on the north side of the D11, a sign guides you down a lane that leads, eventually, to the beautiful farm of bee-keepers Odile and Roger Charozé, producers of prize-winning honey. The smart farm shop sells every kind of honey and bee-related product: pollen, beauty products, biscuits and cakes, royal jelly, mead and even honey-based wood polish. Visitors can tour the farm (charge for large groups), including a talk by M Charozé (in English if required), visit the hives and see an exhibition on beekeeping. *Closed Sun.*

Brigitte Monroty, Route de St-Lô (D11), **t** 02 31 77 46 85. A farm dedicated to angora rabbits. Visitors can tour the farm, see an exhibition, and buy made-up pieces or raw wool. Sweaters and so on can also be made to measure. *Open Mon–Sat pm only.*

Where to Stay

Balleroy ✉ 14490

Les Biards, 1 Place du Marché, **t** 02 31 21 60 05 (*rooms 200–260F/€30.49–39.63*). Excellently placed on the square opposite the château, this establishment has done nothing to keep up with modern trends in décor or hotel styles – the rooms are distinctly elderly – but this quirky charm seems to please the devoted (mostly British) regulars. Michel and Marie-Claire Briard are a tad eccentric, but very sweet, and he speaks very good English.

Tournières ✉ 14330

La Ferme de Marcelet, **t/f** 02 31 22 90 86 (*rooms 220F/€33.54 for two, 300F/€45.73 for four*). An attractive *chambre-d'hôte* in a massive dairy farm just outside Tournières, a little way north of Cerisy, with its own signpost down a narrow lane on the south side of the D15. It was originally a fortified manor, parts of which date back to the 12th century. The five rooms are extremely cosy. Breakfast is served in the farmhouse kitchen, and there is lots of home produce; Mme Isidor cooks ample evening meals (*90F/€13.72*), with prior notice.

Tilly-sur-Seulles ✉ 14250

Hôtel Jeanne d'Arc, 2 Rue de Bayeux, **t** 02 31 80 80 13, **f** 02 31 80 81 79 (*rooms 230–280F/ €35.06–42.68*). A reliably comfortable Logis hotel, on the central crossroads. Its rooms have good facilities and, as the only hotel in town it's an important meeting point, with a popular restaurant (*see* below).

Cahagnes ✉ 14240

Le Mesnil de Benneville, Benneville, **t** 02 31 77 58 05 (*rooms 200F/€30.49 for two, 300F/ €45.73 for four*). A pretty, convivial farm B&B between Caumont and Aunay-sur-Odon. Generous *table-d'hôte* meals are a speciality (*80F/€12.2*). M and Mme Guilbert's hospitality is renowned, and they can show you where to walk, ride, fish or play golf nearby. The house has its own sign on the N175, just east of the junction with the D54 south of Cahagnes; despite the addition of the *autoroute*, it's still very peaceful.

Montfiquet-Balleroy ✉ 14490

Le Relais de la Forêt, L'Embranchement on the D572, **t** 02 31 21 39 78, **f** 02 31 21 44 19 (*rooms 200–300F/ €30.49–45.73*). The only sizeable building near the Embranchement in the Forêt de Cerisy, this is a big, curiously motel-like place, with stags' heads on the walls and huge function rooms for the essential ceremonies of French country life. The rooms are functional, comfortable and decent value.

Villers-Bocage ✉ 14310

Au Vieux Puits, 20 Rue Georges Clémenceau, **t** 02 31 77 00 03, **f** 02 31 77 30 42 (*rooms 200–280F/€30.49–42.68*). A classic French small-town hotel on the main street, with a certain extra friendly brio and a fun restaurant (*see* below).

Eating Alternatives

Le Molay-Littry ✉ 14330

Brasserie de la Forêt, Route de Balleroy, **t** 02 31 22 95 15 (*dishes c. 30–60F/€4.57–9.15*). A handy little brasserie on the road south towards Balleroy, with country versions of standards: grills with *frites*, omelettes, *croques*, sandwiches, and so on. *Closed Sun.*

St-Georges-d'Aunay ✉ 14260

Ferme-Auberge de Saulques, Les Saulques, **t** 02 31 77 03 51 (*menus 85–165F/€12.96–25.15*). In a big farm that's easy to find on the west side of the D54, a little south of the A13, not far past the turning for St-Georges-d'Aunay, Mme Claudine Louis' *ferme-auberge* offers ample menus of classic local dishes using wonderful fresh produce from the farm itself: *rillettes*, foie gras (a speciality), chicken, guinea fowl or duck *au cidre*, salads, *feuilletés* of *chèvre* or Camembert, and hefty desserts like *teurgoules* and Norman fruit tarts. Booking essential. *Closed Sun eve and Mon, and two weeks in Jan.*

Tilly-sur-Seulles ✉ 14250

Hôtel Jeanne d'Arc, *see* above (*menus 94F/ €14.33 and 140F/€21.34*). The dining room has big, curving windows overlooking Tilly's crossroads, and there's a little garden alongside. It's a comfortable, lively place, serving traditional local fare – chicken *vallée d'auge*, grilled fish, and excellent cheeses.

Montfiquet-Balleroy ✉ 14490

Le Relais de la Forêt, *see* above (*menus 90–158F/€13.72–24.09*). The big, cheerful dining room, fronted by a terrace (decorated with several garden gnomes), is a friendly place, and offers loads of good-quality choices: *flambéd* prawns and *magret* of duck in *pommeau*, and an excellent range of brasserie-style dishes and mixed salads.

Villers-Bocage ✉ 14310

Au Vieux Puits, *see* above (*menus 85F/€12.96 and 115F/€17.53*). The brasserie-bar-*tabac* at the Vieux Puits has a cast of characters straight out of a 1960s Claude Chabrol picture, is friendly and great value, with a brasserie menu and even pizza.

Seafood on the Rocks:

Barfleur

28

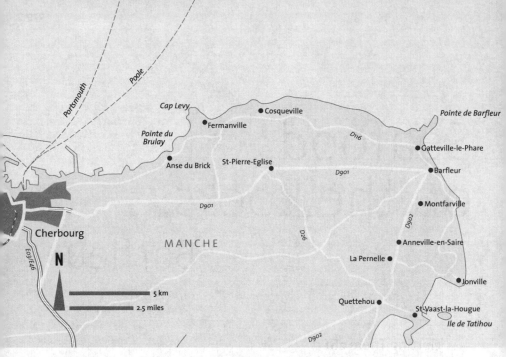

Oysters, mussels, prawns, clams and lobster, and fish such as sole, sea bass and monkfish are the most renowned produce of the northeast Cotentin, the rugged coastline that winds round from Cherbourg to meet the flatlands and beaches of the central Normandy coast. Barfleur is particularly known for lobster, St-Vaast-la-Hougue for oysters – renowned for their unique, vaguely nutty flavour.

The northeast corner of the Cotentin is often referred to as the Val de Saire, after the little river valley that runs through the middle of it, but this soft green valley is not necessarily its most prominent feature. The old fishing harbours of the area are built of granite like the rest of the tip of the Cotentin. Small and full of character, they have an airy tranquillity and relaxed pace that belies their proximity to Cherbourg. They were once centres of much greater activity, closely associated for good or bad with England: after 1066 Barfleur was the main port linking the two halves of the Anglo-Norman empire, and this coast later saw major battles during the centuries of Anglo-French warfare. Today its harbours are favourite ports of call for cross-Channel yachters, many of whom come across specifically to eat.

Between the villages the shoreline is a succession of rocky headlands, cliffs and crags, interrupted by beautiful little coves and some fine beaches, with great walks and views along the way. Inland, the countryside becomes surprisingly leafy and lush, with rich pastures and pockets of thick woodland that produce excellent vegetables, beef and hams, which are almost as highly regarded as the local fish and seafood. For a really memorable display of local produce, make your way to the **Moderne** in Barfleur, an unassuming local hotel-restaurant where Evrard Le Roulier prepares food which combines fine ingredients with attention to detail, skill and inventiveness.

Getting There

Barfleur is easy to reach on the D901 from Cherbourg (27km), or from the south on the D902 via Quettehou. About half-way down the main street, Rue St-Thomas-Becket, on the right looking towards the sea, there is a side street with a large *boulangerie-pâtisserie* on the corner: turn up this street and after about 200m you will come to the Hôtel Moderne.

The nearest stations are in Cherbourg, the end of the line from Paris (St-Lazare) via Caen and Bayeux, and Valognes, on the same line. Local buses run from Cherbourg to Barfleur and St-Vaast.

Tourist Information

Barfleur: 2 Quai Henri Chardon, t 02 33 54 02 48. The office is at the end of the quay to the left, looking out to sea, by the church.

Fermanville: 20 Vallée des Moulins, t 02 33 54 61 12.

Quettehou: 1 Place Général de Gaulle, t 02 33 43 63 21.

St-Pierre-Eglise: Place Abbé St-Pierre, t 02 33 54 37 20.

St-Vaast-la-Hougue: 1 Place Général de Gaulle, t/f 02 33 54 41 37, *www.st-vaast-reville.com*. The office is in the square on the harbour, to the right, looking out to sea.

L'Hôtel Moderne

1 Place Charles de Gaulle, t 02 33 23 12 44, f 02 33 23 91 58.
Open mid-Sept–mid-Jan and mid-Mar–June Mon, Thurs–Sun
12–1.30 and 7–8.30; July–mid-Sept daily 12–1.30 and 7–8.30;
closed 15 Jan–15 Mar. Book weekends. Menus 85F/€12.96 (Mon–Fri only),
105F/€16.01 (Mon–Fri midday only), 144F/€21.95, 170F/€25.92
and 199F/€30.34; à la carte average 240F/€36.59.

The Moderne looks just as a well-established small French harbour-town hotel should look, with a little outside terrace and a Mansard roof. Inside, beyond a round hallway with some interesting art deco touches and the odd fish tank, the dining room is bright and airy, with a few Norman coastal scenes around the walls. The atmosphere is comfortable, quiet and traditional, with a certain air of timelessness. While M Le Roulier is at work in the kitchen his wife is in charge front-of-house, and chats away with the many locals and regulars, who on weekends slip behind the tables with complete familiarity and give the restaurant a distinctly homelike feel.

The menu promises *une cuisine traditionelle*, but M Le Roulier makes quite a few distinctive departures of his own. Once you'd been here a few times you would probably try some of the house terrines, foie gras or other *charcuterie* for a first course, but on an initial visit it has to be the seafood, and above all oysters from St-Vaast. They're offered on all the set menus, either *farcies* with a light, crispy *gratin* or *au naturel*, as simple as they could be, with some great home-baked bread. Around you, fellow diners provide a complete survey of the different styles of oyster-eating: some grab the shells like trowels and swallow the flesh in a vigorous gulp, with a healthy bout of slurping, picking up one oyster after another at a fast pace; others set about them far more delicately, and attempt to use cutlery until the very last possible moment. Another star dish of long-standing has been *crevettes de la côte*, a wonderful platter of plain-boiled local prawns; sadly, in the last few years they have become far harder to find, but if they appear on the menu they're definitely worth choosing.

Choucroute de Poissons (Sauerkraut with Fish)

Serves 4

The chef serves 3 different varieties of fish, such as sea bass, bream and red mullet, depending on what the market offers.

12 fish fillets, about 80g/3oz each (3 kinds if possible)
800g/1¾lb prepared sauerkraut, well rinsed and drained
olive oil, for cooking
2 pieces smoked salmon, cut in half
salt and pepper
For the beurre blanc:
120ml/4oz white wine
1 tablespoon finely chopped shallot
1 heaped tablespoon crème fraîche
100g/3½oz cold butter, diced

Season the fish fillets. Heat the sauerkraut in a steamer until thoroughly hot.

To make the beurre blanc sauce, put the wine and shallot in a small saucepan. Bring to a boil over medium heat and boil until the wine is almost evaporated. Whisk in the crème fraîche, and when it comes back to a boil reduce the heat and whisk in the butter by bits. Taste and season as needed; keep warm, off the heat.

Heat olive oil in a large frying pan over medium heat until it shimmers. Add the fish and cook quickly on each side.

Divide the sauerkraut between 4 warm plates, place a piece of smoked salmon on top and arrange the fish around. Pour over the sauce, dividing it evenly, and serve.

When the starters have been sent on their way, some diners don bibs to engage in the ritual of consuming the local lobster, in which case the beasts of the day may be brought to your table still kicking for you to have an informed discussion of their qualities and make your choice. They can then be served plain with mayonnaise, in a *beurre blanc* or flambéd in calvados. Equally hands-on is a speciality dish that appears on the 199F menu, M. Le Roulier's magnificent Cocktail Royal de la Mer, a superb assortment of mussels, clams, scallops, more oysters and deliciously sweet *langoustines*. Some dishes are less traditional, such as the homemade tagliatelle with *fruits de mer* or the fabulous *choucroute de poissons*, which is delicately buttery and served with a fish-eater's orgy of salmon, different kinds of white fish – perhaps sea bass, monkfish or mullet – and even some mussels and oysters, all in a perfect *beurre blanc*. It's quite a feast, but you'll be loath to leave any.

To help this go down smoothly the wine list offers an ideal selection of light sancerres and muscadets for around 100F/€15.24 a bottle. Another leisurely pause is provided before you finish with the usual fine Norman cheese course, and homemade desserts such as a light crème caramel, or an excellently fruity warm apple tart with crème fraîche. M. Le Roulier emerges to make his customary tour of the tables a little after 2pm, to catch up on local conversation and receive the thanks of all present.

Touring Around

Largest of the northeast Cotentin ports is **St-Vaast-la-Hougue** (from Cherbourg, take the D26 south from the D901, through one of the greenest, lushest stretches of the Val de Saire). It's a broad, attractive harbour, with plenty of bars and restaurants around the waterfront, and in the centre of the view an eccentric 19th-century Mariners' Chapel and much more imposing granite lighthouse. There's still a sizeable fishing trade, and an unmissable street market on Saturday mornings. The famous oyster beds are just south of town, and there are visits and tastings on some days in July and August (*by reservation only; for information contact tourist office*). Almost as prominent a part of modern St-Vaast is the well-equipped marina, which is well patronised by both the French and British yachting communities. South of the port a narrow spit of land runs down to La Hougue point, and the dramatic pile of **Fort de la Hougue**, looking as if it rises straight out of the sea, and still a military installation closed to the public. On either side of the spit there are coves and beaches that, weather and tides permitting, are good for paddling around or even swimming.

The seas offshore were the scene of a famous naval encounter, the battle of La Hougue, a clash that saw France's own nautical Charge of the Light Brigade. In 1692 Louis XIV hatched a plan for his greatest admiral, Tourville, to sail with his squadron from Brest, rendezvous with reinforcements from the Mediterranean, pick up 30,000 mostly Irish soldiers encamped at St-Vaast, and carry them across the Channel before the English and Dutch fleets could join together to oppose him. Once there, in association with English Jacobite plotters, they would restore James II to the British throne. However, bad weather prevented the French Mediterranean fleet from making its way up the coast; Tourville calculated that the same winds would make it much easier for the Anglo-Dutch fleet to join forces, and pointed this out to his superiors, but was told not to question the King's orders. Once the Admiral had set sail, Louis received news that, as predicted, the Allied fleet had made their rendezvous, and that the Jacobite conspiracy in England was no more than a damp squib. A fast boat was sent to call Tourville back, but failed to find him in the bad weather. On 29 May 1692, Tourville with his 44 ships rounded Barfleur point, to find an Anglo-Dutch fleet of 100 ships in front of him. In a scene drawn from pure romantic literature, the French commanders all agreed that the only sensible course was to turn back to Brest; however, Tourville read them the King's orders to engage the enemy, they accepted they had no choice, and then continued to sail onwards, to the amazement of their opponents. To everyone's still greater astonishment, in the fighting that lasted the rest of the day the French actually came off slightly the better. During the night and the following day, though, part of the French fleet was scattered by the winds, while the rest took refuge in the harbours of the Cotentin, where there was no protected naval port, a shortage that had often been lamented by French admirals. The English fleet were able to sail into St-Vaast and set fire to many of Tourville's best ships, ending any possibility of a French invasion in support of James II.

Following the battle, somewhat after the horse had bolted, a team of Marshal Vauban's engineers was sent to St-Vaast to build defences at Fort de la Hougue and on the low green island of **Tatihou**, which looms in the background of the harbour of St-Vaast and adds much to the interest of the view. It remained a military base into the 20th century, but since 1992 the island has been open to the public, and is now one of the most attractive places to visit around the coast. You normally get there by amphibious vehicle, tickets for which are bought at Accueil Tatihou on the quay in St-Vaast (*crossings every 30min: Easter–Sept daily 10–4.30; Oct–Easter Sat and Sun 10–4.30; return tickets including museum entry 50F/€7.62, 10F/€1.52 under-11s; return boat ticket only 30F/€4.57, 5F/€0.76 under-11s*). It's advisable to book in mid-summer, and, if you're planning to have lunch in Barfleur, to arrive early.

As well as a chance to wander around one of the largest and most complete of France's many Vauban-style fortifications, Tatihou offers a very varied range of other things to do. There's a **maritime museum**, centred around artefacts, from weapons to plates, recovered from ships sunk in the 1692 battle, and a workshop that builds and restores traditional Norman fishing craft; it's also possible to stay on the island, and there's a recently improved restaurant. Each summer, too, the island hosts an imaginative series of exhibitions, theatre shows, concerts and events, especially the **Traversées du Tatihou-Musiques du Large** music festival in August, centred on folk, world and 'maritime' music (information **t** 02 33 54 33 33, *www.tatihou.com*). One of the most popular parts of the festival is the Traversée, the walk across to the island at low tide (with guides), although you can also get the boat in the normal way. One of the island's primary permanent attractions, though, is that, since it was kept isolated by the military for centuries, most of it is a pristine expanse of grassy moorland, rocks and dunes, great for walking and a conservation area especially rich in sea birds such as cormorants, terns and gulls. Free guided historical and birding tours are available in July and August.

North of St-Vaast there is a pretty road that runs right along the shore to Jonville and the Pointe de Saire, past some more good beaches, especially towards the point. Inland from here, just across the D902 about halfway between St-Vaast and Barfleur, is one of the Cotentin's most renowned beauty spots, the remarkable village of **La Pernelle**. Its main street improbably runs almost straight up a near sheer-sided ridge to a little granite church at the top, from alongside which there are limitless views that have been eulogised by a whole host of local literati, over the Cotentin, down the coast and out to sea. This is an ancient pilgrimage site, and in a grotto a little below the crest there is an image of the Virgin of Lourdes, installed in the 1920s. During the Second World War the heights of La Pernelle also naturally attracted the attention of the Germans, who installed an observation post, which is still there, and a long-dismantled gun battery that in June 1944 caused considerable trouble to the US troops landing at Utah Beach, 30km to the south. This drew down massive bombardment in turn, and ownership of the hill was fiercely contested. Of the church only the unbreakable 14th-century stone tower really survived, and much of the present building is a reconstruction; in the entrance there's a curious watercolour, painted by a German prisoner-of-war in 1947, which shows what the restorers had to work with. Nowadays there's also a very pleasant bar-restaurant on the crest of the ridge, should you wish to study the view at a leisured pace.

Anneville-en-Saire, just north of La Pernelle along the Barfleur road, is known as the home of the Cotentin's best vegetables, and there are very pretty walks between there and **Montfarville** a little to the northeast, one of the most beautifully tranquil of all the Val de Saire villages, with leafy, winding little streets that are only just car-width. It also has a very unusual church, built in the 1760s to replace an earlier medieval one, still in a traditional, stone-box Norman style, but with details in carved stone and wood that seem very grand for a small village church. Its greatest surprise is in the choir, a series of vividly coloured wall-paintings on the *Life of Christ* painted in 1879 by a local artist, Guillaume Fouace.

Barfleur itself is a charming, uncommercial little granite fishing port that's noticeably less busy than St-Vaast, even though there's usually a fair number of yachts and dinghies sharing space with the fishing boats in the harbour. There's rarely much traffic to disturb the people chatting in the middle of the street, but part-way round the apparently unnecessarily wide arc of the waterfront there's an attractive quayside café, the **Café de France**, where you can grab a table and take in the activity after lunch. A squat 17th-century church dominates the vista at the end of the harbour, next to the tiny beach amid the rocks where some brave souls occasionally take to the waters.

The population of Barfleur is now something over 600. There is little in the town to indicate that 900 years ago it was well over ten times that number, and that this was then one of the largest, busiest harbours in Europe. William the Conqueror himself first set out from here on his voyage towards Hastings, in his Barfleur-built ship the *Mora*, and it became the Norman monarchs' principal port for communications with their new possessions in England, with constant traffic in both directions. The main street is now named after Thomas à Becket, another frequent traveller, and Richard the Lionheart passed through here in 1194 on his long journey back to reclaim his throne after the Third Crusade. Earlier, Barfleur was also the site of another famous nautical disaster, in 1120, when the *Blanche Nef* (the White Ship) sank just outside the harbour, taking with it William Atheling, only son of Henry I, together with several royal bastards and many of the élite of the Anglo-Norman court, church and aristocracy. This was an early incident of Hooray-Henryism: according to the only survivor, a Rouen butcher, passengers and crew were all very drunk, and attempted to overtake ships that had left harbour ahead of them, thus straying out of the channel and on to the Barfleur rocks. The death of the King's heir would lead to civil war between Henry's daughter, Matilda, and a rival claimant, Stephen.

The Anglo-Norman empire was the making of Barfleur's brief fortune, and when Normandy was absorbed into France in 1204 the town's trade and prestige suffered a rapid downturn. Barfleur remained a significant port into the following century, however, sufficiently so for it still to be an important objective for the English in the Hundred Years' War. In 1346 Edward III's son, the Black Prince, landed with a raiding army at St-Vaast, and sacked and burnt Barfleur. A few years later came the Black Death, and Barfleur never really recovered its stride. By the 16th century it was only a small village of some 150 people. More recently, the development of Cherbourg, begun under Louis XVI and continued by Napoleon, definitively consigned both Barfleur and St-Vaast to peaceful obscurity.

Owing to its treacherous rocks, however, Barfleur does have the distinction of possessing France's oldest lifeboat station, opened in 1865, and one of its tallest lighthouses, on **Pointe de Barfleur**. A footpath runs all the way to the point (4km) from beside the church on Barfleur harbour. Whether you go by road or footpath you also pass through the interesting old village of **Gatteville-le-Phare**, with a huge open square alongside one of the most remarkable of Norman monumental churches. Much of it was rebuilt in the 18th century, but it still has its near-unique 12th-century tower, surmounted by a strange balustrade, which from a distance, especially on the lighthouse road, can look as much like a fortress or even a mosque as a church. Just across the square there is also a tiny Norman Romanesque sailors' chapel, the Chapelle des Marins, built during the reign of Henry I in the early 12th century. Gatteville is also a good jumping-off point for the GR223 footpath, which can take you – perhaps via a bus-ride to get through Cherbourg – all the way round the Cotentin to Cap de la Hague on the other side, and down to Avranches. The **Phare de Gatteville** (*normally open April–Sept daily 10–12 and 2–9; Oct–mid-Nov and mid-Dec–Mar daily 10–12 and 2–6; closed mid-Nov–mid-Dec; adm*), the lighthouse, is an impressively stark monument in an isolated, wind-blasted spot, where the air can clear most headaches, and which is also popular with adventurous fishermen. Extraordinarily tall and thin, the lighthouse may be closed for security reasons when gales are up. There is one step up for every day of the year, and those who reach the top are rewarded with wonderful seascapes and views, on a good day, round the peninsula from La Hague and down to Grandcamp at the mouth of the Vire.

From Barfleur point, if you're in a hurry to get to Cherbourg, you can cut back on to the D901 and be there in not much over twenty minutes. More entertaining, though, is the winding D116 west from Gatteville. The road runs a little inland, through tiny, close-clustered villages between hedges and still-narrower side lanes that run down to the sea, with every so often some more beautiful views of rocky inlets between cliffs. From **Cosqueville**, one of the prettiest villages and home to one of the area's best restaurants, a steeply dipping lane leads down to one of its best beaches, the **Plage du Vicq**, in a broad inlet, sheltered and windswept by turns, that catches the sun wonderfully on summer evenings. At Fermanville, the next village west, a road turns off to the right for **Cap Lévy**, with another fine lighthouse and Fort Lévy, a Napoleonic-era fortress that's now been converted into an unusual hotel (*see* below), above a minute beach and harbour. The Cape is another great place for a windswept walk, with a choice of views in two directions, into Cherbourg Bay or back to Barfleur.

West of Cap Lévy you enter the Bay of Cherbourg, first seen to full advantage at Pointe du Brulay. Just below it is **Anse du Brick**, a little seaside resort in its own right, where the coast opens up to leave a well-sized beach that's popular with surfers, and which often gets packed in summer. Perched on the cliffs above there's a selection of bars and restaurants, all with the same great view. West again, and the road runs straight into Cherbourg through a string of little towns each with their own *plage*, where people take to the sands on hot July weekends.

Shopping

The Saturday market in **St-Vaast** is by far the best in the area, and for food it's one of the best in Normandy. The presence of the holiday and yacht clientele attracts fine food producers from a very wide area: particularly excellent, apart from the seafood, are the vegetables, hams and *charcuterie*, and superb fresh *brioches* and breads. The fresh flower stalls are beautiful too. **Barfleur**'s market is a more modest affair (*Tues and Sat*).

St-Vaast-la-Hougue ✉ 50550

Epicerie M. Gosselin, 25–27 Rue de Verrüe, t 02 33 54 40 06. Just about anything you can't find at the market you can get in this St-Vaast institution, founded in 1889. It has every kind of luxury foodstuff, from the many that are exclusive to the shop – terrines, coffees, jams, cheeses – to others from around the world. There's a renowned wine selection, and a whole room dedicated to calvados and whiskies. *Closed Mon.*

Poissonnerie Le Barbenchon, 4 Rue de Verrüe, t 02 33 22 21 00. Multi-prize-winning fish-monger, with a spectacular display of superbly fresh oysters, lobsters, sea bass, etc.

Where to Stay

Cosqueville ✉ 50330

Au Bouquet de Cosqueville, Hameau Remond (Plage du Vicq), t 02 33 54 32 81, f 02 33 54 63 38 (*double rooms 190–320F/ €28.97–48.78*). Best known as a restaurant, in a big, seaside granite house near one of the Val de Saire's most attractive beaches. The rooms vary in quality, but all are comfortable, and the best are bright, well fitted-out and have wonderful sea views. To find it, take the road signposted to Plage du Vicq, just east of Cosqueville village.

Fermanville ✉ 50840

Fort du Cap Lévy, t 02 33 23 68 68, f 02 33 23 68 69, *musee.fermanville@wanadoo.fr* (*double rooms 260F/€39.64, breakfast 30F/ €4.57*). The fortress at the end of Cap Lévy, built on Napoleon's orders to defend Cherbourg against British attack, has been

turned into a very unusual *chambre-d'hôte*, with six guest rooms which reveal the 'official' origins of the project in their rather functional fittings, but are well equipped, with all mod cons. The great draw of the Fort, however, is its extraordinary location, above all of its breakfast room, in a veranda high on the walls, with truly fabulous 180° views out to sea, just in the right place to catch the sunset.

Barfleur ✉ 50760

Hôtel le Conquérant, 16–18 Rue St-Thomas-Becket, t 02 33 54 00 82, f 02 33 54 65 25 (*rooms 200–400F/€30.49–60.98*). A very pleasant hotel in a big, four-square granite mansion, the main parts of which date from the 17th century, right on Barfleur's tranquil main thoroughfare. There's a beautiful little French-style garden at the back, where breakfast can be served in summer. The traditional rooms are airy, with a good range of comforts and some great views over the garden or on to the quiet street. The owners are very friendly, and there's a similarly good-value **restaurant** (*menus 80–125F/ €12.20–19.06*) that mainly offers crêpes and lighter dishes. *Closed mid-Nov–mid-Mar.*

Hôtel Moderne, 1 Place Charles de Gaulle, t 02 33 23 12 44, f 02 33 23 91 58 (*rooms 220–240F/€33.54–36.59, breakfast extra*). The Moderne has four, quite plain but cosily comfortable old-fashioned guest rooms, with decent bathrooms.

St-Vaast-la-Hougue ✉ 50550

Hôtel de France–Restaurant des Fuchsias, 20 Rue Maréchal Foch, t 02 33 54 42 26, f 02 33 43 46 79, *www.france-fuchsias.com* (*double rooms 165–460F/€25.15–70.13; demi-pension usually obligatory in July and Aug*). St-Vaast's classic hotel, snugly tucked into a street running away from the harbour, offers unchanging comfort. Beyond the pretty entrance patio lies a delightfully leafy garden, with the eponymous giant fuchsias. Chamber music concerts are played in the garden in August. The rooms are traditional and slightly chintzy, and vary in standard: the newer, larger ones in a garden annexe are the best. The restaurant is equally popular (*see below*). *Closed Jan and Feb.*

Tatihou Accueil, Quai Vauban, Tatihou, **t** 02 33 23 19 92, **f** 02 33 54 33 47, *www.tatihou.com* (*290F/€44.21 per person half-board, 335F/ €51.07 full-board; there's nowhere else to eat on the island, and at night you can't leave*). 35 guest rooms, in a converted small barracks built in 1818 – mainly orientated towards groups, but available to anyone. Rooms, mostly twins, are functional but quite comfortable, and the great thing is of course the location, location, location.

Montfarville ✉ 50760

Le Manoir, **t/f** 02 33 23 14 21 (*double 300F/ €45.73; suite 350F/€53.36 for two, 400F/ €60.98 for three*). A sombre-fronted 16th-century Cotentin granite manor house, beautifully decorated with antiques and personal mementoes to complement its giant fireplaces, and air of comfort. The rooms are large and full of light, and the breakfast room has a sea view; outside, there's a luxuriantly flowery garden. It's only about 2km south of Barfleur, and a short walk from the centre of Montfarville village.

Gatteville-le-Phare ✉ 50760

La Maison de Fourmi, Village de Roville, **t** 02 33 43 78 74, *maisonfourmi@voilà.fr* (*rooms 250F/€38.11 for two; one can be rented as a full-sized suite with ample space for four, 480F/€73.18*). A delightful B&B in a typical 18th-century farmhouse, run with great flair by Raymonde Roulland (known as Fourmi) and her husband Joseph. The rooms are decorated with photographs and artefacts from their many trips. In summer you can have breakfast in the pretty garden.

Eating Alternatives

Cosqueville ✉ 50330

Au Bouquet de Cosqueville, *see above* (*menus 110–210F/€16.77–32.01*). Eric Pouhier is one of the most highly regarded younger chefs in the Cotentin area. Seafood is naturally a speciality: some dishes are based on Norman cuisine, others, such as the trade-mark *cassolette de joue de raie aux cèpes* (a casserole of skate with cep mushrooms), are very much his own.

St-Vaast-la-Hougue ✉ 50550

Restaurant des Fuchsias, *see* Hôtel de France, above (*menus 85–300F/€12.96–45.73*). The menu is, of course, especially strong on seafood: local oysters, monkfish, sea bass, turbot, etc. in imaginatively light sauces. Fruity desserts are other highlights. For much of the year about half your fellow diners are likely to be English. *Closed Jan and Feb; Mar–June and Sept–Dec Mon.*

Le Débarcadère, Place de Gaulle, **t** 02 33 54 43 45 (*30–90F/€4.57–13.72*). A bright restaurant-brasserie with a big terrace looking on to the harbour, a laidback, buzzy atmosphere and a largely local clientele. Inside, there's a neat little dining area on one side, and a big screen for watching sports on the other. The menu offers plenty of choice, and is a real bargain, including pizzas and big plates of *moules-frites*.

Restaurant du Fort-Tatihou Accueil, *see* above. The café-restaurant on Tatihou has been expanded in the last few years, and offers a range of mixed salads, omelettes, crêpes and other light meals, with a few larger *plats du jour* (*c. 40–90F/€6.10–13.72*). Evening meals are only provided for residents. *Open April–Sept daily 12–3.*

La Pernelle ✉ 50360

Le Panoramique, **t** 02 33 54 13 79 (*menus from 100F/€15.24*). Right next to the church and the old German gun battery at the very top of La Pernelle hill, 123m up, this is a big, modern restaurant with giant panoramic windows and an ample outside terrace. The brasserie-style menu offers a wide choice of good value, fairly standard local fare – *moules* (*c. 40F/€6.10*), crêpes and *galettes* (*55F/€8.38*).

Montfarville ✉ 50760

Restaurant T'Cheu Suzanne, Rue de la Poste, **t** 02 33 54 04 54, **f** 02 33 54 60 63 (*menus 68–140F/€10.37–21.34*). A friendly bistro-bar-*tabac* in the centre of Montfarville, very near the church. The bargain menus offer a healthy range of local classics such as oysters, mussels, Normandy smoked ham or chicken in cider, fish grills, crêpes, *galettes* and salads.

The End
of the World:
Cap de la Hague

29

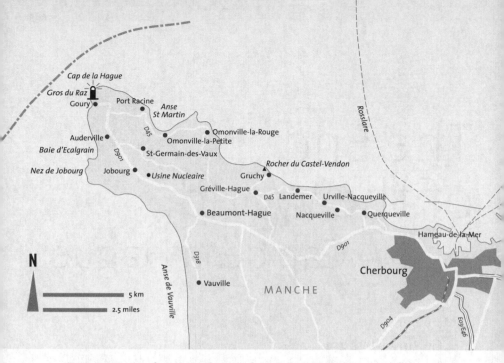

La Hague peninsula is a 15-mile arm of granite reaching out into the sea west of Cherbourg. From the very edge of the city's harbour, you enter a world of increasingly narrow lanes, sometimes virtually enclosed by towering hedgerows, and then opening up into bog and moorland running right to the rim of the massive cliffs that fall away into the surf. Intermittently, you come across little, huddled stone villages, built to withstand severe weather, that look as if they might house communities of Celtic Methodists were it not for the stout old Norman Catholic churches in the middle of each of them.

Another key feature of this landscape is its remarkable and surprising variety, for towards the centre of the peninsula, wherever there are valleys and corners sheltered from the wind, there are microclimates that are often astonishingly lush, soft and leafy. La Hague is exceptionally beautiful when the sun shines, when the wild flowers are out along the cliffs and you can watch the changing colours of the sea below; it's also a great and wild place to visit even if the weather is less favourable, when giant waves crash against the rocks and the Atlantic blasters are enough to clear anyone's head.

At the very end of the peninsula, where the landscape is at its most rugged, there is a little rocky inlet, long a refuge for endangered mariners, with a lighthouse that looks exactly how a lighthouse ought to look. This is Goury. There is a lifeboat station, a shingle beach, a few boats, about six or seven houses and, sometimes, a van selling sandwiches. There's also a surprisingly large tourist office, for the Cape attracts its share of visitors in summer. Still, it is the sense of isolation that predominates, and this seems an unlikely location for a fine-quality restaurant.

Getting There

There is a relatively quick route from Cherbourg to the end of La Hague, along the D901, which runs along the south side of the peninsula and will take you there in about 30–45mins.

To make a trip of it, though, take the much smaller D45, a right turn off the D901 on the way out of Cherbourg in Hameau-de-la-Mer (signposted to Querqueville), and then return by the south route. For most of its length the D45 winds along the north side of La Hague, with a few hairpin bends along the way. Most people will want to stop at a few points along the road, but if you drive straight down you should reach the Cape in a little under an hour. Both roads meet in Auderville, the last real village on the peninsula where, on one side of the widening of the roads that could be called the village square, there is a narrow lane signposted to Goury.

Alternatively, the energetic might take the GR223, the long-distance footpath which runs all the way round La Hague peninsula. It's clearly marked.

The nearest train station is in Cherbourg, from where there are frequent buses to Beaumont-Hague which less frequently continue on to Auderville.

Tourist Information

Beaumont-La Hague: Office de Tourisme de la Hague, 45 Rue Jallot, **t** 02 33 52 74 94, **f** 02 33 52 09 64, *Tourisme@lahague.org*.
Goury: **t** 02 33 04 50 26. *Open April–Oct and school hols.*

However, at the centre of the clutch of grey granite cottages is the **Auberge de Goury**, where owner Pascal Retout has presided since the end of the 1970s with amiable hyper-activity, throwing out rapid snatches of conversation to regulars in between attending to some of the cooking and much else. The style is casual and straightforward, but devotees often make their way here all the way from Cherbourg and beyond just for midweek lunch. When the weather's fine you can sit outside and watch the waves; at other times, when the wind is up, stout stone walls and the smell of the log fire on which the grilled fish is prepared, make you feel snug and sheltered, in a place once considered one of the ends of the known world.

L'Auberge de Goury

*Port de Goury, **t** 02 33 52 77 01. Open Tues–Sun 12–2 and 7–9.30; closed Mon. Book a day in advance, earlier for weekends. Menus 95F/€14.48, 115F/€17.53, 145F/€22.11, 190F/€28.97, 280F/€42.69 and 305F/€46.50; à la carte average 230F/€35.06.*

The menu at Goury now carries a poetic note that thanks everyone for coming, whoever they are and however they got here – by car, boat, through fog and Atlantic gales or by trekking along the footpath. This is of course a literary flourish, but once you're inside it does feel a little as if you've reached a refuge on some distant shore. All of which only encourages you to settle in, get comfortable and take your time, which is all to the good, since to be enjoyed properly a meal here can take a while. This is not due to any breakdown in organisation, but a reflection of the fact that this kind of food often takes some time to eat, and also that the goodness of the food stems above all from the sheer freshness and quality of the basic ingredients, and the

Douillon aux Pommes

The Douillon Normand is one of the simplest of the region's many classic fruit desserts, which can equally be made with pears (a *douillon aux poires*). For each person, take a large green apple, core it, and wrap it entirely in puff pastry; brush with beaten egg, place on a baking sheet and put in a hot oven, 200°C/400°F/Gas mark 6. Cook for 30 minutes or until the pastry is golden and the apples are tender (test with a skewer). Once cooked, serve them quickly on top of *crème fraîche* sprinkled with sugar, and, just before serving, add some apple compote on top of each *douillon* and flambé them with a dash of calvados (or if preferred just add the calvados to the apple compote).

attention to detail shown in the individual preparation of each dish. So, if there is any delay, it's as well to accept the offer of, maybe, a glass of champagne or kir and a plate of *crevettes grises*, and sit back at your table or stand at the little wooden bar for a few minutes while examining the décor, your fellow diners, and the lobsters and crabs manoeuvring in their tank.

The restaurant is comfortably characterful and traditional. Some parts are genuinely old, such as the main dining room with its plain stone walls and open fireplace, while others, such as the larger extension, are simple and modern. The clientele, similarly, are a broad mix – a few foreigners, local couples and families, and during the week groups of workmates who have probably converged from miles around.

If you eat just one course here, it has to be the grilled fish (red mullet, sea bass, sole, turbot, john dory or monkfish, according to what's best that day), cooked by Pascal Retout himself on the wood fire in the main dining room. Tinged with subtle flavours from the wood smoke, it's a revelation of how good simply but perfectly cooked fresh food can be. He uses mainly chestnut and hazel for the fire, and complains that it's increasingly difficult to find wood of sufficient quality, but fortunately seems to be assured of a supply for some time to come. There's some grilled fish (often sea bream) and a selection of smoked fish among the choices in the 95F four-course menu, while the 115F *menu du terroir* offers grilled lamb, as well as crab mayonnaise; if you can, though, go for the five-course 145F *menu gourmand*.

There are several choices for first course, including homemade duck terrine and a smooth fish soup, but the star must be the *assiette de fruits de mer*, a giant pile made up of oysters, a lobster claw, *langoustines*, half a large crab, clams, superlative prawns, *bulots* (large whelks), *bigorneaux* (winkles) and other things you may never have seen before, with a bowl of fabulous fresh mayonnaise on the side. This brings you into the meal gradually by forcing you to take your time and get to grips with your food, literally. Once you've finished, it's time to sample the grilled fish, or perhaps a *feuilleté* of monkfish, served with a deliciously delicate leek purée. There's also a daily fish *surprise du jour*, which might be a superb bowl of *moules à la crème*, the sauce of which is easily good enough to be offered separately as a soup.

After that the meat course might be expected to come as a bit of a letdown, but the grilled lamb, cooked on the other side of the fire from the fish, is of the highest quality, and the dish of the day might be an excellent version of a local classic such as *magret de canard*, served with vegetables and tasty *frites*.

The final courses are just as fine. In a region where competition is not exactly lacking, M. Retout also has an especially excellent cheese selection, which recently included a whole range of unusual varieties – Vieux Lisieux (rather like Pont l'Evêque, washed in calvados and spices), Cabourg, Ecstase, fine *chèvres* – as well as fine examples of all the Norman standards such as Camembert and Livarot. And there's still one more house favourite to come: one of the range of often boozy Norman apple or pear desserts, or maybe a sorbet, or the rich and pure chocolate mousse, before you round off your meal, well into the afternoon, with a good strong coffee.

The more expensive menus prominently feature lobster, hence the price. To drink, there's a reasonably priced wine list, with a fine refreshing saumur at 140F/€21.34 and muscadets at around 90F/€13.72. All this might seem rather a *grande bouffe*, but each course is so well executed, and each presented at such a comfortable pace, that you never feel overwhelmed. But you're unlikely to feel any need to eat again for the rest of the day.

Touring Around

The greatest glory of La Hague is the scenery. As you travel west along its northern flank you begin to get dramatic views over the sea from the fern- and heather-covered cliffs, while in between the road snakes back inland around abrupt narrow bends encased by dense hedgerows. One of the most beautiful routes around the Cape is the **GR223 footpath**, which is also known here as the Sentier des Douaniers, the Customs Officers' Path, since it originated as a track used to keep a check on smuggling among the rocks. It stays close to the shore and the cliff edge all the way around the peninsula from Querqueville, just outside Cherbourg, and only turns a little inland as it leaves La Hague beyond Vauville, in the south. Even if you don't want to take on the whole footpath, it's still easy to walk along it for a kilometre or so, as access to it is well indicated at several points along the D45 with the sign **Sentier Littoral**.

La Hague was also one of the areas of strongest Viking settlement in Normandy, and most of the place names ending in -ville indicate villages founded by Norse chieftains (Querqueville, 'Koki's ville', Auderville, 'Odern's ville', and so on). In **Querqueville**, almost before you have properly left Cherbourg, and with a lovely view back across the harbour, there is the tiny 10th-century, pre-Romanesque **Chapelle de St-Germain**, possibly the oldest church or chapel anywhere in western France and almost certainly the oldest still in use. It's a beautifully simple little building with bare rough-stone walls, almost hidden in the shadow of the much larger later village church. Many other villages around the peninsula – Gréville-Hague, Auderville, Jobourg and others – have churches dating back to the era of William the Conqueror and his immediate descendants in the 12th century.

A little to the west of Querqueville there is a turning for the mainly 16th-century **Château de Nacqueville** (*guided tours only; Easter–30 Sept Mon, Wed, Thurs, Sat and Sun every hour 2–5; adm*). A very elegant combination of French Renaissance château and local granite, it was built for the Grimouville family between 1510 and 1570, and later passed via various inheritances and marriages to the brother of the great 19th-century political writer and essayist Alexis de Tocqueville, author of *Democracy in America*, who wrote many of his works during summers here. It stands in one of the peninsula's sheltered valleys, and is surrounded by a luxuriant 'English-style' garden that was created for the anglophile de Tocquevilles by an English landscape artist in the 1830s. With broad lawns, artificial streams and ponds, and great beds of azaleas and rhodedendrons, it explodes into flower in May (note, though, that the staff do not share the garden's charm, and while there is no official minimum limit for the guided tours, if fewer than ten people turn up on a weekday or at the end of the day they may find the tour is cancelled).

Below the château, **Urville-Nacqueville** is a plain little village, but has a great, broad and breezy stone and pebble beach, interrupted by a few concrete remains of Second World War German blockhouses, that's very popular with kite-flyers and is good for playing in the waves.

Further west again, near the old hotel and viewpoint at Landemer (*see* p.295), there looms beside the D45 the much older-style manor of **Dur-Ecu** ('Strong Shield'; *open July and Aug: manor daily 3–7, maze daily 11–1 and 2–7; adm*), a massive, turreted granite pile that looks as if it could easily have been designed for a movie of a Poe story starring Vincent Price. A few years ago it was a closed-up, romantic semi-ruin, but it has now been restored and is open to visitors in summer. Its giant upper walls are 16th-century, but parts of the foundations date back to a 9th-century Viking stronghold; as well as the fortified manor itself and its attached manor farm there are watermills, a grand dovecote and a thickly wooded park.

Dur-Ecu's most unusual feature, though, is a recent addition, the **Labyrinthe** or 'Maize Maze' created in maize (corn) by British specialist maze designer Adrian Fisher, which is carefully replanted each year to keep it as intriguing and difficult to escape from as possible.

The Hague peninsula may feel remote even today, but it has certainly played its part in *la vie française*. **Gréville-Hague**, in a loop in the D45, was the birthplace of Jean-François Millet, and he painted its squat, typically Norman stone church and other parts of the village many times both before and after moving on to his more familiar themes of peasant life in the Seine valley.

The house where he was born in 1814, a short way back towards the sea in the beautiful little hamlet of Gruchy, has now been restored as the **Maison Natale du Jean-François Millet** (*open Mar Sun 1–6; April–May and Oct daily 1–6; June–Sept daily 11–7; adm*). It's an atmospheric old cottage, and an imaginative museum, centred on the one big room that was home to Millet, his parents, his eight brothers and sisters and their grandmother. Given that they were among the more prosperous inhabitants of Gruchy this is an eloquent indication of the simplicity of life on La Hague at that time. In other rooms there are paintings by him of scenes around the village, and exhibits on his moves to Paris and Barbizon, and the enormous influence he had on other painters, especially Van Gogh. Millet is much more than just one more artist in France: for many decades his work was more frequently reproduced than that of any other French painter, and it used to be said that there was a print of his *Angelus* (a peasant couple praying in the fields) in every home in the country. There's a room which shows some of the many uses made of his most familiar images, from plates, pepper-pots and kitsch gifts to packaging and beer-labels. From the house there's a fine short walk downhill along the narrow lane on to a footpath and then to a view-point above the sea, with a dramatic vista of Castel-Vendon, the huge, glowering mountain of rock just to the east. This was one of Millet's favourite walks, and he must have come here time and time again as a boy – he later did several paintings of the rock from this same spot, as you'll instantly recognise from the reproductions in the museum.

Omonville-la-Petite is further along the peninsula and inland, almost lost in another steep, sheltered valley. The contrast with the bleak and windblown moorland by the sea cliffs is extraordinary: the village and its little hollows are exceptionally quaint and lush, and are covered in bright flowers in summer.

Omonville was the last home of one of the great figures of modern French culture, the poet Jacques Prévert, author of *Paroles* (a fixture on the school syllabus in France), and of the scripts for many of the classics of the golden age of French cinema such as *Le crime de Monsieur Lange*, *Le jour se lève* and *Les enfants du paradis*. He died here in 1977, and his widow Janine stayed on in their house, an extremely pretty cottage with an exuberant garden, until her own death in 1993, since when it has been opened up as the **Maison de Jacques Prévert** (*open Mar Sun 1–6; April–May and Oct daily 1–6; June–Sept daily 11–7; adm*). Visitors must park next to the village churchyard, where both Préverts and their daughter Michelle are buried, and then walk up a quiet lane.

Rather than a display of Prévert effects, much of the house has been made into an exhibition space that each year hosts a single exhibition devoted to a related theme of one or other of his activities or acquaintances – painters such as Miró and Max Ernst, photographers like Robert Doisneau, other poets and his cinema work.

The museum's director says that given the range of Prévert's contacts and interests they have material for several years without repetition. There are also videos and many photographs of Prévert, which allow us to conclude that he shared with Jean Gabin the distinction of having perfected the well-known French technique of talking, eating and generally living with a cigarette clamped permanently in one side of the mouth at a 45-degree angle.

Still intact on the upstairs floor is his airy, comfortable living- and writing-room, which looks as if he might walk in at any moment; sometimes a tape is played – maybe of Juliette Gréco, or of Yves Montand singing another Prévert creation, 'Les Feuilles d'Automne', for which he wrote the lyrics – and the evocation of a certain period of French life couldn't be more complete.

Omonville-la-Rogue is an attractive little fishing port, the existence of which was first recorded in 1026. Here the road rejoins the coast, and from here west the terrain loses much of its leafiness and becomes much more wind-blasted and moor-like. Before reaching St-Germain-des-Vaux and Auderville, near the Cape, the road comes upon tiny **Port Racine**, an inlet of grey shingle with a few boats usually tied up, which a sign proclaims to be '*le port le plus petit de France*'. Since there are only two reasonably substantial buildings in the whole place nobody's likely to argue. There is also a special **garden** (*open Easter–Sept*) created in homage to Jacques Prévert by his friend Gérard Fasberti.

The coastline on the south side of La Hague is less inhabited and more open than the north, with sweeping bays of giant cliffs above empty, sandy beaches. If coming from Goury, take a sharp turn off the D901 in Auderville, signposted to Ecalgrain and Jobourg. This will take you to the viewpoint overlooking the **Baie d'Ecalgrain**, a magnificent arc of sand and surf, and then to the **Nez de Jobourg**, at 128m often described as the tallest cliffs in Europe. From both points you can easily see Alderney on a clear day, although at other times the wind may be enough to knock you straight back inland instead. Again, there are plenty of opportunities for walking along the GR223 footpath.

After you rejoin the main road at Jobourg village it soon becomes surprisingly wide. This indicates that you are about to pass the truly vast bulk of the Beaumont-La Hague **nuclear reprocessing plant**, also known as COGEMA, one of the symbols of official France's notorious modern love affair with all things nuclear. It's hard to know what to say about this giant carbuncle, which looms into the view at certain points around the peninsula; local opinion, in line with a traditional French gung-ho attitude towards technology, was for years quite accepting of it, but lately has become much more critical. As in all such installations, the administration are falling over themselves to invite the public in to have a look around, and anyone interested will find leaflets at all local tourist offices.

From Beaumont, the only town on the peninsula, you can continue on the D901 straight back to Cherbourg, or turn south on to the D318, a precipitously steep road that runs down a deep heather-lined valley to reach another wonderful, open bay, the **Anse de Vauville**, where there are miles of cliffs, an immense sandy beach, a campsite that's open in summer, a pizzeria and a bird sanctuary (*guided tours only; contact local tourist offices for details*).

Vauville itself is another of the more extraordinary villages of La Hague, with centuries-old stone houses, a Neolithic dolmen and an 11th-century priory, and a feel of being very far from the world amid its giant landscape.

Around the old stone manor of the **Château de Vauville** (*guided tours only; May and Sept Tues and Sun 2–6; June Tues, Sat and Sun 2–6; July and Aug daily 2–6; adm*) there's also a very unusual, semi-tropical botanical garden, which is rich in southern hemisphere plants. And, at the south end of the bay, there are stretches of beach where – unusually – it's actually suggested you can swim or windsurf as well as just watch the breakers.

Where to Stay

Urville-Nacqueville ✉ 50460

Hôtel-Restaurant Le Landemer, Landemer,
t 02 33 03 43 00, f 02 33 03 45 42 (*top-floor
rooms 280F/€42.69 with view, 260F/€39.64
without; first-floor rooms 135F/€20.58*). The
oldest hotel on La Hague peninsula, opened
in the 1850s, with one of the best possible
locations, on a bend in the coast road almost
jutting out above the cliffs. Millet painted
from its terrace, which has a famously
beautiful view along the red-green flanks of
the coast. Today the Landemer is a rather
eccentric, scruffy old hotel but it makes up
for the condition of its rooms with its location, loads of character, the amiably laidback
way it is run and low prices. There are nine
old-fashioned-cosy rooms, of which the four
on the top floor with their own bathrooms
are the most attractive, especially the two
with a sea view. The five on the first floor are
very simple, share bathrooms and are
among the cheapest around. The popular
restaurant has the same quirkiness as the
hotel (*see* below). Landemer is about half-
way between Urville-Nacqueville and
Gréville-Hague.

La Blanche Maison, 874 Rue St-Laurent, t 02 33
03 48 79 (*double room 220F/€33.54, extra
single bed 50F/€7.62*). A very pretty B&B in a
converted old farm on the north coast road
along the Hague peninsula, between Urville-
Nacqueville and Dur-Ecu manor. Thick
hedges on the land-side of the road make
the entrance hard to find: the house is actually quite near the road, but once you make
the sharp turn into the steep driveway you
enter one of the Hague's little pockets of
lushness, with an exceptionally dense, varied
and leafy garden. As you climb up the crest
you also get a fabulous view of the sea.
There's only one guest room, almost a self-
contained *gîte* in a separate part of the
ancient granite farm, with access to a kitchenette, and reached by a stone staircase.
Though only 10km from Cherbourg, it feels
very hidden and peaceful, and it's very close
to the GR223 footpath and Urville-
Nacqueville beach.

Gréville-Hague ✉ 50440

M and Mme Dumoncel, Hameau aux Fèvres,
t/f 02 33 52 75 80 (*room 200F/€30.49 for
two*). The spectacular location is the great
draw of this very peaceful B&B. The Hameau
aux Fèvres is a tiny cluster of houses above
the main village of Gréville-Hague, reached
via a very steep, winding lane that turns off
the coastal D45 near Landemer. Once at the
top, maybe after thinking more than once
that you must be on a road to nowhere,
you'll find a few granite cottages scattered
among trees and gardens, of which this
farm is the largest; turn around, and laid out
far below you is the sea, and an almost infinite horizon. The one guest room is more
like a suite, with one double room and a
possible annexe room with twin beds; it's
simply and comfortably decorated, and gets
loads of light. The hamlet is great for
walking, although getting there without a
car is very difficult.

Auderville ✉ 50440

Hôtel du Cap, t 02 33 52 73 46, f 02 33 01 56 30
(*double rooms 230–240F/€35.06–36.59,
breakfast 27F/€4.12*). Occupying a very solid
old Norman farmhouse with a large farmyard on one side – now made into a pretty
garden – and fields falling away to the sea
on the other, this pleasantly relaxed hotel
has eight big, fairly modern and comfortable
rooms. Seven have fine sea views through
the eaves; the room on the ground floor is
fully adapted for disabled guests. The staff
are quietly charming and helpful.

Omonville-la-Petite ✉ 50440

Hôtel La Fossardière, Hameau de la Fosse,
t 02 33 52 19 83, f 02 33 52 73 49 (*double
rooms 260–370F/€39.64–56.41*). One of the
most comfortable options on La Hague, in a
delicious location. The tiny hamlet of La
Fosse seems like a micro-climate within the
micro-climate of Omonville-la-Petite, a snug
little dip in the ground where all kinds of
plants and flowers almost leap out of the
granite walls. The hotel's ten rooms are
distributed between two almost-adjacent
former cottages. The conversion is ingenious
but cannot work miracles, and some rooms

are a bit dark. All the rooms are attractively decorated and have good bathrooms and other comforts. Breakfast is served in the former village bakery, which is also used as a bar. The English-speaking owner, Gilles Fossard, runs the hotel with a certain flair, and among the other extras is a small sauna. *Closed 15 Nov–15 Mar.*

Hôtel St-Martin des Grèves, t 02 33 01 87 87, **f** 02 33 01 87 88 (*double rooms 220–290F/ €33.54–44.21*). In a big granite house by the D45 west of Omonville-la-Petite, overlooking Anse St-Martin bay and Port Racine, the St-Martin has 22 rooms distributed between the main house and a garden annexe. They have all been renovated in the last few years, and are simple and pleasantly comfortable. The five rooms at the front have a great sea view, and there's a large garden.

Eating Alternatives

Auderville ✉ 50440

Auberge d'Auderville, t 02 33 52 77 44 (*menus 59–95F/€8.99–14.48*). An unfussy restaurant-brasserie-*tabac* in the middle of Auderville village, with straightforward menus of Norman classics such as grilled fish, mussels or ham in cider, appley desserts and lighter options like omelettes and mixed salads. When weather permits there's an outside terrace.

Le Nez de Jobourg ✉ 50440

Auberge des Grottes, t 02 33 52 71 44 (*menus 99–340F/€15.09–51.83*). Location is everything for this much-loved restaurant, high up on the cliffs of Jobourg, with a fabulous view, on a clear day, out to Alderney and beyond. When the weather closes in, it's romantically windblown and isolated, a capsule far from the world. It also gains from the welcoming personality of chef and owner, Henri-Paul Fauvel. The menu offers Norman and seafood specialities, but the star choice is the speciality *menu haguard*, highlighting lobster, *gigot d'agneau* and *crêpes au calvados*. In the afternoons the Auberge remains open as a *salon de thé-crêperie* (*sweet and savoury crêpes 20–25F/ €3.05–3.81*).

Urville-Nacqueville ✉ 50460

Hôtel-Restaurant Le Landemer, *see* above (*menus 89–165F/€13.57–25.15*). The hotel's ground-floor restaurant offers generous meals of local seafood and classic Norman dishes, and is a popular local call-in with as much of a casual, no-frills feel as the hotel, rather like a hillside bistro. Its most popular attraction, though, is the wonderful view from its panoramic dining room and celebrated terrace, as enjoyed by Millet in the 1870s.

St-Germain-des-Vaux ✉ 50440

Le Moulin à Vent, Hameau Danneville, **t** 02 33 52 75 20, **f** 02 33 52 22 57 (*menus 98F/€14.94 (Mon–Fri), menu du terroir 170F/€25.92, children's menu 45F/€6.86*). One of the most highly regarded restaurants on La Hague, in another remarkable location high up above Port Racine on the road inland to St-Germain-des-Vaux, with an old disused stone windmill alongside it. The view and the freshness of the air are fabulous, and there's a very pretty garden and summer terrace for making the most of them (look south from the mill, unfortunately, and you see the Beaumont-Hague nuclear facility, but this can be avoided). The food is as renowned as the setting. Fish and seafood *'cuisine de la mer'* are chef Michel Briens' specialities, especially lobster, grilled over a wood fire and served in various different ways, and platters of oysters and mussels, which feature in the *menu du terroir* along with superbly fresh fish, maybe red mullet or John Dory, chosen entirely according to the day's catch. The wood-baked bread and the excellent range of Norman cheese and rich desserts are as impressive as the main delicacies. *Closed Sun eve and Mon.*

Vauville ✉ 50440

Les Tamarins, Belle Rive, **t** 02 33 04 74 04 (*dishes 60–100F/€9.15–15.24*). A handy and welcoming pizzeria-grill near the beach in Vauville, in an old Cotentin stone cottage with a pleasant outside terrace at the bottom of the giant hill. It offers excellent pizzas, salads, sandwiches, drinks and occasional fish or meat grills.

Castles and Dunes:
the Western Cotentin Coast

30

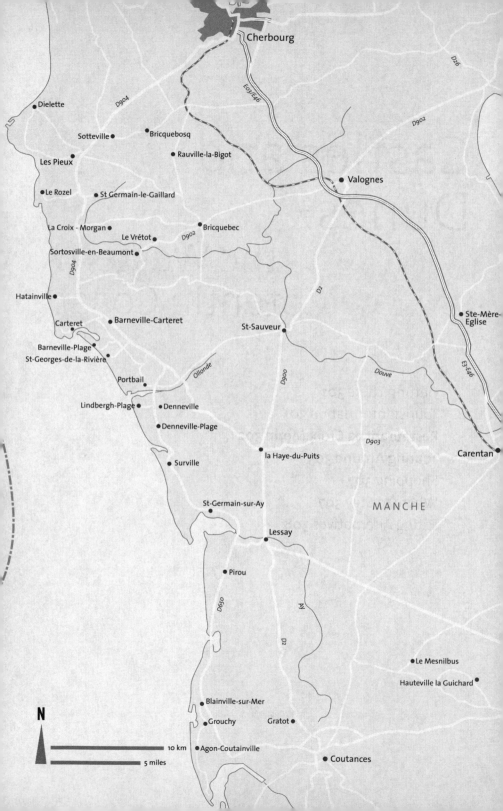

Getting There

From Cherbourg the D904 – signposted to Barneville-Carteret – will take you into the *bocage* countryside and towards the coast. From Caen and the east, leave the N13 at Carentan for the D903 westwards via La Haye-du-Puits to Portbail and Barneville-Carteret. The coastal footpath, the GR223, hugs the shoreline all the way down to Mont St-Michel.

To get to La Croix Morin from Barneville Carteret, take the D902 towards Bricquebec and, after about 10km, look for a sharp turning left for Le Vretot; instead of going into Le Vretot village, look for a little sign to the left for La Croix Morin. From Cherbourg on the D904 look for a lane signposted to Bricquebec, opposite a turning off coastwards to Surtainville, which eventually meets the road from Le Vretot at La Croix Morin crossroads. Don't be put off if either road seems to be going nowhere: they do.

The nearest mainline station is in Valognes, but a private Train Touristique runs along the old line between Carteret and Portbail (*June–Sept Tues, Thurs and Sun*). Coutances has train connections with Avranches and Paris (Gare Montparnasse), and there is a bus service between Coutances and Cherbourg.

There are ferries to the Channel Islands (passenger-only): from Carteret and Portbail to Jersey (*mid-April–mid-Oct*), and from the tiny port of Dielette, just north of Les Pieux, to Guernsey (*mid-April–mid-Oct*). There is also an infrequent service to Alderney (*May–Sept*). For information, call Carteret, t 02 33 52 61 39.

Tourist Information

Barneville-Carteret: 10 Rue des Ecoles, Barneville, t 02 33 04 90 58, f 02 33 04 93 24, *tourisme.barneville-carteret@wanadoo.fr* (*closed Sun*). There is also an office in Place Flandres-Dunkerque, Carteret, t 02 33 04 94 54 (*Easter–Oct daily*).

Coutances: Place Georges Leclerc, t 02 33 19 08 10, f 02 33 19 08 19.

Lessay: 11 Place St-Cloud, t 02 33 45 14 34.

Les Pieux: 6 Rue Centrale, t 02 33 52 81 60, f 02 33 52 86, 79.

St-Sauveur-le-Vicomte: Place Auguste Cousin, t 02 33 21 50 44.

The west coast of the Cotentin peninsula – sometimes called the Côte des Iles because it faces, and has a good deal of contact with, the Channel Islands – contains a whole collection of contrasts and characteristics: an individual mix of cragginess and gentility. Its shore is one of the wildest shores on France's Atlantic coast – a long line of windswept grassy dunes beside immense sandy beaches and crashing surf, with fierce currents that often make swimming hazardous. Every so often there are inlets leading to old fishing villages, or small family seaside resorts, with seafront restaurants and *crêpe*-stands. Scattered among the dunes, rather overwhelmed by the landscape, are clutches of eccentrically ornate Belle Epoque villas, or more contemporary holiday cottages. Inland, there are some of the most untouched and rustic villages and unspoilt countryside you'll find anywhere in France.

The Western Cotentin's role in world affairs peaked a long time ago. It was one of the most important areas of early Viking settlement in Normandy, and men from here travelled with William the Conqueror to England, and set out on the still greater adventure that would see a Norman kingdom established in 12th-century Sicily. Since this flurry of activity nearly a thousand years ago, and apart from a few wartime interludes, the region has generally kept to itself. Its early prominence, however, is reflected in the presence of some of the finest works of Norman Romanesque architecture: great monuments such as the abbey at Lessay and Coutances Cathedral, and fortified village churches. There are also many early medieval warrior castles, with battlements, turrets and crumbling walls.

In food the Western Cotentin shows as many contrasts as in anything else. In the little resorts on the coast there are simple *crêperies*, and restaurants that serve freshly caught fish and seafood with all the subtlety and niceties associated with metropolitan catering. Inland, restaurants are surprisingly thin on the ground, and the fare tends to stay close to its straightforward Norman roots. For anyone who really wants to get in touch with the remote, rural side of the area, a rare experience awaits at La **Croix Morin**, a little inn at a lonely road junction deep in the fields between Bricquebec and the coast.

La Croix Morin

Le Vretot ✉ 50260, t 02 33 52 22 64. Open Mon–Fri and Sun 8am–8pm; mid-Nov–mid-Mar also open Sat from 7pm by reservation; always book for evening and Sunday meals, as the opening hours can be a little eccentric. Menus 57F/€8.69, 65F/€9.91 and 85F/€12.96 (Sun midday); à la carte average 70F/€10.67.

Many people still have a Stella Artois or Jean de Florette fantasy of France at the back of their minds. That is, the hope of walking into an utterly basic village inn with stone walls and gnarled wooden tables, wholesome country cooking and the local brew served in jugs – costing next to nothing and soaked in authenticity. This is pretty hard to find, and La Croix Morin may not entirely fit the bill, but – due to its simplicity – even locals speak of it with a certain awe, as if they're surprised to find it still exists.

The 'Croix Morin' itself is an isolated crossroads in one of the wilder parts of the Cotentin countryside, and the restaurant is a small, whitewashed old inn beside it. Inside there's an old-fashioned country dining room, with benches and long communal tables topped with plastic cloths running away from the fireplace, where Mme Lefey, a charming, if matter-of-fact, Norman woman, will be tending the day's grilled meats. There's also a larger but less atmospheric room that's used in the evenings and on Sundays. Outside there's a luxuriant vegetable and herb garden.

The basic lunch menu begins with an '*hors-d'oeuvre* of the day', which might be a bowl of thick pieces of smoked herring (ie kippers) with boiled potatoes in a vinai-grette. To follow, there's grilled meats, the house speciality: sausages, *côte de porc*, lamb chops and more, all beautifully cooked over the wood fire, and served with *frites* or a bowl of garden peas. The Sunday lunch menu might include starters such as *jambon au porto*, as well as a still wider range of chargrilled meat.

These are followed by Camembert and other classic Norman cheeses, served on a big slab of wood. For dessert there might be a classic *tarte aux pommes*, or maybe *riz au lait* (rice pudding). The weekday menu includes a choice of wine or, for preference, a generous bottle of dry local cider, drawn from the barrel.

La Croix Morin's renowned speciality, though, is its kippers. Fat, flavour-rich herrings are available from November to March, and are freshly smoked over the fire and served up with *frites* and a few veg in *soirées harengs* (kipper-feasts), evening sessions that have something of a legend about them (and must be booked well in advance).

Touring Around

The D904 that cuts across the top of the Cotentin turns south to follow more or less the line of the coast at Les Pieux, a business-like little country town. All along it narrow lanes run off between the hedgerows toward the sea. At **Le Rozel**, as well as an extraordinary château that's now a B&B (*see* p.307), there is a majestic rocky crag, the **Pointe du Rozel**, which looms over the sands on either side. Immediately to the south, **Surtainville** has one of the most beautiful beaches on the whole coast, almost 3km long, an immense, empty space of open dunes, full of birds, and limitless skies framed on one side by the red cliffs of the Pointe du Rozel. **Hatainville**, further south, is another great, wild beach, and has a semi-official nudist section at its southern end. Note, though, that these beaches are unsupervised by life guards, and strong currents and shifting sands mean that you should not attempt to swim here, nor go out of your depth; and neither beach has much in the way of shops or bars.

Inland the countryside is as impressive in a different way. To the north, around Bricqueboscq and Rauville-la-Bigot – only a few kilometres outside Cherbourg – there is one of the densest patches of *bocage* **country** in Normandy (for an explanation of *bocage, see* p.310), a world of steep hills, huge hedges and lanes so narrow they barely let tractors pass. Further south, this gives way to stretches of unbroken forest or moorland. Villages pop up unexpectedly, making it an intriguing area to explore, especially if you're looking for cider and other traditional produce from small-farm producers.

The market hub of this part of the *bocage* is **Bricquebec**, an engaging country town with a pleasantly relaxed pace. The centre of town is still very much its Norman motte-and-bailey castle, the Vieux Château, the giant keep or donjon of which, begun in the 11th century and last rebuilt in the 14th, dominates the view from miles around, while the walled courtyard forms the town's most attractive square. In the clock tower next to the main keep is the **Musée Municipal** (*open for guided tours mid-June–Aug Mon, Wed–Sun 10–12 and 2–6.30; closed Tues; adm*), which mainly deals with Cotentin folk traditions and rural life, although you can also climb up part of the donjon and descend into a 13th-century crypt. Another part of the castle is occupied by the Auberge du Vieux Château (*see* p.307). Bricquebec has some attractive small shops, and hosts the largest country market in the northern Cotentin (*every Mon*), and its biggest festival, the Fête de Ste-Anne (*last weekend in July*). Just north of town is the **Abbaye de Notre-Dame-de-Grâce**, a Cistercian Trappist monastery 'refounded' after the Revolution in 1824. It has a retreat centre, and a visitor centre with a video-exhibit on the life of the community (*open pm only*).

Southeast of Bricquebec, a very pretty, wooded road leads to **St-Sauveur-le-Vicomte**, another rather sleepy, historic country town centred on a still more impressive castle, also called the **Vieux Château** (*guided tours June–Sept daily 2–6; adm*). Begun in around the year 1000, it was rebuilt and extended in the 14th century by the English during the Hundred Years' War, when it was a major stronghold that was fought over several times; today, its massive grey and yellow stone towers seem to dwarf the rest of the town.

Barneville-Carteret, back on the coast, is the main resort centre of the Côte des Iles, although it's still rather modest by the standards of Trouville or other places further south. It consists of three parts, united in one municipality since 1965: **Barneville**, a historic old village on a hill overlooking the narrow estuary of the River Gerfleur; **Carteret**, a fishing port on the north side of the estuary that's now at least half-used by yachts; and **Barneville-Plage**, to the south, a seaside suburb of neat holiday villas in lines parallel to the beach.

Barneville still has very much a casual, country-village feel. It also has a very fine Norman-Romanesque church, **St-Germain**, built in around 1140 but subsequently altered many times, most strikingly with a castle-like battlemented tower from the 15th century – this would have served as a watch-tower against English marauders during the Hundred Years' War; similar examples can be seen all along the peninsula.

Barneville-Carteret is a low-key little resort, with two good beaches which are sheltered and have lifeguards: Barneville-Plage is the largest, the family beach, while the one beyond the end of the harbour in Carteret is prettier. Carteret is the main focus of animation in town, with its yachting marina and an attractive port-side promenade, but only one street that's a little chic, the **Rue de Paris**, with the local gourmets' favourite, the Hôtel de la Marine, and a few smartish shops. Above the harbour, roads lead past balconied Belle Epoque villas to peter out by the lighthouse at the top of Cap de Carteret, a magnificent rocky point from where you get superb views over the coast to the north and south, and of cormorants on the rocks below. North of the cape you can walk down to another beach, which joins up with the dunes at Hatainville.

St-Georges-de-la-Rivière, a summer seaside village just below Barneville-Plage, has some of the most impressive dunes along the whole coast, and contains the **Maison de la Dune information centre** (*usually open June–Sept only; closed Sun*), which has good information on local birdlife. **Portbail**, a few kilometres further south at the mouth of the River Ollonde, has a particularly lovely harbour. Each side of the bay is very flat, and the quality of the light is as striking as the crisp air. On a spit of land at the mouth of the inlet are the quay for the Jersey ferries and the beach, a great bank of sand and shingle; they are joined by a long, low causeway to the original village on the mainland, a classic Norman fishing village with a few restaurants around the harbour. Unmissable from every angle is the almost bizarre, pyramid-topped monolithic tower of the church of **Notre-Dame**, one of the oldest Norman churches, begun in the early 11th century but with fortifications added in the 15th. Alongside are the remains of a 4th-century AD **Gallo-Roman baptistry** (*open for guided tours July–Aug Mon–Sat 10–11.30 and 3–6.30; at other times enquire at tourist office; adm*), the only one of its kind in France north of the Loire.

A detour inland, up the D15 towards St-Sauveur-le-Vicomte, quickly leads to the delightful *bocage* village of **Canville-la-Rocque**, with its impressive 12th-century church. The church's greatest treasures are some rare 16th-century naive frescoes (only discovered in the 1980s), evidently dating from the time when this was a stop on the pilgrim route to Santiago de Compostela. They tell in fascinating and moralistic detail the legend of a pilgrim who was distracted from his goal by a deceitful woman.

South of Portbail, along the coast, many of the beaches are completely and atmospherically empty (and you need to be wary of the current). **Lindbergh-Plage** is a very open, deserted spot, so named because this is where Charles Lindbergh crossed the French coast on his solo Atlantic flight in 1927; **Denneville** is a little more built up, with an hotel and shelter provided by a plantation of pines; **Surville** has miles of empty dunes, and a small *crêperie* at one end in summer. A little further on the road bends inland around the estuary of the River Ay, and the old Norman village of **St-Germain-sur-Ay**, with its dark, very remote church founded in 1190. South of the Ay, **Pirou-Plage** is almost a little seaside town, with seafront restaurants; **Anneville** and **Blainville** are two of the most attractive, undisturbed points along this stretch of coast; while **Agon-Coutainville** is a not especially attractive mini-resort of holiday homes.

Inland, a road cuts off the coast road near St-Germain-sur-Ay to **Lessay**, an important centre for the marketing and processing of the products of the Cotentin's farms, with some interesting traditional food producers (*see* p.307). Its greatest attraction is the massive **Abbatiale de la Ste-Trinité** (*church open daily 9–7; abbey buildings open for guided tours only July–Aug daily 10–12 and 2.30–6.30; adm for tours*) in the middle of town. Its current state of completeness is somewhat deceptive, for Lessay saw some of the heaviest fighting in Normandy in 1944. After the war the abbey underwent a remarkable 12-year restoration programme, making use as much as possible of stone from the same sources as the original. With its immensely long nave, the abbey church must be among the very finest in Normandy for sheer, awe-inspiring beauty. It was founded in 1056, and was the first ever Norman building to have Gothic-transition ogival vaults, but it is the effect of its plain, soaring simplicity that is completely timeless. The other abbey buildings are closed to visitors for most of the year, but were in any case mostly built in the 18th century, and are far less interesting.

To the south is the **Lande de Lessay**, a flat plain with a mixture of *bocage*, moorland and marsh. Still half-unnoticed within it are two unmissable castles. Because the Cotentin was left poor and unfashionable throughout France's golden era from the 16th to the 18th centuries, few fundamental alterations were ever made to them, and they remain as extraordinarily intact monuments to the Middle Ages.

The **castle of Pirou** (*open Nov and Dec, Feb–Easter Mon, Wed–Sun 10–12 and 2–5.30; closed Tues; Easter–Oct Mon, Wed–Sun 10–12 and 2–6.30; closed Tues exc July and Aug; adm; joint ticket available with Abbaye de La Lucerne*), reached via a winding lane off the D650 coast road south of Lessay, was actually entirely forgotten until the 1960s, overgrown amid the fields. Since then it has been cleaned and opened up, but still retains an extraordinary sense of ancientness. In its origins Pirou is the oldest of all the castles in Normandy, for there was almost certainly a stronghold here that resisted Viking attacks in the 9th century. By the 11th century it had passed by marriage to the Norman lord Serlon, son of Tancrède de Hauteville, founding patriarch of the Norman conquerors of Sicily. As the eldest son Serlon remained in Normandy when his father and brothers went off to Italy. The castle saw a great deal of action during the Hundred Years' War, and subsequently was inhabited by various families of minor nobles. By the 19th century it was semi-abandoned, supposedly full of ghosts, and used by smugglers from Jersey.

The main structure of the existing castle is 12th-century, upon an older base. As you approach it along a leafy farm track, there is a remarkable perspective through three successive entrance gates, beyond which you have to do almost a complete circuit of the moat before reaching the bridge to the castle itself. Pirou looks exactly like a child's drawing of a castle, with its moat, giant slate and granite walls, turrets and battlements. The guardhouse is one of the oldest parts of Pirou, with a huge fireplace with a one-piece stone lintel. Beyond it there is a cramped inner courtyard, with tumbledown houses built in the 17th and 18th centuries. From one corner of the courtyard you can climb to the battlements, up precipitous staircases and through narrow doorways. From the very top of the tower you can clearly appreciate Pirou's domination of the plain, with wonderful views right out to sea.

The other castle, **Gratot** (*unlimited access; honesty box for donations*), nearer Coutances, looks just like a picture-book castle, with pepperpot turrets, massive granite walls and a wide moat. The main part of it is 14th-century, although additions continued to be made until the 18th. It was the stronghold of the Argouges clan, the most celebrated of which was the maverick Chevalier Jean d'Argouges, who played a double game in the Hundred Years' War and won eternal opprobrium in France by handing over Granville to the English for hard cash. The last scion of the Argouges, a humble artillery captain, sold his château in 1777. Gratot then passed through various owners, but was still occupied, as a farm, at the turn of the 20th century. A wedding was due to be held there in 1914, when part of the roof fell in on the banqueting tables, fortunately before the guests had arrived. This finally convinced the last owner to give it up as a bad job. It was entirely derelict by 1968, when restoration was begun by local volunteers. Today Gratot is used in summer as a venue for festivals and other cultural events. At other times, you may well have it to yourself.

East of here is a beautiful stretch of sometimes almost impenetrably dense *bocage* countryside. The pretty, little village of **Le Mesnilbus** has an enjoyable country *auberge* (*see* p.308) and is a good place to find footpaths or go pony trekking through the woods. It also contains a very odd little war memorial, the tail and engine of a US Thunderbolt aircraft that crashed nearby in July 1944.

Coutances, capital of the central Cotentin, is a quiet town built, like Avranches, on one of the tallest hills the Normans could find. It's a town of fine churches, and has a wonderful **cathedral**, whose enormously tall twin spires dominate all approaches to the town – and can even be seen from Jersey on a good day. First built in plain Norman style in the 11th century, it was rebuilt in the 13th, but its Gothic façade is unlike any other – an entirely unique Norman combination of elaborate traceries and strangely modern, almost rocket-like false towers. Around the outside there are some great gargoyles, of smiling sheep and growling dogs. Another of the sights of Coutances is the Second-Empire **Jardin Public**, which stands out among the many similar French formal parks for its superb view and the dazzling colours of its lush and intricate flower beds.

Shopping

The largest country market in the Cotentin is in **Bricquebec** (*Mon*): **Coutances** has a street market (*Thurs*). There is a market in **Barneville** village (*Sat*), and in summer there are also markets in **Carteret** (*Thurs*) and **Barneville-Plage** (*Sun*). Several of the traditional food and craft establishments in the Cotentin form part of a semi-official Route de la Table (details from all tourist offices).

Bricquebec ✉ 50260

Charcuterie Artisanale Guilbert, 18 Rue Armand Levéel, **t** 02 33 52 20 65. A tiny shop near the château, selling traditional Norman pork products – *boudin noir* (black pudding), *andouilles*, pork terrines and *rillettes*, and smoked hams – and is best known locally for superb smoked sausages. *Closed Tues.*

Lessay ✉ 50430

Fromagerie du Val d'Ay-Fromagerie Réo, Rue de la Laiterie, **t** 02 33 46 41 33, **f** 02 33 46 07 54. Better-known simply as Réo, from its most-used label, this small, modern dairy produces high-quality Camembert, butter and crème fraîche. It is signposted (just Réo) off the D2 through Lessay, but it takes a few turns to find it. *Tours with free tastings July–mid-Sept Mon–Fri 10–12 and 2–4; shop open April–Sept Mon–Fri, at other times Fri am or by appointment.*

Bricqueboscq ✉ 50340

M Emile Mahieu, Hameau Les Mesles, **t** 02 33 04 41 19. A small-farm cider producer in a knot of very dense *bocage* south of the D904, a little north of Bricqueboscq. The unfermented apple juice, *pommeau* and ciders are crisp and fresh, and the fragrant calvados is superb. You can also buy apple jam and *confiture de lait* (ie toffee spread).

Sortosville-en-Beaumont ✉ 50270

Maison du Biscuit, **t** 02 33 04 09 04. A company dedicated to craft biscuit-making, with a big shop and a pretty little *salon de thé*. Their own range includes delicious handmade *palets* and *galettes normandes*, ladies fingers, cookies, *petits-fours*, *pains d'epice*, etc. They also sell jams, vinegars, soaps, gourmet foods, and other goodies. *Closed Jan, and Oct–May Mon.*

Le Rozel ✉ 50340

La Mielle, **t** 02 33 52 41 62. A small farm near the dunes by Le Rozel, where M and Mme Connefroy produce and sell award-winning crème fraîche, cottage cheese, butter and yogurt, and also asparagus in summer. It takes a bit of finding. *Open Sept–June Mon–Sat am only; July and Aug daily.*

Where to Stay

Bricquebec ✉ 50260

Auberge du Vieux Château, **t** 02 33 52 24 49, **f** 02 33 52 62 71 (*double rooms 300–495F/ €45.73–75.46*). One of Normandy's first 'château-hotels', inside the massive, half-ruined Norman keep, in the manor house built on to the castle in the later Middle Ages. It has a lot of old-fashioned charm, and Queen Victoria slept here in 1857.

Canville-la-Rocque ✉ 50580

Les Buttes, La Rue, **t** 02 33 53 03 06 (*rooms 250F/€38.11 for two, 350F/€53.35 for four*). A delightful *chambre-d'hôtes* in a distin-guished old Cotentin-granite farmhouse finely restored and filled with an impressive antiques collection. One of the rooms has an old Norman box-bed in carved wood, with doors for you to shut yourself in at night, and M and Mme Frugier are friendly hosts.

Le Rozel ✉ 50340

Le Château de Rozel, **t** 02 33 52 95 08 (*rooms 480F/€73.17 for two, 680F/€103.66 for three*). One of the most extraordinary B&Bs in the Cotentin; the shape of this fortified castle-farm is still that of a Norman keep: around it there's a 14th-century turret and walls, 16th-century pepperpot towers and an 18th-century main house. The huge suite has a double bedroom, antique furniture, and an extra room if you need it.

Barneville-Carteret ✉ 50270

Hôtel de la Marine, 11 Rue de Paris, **t** 02 33 53 83 31, **f** 02 33 53 39 60 (*rooms 440–620F/ €67.07–94.51 for two*). Plush, traditional comforts and a great location: at high tide, the harbour-side rooms – some of which have balconies – are right above the water. The rooms are quiet and comfortable, with excellent facilities. *Closed mid-Nov–mid-Feb.*

Hôtel de Paris, Place de l'Eglise, **t** 02 33 04 90 02, **f** 02 33 04 01 13 (*double rooms 190–300F/€28.96–45.73*). A straightforward, friendly Logis hotel on the main square in Barneville village. It has a pleasant **restaurant** (*menus 89–125F/ €13.57–19.05*) which serves local seafood and Norman classics, and has a charming pavement terrace.

Surville ✉ 50250

La Huberdière, t 02 33 07 97 24 (*rooms 300–390F/€45.73–59.45 for two, 450F/€68.6 for four*). An attractive B&B near the beach in an ivy-clad, Belle Epoque villa, surrounded by a lovely garden. Although quite near the coast road, in general it's a peaceful spot.

Blainville-sur-Mer ✉ 50560

M and Mme Sebire, 11 Rue du Vieux Lavoir, Village Grouchy, **t/f** 02 33 47 20 31 (*rooms 230/€35.06 for two, 280F/€42.68 for three*). In a converted 17th-century house in the former fishing hamlet of Grouchy, between Blainville and Agon-Coutainville. The B&B rooms are comfortable, and there's a lounge. It's only a kilometre from the beach, and guests have free use of bikes.

Eating Alternatives

Le Mesnilbus ✉ 50490

Auberge des Bonnes Gens, t 02 33 07 66 85 (*menus 95–140F/€14.48–21.34*). A very popular *auberge du terroir* in a giant old granite inn. Local produce and seafood are used to create hearty feasts of Norman classics, and there's a decent choice of beers and wines, as well as cider and calvados. It also has four simple **rooms** (*140F/€21.34 for two*). *Open Oct–Easter by reservation only; closed Sun eve and Mon.*

Bricquebec ✉ 50260

Auberge du Vieux Château, *see above* (*menus 80–170F/€12.2–25.91*). Meals are served in the former Knights' Hall, between stone pillars

and baronial fireplaces. The food – Norman classics like *moules à la crème, lapin au cidre* or roast lamb – is not as impressive as the setting, but still enjoyable.

Sortosville-en-Beaumont ✉ 50270

Le Berlingot, t 02 33 53 87 16 (*menus 78F/€11.89 and 98F/€14.94*). This unassuming restaurant-*crêperie*, off the D902, is very popular for its quality food at low prices: steaks and other meats grilled on an open fire, salads, crêpes and *galettes* (*under 50F/€7.62*). Service is charming and it's often necessary to book. *Closed Tues, Wed and mid-Nov–Mar.*

St-Germain-le-Gaillard ✉ 50340

Ferme-Auberge de Bunehou, t 02 33 52 80 69, **f** 02 33 52 84 29 (*menus 85–135F/ €12.96–20.58, children's menu 45F/€6.86*). A popular *ferme-auberge* 4km inland from Les Pieux. Meals are served in two large dining rooms, and outside there are ponds, and a kids' play area. Classic Norman country cooking uses farm produce – chicken *au cidre* or roast duck, local cheeses, *teurgoules* and homemade ice-cream. In theory it's for groups only (*exc Fri–Sun*), but check when calling and they might fit you in. *Closed Feb–mid-Mar; booking essential.*

Barneville-Carteret ✉ 50270

Hôtel de la Marine, *see above* (*weekday and Sat lunch menus 150–450F/€22.87–68.6; otherwise, à la carte c. 350F/€53.35*). The premier restaurant along the Côte des Iles in a wonderful location, right on the harbour's edge. Chef Laurent Cesne's best dishes feature fresh local seafood, often in elaborate combinations, and his lobster and *coquilles St-Jacques* dishes are renowned. *Closed mid-Nov–mid-Feb; Feb–Mar and Oct Sun eve; Mon midday exc July and Aug.*

Le Gohan, Rue des Rivières, Hameau de Bas, **t** 02 33 04 95 33, **f** 02 33 04 27 75 (*menus 75–135F/€11.43–20.58, children's menu 33F/ €5.03*). A popular restaurant-grill-*crêperie* in a converted farmhouse between Barneville and Barneville-Plage. Meats and fresh fish are grilled over an open fire; or there are seaside favourites and traditional Norman dishes. *Closed Mon, and Nov–Easter Wed.*

Far Away among the Hedgerows:
The Cotentin *Bocage*

31

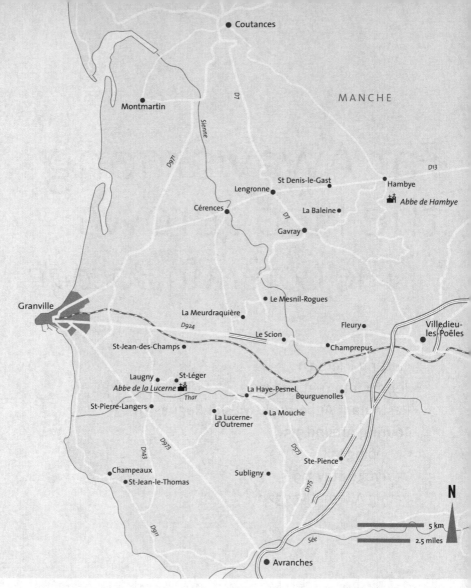

The *bocage* country of Normandy stretches across the Cotentin peninsula and much of western Calvados and the Orne, a countryside of innumerable villages, solid stone houses, small, scattered farms, and fields separated by giant, stone-bottomed hedgerows, all spread over rolling hills between patches of thick woodland. The fields are rarely more than a hundred yards wide, and at times so small that their grass becomes almost invisible between the hedges. The word *bocage* is probably best known in English to those with an interest in the Second World War, for this is also the countryside that caused such utter misery to the US Army following the D-Day landings, when the region's trademark hedgerows gave the Germans ready-made defences that had to be taken one by one. It takes a real leap of the imagination to conceive of these horrors here today. The southern Cotentin, inland from Coutances

Getting There

The main roads from Cherbourg southwards meet at Coutances, to divide again just south of the town; take the turning off to the left, the D7 inland, signposted to Gavray and Villedieu. From Caen and the east, leave the A84 at the main St-Lô exit, cut westwards on side roads to Domjean to get on to the D13, and then turn left on to the D7 at Lengronne. At Gavray, the D7 veers to the southwest and runs through a particularly pretty stretch of rolling bends through the hedges. After about 5km, look out for the turn for Le Mesnil-Rogues off to the left – it's quite well signposted, but it's a sharp, narrow turn. In the village, a short way from the main road, it's impossible to miss the Auberge, right by the roadside. If you're coming from the south, the turn off the D7 is less abrupt, to the right about 2km north of the crossroads at Le Scion.

Trains run to Granville and Villedieu-les-Poêles from Avranches and Paris (Gare Montparnasse), but local bus services to the villages are pretty infrequent.

There is a fast passenger-only ferry service between Granville and Jersey, taking about an hour in each direction (*mid-April–Oct daily one sailing each way*), and from Granville to the Iles Chausey, the tiny French islands off the coast (*more limited schedule*). For ferry information call Granville **t** 02 33 50 16 36.

Tourist Information

Gavray: Mairie, **t** 02 33 50 10 10.
Granville: 4 Cours Jonville, **t** 02 33 91 30 03, **f** 02 33 91 30 19.
La Haye-Pesnel: Rue de la Gendarmerie, **t** 02 33 90 75 02.
Villedieu: Place Costils, **t/f** 02 33 61 05 69.

and Avranches, is one of the most beautiful parts of the *bocage*. In the early Middle Ages, when most of the region was still covered by forest, several monasteries were founded here, their monks attracted by its very remoteness and isolation.

This is one of the best areas in Normandy to sample farm ciders and other traditional foods and crafts. Cheese, for once, is not foremost among the region's products, but there are plenty of small cider producers that welcome visitors, and the Cotentin's ham, duck, lamb, beef and their derivatives are renowned. And, when it comes to exploring the very French concept that food is always better at source, where better than an *auberge du terroir*, officially recognised as serving only local produce. The welcoming **Auberge du Mesnil-Rogues** occupies a granite building in a tiny village in the heart of the *bocage*, with a small bar by the door and the restaurant just beyond. Presided over by the aptly named Joseph Cotentin, the Auberge is dedicated to presenting country produce at its best.

L'Auberge du Mesnil-Rogues

*Le Mesnil-Rogues, **t** 02 33 61 37 12, **f** 02 33 50 85 63. Open May–June Mon and Tues 12–3, Wed–Sun 12–3 and 7–9; July–mid-Sept daily 12–3 and 7–9; mid-Sept–April Wed–Sun 12–3 and 7–9; closed Mon and Tues, four weeks Jan and Feb, and three weeks late Sept and Oct. Book a day in advance, more for weekends. Menus 58F/€8.84 (Mon–Fri midday), 98F/€14.94, 142F/€21.65, 180F/€27.44 and 198F/€30.18; children's menu 44F/€6.71; à la carte average 160F/€24.39.*

The centrepiece of the main dining room at the Auberge is the massive old, distinctly manorial stone fireplace, which Mme Cotentin visits every so often to check on the meat grilling over beech logs – every Friday a whole ham is slowly spit-roasted there, ready for the night's special of *jambon façon York cuit à la broche*. There's no deliberate rusticity here, though, for this is something to which few French restaurants aspire; the rest of the room is perhaps surprisingly neat and smart, with striped and flowery wallpaper, pretty tablecloths and flowers on the tables. M Cotentin's staff are young, bright and smart. There's also a large additional dining room that is positively ornate, but which regularly fills up with the big, noisy family groups that home in on the Auberge from miles around for Sunday lunch. This is a family restaurant in more ways than one – outside, across a small garden, there's a well-equipped play area, with slides and climbing frames, and requests for high chairs and other infant accessories are happily answered.

An *auberge du terroir* this may be, but this doesn't mean the food here is unsophisticated. M. Cotentin worked for several years around the Paris region before returning to his particular *terroir* and, as well as Norman tradition, there are well-developed skills evident in his cooking. Like any good French chef he also experiments, and, while superb traditional grilled meats remain his most renowned forte, he has recently developed a variety of *terre et mer* dishes, alias mixed meat and seafood or surf'n'turf, as is now very fashionable in France. His range of menus, moreover, provides an opportunity to sample all the dishes for an exceptionally reasonable outlay; for anyone who only wants a smaller, lighter meal, there's also an excellent choice of one-course *assiettes du terroir*, including local classics such as braised ham *à la normande* (in cream and cider sauce), *poule au pot*, or assorted Normandy cheeses with farm-fresh salad (*all around 40–60F/€6.1–9.15*). The wine list is short but satisfying, with several good classic French reds for around 90F that make an excellent match for the meats.

Among the starters, as well as salads and local river fish, there are plenty of homemade terrines and foie gras. From June to September, when *langoustines* are available in Granville, the waitresses may take up position behind many of the diners, young and old, to tie on rather cute little pink bibs in preparation for slurpy dishes such as *langoustines à la crème de calvados*. With a sweet and richly buttery finger-licking sauce, this could be called the essence of slightly over-the-top Norman cooking, but it's hugely enjoyable, and, coming in a 142F menu, is unquestionably a luxury (from autumn into spring, similar dishes may be made with *coquilles St-Jacques*). Main courses include variations on duck, lamb and cider, many with traditional Norman cider, cream or cheese sauces, fish dishes such as smoked pollack, and the *terre et mer* alternatives that are entirely Joseph Cotentin's own creation. Serious carnivores, though, will wish to try the grilled meats, such as the *pièce de bœuf grillée* that's more or less a fixture on the menu – and a definitive version of the classic *steak-frites*. The English are well-known in French restaurants for liking their meat well- (meaning over-) done. In this case, however, try to overcome any prejudices and ask for it *saignant* or even *bleu*. Meat of this quality scarcely needs any cooking at all.

After some Livarot from the excellent cheeseboard, desserts present a difficult choice. If you're looking for comfort food, there's an excellent *teurgoule*, the Norman rice pudding, with fine cinnamon flavours and a thick, crispy crust on top, although it's hard not to choose the homemade *pâtisserie* of the day, which might be a tart of

Magret de Canard, Sauce Camembert

Serves 4

150g/5oz Camembert
4 duck breasts
200ml/7fl oz sweet white wine
150g/5oz crème fraîche
salt and pepper

Remove the rind from the Camembert and cut the cheese into 1cm/½in cubes.

With a small knife, lightly score the skin of the duck breasts in a criss-cross pattern. Just before cooking, season with salt and pepper.

Take a cast-iron casserole dish, or a very heavy frying pan; preheat it dry. When the pan is very hot, lay the duck breasts in it, with the skin side downwards. The heat will immediately melt the fat; lift the breasts up gently so that it can penetrate underneath. Cook this side for 5–7 minutes, making sure that the skin doesn't get too brown (and do not prick the meat). Then turn the breasts over and cook on the other side for 4–5 mins. Transfer the breasts to a plate, skin side downwards, to keep warm.

To make the sauce, pour off the fat from the pan, and then put it back on the heat. Pour in the white wine and bring to the boil, stirring to scrape up the sediment from the base of the pan, and then add the Camembert. Allow it to melt, and then add the crème fraîche. Reduce the mixture until it reaches the desired consistency. Taste, and add seasoning if required.

Serve the duck breasts whole or in slices, with the sauce poured around.

utterly smooth apple mousse topped with minutely fine apple slices and soaked in yet more calvados. At the end of the meal M Cotentin emerges from his kitchen to tour the tables with a very genuine beaming smile.

Touring Around

Around 15km south of Coutances the D7 enters the Valley of the Sienne. At Lengronne, on the north side of the main valley, a turn off to the left (D13) leads to the large village of **Hambye**, from where a turning south, to the right, will take you to one of the region's best-known monuments, the ruins of the Benedictine **Abbaye de Hambye** (*open Mar Sun 1–6; April–Oct daily 10–12 and 2–6, guided tours 10–11.30 and 2–5.30 (1–1½hrs; in French only – English-speakers must tag along with an information sheet); chapter house and some other sections closed Tues; Nov–Feb open local school hols only; adm*), looming lichen-clad above the trees. Founded in 1145 by Guillaume de Paynel, Lord of Hambye, and much-favoured by Henry II of England and Normandy, it was still occupied until the Revolution, after which it rapidly fell into dereliction, thanks mostly to its being used by locals as a stone quarry. It is the largest complex of medieval monastic buildings in Normandy after Mont St-Michel. Though battered and roofless, the abbey church still stands as one of the finest examples of Norman

Gothic, for the soaring simplicity of its unusually tall, narrow arches and its massive tower, still improbably perched almost intact on top of the giant arches, a full 100ft above the nave.

Some of the monastic buildings are still more intact, and extensive restoration work has been undertaken in the last few years, particularly in the kitchens, the cider press and the scriptorium, or room for the copying of manuscripts. The Monks' Parlour has a remarkable 13th-century decorated ceiling, painted very simply with flowers, while the kitchen has a truly magnificent giant fireplace; the Chapter House, virtually undamaged, is similar in shape and vaulting to that in Norwich, with which Hambye had close links during the Middle Ages. You can wander around on your own, but unless you join the tour you will not have access to many interesting parts of the abbey, such as the Chapter House and the Parlour (this is not made clear at the entrance, and the admission charge is the same).

The setting of Hambye, next to the Sienne in a small, flat bend in the valley surrounded by woods, is as beautiful as the ruins themselves. Within walking distance, too, is one of the *bocage*'s most widely appreciated hotel-restaurants, the Auberge de l'Abbaye (*see* p.320).

From Hambye a string of lanes lead back westwards up hill and down dale towards Gavray and Le Mesnil-Rogues. The *bocage* countryside can seem like a dense green web, in which the towering foliage of trees and unkempt hedges could be gently closing in around you – especially if you wander up any of the narrower lanes that follow the most apparently incomprehensible twists and turns. This overpowering greenness all adds to the area's fascination, and to its noticeable feeling of remoteness. This is a man-made landscape – in the shape of the hedgerows, built up over centuries – but it's one in which nature seems very much the most powerful factor.

Around you there are also plenty of opportunities for cider-tasting and investigating other local specialities. One of the most spectacularly pretty of all the *bocage* villages is **La Baleine**, a little cluster of houses on a particularly narrow and steep-sided bend in the Valley of the Sienne, with an old humpbacked bridge across the river. It has what must be one of France's smallest *mairies*, next to the much larger, four-square stone *auberge*. Right beside the bridge on the north side is the **Andouillerie de la Vallée de la Sienne**, which produces high-quality examples of the Norman versions of *andouilles* and *andouillettes*, gut and offal sausages, using entirely traditional, craft methods, smoking them over forest woods. Charcuterie enthusiasts can also go on guided tours of the Andouillerie (*see* p.318). In **Le Mesnil-Rogues** itself, look for the farm **La Pinotière**, which has good, subtly flavoured *chèvre*.

After lunch, perhaps, turn back from the Auberge in Le Mesnil-Rogues towards the main D7 and go straight across it on to the little narrow road downhill to **La Meurdraquière**, site of two impressive old farms, their driveways one either side of a crossroads like bookends, M Bruno Vastel's Ferme de la Grenterie, which offers *chambre-d'hôte* rooms and occasionally cider, and M Roland Venisse's La Butte, with B&B rooms, cider and calvados at all times. The Cotentin ciders, though still nothing like rough cider, are in general a little drier and not quite so smooth as those from the Pays d'Auge. The best time to try them is from April to September, for the region's cider farmers are small producers, and may have sold much of their stock by October, although most will have some bottles for sale at least until Christmas, and calvados is available at all times. Also in La Meurdraquière there is another farm, La Percehaye, which specialises in beekeeping, and offers farmhouse honeys. A little southwest of La Meurdraquière, well-signposted off the main D924 Granville road near **St-Jean-des-Champs**, is the Ferme de la Hermitière, one of the larger cider farms in the area, where as well as offering ciders and calvados for sale owner Jean-Luc Colombier gives guided tours of the centuries-old farm, its orchards, still and cider presses, with a video (shown in English on request) on cider-making and a year in the life of the farm (for details, see p.318).

From La Hermitière, presuming you've had enough cider-tasting for a while, look for the road, a little way east towards Villedieu on the south side of the main road, signed for St-Jean-des-Champs and the Abbaye de la Lucerne. This can seem almost deliberately deceptive, for, despite something of a recent signing-offensive, having got you on to this leaf-shrouded lane the authorities then omit to place many more signs to the abbey. It's best to accept the occasional false turning, appreciate the scenery, and more or less follow the signs towards St-Léger. Then, just when you think you're totally lost, you roll around a hill and there, nestling in a wood-clad valley like a medieval monastic vision, is the **Abbaye de la Lucerne d'Outremer** (open Easter–Oct daily 10–12 and 2–6.30; Nov and Dec daily 10–12 and 2–5.30; Feb–Easter Mon, Wed–Sun 10–12 and 2–5.30, closed Tues; closed Jan; adm; joint ticket with castle of Pirou).

La Lucerne is less well-known than Hambye (possibly because it's harder to find), but, if you want to visit only one of the Cotentin's ruined abbeys, this should be it. It's more atmospheric, and you're left to wander around it on your own; it's also less of a ruin, both because it survived the post-Revolutionary destruction better, and because La Lucerne is now the centre of a remarkable project. The abbey is not just being restored in certain details or shored up against any future collapse, it is being rebuilt. Since 1959 it has been in the care of a private foundation, the ultimate goal of which is to rebuild the abbey and re-establish a monastic community here. This was little more than a pious hope until the mid-1990s, but since then work has proceeded at a steadier pace.

The abbey's sub-title 'd'Outremer' stems from its persistent loyalty during the Middle Ages 'across the sea', to England. Its site was chosen in 1161 by the Blessed Achard, then Bishop of Avranches, a major figure in the Anglo-Norman church who had also been Canon of Bridlington in County Durham. In 1204, when Philippe Auguste of France seized control of the Duchy of Normandy, the monks of La Lucerne remained stubbornly loyal to their former Duke, King John, in opposition to the French ecclesiastical stronghold of Mont St-Michel. Later, moreover, when the English reappeared in the area during the Hundred Years' War, the abbey again offered them its allegiance, providing a chaplain for Edward III. However, this did not prevent it later becoming one of the largest religious houses in France.

The main **church** was built between 1164 and 1178. Given that by this time Notre-Dame in Paris and the other great works of early French Gothic were under construction to the east, the style – which has been faithfully respected in the current restoration – is remarkably simple and conservative, an unadorned Norman Romanesque little changed since the Conqueror's time. The building's very plainness gives it strength; alongside the church there is the even simpler **Chapel of the Blessed Achard**, a beautifully plain space that is one of the oldest parts of the abbey. Towards the back of the church a door leads through to the slightly later, more **Gothic Chapter House** and **Cloister**, still in ruins but earmarked for work at some point in the future. Clearly visible and in much less need of any restoration is the **Lavatorium**, the monks' washing area, with classic Norman-style carving. Another door off the cloister leads to the giant 18th-century **refectory**, built on top of an impressive 12th-century vaulted cellar. Only recently opened to visitors, the refectory has as its centrepiece a truly spectacular, worm-eaten but still intact, original timber staircase.

Another feature of La Lucerne is that, in its valley, the abbey seems always close to water: at the back of the church there is a small aqueduct, and alongside there is a near lake-sized pond, separating the main buildings from the 18th-century Bishops' Palace. This is now a private house, and visitors are asked not to go too close, but there doesn't seem to be any problem in sitting by the pond on a sunny afternoon.

The restored church already contains a superb 1780s organ – originally built for the Cathedral in Chambéry, near the Alps, and brought here in the 1970s – and Mass is said every Sunday at 11.15am. During July and August a series of performances of organ music, Gregorian chant and other religious music takes place in the church, and exhibitions on suitably related themes are presented in the abbey buildings. Behind the abbey to the east is a substantial stretch of the **Forêt de la Lucerne**, the thick deciduous wood that once covered most of the valley of the Thar, one of the Cotentin's fast-flowing rivers. Through the forest and beside the abbey there runs the well-marked GR226 long-distance footpath, which follows the line of one of the **Chemins aux Anglais**, the old tracks used by medieval English pilgrims on their way to Mont St-Michel and Santiago de Compostela, and which to the west runs to St-Pierre-Langers and then down to the Bay of Mont St-Michel. Using the footpath and side-tracks off to the south (free local maps are available at the abbey) it's an easy 3km-walk to the pretty village of La Lucerne d'Outremer, where there is a good *auberge* restaurant (*see* p.320).

East of La Lucerne is the capital of the southern *bocage*, **Villedieu-les-Poêles**. The 'City-of-God-of-the-Cooking-Pots' is so-called because since the 12th century the town has been single-mindedly dedicated to the working of copper, pewter and other metals. It became so because in the 1100s Henry I of England gave the town to the Knights of St John, with trading privileges that encouraged industry; the surrounding *bocage* was for centuries poor and over-populated, and unemployed farm boys flocked into Villedieu to work in the metal trades and other crafts that developed.

The stone and slate medieval town is classically pretty, with a special architectural style of its own. It is centred on one long main street along a ridge, called **Place de la République** at the lower end, narrowing into **Rue Général Huard**, on either side of which narrow alleyways run away into courtyards of grey stone houses, the old copperworkers' homes and workshops. It's also much visited, with shops selling copper, kitchenware and other crafts almost end to end along the main street.

The town also has several museums and open workshops to showcase its trades, notably the **Fonderie des Cloches** (*Rue du Pont-Chignon; tours Tues–Sat 9–12 and 2–5.30; 15 Jun–31 Aug also Mon; adm*), one of the last completely traditional bell-foundries in Europe; the **Atelier du Cuivre** (*54 Rue Général Huard; open Mon–Fri 9–12 and 1.30–6, Sat 9–12 and 2.30–5.30; adm*); and, in a fine 18th-century copperworkers' courtyard, the **Musée de la Poêlerie et de la Dentelle** (Museum of Copperworking and Lacemaking; *25 Rue Général Huard; open Easter–31 Oct Mon, Wed–Sun 10–12 and 2–6.30, Tues 2–6.30; adm*).

A radical contrast is offered by the other substantial town in this area, 2 8km directly west of Villedieu down the D924, **Granville**. The largest and one of the most characterful and engaging of the harbour towns along the Cotentin coast. It was actually founded by the English, in the 15th century, as a base from which to attack the French in Mont St-Michel, and the old town, the **Haute-Ville**, reflects its military origins in its spectacular location, on a giant spit of rock jutting out into the Atlantic, a natural fortress. There is a great walk around the line of the old ramparts encircling the Haute-Ville, with limitless sea views. Within its tight space old Granville is an atmospheric and distinctive town of verticals, with steep cobbled streets climbing between strangely tall, thin 16th- and 17th-century buildings perched on the hillsides, and impressive interconnecting squares. In the middle of the old town there is a massive 15th-century church, Notre-Dame, and the main commercial thoroughfare, Rue des Juifs, contains some interesting old shops. The Haute-Ville also contains two attractive museums, the **Musée du Vieux Granville** (*open April–Sept Mon, Wed–Sun 10–12 and 2–6; Oct–Mar Wed, Sat and Sun 2–6; adm*), a display mainly on maritime history in a fine old stone house; and the **Musée d'Art Moderne Richard Anacréon** (*open July–Sept daily 11–6; Oct–June check with the museum, t 02 33 51 02 94; adm*), an intriguingly personal museum containing the varied collections of a Paris bookseller.

Granville's lower town, the **Basse-Ville**, is very different, a much more modern, workaday place with all the standard features of a French provincial town, centred on the lively fishing port. It also contains the Gare Maritime, for ferries to Jersey, and a line of renowned seafood restaurants on the harbourside below the Haute-Ville, which make full use, naturally, of fabulously fresh ingredients. Across on the other flank of the Haute-Ville spit to the north, meanwhile, you can find a third side to Granville that is different again, its **seaside** town, with a casino, and a long, narrow beach that's still popular in summer. In the late 19th century Granville became one of the places around the French coasts where it was fashionable for respectable people to spend their summers, and on the heights above the beach there are neat lanes of opulent Belle Epoque bourgeois villas, most of them still in very good shape. One of the grandest is the **Musée et Jardin Christian Dior** (*open late-May–Sept Tues–Sun 10–12.30 and 2.30–7; closed Mon; adm*), the pink mansion that was the summer home of the great couturier's family when he was a child. Surrounded by perfectly trimmed (even chic) gardens, it contains designs and memorabilia mainly drawn from Dior's early years, as complete a contrast with the blue-overalled world of the *bocage* as you're likely to get.

Shopping

The largest market in this area is in **Villedieu** (*Thurs and Fri*). There are also markets in **Granville** (*Wed and Sat*) and an interesting little local market in **La Haye-Pesnel** (*Wed*). Several of the traditional food and craft establishments in the Cotentin form part of a semi-official Route de la Table; visit four or more of them and you qualify for a *cadeau surprise* of goodies (details from all tourist offices). Among those that take part are the Fromagerie du Val d'Ay (*see* chapter 30, p.307), and the Andouillerie de la Vallée de la Sienne, the Ferme de l'Hermitière and the Atelier du Cuivre metal workshop in Villedieu. For general notes on cider buying, *see* p.11.

St-Denis-le-Gast ✉ 50450

L'Andouillerie de la Vallée de la Sienne, Pont de la Baleine, **t** 02 33 61 44 20, **f** 02 33 61 84 53. Deep in the forest is this tiny workshop, in a fairytale site next to the humpbacked bridge in La Baleine (so it's easy to miss it completely, if you're concentrating too hard on the winding bends). Inside it are M Bernard Boscher and his six staff, dedicated to making the finest *andouilles* – Norman smoked gut sausages – using entirely traditional techniques. Recent food scares have put this most traditional of local products under severe pressure, but the superior models on sale here are made with very carefully selected ingredients. As well as basic *andouilles* and *andouillettes* you can buy *rillettes*, bacon and other smoked meats, and some locally made fruit liqueurs. *Guided tours July and Aug daily 11am and 2.30–5.30, at other times by appointment. Closed Mon.*

La Meurdraquière ✉ 50510

Ferme de la Butte, **t** 02 33 61 31 52, **f** 02 33 61 17 64. Wander into La Butte and M. Roland Venisse will bluffly leave his apple-crusher to open up his shed and sit at a massive log table with you while you try out his especially fine *brut* cider and fairly ferocious calvados. He has won many awards for his ciders and other products; he and his wife sell all of it either directly from the farm or to a few local *auberges*, the Auberge du Mesnil-Rogues among them, but not to

shops. They also have attractive B&B rooms (*see* below).

St-Jean-des-Champs ✉ 50320

Ferme de l'Hermitière, **t** 02 33 61 31 51, **f** 02 33 61 87 27, *www.ferme-hermitiere.com*. Jean-Luc Colombier's guided tours (*c. 1½hrs*) of his big farm outside St-Jean-des-Champs give you a very good idea of all the traditional processes used in making cider, *pommeau* and calvados. Included is the 'eco-musée' farm museum. All tours end with a tasting. Despite all this organisation, this big, rambling place still feels very much like a farm. At the farm shop you can buy their fine sweet and dry ciders, unfermented apple juice, *pommeau*, excellent, not overly sweet *poiré* (pear cider) and a superior range of calvados. *Tours Easter–June Mon–Fri 2–6; July and Aug Mon–Sat 10–12 and 1.30–6; Sept Mon–Fri 10–12 and 1.30–6; adm. Shop open daily exc Sun.*

Champrepus ✉ 50800

Au Fournil d'Antan, Village de l'Eglise, **t** 02 33 90 01 86. Best identified by the board outside offering 'Pain Levain', this traditional bakery in the village of Champrepus between Villedieu and Granville – on the D924, right opposite the church – is renowned for its superb country breads, baked in an historic wood-fired oven. As well as breads from *baguettes* to *pains de campagne* it offers delicious *teurgoules* (Norman rice puddings), a traditional by-product of the baking process, cooked in the bread oven as it cools down.

Cerences ✉ 50510

Le Manoir de Guelle, **t** 02 33 51 99 06, **f** 02 33 51 20 55. Products of the duck: terrines, *rillettes*, *confits de canard*, smoked duck breasts and foie gras, all made right on the farm, the same specialities that are used in the *ferme-auberge* (*see* below). *Open daily 2–8.*

Le Mesnil-Rogues ✉ 50450

La Pinotière, **t** 02 33 61 38 98. Amid the *bocage* cider farms, Mme Legallais' farm is dedicated to raising goats, and producing high-quality *chèvre*. The farm shop also has other local produce – preserves and ciders – and on the farm there are four simple *chambre-d'hôte* rooms (*200F/€30.49 for two*). It's less than a kilometre walk from the Auberge du Mesnil-Rogues: to find it, follow the Fromages de Chèvres signs from the centre of the village.

Where to Stay

Hambye ✉ 50450

Auberge de l'Abbaye, Route de l'Abbaye, t 02 33 61 42 19, f 02 33 61 00 85 (*rooms 300–320F/ €45.73–48.78*). A much-loved Logis hotel in a delightful location, next to the River Sienne and very near the abbey. The seven rooms are comfortable, and there's a pretty garden from where you can see the abbey tower poking out above the trees. What wins most praise, though, is the warmth and enthusiasm of the Allain family. Equally popular is the excellent restaurant (*see below*). *Closed two weeks late-Feb and late-Sept.*

St-Pierre-Langers ✉ 50530

La Cocquetlère, t 02 33 48 37 54 (*rooms 190F/ €28.97 for two, 250F/€38.11 for three*). Only a few kilometres inland from the Bay of Mont St-Michel, this old Cotentin granite farmhouse surrounded by a dense garden of fruit trees feels almost hidden among the woods and hedges. M and Mme Gabeloux have two B&B rooms, one double and one with three single beds. It couldn't be more peaceful. It's also very near the GR226 footpath, which allows you to walk towards Granville or the Bay in one direction or (more easily) La Lucerne in the other. There are signs to the farm a little north of St-Pierre-Langers village, on the D143 towards Laugny.

La Meurdraquière ✉ 50510

La Grenterie, 10 Route de St-Martin, t 02 33 90 26 45, f 02 33 91 96 32 (*rooms 230F/€35.06 for two, 300F/€45.73 for three; extra beds available*). A giant 17th-century farmhouse, like something out of Balzac, in the middle of a similarly rambling farm. Bruno and Delphine Vastel have three comfortable B&B rooms, with plenty of farmhouse character and good bathrooms, and guests have the use of a living room and kitchen, although Mme Vastel can provide evening meals with prior notice (*90F/€13.72*). The farm's magnificent

cider shed, dating from 1689, is still occasionally put to use.

Ferme de la Butte, *see* 'Shopping', above (*rooms 200F/€30.49 for two, 300F/€45.73 for four*). M and Mme Venisse have three very well-equipped *chambre-d'hôte* rooms in a separate, converted barn alongside their main farm. The ground floor room is fully adapted for disabled access; the large, family room has ample space for four people, and all the rooms have the use of a well fitted-out, shared kitchen.

Subligny ✉ 50870

La Grande Coquerie, t 02 33 61 50 23, f 02 33 61 18 24 (*rooms 260F/€39.64 for two*). Superior *chambre-d'hôte* in a very large farm surrounded by lawns and beautiful gardens. Owners M and Mme Dulin run the Coquerie as a stud farm, so the house is surrounded by horses (which are, though, much too valuable for guests to be allowed to ride them). Breakfast is served in a fabulous old room with fireplace, timber table and lots of flowers. The Dulins also have two self-contained *gîtes*, each with room for four. The farm is some way from Subligny village, off the tiny D573 to the hamlet of La Mouche.

Villedieu-les-Poêles ✉ 50800

Hôtel St-Pierre et St-Michel, 12 Place de la République, t 02 33 61 00 11, f 02 33 61 06 52 (*rooms 240–260F/€36.59–39.64*). A traditional Logis hotel restaurant on Villedieu's main square, with a typical country-town-hotel three-storey frontage and flower boxes. The 21 rooms have simple, quite pretty décor and decent bathrooms. Those at the front can be a little noisy, especially during the Tuesday and Sunday markets. The **restaurant** is one of the town's most popular, serving good Norman fare (*menus 85–195F/€12.96–29.73*). *Closed Jan.*

Ste-Pience ✉ 50870

Manoir de la Porte, t 02 33 68 13 61, f 02 33 68 29 54, *manoir.de.la.porte@wanadoo.fr* (*rooms 280F/€42.69 for two, 370F/€56.41 for three*). Another of the *bocage*'s exceptional B&Bs, in a 16th-century priory with fairytale pepperpot turrets, surrounded by a lovely wooded park with pond that makes it deliciously peaceful. The owners, M and Mme

Lagadec, are a retired couple who are very proud of their house. The two exceptional-value guest rooms, each with a double and a single bed, are spacious, with a mix of antiques and modern touches. In the grounds there's also a large separate *gîte*, with room for as many as 12. The house is on the D175 north of Ste-Pience on the way to Bourguenolles, but it's not well signposted, so ask for directions. *Closed Nov.*

Eating Alternatives

Hambye ✉ 50450
Auberge de l'Abbaye, Route de l'Abbaye, **t** 02 33 61 42 19, **f** 02 33 61 00 85 (*menus 110–300F/ €16.77–45.73*). The restaurant at the Auberge in Hambye has an international fan club all of its own, both for Jean Allain's imaginative and enjoyable food and for the friendly, individual style with which it is served. He features dishes from other parts of France as a change from all-Norman cooking, all prepared with care and using excellent ingredients. The wine list is similarly impressive, and wide-ranging. *Closed Sun eve and Mon, and two weeks late-Feb and late-Sept.*

La Baleine ✉ 50450
Auberge de la Baleine, **t** 02 33 90 92 74 (*menus 98–146F/€14.94–22.26*). A big, plain old inn in a superb location in the village of La Baleine, near the River Sienne and with terrace tables outside on sunny days. This is another *auberge du terroir*, so the superb sausages from the *andouillerie* just across the bridge (*see* above) feature strongly, but a wide range of other local produce – and Granville seafood – is used too. There are also three very simple and very cheap guest **rooms** (*150–180F/€22.87–27.44*).

La Lucerne d'Outremer ✉ 50320
Le Courtil de la Lucerne, **t** 02 33 61 22 02, **f** 02 33 61 22 15 (*menus 88–204F/ €13.42–31.10*). This imposing 18th-century former Presbytery, in Cotentin granite and slate, surrounded by a well-tended garden, is – after the church – about the largest building in the village of La Lucerne, a few kilometres east of the abbey. It's one of the smarter *auberges du terroir*, with a neat

dining room and four extensive set menus. Dishes may have their sophisticated touches, but the cooking style is still hearty, with lots of cheese and calvados, and meals finish up with rich and indulgent desserts like the speciality calvados ice-cream soufflé. *Closed Wed and Feb.*

Cerences ✉ 50510
Ferme-Auberge du Manoir de Guelle, **t** 02 33 51 99 06, **f** 02 33 51 20 55 (*menus 95–195F/ €14.48–29.73*). A *ferme-auberge*, using only produce from the farm itself, in a fine old 18th-century manor-farm by the Sienne near Cerences, a little west of Gavray. Duck in its many forms is the great speciality, particularly *magret* grilled on a wood fire in the big fireplace at one end of the room, and there are delicious, fruity and creamy farmhouse desserts. *Closed Mon and Tues.*

Granville ✉ 50400
Le Phare, Rue du Port, **t** 02 33 50 12 94 (*moules and wine 45F/€6.86; menus 89–210F/ €13.57–32.01; children's menu*). Of all the seafood restaurants on the harbourside in Granville, it's the Phare that has the most return visitors. Granville is a working harbour and this is a bustling, straightforward restaurant, with the luxury of a first-floor *salle panoramique* for taking a more leisurely view of all the movement in the port. The fish and seafood, naturally, couldn't be fresher. It's by the very end of the quay on the right side of the harbour, looking seawards. *Closed Tues eve, Oct–May Wed, and most of Jan.*

Fleury ✉ 50800
La Pommerie, Route de Granville, **t** 02 33 51 23 12 (*menus 55F/€8.38 and 65F/€9.91*). A great little café-*tabac*-restaurant beside the Granville road in Fleury, just west of Villedieu. Ultra-bargain menus might include grilled meats, salads, chicken in cider or other local favourites, made with no frills but good fresh ingredients. The bar has a friendly buzz about it, and there's even an outside terrace for good weather. The shop, as well as the usual cigarettes, papers and postcards, has a variety of local products and souvenirs, such as cider, Villedieu copper pots and honey. *Closed Sept–May Sun.*

Mystic Mountain:
Mont St-Michel and its Bay

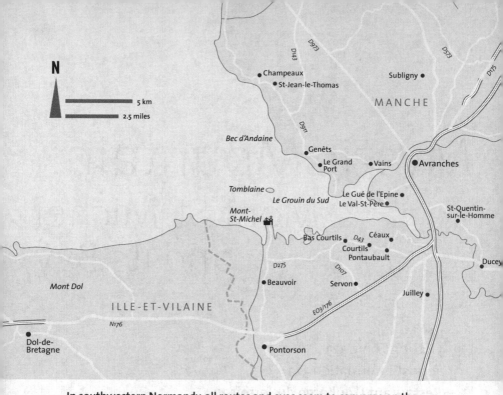

In southwestern Normandy, all routes and eyes seem to converge on the extraordinary giant pinnacle of Mont St-Michel. Like a natural extension of the tiny rock on which it stands, the abbey can be seen from all angles towering above the surrounding empty wastes of sand and water, whether first seen sharply outlined from miles away on a clear day, or dimly glimpsed in silhouette through mists and the not-infrequent rain. First built to embody a particularly intense ideal of Christianity, it can still suggest a celestial vision against the sky. Even the giant arc of the bay itself seems to have been created as a great amphitheatre for the glory of the abbey.

The Merveille de l'Occident, the 'Wonder of the Western World', as it has often been called, is also France's greatest tourist attraction outside Paris. Pilgrims have been flocking here for well over a thousand years, and when people began to travel for pure pleasure in the 19th century it immediately became an obligatory stop. Consequently, as with the Vatican, St Mark's in Venice or any other site that's beyond mere fame, to see Mont St-Michel is usually to see it together with hundreds of other people. This can be disheartening, and to avoid most of the crowds it's advisable to visit in spring, autumn or winter. However, even with the crowds and for all its arch-familiarity, the holy mountain is still extraordinary. The abbey looks astonishing from a distance, and is truly staggering from close up. If it were not so well-known, perhaps no one would quite believe it was there.

And all around it is the bay, a mysterious expanse of constantly shifting sands, channels and salt marshes every bit as strange and enigmatic as the Mount, known

Getting There

All roads from Cherbourg, the Caen area and Paris via Alençon converge at Avranches to form the N176, a motorway-standard road that sweeps around the Bay of Mont St-Michel into Brittany, while the A84 *autoroute* heads off south to Rennes. South of Avranches, by Pontaubault, look for an exit clearly signposted Mont St-Michel to get on to the D75, the most attractive route to the Mount, which skirts the south side of the Bay. To go direct to Servon, stay on the N176 for about another 5km and look for a turn off to the right, signed to Servon. The Auberge is very easy to find in the middle of the village.

If you are driving from Mont St-Michel, turn left on to the D275-D75 Bay road at the south end of the causeway, and then turning right on to a narrow lane signed to Servon; if you're coming from St-Malo, stay on the N176 past Pontorson and look for a left turn to Servon.

Trains run to Avranches and Pontorson from Cherbourg and Paris (Gare Montparnasse, c. 3hrs). The most direct way to get to Mont St-Michel by train is to get off in Pontorson, and take a bus or cab from there.

Tourist Information

Some information is also available on *www.manchetourisme.com*.

Maisons de la Baie

Maison de la Baie de Courtils, Route de Roche Torin, t 02 33 89 66 00, f 02 33 89 66 09 (south side); and **Maison de la Baie de Genêts**, Place de la Mairie, t 02 33 89 64 00, f 02 33 89 64 09 (north side). The two Maisons de la Baie are the best sources of information on walks, other nature- and wildlife-related activities and the ecology of the Bay in general. Genêts is also the main place to find out about walking to Mont St-Michel across the sands (*see* below). A third Maison de la Baie is due to open shortly in Vains, between Genêts and Avranches.

Tourist Offices

Mont St-Michel: t 02 33 60 14 30, f 02 33 60 06 75. The tourist office is impossible to miss, next to the main gate into the old town at the end of the causeway.

Avranches: 2 Rue du Général de Gaulle, t 02 33 58 00 22, f 02 33 68 13 29.

Champeaux: Mairie de Champeaux, t 02 33 61 90 38, f 02 33 61 75 77.

Dol-de-Bretagne: 3 Grande Rue des Stuarts, t 02 99 48 15 37, f 02 99 48 14 13.

Pontorson: Place de la Mairie, t 02 33 60 20 65, f 02 33 60 85 67.

St-Jean-le-Thomas: Mairie, t 02 33 48 86 09, f 02 33 48 48 51.

for its unpredictable weather, and where the horizon sometimes seems infinitely far away to the west and at other moments is impossible to make out in the mist. It has the longest, deepest tides in Europe, with the sea a full 15 kilometres away at low tide. This immense flatness contains an abundance of birds and shellfish, while the marshes around the bay's edge are used to graze the much-prized *pré-salé* or salt-marsh lamb.

A century ago Henry James and other luminaries who made their way to Mont St-Michel invariably slept and ate at the hotel of Mère Poulard, sampling her famous omelettes (with crème fraîche whipped into the eggs). You can still eat there today, for a price, but meals on the Mount nowadays rarely justify the restaurants' inflated charges. For a meal that doesn't disappoint it's much better to eat away from the rock, and one of the best of all the choices near the Mount is the simply named **Auberge du Terroir** in Servon, just 10km away in the countryside on the south side of the bay, an exceptional and very comfortable village restaurant with sophisticated cuisine based entirely on wonderfully fresh local produce.

L'Auberge du Terroir

Servon, t 02 33 60 17 92, f 02 33 60 35 26. Open mid-June–mid-Sept daily 12–2.30 and 7–8.30; mid-Sept–mid-June closed Wed and Sat midday; closed late Nov and late Feb. Booking advisable. Menus 90F/€13.72, 135F/€20.58, 175F/€26.68 and 240F/€36.59; à la carte average 240F/€36.59.

The label *auberge du terroir* tends to bring to mind images of sturdy country cooking, and indeed in western Normandy there are many such *auberges* that always include on their menus things like farmhouse terrines, *jambon au cidre* and *tarte tatin* or *teurgoule* (rice pudding) with lashings of crème fraîche. The name in fact simply means that all the ingredients used are from the local *terroir*, and, French chefs being French chefs, it's very hard for many of them to be left alone with even the most traditional local products without trying out their own ideas and new ways of cooking them. Anyone expecting old-fashioned rustic fare here will be very surprised.

First, the setting. It looks rural enough, in one of the larger old houses in Servon, a very pretty, calmly peaceful granite village typical of those on the solid ground around the south of the bay, with beautifully fresh, clean air. Inside, the dining room has bright décor in light colours, lots of light through the stone-sided windows, crisp linen, tasteful flower arrangements and an air of serenity. Mme Annie Lefort is in charge of service front-of-house and, with her young, all-female staff, sees that every detail is attended to with similarly quiet charm. As you wait to order, some superbly crusty homemade bread arrives, along with a notably refined wine list.

Neither chef Thierry Lefort nor his wife are actually from this area, but came here in the early 1990s from Limoges. He is, though, an enthusiast for the produce of the bay of Mont St-Michel, and especially its *agneau de pré-salé*, or salt-marsh lamb. Mont St-Michel lamb is often considered the finest of the similar meats from around France (although inhabitants of the Baie de la Somme would obviously not agree). Like all *pré-salé* lamb, it of course has a higher salt content than ordinary lamb, but also has a more delicate flavour. M Lefort also maintains his own wonderful herb garden, at the end of the garden where hotel guests can have their breakfast (*see* p.331), which he planted and tends with great pride himself – and which gives him access to a constantly changing range of seasonings, which he uses with great inventiveness.

A starter of *flan de poisson aux herbes fines* is a superbly subtle, savoury mix of fish, *langoustines* and herby flavours; to follow, *confit de canard* is a perfect version of a more conventional classic, with wonderfully crispy duck full of deep, rich flavour, served with a fabulously creamy potato cake, apple *frites* and a rich sauce. *Dos de cabillaud au jus de persil*, fresh cod in a butter sauce with parsley and a potato *gratin*, is equally delicious. And M Lefort definitely has a way with mash.

The menu naturally changes a great deal with the seasons, but local seafood is a regular feature, whether bay oysters, the speciality *mouclade du chef* (mussels cooked in a wine and cream sauce with turmeric and saffron), sea bass, and platters of mixed *fruits de mer* or lobster (which need to be ordered ahead). To finish, after the fine local cheeses, there are no winners in the contest between a very clever saffron crème brûlée and ideally refreshing, homemade lime and raspberry sorbets.

Touring Around

The city of **Avranches** sits atop a clutch of giant granite hills that on one side fall away almost precipitously down to the great flat plain of the Bay of Mont St-Michel. Its history is inextricably bound up with that of the Mount. According to medieval manuscripts, in the year 708 the Archangel Michael appeared to St Aubert, Bishop of Avranches, and commanded him to build a shrine on what was then just a rocky outcrop covered in trees in the middle of the bay. Aubert, evidently an early rationalist despite his saintly status, dismissed this as a dream, and what's more did so again when Michael came a second time. The third time the angry Archangel gave him a sharp prod in the side of the head, and so the Bishop, duly called to attention, built the first small oratory on the Mount. The 19th-century church of **St-Gervais** in Avranches contains as its greatest relic the skull of St Aubert, with a small hole supposedly left by the Archangel's finger.

Also in Avranches is the **Plate-forme**, the small square (also called Square Becket) where in 1172, at the instigation of Robert de Torigni, Bishop of Avranches and abbot of Mont St-Michel, Henry II of England and Normandy knelt for a whole day dressed only in his shirt in penance for the murder of Thomas à Becket. This is also a vantage point from where, coming from the north, you have the first great views out across the vast expanse of the bay, and of Mont St-Michel itself at its centre. Henry knelt in front of Avranches Cathedral, which was then being built to a design by De Torigni himself; however, like much of the same abbot's building work on Mont St-Michel, this church proved over-ambitious, and collapsed through decay during the 1790s, helped along by the destructive activities of local Revolutionaries.

A few streets away is Avranches' **Hôtel de Ville**, which contains a matchless treasure, the surviving books and documents from the library of Mont St-Michel, saved from the abbey during the Revolution. A spectacular selection of these Manuscrits du Mont St-Michel, some of the finest medieval illuminated manuscripts in the world, is put on display each summer in the newly renovated **library** (*open June and Sept daily 10–12 and 2–6; July and Aug daily 10–6; adm*). Almost next to it is the **Musée Municipal** (*open Easter–mid-Oct daily 9.30–12 and 2–6; adm*), which contains a reconstruction of a medieval manuscript workshop as well as displays on more recent local traditions. More recently still, Avranches was also the jumping-off point for General Patton's breakout from Normandy in 1944, and accordingly south of the town beside the N176 there is a war museum, the **Musée de la Seconde Guerre Mondiale** (*open April–mid-Nov daily 9–7; mid-Nov–Mar Sun 10–6; closed Jan; adm*), an eccentric private collection very much of the shop dummies-in-old-uniforms kind.

Avranches is also a good point from which to explore the **north side of the bay**. Traditionally, pilgrims and other travellers from England and the north got their first, extraordinary sight of Mont St-Michel from one of the most spectacular places of all, the top of the towering cliffs at **Champeaux**, dubbed the '*plus beau kilomètre de France*' because of the lush stretch of rare coastal forest that lines the lower slopes. All along the narrow road that follows the bay shore you get astonishing views, in snatches or long stretches, as you seem to circle the Mount, as if it were an object of worship in itself. A contemplation of the extraordinary, ever-present silhouette of Mont St-Michel is as much a part of any visit as a tour of the abbey buildings, above all at sunset, when you can well imagine medieval pilgrims thinking they had come within the presence of the divine. When the weather closes in (as often happens) you see a different but equally awesome sight, for, even when little else is distinguishable, the misty spire rises up out of the murk.

Along the **Bay road** – which often runs a little inland – there are tracks and paths that run to the shoreline, to beautifully peaceful, often deserted spots, with sheep grazing in the salt marshes, and the Mount and the shifting horizons of the bay away in the distance – the point of Le Grouin du Sud and Le Gué de l'Epine, just south of Avranches, are two of the most atmospheric. All make fine points from which to appreciate the remarkable shape and ecology of the bay, which is in effect a vast, unique area of unstable, shifting territory, neither sea nor land, between the granite solids of the Cotentin and Brittany. Scattered in the sands, like three pebbles, there are three immovable granite rocks: Mont St-Michel, the little island of **Tombelaine** to its north, and **Mont-Dol**, long swallowed up by the land and which now forms a curious mountain near Dol-de-Bretagne, on the Breton side of the bay. According to one of the many bay legends, until around AD 700 the whole area consisted of a dense wood, the Forest of Scissy; then in 709 some hermit monks who lived there returned from a pilgrimage to Italy to find that a specially high tide had swept the whole forest away, leaving Mont St-Michel behind for St Aubert and the Archangel to found their monastery. This is impossible, but it is believed that the bay may well have been covered by a lost forest thousands of years earlier.

The **south side of the Bay** has been notoriously volatile, and much of the land here has been reclaimed from the sea. The river Couesnon, the frontier between Normandy and Brittany, was for centuries regarded as the region's curse because of its flooding and erratic course, until Dutch engineers established its present banks and began to drain the 'polders' west of the river in the 1860s. This drainage work, however, and the causeway that followed in 1877, have greatly aggravated the problem of silting up in the bay, and it is now likely that the long-disputed proposal to cut the Mont St-Michel causeway again will be carried out in the next few years.

Back on the north side of the bay, **Genêts** is a very attractive village, with another wonderful view, which like Avranches is inseparable from the Mount, for it grew up as the foremost departure-point for pilgrims walking to the abbey in the centuries when there was no causeway linking it to the mainland. It is still the main centre today for anyone seeking the unforgettable experience of getting to Mont St-Michel on foot across the sands, especially the **Maison de la Baie** just behind the Mairie (*see* 'Activities'). On no account should anyone attempt this journey without a guide. Legends abound about the giant tides and quicksands of the bay, and during the Middle Ages, when the major pilgrimage routes to the Mount ran through Genêts and Le Grand-Port, thousands of unwary pilgrims were lost to the sands, mists and the sudden arrival of the sea.

South of Avranches, the main road runs down to **Pontorson**, a pleasant town, with two outstanding hotels, that makes a good base for visiting the Mount. On the way it may be a good time to stop at Servon for lunch. Afterwards, head back to Pontaubault to get back on to the coast road for Mont St-Michel, now the D43. As the road winds across the flat, marshy fields, the abbey appears once again like a lodestar, sometimes hidden from view, at others re-emerging suddenly around a bend in the hedgerows. Along the way is Courtils, a lovely village on the very edge of the salt flats, with more superb views and great possibilities for walks on the bay shore. It also contains the southern **Maison de la Baie** (*open April–Oct; adm*), which doesn't organise so many walks but has a much larger exhibit on every aspect of the bay's ecology.

As you finally come up to the **causeway** to the Mount you are reminded with a thump that you are entering one of the world's great tourist sites, as the base of the causeway resembles nothing so much as an American small-town motel strip, with ranks of shiny new hotels, petrol stations, souvenir shops and fast-throughput restaurants. Apparently, though, this is no novelty: in the *Roman du Mont St-Michel*, written some time around 1160–1180, the monk Guillaume de St-Pair describes the annual September pilgrimage for the Feast of St Michael, when huge crowds converged on the bay from all directions, in procession with musicians, and bringing their livestock with them. All along the routes to the Mount there were tents with entertainments, and vendors selling wines, cakes and every other kind of food:

De lules parz aveit a vendre
Assez en out qui ad que tendre
('On every side there were things for sale
They had plenty enough, those who had the means to pay')

After this interlude you come on to the causeway proper, undeniably one of the greatest approaches in the world, with the Mount towering ever larger at the far end. Drivers are obliged to stop short of the rock and turn into one of the causeway car parks; if you are staying overnight on the Mount, resist any suggestions to do otherwise and continue to car park 1, nearest the entrance. From there a very narrow walkway leads to the first gate in the 15th-century ramparts, and the tourist office. Carry on through the massive Porte du Roi, the very model of a medieval citadel, into Mont St-Michel's only real street, the **Grande Rue**, which winds anti-clockwise around the rock. Tourist office literature optimistically refers to the shopkeepers of the Grande Rue 'maintaining a tradition born in catering to pilgrims in the Middle Ages'. This means in effect that they have been peddling junk for centuries. As well as the cutting of the causeway, another recent official proposal has been a rather sniffy suggestion that the shops of the Grande Rue lower the tone, and should be replaced with something more tasteful. However, with their Archangel-Michael thermometers, model boats, daft T-shirts, crêpes and Breton biscuits, the Grande Rue traders do maintain something of the all-life-is-there feel of a medieval pilgrimage, and reinforce the original imagery of the Mount, in which the climb up is supposed to lead out of the dross of worldly life towards God. It's possible to find some quite good, if expensive, craft jewellery and ceramics, mostly in the shops away from the main street along the ramparts.

Mont St-Michel is proud of still being officially a town, with a Mairie in the former Governors' residence above the Porte du Roi, even though its permanent population is less than a hundred. As well as the abbey it has some other museums and exhibits, none of them especially impressive (the **Logis Tiphaine**, a 14th-century house that belonged to the wife of Bertrand du Guesclin, French hero of the Hundred Years' War, is closed indefinitely for renovation). The **Musée Maritime** has old boat models and exhibits on the development of the bay, and the **Archéoscope** is a multi-media show on the history and legends surrounding the Mount; as part of the local taste offensive the very silly wax museum has been removed and replaced by a more worthy **Musée Historique** (*museums and Archéoscope open Feb–mid-Nov and Christmas week daily 9–6; adm exp; joint ticket available for all three museums*), dealing with the history of the abbey. More interesting is the town itself. Although the Grande Rue can seem Disneyfied, it is nonetheless an extraordinary image of a medieval street that's only a few feet wide for much of its length, with remarkably tall half-timbered gables that appear impossibly narrow and close together. Away from the Grande Rue, the town is a fascinating labyrinth of passages, stairways and ramparts.

The Grande Rue eventually winds up and round into the **Grand Degré** or great stair-case up to the abbey. Maupassant wrote that from different angles Mont St-Michel can look like a cathedral, or a fortress. It has also been called France's Pyramid, and has distinct similarities to the Potala Palace in Tibet. Vast quantities of granite were brought across the water from the Chausey Islands to build it; if nothing else it was an astonishing feat of structural engineering, in an era when only very simple tools were available. No one knows how many of its builders died at their work. Neglected after the 16th century, the Mount was rediscovered and venerated by Romantics such as Chateaubriand and Hugo, and from there entered the universal Gothic imagina-tion. Particularly striking are the abbey's proportions – some walls and windows are enormous beyond expectations, while other rooms are quite intimate. One of the most imposing sections is the Grand Degré itself, rising remarkably steeply between awesomely high walls.

The **Abbey** is a complex building in which rooms and wings from different periods and styles are all intertwined, so that it is impossible to look at it in chronological order. St Aubert's oratory was succeeded by the first substantial church on the rock in the early 10th century, but building really accelerated after the Benedictines took over the Mount and founded an abbey in 966. The main church was begun in 1017 by Abbot Hildebert, and the most important parts of it were completed in 1058, under William the Conqueror. One of the greatest periods for the abbey was the late-12th century, under Robert de Torigni, who made it a major centre for the production of manuscripts, and altered and extended the buildings in a Gothic-Transition style.

Part of the legend of Mont St-Michel is that it has never been captured in war. This really only applies to strictly non-French armies, for in 1204, when Philippe Auguste of France was struggling to wrest Normandy from King John, Breton soldiers allied to the French king took the Mount and severely damaged it in a fire. In atonement the king commissioned an entire new wing on the north side of the Mount, the master-piece of high Gothic known as the **Merveille** or Marvel. In return, Mont St-Michel became a bastion of French power in Normandy, and later resisted the English throughout the Hundred Years' War. Alterations were still being made to the buildings up until the 18th century, but the abbey was closed and badly damaged during the Revolution. It was made into a prison, remaining so until it became one of France's first national monuments in 1874.

It is theoretically possible to visit the abbey (*open May–Sept daily 9–5.30; Oct–April daily 9–4.30; also open French school hols daily 9–5; adm*) without a guide, but if you do you will find many sections closed to you. Mont St-Michel is, in any case, very difficult for first-time visitors to find their way round alone, so it's worth following the official tours (*for no extra charge, and in different languages*). The basic tour lasts about an hour, but still does not visit all the abbey; extended tours are available by appointment, for an extra charge. Since 1966, the abbey's millennium, there has again been a token religious presence of five or six monks and nuns on the Mount. Mass is celebrated in the church every day at 12.15pm, and they also organise retreats.

When you finally reach the top of the Grand Degré, you emerge via another gatehouse on to the **Western Platform**, with a fine view of the bay across to Cancale, and where the guides begin their tours. Surprisingly, the abbey church has a plain neoclassical façade, dating only from the 1770s. It once had a massive Gothic-Transition frontage designed by Robert de Torigni, but like his cathedral in Avranches this was not structurally all it should have been. It began to crumble in the 1300s, and when it finally fell beyond repair in the 18th century it took with it three of the seven arches of Abbot Hildebert's original 11th-century nave. **Inside** the church, you are immediately made aware of the extraordinary, mystical ambition of the abbey's builders. It was not built against the Mount, but on top of it, with the peak of the original rock precisely beneath the centre of the church's cross, so that the whole thing is actually a cathedral suspended in mid air. Around the centre are Hildebert's original four massive columns, the basis of the whole structure. They and the remaining arches of the nave form a classic if severe, plain Norman Romanesque. The choir, on the other hand, is in a light, graceful Flamboyant Gothic style, completed only in 1521, and built after the original choir had also given way, in the 15th century. The church thus contains both the first and final phases of medieval architecture.

The tour route runs in a rough spiral downwards, in a way that broadly mirrors the way the abbey was conceived, with the church at its apex, the monastic and official apartments below, and rooms for the reception of poor pilgrims at the bottom. On the same level as the church is one of the most beautiful and famous parts of the Merveille, the wonderful **Cloister** (1218–28), another monument suspended in space with sheer walls beneath it on two sides. In the middle there is now a large sculpture of a book in a glass case, a typical Mitterrand-era combination of the revered and the contemporary. The Cloister leads to the **Refectory**, from the same period, famed for the complex diffusion of light through its windows. Today, like the church, it can appear very austere and granite-grey – colour is the one major feature of the abbey that is now entirely missing: the main halls of Mont St-Michel were so large precisely because the abbots entertained exalted guests frequently, and they and the church would have been decorated throughout with frescoes, tiles and tapestries in lavish hues. Today, about the only place where one can get an idea of the colours of Mont St-Michel is in the manuscripts kept at Avranches.

As you descend, the intricacy with which rooms lead into each other is constantly surprising. Beneath the Cloister is the rib-vaulted **Promenoir** from 1115, one of the finest examples in existence of the Romanesque-Gothic transition. It was built as a place for monks to take exercise, but was also used as a refectory before the building of the one above, and Robert de Torigni entertained Henry II, Eleanor of Aquitaine and their court here in 1158. Nearby there is a human treadmill, used to haul supplies up an extraordinarily tall chute, which was installed as part of the prison in the 19th century but now seems one of the most Gothic parts of the whole edifice. Beyond is the mysteriously atmospheric crypt of the **Gros Piliers** or 'Great Pillars', a thicket of giant granite columns. Look up through a little hole in the centre of the ceiling and you suddenly realise you are underneath the choir of the church.

The most elegant room in the abbey is the **Guests' Hall**, part of the Gothic Merveille, with one row of delicate columns down the centre. Here late-medieval French Kings were received on their visits to the abbey. The contemporary **Knights' Hall**, on the other hand, is much larger. Despite its name it was most usually the main working room of the abbey, where the monks copied manuscripts, with two giant fireplaces to keep them warm. The last room visited on the main tour is the 12th- and 13th-century **Almonry**, where charity was distributed to poor pilgrims.

After leaving the abbey buildings walk around the wind-blown **gardens** on the north side of the Mount, a great place from which to look at the bay and admire the truly giant outside walls of the abbey, supported on buttresses that seem to soar up hundreds of feet out of the rock. You can also see the most modern part of the whole complex, the **spire**, only completed in the 1890s as part of the French government's post-prison restoration work. Another thing to look out for from the gardens, or the town ramparts with which they connect, is the incoming tide. The speed of the tides in the bay, which so terrified medieval pilgrims, has often been compared to a galloping horse, and the sight of the encroaching waters is undoubtedly spectacular, especially during the spring and autumn high tides. Tide tables are provided at the tourist office.

If you're here in summer (and don't mind paying to visit again), try to return to the abbey at night for the *son et lumière* performance. Inexplicably, the very popular **Les Imaginaires** that had run for several years was brought to an end in 2000, and is due to be replaced by a new presentation. The great attraction of Les Imaginaires, apart from the fact that the abbey was much less crowded than by day, was that you were free to wander at will, or stay for hours examining the shadows in one room if you wished, a superb way of experiencing the atmosphere. You could also see parts of the abbey not included in the main tour, notably **Notre-Dame-sous-Terre**, the wonderfully simple 10th-century first church of Mont St-Michel, which actually supports the nave of Hildebert's church. It's not clear what form the new night-time exhibit will take, but it's to be hoped that it will retain the prime virtues of the old one. It will originally only be presented in July, nightly, but from 2002 it should function from June to September.

Activities

Guided walks are run from the Maison de la Baie in Genêts (*April–Oct; the schedule varies according to weather and tides*). They actually set out from the traditional starting-place of the Bec d'Andaine, just north of the village. The walk (barefoot, and in shorts) takes about 1hr 45mins in each direction, with an hour or so on the Mount in between; commented walks (in French unless with special reservation) are also organised that include Tombelaine or explore the different historic pilgrims' paths, or deal with different aspects of the Bay's intricate history.

Walks are also run from the Maison du Guide on the Grande Rue in Genêts (**t** *02 33 70 83 49; April–Oct Sat and Sun; July and Aug daily*), and it's also possible to cross over on horseback (**t** *02 33 70 83 67*).

Shopping

The best local market around the Bay is in **Pontorson**, on Wednesdays, while in **Avranches** market day is Saturday. In summer, there's also a market on Sundays in **Genêts**.

Juilley ✉ 50220

La Lande Martel, t *02 33 60 65 48*, **f** *02 33 58 29 73*. Bernard and Marie-Hélène Cocman make only traditional dry and sweet ciders on their small farm south of the Bay, as well as offering *chambre-d'hôte* rooms (*see below*). In their farm shop, though, they also sell foodstuffs from other farm producers in the area, including *charcuterie*, butter, preserves, and dry calvados which will put hairs on your chest.

Le-Val-St-Pierre ✉ 50300

La Nonnerie, t *02 33 58 20 28*. A small farm in Le-Val-St-Pierre, between Avranches and the Bay shore near Le Gué de l'Epine, where Etienne Bechet raises goats, and produces several different varieties of fine *chèvre*.

Where to Stay

Ducey ✉ 50220

Auberge de la Selune, 2 Rue St-Germain, **t** *02 33 48 53 62*, **f** *02 33 48 90 30*, *www.selune.com* (*rooms 295–315F/ €44.97–48.02*). A four-square country hotel, in this attractive village just south of Avranches, which has been thoroughly renovated in the combination of modern and traditional style that you will find is much favoured in French hotels. Beyond the reception desk there is a lovely garden beside the fast-flowing River Selune, the winner of awards as the *plus fleuri* and best kept hotel garden in Normandy. The nineteen rooms are as brightly comfortable as the public areas, and the restaurant is one of the area's best (*see below*). A very relaxing, if slightly formal, place. *Closed Nov.*

Servon ✉ 50170

Auberge du Terroir, t *02 33 60 17 92*, **f** *02 33 60 35 26* (*rooms 290–340F/€44.21–51.83 for two, 420F/€64.03 for four*). The Auberge has six very attractive guest rooms, three in the main house and three in an adjacent annexe. All the rooms have been thoroughly renovated as the Leforts have expanded the hotel side of their business: each room is decorated in a pretty, colourful, neatly flowery style, each with different colours and details, and identified by a name rather than a number. Very comfortable with good facilities. They vary in size and one room is fully adapted for disabled guests. The village is very peaceful and, of course, there's the restaurant (*see above*).

Beauvoir ✉ 50170

Hôtel Le Beauvoir, 9 Route du Mont St-Michel, **t** *02 33 60 09 39*, **f** *02 33 48 59 65* (*rooms 310–340F/€47.26–51.83*). The most attractive of the hotels at the foot of the causeway, a cosy traditional Logis on Beauvoir's main street with a warm and friendly atmos-phere. Its 18 rooms are quite simple, but pleasantly comfortable and decent value. On the ground floor there's a similarly traditional, cosy **restaurant** (*menus 75–280F/€11.43–42.69*).

Pontorson ✉ 50170

Le Montgomery, 13 Rue Couesnon, **t** 02 33 60 00 09, **f** 02 33 60 37 66, *www.hotel.montgomery.fr* (*double rooms 320–750F/ €48.78–114.34*). The correct name of this hotel on Pontorson's main street is now in fact 'Best Western Montgomery', but it's still one of the most historic and characterful places to stay around the Bay. It occupies the 500-year-old former mansion of the Counts of Montgomery, distant relatives of the British Field Marshal, and the original 1550s main staircase, carved wood fittings, fireplaces and rambling corridors are spectacular: lovers of historic houses adore it. Some of the 32 rooms are in the same style, with four-poster beds and dark-timbered ceilings, others are more conventional, but all are very comfortable, and have especially big and well-equipped bathrooms (above all no.7, the 'Grand Luxe' room); from two rooms you can also, on a good day, see Mont St-Michel. Prices are reasonable for the standard. There's also a pretty garden terrace, and a **restaurant** (not open to non-residents). The Duchesne family and their staff are charming and run the hotel with a notable flair.

Hôtel de Bretagne, 59 Rue Couesnon, **t** 02 33 60 10 55, **f** 02 33 58 20 54 (*rooms 250–400F/ €38.11–60.98*). Pontorson's 'other' star hotel is not as historic as the Montgomery – it was built in 1903, and is more of a monument to the Belle Epoque – but lacks for nothing in character and quirky charm, as is soon apparent when you see its purple-painted front woodwork. A lot of this individuality – and the very personal attention given each guest – comes from its owner, Mme Carnet, in charge for nearly 40 years and a local legend. Hugely welcoming and as French as Edith Piaf, she has extended her original style through the whole place, from the figures in the lobby

to the décor (including that paint). Some of the 15 rooms are older and rather plain, with shared bathrooms, some are larger *chambres modernes* with full facilities; all are pleasant. There's also an excellent restaurant, and a great little lounge bar. *Closed Jan.*

Juilley ✉ 50220

La Lande Martel, **t** 02 33 60 65 48, **f** 02 33 58 29 73 (*rooms 210F/€32.01 for two*). Although it's only a few kilometres from the N175 and A84, this farm in deep-green countryside south of Avranches, 15km from Mont St-Michel, feels very far away from the urban world (and takes a little time to find). M and Mme Cocman have three simply decorated B&B rooms, all with bathrooms, which have their own entrance and access to a small living room and kitchen. And since this is a cider farm (*see* above), there is as much of the local speciality as you could possibly wish.

Courtils ✉ 50220

Manoir de la Roche Torin, **t** 02 33 70 96 55, **f** 02 33 48 35 20, *www.manoir-rochetorin.com* (*rooms 480–870F/ €91.47–132.63 for two; suite 910F/€138.73*). One of the most luxurious options around the Bay, in a grand, rather English-looking ivy-clad 19th-century house in a superb location right on the edge of the marshes north of the village of Courtils. Of the 13 elegant, traditionally styled rooms the ones really to go for are the three that actually have views of the Mont, one on the first floor and two with garden terraces. Other luxury-standard rooms and a three-person suite have larger terraces, while other rooms are smaller, but still attractive. And you get the same wonderful view by walking just a few steps beyond the end of the lush garden. Public rooms are plushly comfortable, and there is a fine restaurant (*see* below).

Champeaux ✉ 50530

**Au Marquis de Tombelaine-Hôtel les
Hermelles**, Route de Carolles, **t** 02 33 61
85 94, **f** 02 33 61 21 52 (*double rooms
280–320F/€42.69–48.78, with a 10% discount
Nov–Mar*). The very popular Marquis de
Tombelaine restaurant (*see below*)
has a six-room hotel above it. The rooms are
light and comfortable, but their greatest
draw is that in those at the front you wake
up to a superb view across to Mont
St-Michel.

Céaux ✉ 50220

Le Mée Provost, **t** 02 33 60 49 03 (*rooms 210F/
€32.01 for two, 310F/€47.26 for four*). A real
farm B&B in the countryside right in the
'corner' of the Bay, outside the village of
Céaux. When the Delaunay family began
renting rooms in the early 1980s it
was the first *chambre-d'hôte* in the area:
they now have five guest rooms, two family
rooms in the main house with space for up
to four, and three doubles in another
building. Comfortably equipped and with
old-fashioned décor, they're cosy, and
wonderful value. Guests also have
access to a kitchen, but this would mean
missing out on Mme Delaunay's breakfasts,
which use produce straight from the farm
and are served in a beautiful old room in the
main house. The Delaunays are very
friendly, one of the sons speaks English, and
the farm is only about a 1km walk from the
bay shore.

Genêts ✉ 50530

Le Moulin, **t** 02 33 70 83 78 (*rooms 200F/
€30.49 for two*). A spectacular old watermill
in Genêts, with burbling mill-race still alongside, where M Louis Daniel offers four B&B
rooms, three doubles and a twin.
They're simply decorated with nice bathrooms; extra children's beds can be
added, and there's a lounge for guests'
use. The location is wonderful, a short walk
from the quiet country village of Genêts,
the starting point for Bay walks.

Eating Alternatives

Mont St-Michel ✉ 50116

Auberge St-Pierre, Grande Rue, **t** 02 33 60
14 03, **f** 02 33 48 59 82, *www.auberge-saint-
pierre.fr* (*menus 95–320F/€14.48–48.78*). One
of the more attractive places to eat on
Mont St-Michel itself, thanks to its location
in one of the peculiarly tall and thin 15th-
century houses along the Grande Rue, and
its decent if not especially original classic
Norman dishes at reasonable prices. There's
a certain amount of Mont-kitsch (such as
the waitresses' obligatory peasant outfits),
but it's not overpowering, and the flowery
terrace at the back is pretty and tranquil. It's
also a Logis **hotel** (*rooms 490–620F/
€74.70–94.52*), with 21 small, snug rooms.
Closed Jan.

Ducey ✉ 50220

Auberge de la Selune, *see above* (*menus
84–208F/€12.81–31.71*). The Auberge's light
and airy dining room has a certain feel of a
classic restaurant *bourgeois*, with ultra-
smooth service and utterly snug seating.
The impressive cooking of chef-owner
Jean-Pierre Girres, however, offers
imaginative surprises: proper French and
Norman tradition is still the base, but
among the specialities are a wonderful crab
pie, *truite soufflée* – a complex, fragrant
concoction using trout from the river right
alongside – and even a vegetarian
aubergine *gâteau* with red pepper coulis.
It's superb value. *Closed Mon, and Oct–Feb
and Nov.*

Genêts ✉ 50530

Chez François, Rue Jérémie, **t** 02 33 70 83 98
(*there might not be a set menu; full meals no
more than 100F/€15.24*). A bit like a brick-
and-stone cave, this is a great village
café-bistro with a speciality of grilled
meats – pigs' trotters, pork chops, *andouillette* sausages, local lamb – and some fish,
cooked on an open wood fire in the massive
old fireplace. As accompaniments, there are
fresh salads, wonderful bread, occasional

bowls of shellfish and the usual rich desserts, and straightforward wines, beers and ciders. You can find it on a street that runs off Genêts' 'Grande Rue', very near the Mairie and Maison de la Baie. It's as simple as they come, but very enjoyable, and a favourite place to finish up after the over-the-Bay walk to Mont St-Michel. It's also very popular, so get there early for lunch. *Closed Thurs.*

St-Quentin-sur-le-Holme ✉ 50220

Le Gué du Holme, 14 Rue des Estuaires, **t** 02 33 60 63 76, **f** 02 33 60 06 77, *gue.holme@ wanadoo.fr* (*menus 150–390F/ €22.87–59.46*). One of the most prestigious restaurants around the Bay, in an imposing old stone building in the middle of the busy village of St-Quentin, south of Avranches, and with an elaborate *haute-cuisine* menu. It changes frequently, but among the refined offerings there might be mackerel in muscadet, grilled sea bream with an infusion of dill and a fennel fondue, stuffed leg of hare with a mustard vinaigrette and exquisite creations with duck. To go with the food there's a suitably proper, flower-decorated dining room, and a distinguished wine list. This is also a superior-standard Logis **hotel** (*rooms 400–500F/ €60.98–76.22*), with 10 spacious rooms. *Closed Fri and Sat lunch.*

Pontorson ✉ 50170

Hôtel de Bretagne, *see* above (*menus 89–215F/ €13.57–32.78*). The restaurant at the Bretagne is as individual as the rest of the hotel, with a beautiful art nouveau dining room at the front – with wonderful Edwardian-era radiators and plate-warmers – and a large, almost country-courtyard-like space within. The enjoyable food includes plenty of local classics – chicken braised in cider, oysters in a Camembert *gratin*, Bay lamb and mussels, fruity desserts – and is great value. It's a local favourite, with many regulars who have obviously been coming in and chatting to Mme Carnet for years. *Closed Mon, Oct–Mar, and Jan.*

Courtils ✉ 50220

Manoir de la Roche Torin, *see* above (*menus 130–320F/€19.82–48.78*). The big and neatly pretty dining room has a superb outlook through its conservatory-style windows, across gardens, fields and salt marshes to the Mont. On the inland side, there are tables in the garden. Its cooking has a high reputation: mainstay of the menu is *pré-salé* lamb, served several different ways, along with often-opulent variations on Norman classics and local seafood dishes. One of its greatest attractions, though, has to be the chance of a post-lunch stroll along the Bay's edge.

Champeaux ✉ 50530

Au Marquis de Tombelaine, *see* above (*menus 98–260F/€14.94–39.64*). One of the best culinary stops on the north side of the Bay, in a fabulous location on top of the cliffs just north of Champeaux – although from inside the old-world, stone-walled dining room you may not always get a view of the Sacred Mount. Chef-owner Claude Giard offers classic French cuisine with Norman touches – the great speciality is local lobster, available several different ways, but equally fine are the dishes featuring sea bass, Bay lamb and pork, and creamy desserts. The atmosphere is welcoming. *Closed Sept–June Tues eve and Wed.*

A Fortress on
the Ocean:
St-Malo

33

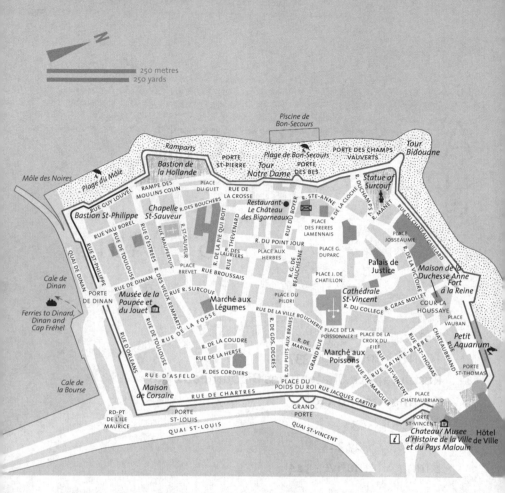

St-Malo, with a walled city still at its centre, has the most spectacular location of any of the ports along France's north coast. The old city looks almost as much a part of the sea as the land, its spires and giant ramparts filling up completely a spit of earth jutting out into the Atlantic at the mouth of the River Rance. Around it, the eye follows surf breaking over a scattering of tiny rocky islands, across to the green banks on the other side of the estuary. Its life has inevitably been tied to the sea. Mariners from St-Malo, called Malouins, sailed to every corner of the earth: to Canada, the Indian Ocean, and Polynesia, and the French and Spanish names for the Falkland Islands, the Malouïnes or Malvinas, stem from the fact that they were first discovered by men from here. This was the home port of many of France's greatest explorers.

The Malouins were also known for their bellicose independence. When the Duchy of Brittany was still independent in the Middle Ages, St-Malo appealed to the authority of the kings of France against their duke; at other times, they did the same thing in reverse, and at one point in the 16th century announced that they were 'neither Frenchmen, nor Bretons' and declared an independent republic. The city was

Getting There

The ferry terminals for boats from Britain, Ireland or the Channel Islands are just south of the old walled city of St-Malo, between it and the beaches of the Aleth peninsula. As you leave the terminals, turn left along Quai St-Louis, and the city walls are within easy walking distance. Coming into St-Malo from anywhere inland, follow the signs for *centre ville*, and more specifically Intra-Muros (the old city). Both routes will eventually bring you to Porte St-Vincent, the main entry for vehicles into the walled city. Just outside it is the tourist office, and a large free parking area; for drivers it's often the best idea to use it, as parking inside the walls can be difficult and expensive, while nowhere within the old city is very far to reach by foot.

Walk through the gate, and you come directly into Place Châteaubriand, the main square of the old city. To get to the Château des Bigorneaux, turn left in the square and follow Rue Jacques Cartier along the ramparts to Place du Poids du Roi, then turn right into Rue du Puits aux Braies, which leads through a few changes of name across the old town to the Rue du Boyer, and the restaurant. If you want to try driving there, turn immediately left in the square after you come through Porte St-Vincent and follow the ramparts (Rue de Chartres) almost to the southeast corner, then turn right up Rue de Toulouse. Follow this street almost to its end, and then turn right into Rue Vau Borel, which eventually leads to Place du Guet near the top of Rue du Boyer. If you see a parking place, grab it.

Tourist Information

St-Malo: Esplanade St-Vincent, Port des Yachts, t 02 99 56 64 48, f 02 99 56 67 00, *www.ville-saint-malo.fr*.

already notorious in the 13th century for its pirates, who demanded tribute from ships in the channel, and from the 17th century for close on 200 years St-Malo carried on world-wide wars virtually all of its own against England, Holland, Portugal and any other challengers, through its legendary privateers or Corsairs, whose names – Duguay-Trouin, Surcouf – crop up all over the city today as favourite sons. This privateering led to retaliation, and St-Malo was attacked several times by British and Dutch fleets. To resist them, small forts were built on many of the islands offshore.

Today, these forts and the ramparts still give the city something of the air of a bristling maritime stronghold. Inside, the atmosphere is now entirely peaceful. Within the walls of the old city, known as Intra-Muros, chasm-like narrow streets between tall granite houses open up into ample squares, lined with cafés for watching the town go by. Outside, at the very foot of the ramparts, there are beaches that fill up with Malouins and visitors each summer. Miraculously restored after the Second World War, it's a city that has retained its old character but has a vigorous modern life as well, visible in its shops, markets, café life, theatres and festivals. Away from the walled city, there are the basins of the port and the broader streets of modern St-Malo, but also small, wooded promontories and sheltered, rocky coves ideal for sailing.

In culinary matters, St Malo, as might be expected, has always relied heavily on fish and seafood, and also shown an open-minded willingness to mix Breton tradition – *galettes*, lobster, mussels – with other elements from Normandy, the rest of France and further afield. The **Château des Bigorneaux** is a little restaurant in one of the cobbled streets Intra-Muros where a very able young chef offers light, imaginative variations on local cuisine incorporating a wide range of contemporary influences.

Le Château des Bigorneaux

*14 Rue du Boyer, t/f 02 99 56 61 93. Open Sept–June Tues–Sat
12–2 and 7.30–10; July and Aug daily 12–2.30 and 7.30–11.30;
closed one week end Jan and one week June. Booking advisable.
Menus 68F/€10.37 (midday only) and 98F/€14.94;
à la carte average 180F/€27.44.*

Château in France can mean many things, from giant stately mansions to crumbling overgrown farms, but it can rarely ever have been applied to anything quite so small as this intimate little street-corner restaurant of just 25 covers, at the foot of one of the more historic old buildings in Intra-Muros St-Malo, one street away from the ramparts by the Porte des Bés. The low-ceilinged interior is prettily decorated, with stylishly modern greens and ochres and bunches of fresh flowers. The wooden tables and seats are necessarily close together, but it doesn't feel cramped. Tables here are in great demand, from a wide range of locals – families, friends of the owners, ladies who lunch, workers from the post office across the street – who all appreciate an imaginative, high-quality meal of exceptional value. Table space may be at a premium, but you'll be more than welcome to settle in for a relaxing afternoon.

The young couple who do everything at the restaurant, Stéfan and Natalie Vaugeois, hail from Rennes and have built up the Château's reputation over five years. Naturally Stéfan Vaugeois' most favoured dishes involve fish and seafood; the 98F/€14.94 menu includes a *retour du marché* special featuring the best from the fish market that day. Dishes are light, full of fresh, enjoyable flavours, and made with care and skill.

First courses might include stuffed *fruits de mer* in garlic butter, or maybe a refreshing *tartine* of Fourme d'Ambert cheese with a roast pear. Regulars among the main courses include a very smooth version of the classic *choucroute de mer*, including star anise and apple juice as well as salmon, *langoustines*, haddock and other fish, and a delicious *feuilleté* of salt cod with finely chopped vegetables. On the meat side, there might be a rich *brochette* of beef with pasta, or *magret* of duck with a pepper and honey sauce. Desserts often feature a very moreish, thick *tarte au chocolat* or a simple plate of *fromage blanc* with red berries. There's a simple, unfussy wine list which includes some excellent bottles such as a fine and light Nicolas de Bourgueil red (*c. 100F/€15.24*).

Bigorneaux are winkles, and the restaurant's name refers to an old St-Malo legend that was attached to a big old house that stood in one of the streets nearby until it was destroyed in the Second World War. In it there lived an old woman, who had a son who went off to do the *grande pêche* – deep-sea fishing off the Newfoundland Banks. On one voyage, on Christmas night, he was lost at sea; and at the very same moment, thousands of miles away, his mother saw in a dream that he had been killed. The next day she woke up to find *bigorneaux* covering her entire house. She sold them along with oysters outside the cathedral as people came away from Mass, and made her fortune. Her house then became known as the Château des Bigorneaux, Castle Winkle.

Touring Around

Although St-Malo has a substantial 19th- and 20th-century sprawl, its heart is still the walled city, surrounded by **ramparts** which are regularly interrupted by giant gates and bastions. The **Porte St-Vincent**, with the arms of St-Malo and Brittany above the gates on the outer façade, has been the old city's main entrance since the 18th century. In the pedestrian passageway alongside the main gateways is a tiny, barred chamber where anyone who tried to enter the city after the ten o'clock curfew, in force until 1770, was locked up for the night.

To the left of St-Vincent, looking towards the city, is the **Grande Porte**, formerly the principal entrance, with two massive 15th-century drum towers. The long, straight south side of the ramparts that crosses the **Porte de Dinan** has great views over the ferry terminal and the Aleth peninsula, while the **Bastion de la Hollande** on the sea-side of the walls contains the kennels of the famously ferocious watchdogs, released on to the beach every night during the 18th century to deter any nocturnal interlopers. The **Porte des Bés**, the next gate along going clockwise, has a large round tower next to it, the **Tour Notre-Dame**, and makes a good point to pause as it is the only gate with a crêperie on top (the Corps de Garde, see p.344). At each corner of the ramparts there are statues of doughty St-Malo seafarers; and of course there are the views: by the main gates you overlook the basins of the modern port, with the yachts down below; further round, look across to the harbour islands and the green shore of Dinard across the bay, which make the Rance estuary one of the most beautiful in the world.

The broad and sandy **beaches**, where people paddle, swim and windsurf, extend around the western and northern sides of the ramparts, continuing into the long Grande Plage along the sea front of the modern Paramé district. On the west side, the Plage de Bon-Secours, there is a walled-off salt-water swimming pool. Water buses to Dinard leave from the Cale de Dinan, by the southwest corner of the ramparts. Another favourite excursion is to paddle across at low tide to the **Fort National** (*open June–Sept daily; times depend on tides; adm*), one of the small bastions built on a rocky outcrop: slightly further out (so, once again, keep an eye on the tide), is the island of **Le Grand Bé**, with superb views back towards the city. This is the burial place of the writer Chateaubriand, the arch-romantic, sometime Foreign Minister and egomaniac who demanded to be buried here, and was given a virtual state funeral by his home town in 1848.

The present configuration of the ramparts is due to Marshal Vauban, the ubiquitous military engineer. Whether through conventional trade, slaving or piracy (*see* below), St-Malo had become France's most important commercial port, and in 1689 Vauban was sent here to provide the city with a comprehensive system of defences. They are among his greatest work, and, interrupted several times by ferocious Anglo-Dutch attacks, were only completed after his death by one of his assistants, Siméon de Garengeau. The old city was considerably extended, especially towards the Porte St-Louis on the south side. After a disastrous fire in 1661 the city council had banned the use of wood, and made stone – usually granite – obligatory for all buildings within the walls. It is thanks to this, and the plain, rather severe lines favoured by

Vauban's soldier-architects, that St-Malo sometimes has the look of a Gallic Aberdeen. Good examples of the distinctly military-looking *hôtels* erected during that era, built unusually high to maximise space within the confines of the walls, can be seen in Place Chateaubriand, Rue de Chartres and Rue des Cordiers, near the Grande Porte.

However, old St-Malo today is not really as the 18th-century architects left it. Look twice at many of the buildings Intra-Muros and you see that the stone is too clean, the edges too sharp, for them to be that old. The modern walled city is, in fact, a very clever replica. In August 1944, when General Patton's army broke out from Avranches across Brittany to the Loire, several thousand German soldiers retreated into St-Malo, determined to deny the allies the use of the port. They were led by one Andreas von Aulock, a caricature of a Prussian General complete with monocle, who during truce negotiations alternately infuriated and astonished his American opponents with his supercilious manner and habit of being immaculately turned out even at moments of ultimate crisis. He did have the good grace to order the civilian population out of the city, saying 'I prefer to have my enemies in front of me'; this, though, only encouraged the US commanders to try and batter their way in with all the means at their disposal, with bombardments from artillery, aircraft and ships offshore. Even so, it still took two weeks of ferocious street-by-street fighting before Von Aulock finally gave up resistance, in suitably Wagnerian style in the castle of the old city. By then, an estimated 80 per cent of Intra-Muros St-Malo had been destroyed and the port so comprehensively sabotaged that it would be unusable for months – although Vauban's ramparts withstood 20th-century technology as well as they had repelled cannonballs. Photos in the castle museum show the extent of the devastation.

Post-war, the city fathers of St-Malo did not tinker with any modernistic reconstruction plans, but with great determination set about getting their city back as they remembered it. Any buildings that could be were painstakingly restored; others, irredeemably lost, were replaced with new creations in matching style and materials. The resulting restoration is remarkably successful, and a model of its kind. Intra-Muros St-Malo doesn't feel like an artificially preserved city, and even locals can be hard put to identify which buildings are genuinely old and which are not. Its cobbled streets remain atmospheric and engaging places to wander around, and you can discover corners such as the Cour de la Houssaye, near the meeting-point of Rue de la Corne de Cerf and Rue Chateaubriand, where there's a relic of St-Malo from before Vauban's time, the **Maison de la Duchesse Anne**, a fine example of a 15th-century Breton stone townhouse. In the Rue d'Asfeld, in the southeast corner of the old city near the Porte St-Louis, there is the **Maison de Corsaire** (*open Feb–Nov Tues–Sun 10.30–12 and 2.30–6; adm*), also known as the Demeure des Magon de la Lande or Maison Asfeld, an imposing 18th-century townhouse built for the Magons, one of the city's wealthiest merchant dynasties. It was long ago converted into apartments, but parts of it have now been opened up as a private museum in which an enthusiastic guide takes tours (in French) around some of the rooms that have remarkably survived unchanged, including the original dining room.

The streets of Intra-Muros also attract thousands of visitors, which can make the main squares overpowering in high summer, but other streets stay much more tranquil. St-Malo's old city also has a lively, quite trendy and studenty nightlife, with two little hubs around Rue de la Corne de Cerf and Rue de Dinan; a less fashionable crowd gravitates to Rue Jacques Cartier by the ramparts, while all and sundry meet up in Place Chateaubriand. By day the old city still hosts vigorous **markets** (*Tues and Fri mornings*) that are great places to stock up on every kind of food (there are also markets in districts outside the walls on other days, *see* p.343). More static shopping is concentrated around Rue Broussais and Place du Pilori, where there are some smart fashion and food shops, and plenty of opportunities to buy Breton knick-knacks and other souvenirs.

Here and there in the old town there are sections that retain a raffish, port-city air, such as the lines of touristy bars and restaurants set into the ramparts along Rue Jacques Cartier and Rue d'Orléans, or the waterfront dives on Rue de Chartres. The main social focus of old St-Malo, however, is **Place Chateaubriand** by the Porte St-Vincent, site of a clutch of grand cafés that are the prime places to secure a table for an afternoon, and well justify their slightly above-average prices with celebrated 19th-century interiors that post-1945 were restored more lovingly than the city's (not especially striking) Gothic cathedral. Around the corner, at 3 Rue Chateaubriand, is the house where the great writer was actually born, in 1768.

Overlooking the cafés on one side of the *place* is the castle, now housing the **Musée d'Histoire de la Ville et du Pays Malouin** (*open Oct–Easter Mon, Wed–Sun 10–12 and 2–6, closed Tues and hols; Easter–Sept daily 10–12 and 2–6pm; adm*). A visit to the museum also allows you to explore the inside of the castle, built in the 1420s and then modified by Vauban, and take in the great views from the top ramparts, with their low galleried roofs. The museum collection is a corker: it makes scarcely any concessions to progressive notions of history or modern museum techniques, and is for the most part an unabashedly old-fashioned and gung-ho celebration of local heroes, especially mariners and pirates. Piracy had long been practised by the seamen of St-Malo, but it was not until the 1660s that Louis XIV's minister Colbert followed England and Holland in authorising French captains to engage in privateering, as long as part of the booty was passed on to the state. For much of the next century, privateering employed as many men in St-Malo as did conventional trade, and its profits did much to build the post-Vauban city (St-Malo's ships also played their part in the slave trade, something the museum conveniently makes little of). The legendary privateer or corsair captains, though, are fully commemorated: there's **Duguay-Trouin**, who plundered Rio de Janeiro in 1711 and ended up as one of the town's wealthiest citizens; **La Bourdonnais**, taking Madras from the British in 1746; and **Robert Surcouf**, who privateered for Napoleon and seized HMS Kent in 1803. Needless to say, these Gallic sea-dogs have never rated much of a mention in standard British history books. Also present in the museum are less martial heroes such as the explorer Cartier, the inescapable Chateaubriand and the Catholic writer Lamennais, and a mixed bag of displays on aspects of St-Malo's history such as the lives of fishermen, local customs and the reconstruction after 1945.

There are also attractive parts of St-Malo outside the walls. From any of the gates on the harbour side of the ramparts, turn right and walk around the quays, past the ferry terminal, from where boats also depart on excursions around the Rance and the bay of Mont-St-Michel. Cut right at Rue Clémenceau and Rue Dauphine, and you will come to the **Plage des Sablons**, a sheltered beach on a neatly arc-shaped cove that's now full of yachts and dinghies. Beyond it, clad in trees and standing out into the estuary, is the promontory of **Cité d'Aleth**. This was actually the site of the first city of St-Malo, a Gallo-Roman and then an early Breton settlement, and contained the hermitage of Maclow, or Maclou (from whence comes St-Malo), a Christian monk and mystic, believed to have been Welsh, who came here from Britain in the 6th century. However, the erosion of the peninsula led to the main community transferring to the Intra-Muros area in 1146. There is a beautiful walk on the Corniche path around the Aleth peninsula, with great views of Dinard and the Rance. At the other end of the path, winding, narrow streets and snug, rocky inlets with shingle beaches create the feel of a small harbour town; this, like several other outlying parts of town, was only incorporated into St-Malo in 1967. On a spit of rock stands the Tour Solidor, a 14th-century fortress that now contains St-Malo's other main museum, the **Musée International des Cap-Horniers** (*open Oct–Easter Mon, Wed–Sun 10–12 and 2–5, closed Tues and hols; Easter–Sept daily 10–12 and 2–6; adm*), dedicated to the sailing ships that went to fish the Newfoundland banks and to round Cape Horn.

St-Malo also has another nautical attraction, the **Manoir de Jacques Cartier** (*open Oct–May Mon–Fri, tours 10 and 3; June and Sept Mon–Fri 10–11.30 and 2.30–6; July and Aug daily 10–11.30 and 2.30–6; adm*) at Limoëlou, away on the eastern edge of the city in the suburb of Rotheneuf. Cartier discovered the St Lawrence river, and founded Montreal and French Canada. The house is a little hard to find – probably the best way to get there is to follow the beach road and Avenue Kennedy straight out of St-Malo, and then look for signs when you get to Rotheneuf – but this plain little Breton manorhouse, with its drains, marriage chests and simple kitchen, gives a fascinating insight into the life of a none-too-prosperous gentleman of the time. (None of the articles actually belonged to Cartier, as the manor-farm had passed through many owners before its restoration by a Canadian foundation in the 1970s.) Cartier first sailed to Canada in 1534, and then again the next winter when he lost most of his crew to cold or scurvy. Before his third voyage in 1542 he was told by François I that, as a commoner, he had to go as second-in-command to a nobleman; the irascible Cartier refused to accept this and sailed off in his own ship, hoping to reinstate himself with the King by returning with some gold given to him by Indians. However, this turned out to be no more than iron pyrites or 'fool's gold', and Cartier retired to his basic house in disgrace. He died of the plague in 1557; it has been believed that he was buried in the cathedral in St-Malo, but during restoration of the house a body was discovered buried beneath the kitchen, so he may in fact have been buried here.

East of St-Malo, beyond Rotheneuf, the D201 coast road will take you past head-lands, lighthouses, and a succession of beautiful coves with open seas and scudding surf to the fishing harbour of Cancale, a favourite holiday town of Colette, and famous throughout France for its oysters. On a good day, there are also views all the way across the bay to Mont-St-Michel.

Shopping

There are markets on Tuesdays and Fridays: Place de la Poissonnerie is still a fish market and there are stalls in the streets around Place du Pilori; the main market by Place du Marché aux Légumes is now under cover. There are also markets outside the walls in Paramé (*Wed and Sat*), and St-Servan (*Tues and Fri*).

As well as fish, seafood and crêpes, St-Malo's food speciality is its traditional confectionery – *specialités malouines* – produced in a bewildering range of shapes, sizes and ingredients.

St-Malo ✉ 35400

Arts et Créations, 9 Rue des Cordiers, **t** 02 99 40 16 48. A little workshop, in an old stone-walled storehouse, which produces hand-crafted paper and fine stationery.

Cave de l'Abbaye St-Jean, 7 Rue des Cordiers, **t** 02 99 20 17 20, **f** 02 99 20 17 18. Excellent, individual wine merchant in another old storehouse, with over 1,000 French wines, plus local ciders and beers. The young staff (several English-speaking) are very helpful.

Maison Guella, 8 Rue de Porcon, **t** 02 99 40 83 43. St-Malo's most renowned *chocolatier* and confectioner: a giant stall at the eastern end of the cathedral, selling every kind of *spécialités régionales* in chocolate, nuts and sugar – highlights are the buttered caramels and the *patates malouines*, little fried balls of potato, almond and sugar, which seem a little dull at first but get more interesting as you work your way through the bag.

La Savonnerie, 12 Rue de Dinan, **t** 02 99 40 30 20. Utterly French little shop selling fragrant soaps, gels, shampoos, body milks, etc. – all handmade using fine natural ingredients – and plenty of other gift ideas.

Spirale, 5 Place aux Herbes, **t** 02 99 40 84 48. A stylish contemporary design shop tucked away on a quiet square. It has great lamps, ceramics, etc., as well as vibrantly inventive textiles, especially towels.

Taffin Chocolatier, 4 Rue Broussais, **t** 02 99 40 93 53. A more traditional purveyor of chocolate, sweets and pastry, with its Malouin and Breton specialities. Breton *gâteaux*, *Kouign Amann* (puff-pastry cakes), *galettes*, crêpes, homemade ice-cream. There's a whole range of often-ornate gift presentations.

Where to Stay

Hotels within the old city are a little expensive, but you gain enormously in atmosphere. Since the old houses tend to be rather tall, having a lift can be a significant consideration.

St-Malo ✉ 35400

Hôtel Elizabeth, 2 Rue des Cordiers, **t** 02 99 56 24 98, **f** 02 99 56 39 24 (*rooms 500–780F/€76.22–118.9*). In one of the oldest stone buildings in St-Malo, built in 1558 (the year of the accession of Elizabeth I, hence the name), on the south side of Intra-Muros; three rooms at the very top (there's a lift) have harbour views. All are very spacious, and the décor is semi-17th-century opulence. Breakfast is served in a wonderful cellar.

Hôtel de France et de Chateaubriand, Place Chateaubriand, **t** 02 99 56 66 52, **f** 02 99 40 10 04, *www.hotel.fr.chateaubriand.com* (*rooms 360–432F/€54.88–65.85 for two*). St-Malo's most historic grand hotel, lovingly rebuilt after 1944, retains a great deal of period charm and brio. The lobby, Second-Empire dining room and terrace are all stunning; the 80 rooms have much less character, but offer traditional plush comfort. Some have a lovely view of the sea or the *place*. The **restaurant** (*menus from 95F/€14.48*) serves classic local cuisine, with lobster and mussels as specialities.

Hôtel Le Nautilus, 9 Rue de la Corne de Cerf, **t** 02 99 40 42 27, **f** 02 99 56 75 43, *nautilus-st-malo@wanadoo.fr* (*rooms 350F/€53.35 for two*). A hip small hotel in one of the city's most vertical buildings – with a lift. Some of the 15 striking rooms are decorated in bright modern colours, some are more traditional; some are tiny, inserted into the eaves, but all have excellent facilities. (Rooms on the first floor can be a little noisy.) The hotel is run with style and imagination, and at street level there's an equally stylish bar, with some outside tables, where you can descend for excellent breakfasts in the morning and cocktails at night.

Hôtel-Restaurant de la Pomme d'Or, 4 Place du Poids du Roi, **t** 02 99 40 90 24, **f** 02 99 40 58 31 (*double rooms 265–350F/€40.4–53.35*). A rather old-fashioned hotel, with 13 well-maintained rooms and fine views over the harbour from the top floors. The atmosphere is cosy, and the lady who runs it has several cats and other animals. There's a similarly cosy **restaurant** (*menus 69–215F/ €10.52–32.77*), with some outside tables, serving good fish and seafood. *Closed Jan.*

Hôtel San Pedro, 1 Rue Ste-Anne, **t** 02 99 40 88 57, **f** 02 99 40 46 25 (*rooms 280–320F/ €42.68–48.78*). An unassuming small hotel in one of the granite-tower buildings on the north side of Intra-Muros, so rooms on the upper floors have great sea views. The 12 rooms have good facilities, and there's a lift.

Hôtel de l'Univers, Place Chateaubriand, **t** 02 99 40 89 52, **f** 02 99 40 07 27, *www.st-malo.com/hotel-de-lunivers* (*double rooms from 290F/€44.21; family rooms from 475F/ €72.41*). The Univers is a monument to the 1890s, the Belle Epoque, with some original features that survived the 1944 siege. The 61 rooms have an old-world stylishness; nine rooms have views over the square. The restaurant is equally enjoyable (*see below*).

Hôtel-Bar Le Valparaíso, 9 Rue de la Pie qui Boit, **t** 02 99 40 94 63 (*rooms 180–240F/ €27.44–36.59 for two*). An easygoing hotel in the heart of Intra-Muros St-Malo that's one of the best budget choices in town. The nine rooms are simple and comfortable, but there's no lift. Downstairs there's a laidback little bar, popular with the local bohemians.

Eating Alternatives

As in the rest of Brittany, St-Malo has lots of crêperies, which always offer savoury *galettes* and sometimes salads as well as sweet crêpes. Note, however, that while crêperies are generally open all day, they often close quite early in the evening.

St-Malo ✉ 35400

Le Chalut, 8 Rue de la Corne de Cerf, **t/f** 02 99 56 71 58 (*menus 115–270F/€17.53–41.16; fabulous five-course 'all-lobster' menu 370F/ €56.40*). One of St-Malo and Brittany's premier seafood restaurants. Chef Jean-Philippe Foucat's menus vary considerably to make the most of the best fresh fish and shellfish each day; main courses might include brill pan-fried with coriander and a *langoustine* sauce, or a superb John Dory with *girolles* mushrooms. *Closed Mon and Tues; reservations essential.*

La Corderie, 9 Chemin de la Corderie, Cité d'Alet, **t** 02 99 81 62 38, **f** 02 99 81 25 14 (*menus 98–250F/€14.94–38.11*). In a big old house, with fabulous views of Tour Solidor and over the Rance estuary to Dinard. A little hard to locate, near the point where the road ends by the Corniche path around the Aleth peninsula. Market-fresh local produce is the highlight: oysters and *moules à la crème. Closed Mon exc July and Aug.*

Hôtel de l'Univers, *see above* (*menus 75–200F/€11.43–30.49*). The terrace and ornate 1890s dining room are among the most stylish and atmospheric places on Place Châteaubriand, and are also very good value. There are no great surprises in the fare: *plateaux de fruits de mer*, mussels, etc. in the restaurant; crêpes, *croques* and salads in the bar and on the terrace.

La Coquille d'Oeuf, 20 Rue de la Corne de Cerf, **t** 02 99 40 92 62 (*menus 68–148F/ €10.37–22.56*). An attractive modern restaurant with good-value menus and a big range: from interesting salads and pasta through light fish or meat dishes to more hefty classics like a seafood *choucroute*. Service is friendly and efficient. *Closed Mon.*

Crêperie Ty-Nevez, 12 Rue Broussais, **t** 02 99 40 82 50. The longest-running crêperie in St-Malo, owned by the same family for over 40 years. Wonderful crêpes and savoury *galettes* in a full range of flavours (*from c. 20F/€3.05*) plus speciality crêpes and Breton cider. *Open till c. 7.30pm. Closed Wed.*

Le Corps de Garde, 3 Montée Notre Dame, **t** 02 99 40 91 46. A pleasant little bar-crêperie, and the only place to eat on top of the walls, with an invigorating view out to sea. It occupies a former guardhouse on top of the Porte des Bés, hence the name.

Le Bouff'tard, 13 Rue de Chartres, **t** 02 23 18 10 28. Not the most elegant restaurant in town, the Bouff'tard (a pun that could be translated as the 'late blow-out') is a battered little place that serves cheap (*25–50F/€3.82–7.62*) crêpes, *galettes* and pizzas until around 3am every night. Conversely, it isn't usually open during the day.

Glossary

The full French culinary vocabulary is enormous, and several pocket guides are available that give extensive lists of the many terms and phrases. The following should, though, provide some of the necessary basics. For more information on specific dishes and cheeses, see The Food and Drink of Northern France, pp.5–12.

Useful Phrases

I'd like to book a table (for two/at 12.30pm)
  Je voudrais réserver une table (pour deux personnes/à midi et demie)
lunch/dinner *le dejeuner/le dîner*
Is it necessary to book for lunch/dinner today?
  Est-ce qu'il faut réserver pour déjeuner/dîner aujourd'hui?
Waiter/Waitress! (to attract their attention)
  Monsieur/Madame/Mademoiselle! S'il vous plaît
The 130F menu, please *Le menu à cent trente francs, s'il vous plaît*
Which are your specialities? *Quelles sont les spécialités de la maison?*
What is (this dish), exactly? *Qu'est-ce que c'est exactement, (ce plat)?*
The wine list, please *La carte des vins, s'il vous plaît*
Another bottle of wine, please *Une autre bouteille, s'il vous plaît*
water (from the tap, perfectly good in France, and usually given as a matter of course)
  une carafe d'eau
mineral water/fizzy/still *eau minérale/gazeuse/plate*
coffee (espresso) *café*
white coffee *café au lait /café crème*
That was wonderful *C'était formidable/délicieux*
We've enjoyed the meal very much, thank you
  Nous avons très bien mangé, merci
The bill, please *L'addition, s'il vous plaît*

Poissons et Coquillages (Fish and Shellfish)

bar sea bass
barbue brill
bigorneau winkle, sea snail
bulot whelk, large sea snail
cabillaud fresh cod
calamar squid
colin hake
coques cockles
coquilles St-Jacques large scallops
crabe crab
crevettes grises shrimps
crevettes roses prawns
daurade sea bream
écrevisses freshwater crayfish
escargots snails
espadon swordfish
flétan halibut
fruits de mer seafood
gambas large prawns
hareng herring
homard lobster
huîtres oysters
langouste spiny lobster or crawfish
langoustine Dublin Bay prawn
lieu pollack or ling
lotte monkfish
loup de mer sea bass
maquereau mackerel
merlan whiting
morue salt cod
moules mussels
mulet grey mullet
ombre grayling
oursin sea urchin
palourde clam
pétoncle small scallop
poulpe octopus
raie skate
rascasse scorpion-fish
rouget red mullet
St-Pierre John Dory

saumon salmon
saumonette dogfish
sauterelles shrimps in Picardy
sole sole
thon tuna
tortue turtle
tourteau large crab
truite trout
truite saumonée sea/salmon trout
turbot turbot

Viandes, Volaille, Charcuterie (Meat, Poultry, Charcuterie)

battis/abats giblets/offal
agneau (de pré-salé) lamb (raised on salt marshes)
andouille large sausage made from offal, served cold
andouillette smaller than an andouille, eaten hot
ballotine boned, stuffed and rolled meat (cold)
biftek, bifteck steak
bœuf beef
boudin blanc white pudding, a sausage made with veal, chicken, pork
boudin noir black pudding
caille quail
canard, caneton duck, duckling
cervelas garlic pork sausage
cervelles brains
chapon capon
chevreau kid
chevreuil roe deer; also venison in general
civet stew (rabbit or hare)
colvert mallard
daguet young venison
dinde, dindon turkey
dindonneau young turkey
estouffade braised meat stew
faisan pheasant
foie liver
foie gras fattened goose or duck liver
galantine meat stuffed, rolled, set in its own jelly
gésier gizzard
gibiers game
grive thrush

jambon ham
jambon cru salt-cured, raw ham
langue (de veau, de bœuf) tongue (veal, ox)
lapereau young rabbit
lapin rabbit
lard (lardons) bacon (diced)
lièvre hare
marcassin young wild boar
merguez spicy red sausage (North African)
moëlle beef marrow
navarin (d'agneau) lamb stew with spring vegetables
oie goose
os bone
perdreau young partridge
perdrix partridge
petit salé salt pork
pintade guinea fowl
pintadeau young guinea fowl
porc pork
poularde fattened chicken
poulet chicken
poussin spring chicken
queue de bœuf oxtail
rillettes potted meats (duck, goose, pork, rabbit)
ris (de veau) sweetbreads (veal)
rognons kidneys
sanglier wild boar
saucisses sausages
saucisson salami-type sausages, cold
tête (de veau) head (of veal)
tripes tripe
veau veal
venaison venison

Meat Cuts

aiguillette long, thin slice
carré (d'agneau) rack (of lamb)
châteaubriand double fillet steak, usually with a béarnaise sauce
contre-filet, faux-filet sirloin steak
côte, côtelette chop, cutlet
cuisse leg or thigh
entrecôte rib steak
épaule shoulder
escalope thin fillet
gigot (d'agneau) leg (of lamb)
jarret shin or knuckle
magret, maigret (de canard) breast (of duck)

noisette (*d'agneau*) small round cut (of lamb)
onglet flank of beef
pavé thick, square fillet
pieds trotters
râble (*de lièvre, de lapin*) saddle (of hare, rabbit)
rôti roast
selle (*d'agneau*) saddle (of lamb)
tournedos thick round slices of steak
travers de porc pork spareribs

Cooking Terms for Steaks and Grills

bleu very rare
saignant rare
à point medium rare
bien cuit well done

Légumes, Herbes, Epices (Vegetables, Herbs, Spices)

ail garlic
algue seaweed
aneth dill
aromates aromatic herbs
artichaut artichoke
asperges asparagus
aubergine aubergine
avocat avocado
avoine oats
badiane star anise
baies roses pink peppercorns
basilic basil
betterave beetroot
blette swiss chard
cannelle cinnamon
carotte carrot
céleri celery
céleri-rave celeriac
cèpes wild, large, brown, fleshy mushrooms
cerfeuil chervil
champignons mushrooms
chanterelles wild, yellowish mushrooms (*girolles*)
chicorée frisée curly endive lettuce
chou cabbage
chou-fleur cauliflower

chou-frisé kale
chou de mer seakale
choux de Bruxelles Brussels sprouts
ciboulette chives
citrouille pumpkin
cœur de palmier palm hearts
concombre cucumber
coriandre coriander
cornichons gherkins
courge pumpkin
cresson watercress
échalote shallot
endive chicory
épinards spinach
estragon tarragon
fenouil fennel
fèves broad beans
flageolets white, dried beans
frites chips
genièvre juniper
gingembre ginger
girofle clove
girolles same as *chanterelles*
haricots (*rouge, blanc, vert*) beans (kidney, white, green)
laitue lettuce
laurier bay leaf
lentilles lentils
maïs (*épis de*) sweet corn (on the cob)
marjolaine marjoram
menthe mint
morilles morel mushrooms
muscade nutmeg
navet turnip
oignons onions
oseille sorrel
panais parsnip
persil parsley
petits-pois peas
piment pimento, hot red pepper
piment doux (*poivron*) sweet red or green pepper
pissenlit dandelion
pleurotes soft-fleshed wild mushrooms
poireau leek
pois chiche chickpea
poivron sweet red or green pepper
pomme de terre potato
radis radish
raifort horseradish
riz rice
romarin rosemary

safran saffron
salade salad (often just lettuce)
salade Lyonnais green salad together with eggs, diced bacon, shallots, fish (herring, anchovies) and maybe sheep's trotters or other meat cuts
salade Niçoise substantial salad: a combination of lettuce, tomatoes, hard-boiled eggs, tuna, potatoes, olives, capers, artichokes and anchovies, with a herby vinaigrette
salade verte green salad
salsifis salsify
sarriette savory (the herb)
sarrasin buckwheat
sauge sage
scarole escarole
seigle rye
thym thyme
tomate tomato
truffes truffles

Fruits, Noix, Desserts (Fruits, Nuts, Desserts)

abricot apricot
amande almond
ananas pineapple
banane banana
bavarois made with whipped cream, egg custard
bombe ice-cream dessert in a round mould
brugnon nectarine
cacahouètes peanuts
cajou cashew nut
cassis blackcurrant
cerise cherry
charlotte dessert in a mould with ladies' fingers
citron/citron vert lemon/lime
clafoutis black-cherry tart
coing quince
corbeille de fruits basket of fruits
coupe ice-cream cup
crème anglaise very light custard
crème Chantilly sweet whipped cream
crème fleurette double cream
crème fraîche sour cream
crème pâtissière custard filling
dattes dates
figues figs
figue de Barbarie prickly pear

fraises (des bois) strawberries (wild)
framboises raspberries
fruit de la passion passion fruit
génoise sponge cake
glace ice cream
grenade pomegranate
groseilles red currants
macarons macaroons
madeleine small sponge cake
mandarine tangerine
mangue mango
marrons chestnuts
miel honey
mirabelles small yellow plums
mûres mulberries, blackberries
myrtilles bilberries
noisette hazelnut
noix walnut
œufs à la neige light meringue in a vanilla custard
pamplemousse grapefruit
parfait chilled mousse
pastèque watermelon
pêche peach
pignons pine nuts
pistache pistachio
poire pear
pomme apple
prune plum
pruneau prune
reine Claude greengage
raisin grapes
raisins secs raisins
sablé shortbread biscuit
savarin ring-shaped cake, in rum- or kirsch-flavoured syrup
tarte Tatin caramelised apple pie, upside-down
truffes chocolate truffles

General Terminology

aigre-doux sweet and sour
allumettes strips of puff pastry or potatoes
amuse-gueules appetisers
(à l') anglaise plain boiled
barquette small pastry boat
béarnaise classic sauce of egg yolks, white wine, shallots, butter, tarragon
béchamel white sauce of butter, flour, milk
beignets fritters
Bercy similar to a *beurre blanc*, but thicker

beurre blanc reduced sauce of butter, white wine, vinegar, shallots

beurre noir browned butter, lemon juice, capers and parsley

bisque thick soup, usually of seafood

blanquette thick creamy stew

bouchée tiny mouthful, or *vol-au-vent*

bouillon stock or broth

brébis sheeps'-milk cheese

braisé braised

brioche sweet bread or roll

(à la) broche spit-roasted

brouillé scrambled

brûlé caramelized ('burnt')

chasseur white wine sauce, mushrooms, shallots

chausson pastry turnover

chèvre goats'-milk cheese

cocotte round ceramic dish

confit meat preserves

confiture jam

coulis thick sauce, purée

court-bouillon stock

croustade savoury pastry case

(en) croûte in a pastry crust

cru raw

cuit cooked

demi-glace basic brown sauce, reduced meat stock

diable peppery sauce: mustard, vinegar, shallots

Duxelles mushrooms and shallots sautéd in butter and cream

émincé thinly sliced

épices spices

farci stuffed

(au) feu de bois cooked over a wood fire

feuilleté flaky pastry leaves

forestière with mushrooms bacon and potatoes

(au) four oven-baked

fourré filled or stuffed, usually sweets

frappé with crushed ice

fricassé braised in sauce of white wine, butter, and cream

frit fried

friture mixed platter of small fried fish

fumé smoked

galette buckwheat pancake

garni garnished; served with vegetables

gelée aspic

glacé iced

grillade mixed grill

hachis minced or chopped

hollandaise sauce of egg yolks, butter, lemon juice

jardinière with diced garden vegetables

marmite small casserole

matelote fish stew

meunière fish: floured, fried in butter, with lemon and parsley

mijoté simmered

Mornay cheesy béchamel

mousseline hollandaise sauce with egg whites and whipped cream

moutarde mustard

(à la) nage poached in an aromatic broth (fish)

nature, au naturel simple, plain

panaché mixed, a mixture

pané breaded

(en) papillote baked in buttered paper or foil

Parmentier with potatoes

pâte pastry, dough

pâte à chou choux pastry

pâte brisée shortcrust pastry

paupiettes thin slices of fish or meat filled, rolled, wrapped to cook

paysan, paysanne country-style; with bacon, potato, carrot, onion, turnip

poché poached

poêlé pan-fried

poivrade peppery sauce: a demi-glace, wine, vinegar, vegetables

potage thick soup

primeurs early-season vegetables

printanière garnish of spring vegetables

quenelles dumplings made with fish or meat

râpé grated, shredded

rémoulade mayonnaise with capers, mustard, gherkins, herbs; also shredded celery

roulade rolled meat or fish, often stuffed

sabayon whipped up wine, egg-yolks and sugar (zabaglione)

salé salted, spicy

sauvage wild

Soubise white onion sauce

sucré sweet, sugared

suprême boned breast of poultry; fish fillet; a creamy sauce

tiède lukewarm

timbale small pie cooked in dome-shaped mould

tranche slice

(à la) vapeur steamed

velouté white sauce flavoured with stock

Véronique garnished with grapes

Index

Page references to maps are in *italics*.

Acknowledgements

First of all, my very sincere thanks to all the chefs and restaurateurs featured in this guide, and to their families, for their great hospitality, courtesy, enthusiasm, generosity with their time and, of course, their cooking. My appreciation, too, to all the chambre-d'hôte proprietors who welcomed me into their homes, and to the many shopowners, museum staff, farmers, foodproducers and others mentioned in this book, for responding so well to so much tedious questioning from a dumb foreigner. Enormous thanks go also from the publishers and myself to the representatives of the various Comités Départementaux du Tourisme and other local authorities for indispensable assistance, and for their unfailing courtesy, professionalism, friendliness, interest in and knowledge of their area: Diana Hounslow and Nicolas Célie of the CDT Pas-de-Calais; Judith Richard and Katia Breton of the Comité Régional Nord-Pas-de-Calais; Anne-France Rouxel of the CDT de la Somme; Armelle Baudrier and Geneviève Muller of the CDT-Seine-Maritime; Capucine d'Halluin of the CDT-Eure; Armelle Le Goff of the CDT-Calvados; Isabelle Chollet of the CDT de la Manche; and the staff of the Offices de Tourisme in St-Malo and Lyons-la-Forêt, and Magali Thuillier in Etretat. Special thanks are due too to Michel Agodi in Dieppe, Sophie Osouf in St-Valéry-en-Caux and above all Chantal Atamian in Eu, for their charm and especially warm enthusiasm. In Britain, I have to thank Marie-Thérèse Smith of the Maison de France in London.

Many, many thanks also to my editor at Cadogan, Catherine Charles, for her patience, and for being so optimistic and encouraging, which I very much appreciated. To Jo Taborn and her father David, for letting us into their Cotentin cottage. To Vicki Ingle and Linda McQueen at Cadogan, for letting me do the book, and for their understanding. And most of all to Ethel for coming along with me, culinary advice, picking up on things I never even noticed, putting up with it, and for everything.

Also Available from Cadogan Guides...

Country Guides

Amazon
Antarctica
Central Asia
China: The Silk Routes
Germany: Bavaria
Greece: The Peloponnese
Holland
Holland: Amsterdam & the Randstad
India
India: South India
Ireland
Ireland: Southwest Ireland
Ireland: Northern Ireland
Japan
Morocco
Portugal
Portugal: The Algarve
Scotland
Scotland: Highlands and Islands
South Africa, Swaziland and Lesotho
Tunisia
Turkey
Yucatán and Southern Mexico
Zimbabwe, Botswana and Namibia

The France Series

France
France: Dordogne & the Lot
France: Gascony & the Pyrenees
France: Brittany
France: The Loire
France: The South of France
France: Provence
France: Corsica
France: Côte d'Azur
Short Breaks in Northern France

The Italy Series

Italy
Italy: The Bay of Naples and Southern Italy
Italy: Bologna and Emilia Romagna
Italy: Italian Riviera
Italy: Lombardy and the Italian Lakes
Italy: Rome and the Heart of Italy
Italy: Tuscany, Umbria and the Marches
Italy: Tuscany
Italy: Umbria
Italy: Northeast Italy

The Spain Series

Spain
Spain: Andalucía
Spain: Northern Spain
Spain: Bilbao and the Basque Lands

Island Guides

Caribbean and Bahamas
Corfu & the Ionian Islands
Crete
Greek Islands
Greek Islands By Air
Jamaica & the Caymans
Madeira & Porto Santo
Malta
Mykonos, Santorini & the Cyclades
Rhodes & the Dodecanese
Sardinia
Sicily

City Guides

Amsterdam
Barcelona
Brussels, Bruges, Ghent & Antwerp
Bruges
Edinburgh
Egypt: Three Cities – Cairo, Luxor, Aswan
Florence, Siena, Pisa & Lucca
Italy: Three Cities – Rome, Florence, Venice
Japan: Three Cities – Tokyo, Kyoto and
    Ancient Nara
Morocco: Three Cities – Marrakesh, Fez, Rabat
Spain: Three Cities – Granada, Seville, Cordoba
Spain: Three Cities – Madrid, Barcelona, Seville
London
London–Amsterdam
London–Edinburgh
London–Paris
London–Brussels
Madrid
Manhattan
Paris
Prague-Budapest
Rome
St Petersburg
Venice

Cadogan Guides are available from good bookshops, or via **Grantham Book Services,** Isaac Newton Way, Alma Park Industrial Estate, Grantham NG31 9SD, **t** (01476) 541 080, **f** (01476) 541 061; and **The Globe Pequot Press,** 246 Goose Lane, PO Box 480, Guilford, Connecticut 06437–0480, **t** (800) 458 4500/**f** (203) 458 4500, **t** (203) 458 4603.

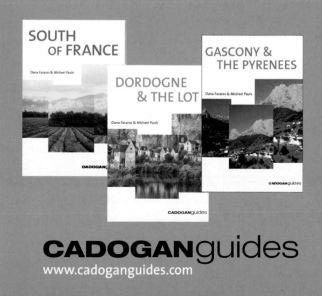

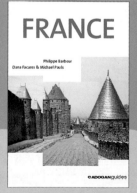

It can take a life time to see France. The sooner you start the better.

WHY SPEND
HOURS DRIVING,
WHEN YOU CAN SAIL
DIRECT TO HOLIDAY FRANCE?

Make a start with our brochure *The Ferry Guide & Short Breaks.* You'll find the perfect place to escape to for a weekend or longer, from fairytale châteaux to charming chambres d'hôtes.

Then sail with us in comfort and style to the historic channel ports of Western France.

Before you know it, you'll have escaped to a more relaxed way of life.

Brittany Ferries
The Holiday Fleet

Call now for a brochure
08705 360 360

www.brittanyferries.com or see your travel agent.

short breaks in **Northern France**
touring atlas

20 km
10 miles

N

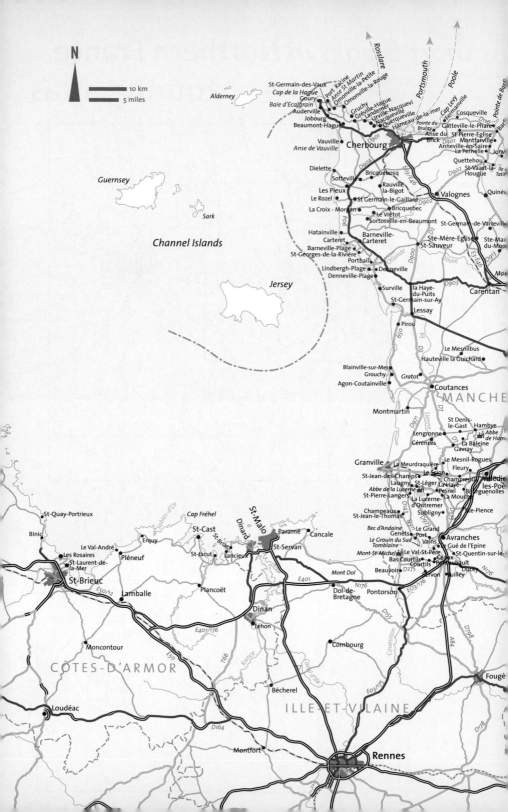

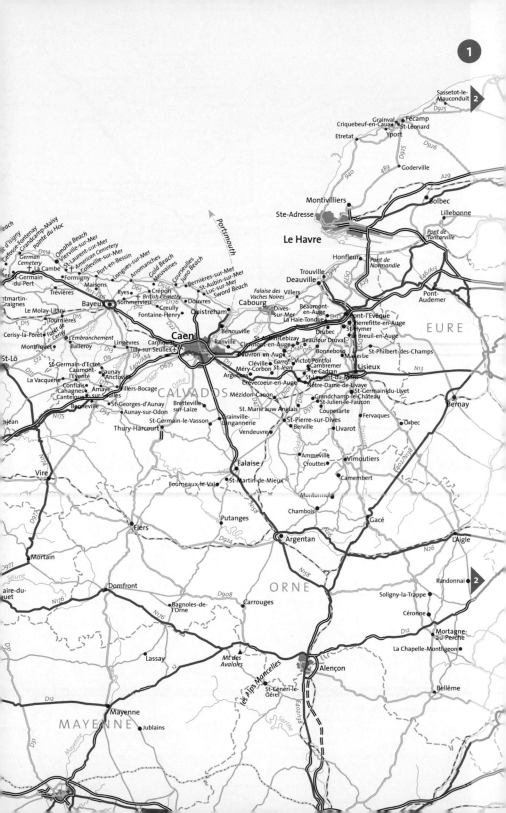

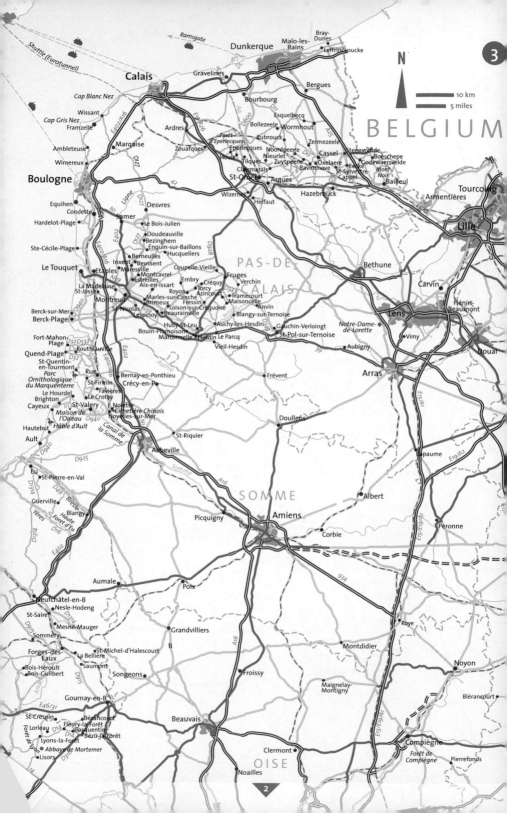